DIGENES AKRITES

DIGENES AKRITES

EDITED WITH AN INTRODUCTION
TRANSLATION AND COMMENTARY

BY

JOHN MAVROGORDATO

FORMERLY BYWATER AND SOTHEBY PROFESSOR
OF BYZANTINE AND MODERN GREEK LANGUAGE
AND LITERATURE IN THE UNIVERSITY OF OXFORD
AND FELLOW OF EXETER COLLEGE

OXFORD
AT THE CLARENDON PRESS

OXFORD
UNIVERSITY PRESS

Great Clarendon Street, Oxford OX2 6DP

Oxford University Press is a department of the University of Oxford.
It furthers the University's objective of excellence in research, scholarship,
and education by publishing worldwide in

Oxford New York

Athens Auckland Bangkok Bogotá Buenos Aires Calcutta
Cape Town Chennai Dar es Salaam Delhi Florence Hong Kong Istanbul
Karachi Kuala Lumpur Madrid Melbourne Mexico City Mumbai
Nairobi Paris São Paulo Singapore Taipei Tokyo Toronto Warsaw

with associated companies in Berlin Ibadan

Oxford is a registered trade mark of Oxford University Press
in the UK and in certain other countries

Published in the United States
by Oxford University Press Inc., New York

British Library Cataloguing in Publication Data
Data available
ISBN 0-19-924020-5

1 3 5 7 9 10 8 6 4 2

Printed in Great Britain
on-acid free paper by
Bookcraft (Bath) Ltd.,
Midsomer Norton

PREFACE

MANY years ago my friend Petros Petrides, himself born at Nigde in Kappadokia, used to tell me about the stories of Digenes, which were to inspire his own dramatic symphony first performed in Athens in May 1940. When at last I started to read for myself this heroic poem of *Twyborn the Borderer*, who guarded the marches of the Byzantine Empire in the tenth or eleventh century, I was alone in the country, and found my way through the text as best I could; if some of the notes now published sound like an ingenuous soliloquy, it is from that early period they must have survived— *excusata suo tempore, lector, habe; exsul eram.* Later on I was back in London, and there enjoyed the advice and encouragement of Norman Baynes, of F. H. Marshall, and of Romilly Jenkins; somehow or other my translation and a few lectures were on paper in 1938; and not long afterwards, thanks perhaps largely to their continued interest, I found myself living in College at Oxford and on the same staircase as my friend R. M. Dawkins. Many were now the anxious days and black nights in the course of which we talked about nearly everything in the world. I do not remember that in fact we ever talked about the Warden of the Marches. But Dawkins had such a lively knowledge of the land and the people and the language of Greece, and such an affection for them all, ancient, mediaeval, and modern, that his talk and his example were a university; and this is the place in which I must say how much I owe consciously and unconsciously to his learning and judgement.

It was some years later, and I was no longer living in Oxford, when the Delegates of the Clarendon Press gave me one of the pleasantest surprises of my life by undertaking the publication of this work. By this time most of my books had had to go into store; and as I had been brought up to fill every margin with notes—not to mention several cardboard boxes full of half-sheets of paper—many of my cherished references had now become inaccessible. Perhaps that does not matter as much as I thought it did. But it has taken a long time to reconstitute the commentary and do all that was necessary; and I am immensely grateful to the readers and experts of the Press whose patience and skill have been at my service on every page.

iii

The Greek text here printed is that of the Grottaferrata MS. of *Digenes* edited by Emile Legrand and published in Paris (by Maisonneuve) in 1892. A few passages to fill up gaps in the narrative have been borrowed from the Trebizond MS., edited by C. Sathas and Legrand and published in Paris in 1875; and from the Andros MS., edited by A. Mêliarakes and published in Athens in 1881, these passages amounting to 117 and 26 lines respectively. A second edition of Legrand's text *revue et corrigée* was issued in 1902, but all the errors I have noticed appear in both editions. Legrand can never be sufficiently honoured for his great services to the study of post-classical Greek, and above all for his two large collections of *Monuments pour servir à l'étude de la langue néo-hellénique*, but much of his work contains small inaccuracies. Some light may be thrown on these by an affectionate tribute he pays to his wife in the preface to the third edition (Paris, 1900) of the Cretan pastoral *The Fair Shepherdess*. He there tells us that in order to lighten his labours she had learned to read and write the Greek characters and so for many years had copied out all his Greek texts for him: 'ma femme transcrivait avec une exactitude d'autant plus surprenante (ce qui peut sembler paradoxal) qu'elle savait moins la langue.' Of the slips in his Grottaferrata text and *apparatus criticus* a few erratic punctuations and accents have been silently corrected. Otherwise his text and *apparatus* have been exactly reprinted and any emendations I have been obliged to make are recorded only in my own notes.

In his introduction Legrand recalls that on the publication in 1875, edited by Constantine Sathas and himself, of the Trebizond MS.—the first to be discovered—the interest excited had led to the publication of the Oxford MS., which was included by S. P. Lampros in his *Romans grecs en vers* (Paris, 1880), and of the Andros MS., edited by Mêliarakes (Athens, 1881). Lampros in his introduction (pp. xc—ci) describes the manuscript which he had seen in the autumn of 1879 in the library of the Greek monastery at Grottaferrata near Frascati. It is a manuscript of the fourteenth century written on 79 leaves of paper ($5\frac{1}{2} \times 8\frac{1}{4}$ inches—14×21 cm.) of which the first 73 contain the text here printed.

Joseph Müller of the University of Turin had already called attention to this manuscript, and had himself made a copy of it which he had shown to Legrand and had subsequently presented to the German scholar Wilhelm Wagner (editor of *Medieval Greek*

Texts, London, 1870; *Carmina Graeca Medii Aevi*, Leipzig, 1874; and *Trois poèmes grecs*, Berlin, 1881). After Wagner's premature death in 1880 this copy had been returned to Müller and has never been heard of again.

Meanwhile Nicolas Polites in Athens, fired by the description given by Lampros, had asked the librarian at Grottaferrata to have the manuscript copied for him; and Legrand through the French Ministry of Foreign Affairs had asked for a loan of the precious volume which in due course reached him in Paris. Lampros and Polites withdrew in his favour, and Legrand with his friend Jean Psichari read over together the copy which he had made, and certified its accuracy, in May 1887.

The most important thing about my translation is that it follows the Greek line for line, so that the original can always be referred to without delay. This has involved a good deal of compression but few, if any, sacrifices. On the rare occasions on which some Greek word has had to be omitted the fact has been recorded in the notes. This does not apply to particles which the Greek author uses almost indiscriminately in order to fill up his line. In order to empty the English line I have omitted 'fors', 'howevers', and 'yets' by the bushel, and 'buts' by the load; thus not only lightening the metre but improving the style. In English a minimum of such words is a condition of good writing as a minimum of gestures is a condition of good speaking.

Secondly, this translation has been kept as literal as possible. First finished in December 1938, it had to be copied out. In the first ten weeks of 1939 it was not only copied out but completely rewritten from beginning to end, because almost every line as it came up for approval was changed so as to give a more literal representation of the Greek, even if it produced less tidy metre and less conventional English. One result of this insistence on literalness has been an occasional loosening of the metre; so that instead of five feet and ten syllables some lines (e.g. 3314) have three beats each followed by a varying number of unaccented syllables.

Thirdly, I have never tried to improve the Greek original. (Well, hardly ever.) Clumsy Greek has often been turned into clumsy English. I have resisted the temptation to conceal silliness or bathos, and to make the English line more poetical than the Greek line which it is supposed to represent.

Generally speaking I have used a basis of ordinary conversational English; the fundamental rule for the structure of this groundwork being that there shall be no inversion of the natural order of words. To reinforce this natural order there has been an avoidance of conventionally poetical usages. I have never used the second person singular, except where God is addressed. The heroine, when she is referred to, perhaps with some mystical significance, as *Korê*, is called the Girl rather than the Maiden or the Virgin.

On the other hand, although based on natural speech the diction is one definitely removed from that of common talk. It is what Aristotle in his *Poetics* calls *exêllagmenê*; it is changed over from the customary *dialektos*, the conversation of ordinary life. This translation in fact uses a written language and not a spoken language. And why not? Does anybody suppose that the Greek was not an artificial language? It is only as a result of contemporary fashions, English as well as Greek, that one has to defend the perfectly natural division of the written from the spoken language. This division connotes the artificiality of the written language. But all writing is an artifice and it can never be anything else. The words commonly used in streets and fields are often better than others, but they are not in themselves patterns laid up in heaven.

Having laid down the ground, a written language free from inversions and poetical conventions, based on ordinary speech but clearly divided from it, we proceed to colour it with reminiscences of the Bible, of Shakespeare, of Milton, and of the Ballads; inevitable reminiscences, not because they are beautiful English, and recall beauty by association even when they have it not in the immediate use; but because these exactly represent the Greek of the ancient classics, which the redactor of this version was attempting to revive, with painful but with loving artifice, in the middle of the eleventh century. His is certainly an artificial language. There is only one characteristic of his style which he shares with the good conversationalist and the good letter-writer: that he often begins a sentence without knowing how he is going to end it.

This is not the place to examine other characteristics of his style, notably his mixture both in vocabulary and in syntax of elements from every period, from Homer, from the Septuagint, and from contemporary folk-song. This eclecticism shocks the grammarians, and it shocks the Athenian demotics; but it does not shock anyone who has a sense and a love of the Greek language as a whole, to whom no part is unclean. It does not shock me, and I have sometimes even attempted to reproduce it in English. In passages where the Greek is peculiar, and possibly corrupt, or the words rare or remarkable, or the meaning doubtful, the original was sometimes quoted in the notes, without comment, so as to call attention to the fact that further elucidation was required. But many of these mere exclamation marks were afterwards left out in order to save space.

The lines of this edition are numbered on two systems. The numbers in the margins of the right-hand pages, that is of the English version, include not only Grottaferrata but also the passages borrowed from the Trebizond and Andros versions to fill up gaps in the narrative. This numeration, running from 1 to 3850, is used in the notes and in the index. The Greek text of the Grottaferrata and other versions on the left-hand pages have each book numbered separately— (GRO Book I, 337 lines; Book II, 300 lines; Book III, 343 lines; Book IV, 1093 lines; Book V, 289 lines; Book VI, 845 lines; Book VII, 229 lines; Book VIII, 313 lines; TRE and AND, Books I to X); this numeration given on the left-hand pages is to be associated with the number of the book in Roman figures given at the top of the page, and both the line-numbers and the Roman book-numbers must be used for reference to the Greek text. (Note, however, that the TREbizond and ANDros versions, each divided into ten books, are not numbered by separate books but straight through from beginning to end—3182 and 4778 lines respectively.)

J.N.M.

CONTENTS

INTRODUCTION

1. DISCOVERY

In the middle of last century nothing was known of the Byzantine epic of *Digenes Akrites*; but the atmosphere had been prepared by the publication of several ballads of what is now called the Akritic Cycle (a name first used by Legrand in 1874). The discussion of these—(in particular a paper by Büdinger who had used the headline 'A Greek Mediaeval Popular Epic', although the Song in question, *The Sons of Andronikos*, was only seventy lines in length)—had opened the way for further revelations of an heroic age of mediaeval Greece.

(i) The discovery was made at Trebizond. Manuscripts could not be photographed at Trebizond, and after considerable correspondence the precious work was sent to Paris by post; and in 1875 Sathas and Legrand published *Les Exploits de Digénis Akritas—épopée byzantine du dixième siècle . . . d'après le manuscrit unique de Trébizonde*. The manuscript is said to be not earlier than the sixteenth century. There are several gaps in it. The poem is divided into ten books of which the first and the last are missing altogether; there remain 3,182 lines of it.

This manuscript was afterwards returned to the hands of Savvas Ioannides, the Trebizond schoolmaster, author of a statistical history of Trebizond, who in May 1868 had received it from a monk at the monastery of Soumelá. (For the present state of the monastery of Soumelá see D. Talbot Rice in *Byzantion*, v. 72 ff.) He published another edition of it at Constantinople in 1887,[1] and then deposited it in the library of the *Filologikos Syllogos*. All the archives of this institution are said to have been removed to Angora by the Turkish Government and the fate of the Digenes manuscript is unknown; but in the opinion of Kyriakides (conveyed in a private letter 7 April 1936) it must, for the present at least, be regarded as lost.

(ii) Before the learned world had had time to digest this, several

---

[1] Epos Mesaiônikon / ek tou kheirografou Trapezountos / O Basileios Digenes Akritês / O Kappadokês / ypomnêmatisthen ekdidotai / ypo / Sabba Iôannidou / . . . en Kônstantinoupolei / . . . 1887.

The text is fairly correct and is supplemented by about 700 lines from the OXF and AND versions. Ioannides regards Digenes as a fully historical figure of the Kappadokian aristocracy who lived from 936 to 969 against a background slightly adjusted from the chronicle of Kedrenos.

other manuscripts were discovered; beginning with the version found in Andros in 1878 and published by Mêliarakes in 1881, a manuscript of the sixteenth century practically complete in 4,778 lines, conveniently filling the gaps in the Trebizond manuscript which it closely follows. The Mêliarakes edition was reprinted in 1920. This Andros manuscript is now in the National Library at Athens, and is referred to by Kalonaros as the Athens version (which he prints first in his collection).

The Mêliarakes introduction refers to a Greek newspaper of 23 November 1880, reporting that Legrand had discovered in Constantinople, and proposed to publish, another version, the oldest known, written in iambics and containing the name of the poet. At that time (towards the end of 1880), Legrand must have known of the existence of the Grottaferrata and Oxford manuscripts besides the Andros manuscript, which was still in the press; he may also have heard about the description of other versions in an unpublished Athos manuscript of the monk Dapontes just then discovered (see below). Legrand, discussing his hopes of one or all of these in a conversation with reference to his own edition of the Trebizond manuscript, may have originated this newspaper paragraph of which nothing more seems to be known.

Another short version, in prose, said to have been discovered in Constantinople by Dr. Mordtmann, is mentioned in Legrand's preface to Grottaferrata (pp. xi, xxii—'signalée par le Dr. Mordtmann à Sabbas Ioannidis'); and is also referred to hopefully by Polites (*Peri tou Ethnikou Epous*, p. 5); by Hesseling in his introduction to ESC (*Laografia*, iii. 551); and by Ioannides himself in the introduction to his Constantinople edition of 1887.

(iii) Next came a manuscript of the fourteenth century discovered at the Greek monastery of Grottaferrata near Frascati in 1879, which was published by Legrand in 1892 (reprinted 1902).

(iv) The incomplete 'Madrid' version of only 1,867 lines was discovered by Krumbacher in the Escorial library in 1904 and was published by Hesseling in 1912.

(v) A rhymed version was published by Lampros in 1880 from a manuscript at Lincoln College, Oxford, which had the advantage of being signed by the writer, a monk of Chios, by name Ignatios Petritzes, who finished his task on 25 November 1670.

(vi) A prose version, written by Meletios Vlastos of Chios in 1632, discovered by Mr. D. Paschales in Andros in 1898, was not published till 1928; it is now in the library of the department of Folk-lore at the University of Salonica.

(vii) Finally there is a very incomplete Russian version— fragments of a (linguistically) thirteenth-century version assembled from two different eighteenth-century manuscripts and from the quotations of the historian Karamzin (the third manuscript, from which he took his quotations, was burned in Moscow in 1812). This version was published by Speransky in 1922 and reproduced in a French translation by M. Pascal in 1935; and in a Greek translation in the edition of Kalonaros in 1941. A third and fuller eighteenth-century manuscript of this version was recently discovered in Russia and was published in 1953.

We thus have now manuscripts of five metrical versions of the Digenes Epic:

TREBIZOND	. MS. sec. XVI,	3,182 lines,	10 books	
ANDROS . .	„ „	4,778 „	„ „	
GROTTAFERRATA	„ XIV,	3,749 „	8 „	
ESCORIAL . .	„ XVI,	1,867 „		
OXFORD . .	MS. 1670,	3,094 „	„ „	

One prose version:

PASCHALES. .	MS. 1632,	10 books

And one Russian version:

SPERANSKY	. MSS. sec. XVIII
KUZMINA .	. MS. 1761.

I usually cite these versions by the first three letters of these titles (TRE, AND, GRO, ESC, OXF, PAS, SPE), giving the number of the line and of the book where necessary for the metrical versions, and for the prose versions the number of the page of the volumes of *Laografia* and *Byzantion* in which the Greek prose version and the French translation of the Russian version were first published.

The Ballads of the Akritic Cycle are more difficult to deal with because no approximately complete collection has yet been published and they must be hunted out in various journals and anthologies. Polites once said that his own private collection contained more than 1,300 ballads; but after eliminating versions which differ in only a few words or only by combination or contamination with fragments of other versions, it might be permissible to guess that the number of ballads deserving consideration as 'Akritic' must be less than a hundred; of which not more than fifty have any great significance.

Each version includes some details or names which must have been added by the author or transcriber of the version in which they occur, and could not have formed part of the supposed archetype, the original *Digeneid*, which is generally believed to have been put together from a great variety of sources in the tenth century.

The *Digenes Akrites* is a romantic epic of between 3,000 and 4,000 lines, narrating and celebrating the parentage, education, exploits, and death of its eponymous hero—whose name implies the burden of the story, for it may be translated as *Twyborn the Borderer*. His father was a notable Arabian emir who in a raid over the Byzantine frontier carried off the daughter of a Greek general; after embracing Christianity he was permitted by the family to marry her; and settled down as a law-abiding subject of the 'Roman' Empire. The son of this union of two races and two religions soon showed in the chase signs of exceptional heroic ability—hunting and athletics having been in the Greek Empire the pride and privilege of a ruling class. He imitated his father by carrying off—but single-handed—the daughter of a Greek general. After his marriage he left the parental castle, and with his bride and a few personal attendants lived a nomadic life among the lonely places of the border; making it his special business to exterminate the bands of robbers and cattle-drivers who haunted it (all of whom seem to have been Greeks, and one of whom was a woman). He built himself a palace on the Euphrates (although the earlier books seem to imply an imperial frontier in Kappadokia, where his parents had their castle till they came, before their death, to live with him). There he soon fell ill and died surrounded by the honours of the whole empire in Asia.

The epic can hardly have been officially inspired for it seems to embody no definite propaganda. If the imperial authorities had wanted to promote a new ideal of peace they would have displayed it in a less indefinite and more popular form, and would have employed a more accomplished and a more metropolitan poet. The bare outline just given suggests an attempt to arrange a bunch of local adventure stories into the likeness of an epic embodying ideals of tolerance and peace. It is not a romance in spite of many borrowings from Hellenistic romances; and it is untouched by Western influences in spite of many reflections, through such Hellenistic writers, from the Mediterranean world which was later to inspire any number of Italian and French storytellers. J. B. Bury (*Romances of Chivalry*, pp. 18, 19) praises the epic comprehensiveness of *Digenes*, 'which justifies us in naming it along with Homer and the *Nibelungenlied*'.

It is a heroic poem of provincial origin intended for private reading or for recitation not in the market-place but in banqueting hall or refectory.

2. VERSIONS

I

The Grottaferrata version is probably the earliest we possess. The narrative is clear, simple, and concise. Irrelevancies are omitted and effective detail often added. It omits altogether the rather silly story about Ankylas. It begins with the Emir instead of with the once-upon-a-time King and Queen who had a beautiful daughter. It omits the earlier visit of Digenes to Philopappos. In the episode of the Emperor's visit it names the Emperor Basil (instead of Romanos as in TRE and AND) and it adds the detail that Digenes catches a wild horse and kills a lion by way of display for the Emperor's entertainment; it also names the Emperor Basil (instead of Romanos) in the passage in Book IV which refers to the banishment of Eirene's father, and in the same passage, by a sort of attraction or association set up by the name Basil, gives the Emperor himself the surname of Akrites, calling him 'Basil the blessed, the great Borderer' (cf. GRO iv. 55 with TRE 835 ff.). It omits the later references to honours conferred on Digenes by the Emperor Nikeforos which appear in the penultimate books of AND and TRE. From the same part of the narrative it also omits many redundant details of his wealth and daily life, and it omits the excessive lamentations on the death of his mother. It mentions that his final illness was the result of a chill after bathing; and it specifies that his tomb was built on a hill near Trôsis. It develops at greater length than the other versions the incidents of his courtship and marriage.

There is more Moslem colour in GRO than in other versions (e.g. a knowledge of Moslem miracles (GRO iii. 139) and of the Moslem shrine at Palermo (GRO i. 101)); but there is also a greater sincerity, one might almost say a greater savagery, of Christian morality.

The language is fairly correct literary Greek of, probably, the eleventh century, with a noticeably large number of words from the Septuagint. Such, however, is the unity of the Greek language, and so insufficient is our present knowledge, that, if allowance be made for ecclesiastical and literary influences (for familiarity with the Septuagint and with historical sources) on the one hand, and for the revisionary habits of later copyists on the other, it would be difficult, judging by language alone, to say much more than that the Grottaferrata version was written between the tenth and fourteenth centuries.

II

TRE and AND are a pair and follow the same story in all its details so that AND is useful for filling up the numerous gaps in TRE (especially the whole of the beginning down to the pursuing brothers' search for their sister's body in the Emir's camp, and the whole of the end from the speech of Digenes to Eudokia on his deathbed).

The language of TRE is also inclined to be literary but is distinctly less correct than that of GRO; the syntax is often in a state of dissolution so that the semi-classical manner seems less natural.

III

AND tells exactly the same story as TRE and has many identical passages. But it has been written up in a later and more romantic manner; many passages suggest that it was copied and rewritten as late as the fifteenth or sixteenth century. (The writing of the manuscript is said to be of the sixteenth.) The end of Book I from line 247 onwards actually breaks into rhyme and produces a lyrical peroration in roughly rhymed octosyllables. Although the extant parts of TRE are, as has been said, identical in incident with AND, it is permissible to suspect that the beginning of TRE, if we had it, might differ considerably; for the first book of AND ('once upon a time a King and Queen'), while consistent with the romantic manner of the AND narrative and language, would have seemed incongruous in the distinctly more epic manner of TRE. A romantic monk of the fifteenth century seems to have been rewriting a more learned text which was almost that of TRE, and often took over its lines as they stood. (For the introduction of rhyme see Krumbacher, p. 700.)

Perhaps this romantic monk was Eustathios, who is said in the opening lines to be writing the story for a dear young friend called Manuel. It has been surprisingly believed that these lines do in fact give us the name of the original author of *Digenes*. A Greek scholar, A. Hatzês, has tried without much success to prove by linguistic arguments that the *Digenes* was written by Eustathios (or Eumathios) Makrembolites, author of the Byzantine prose romance *Hysmine and Hysminias*. (See *Byz. Neugr. Jahrb.* ix (1931), pp. 256 ff.; and for Grégoire's criticism and list of Hatzês's works, *Byzantion*, vi. 482.) It ought to have been impossible for anybody to suppose that the heading of AND implies that Eustathios was the original author. Petritzes, the writer of OXF, uses even more definite language— *esyntaxa kai 'synthesa to*, he says—yet we know that he was only the versifier. Eustathios may have been the redactor who added the rhymes and other romantic embroideries. As for the author of *Hysmine and Hysminias*, he lives in quite a different world of literary preciosity.

IV

The ESC version is extremely incomplete, beginning at about the same point as TRE and omitting altogether many incidents and innumerable details, while many of the episodes and lines are in the wrong order. It is written in an extremely but not uniformly popular style, with a Cretan flavour, which combines with many repetitions and confusions to give it a striking if superficial resemblance to some of the Akritic ballads. It has become a commonplace, started by N. G. Polites, to say that the Ballads are more 'poetical' than the Epic, because they are full of magic and confusion. Consequently Kyriakides and others declare that the 'breath of life' blows through the muddle of the ESC because it resembles the Ballads. It has even been argued that, assuming the Epic to have been assembled from scattered Ballads or Lays, the fact that ESC most resembles the extant Ballads shows that it is nearer to the source and consequently earlier than all the other versions. A similar argument was at one time (October 1941) produced by Grégoire in support of the Russian version. This argument ignores the considerations that the qualities of an Epic are not the same as those of a Ballad; and that we cannot conclude that an epic text is closer in time to its component lays because it resembles what other lays or ballads have become after a thousand years of oral transmission. So much *a priori*. But Grégoire has now shown (*Byzantion*, v. 339) that the details of Arab raids borrowed by GRO from the chronicles of Genesios are not absent from ESC; and ESC even exceeds other versions in bookishness by borrowing the tomb of Digenes from Arrian's description of the tomb of Cyrus (*Anabasis*, vi. 29. 4–8) and the parrots in the garden from Achilles Tatius.

Actually the disorder of the ESC version, the innumerable omissions, the innumerable additions of irrelevant tags out of ballads, the repetitions of the same line, the duplications, the phonetic confusions (e.g. 719, *améras*, 'the emir', for *Oméros*, Homer), the way the words continually overflow the metre, and the metre breaks off into half-lines or into the rhythms of a chanted speech—all these lead to the conviction that this was taken down, not before the end of the fifteenth century, the date of the manuscript, from the dictation of a wandering Cretan ballad-monger who was trying to recite from memory in the musical recitative which still survives in Crete a version which contained a few original details (e.g. that Digenes made a bridge over the Euphrates). (The same overflowing of the metre is noted by Kyriakides (p. 119) as a sign of dictation in the *Ballad of Armoures*.) Whenever his memory fails he repeats as a catchword one of the characteristic or operative lines of the episode he is trying to recall, or he improvises, or marks time with a tag or two out of his repertory; and his version certainly contains vestiges of a literary original. Anyone who doubts the possibility of memorizing even imperfectly the whole of the *Digenes* may be reminded that only a few years ago villagers could be found in Crete who professed to know by heart the whole of the *Erotokritos* which is nearly three times as long as this (9,956 lines).

Kyriakides (op. cit., p. 75) compares three extracts—ESC 806–23, TRE 1207–37, GRO iv. 380–95—with a view to showing that ESC, allowing for a lacuna, follows the fullest tradition. He argues that there must be a lacuna because the mother of Digenes prays to the Virgin twice; and that therefore something to account for her second prayer—actually, as we see from TRE, the fact that Digenes couldn't eat his supper—must have been lost. But the whole passage shows that ESC doubles nearly everything; he repeats things because he is trying to remember what comes next; e.g. 831, Digenes plays his *tampouri* as well as his *labouto*; 918, 919, he calls out to Doukas to arouse him, but Doukas is aroused by hearing the gallop of the horse; there is another repetition in 836, 845, and another muddle in 844, again defended by Kyriakides in a long note (p. 79) on the kailyard principle that whatever is *laïkôteron* must be *poiêtikôteron*. It is true that this version has beauties and originalities of sound and surface that have been produced by oral transmission; but they are the qualities of a seventeenth-century ballad, not of an eleventh-century heroic poem.

The ESC manuscript which contains this version also contains a version of the *Lybistros and Rodamne* romance written in the same hand and disfigured to a smaller extent by faults of the same kind. The latest editor of *Lybistros and Rodamne* (Mme J. A. Lambert, Amsterdam, 1935) dismisses the hypothesis of dictation in the case of the *Lybistros*, in spite of the phonetic evidence, on grounds which seem insufficient.

V

There is no such problem when we come to the OXF version. We know that it was composed in 1670 by the monk Ignatios Petritzes of Chios, who puts into rhyme a version which substantially resembles that of AND; but as it is in eight books instead of ten he may have been working from one of the versions seen on Mount Athos by Dapontes (see below, p. xxi). In so doing he humanizes and to some extent rationalizes the story. His tale is well-proportioned and not savage or sanctimonious; it is set in a world which is more 'civilized', or at least less mediaeval. He brings in priests and bishops to celebrate weddings and funerals. The Arabs become Turks; the emir Haplorrabdes becomes Abdullah; and Petritzes is the only redactor who bothers to give Abdullah's wife and daughter Moslem names, Aissé and Fatouma—names easily found, for these were the favourite wife and youngest daughter of Mohammed. In the same episode he explicitly denies that Digenes, after rescuing the deserted bride, helped himself to his own reward, as the earlier versions allege, or did anything to be ashamed of. When he comes to Maximo the Amazon, whom he calls Maximilla, he remarks that a woman's place is in the home; and now he allows Digenes to yield to temptation, thus distinguishing Fatouma from Maximilla, who had, literally, asked for it. The name Maximilla may have been familiar to him as that of a prophetess who was head of the Montanist heresy at the end of the second century.

The fact that the earlier versions seem to see no difference between the treatment of the unwilling Fatouma and that of the willing Maximo, may be connected with the oriental seclusion of Evdokia (who was never seen by any of the servants; only a little boy waited on them at table) to show that the author of Digenes was exceedingly provincial in his outlook; there was nothing like this at Constantinople (or in *Hysmine and Hysminias*); but the author of Digenes was Asiatic; he seems never to have heard of Europe; and only mentions one place in Europe—the Moslem shrine of Palermo (except for AND 2419, *sta merê Ahaias*).

Ignatios Petritzes was not only six hundred years later; he was writing in Chios. The whole is written in good popular Greek of the seventeenth century without pretentiousness or affectation.[1] We are surprised only by quotations from Aristophanes (*Plutus*), Theocritus, *The Song of Songs*, Bion, and Euripides (*Hecuba*). (OXF 237–42 = Aristoph. *Plut.* 3–7; OXF 1563–6 = Theoc. iii. 15, 16; OXF 1576–80 = Bion, 1. 7–20; OXF 1052 ff. = Song of Solomon vi. 8; OXF 1593–6 = Eur. *Hec.* 600, 601.) The chief interest of this version is in the personality of the author Ignatios Petritzes. (There are four other manuscripts copied by him in the library of the Greek patriarchate at Jerusalem. See GRO, introd. p. xii.) His humble lines of dedication at the end of his work, and his hopes that it may some day be printed, are modest and attractive.

VI

D. Paschales who discovered the prose version in Andros in 1898 waited thirty years before he published the manuscript. When at last it appeared in 1928 it was a sad disappointment. It had been hoped that a prose version might throw some light on problems of date and origin; or at least that it might correspond to one of the versions which the eighteenth-century monk and polygrapher Caesar Dapontes (1714–84) describes as then existing in the library

---

[1] Ioannides (p. 22) says it is written in the dialect of Chios, presumably because it is too demotic for his taste.

of the monastery of Xêropotamou on Mount Athos. (This reference was first discovered by M. Gedeon in the manuscript of a Byzantine chronicle in verse called *Biblos Basileiôn*. See Lampros, *Romans grecs en vers*, introd. p. xcix. For a notice of Dapontes see R. M. Dawkins, *The Monks of Athos* (1936).)

Dapontes gives in twenty lines a summary of the story which he unfortunately breaks off at the point where the hero's parents have been introduced; up to this point, that is to say up to about the end of the first book, he appears to follow closely the story as given in AND—except that the father of Digenes is said to have been an 'emir of Egypt' or 'Sultan of Misir' (Cairo): this difference is probably without significance: the Emir is actually called *Soultanos* in AND 307—and a *Syrias* may have been confused with *Misiriou*. Then interrupting his summary he adds:

'The story is very long but interesting and sweet as sugar. It is a book of eight or ten quires and contains all his exploits. I have seen it in two forms with illustrations and without pictures. It is divided into eight books and it is very rare and difficult to find. At the beginning of each book it has five lines of verse containing the argument of each book: and it is always in manuscript. I have not seen a printed copy and it seems never to have been printed. They have printed *Erotokritos*, *Sôsanna*, *Erofile* and others: what a pity they have never printed Basil. If it is given me to live I mean to put this story into verse and send it straight to Venice. Happy the printer who prints it for it will bring him both profit and honour.'

Two points should be noticed in this quotation. First of all his intention of putting it into verse before having it printed, which implies that both the manuscripts he saw were prose versions. (It cannot be assumed that he saw two different versions. He may have seen two copies of the same version, one of them illustrated.) It has been suggested, quite untenably I believe, that he only meant to put it into rhyme, to add rhyme to blank verses. But his mention of the five lines of verse (and if they were five lines they were almost certainly unrhymed lines) prefixed to each book implies that the rest of the work was in prose. It is curious, however, that the library should have had two copies in prose and none apparently in verse. If Dapontes had succeeded in producing his own versified edition, we may be sure it would have resembled closely the Oxford version written a hundred years earlier by that other monk from Chios,

Ignatios Petritzes, whose character, gentle, literary, and unheroic, must have been very much like that of Dapontes.

It was the curious habit of those who enjoyed and transmitted to us the works of middle Greek literature to rewrite, apparently each to his own taste, any work which they thought worthy of preservation. The Cretan play *Erôfile* even after it was printed is said to have been rewritten for the second edition by a patriotic Cretan. Of the *Cypriot Chronicle* of Mahairas the two sixteenth-century manuscripts (Venice and Oxford) differ so much, and yet are so much alike, that Professor Dawkins felt himself obliged to conclude—rather unsatisfactorily—that they were written by two independent authors working from identical materials.

This rewriting habit must have begun early. The text of *Chaireas and Calliroe*, a romance of the second-century novelist Chariton of Aphrodisias, depended on a single Florentine manuscript until the recent recovery from Egypt of three small fragments. Of these fragments two papyri of the second or third century generally confirm the Florentine text. But a seventh-century parchment palimpsest discovered near Thebes in 1898 differs so widely that in the words of the latest editor (W. E. Blake, Oxford, 1938) 'rationem inter Thebanum et Florentinum haud aliter definire se posse crediderit vir doctus quam si duas memorias omnino inter se diversas poneret, quarum utraque suo modo ex ampliore exemplari contracta esset'. Before the discovery of these fragments the romance was usually attributed to the fourth century.[1]

Be that as it may, when D. Paschales at last published the PROSE version associated with his name, it turned out to be another seventeenth-century version which had little interest either as a prose romance of Digenes or as a specimen of the seventeenth-century language, because it was obvious that the writer had taken the trouble to turn into flat and literary prose a version very closely resembling that of AND, leaving embedded in his periods many undigested fragments of the original verses.[2] The editor claims (*Laografia*, ix. 312) that it represents an independent tradition, and it is true that

---

[1] Achilles Tatius has also been shown by a papyrus fragment to have written at the end of the third century, though he had formerly been placed in the fourth or fifth (see *Ach. Tat.*, ed. S. Gaselee, pp. xiii–xv).

[2] It should be noted here that all the metrical versions of Digenes are written in the well-known 'political' metre, the *politikos stichos*, the fifteen-syllable ballad

in numerous unimportant details he seems to follow TRE rather than AND and in a few details to have been following a version which differed from both. (See, for example, *Laografia*, ix. 350, compared with TRE 1128, 1133, lines which are different in AND; p. 358, where the name of the Saracen Soudales is omitted but details are inserted which are not in AND or TRE (lacuna), or GRO (where the Saracen is omitted altogether), but which are in ESC 930, 931; p. 359, where the detail of the girl's father and her two brothers pursuing does not agree with TRE 1267 or AND 2075 or OXF 1957 (where the three pursuers are her three brothers), or with ESC 969 (five brothers) but with GRO iv. 610, iv. 657; PAS p. 361, the twelve eunuchs, who are to be found in GRO iv. 925 but in no other version; p. 366, a detail which is in no other version about the confusion in the house of Haplorrabdes when his wife fell ill; p. 406, the doctors feel his pulse; and a few other details and misunderstandings.)

The writer gives his name as MELETIOS VLASTOS and the date 1632. The editor on insufficient linguistic grounds says that he was a native of Chios. A Cretan monk of this name is said to have been one of the teachers of Cyril Loukares. Why did Meletios want to turn the story of Digenes, of which he had in his hands a perfectly good

metre, which has become almost universal in Greek popular poetry. (See my note in F. H. Marshall's *Three Cretan Plays* (Oxford, 1929), p. 2, and add refs. to Wagner, *Mediaeval Greek Texts* (1870), pp. ii–viii; Schmitt, *The Chronicle of Morea* (1904), pp. xxxiii–xxxvi; W. P. Ker, *The Dark Ages* (1904, n.e. 1955), pp. 343, 344; Heisenberg, *Dialekte und Umgangsprache im Neugriechischen* (Munich, 1918), pp. 44–55; and Ducange, s.v. *politikoi stichoi*.) This metre, although it is now of course accentual, seems to be the same as the ancient (quantitative) iambic tetrameter catalectic which is to be found fairly often in the tragedians as well as in Aristophanes. See, for example, Aristophanes, *Plutus* 288, *Nubes* 1433, which are both quantitative and accentual; *Nubes* 1399, which is quantitative but cannot be read accentually. Aeschylus, *Persae* 155, and Soph. *O.T.* 1524, are examples of quantitative trochaic tetrameters catalectic which can be read accentually as iambic tetrameters catalectic, and many more could no doubt be found; even Homeric hexameters can sometimes be read as accentual fifteeners, though usually without caesura: e.g. *Od.* ix. 106, *Iliad* vii. 59. The beginnings of the accentual fifteener are obscure, but Professor D. S. Robertson has shown that it can be discovered in Procopius' *Anecdota* xv. 34 by substituting for the discreet *ho deina* ('so-and-so') the vocative of a proper name such as *Theódôre*. This would take it back to, say, A.D. 550. In English it is less common than in Greek, and is seldom heard except in ballads like 'In Scarlet town where I was born there was a fair maid dwellin'', or better still in the song of the London Apprentices in *The Knight of the Burning Pestle*:
The rumbling rivers now do warm for little boys to paddle:
The sturdy steed now goes to grass and up they hang his saddle.

redaction in verse, into indifferent prose? His motive was not the same as that of the gentlemen who translate the New Testament into 'modern English'. Verse is the natural speech of the peasant culture (cf. the story of Mrs. Flecker's cook in *J.H.S.* liii (1933), 1); verse aids the memory in recitation, and is no longer necessary when recitation gives place to reading.[1] There are many French prose romances (e.g. *Balin and Balan*) made from earlier verse romances; and various prose versions of the *Roman de Troie* of Benoît de Ste-Maure from the twelfth century onwards. To Meletios there was something vulgar and uneducated about a story in verse; he wanted to have a good story in a form fit for a gentleman to read.

VII

The Russian version (SPE) is composed of three fragments of a (linguistically) thirteenth-century prose romance, two from manuscripts of the eighteenth century, and a third quoted by the historian Karamzin from a manuscript probably of the thirteenth century which was burned in Moscow in 1812. These fragments were assembled and published by Speransky in 1922, and were edited in a French translation by Pascal in 1935 (in *Byzantion*), and in a Greek translation by Kalonaros in 1941.

Here, combined with many folk-tale elements—a book of fate, a magic horse, a spring of water with a light burning in it,[2] and other fairytale wonders which suggest oral transmission—we can recognize the chief incidents of the Greek story.

Maximo the Amazon becomes Maximiana the daughter of Philipap, and Devgeny after pole-jumping over the river[3] easily defeats them both and sends them home to his parents. He refuses to marry Maximiana because the Dream Book says that if he marries her he will live sixteen years but if he marries Strategovna (the

---

[1] This is explicitly stated in a Greek song published by Firmenich (*Tragoudia Rômaïka*, 1840, p. 122).

> *Ta grammata den éxevra, kai na mên tên xehasô*
> *Tragoudi tou tên ekama, kala na tên fylaxô,*
> 'To keep the story safe, because I could not read,
> I made a song of it, that he who hears may heed.'

[2] There is a magic spring with fire in it in *Belthandros and Hrysantza* (240 ff.); and in view of the geography of *Digenes* it is curious that the magic water in *Belthandros* should be situated *plêsion Armenias . . . eis tês Tarsou to kastron.* (*Belthandros*, 104, has the word *apelates.*) 'A spring in Sicily which has fire mixed with its waters' is described in Achilles Tatius ii. 14. 7.

[3] For the pole-jumping over the river cf. *Kallimachos and Khrysorroe*, 2532.

daughter of the General) he will live thirty-six years. So he carried off and, after several bachelor parties, married the General's daughter, and settled down to a life of fame and hunting, until he was attacked by a certain Caesar called Basil; and then he jumps over the river again, defeats him, enters into the town (not named), and ascends the throne.

Grégoire accepts this rebellion as the first nucleus of the poem, and argues that we must see in it a revolutionary manifesto issued by the Paulician heretics of the Armenian border and their Arab allies against their arch enemy the Emperor Basil I the Macedonian (867–86)—from whom the hero was given his first name—and that all the Greek versions are descended from a loyalist revision of this seditious original officially prepared and circulated at the beginning of the tenth century. Grégoire's arguments, too numerous to be examined in detail, would be convincing only in an unreal society. (He has not noticed by the way that Philipap's army—SPE 318—are said to be 'brave as Macedonians'.)

These arguments were strongly contested by Wartenberg (in *Byzantion*, xi (1936), pp. 320 ff.); it must be added, however, that they seem to have been largely accepted with other Gregorian hypotheses by Professor Arnold Toynbee (*A Study of History*, v. 252 ff.). The evidence leads us rather to believe that the Russian is descended by oral transmission from a sophisticated Greek version already combining the later Euphrates frontier—quite inconsistent with the reign of Basil I—with the earlier Kappadokian frontier; the Russian includes even the eulogy of the month of May which seems to derive from the eulogy of the Rose in the second book of Achilles Tatius. It is reasonable to suppose that the Hero of the Borders becoming Emperor in the City is a fairy-tale ending tacked on in the course of transmission—a common form of contamination in popular literature of any period. This conclusion seems to have been finally confirmed by the discovery of a third Russian manuscript dated 1761. It closely follows the earlier of Speransky's two eighteenth-century fragments, but is much fuller and preserves traces of an earlier text and vocabulary.[1] It begins

[1] See V. D. Kuzmina, *Novy Spisok 'Devgeneva deyaniya'*, in *Trudy otdela drevnerusskoi literatury*, ix, Moscow and Leningrad, 1953. For all information about this third Russian version I am indebted to the great kindness of Mr. John W. H. Smith of Merton College, Oxford.

with the Emir and completes the story of the abduction of the daughter of Strategos, but omits altogether the final episode of the overthrow of the Emperor Basil. If, as seems probable from the superior text and archaic vocabulary, this new version in fact preserves the oldest Russian tradition, it follows that the Emperor's defeat must be the addition of a later copyist, and does not preserve any early Greek original put about by rebellious Paulicians. It was already impossible to understand, on Grégoire's hypothesis, why no version, Russian or Greek, shows any trace of feeling either for or against the Paulicians.

VIII

Before leaving this review of the various versions of the Digeneid and passing on to consider the story they present, something must be said about the Ballads, the Akritic Cycle of Folk-songs or TRAGOUDIA.

These ballads have been found to some extent in all parts of the Greek world (as have also 'Castles' or 'Tombs of Digenes'), and it was clear that they belonged to the Byzantine period and to Asia Minor, on the fringes of which, and especially in Pontus and in Cyprus, the best of them have been collected. Their nature is well indicated in the well-known scholion, on a passage in Philostratus' *Life of Apollonius of Tyana*, written by Arethas (850–932), Bishop of Cappadocian Caesarea,[1] which speaks of 'wandering beggars, like the cursed Paphlagonians who now make up songs about the adventures of famous men and sing them for pennies from door to door' (see Kougéas, in *Laografia*, iv. 236). This brings us at once to the place and also to the time of the Akritic ballads: the period which, as Grégoire has shown, is peculiarly the Heroic Age of Mediaeval Greece: the ninth and tenth centuries which produced the adventurers of the Amorian and Macedonian dynasties, the Andrónikoi and Constantines of the Doukas family, the Nikefóroi of the Fokâs family, and many others whom he has convincingly identified in the fragments of the existing ballads.

Many of the early investigators thought that the poem of Digenes had been made by a 'rhapsode' who stitched together short lays or ballads of this sort which celebrated the glories of individual heroes,

[1] Whose copy of Plato, found in Patmos, is now in the Bodleian Library (Harvey).

a method of composition once supposed to have produced the *Iliad* and the *Odyssey*, and the French *Roland* (as Lönnrott in fact produced the Finnish *Kalevala* in modern times (1835-49) from traditional lays collected by Topelius in 1822).

Here, then, we say as we approach the Greek songs of the Akritic Cycle, here is a wonderful chance to study in their raw state the materials of an epic poem. In these ballads we might expect to find, distorted perhaps by oral tradition but still easily recognizable, many of the episodes of *Digenes*. We are surprised to discover an entirely different world: a world of supernatural feats, magic weapons, and talking birds; in which Digenes is only one of a number of heroes we have never heard of before—Andronikos, Porfyrios, Armouropoulos, Konstantas, Theophylaktos, Xantinos—and is not by any means the most popular. Digenes indeed hardly appears at all except in the series of ballads describing his death,[1] foretold by talking birds, his iron death-bed, and his wrestling with Death who comes to fetch him. This connected series and one or two which seem to refer to his carrying off, in entirely different circumstances, of Evdokia, are the only ones that can be fitted into the story of our Digenes at all; and a great number are commonly called 'Akritic' only because of their obvious antiquity. Some of the other heroes have been plausibly identified by Grégoire as historical figures, emperors or generals or pretenders; or as the eponymous heroes of imperial themes or regiments. But he has had less success in rationalizing the incidents.

A son of Andronikos born in captivity, his mother having been carried off before his birth, escapes from the Saracens and goes in search of his father and brothers. (In this episode it is worth noting that the hero is *digenes*, twy-born, in another sense, as being the son of a Christian father Andronikos as well as the putative son of the Emir at whose court he is born and brought up (see Passow 482, Kyriakides, *Dig. Akr.*, pp. 35 ff., and Legrand, *Chansons pop. grecques* (1874), no. 87, esp. lines 7, 8).) A gargantuan Porfyres falls in love with the king's daughter and no chains are strong enough to hold him. The equally monstrous Xantinos liberates his son who has

---

[1] *Laografia*, i (1910), pp. 169-274. Polites has here edited 72 songs including 14 which are only slightly, and in some versions, contaminated with Akritic matter; but not including, he says (p. 171), innumerable wrestling matches of an unnamed man with Charon.

been yoked to the plough with a buffalo. Most of the songs which are not in the Pontic or Cypriot dialect have almost lost their narrative character and have been so contaminated with later ballads that they are only recognized as Akritic by the names of the heroes and by their obvious antiquity. It is sometimes suggested that Digenes was only one among a number of ballad-heroes and that the author of the epic took up the Digenes cycle and left the other heroes to the wandering ballad singers. But why should adventures which were good enough to attract the epic-maker in search of material have completely disappeared from ballad circulation? It must be understood that the relation between ballads and epic is not one between successive stages of composition, or between different treatments of the same materials, adapted in one form for street singing and in another for ceremonial recitation or private reading. It is rather a relation between different levels of interest in the same community. The study of one does not necessarily throw any light on the other; although a knowledge of both is necessary for an understanding of the society in which both were produced and developed.

What nearly all editors call the poetical vigour of the ballads as distinguished from the epic is really a radical difference of theme and treatment. A fourth-rate ballad, especially if it is recorded in the surprising dialect of Pontus, may be superficially more attractive than a second-rate epic. The songs as we have them today, after 900 years of oral transmission, cannot be regarded as the sources of the epic, and cannot be used as standards by which to judge the relative ages of the various versions or the various episodes of the epic. We do not know what these ballads were like when they were first sung. If they were recognizably the same as they are now, then they obviously have nothing to do with our Digenes; even the death-bed series are disqualified for comparison by their association with miraculous incident; and if they were entirely different—still less can we be allowed to draw any critical information from their present derivatives.

Only one of the ballads, the *Son of Armoures* (first published by Destouny in Russia in 1877 with a facsimile and reprinted by Kyriakides, p. 119), exists or used to exist in a manuscript said to have been of the fifteenth or sixteenth century. All others have been collected in modern times, although the sources are not always known. (See, for example, the obscure history of the *Sons of Andronikos* ballad, first published by Zampelios (1859) who says the manuscript was given him by Brunet de Presle,[1] who had it from the unpublished part of the collection of Fauriel, who had copied it from a manuscript in the Bibliothèque Nationale; this is flatly denied by Legrand who says that Brunet de Presle when a student took it down from the dictation of Professor Hase (Zampelios, *Pothen hê Koinê Lexis Tragoudô?* (1859), p. 37; Legrand, *Chansons pop. grecques*, p. 183). Büdinger, who reprinted the text given by Zampelios, refers to his vain efforts to trace the supposed manuscript in Paris (*Ein mittelgriechisches Volksepos* (Leipzig, 1866), p. 3); see also Wagner who again reprinted it (*Medieval Greek Texts* (1870), pp. x, xiii n. 34, xxii). Legrand implies that his own text was taken from the same manuscript of Brunet de Presle as that which Zampelios had copied and 'improved'.)

Not one of the Akritic ballads or fragments can be regarded as belonging to the category of Folk-chronicles or Historical Ballads, a class represented by the Cretan historical ballads of the eighteenth century like the well-known *Daskalogiannes*; and it is from the historical rather than from the romantic ballad that we should expect the maker of the Digenes epic to have drawn some of his materials.[2] The strange absence from the extant Akritic ballads of any recognizable incident of the epic is paralleled to some extent in English ballad literature. *The Gest of Robyn Hode* is a small epic of 1,824 lines divided into eight 'fyttes', first published in the middle of the sixteenth century, and said to have been composed 'by a poet of a thoroughly congenial spirit' from ballads which had begun to circulate about a hundred years earlier. Not one of the ballads from which it was made up is extant in a separate shape, and 'some portions of the story may have been of the compiler's own invention' (Child's *Popular Ballads*, ed. Sargent and Kittredge, p. 225).

[1] With special permission from Fauriel's widow to take a copy of it; see Zampelios, *Pothen hê Koinê Lexis Tragoudô?* (p. 37, footnote).

[2] Note that neither ballads nor epic present Digenes as typically a Dragon-slayer; yet Grégoire sees Digenes on some fragments of pottery, said to be of the thirteenth century, discovered at Athens by the Agora Excavation (see *Byzantion*, xv (1940–1); and *Hesperia*, x (Jan.–March 1941) and *Dig. Akr.* (New York, 1942), pp. 3–5). For knowledge of these fragments and photographs of two of them I am greatly indebted to Prof. J. M. Hussey and Dr. Alison Frantz. They seem to be typical figures of St. George and may be compared with the fresco of St. George and the Dragon from Stratford-on-Avon, used as frontispiece in E. K. Chambers, *The English Folk-Play* (1933).

3. STORY

Once upon a time (so begins the first book, which is found only in AND and PAS) there lived in Kappadokia in the Roman Empire (Rômania) a certain prince called Andronikos, or Aaron, of the Doukas family. He and his wife Anna (of the Magastrean or Kinnamos family) had five sons, but they wanted a daughter. (The wanted daughter is a very rare theme in oriental folk-lore.) So they prayed and in due time a little girl was born to them, a lovely child called Eirene. The soothsayers foretold that she should be carried off by an (Arabian) Emir—who would, however, become a Christian—so when she was seven years old she was put in a palace in a garden attended by a company of guards and nursemaids, so that she should never think of love. When she was twelve years old and more beautiful than the moon she saw in the palace a picture of Love painted in the likeness of a little boy shooting with a bow, and one of her maids told her that this was the strong and terrible one, armed with arrows and fire, the conqueror, the slave-driver, bearing inkhorn and paper to enrol his victims.[1] She only laughed and said she was not afraid of his arrows or his lions or his fire or his ink and paper. But that night Love himself appeared to her in a dream and she was terrified and begged him to have mercy on her and had to run to her maids to be comforted. From this point (AND 261) the writer breaks into rhyming octosyllables in attempting to describe her loveliness and her nobility. The last thirty lines of the book can hardly be earlier than the fifteenth century and must have been added by one of the later transcribers. PAS says only that 'her heart was on fire'.

Then one day when her father was away on an expedition she went out with her maids and her nurses into the country for a picnic. Now at this time there was a great Emir called Mousour who had been made prince of Syria; and one day when he came raiding into Rômania he happened to come to the place where the picnic was going on and he carried off the girl and her young companions.

When her five brothers heard of it and told their mother she charged them on pain of a mother's curse[2] to go after the Emir and bring back their sister or not to return alive. They arm and go in pursuit, and Konstantine, who is either her eldest brother (AND

---

[1] Cf. the painting of Love in Eustathius's *Hysmine and Hysminias*, ii. 7.
[2] ESC opens at this point: ESC 2 = AND 324.

320; PAS p. 320; TREB 303; OXF 741) or her twin (GRO i. 132; SPE p. 307), fights the emir while the others look on.

The Emir is outfought, surrenders, gives them his ring, and allows them to search the camp for their sister. They cannot find her, and a helpful Arab suggests that she may have been killed with a lot of other girls whose bodies have been thrown into the ditch. There is a search among the mutilated bodies of her companions. (TRE begins at this point.) Finally they return to the Emir and threaten him. He asks them who they are, and when they ask him about his own family he replies proudly, 'I am the son of Chrysoherpes and Spathia (or Panthia, GRO i. 284). My father is dead, so I was brought up by my Arabian uncles as a Mohammedan. My grandfather was Ambron and my uncle Karoes. I have conquered all Syria and beyond and have never been defeated, but now I surrender to your sister's beauty. She is alive and unharmed, and if I may marry her, I am willing to become a Christian and come over with all my people into Rômania.'

(These genealogies must be noticed.[1] The study of the historical vestiges in the poem really begins with the identification of Chrysoherpes, father of the Emir Mousour, with Chrysocheir a leader of the Paulician (Christian) heretics, who in the ninth century rebelled against the empire, ravaged Asia Minor, and compelled Basil I the Macedonian to sue for peace, but in a later expedition in 873 was surrounded and beheaded (see below, p. xxxii). 'In their hostile raids', says Gibbon (vol. vi, p. 126) 'the disciples of St. Paul were allied with those of Mahomet'; and after the defeat of Chrysocheir, 'the glory of the Paulicians faded and withered;[2] but the spirit of independence survived in the mountains; the Paulicians defended above a century their religion and liberty, infested the Roman limits, and maintained their perpetual alliance with the enemies of the empire and the gospel'. In those words Gibbon has recorded the circumstances which produced the background of the present poem. He has even defined by that phrase 'infesting the Roman limits' the name or rather the profession of our hero. For AKRITÊS means

---

[1] See Genealogical Table, Appendix A.
[2] *synapemaranthê pasa hê anthousa tês Tefrikês euandria* (Cedrenus, Bonn, ii. 212), quoted by Gibbon—'How elegant is the Greek tongue, even in the mouth of Cedrenus!'

a BORDERER, a *miles limitaneus*, a frontier guard, or Warden of the Marches: but the office had been so notably illustrated by the pacifying achievements of Digenes or one of his prototypes that already in the twelfth century it had become almost a proper name and the poet Ptôhoprodromos tried to flatter the emperor Manuel Komnênos by addressing him as 'a second Akritês' and again used the phrase much as one might say 'a new Achilles'; and as GRO 1036 refers to 'the Emperor Basil the Blessed, the mighty Borderer' (see Mavrofrydes, *Eklogê Mnêmeiôn* (1866), pp. 45, 65, for the two Prodromic verses). Neither Mavrofrydes nor Koraês (*Atakta*, i. 256) knew the meaning of the word *akrites*; and Legrand when he first quoted the two verses in his introduction to the ballads which he was the first to call the Akritic Cycle (*Chansons pop. grecques* (1874), p. 184) still thought it was a proper name. (See Krumbacher, p. 832, for quotation from Const. Porph., *de Cerim.* (Bonn, p. 489), describing duties of *akritai*.)

So after making peace they all returned to Roman territory, and there at the castle the *Stratêgissa*, the General's wife, welcomed her sons returning with their sister 'as a mother that rejoiceth over her children' (a quotation from the Septuagint version of the Psalms: LXX, Ps. cxii. 9; A.V., Ps. cxiii. 9). The Emir was baptized and married the princess Eirene and in due time a child was born who was called Basil Digenes Akrites.

All versions report the baptism, the marriage, and the birth of the child very briefly, and at this point give no explanation of the child's names. It is only later that we learn that he was called Digenes because he was born of two races, a happy union of Roman and Arab, and Akrites because his task was to bring peace to the border between the two. (See TRE 835 ff.; GRO iv. 50 ff.; AND 1357 ff.)

The Emir's mother, hearing what had happened, wrote to him from Syria a letter of bitter reproaches. She reminded him of the achievements of his father Chrysocherpes, who had defeated many Roman generals, and when at last he was surrounded and offered an honourable and even a glorious peace, who had preferred to be cut to pieces rather than surrender. And his uncle Mousour of Tarsus, what raids he had made as far as Ankyra and Smyrna! (GRO ii. 78, where cf. Procop. *Buildings*, ii. ix. 10, for 'Pentakomia near the Euphrates'). She tells him of the danger she herself is in as a result of her son letting himself be seduced from glory by a pretty eater of pork. (She even reminds him rather surprisingly—the reference is omitted in the later versions—of the wives of his harem and his children left behind in Syria. In GRO iii. 127 these damsels and their children go to meet him on his return to Edessa.) He must return at once and bring the girl with him if he likes.

She sends the letter by swift horsemen who camp outside the Doukas castle at a place called Whitestone (*Leukopetra*, TRE 230, AND 680; *Asprê Petra*, OXF 635; but *Lakkopetra*, GRO ii. 101, *Halkopetron*, ESC 321—evidently by a mnemonic confusion with Halkourgia in GRO v. 238). When the Emir receives his mother's letter he tells Eirene, who is quite willing, though distressed, to go away with him.[1] There follows a rather complicated quarrel which is developed with much originality in ESC 405 ff.

However, all ended happily. Eirene declared that she had not told her brothers anything and then she ran and explained to them that the Emir only wanted to go to Syria to see his mother, because she had written to him, and would then return again; and they themselves not long ago had been afraid of a mother's curse. So there was a general reconciliation and the Emir set off with all their good wishes for a speedy return. But he went, rather unexpectedly after what had been said, without Eirene. The incident illustrates the sensitivity of brothers about their sisters' 'honour' in the Greek world: Psichari has a pungent note on the selfish tyranny of Greek brothers and quotes an even more pungent proverb (Psichari, *Quelques Travaux* (Paris, 1930), p. 45).

The Emir sings to his men on the journey to cheer them on, for he makes them travel fast, covering three stages in one day in his longing to return to his love. He reminds them how they had been in a desperate battle together and how—at Mellokopia, GRO iii. 67; Mylokopodi, AND 956; the passage is missing in TRE; the modern Malakopi in Kappadokia, south of the Halys[2]—he had cut a way for them through the Roman forces that had surrounded them.

This battle is identified by Grégoire with that in which Omar of

---

[1] There is a similar episode in *Imperios and Margarona*, 455 ff. Imperios proposes to his bride that they should go off secretly to visit his father, without the knowledge of her parents.

[2] For the modern village see R. M. Dawkins, *Modern Greek in Asia Minor* (1916), pp. 23 ff.

Melitene was defeated and killed by the Roman General Petronas, as described in the histories of Genesius and the Continuation of Theophanes; it took place in 863, but not at Malakopi (see Bury, *Eastern Rom. Emp.*, p. 283). After comparing the accounts of this Byzantine victory with the passages in GRO and in ESC 500 ff., he claims, not without reason, that the 'historical' elements in the poem are simply borrowed from the chroniclers (*Byzantion*, v. 334 ff.).

On the road through the mountains the Emir kills a lion and takes its teeth and the claws of its right foot as a present for his little boy, Basil. No river crossing is described but they soon arrive at Edessa, capital of Osroëne in Mesopotamia (*tou Rouhâ to Kastron*, TRE, AND; *to Rahab to Kastron*, GRO), and there after dinner he preaches the Christian faith to his mother with such success that she and all her household are immediately converted; and after loading up apparently most of the treasure of Edessa they all return to Kappadokia to be baptized. (Edessa took its Greek name from the ancient capital of Macedonia. From the Arabic name, Er-Ruha, was developed the Greek adjectival name of the province of Osroëne).

In GRO, however (iii. 135–57), but not in the other versions, the Emir's mother anticipates his preaching by challenging him again about the cause of his absence. Had he ever seen, she asks, in Rômania any wonders to compare with the miracles which are performed at the tomb of the Prophet, the light that there descends by night from on high, the bears and lions, the wolves and sheep together, one not hurting the other that there bow down together during the prayer? 'And have we not', she continues, 'the Kerchief of Naaman who was king among the Assyrians and for his virtues was found worthy of miracles? How could you overstep all these, my son, and even despise the greatest honours when all thought you would be lord of Egypt, standing in the way of your own destiny, all for the sake of this Greek girl?'

Now, says Grégoire, what is this Kerchief, or Towel, of Naaman? It must be the Sacred Image of Edessa—'one of the most precious of Christian relics . . . an authentic portrait of Christ, the Towel on which He had dried his face, leaving on it the Impression which he had sent to King Abgar of Edessa' (Runciman, *Romanus Lecap.* p. 145). But this relic was surrendered by the Arabs of Edessa to the victorious Kourkouas and triumphantly carried to Constantinople in 944. Therefore, says Grégoire, the poem which refers to its beneficent presence at Edessa must have been written before that year. *Digenes* (presumably he means the hypothetical orthodox anti-Paulician revision he has been talking about) must have been written between 930 and 944. But if we refuse to be bluffed or hypnotized we will find it difficult to suppose that a poet writing in the immediate neighbourhood, with a good knowledge of the Septuagint and of local tradition, could possibly confuse—just because they were both lepers—Naaman the Syrian lord healed by Elisha with Abgar the King of Edessa to whom Christ was said to have sent firstly a Letter and secondly 'the perfect impression of his Face on a Linen' (Gibbon, v. 265). This Holy Image (or *ekmageion*, 'impression', as it was called) was certainly brought from Edessa to Constantinople in 944, after the victorious advance of Kourkouas to the Euphrates. But much the more famous of the two treasures of Edessa, the Letter and the Image, both associated with the Christ–Abgar story, was the Letter. Only the Letter is mentioned by Saint Sylvia (*Peregrinatio ad Loca Sancta*) who visited Edessa in the fourth century. Both Letter and Image are referred to on the capture of Edessa by the Arabs in 637 (Gibbon, v. 471). The Image seems to have been a later discovery. The more famous relic of the two, the Letter, did *not* leave Edessa in 944, but remained there until the town was again captured by Maniakes in 1031. Of course *mantéli*, 'Kerchief', might be a mistake for *mantato*, 'letter'. But we should still wonder why Naaman should have been written for Abgar. If the name Naaman is retained, as I think it must be, either Letter or Towel would make sense, for both a Letter and a Towel (i.e. the towel on which Naaman dried himself after bathing in Jordan) would suit the Elisha–Naaman story (2 Kings v; LXX, 4 Kings v); and Edessa was such a well-known clearing-house of religious legend (cf. Hasluck, *Christianity and Islam*, p. 37) that there may have been many relics there we have not heard of.

On the Emir's return to Cappadocia with his mother and her household there is a scene of reunion, and when he embraces his Eirene they faint for joy in the fashion of the later romances. Then the little boy Digenes was brought in and the Emir took him in his arms and said, 'My little hawk, and when will you spread your wings and go after the partridges?' (GRO iii. 307.) And so the third book ends in a scene of happy family life among the Cappadocian nobility.

The fourth book in the three oldest and most complete versions (GRO, TRE, AND) opens with a recapitulation of the life and exploits of the Emir which would be a suitable introduction to the Tale of Digenes if it were only just beginning. In the course of this introduction we are told explicitly for the first time why Basil was called Digenes and why he was called Akrites. 'To these a child was born and from his birth he was named Basil; and he is also called Digenes as from his parents, being a gentile (*ethnikos*) by his father and by his mother a Roman; and becoming terrible, as the tale shall show, he is named Akrites the Borderer as having subdued the Borders.' (GRO iv. 50–53; TRE 825–34, a slightly different version; AND 1356–64 again slightly different.)

When at last the hero does begin to grow up he grows up very quickly. For three years he learned letters. Then he learned arms, the uses of spear and sword, the arts of running and wrestling. When he was twelve years old he asked if he might go with his father and his uncle to the chase. The Emir said he was too young but he insisted; and next morning he rode off into the forest with his father and his uncle Constantine. He kills two bears, and catches a running deer on foot and kills it with his hands. When a lion springs at him he draws his sword and kills it with one stroke. Afterwards they go to a spring in the forest and wash him and give him clean clothes of silk and gold; and a curious piece of folklore has survived in the account in GRO iv, 217, 218 (not in TRE 990 ff. or AND 1530 ff.). The boy was anxious to ride home to his mother: so they mounted him on a white horse, its mane plaited with turquoises and little bells of gold, with a saddlecloth of rose and green silk, and a bridle embroidered with gold and pearls. The horse was spirited but he let it play to his own desire and sat in the saddle 'like a full-blown rose' (TRE 1019, AND 1557), or 'like an apple on a tree' (GRO iv. 245). So he grew up strong and beautiful, and as the Emir his father grew old he left all adventuring to his son.

One day when he became a man Digenes rode off with his company and in one of the passes succeeded in finding a band of the Brigands or *Apelatai* whom he had been longing to meet.

This is the first appearance on the scene of a class of freebooters or highwaymen who with their enemies the *Akritai* or Wardens play a great part in the action. In fact all the action of the poem is a conflict between *Akritai* and *Apelatai*. The name by which they are called, *apelatai*, has given occasion for many notes, although it is fairly common in Byzantine literature (e.g. *Belth. Chrys.* 104; see Krumbacher, p. 832; Lampros, *Romans grecs*, gloss.; and Sophokles, s.v.) and has even given its name *apelatiki* to the mace or club which seems to have been their characteristic weapon (see Ducange and Meursius, s.vv.). It is the exact equivalent of the Latin, and obsolete English, *abactor*, and means simply drivers-away, reivers, rustlers, cattle-drivers, or horse-thieves. St. Theodore, in whose name Digenes vows to his lady in ESC 891, AND 1921, is there called 'the great Apelates'.[1] But nearly all commentators before Krumbacher, including Lampros, Legrand, Gidel, and Rambaud, took the word *apelatês* in a passive sense and explained it as meaning one who had been driven away, that is an 'outlaw'; and Ioannides (in his Constantinople edition of TRE, p. 49) suggests that it means one who is not any man's dependant (*a* privative + *pelatês*).

Digenes finds their water-carrier and by him is guided to their chief, the old brigand Philopappos, who is lying in his tent on a heap of wild beasts' skins, and tells him that he wants to join the band. The old man answered and said (AND 1609–20): 'Young man, if you think yourself good enough to be a Reiver take this club and go on guard: and if you can fast for fifteen days, and let no sleep close your eyes, and then go off and kill lions and bring me their skins; and after that go and watch again, and when the princes go by with a caravan and the bride and bridegroom with them, if you can take the bride from the midst of them all and bring her here to me, then indeed you may call yourself a Reiver.' Digenes answers that he had done all that when he was a little boy: now he can overtake a hare running uphill, or catch a low-flying partridge in his hands. The Reivers invite him to dinner, and when they are boasting he challenges them, all of them, to a bout with quarter staves, disables the whole company and presents their weapons to old Philopappos saying, 'If you don't like it I will do the same to you.' And so he rejoined his young men and they rode home.

This disconnected episode, well developed in ESC 622–701, is omitted by the GRO version which passes directly from the Hunting

[1] See also Maigne d'Arnis, s.v. It is worth recording that one evening in 1917 when there had been a Turkish raid on one of the islands off the coast of Asia Minor in allied occupation, I think Astypalaia, a newspaper paragraph about it was adorned with the memorable headline INSULAR ABACTORS OF THE LEVANT.

to the Courtship. The omission is not an unmixed advantage. For the incident not only represents a preliminary challenge from the youthful hero to the forces of lawlessness and the standards of violence (it is perhaps not by accident that Digenes in his reply to Philopappos suggests that the skill of the athlete is better than the violence of the brigand); it also serves a purpose in the narrative of representing the years of adolescent adventure which must have elapsed between the boy's first hunting and the young man's lovemaking. In fact there is little doubt that there is a lacuna in GRO after line iv. 253; a lacuna easily explained by the fact that the Hunting ends as the Courtship begins with a Homecoming from the Chase, and easily filled by TRE 1027–1109 or AND 1566–1674.

Now there was a famous general in that part of Rômania called Doukas and he had a lovely daughter called Evdokia. (Here there seems to be a curious doublet of the Emir's courtship of Eirene, also the daughter of a Doukas, a doublet which the poet has tried to explain by making Evdokia remark (GRO iv. 325; AND 1740; TRE 1179) that Digenes, through the Doukas family, must be a relation.) One day when he was hunting in that country Digenes sang under her window, and she looked out and saw him, and sent her Nurse with a ring and a message of warning; her father the General had a cruel way with suitors, however noble and brave they were. He rode home, praying for the sun to set and the moon to rise, and told his groom to have his black horse ready at nightfall with double girths and double martingales and sword and mace at the saddle; and at dinner he could not eat, so that his mother was anxious, and asked him what was the matter,[1] even quoting Homer to him (*Iliad* i. 363, in TRE and AND but not in GRO), and began to pray. But he only went up to his room and put on his riding-boots and tuned his lute as he liked it, and as he rode through the night he sang a song.

It is a real folk-song with rather magical words about loving far and roving late which do not make much sense (ESC 839; AND 1844; GRO iv. 401; TRE 1249 has a lacuna as it often does where a song is indicated, and also omits the whole following scene at the window corresponding to AND 1839–2057). The words are slightly and suspiciously less obscure in GRO than in AND.

[1] There seems to be an echo of this in an Epeirotic folk-tale in Pio, *Contes pop. grecques* (Copenhagen, 1879), no. 4, p. 14.

When he arrived at the castle it was nearly daybreak and Evdokia had fallen asleep waiting for him, and when he played under her window to wake her up she is rather cross at first and frightened—'if they do see thee they will murder thee'. But they talk at the window and exchange many vows—'if that thy bent of love be honourable, thy purpose marriage'—and 'all my Fortunes at thy foote Ile lay and follow thee dear lord throughout the world'—and then at last he stands up in the saddle and catches her as she jumps down from the window.

He would not let it be thought that he had stolen her secretly, but shouted and awakened the whole castle. One of the leading pursuers whom Digenes crushes with a single blow is named as Soudáles the Saracen (AND 2024; ESC 928).

It seems strange that a Saracen should have been fighting among the retainers of Doukas; and this appears to be the only occasion in the poem on which Digenes kills an opponent who is specified as an Arab. But Soudáles is not an Arab name. It is actually the name of a Byzantine general sent with Andronikos Doukas into Asia Minor by the Empress Theodora in 855 against the Paulicians, whom he persecuted with a ferocity which provoked their subsequent rebellions under Karbeas and Chrysocheir (see TRE introd. p. lxxx, and Kyriak. p. 85 and below). So the death of Soudáles here may be a trace and apparently the only trace of Paulician prejudice in the story.

So Digenes easily defeated all the pursuers: he was careful not to hurt her three brothers (TRE 1275; AND 2075; but two of them in GRO iv. 610 and PAS, p. 359) but only knocked them off their horses. He shook hands with the General and congratulated him on having found such a fine son-in-law. But he insisted on taking the Girl—she is usually called simply *Kore*, the girl and, in ESC, *Korasion*—back to his own father's house for the wedding. The celebrations lasted three months, and there is a long list of remarkable wedding presents from the bride's father, which included hawks, leopards, embroidered tents, maid-servants, two ikons of the two saints Theodore, the sword of Chosroes, a tame lion, and (only in PAS and GRO) twelve eunuchs.

Thereafter Digenes rode out with Evdokia in the borders and he destroyed many reivers and freebooters and made peace on all the

Roman limits. He loved to ride about alone in the wilderness. He had one tent for himself and the Girl, and for his men and the maid-servants he had two separate tents at a distance. These details about his servants are in all primary versions (see AND 2312 ff., TRE 1448 ff., GRO iv. 960 ff. repeated AND 3737, TRE 2555, GRO vi. 725); but the story of how Digenes blinded one of his cooks is only in AND (2324) and TRE (1460). This is a reflection of Alexander's quarrel with his cook Andreas who found, and lost, the Water of Life. The birth in captivity of Digenes (not in the epic but in some of the Akritic ballads) may also be a reflection from the *Shah Nameh* version of the birth of Alexander.

And the Emperor of the Romans hearing his fame and being then in Kappadokia[1] wrote that he was anxious to see him. Digenes answered that if the Emperor wanted to see his worthless servant he should ride down to the Euphrates with only a few men—'I am afraid that if you were to come with a large army your men might find fault with me, and I am so young and foolish I might pay them with my fists' (TRE 1501–4). So the Emperor came to the river with only a hundred men and greeted Digenes affectionately and asked him to name his reward. Digenes replied with a short lecture on the duties of empire—*parcere subjectis et debellare superbos*—among which GRO (iv. 1037), but not AND or TRE, includes the task of 'scatter-ing the heretics and fortifying the orthodox'—which perhaps might be taken as a reference to the Paulicians.

The Emperor, wishing he had four such men in the empire (GRO iv. 1025), restores to him all the possessions which had been con-fiscated from his grandfather (an obvious reference to the mysterious disgrace and exile of Eirene's father Doukas, to which there have been some allusions: e.g. GRO iv. 55; and which explained his absence from home when Eirene was carried off by the Emir (GRO i. 63) where the word *exoria*, exile, seems to have been misunder-stood by the redactor of AND 290, as equivalent to *taxeidi*, expedi-tion); and confirmed with a Golden Bull his authority over the Border.

The GRO version here introduces a new incident not found in

---

[1] According to TRE 1476 ff. the Emperor was campaigning in Kappadokia and Digenes was at the frontiers on the Euphrates. According to GRO iv. 971 ff. the Emperor was campaigning against the 'Persians' when Digenes invited him to come to the Euphrates.

any other version. Digenes entertains the Emperor by an exhibition of strength: he catches and, on foot, turns and throws with his hands at the Emperor's feet, a wild unbroken horse; and a second item on the programme is provided by a lion which at that moment jumps unrehearsed out of the undergrowth. Digenes seizes it by one leg, dashes it on the ground, and presents it to the delighted Emperor. From that time, concludes the incident (GRO iv. 1087), 'they called the lad Basil Akrites the Borderer because of the Golden Bull which appointed him to rule over the Borders'.

Whether or not this implies that he was given the name Basil after the Emperor Basil (who is himself named at the beginning of this book (iv. 56) as the Emperor who had banished the grandfather of Digenes), it certainly states that his name Akrites was taken from the appointment officially conferred by the Emperor on this occasion, which is in direct contradiction to the statement at the beginning of the book (iv. 49–53); and this seems to make it more probable than it already appears that this whole passage of the demonstration of strength before the Emperor is a later interpolation (whether or not we believe in the general theory of a Basilian recension), and that the interpolator, as Grégoire points out (*Byzantion*, vi. 491), appears to have copied from the chronicle of Theophanes Continuatus the description of Basil the Macedonian exhibiting his prowess in order to gain the favour of the Emperor Michael III.

In this remarkable incident the name of the Emperor concerned is given in four versions (AND, TRE, OXF, PAS) as Romanos——presumably Romanos Lekapenos (919–44). But in one version, and that perhaps the best and oldest (GRO), as well as in the Russian version (SPE), the Emperor's name is given as Basil. The GRO version also has Basil in the passage of recapitulatory introduction at the beginning of Book IV which refers to the banishment of Doukas the grandfather of Digenes (GRO iv. 55). Here, where both TRE (836) and AND (1369) speak of *Rômanou tou paneutyhous*, GRO has *Basileiou tou eutyhous akritou tou megalou*. This Emperor, who is here also called the Chief Warden of the Frontiers, must be, says Grégoire, Basil I, the Macedonian (867–86), himself an athlete of prodigious strength, who might well have been chosen by a court poet to banish his hero's grandfather as well as to honour his hero. Two of the three Russian manuscripts go on to tell how Digenes, or as he there appears

Deugeny, instead of greeting the Emperor Basil as a respectful vassal, proceeds to fight him, defeats him, and seizes his throne. Grégoire, as noted above, accepts this with delight, and argues that in this Russian version we have fragments of the earliest nucleus of the poem, which was nothing less than a revolutionary manifesto, issued by the Paulician heretics of the border, and their Arab allies, against their arch enemy the Emperor Basil the Macedonian. He believes that after the defeat of the Paulicians the imperial government produced a revised and loyalist version of the poem, suppressing, naturally, the wish-fulfilment scene of the Emperor's defeat, giving Digenes the name of Basil in honour of the victorious Emperor— he is never called Basil in the Russian version—and representing him as a loyal vassal devoted to peace and conciliation. We are to suppose that all extant Greek versions are descended from this loyalist revision; and that the versions in which Romanos is named, that is, all versions except GRO, including the three versions which in the ninth book, in a death-bed recapitulation of his achievements, *also* mention as having honoured him the Emperor Nikêforos (presumably Nikêforos Fôkas, 963–9) (TRE 3107; AND 4344; PAS, p. 405), are all later rehandlings intended to bring up to date the first loyalist edition which has reached us as the Basilian version of GRO.

Without going into all the details of Grégoire's conclusions it may first of all be accepted as axiomatic that the poem reflects the Arabian alliances during the ninth century of the Paulician heretics on the Armenian border. Even if we could accept Grégoire's argument that the original poem must have been produced *after* certain battles of the ninth century to which it seems to refer, and perhaps after certain Arabian conversions of 928, but *before* 944 because the Sacred Towel seems to be still at Edessa, and this famous Christian relic, the 'Image of Edessa', was surrendered to Kourkouas and transferred to Constantinople in that year; even if we accept all this, and accept, too, the supposition, which is extremely probable for other reasons, of which those of language and style may be thought conclusive, that GRO is the earliest of the Greek versions; accepting all this it is still not possible to be convinced by Grégoire's arguments that the Russian version (as it exists in the two manuscripts published by Speransky in 1922) represented an archetypal form of the poem preceding any of the existing Greek versions.

(1) It is conceivable that the fact that the Emperor is named

Basil in GRO iv. 973 and in no other Greek version may be due to a simple error or misunderstanding. (GRO does not mention any emperor at all where other versions mention Nikeforos, for it omits the death-bed recapitulation altogether and treats the conclusion with refreshing brevity.) It may be noticed that both TRE (1483) and AND (2349), in the middle of the passage describing the arrival of the Emperor (Romanos) in Kappadokia, have a line saying that the 'wonderful Basil' was on the border; this line refers of course to Digenes, but from its position a careless copyist might easily suppose that it referred to the Emperor, and that therefore the Emperor was not really Romanos but Basil. Although this ambiguous line does not occur in GRO, which in fact is careful to inform us that Digenes Akrites was only called Basil after the Emperor Basil's visitation, yet the possibility of an error of this sort should warn us against giving any overwhelming significance to the variation of the Emperor's name in one version out of five. (No Emperor is mentioned in ESC, perhaps another sign of the lateness of this version.)

(2) It is also possible that in the Russian version the name Basil is the result of a misunderstanding. In the Greek versions the Emperor is always called by his usual title of *Basileus* which in the course of transmission into Russian may easily have been mistaken for the proper name *Basileios*: and the proper name *Rômanos* may even have been mistaken for the adjective *Rômaios*, Roman, i.e. Greek; so that 'Romanos the Basileus' passed into the Russian tale as 'Basil the Roman (King)': although in the fragments extant he is only referred to as a 'certain Tsar called Basil' who held 'all the country of Kappadokia' (SPE, p. 331).

It is quite another point, to which we may return, that the definite placing of this incident in Kappadokia suggests a time when the frontiers of the empire were in Kappadokia, whereas later incidents imply a time when the frontiers of the empire were on the Euphrates so that two distinct layers may be traced here.

(3) The Russian version contains so many evidences of folk-story and popular transmission that it is not necessary to see in the defeat of the Emperor by Digenes, who has just jumped over the river Euphrates on his lance,[1] anything more than a climax of popular exaggeration. (SPE, p. 332; Kalonaros, ii. p. 290.)

---

[1] Professor W. J. Entwistle told me that the Dnieper is jumped in a Russian ballad; but such pole-jumping is also to be found in *Kallim. and Khrysorroe*, 2532.

(4) Over the Euphrates? (SPE, p. 332.) But what is the Euphrates doing in Kappadokia? Surely this combination in the Russian version of the Euphrates frontier and the Kappadokian frontier in the same incident can mean only that the Russian was transmitted from a Greek version in which the two frontier-periods were already combined; that is to say it must have been derived from a late and sophisticated conflation rather than from a primitive and revolutionary manifesto. TRE and AND combine Kappadokia with Euphrates, but not GRO.

(5) It may be true, as Grégoire argues, that the Russian version is nearer to the Songs than any other. But this means little more than that both show the same rustic deformities which are the result of oral transmission.

(6) If a loyalist or expurgated revision of the poem was formally put into circulation it seems very unlikely that the revisers would have left in their hypothetically wholesome version the insolent answer which Digenes returns to the Emperor's invitation; nor, it may be thought, would they have allowed him to lecture the Emperor on his proper duties.

(7) It is difficult to imagine the activity or believe in the efficiency of an Imperial propaganda which would have to discover all the manuscript copies of a heroic saga which was being chanted in the revolutionary centres along a mainly illiterate frontier, and substitute for them a sophisticated epic fit only for the appreciation of the capital.

We come now in Book VI (V in GRO) to a rather more than ordinarily episodic part of the poem. The poet seems to have been conscious that there was little left in his book but a collection of anecdotes, which could not be jettisoned because there was not only a general shortage of material but also a shortage of romantic relief. In order to make a suitable setting for these he would put them all into the first person and represent them as spoken by the hero himself to his friends after dinner. Accordingly the next two books (vi and vii in TRE and AND, v and vi in GRO) are spoken by Digenes in his own person;[1] and although it has been previously stated that he had no friends, he is now represented as illustrating the temptations to which a young man is exposed by telling his friends at table

---

[1] The first person narrative also breaks in at ESC 1115.

some of his own youthful experiences. The episodes in fact become examples of formal boasting, which is a feature of much heroic poetry of every age, like the 'Gabs' of Charlemagne and his knights (Chadwick, *Heroic Age*, p. 326; see, for example, *Iliad* xx. 83 ff.; and *Beowulf* 480, 636). The opening of GRO Book V, is careful to add that it was not for the sake of boasting but as a manner of repentance that Digenes once told the following story to a passing Kappadokian.

He begins with the strange tale of the daughter of the great Emir Haplorrabdes, who lived with her father and her mother Melanthia at the city of Meferkeh (GRO v. 66; TRE 1665).

Digenes was fifteen years old at the time (GRO v. 24), or eighteen (TRE 1610), and living with his love on the borders. [GRO, although it retains the detail at the beginning of Book V that he was living apart from his parents on the frontiers, omits the detail that he was living with his beloved Evdokia. It might have been thought that the redactor of GRO had omitted his marriage deliberately, in order to minimize his fall from Christian chastity; and had then perhaps been obliged to reduce his age from eighteen to fifteen in order to be more consistent with his celibacy; but a little farther on (GRO v. 57) he has inadvertently allowed Digenes to say that the daughter of Haplorrabdes seemed *deutera tês emês*; and he records the return of Digenes to his own love at the end of the book (GRO v. 281).]

The daughter of Haplorrabdes had the common fortune to fall in love with one of her father's captives (Eudoxios he is called in OXF 2233: OXF also gives the girl an oriental name, Aïssé, and calls her mother Fatouma instead of Melanthia), son of the Roman general Antiochus. They eloped together with horses and treasure but at their first encampment beside a well he deserted her and rode away. He was, however, attacked by the highwayman Mousour, who would have killed him if Digenes had not just then ridden over the border on his black charger. 'I killed Mousour', says Digenes, 'and gave the young man into the keeping of my friends.' (Mousour is the only person killed by Digenes who is given an Arab name; and he is not an *apelates* but is described as a *lêstês hodostatês*.) 'I rode on and soon came to the Emir's daughter weeping beside the water under the tree. I was at first frightened and thought I saw a ghost' (these two lines TRE 1641–2 (AND 2528–9) seem to be imitated according to

Legrand in the allegorical poem of Meliteniotes[1] 141–2), 'but she asked me to stay and rest and told me her story.' She repeats, without much verbal repetition, in greater detail and in character, the account which has already been given of her parentage, her elopement, and her desertion, after she and her lover had been three nights at the well. She had been here alone in the desert for ten days. The day before, an old man crossing the desert on his way to Arabia had told her how he had five days before seen her husband rescued from the brigand Mousour at a place called *Blattolibadi*, by the young Akrites.

At this moment a band of a hundred Arabs attacked them and attempted to carry her off, but Digenes soon scattered them. (The incident is omitted in TRE 1774 but the lacuna can be filled by AND 2671–2720 or GRO v. 177–97.) She recognized him as the Akrites who had rescued her lover and he offered to lead her back to him if she would renounce 'the faith of the Aethiopians'. She replied that she had already been converted by her husband, and he took her on his own horse to take her back to her husband at Halkogourna (TRE 1810; but GRO v. 238 Halkourgia; AND 2768 Hohlakoura). But on the road he was inflamed by her beauty, and did not resist the temptation. (This is the incident which deeply shocked W. P. Ker (*The Dark Ages*, p. 345). Perhaps more shocking to modern sentiment are the confessional phrases of the narrator.) He returned her to her husband—whose father had been killed long ago in subduing the Persians—and no more was said about it; but he gave him plenty of good advice; 'and still bitterly ashamed and repentant I returned to my own beloved in the middle of April.'

The narration of this incident which fills nearly the whole of the sixth book in AND and TRE and of the fifth in GRO is carried through with skill and liveliness. It should be noted that the episode

---

[1] For Melitêniotes see Krumbacher, p. 782, and Grégoire and Goossens in *Ant. Class.* ii. 2 (1933), p. 470, n. 5, according to whom Dölger has identified the author of this '*Poème Moral*' as Theodore M. and decided that the poem must have been composed between 1355 and 1395. This date cannot be regarded as certain; all that is certain is that all four authors of this name must have come from Melitene (Malatiyah), the history of which in the tenth century is closely associated with the background of *Digenes*. For other close verbal parallels between *Digenes* and the *Poème Moral* see Appendix D.

is yet another treatment of the major theme of the poem, that of a runaway marriage between an Arabian and a Greek, a treatment in which it is the Greek who appears in an unfavourable light; while one incident, the desertion of the bride, may be regarded as a pale reflection of the Emir's return to Syria; and another incident is a doublet of another favourite theme, that of a young couple at an oasis attacked by a band of robbers, a theme the major treatment of which we shall find in the next book. The spring under a palm-tree is a commonplace which becomes an obsession in ESC.

After this April repentance, Book VII (VI in GRO) opens in the month of May, the year's pleasant King, the loveliness of which moves Akrites, who is still the narrator, to set up his tent in a flowery meadow by a running pool. In the heat of the day he lay down to sleep while Evdokia, not less lovely than the flowers, went down to the water.

The set piece on the month of May (TRE 1860–1920) is in a lifeless and artificial style and is almost certainly a redactor's embroidery. Several phrases in it seem to be copied in the still more elaborate picture of May at the beginning of the allegorical poem of Meliteniotes (e.g. Mel. 37, 38 = TRE 1866, 1867—one of a large number of parallels, to some of which Sathas and Legrand first called attention in their introduction to TRE, introd. pp. cxli ff., and of which a fairly complete list will be found in Appendix D). The month of May has a proverbial quality in all European languages, and in Greece came to be known as *Kaloménas*; 'tears falling like Goodmonth hail' will be found in the Kerasund version of the *Sons of Andronikos* ballad (Polites, *Eklogai*, p. 298).

And so the Girl—she is always referred to simply as *Kore* (the name is used almost in a mystical sense; so Meliteniotes always calls the prophetess of his allegory 'the Maiden' *Kore*)—after sprinkling him with rosewater, and he asleep with the nightingales singing, went down to the water to drink and paddle. There she was attacked by a serpent in the form of a beautiful youth. She screamed, and Digenes sprang up and seized his sword and had soon slain the monster which now had three fire-breathing heads—(which ESC 1110 characteristically fantasticates into an old man's head, a young man's head, and in between them the head of a serpent).

This seductive dragon is remarkable as being the only instance in the poem of a definitely supernatural appearance: there is a sense in which the defeat of three hundred armed men by one unarmed hero is a natural occurrence when compared with the appearance of a fire-breathing dragon or a talking bird. MM. Grégoire and Goossens note that serpents in human form are definitely an Indo-Iranian theme. I cannot help thinking that for the suggestion of such an incident the author need not have gone farther than the garden of Eden. A serpent with four human heads also appears in the Russian version (SPE, p. 317) by the side of the magic spring in which a light seems to burn; but it is the spring in the forest in which the young Digenes is washed after his first hunting. The Russian version also contains a brief praising of the month of May (SPE, p. 319), but again it is in an entirely different context—in a letter to Digenes from Maximo (Maximiana).

So the Girl laughed at her fears, and Digenes lay down to sleep again; and the next time she called him from sleep it was to kill a lion which came out of the undergrowth and was preparing to spring at her. He killed it easily with his club without damaging its skin. This time she was cast down by her fears and asked him to play to her to raise her spirits. 'So I took my lute from the peg. . . . And the sound of the lute and the sound of her voice sent up a pleasant noise into the air and resounded in the mountains' (TRE 1986). It is almost as if the author were feeling for an effect which was recorded by a greater poet about eight hundred years later:

> O listen! for the Vale profound
> Is overflowing with the sound.
> No nightingale did ever chaunt
> More welcome notes to weary bands
> Of travellers in some shady haunt,
> Among Arabian sands. . . .

After this idyll by the pool—the Serpent and the Lion and the Song—the rest of the book is given up to fighting. First of all a band of three hundred Reivers, attracted by the sound of the lute and the Girl's singing, came down from the mountains and attacked them, trying to frighten him away from her: but he drove them away with his club and returned to the tent 'shaking his sleeves' (*seiôn ta*

manikia, TRE 2048, AND 3013; *to manikin eseion,* GRO vi. 158;
ehysa ta manikia mou, ESC 118).[1]

In OXF 2429 ff. there are only one hundred of them; and in
GRO vi. 115 ff. they are only forty-five soldiers 'passing by a way
called Trôsis': a place also mentioned later, TRE 2289, when
Philopappos is reporting to Maximo his encounter with Digenes;
and notable as one of the place-names identified by Grégoire.

Next morning when Digenes went down to the river to wash he
met Three Armed Horsemen, who asked him if he had seen the band
of Reivers. (There is a lacuna here in TRE 2053, which can be
filled by AND 3018–50 or GRO vi. 163–87.) He said they had indeed
come along and wanted to carry off his Bride; but he had not even
had to get on a horse to deal with them; they should soon know what
had happened to the Reivers; for they fell into the pit they themselves had dug. The Three Horsemen whispered together saying,
'Can this be Digenes the Borderer?' And to him they said, 'You
must prove your words: choose one of us and fight, and we shall
soon know.' 'But I only smiled and said, I am an only-begotten son,
and I live one and alone—*egô monogenês eimi kai monos diatribô*—but
with one man alone I have never yet fought.' (TRE 2069, AND
3066, cf. OXF 2442, but not in GRO which also omits the story of
Ankylas which Digenes now tells.) The washing on the banks of the
river suggests a reflection of the later scene on the banks of the
Euphrates. In fact the scene has suddenly shifted from somewhere
near the Kilikian Gates (Blattolivadi, TRE 1763) to the banks of the
Euphrates (Trôsis); and the story of Ankylas is placed in Mesopotamia (TRE 2073). The curious emphasis on his being an Only Son
and a Lonely Knight suggests that the line which is repeated more
than once (AND 3066, 3221; TRE 2223; ESC 1299; and GRO vi.
289, inf.) is meant to have some symbolic significance. It is to be
noticed in this connexion that to his great sorrow he had no children
(TRE 2950; GRO vii. 180); and that he was thirty-three years old
when he died. (Only in AND 1299 and in one of the Death-songs;
Laografia, i (1910), p. 232; also quoted TRE, introd. p. lxiii.) So also
were Jesus Christ and Alexander the Great. Digenes proceeds to tell
the story of Ankylas which is only found in TRE 2071–2123, AND
3068–3120, OXF 2495 ff., and PAS, pp. 379–81. It is a story within

---

[1] See *Laografia,* iii. 701; iv. 327; and N.T., Acts xviii. 6; Luke x. 11; Mark, vi. 11,
&c.; and cf. the modern proverbial phrase *makrya ta rouha sou.*

a story told by Digenes as a warning to the Three Horsemen, and although evidently interpolated and not included in the text printed below is fairly appropriate to the context.

One day riding down into the plain he had met a young man in Mesopotamia called Ankylas, who had unhorsed and disarmed him, and had written on his club an insulting message—you can tell all the other Reivers that you have fought with Ankylas and escaped alive. But a year later he says, 'I rode out to his abode and sang a musical challenge to my lute. When Ankylas rode out at me I just tapped him on the head and when I picked him up he was dead.'

So after some more challenging Digenes fights with the Three Horsemen, who are revealed as the *Apelate* (Reiver) chiefs, old Philopappos (he is fifty-two years old, TRE 2227), with Kinnamos and Iôannikios who appear to be his sons (GRO vi. 396; TRE 2276; AND 3366). When he had knocked the 'old man' down, the other two attacked him together 'like barking dogs' (TRE 2176), and there is a good long fight before, encouraged by the cries of his Girl, he defeats them, and spares their lives. Then Philopappos asked him to make peace and accept the leadership of all the Abactors. But Digenes replied (nothing about fighting to serve the imperial peace or anything of that sort): 'I do not want to command but to live alone; for I was an only son' (TRE 223; AND 3221; and this time the curious reason is repeated in GRO vi. 289).

At this point there is a lacuna in TRE, which can be supplied from AND 3225—3303 or GRO vi. 293–354. The Three Chiefs thank him and depart, but soon begin to wonder and murmur among themselves at their own defeat: fortunately no one had seen it. This Digenes had passed unhurt among their swords, as if he had been a spirit of the place (*stoiheion tou topou*, AND 3273, GRO vi. 326; ESC 1328 *thêrion ton topon tou blepei*—a characteristic muddle). Not less astonishing had been the beauty of his Girl: she had been like a living statue (*stêlê empsyhos*, AND 3277, GRO vi. 330; cf. below—TRE 2296, AND 3385, GRO vi. 413—where she is said to be like an *eikon empnous*; cf. Anna Comnena's description of her mother Eirene (Alex. iii. 3)).

They decide on the advice of Philopappos to summon their friends by lighting beacons, and then attack Digenes again at night. As for the Girl, of whose dazzling loveliness he had never seen the like, she should be given to Iôannikios.

1

The whole passage in AND 3234–3353 is muddled and corrupt with numerous repetitions. The offer of the Bride of Digenes to Little Johnnie (Iôannikios) as his share of the spoil is claimed by Grégoire, as formerly by Polites, to be a trace of an earlier story, which survives in some of the Akritic songs, according to which it was Digenes who carried off the bride of a hero called Iannakos. Grégoire's arguments are not fully convincing, however eager we may be to discover in the epic some trace of the *tragoudia* used in its composition. The songs dealing with the Rape of the Bride, which are reprinted by Kyriakides, Kalonaros, and Grégoire, may be described as variations of the Lochinvar theme, with contaminations from numerous other sources; they record a story that Digenes married by capture not the daugher of Doukas but the betrothed of a certain John. It is not true that GRO vi. 415 means that 'la femme de Digenis a été la fiancée de Ioannakes'. A comparison with TRE 2298 and AND 3387 shows that Eudokia was wanted for Ioannakes or Ioannikios only in some vague and distant manner: there is no suggestion of betrothal—even if we suppose that the words of Philopappos are meant to have any truth in them at all, in view of the fact that we are definitely told that he was lying in order to interest Maximo (TRE 2309, GRO vi. 425, AND 3367; cf. ESC 1365 *psevdeîs lôgous tês légei*). GRO adds the significant detail that Maximo did not even bother to ask who was the present husband of the Girl. It must also be remembered that the natural confusion of the Songs is complicated by the fact that in transmission the names Digenes and Giannes are interchangeable; and that in popular story such a hero as Digenes would have been credited with as many adventures in love as in war. (For the Lochinvar theme see also Polites, *Eklogai*, no. 75, p. 106.)

The lighting of the beacons fails to assemble the expected gathering of Abactors, so Philopappos is advised to 'go and see our kinswoman Maximo'. She was a maiden warrior descended from those Amazons whom King Alexander brought back from India (*ek Brahmanôn*, TRE 2270). (See the letter from the Amazons to Alexander in the Pseudo-Kallisthenes *History of Alexander*—they promise to send him 1,500 picked Amazons to be renewed every year.) Maximo seems to be some relation to Philopappos (GRO vi. 375; TRE 2259. In the Russian version she is his daughter; SPE, p. 31). So Philopappos goes to Maximo, and tells her that his sons are gone off to the borders to fight the irregulars. (It is not clear why *apelatai* should have to fight against *ataktoi*, unless these 'irregulars' were a rival band.) While he was riding along the frontiers, he tells her, he saw in a meadow at a place called Trôsis (TRE 2289; AND 3378; GRO vi. 406) the loveliest girl in the world: let Maximo prove her affection and kinship by helping to capture this girl for her dear Iôannikios. Maximo falls into the trap (the suggestion is that she would never willingly have had anything to do with an attack on Digenes if she had known that he was concerned). She called for Melementzes the leader of her own band of *Apelatai* and chose a picked troop of a hundred men. They are joined by Kinnamos with his own band, and come down to the bank of the river. (The scene now and for the rest of the poem is definitely on the banks of the Euphrates.)

On the advice of Philopappos he alone with Kinnamos and Melementzes advanced along the bank to spy out the position. 'And I', says Digenes, still the narrator, 'was sitting on a rock, holding my grey horse by the bridle, watching for them.' 'There he is,' said Philopappos; 'we must keep at a safe distance, but find out where the Girl is.' Melementzes thought this was ridiculous: he had never been afraid of a thousand men; and now was he to run away from one? (There is a lacuna here in TRE corresponding to AND 3474–3551 and GRO vi. 492–550.) So Melimentzes advanced alone to the attack (they had crossed the river though their passage is not mentioned). 'I knocked him off, saddle and all, but while I was watching to see if he would get up, Philopappos came from one side and wounded my horse in the thigh. I chased them only down to the water's edge, seeing their people all around on the other side and with my horse lamed, and unarmed as I was.'

(It is clear from the passages preceding that Digenes was armed only with sword and mace and dressed in a silk tunic while the others were armed with lances besides wearing body armour and helmets. This is a good example of the fact that in the Greek poem in the standard versions (TRE, AND, GRO, OXF) Digenes is a human warrior, not a giant or a magician as in the Russian version and in the Songs.)

'I returned to my camp, took arms and a fresh horse, then took the Girl and put her on my horse and hid her in a cave on a hilltop, with provisions, where she could watch without being seen.' (In OXF 2765 she is hidden in a wood where she can *not* see the fighting—a change very characteristic of the gentle monk who wrote it: he also silently drops the 'Amazon' story: Maximilla is just a modern young woman.)

'When I came down again, there they were on the other side looking for the ford, Maximo in the middle of the four others—Philopappos, Kinnamos, Ioannakes, and Leander.'

(Leander here makes his appearance for the first time and not for long; in AND 3552 alone five warriors were with her, Melementzes being one of them, the redactor of AND having apparently forgotten that Melementzes had already been disposed of (though he may have been only stunned). Or possibly his reappearance arose from a version from which the first unhorsing of Melementzes was missing owing to a lacuna as in TRE 2384. Melementzes reappears in the final battle in both AND 3634 and TRE 2465; GRO alone consistently presents the Big Four, instead of the Big Five, Leander appearing after the unhorsing of Melimitzes.)

Melimentzes, whose name appears as Melimitzes in GRO, and as Melema in OXF, has been plausibly identified by Adontz and Grégoire as the Armenian general Melias or Mleh the Great, who supported Kourkouas in many of his victories and was granted the frontier fief of Lykandos by Constantine Porphyrogennetos about 914. (See Const. Porph. *de Adm. Imp.* (Budapest, 1949), 50. 135 ff.) They have not noted the curious fact that according to Hasluck (*Christianity and Islam*, pp. 478, 482, quoting Langlois and Grothe) there are still heterodox tribes in the districts of Adana and Tarsus bearing the name of Melemenji.)

Now Lykantos or Liskantos occurs in *Digenes* as a place name, though not in connexion with Melimentzes. It seems to be referred to, in two versions only, in the passage in which Old Doukas, discovering the loss of his daughter—'It is too true an evil. Gone she is'—calls out the guard to summon his feudatories and send them in pursuit. ESC 920:

> agouroi apo tou Lykantos agouroi apo tên biglan
> boêthêsate eis tên pankopelon epêren to paidin mou.

AND 2006:

> andreioi ek tou Liskantos kai neoi ek tês biglês
> fthasate 's ton pankopelon, epêre mou tên korên.

It will be noted that AND ordinarily has a more correct text than ESC; but it can hardly be doubted that here Lykantos is the correct reading and must be the frontier town rebuilt by Melias in the first

decade of the tenth century. In the second line it is AND which preserves the obviously correct reading *ton* instead of *tên*. Kyriakides,
however, is so much obsessed with ideas of the antiquity and general
excellence of ESC, and its capacity for preserving geographical
clues, that he prints

> . . . *tên Pankopelon* . . .

and adds a footnote (*Dig. Akr.*, p. 27, n. 3) that a place-name is probably intended. Of course it is AND which preserves the true reading.
Although the word *pankopelos* is not in any dictionary, the meaning
'all-bastard' is sufficiently obvious, even without investigating the
word *kopelos* in the dictionary of Ducange.[1]

Maximo had come forward alone; she was riding a horse black as
a swallow, his mane and tail, his ears and his hoofs dyed with scarlet
('with henna', ESC 1487); and she herself was in cloth of gold with a
gold breastplate and a green turban, and she carried a blue and
gilded lance.

She asked where Digenes had his men, and when Philopappos told
her that he always went about like that, alone with his Girl, she
cursed him for an old fool (and very vulgarly in ESC 1520) for
making all this fuss for one man; she would cross over by herself and
bring them back his head. And she started forward; 'but I', says
Digenes, 'spoke up and said, "Men ought to come to women, and I
will cross over to you." I rode my horse into the deep water and swam
him over to the shallows where she was waiting for me.' In the fight
her lance was broken, and before she could draw her sword Digenes
(who seems never to have used a lance himself) had swung his
sword and, sparing her, cut off the head of her horse. He left her on
the ground crying for mercy, and was immediately surrounded by
her men gathering together like eagles; a battle piece of considerable
style and dignity describes how he killed or scattered her hundred
men-at-arms (TRE 2425–62, AND 3590–3629; but in GRO there is
only the bare record of their scattering and a protestation that he

---

[1] For *kopelos* see particularly Dawkins, *Mahairas*, ii. 250, 333, showing that this
Byzantine sense survives specifically in the Pontic dialect. Although the meaning
of *pankopelos* in this context cannot be doubted, it is difficult to produce any formation exactly like it. The nearest seem to be *pandoulos* (*Anth. Pal.* 5. 22. 3); *panaischros*
and *panaischês* (see L. & S.); *pankalê* (ESC 1738); *panchalepos* (Chariton, vii. 3); and
pantermos (*Erotokritos* i. 842) which is for *panerêmos* (Sofokles, s.v.) and not, as suggested by Xanthoudides, for *penterêmos*. The vulgarity of the language here (ESC
920) is paralleled by ESC 1520, *ho kôlos sou esynkryase*.

does not want to boast and is indeed only mentioning this occasion (as he said at the beginning of Book V) because he required forgiveness for what followed (GRO vi. 600–8)).

And so he was left to deal with the Five, Philopappos, Kinnamos, Ioannikios, Leander, and Melementzes (TRE 2466; AND 3460; but only the first Four in GRO vi. 620), who tried to cut him off from the river, and charged with their lances, but his armour and his sword made them all ineffective. Then Leander alone drew his sword but was knocked into the river, horse and all. The others turned to fly; only Melimentzes in TRE and AND as well as in OXF, which seems to be based mainly on their tradition, tries to turn and fight again but is unhorsed with one blow. He shouted after them but did not pursue them—'I always took pity on the fugitive. One must conquer but not over-conquer, and love one's opponents'— *Nikan kai mê hypernikan, filein tous enantious* (TRE 2510; AND 3679; GRO vi. 642. With these *parcere subjectis* sentiments cf. the lecture on imperial duties GRO iv. 1030 ff., TRE 1525 ff., &c.). He goes to send Maximo away with a warning and she thanks him for his mercy and blesses him for his valour, and asks that they may meet again in the morning in single combat. He accepts gladly and sends her home on one of the many horses now riderless. (GRO vi. 685–711 takes the opportunity to interpolate an explanation that his victory over such a crowd was mainly due to the help of the saints Theodore (both), George, and Demetrios.)

So he crosses the river to his tent, changes arms and horses, dresses in a purple silk tunic with a scarlet hood, and as it is already evening he does not visit Evdokia but sends to her two of his serving men (for they had separate tents for menservants and maidservants at some distance from their own and from each other—a domestic detail which is twice repeated: TRE 1453, 2555; AND 2315, 3737; GRO vi. 725, iv. 962). Then he crosses the river Euphrates and waits for the night to pass while his horse rests in the meadow. 'At dawn I rose up and mounted and rode into the plain and waited: and when the day came, and the daylight, and the sun shone on the heights, then Maximo appeared in the open alone. She was riding a horse white as snow, its hoofs dyed scarlet; and she wore a plated cuirass, and over it a tabard embroidered with pearls, and she carried a gleaming Arabian lance blue and gilded, a sword at her waist and a yataghan at her saddle, a shield of silver with a gilt border, and in the centre the head of a lion in gold studded with precious stones.'

Perhaps the two swords here worn by Maximo are the one-edged and the two-edged sword as worn by Waltharius (*Waltharius* 338) (for whose connexion with Digenes, if any, see below p. lxxiv.)

> Et laevum femur ancipiti praecinxerat ense,
> Atque alio dextrum, pro ritu Pannoniarum,
> Is tamen ex una tantum dat vulnera parte.

After riding round for a little they charged, but neither was unhorsed. When they drew swords, he cut her over the fingers so that her sword fell to the ground; and then to show how completely she was at his mercy he killed her horse, cutting it in two with a single stroke. She begged for mercy and told him that she had kept her virginity for the man who should conquer her. He says that he has a wife of his own; but they sit under the trees by the river where she bathes her wounded hand and puts on it the proper herb which they carried with them in battle. When she took off her armour her body gleamed as if seen in a mirror; the description seems to come mostly from a picture of Europa in Achilles Tatius, but there is another maiden in a gossamer singlet in Eustathius Makrembolites (ii. 4. 3). Afterwards he was ashamed of having yielded to a sinful temptation. He rides away saying 'go in peace and do not forget me' while Maximo, washing herself in the river, tries to make him turn back. But he rode quickly back to his own true love, his 'untroubled fountain set apart'[1] (TRE 2641), who questioned him rather sharply about his long absence. He told her that he had had to attend to Maximo's wounds, and her suspicions were soon allayed. In ESC (1580 ff.), however, the *Korasion* guessed what had happened and seems to have been rather amused.

So ends Book VII to which AND 3853–84 adds a lengthy recapitulation and peroration—and Book VII brings to an end the section which is narrated by Digenes in the first person. In the GRO manuscript there is a leaf missing after line vi. 785, and the editor has filled the lacuna by extracting lines 2632–72 from TRE. The original redactor of this GRO version has added to this incident a savage conclusion which occurs in no other version. On thinking it over, Digenes pretends that he is going for a day's hunting, rides back, and slaughters Maximo for her sin.

In the Russian version (SPE, pp. 319 ff.) Maximiana is the

---

[1] A reference to the Septuagint, Proverbs v. 18, *hê pêgê sou tou hydatos estô soi idia.*

daughter of Philipap, and Devgeny, after pole-jumping over the Euphrates, easily defeats them both and sends them home to his father and mother. But he refuses to join them or marry Maximiana, because the dream book tells him that if he marries her he will live sixteen years but if he marries the fair Strategovna (the daughter of the General) he would live thirty-six years. So he carried off and, after several bachelor parties, married the General's daughter (in a passage which is less unlike the Greek versions than the rest of the poem, SPE pp. 322 ff.) and then settled down to a life of fame and hunting until he was attacked by the 'Caesar called Basil' whom he defeated on the Euphrates and reigned in his stead. But the third Russian manuscript, dated 1761, recently discovered, which seems to provide a better and an older text than the two published by Speransky, brings the story to an end with the abduction of Strategovna.[1]

There is not much more to tell. Book VIII (VII in GRO), returning to narrative in the third person, describes with some elaboration the Garden and Palace which Digenes made for himself and Evdokia on the banks of the Euphrates. The description of the garden is to some extent a doublet of the description of the garden in May at the beginning of Book VII. The architecture of the Palace is described in detail. The tower, square at the base and octagonal above and so high that from the top one could see right over Syria towards Babylon (TRE 2765; AND 3970), recalls some of the tenth-century Persian towers of brick visited by Robert Byron. The decorations of the great hall include mosaics of Samson and the Philistines, David and Goliath, Saul, Achilles, Agamemnon, Penelope and the Suitors, Odysseus and the Cyclops, Bellerophon, Darius, Alexander the Great, Queen Candace (a queen of Tarsus in the Alexander legend, not to be confused with the queen of the Ethiopians of Acts viii. 27),[2] Moses and the Plagues of Egypt, and the miracles of Joshua the son of Nun.

Half-way through this list in TRE, AND, and PAS appear in the company of Kinnamos the mysterious figures of Aldelaga and Olope (TRE 2817; Aldegala and Elope, AND 4022; Aldephaga and Elope, PAS, p. 400), names which are enough to send us hunting through the *Thousand Nights and a Night*, especially if we have been

---

[1] See Appendix C for reference to Kuzmina's article published in 1953.
[2] Perhaps this is the Queen of Persia who appears in ESC 1671.

reading one of Grégoire's articles on Arabian contacts; inspiring names which caused Krumbacher, speaking of lost Byzantine romances, to give as an instance 'eine sonst unbekannte Leidens-geschichte des Paares Aldelagas und Olope' (*Byz. Litt.*, p. 855). Once again the relatively direct descent of GRO from the archetype is suggested by the fact that this manuscript alone has preserved in these lines (GRO vii. 86–88) the identity of Agamemnon, Penelope, Odysseus, and the Cyclops.

In the Allegorical Poem of Meliteniotes, mentioned above as containing expressions apparently copied from Digenes, there is mentioned (line 2218, ed. Miller, p. 105) among other monuments of famous men, one of 'Aderaphas'—a name which is said by Grégoire and Goossens (*Ant. Class.* i. 425) to be copied from the 'Aldelaga' of Andros. On this it may be remarked that this mistake is *not* confined to the Andros manuscript but is also in TRE 2817, PAS, p. 400. Secondly that the name Aderaphas was certainly not copied from any version of Digenes; for Meliteniotes goes on to attribute to 'Aderaphas' the 'bedstead of iron' of Og the King of Bashan (Deut. iii. 11); and it is evident that Aderaphas has taken his name as well as his bedstead from the same passage in the Septuagint, where the name *Raphaein* occurs (translated 'giants' in the A.V.). Cf. Meliten. 2000, *ton tou Raphan apogonon ton apo tôn gigantôn.*

The corresponding passage in ESC (1630–60) produces only a characteristically muddled account of the gardens, in which the bard tries to incite his memory by casting down for the catchword, and drawing up, twice, a line about water springing up at the foot of a palm-tree (ESC 1633, 1646) which rightly belongs to the beginning of the story of the daughter of Haplorrabdes, the Deserted Bride at the Oasis (TRE 1632; GRO v. 33; AND 2519). He skips the palace with a few vague lines about a building surrounded by golden animals spouting water; and then he makes the quite original contribution that Digenes built a Bridge; a Bridge which crossed the Euphrates in a single span,[1] and on it a four-chambered building of white marble to contain his tomb (ESC 1660–77).

[1] There can be no doubt about the meaning of *monokerato* although *keras* is not found elsewhere in the sense of 'arch' or 'span' or 'bow.' But Grégoire (*Ethnikos Kêryx* (Oct. 1941), and *Dig. Akr.* (New York, 1942), p. 94) prefers the astonishing reading *monocherata* which he translates 'built with his hands alone'.

Only two lines are given to the building of a Church of Saint Theodore (TRE 2854; AND 4059; GRO vii. 105). The Theodores seem to be the saints most often mentioned; AND 1920 (where he is called *megas apelates*), 2266, and 4236; with George and Demetrios (GRO vi. 701).

Here by the Euphrates Digenes lived, devoting his wealth to good works and the pacification of the Empire. All the princes and governors of Romania sent him gifts in gratitude for his services; and the *Basileus* every day sent presents to Akrites. Romans, Saracens, Persians, or men of Tarsus on the roads, not one of them dared approach without his order or pass without his seal, for the Apelates who served and feared him would have destroyed them.

Grégoire, having identified the headquarters of Digenes at Trôsis with Trusch near Samosata, clinches the identification and the nature of his activity by adding that on an adjacent hill there still stands a ruined monument of one of the Commagene Kings which may well have been known in local legend as the 'Tomb' of Digenes; while near by is a village bearing the name of Gömrük which clearly marks the site of a Byzantine *kommerkion* or custom house.

When his father the Emir died, in Kappadokia, his mother came to live with them (TRE 2880). Curious details are given about his domestic life: his dislike of having servants about him; they all had to keep out of his way; he would ring a bell when he was ready for dinner, and they would all withdraw before he and Evdokia took their places on one couch, and only one little boy waited in the room as a cup-bearer and was allowed to see her. They stood up when his mother came in last and sat in her own armchair; and after dinner they often had music and Evdokia would dance. The oriental seclusion of Evdokia is again referred to in the next book (TRE 3040 ff.; AND 4279 ff.).

The domestic habits of Digenes, which are described several times in the course of the poem, may be intended as models of feudal etiquette. It seems more probable that they were characteristics of a definite historical personage, and were perhaps copied from some lost imperial biography, or history of Alexander (cf. his entertainment of the wife of Darius).

Five years later (GRO vii. 190) his mother dies, and her death is celebrated in TRE and AND with a conventionally elaborate

moirologi. GRO omits the *moirologi* but celebrates her as the inspirer
of the peace everywhere imposed by Digenes: in fact her authorship
of the policy of peace is so much insisted on (GRO vii. 198 ff.) that
we begin to wonder if she was named *Eirene* with some symbolical
intention. In that case it is curious that GRO does not mention her
name at all, and that the name Eirene is only given to her in the
later versions AND (68) and OXF (67). GRO concludes Book VII
with her death. TRE and AND, closely followed by PAS (but not by
OXF which in the composition of the close is more akin to GRO),
begin their Ninth books with the death and *moirologi* of his mother,
and then have to fill up the rest of the book with a recapitulation of
the glory of Digenes, a list of the line of great Arab raiders whose
exploits were brought to an end when the Emir Mousour, father of
Akrites, called after his baptism *Ioannes* (TRE 3071), was baptized and
kept his faith and settled down in Kappadokia and begat the young
Akrites who wonderfully subdued the Outlaws and Irregulars who
held the passes and the marches so that they paid a tribute to the
Emperor. His successes were suitably rewarded by the Emperor
Nikeforos (TRE 3110; AND 4347).

In Book X (Book VIII in GRO) Digenes falls ill. 'All things in
this vain world come to an end'—a line which is found in every
Greek version (GRO viii. 1; TRE 3130 (as well as 2986, i.e. at the
beginning of each of the last two books); AND 4222 and 4368; ESC
1695; OXF 2975; PAS, pp. 403 and 406). GRO is quite brief and
rationalistic about it; his illness started with a cramp after bathing.
The doctors could do him no good and told him so. He sends them
away and calls Evdokia and makes her sit near him and in a fine
and moving speech recalls all their past life together: how fearlessly
he had carried her off; their lovely life in the desert at Blattolivadi—
the Serpent and the Lion and the Well; and how he fought with
Robbers, and Outlaws; and Maximo (whom he afterwards murdered
secretly, GRO viii. 120); she would have to marry again for protec-
tion and rather than endure the drought of widowhood. She begins
to pray and at the end of her prayer looks up and sees him in the
article of death and herself falls dead; so that he died happy. TRE
comes to an end at line 3182 at the beginning of his last speech; and
unfortunately it is not so satisfactory here to fill the gap from AND,
because AND ends as it began with a piece of rather weak and
monkish writing. The funeral of Digenes and his Tomb built on a

hill at Trôsis (GRO viii. 239) are described briefly in GRO and with much elaboration of lamentation and moralization in AND— which concludes (4727–78) with a final discourse on the vanity of earthly glory.

4. DISCUSSIONS

I

An attempt must be made to summarize the interpretations and estimates of the Poem of *Digenes* put forward by a succession of scholars from the first editors Sathas and Legrand down to M. Henri Grégoire, who, in a series of articles beginning in 1930 (assisted on questions of the relations of Byzantium and the Arabs by the researches of E. Honigmann, A. A. Vasiliev, and Marius Canard), has put these studies on a new foundation. He first entered this field by demonstrating that incidents of Anatolian history not mentioned by any Byzantine historian but known only from Arab sources could be traced in *Digenes*; he was soon showing that the author of *Digenes* was equally conversant with Byzantine sources; and in particular that some of the original details for which the Escorial version had acquired a reputation as a folk-epic of infallible originality were actually borrowed directly from Genesius, and in one detail went back to Herodotus. (See *Byzantion*, v (1930), pp. 327 ff.; and p. 128; ESC 254 ff.; GRO ii. 75 ff.; Genesius, pp. 121–6 (describing the capture of Ankyra by the Paulicians); and id., p. 94; *Theoph. Cont.*, p. 179.)

II

It must be remembered to the credit of Sathas and Legrand that they, the first editors, were the first to see that the historical incidents and background against which the hero was set in motion were the rebellions, in the ninth and tenth centuries, of the Paulician heretics, to whom Gibbon devoted a chapter and Bury an appendix (*Decline and Fall*, ch. liv; ed. Bury, vol. vi, pp. 110, 543). In spite of these attentions their doctrines remain wrapped in considerable obscurity. The publication of an Armenian text *The Key of Truth* (ed. Conybeare, 1898) is said to show that they held the belief, commonly known as Adoptionism, that Jesus was only a man until the entrance of a spirit on his baptism in his thirtieth year. They are said to have rejected the Old Testament, and to have represented generally speaking an advanced form of protestantism: they 'hated monkery, and protested against the superstitious practices and rites of the Church' (Baynes, *Byz. Empire*, p. 88). They are also said to have believed in a dualistic government of the world. A colony of Paulicians had been transported to Thrace in the seventh century and later are said to have spread westward through Bulgaria as far as Provence. They had no priests, and disliked all churches, icons, and relics.[1] On these grounds they have been approximated to, or identified with, the Iconoclasts, the Manichaeans, the Bogomils, and the Albigenses. Anna Comnena, who ought to know, speaks of the Paulicians as a branch of the Manichaeans (*Alexiad* xiv; ed. Reifferscheid, vol. ii, p. 257); and it will probably be safe to suppose that they were to some extent a link between the Manichaeans and the Iconoclasts. 'The Paulicians took refuge in Mesopotamia, and later in the Mohammedan dominions generally', says Conybeare (quoted by Bury (loc. cit.)), 'where they were tolerated, and where their own type of belief, as we see from the (Manichaean) *Acts of Arkelaus*, had never ceased to be accounted orthodox. They were thus lost sight of almost for centuries. . . at last they again made themselves felt as the extreme left wing of the Iconoclasts . . .' (cf. Baynes, *Byz. Emp.*, p. 88; Byron, *Byz. Ach.*, p. 174, is inclined to exaggerate the connexion with Iconoclasm). Of the connexion between Paulicians and Bogomils no doubt is possible, for colonies of Bogomils in Turkey were sometimes called Paulicians; but 'the Paulicians always appear in history as restless and troublesome, . . . the Bogomils, on the contrary, as meek, humble and ascetic'.[2] There seems to be no doubt that the Bogomils were both Adoptionists and Manichaeans, rejecting both the divinity of Christ and the ceremonial of the Church with a severe puritanism which they somehow reconciled with the extravagances of dualistic eschatology.

> These zealots ascribed
> this visible world to the work of a devil,

says Robert Bridges of 'those ancient Manichees' (*Testament of Beauty*, iii. 703 ff.):

[1] See S. Runciman, *The Medieval Manichee* (Cambridge, 1947).
[2] See D. Obolensky, *The Bogomils* (Cambridge, 1948).

from all time Goddes foe and enemy to all good:
In hate of which hellpower so worthy of man's defiance
they had lost the old fear, and finding internecine war
declared twixt flesh and spirit in the authentic script
of Paul of Tarsus, him they took for master, and styled
themselves Paulicians the depositories of Christ.
    Their creed—better than other exonerating God
from blame of evil—and their austere asceticism
shamed the half-hearted clerics, whose licence in sin
confirm'd the uncompromising logic, which inferr'd
a visible earthly Church to be Satan's device. . .

all of which may be accepted as a fair account of the Paulicians
except that they took their name not from Paul of Tarsus but from
Paul of Samosata, as is sufficiently proved by the passage of Anna
Comnena's *Alexiad* already referred to, which also suggests that the
Paulicians were more deeply infected than the Bogomils with
Manichaeanism. Obolensky, however, insists that their name must
be derived from an Armenian *Polik* (a contemptuous diminutive)
and that the connexion with Paul of Samosata 'cannot be justified
either doctrinally or historically' and 'must be finally abandoned'
(*The Bogomils*, pp. 55, 56).

    After the most savage persecution by the imperial armies, especially
under the Regency of Theodora (842–856), the Paulicians revolted
under the Armenian General Carbeas, formed an alliance with
Omar the Emir of Melitene, and fortified Tefrik (which appears as
Afrikê, GRO ii. 78) and other strongholds in the Armenian marches,
whence, says Gibbon, 'in their hostile inroads the disciples of St.
Paul [*sic*] were joined with those of Mahomet'. In 859 Carbeas
defeated Michael III, son of Theodora, under the walls of Samosata.
E. W. Brooks (*Camb. Med. History*, iv. 133) says that this reading in
Genesius should be amended to Arsamosata as 'Omar had nothing
to do with Samosata'; but Samosata was the headquarters of the
Paulicians. Under the Regency of Bardas (862–6) and the general-
ship of his brother Petronas, Omar was defeated and killed at Poson
in 863. But the Paulician rebels under Chrysocheir continued to
pillage Asia Minor till Basil I the Macedonian (867–86) sued for
peace, or at least sent an embassy of conciliation which led to a
renewal of the war. In a later campaign Chrysocheir was defeated
and beheaded (873) and Tefrik and Melitene and Samosata came
definitely under the Byzantine dominion. Yet, says Gibbon, 'the

spirit of independence survived in the mountains; the Paulicians defended above a century their religion and liberty, infested the Roman limits, and maintained their perpetual alliance with the enemies of the empire and the gospel'.

It is impossible to read TRE 187 ff. without accepting the identification of Chrysocheir the Paulician with Chrysocherpes, father of the Emir Mousour and grandfather of Digenes. Chrysocherpes (Chrysoberges in GRO i. 284), marrying Spathia of Rahab-Edessa (called Panthia in GRO i. 284), became son-in-law of Ambrôn who is Omar of Melitene. After the death in battle of Chrysocherpes, his son the Emir Mousour tells us that he was brought up by his 'Arabian uncles' (*theioi Arabitai*, TRE 80, 808; GRO i. 287); and these Arabian uncles must be Mousour of Tarsus, and Karôes, for the Emir's mother, in GRO ii. 75, explicitly calls Karôes her brother. Karôes is to be identified with equal certainty with Carbeas. All these principal identifications, Ambron–Omar, Chrysocherpes–Chrysocheir, Karôes–Carbeas, were originally pointed out by Sathas and Legrand in their edition of Trebizond (introd. pp. lxiv ff.) and have been abundantly confirmed by Grégoire. But I do not think it has been noticed that if the Emir Mousour is son of Spathia and of the Paulician Christian Chrysocheir, he is just as much a Digenes, a child of two races, as his own son who is the Digenes *par excellence* of the poem; and this is what he implies when he emphasizes the fact that he was brought up by his Arabian uncles or kinsmen; he means that if his father had not been killed he would have been a Christian (GRO i. 288 is corrupt, but the emendation is obvious); and if Spathia calls Carbeas her own brother (a point which Grégoire seems to have missed), she is definitely naming as an Arab of the true faith the other Paulician leader of Armenian extraction. What is the explanation? It can only be that the author had very little knowledge of the Paulician heresy. This is exactly what we should suppose from the fact that it is impossible to squeeze out of the poem the faintest trace of Paulician doctrine[1] (unless anyone is optimistic enough to suggest that the name of Digenes symbolizes a Manichaean dualism!). It follows that the poem is not and never can have been a Paulician pamphlet, as Grégoire suggests, of which fragments have survived in the Slavonic

---

[1] But see above p. xxxix for the possible significance of the name Soudales in AND 2024.

version (*Byzantion*, x (1935), pp. 335 ff.). For even if the pamphlet had been submitted as he assumes to loyalist revision before being reissued as imperial propaganda, the orthodox censors would certainly have left some signs of anti-Paulician odium; they would have emphasized the virtues of monasticism or the divinity of Christ or the unity of the creation, or some other points of doctrine on which the Paulicians erred; and they certainly would not have allowed Carbeas and Chrysocheir to be honourably mentioned in the family of the orthodox hero; and Chrysocheir to be openly glorified by his widow for refusing to apostatize before his death (TRE 190–5). The fact remains that the author of the poem as we have it is as surprisingly impartial as between Paulicianism and orthodoxy as he is between Christianity and Islam; if indeed his attitude is not so much impartiality as ignorance; for he does not seem to have ever heard of the Paulician heresy; and names the Paulician leaders only as brave enemies of the Empire, not distinguishable in any way from the Arabs who have now been conciliated. Sathas and Legrand were right in detecting that all the identifiable figures in the poem are connected by family and by locality to a Paulician milieu. They were wrong when they tried to stretch the evidence to prove that one of the objects of the Paulicians was the re-hellenization of the 'Roman' empire of Byzantium (TRE, introd. p. lxxiii), arguing only from a certain 'westernizing' tendency of Constantine Porphyrogennetos. They were unfortunately obsessed at the time with the great idea of producing a hero to lead Greece in a secular crusade against the Turks.

III

In this political obsession they were followed thirty years later by N. G. Polites who presented the poem as the 'National Epic of Modern Greece'. It is difficult to see how anybody capable of reading the poem from beginning to end could be expected to swallow this, seeing that the hero is *ex hypothesi* a happy fusion of Christian and Mohammedan blood. There is little religious fanaticism in the poem, and only the most perfunctory expressions of orthodox Christianity. There is in fact little sign of any real religious feeling at all. It would never have occurred to this 'Gentle Knight y cladd in mightie armes' to spend the hours before battle on his knees. It has already been remarked that all the opponents of Digenes appear to have been at least nominally Christians, with the exception of the highwayman Mousour (TRE 1617), and of 'Soudales the Saracen' (AND 2024; ESC 928); and the latter curiously enough, though called a Saracen, was fighting in the service of our hero's prospective father-in-law Doukas, and bore the name of a Byzantine general; of a Byzantine general who distinguished himself by his persecution of the Paulicians (see above, p. xxxix). Is this a faint trace of Digenes being on the Paulician side? (See refs. to Cedrenus and *Cont. Theoph.* in TRE, introd. p. lxxx.) Or is it only another detail which tends to show that the author was not composing propaganda for either Greeks or Paulicians but was writing romantically about battles long ago? These considerations suggest that theological passion was not as universal in the Empire as has sometimes been supposed. Distant provinces, unless agitated by particular local heresies, were inclined to be less fanatical than the capital not only because the shifting frontiers were natural areas of percolation and tolerance, but also because all bigoted theologians, from a natural love of temporal power, must usually have a centripetal tendency. If the author had any political theories at all, other than a general preference for peace, he may have been hinting that the Paulicians (represented by Chrysocherpes and by Digenes the grandson of Chrysocherpes, who would represent a non-existent but wished-for product of the Paulician-Arab alliance) ought to be used by the Empire to subdue or convert the Arabs. If he held such views, he might have expressed them more clearly. Or was it too dangerous for an Orthodox author to suggest that Paulicians might have their uses?

IV

The nationalism of Polites was a cause of distortion more serious than the linguistic prejudices of his successor S. P. Kyriakides, whose preference for the rustic language makes him overestimate the Escorial version and the Pontic Songs. But his admirable book on *Digenes Akritas* collects from the Byzantine chroniclers many invaluable illustrations of the Akritic life, showing its extraordinary passion for horses, hunting, and feats of strength; and his review (in *Laografia*, x (1928), pp. 623–62) of the first five Gregorian articles is of the greatest importance.

Kyriakides accepts in general Grégoire's dates (928–44) for the production of the original *Digeneid*, and even narrows it down, by the final destruction of Melitene in 934, to the decade immediately preceding 944 under Romanos Lekapenos (918–44). Then, by an extremely detailed examination of modifications which have been introduced into the genealogy of the hero in the various versions of the poem, he goes on to argue that it received two 'Doukas revisions' in the eleventh century under Constantine Doukas (1059–67) and Nikeforos III Botaneiates (1078–81). From the first of these revisions descends our Escorial version, from the second our Grottaferrata; and all our other versions descend from a third or Comnenian revision in the first half of the twelfth century. The endless argument about details seldom carries conviction, and his maintenance of the Escorial version in a position at the top of the tree nearest to the archetype is based on linguistic prejudice; product though it is, says he, of a Doukas revision, it shows signs of independence and of 'earliness', among which he is driven to enumerate, as pointing to the ninth century, the mention of the Emir's victories over 'Romans and Persians' (ESC 150) and of 'Soudales the Saracen' (see above), although Persians are also mentioned in TRE (2868) and Soudales in AND 2026; TRE has a lacuna here.[1]

Finally he notes that it is unnecessary to go back for an origin of the name of Digenes to a turmarch Diogenes killed in 788 (see below, p. lxxi). The epithet *digenes* is applied to Leo V the Armenian (813–20) by Symeon Magister; mixed parentage is a not uncommon attribute of royal or heroic figures as it is of Alexander in the Persian epic of Firdausi (see the *Shah Nameh* of Firdausi, translated by J. Atkinson, 1833, pp. 493 ff.). Sikander is born of the union of Nahid, daughter of Failakus (Philip), with Darab the Arabian general (see also pp. 375 ff. for the marriage of Gushtasp to Kitabun, daughter of the King of Rum, a curious episode with numerous Greek affinities, including the detail that the friend and brother-in-law of Gushtasp is called Mabrun who must be the Mavrianos of the Greek ballad).

---

[1] An examination of all the passages in which Persians are mentioned suggests that the name is used vaguely to indicate any enemies from the East. Add to the passages quoted above GRO iv. 975; GRO v. 260 (= TRE 1830); AND 2439, 1278, 4073.

V

In the train of Grégoire has appeared most notably N. Adontz ('Les Fonds historiques de l'épopée byzantine Digénès Akritas', in *Byz. Zeitschrift*, xxix (1930), pp. 198–227) who, naturally provoked by the Sathas–Legrand–Polites idealization of everything Greek, has proceeded to show that as a matter of fact everybody mentioned in the poem was more or less an Armenian. Indeed 'les hommes d'action à Byzance, soit au palais impérial, soit sur le champ de bataille, étaient principalement Arméniens ou d'origine arménienne'. This may be true of the period, and corresponds of course to the importance of Melitene. But the observation is historically misleading because the Empire habitually disregarded such distinctions: all its subjects were 'Romans' or 'Christians'. He is more convincing when he reminds us, and I believe he was the first to observe the fact, that the emperor Basil I the Macedonian (867–86), whose campaigns against the Paulicians led to the death of Chrysocheir, was himself so famous for his athletic and hunting exploits that Basil Digenes the Borderer might have taken from him both his name and his attributes. He also noted that the three heroines of the poem, Anna, Eirene, and Evdokia, seem to have been named after the ladies of the court two hundred years later, when the emperor, who married Evdokia, widow of Constantine Doukas, was called Romanos Diogenes (1068–71)—suggesting a later or Comnenian recension in the eleventh century. His examination of Armenian epic romances for alleged parallels and originals of incidents in the Greek is interesting but produces results fewer and less convincing than those extracted from the Arabic by Grégoire and his collaborators. That Armenians were unusually active and prominent in the ninth and tenth centuries is undeniable. But it is equally true that at this period men of every descent began to forget their races in the service of the Empire. From the middle of the ninth century, says Diehl, 'there really existed a Byzantine nationality'. By speaking Greek they became consciously 'Romans'.

VI

It was Grégoire who first turned his attention to Trôsis, a place on the Euphrates where Digenes is said to have made his camp in the meadow. He looked for it on the map—and there it was: a place called Trusch, a day's march from Samosata; and Samosata (actually mentioned in ESC 1320 in an incidental boast of the three Apelate leaders among themselves, but in no other version) was the capital of the ancient Commagene Kingdom on the upper Euphrates, the Kingdom of the Philopappi, and later became the metropolis of the Paulicians. Many of the rulers of the Syrian Kingdom of Commagene (suppressed by Rome in A.D. 72) bore the name of Philopappos, and the last of them, dying in exile in A.D. 114, gave his name to a familiar monument in Athens.[1] The name of Philopappos may well have survived in heroic legend round the ancient capital on the Euphrates, and it is at least a curious coincidence that Philopappos should be the name of the chief of the Reivers in the Digenes epic, reappearing in all sorts of mutilated and distorted forms in many of the Songs. But near Trôsis–Trusch on the Euphrates there stands on a hill another ruined monument of the Commagene period, and this seems to answer exactly to the poem's description of the tomb of Digenes (GRO viii. 239; in ESC 1670 ff. the more elaborate description seems to be reminiscent of Arrian's description of the tomb of Cyrus). But that is not all; near by there still stands a Roman bridge crossing a branch of the Euphrates—and this must be the bridge which Digenes (again only in ESC 1660) is said to have built over the Euphrates in a single span (*monokerato*). Grégoire, as mentioned above, cannot leave the single span alone, and produces a preposterous emendation; but it is hard to resist him when he argues that the frontier guards of Romanos Lekapenos, who advanced to the Euphrates after 928, saw these monuments of antiquity, the Bridge and the Tomb, and connected them in their ballads with their eponymous and partly symbolic hero Digenes Akrites. (He does not tell us when these singing soldiers imagined their hero to have lived—the Bridge and the Tomb cannot have looked very new—or what interval of time separated the soldiers' songs from the literary epic made out of them.)

Thus one layer of the poem—although layer is hardly the right metaphor for a tissue of fibres which penetrate the epic in all

---

[1] See E. R. Bevan, *The House of Seleucus*, ii. 268. 'The dynasty of Commagene vaunted it [the blood of the imperial house of Seleucus] and after the dynasty was brought down, [so did] the last members of the family. One of them, Gaius Julius Antiochus Philopappus, put up the well-known monument at Athens about A.D. 115 with a statue of Seleucus Nicator, his great ancestor.' See *Corp. Inscr. Att.* iii. 557; and Pausanias xxv. 8.

directions—derives from Melitene, and another from the Euphrates, which the Byzantine power bordered from 928 to 1071. The line of demarcation in the poem is exactly the front reached by the armies of Romanos Lekapenos, who died in 944. Other elements, as already shown, have led us to the decade 934–44. The Sacred *mandelin* is still in Arabian custody in Edessa whence it was removed in 944; and it must be after 934, Kyriakides has supplemented, for there is no mention of Melitene; Edessa is the headquarters of the Syrian Arabs; it was in 934 that Melitene, after the reconciliation of 928, was again attacked by Kourkouas and wiped out with the help of Melias and his Armenians (Kyriak., *Laografia*, x. 628; referring to *Theoph. Cont.* 416). But there are the unmistakable borrowings from Genesius; and his work is generally believed to have been written between 945 and 959, and can hardly have been in circulation before 944 owing to the dedication to Constantine Porphyrogennetos (Krumb., *Byz. Litt.* 264; Gibbon, ed. Bury, v. 503; Bury, *East. Rom. Emp.* 460; *Byzantion*, v. 346, vi. 495). To this difficulty Grégoire replies that there may have been an earlier edition of the History or an earlier dedication; that Miss A. Werner, a pupil of Heisenberg, has contended that Bury may have been mistaken in thinking that Genesius preceded the Continuation of Theophanes; or that both authors may have drawn independently from a common source now lost.

To these chronographical data must be added the fact that the poem also contains recognizable memories of the raiding of Anatolia by Paulician rebels in alliance with Omar of Melitene a hundred years earlier. Grégoire had first been led to examine the historical substructure of the *Digeneid* by noting that the destruction of Ankyra, which necessitated its rebuilding by Michael III in 859 (known from an inscription), is not mentioned by any Greek historian, and only from Arab sources is known to have occurred in 838; yet it is clearly referred to in the Greek epic (GRO ii. 77; AND 4291). Besides these memories of ninth-century campaigns, which require some expert knowledge to decipher, it is obvious that there is an older layer of the epic localized in Asia Minor before the imperial frontiers were advanced to the Euphrates. The move of Digenes from Kappadokia to the Euphrates is never explicitly referred to; but his parents remained in Kappadokia till his father's death when his mother rejoined him on the river banks; the career of Digenes may itself symbolize the imperial advance, though Grégoire never suggests this. In Kappadokia, Grégoire concludes, historic lays may have preserved and magnified the memory of an officer of the Anatolic theme named Diogenes, described as *tourmarches anêr hikanos,* 'a good regimental officer', who is known from Theophanes (Bonn, p. 718) to have fallen in battle in 788 at Kopidnado (emended by Grégoire to Podando) in the Taurus. (Kyriakides, as we have seen, thinks this supposition unnecessary.) In a later contribution (*Byzantion,* xi (1936), p. 608) Grégoire reaffirms this identification, and also that of Aaron Doukas (TRE 54), with a Bulgarian Aaron, Duke of Mesopotamia, who died about 1070, and is one indication of a Comnenian recension at the beginning of the twelfth century; and in his latest work (*Digenes,* New York, 1942, p. 34) the identification of Digenes with the 'good regimental officer' Diogenes, who was killed in 788, appears to be supported by the fact that Roland, eponymous hero of the French *Chanson,* was killed in the Pyrenees in 788.

A further note must be added about Grégoire's Diogénes; it is not easy to see how such a name could have developed into the adjective Digenés—an adjective of learned formation, and always used as such in the epic; the author of which might seem to have taken it not from any real person but from the Byzantine prose of his day. The adjective *digenés* is not used at all—except by one or two grammarians with the meaning 'of two genders' (as Aristotle *G.A.* iii. 9. 11 uses *trigenés* of a moth which is 'thrice-born')—until it appears in the history of Symeon Magister (Theophanes, Bonn, iii. 603), used of Leo V the Armenian (813–20)—*digenes ex Assyriôn kai Armeniôn* (Symeon was writing about 970). The idea of the double descent of great men, if not the adjective, is familiar in learned literature and in romance. Kyriakides, who gives us this quotation from Symeon, also points out (*Laografia,* x (1928), p. 661) that the Perso-Macedonian descent of Basil I is emphasized in *Theophanes Cont.* and that the idea of the double descent of Alexander and of other great men is common in the Alexander Romance and in Firdausi. But in the ballads Digenés is used only as a proper name; and the idea that a descent from two races is an advantage seems to be unfamiliar to the ballads. They often seem to adopt the name without knowing what it means; and show signs of trying to regularize it as a proper name by shifting the accent back to the penultimate and calling him Digénes. The result of this shift is that the name is very soon corrupted to *Giánnes* (e.g. the ballads on the death of Digenes in *Laografia*, i (1910), nos. 27, 31, 38, 39).

Finally it must be said that even if Diogénes were a more convincing figure, it is apparent that the epic is not about a good officer or even about a successful general of the imperial government, but about a lonely hero of romance; a hero who somehow crystallized social and political emotions and perhaps—like King Arthur or like Robin Hood or like Piers Plowman—was not a reflection of any clear original.

Grégoire's most original and substantial contribution to Digenic research is his dissection and exhibition of the Arabic element in the poem. Digenes has an Arabic counterpart, an historical character named Abd Allah Abu-'l Husain el Antaki el Battal, commonly known as Sidi Battal who was killed in an Arab raid at Akroenos in 740 (see Hasluck, *Christianity and Islam*, p. 709). His apocryphal adventures are enshrined in the Turkish romance of *Sidi Battal* (itself not earlier than the fourteenth century, and most familiar in Ethé's German translation), and his tomb near Eskishehr was still a place of pilgrimage in Asia Minor in the twentieth. He also married a Christian princess and in fact had several Christian wives, one of whom was the daughter of his vizir Akrates—so named, presumably, after Akrites himself. (Hasluck (pp. 706 ff.), from whom most of these details are taken, makes a strange slip when he remarks that 'Digenes Akritas elopes with an emir's daughter'.) This Turkish romance acquires some historical importance when Marius Canard discovers that it incorporates the substance of a tenth-century lay of the Emir of Melitene, an Arabic Gest of Omar of Melitene the existence of which Grégoire had suspected must underlie the earlier part of the Digenes epic, occupied largely as it is with Arabian andragathy and celebrating the gallantry of the Emir (father of Digenes) and his grandfather Ambron (who is Omar of Melitene although Melitene is never mentioned). This Arabic epic material appears most clearly in GRO; more clearly than in ESC which Grégoire usually quotes; it refers openly to the Emir's harem, as in fact do all versions except the seventeenth-century OXF; see TRE 215, GRO iii. 127, AND 669—all references quite as explicit as ESC 236 to the *terpna korasia* he has left behind him. GRO is the only version which refers to the Moslem sanctuary at Palermo, GRO i. 101; although ESC refers to Mecca and the tomb of Mohammed (ESC 537, 564). Sidi Battal himself is fanatically Moslem in spite of his Christian wives, but the romance is a late Turkish recension. It is possible that a Gest of the exploits of Omar of Melitene, the existence of which can be traced not only in the Adventures of Sidi Battal but also in an earlier Arabian epic, the *Dat el Himmat*, was used by the author of Digenes to furnish the exploits of the hero's father and grandfather; but it is more probable that the exploits of Omar were familiar in local tradition.

The conversion of the Emir Musur evidently corresponds, says Grégoire, to the historical submission of an Emir of Melitene to the Byzantine general John Kourkouas in 928. But the dating of all these campaigns is extremely precarious (see Runciman, *Romanus Lecapenus*, pp. 137 ff.); it seems much more likely to correspond with the final capture of the city in 934, when 'only Christians were allowed to remain inside the walls, whereupon the majority of the population hastened to be converted' (ibid., p. 142); and the fact that in this culminating attack Kourkouas was supported by Melias (who has been identified as Melimendzes) shows how difficult and unnecessary it is to follow into extreme detail the historical incidents reflected in the epic. The place which historical detail occupies in the Digeneid must be conditioned by the character of the poem. If it is, as Grégoire appears to believe, a semi-political manifesto, it should have as a background a prejudiced perhaps but at least a recognizable picture of the contemporary scene. If it is a romance enlivened by the occasional appearance of historical characters, it is legitimate to identify these but unnecessary to expect them to coincide in detail with their prototypes.[1]

The fall of Melitene was followed shortly, as the Arab but not the Byzantine chroniclers report, by the conversion of a whole tribe, the Beni Habib, of Syrian Arabs; an incident which strikingly recalls the conversion, in *Digenes*, of the Emir's mother and all his household and their migration to Kappadokia. It is known, however, that similar conversions were not rare. Kyriakides (*Digenes*, p. 69) quotes an edict of Constantine Porphyrogennetos by which Saracen prisoners are encouraged to marry and settle down by three years' exemption from taxation. After the victory of John Kourkouas the

---

[1] It is pertinent to recall the appearance of Charlemagne in the *Chanson de Roland*, and that of Attila (Etzel) in the *Nibelungenlied*.

imperial attitude towards the Syrian Arabs became one of conciliation and peaceful penetration, says Grégoire rather questionably. It
was hoped that the friendly Syrian Arabs might form a buffer against
the darker tribes from the south, the 'Egyptians', and the Arabs
from Baghdad who had failed to come to the help of Melitene. It is
specially noted in *Digenes* (GRO i. 32) that the Emir, whose marriage
and conversion produced the hero, was fair and handsome, 'Not
black like the Ethiopians'.

With the help of Marius Canard, Grégoire follows the Emirs of
Melitene from the Arabian chroniclers into the *Arabian Nights*.
But no useful end seems to be served, as far as Digenes is concerned,
by recognizing their appearance there, or the appearance of other
characters some of whom seem to have come from the Akritic cycle
(as we have already noticed, above, the appearance of Maurianos in
the *Shah Nameh*). We are not impressed by the resemblance, detected
by Grégoire, between the Magic Horse of the Arabian Nights and
the Rape of Evdokia. Even if we were, it would be unnecessary to
deduce any Arabic or any Greek priority, or any specifically literary
influence. In Mesopotamia a common reservoir of folk anecdote,
which is always more local than national, must have been decanted
indifferently into Greek *tragoudia* and into Arabic bazaar stories;
and much later recorded in the literary redactions of *Digenes Akrites*
and of the *Thousand and One Nights*. Difference of language is no bar
to the diffusion of folk-tale. Mesopotamia had been a mixing bowl
and centre of diffusion for a thousand years or more—and nearly
all the inhabitants of Syria must have spoken more than one
language. It is only with the growth of nationalism and the spread
of public education that the ability to speak more than one language
has come to be regarded as the privilege of a minority.

After following Arabic themes eastward to Persia and westward to
France, and after applying the methods which were so successful on
the Euphrates to the upper reaches of the Meuse, Henri Grégoire
was conducted by the Nibelungs[1] to the tenth-century Latin poem
Waltharius. There he finds on a hill-top in the Vosges the hero
Walther spending the night, while his enemies approach, with his
head in the lap of the damsel Hildegunde (*Waltharius*, ii. 490 ff.;
Grimm and Schmeller, *Lateinische Gedichte des X. und XI. JH.*
(Göttingen, 1838), p. 19; see also Raby, *Secular Latin Poetry*, i. 262 ff.).

[1] The last of whom, by the way, was Napoleon; see *Byzantion*, xi (1936), p. 614.

This, cries Grégoire, is exactly what Digenes does in the Russian version after he has carried off Evdokia (SPE, p. 327). In this passage Devgeny, having carried off the daughter of Strategos, says to her, 'Sit down and look in my hair until your father and brothers arrive. If I fall asleep do not wake me in a fright but gently' (see also Kalonaros, ii. 285). It is a passage which shows the contaminating folk element in the Russian version, but otherwise has little significance. The *Waltharius* is a literary exercise written by a schoolboy who knew Virgil and a little Greek and took a German story for his plot. No source, says Grégoire, has ever been discovered for this episode, and this German boy must have seen the primitive Greek original of the Russian version: it is a final proof for him of the existence of a primitive Greek version which followed the fantastic lines of the Russian. But Devgeny was not the first young man, nor was Waltharius the last, to sleep with his head on the lap of a damsel who wakes him *attactu blando* at the proper moment; and whether she cleanses his head while he is asleep, as in the Russian version, or only strokes it to wake him up is an accident of place. We know that head-in-lap is a characteristic position of the dreaming King in Celtic legend, especially before battle;[1] and *Waltharius* is not more relevant to *Digenes* than is the ballad of *Lady Isabel and the Elf-Knight* (Child, no. 4, A.; p. 5):

> 'O sit down a while, lay your head on my knee
> That we may hae some rest before that I die.'
> She stroak'd him sae fast, the nearer he did creep,
> Wi a sma charm she lulld him fast asleep.

After all this it will perhaps seem surprising that although Sathas and Legrand chose to identify Digenes, by appealing to the Porfyrios of the Songs, with an obscure Byzantine general called Pantherios, a relative of Constantine, who is supposed to have deserved some of the glory of Kourkouas whom he replaced in 944 (TRE, introd. p. cxxvi), no one has yet found any connexion between *Digenes* and the Georgian epic *The Man in the Panther's Skin*. Nor has it yet been suggested that Digenes, the Lonely Knight, symbolizes the Monothelite heresy, with Maximo to represent the seventh-century champion of orthodoxy, Maximus the Confessor. But Grégoire has succeeded in tracing Maximo to a Greek inscription of the second

---

[1] See E. Ettlinger, 'Pre-cognitive Dreams in Celtic Legend', *Folk-Lore*, lix (Sept. 1948), pp. 114–17.

century A.D., which was found at Sebastopolis (Sulu-Serai) on the Black Sea, was recorded by Röhl in 1875, and has now disappeared. It was erected to the memory of a woman described as *matrônan stolatan*, and *archiereian*, and wife of a *pontarches*, and she is named as

KESE(NN)IAN MAXIMAN TÊN KAI AMAZONIN.

Districts associated with the cult of Hercules, as was the town of Sebastopolis, were traditionally sites of colonies of Amazons; the same tradition no doubt led one of the great ladies of Sebastopolis to take the surname of Amazonis. This inscription, says Grégoire, must certainly have been seen and misunderstood by some Byzantine soldier of the Charsianian Theme, and gave rise to a local story which suggested the name of Maximo for the Amazon adversary of Digenes.[1]

5. CONCLUSIONS

I

It has been made sufficiently clear that *Digenes* is not a conflict between Greek and Barbarian, Christianity and Islam, or East and West. Partly of course this is because, as Baynes says in a passage already quoted, in the eighth and ninth centuries the heart of the Empire was in Asia Minor and Armenia. There is something more that can be said about the relation of the Christian and Moslem aspects of the poem. Why should a Christian author trouble to include in his work, with very little alteration, the substance of a Moslem epic? An answer to this may be borrowed from another quarter. Recent finds of Byzantine art in Russia have occasioned argument about the priority of Greek and Iranian motives. In reference to these discussions Talbot Rice has remarked that 'it is not possible to speak of the influence of the East upon the West because from the seventh to the twelfth centuries there was neither east nor west'.

This highly relevant remark may be supplemented by a quotation from H. St. L. B. Moss (*Birth of the Middle Ages* (1935), p. 144): 'The culture of Islam was not, as is often supposed, an Asiatic civilization, irreconcilably opposed to that of Europe. It was, on the contrary,

---

[1] See Grégoire, *Dig. Akr.* (New York, 1942), pp. 136 ff. I have to thank M. Grégoire for communicating this discovery to me in a private letter (March 1936) a year before its publication in *Byzantion*, xi (1936), pp. 607 ff. and *Mélanges Cumont*, fasc. 2, pp. 723 ff. There are some good notes on the Female Warrior in history and literature in Hasluck's *Letters on Religion and Folklore*, pp. 204-9.

a product of the same elements as those which formed the back-ground of early Christian thought, the union, namely, of Hellenistic culture which pervaded the near east.' He goes on to remind us with a reference to Vasiliev (vol. i, p. 274) that in the eyes of many medieval writers from John Damascene to Dante (*Inferno*, xxviii. 31) Islam was not a pagan religion but a Christian heresy. This attitude helps to explain the carelessness with which Moslems and Paulicians are confused in the genealogy of Digenes.

If the author had been writing 'historically' about the Arabs and the Empire before 944, would it have been possible for him to avoid mentioning the victorious general John Kourkouas? 'The Greek chroniclers lauded John Kourkouas as the man that brought the frontier to the Euphrates', says Runciman (*Romanus Lecapenus*, p. 148); 'for once they were guilty of underpraising'. Sathas and Legrand (TRE, introd. pp. cxv ff.) suggest that there was a con-spiracy between Constantine Porphyrogennetos and the chroniclers to exalt the Armenian Kourkouas and suppress with silence the achievements of the Greek Pantherios; and that the magnificence of Pantherios is presented in the figure of Digenes, who is in fact the historical Pantherios of whom very little is known except that he was of the imperial family. But now an even greater difficulty arises which does not seem to have been noticed. Our hero Digenes is not a general at all. He never led an army in his life. He chooses his own lonely and errant life on the borders. It is ridiculous, therefore, to look for him in the regular army or in the regular bureaucracy of the Empire. If it is strange to find no mention of Kourkouas, it is equally strange that another Armenian, Melias or Mleh the Great, whose rise to power is recorded in Constantine Porphyrogennetos (*de Admin. Imp.*, Bonn, pp. 227, 228), the constant ally of Kourkouas in his campaigns against the Arabs, should appear in an unflattering light as Melimentzes whom Digenes unhorses with a single blow: Melias who was given the frontier theme of Lykandos in 914 and shared with Kourkouas the triumph of Melitene in 934. (Adontz thinks that Kourkouas himself does appear—as Ioannikios; and Grégoire at one time suggested that Digenes himself represented Melias, and by defeating him assumed his exploits.)

II

Grégoire believes that the poem—that is the archetypal version—

must have been written after 930, when Melitene was destroyed, and before 944. His reason for this is that in GRO iii. 135 the Emir's mother, resisting his attempts to convert her, refers to a famous local relic—'The Towel of Naaman'. He assumes that this must be the famous 'Sacred Image of Edessa', a towel on which Christ had wiped his face, leaving on it an impression or mould (*ekmageion*) which he sent to King Abgar of Edessa.

Unfortunately, as noted above (p. xxxv), Grégoire forgets that there was a second Relic, no less sacred than the Sacred Image, which was not removed from Edessa in 944. This was the Letter from Jesus Christ to the leprous King Abgar; it was more closely associated with Abgar than the kerchief, and more likely to be confused with Naaman than the portrait of Christ; it might even have been described as *tou Naiman to mantato*—the letter of Naaman—and a Greek scribe thinking of the more famous relic may have changed *mantato* into *mantili*. There may even have been a third relic, rightly called *tou Naiman to mantili*, which was the towel on which Naaman wiped himself after bathing in Jordan. Edessa, as Hasluck notes (*Letters on Religion and Folklore*, pp. 129, 172), was a great clearing-house of religious legend. The letters of Christ and Abgar are preserved in Eusebius (*Eccl. Hist.* i, 13), copied from a Syriac manuscript at Edessa. A modern version of the story and the text of the Letter for use as a charm are to be found in a pamphlet of magical formulas from Cyprus now in the Cambridge University Library (pam. 5.91.1434. *Kyprianarion periehon proseuhas kai exorkismous. . .*, K. Belefantou (Leukosia, 1913), pp. 29, 30). Christ, on the appeal of Abgar, sent not only the Letter promising the evangelizing visit of Judas son of Thaddaeus, but also, by the same messenger, Ananias, the self-portrait on a towel, after Ananias, himself an artist, had failed to draw it. This version combines both Portrait and Letter and the Letter is said to have remained at Edessa till it was captured by the Byzantine General Maniakes in 1031, six years after the death of Basil II. Maniakes, by the way, was famous for his herculean strength and stature (Psellos, ed. Sathas, p. 137; cf. TRE 974; AND 1511; GRO 1179). By that time Romanos III Argyros was on the throne, and he started negotiations with the Arabs. Vasiliev says that they resulted in a treaty for the rebuilding of the churches of Jerusalem. In any case the Arabian Wars, which had lasted without any considerable intermission for three hundred years, now came to an end. We have found another Basil, another Romanos, and another Relic of Abgar–Naaman, nearly a hundred years later than the first; and in some respects they are more congruous with the data than the other trio.

III

The poem of *Digenes* is in fact a romance, and a romance destitute of theological or political propaganda; fortunate is the reader who can not only find in it with Grégoire (*Ant. Class.* i. 424) 'des indications géographiques nombreuses et précises' but draw any substantial information from them. It is marked by a complete absence of fanaticism or political urgency because it is based on floating folk-tale; and it is of learned execution because it is written by a monk or scribe with enough education to want to make out of floating folk-story something permanent like '*l'art des musées*', that is to say like Homer, or perhaps like Pseudo-Kallisthenes. We know that it was written when there had been for some time a 'Roman peace' on the frontiers of the Empire and when there was a possibility and a prospect of that peace being maintained. The author is telling a story of the past and not recording contemporary events. He has heard of the Paulician rebellions but knows very little about them, in spite of the fact that he appears to be writing in their own country on the Euphrates. He can suppose without improbability that the funeral of Digenes was attended by delegations from Baghdad and Babylon; and he took apparently from an Arab source a chronicle of the Arab raids of the ninth century as part of his background. He had no difficulty in reading it because as a dweller on the frontier he was certainly bilingual, like the Emir (GRO i. 115). As his poem was intended for Greek readers he was careful to connect his hero with no generals, no armies, and no big cities. Historical characters in romance, like the author's friends in a modern novel, are often difficult to disguise; when he was obliged to name a Greek family he avoided the difficulty by calling them all Doukas.

IV

The author of the original *Digeneid* (and there is no reason to suppose that it was very different from the Grottaferrata version) was a Greek or rather a 'Roman', from the district of Syria Commagene. He was probably a monk. His language is largely drawn from the Septuagint, and he has some pretensions to a literary education, although his knowledge of past history seems to be a pantheon of biblical heroes and Alexander the Great; he is more familiar with Heliodorus and Achilles Tatius than with Homer. (The actual quotations from the *Iliad* only occur in TRE and AND; *Iliad* i. 365—TRE 1218, AND 1808; *Iliad* ii. 489—TRE 504, AND 1018; they seem to have been added as part of a definite writing-up of GRO (see especially GRO iv. 391, a gnomic line identical with TRE 1221, where TRE (followed of course in more popular language by AND) has added the quotation from the *Iliad*). But GRO shares with TRE a reference to Odysseus and the Seirens: GRO iv. 261; TRE 1117.) His literary culture is small. But he has intimations of a highly civilized idea, the idea of imperial peace, the opposite of nationalism; an idea which might come naturally to one who lived on the tidemark of the Byzantine armies, and was not, for all that, any commoner in the tenth century than it is today. It would be pleasant to believe that in the figure of Digenes the author was personifying a new political ideal for the future of the Empire:

ostendent terris hunc tantum fata neque ultra
esse sinent. . . .

And where in the history of the Arab wars are we to find a period of established peace for the author to look back on?

Grégoire finds such a pacific interval in 928 and even discovers that Kourkouas was then following a new policy of 'pacific penetration'. Less optimistic surveyors of the eastern frontier will find it difficult to discover any settled frontiers before the victories of Nikeforos Fôkas (963–9); or any tranquillity before the victories of Basil Bulgaroktonos (976–1025). When Romanos Lekapenos advanced to the Euphrates he had come to the brink of another hundred years of unceasing warfare. It was only the victories of Basil Bulgaroktonos, culminating in the last taking of Edessa, and the capture of the second relic of Edessa, the Letter of Abgar, by George Maniakes, that inaugurated a period of established peace on the Mesopotamian frontiers during the reign of Constantine Monomachos (1042–55).

Reference has been made to the description in the history of Psellos (ed. Sathas, 1899, p. 123) of George Maniakes. Psellos (1018–79) wrote the earlier part of his history about 1060 and gives a personal description of Maniakes the victor of Edessa. He towered over everybody; his voice was like thunder, his hands looked capable of shaking walls and shattering gates of bronze; his spring was like that of a lion; and his fame even surpassed his actual appearance; every enemy of the Empire (*barbaros*) was afraid of him, either from having seen him or from having heard the stories about him. The same historian has also left us a striking description of the beauty of Constantine IX Monomachos (ibid. p. 147) which exceeded in naturally exquisite form, colour, and proportion the poetical descriptions of Achilles and 'Nereus'.[1] His head was ruddy and gleamed like the sun while the skin of his breast and belly was of a dazzling whiteness, so that, in his youth of course, and before he fell ill, one might have looked and said that his head was like the sun surrounded with shining rays of hair and the rest of his body like pure and transparent crystal. Both these descriptions recall the descriptions of Digenes, though none of the details are identical, except that the breast of the youthful Digenes was also like crystal (GRO iv. 199, TRE 974). There is nothing in the least decisive in such descriptions, though the resemblances are certainly greater than those which Kyriakides detects (*Laografia*, x. 656) between the description of the twelve-year-old Eirene (AND 124 ff.) and Anna Comnena's description of her own mother Eirene (*Alex.* iii. 3; ed. Reifferscheid, vol. i, p. 101).[2] But they certainly add to the probability that the middle of the eleventh century was the time when a provincial author, a Syrian or Mesopotamian monk, could have looked back into the past over a considerable period of peace, and attributed its establishment to a fictitious hero who had been honoured by an emperor named Basil, or (in a second edition) by two emperors named Romanos and Nikeforos.

The crystalline torso of Constantine Monomachos had already been noticed by Sathas and Legrand (in their note on TRE 974) who refer to uses of the same simile in later romances (*Florios and Platziaflora* and *Imberios and Margarona*). It is in fact a commonplace in Byzantine authors[3]—but not before the eleventh century.

[1] Psellos says Nereus. But the reference is to the Homeric Nireus of *Iliad* ii. 671. Cf. Propertius iii. 18. 27, 'Nirea non facies non uis exemit Achillem'—where also all the manuscripts read Nerea.

[2] I have mentioned above, p. l, a more striking verbal resemblance from Anna Comnena, and from the same page; and this resemblance occurs not only in AND and TRE, but also in GRO, which, according to Kyriakides, escaped any Comnenian recensions.

[3] And reappears in folk-song: see Polites, *Eklogai*, no. 195: *agoure drosere kroustallobrahionate*.

V

The emperor Basil who delights to honour his namesake *Digenes* in the oldest version (GRO iv. 972) is clearly Basil II, the Bulgaroctone (976–1025), 'who at that time was managing the empire of the Romans, Basil the blessed, the great conqueror, who indeed buried with himself the imperial glory; for he happened to be making his expedition against the Persians in those parts where the Boy was to be found'. His Persian campaign may quite permissibly refer to Basil's Georgian campaign of 1021, although Kyriakides, while accepting the manifest reference to Basil II, decides that *Persón* cannot here mean Persians—*etyhe gar kata Persón poión tên ekstrateian*— but is an anachronism put in in the eleventh century as a compliment to Nikeforos Botaneiates who was proud of his descent from Basil II. (*Laografia*, x. 654.) It is noteworthy that in GRO iv. 56 'Basil the Blessed the Great Borderer' is also given as the name of the emperor who had banished the grandfather of Digenes; and that owing to the length of his reign Basil II is one of the few emperors who might really have lived to honour the grandson after banishing the grandfather. (The corresponding passages in TRE 836 and AND 1369 mention Romanos as the emperor who banished the grandfather, evidently because in those versions it is Romanos who honours the grandson Digenes.) Sathas and Legrand connect the disgracing of the grandfather with the conspiracy against Leo VI in 908 led by the real Andronikos Doukas who strangely enough went over to the Arabs (TRE, introd. p. xcv). All of which goes to show again that the history of *Digenes* while often recognizable is not real history. It is 'typical' history presenting a generalized or abstract picture of the Eastern frontier.

The elaborate theories of Grégoire and Kyriakides, who suppose that successive revisers made genealogical interpolations in order to do honour to various living individuals, require us to think that the author or reviser possessed a mentality which is not to be found in other parts of the poem; and ask us to believe, if we can, that a Doukas at any period within the author's range would have been highly honoured on being related, by an anonymous monk, to the grandmother of a legendary hero. The author undoubtedly took what names he could from the histories available, and he would not have had to look very far to find the names of Doukas or Mouselês: and as for damsels, there are fourteen Evdokias and twenty-one Eirenes in the index of Ducange's *Familiae Byzantinae*. It must have been from a history book that he took the name of Soudales the 'Saracen' who fought for Evdokia's father on the night of the elopement. Soudales, as has been said, was one of three generals sent against the Paulicians by the Empress Theodora in 855; in the *Continuation of Theophanes* their names are given as 'the son of Argyros, and the son of Doukas, and Soudales'; but in the Skylitzes transcription of this chronicle the names are given as 'Leon Argyros, and Andronikos Doukas, and Soudales'. The conjunction of Soudales with Andronikos Doukas suggests that it was from this passage that the author of Digenes took both these names. But this conjunction is found not in the original book but only in the transcription of Skylitzes; and Skylitzes was a contemporary of Psellos writing in the middle of the eleventh century. So the conjunction in the poem of Soudales and Andronikos Doukas is another detail which gives a hint of this date.[1]

VI

Digenes is a symbolic hero; he must accordingly be placed in a symbolical setting. So the poem gives us no history but a composite arrangement of history, in which fragments or aspects of many actual facts are rearranged to give a universalized image of conflict on the eastern frontier; combined with elements of pure romance. This legendary or at least typical period of conflict so far from being contemporary or even conterminous with the time of composition is separated from it by a gap the existence of which is indicated by the word *tênikauta* (GRO iv. 972) which has been often overlooked.

For such a legendary period it was necessary to provide typical emperors; and we may suppose that the author chose as his ideal emperor the not so long departed Basil II; and that the first rewriter of the poem preferred the conquering names of Romanos Lekapenos and Nikeforos Fôkas, without considering or caring whether both these emperors could have honoured a hero who died at the age of thirty-three. Of one thing we may be quite certain, that the emperors named were not the author's contemporaries. Basil II died in 1025.

---

[1] See Bury, *East Rom. Emp.*, p. 278; Gibbon, v. 507. Andronikos (or Aaron) Doukas is named as the father of Eirene, TRE 844, AND 20; see Appendix A.

What are we to regard as a sufficient interval in order that his achievements may be represented as legendary? Shall we guess that the *Digenes* was written during the reign of Constantine IX Monomachos (1042–54) during which 'almost complete peace reigned on the frontier of Syria and Mesopotamia'? It was not only the first period of complete peace but also the latest. In 1048 the Seljuq Turks were already gathering on the Armenian border.

ΒΑΣΙΛΕΙΟΥ ΔΙΓΕΝΟΥΣ ΑΚΡΙΤΟΥ

ΛΟΓΟΙ ΟΚΤω

ΒΑΣΙΛΕΙΟΥ ΔΙΓΕΝΟΥΣ ΑΚΡΙΤΟΥ

ΛΟΓΟΣ ΠΡΩΤΟΣ

Ἔπαινοι καὶ τρόπαια ἐγκώμιόν τε   F. 1 rᵒ.
τοῦ τρισμάκαρος Ἀκρίτου Βασιλείου,
τοῦ ἀνδρειοτάτου τε γενναιοτάτου,
τοῦ τὴν ἰσχὺν ἔχοντος παρὰ Θεοῦ ὡς δῶρον,
καὶ κατατροπώσαντος πᾶσαν Συρίαν,   5
τὴν Βαβυλῶνα, Χαρζιανήν τε ὅλην,
Ἀρμενίαν τε καὶ τὴν Καππαδοκίαν,
τὸ Ἀμόριν τε καὶ τὸ Ἰκόνιν ἅμα,
τὸ περίφημον καὶ μέγα κάστρον ἔτι,
τὸ δυνατόν τε καὶ κατωχυρωμένον,   10
τὴν Ἄγκυραν λέγω τε καὶ πᾶσαν Σμύρνην,
καὶ τὰ παρὰ θάλασσαν καθυποτάξας.
Δηλώσω σοι γὰρ τὰς αὐτοῦ πράξεις ἄρτι,
ἃς εἰργάσατο ἐν τῷ παρόντι βίῳ,
πῶς πολεμιστὰς δυνατοὺς καὶ ἀνδρείους   15
κατεπτόησε καὶ πάντα τὰ θηρία,
ἔχων συνεργοῦσαν τε Θεοῦ τὴν χάριν,
καὶ Θεοτόκου τῆς ἀκαταμαχήτου,
καὶ τῶν ἀγγέλων ἅμα καὶ ἀρχαγγέλων,
τῶν ἀθλοφόρων καὶ μεγάλων μαρτύρων,   20
Θεοδώρων τε τῶν πανενδοξοτάτων,
τοῦ στρατηλάτου καὶ τοῦ τίρωνος ἅμα,
τοῦ πολυάθλου γενναίου Γεωργίου,
καὶ θαυματουργοῦ καὶ μάρτυρος μαρτύρων   1 vᵒ.
ἐνδοξοτάτου Δημητρίου, προστάτου   25
τοῦ Βασιλείου καὶ καύχημα καὶ κλέος
τοῦ νικοποιοῦ ἐν τοῖς ὑπεναντίοις
Ἀγαρηνοῖς τε καὶ τοῖς Ἰσμαηλίταις,

TITRE. Il manque dans le manuscrit.
1 Après ἐγκώμιον, il y avait un mot assez long que l'on ne peut plus lire et qui a dû être effacé à dessein. Je supplée τε, que réclament le sens et la mesure du vers.
10 κατοχυρωμένον.   22 Il y a dans l'original τήρωνος.

1-29 These lines of general introduction are written in semi-accentual iambic senarii. Each line has twelve syllables always with an accent on

OF BASIL TWYBORN BORDERER

FIRST BOOK

GROTTAFERRATA I

HONOURS triumphs and the praise　　　　　1
Of the thrice-blessed Borderer Basil,
The very noble, most brave
Who had his strength as gift from God,
And overthrew all Syria,
Babylon, all Harziane,
Armenia, Kappadokia,
Amorion and Ikonion,
And that famous and great fortress,
The mighty and the fortified,　　　　　10
Ankyra I mean, and all Smyrna
And the seaside subduing.
I will declare his works to you
Which in this present life he did.
How warriors mighty and brave
He overawed, and all wild beasts,
Having to help the grace of God,
And of God's mother unconquerable,
Of the angels and archangels,
Of the prize-bearing great martyrs,　　　　　20
Of both the glorious Theodores,
The host's leader and the recruit,
Of noble George of many trials,
And wonder-working martyr of martyrs
Glorious Demetrios, defender
Of Basil, boast and pride of him
Who had victory on his adversaries
The Agarenes and Ishmaelites,

the penultimate. This is what the Byzantines had made of the classical iambic. See Krumbacher, p. 648. They give very little idea of the contents of the poem, and may be supposed to give a measure of the monkish redactor's powers as an original poet when he had no archetype to guide him.

3

Σκύθοις βαρβάροις τοῖς λυσσῶσιν ὡς κύνες.

* * *

Ἦν ἀμηρᾶς τῶν εὐγενῶν πλουσιώτατος σφόδρα, 30
φρονήσεώς τε μέτοχος καὶ ἀνδρείας εἰς ἄκρος,
οὐ μέλας ὡς Αἰθίοπες, ἀλλὰ ξανθός, ὡραῖος,
ἀνθῶν ἄρτι τὸ γένειον εὐπρεπέστατον, σγοῦρον.
Εἶχεν ὀφρύδιν πεπανὸν καθάπερ πεπλεγμένον,
βλέμμα γοργόν, ἐνήδονον, πλήρης ἔρωτος γέμον, 35
ὡς ῥόδον ἐξανέτειλεν ἐν μέσῳ τοῦ προσώπου,
ὡς κυπαρίσσιν ἔμνοστον τὴν ἡλικίαν ἔχων,
εἴπερ ἄν τις ἰδὼν αὐτὸν εἰκόνι ἐοικέναι·
σὺν τούτοις ἀκατάμαχον τὴν ἰσχὺν κεκτημένος,
καθ᾽ ἑκάστην ἐσχόλαζεν εἰς θηρίων πολέμους, 40
τόλμην πειράζων τὴν αὐτοῦ καὶ ἀνδρείαν θαυμάζων,
ὡς θαῦμα πᾶσι προὔκειτο τοῖς αὐτὸν καθορῶσι.
Δεινὸν δὲ πρᾶγμα πέφηνεν εἰς τοὺς νέους ἡ δόξα.
Τῷ γὰρ πλουτεῖν διεπαρθεὶς καὶ ὄγκῳ τῆς ἀνδρείας,
στρατολογεῖν ἀπήρξατο Τούρκους καὶ Διλεβίτας, 45
Ἀραβίτας τε ἐκλεκτοὺς καὶ πεζοὺς Τρωγλοδύτας·
εἶχε καὶ τοὺς ἀγούρους του χιλίους Γουλαβίους,
ἀδνουμιάτας ἅπαντας ἐπαξίως ρογεύσας·
ἐξέπνευσε πνέων θυμοῦ κατὰ τῆς Ῥωμανίας· 2 r°.
τὰ μέρη δὲ καταλαβὼν χώρας τοῦ Ἡρακλέος, 50
πόλεις ἠρήμωσε πολλὰς ἐρήμους καταστήσας,
καὶ πλήθη ἠχμαλώτευσε λαοῦ ἀναριθμήτου,
ἀπροσφυλάκτων τῶν μερῶν ἐκείνων τυγχανόντων·
οἱ γὰρ ἐκεῖ φυλάσσοντες ἔτυχον εἰς τὰς ἄκρας·
καί, ὡς ἐκ τούτου ἄδειαν μεγάλην συναντήσας, 55

40 καθεκάστην.   43 πράγμα.

---

29 The barbarous Scythians may have been suggested by the 2nd and 3rd chapters of the 8th book of Anna Comnena's *Alexiad* (ed. Reifferscheid, ii, pp. 6, 7). A few other details which will be noted also seem to have been borrowed from this work. This gives a possible date for the present recension.

34 πεπανόν. It is difficult to know what a 'ripe' brow is.

37 ἡλικίαν, as always, 'stature'. See index.

41 θαυμάζων: unusual sense for which cf. below 1730 ὡραΐζουσα.

45 Διλεβίτας. This should certainly be Διλεμίτας, for whom see Honigmann, *Ostgrenze des Byz. Reiches*, p. 164; and Grégoire, op. cit. below.

'Above three thousand Dilemites, who descended by their free choice from the hills of Hyrcania', fought

4

And barbarous Skyths who rage like dogs.

*   *   *

Was an Emir of breed, exceeding rich,   30
Of wisdom seized and bravery to the top,
Not black as Aethiops are, but fair and lovely,
Already bloomed with comely curly beard.
He had a well-grown and rather matted brow;
His quick and pleasant gaze and full of love
Shone like a rose from out his countenance.
The beauty of a cypress was his stature,
That any saw him to be like a picture;
With this he held unconquerable strength;
And every day he pleased to war with beasts,   40
Trying his own daring, making his bravery
A wonder as he was to all who saw him.
Terrible was his glory to the young.
With wealth and load of bravery exalted
He began to enroll Turks, and Dilemites,
And picked Arabians, Troglodytes on foot,
And his companions, a thousand men-at-arms
All on his muster fitly salaried.
Breathing he breathed out wrath at Romania,
Taking those parts, the lands of Herakles,   50
He wasted many cities laying waste,
And captured hosts of people without number,
Happening those places there to be unguarded,
Those there on guard chanced to be on the borders;
He meeting therefore great impunity,

for Chosroes in Justinian's Lazic War. See Gibbon (i. 398; ii. 407) following Procopius, whom the redactor may have read.

46 Τρωγλοδύτας. Perhaps taken from Anna Comnena (*Alex*. ed. Reiff. i. 214) to typify the farthest southwestern confines of the empire; or more probably from Heliodorus, *Aithiop*. viii. 16 and ix. 16.

47. ἀγούρους 'Boys', used regularly of the personal followers who together compose the λαός or company.

Γουλαβίους. See Grégoire (Acad. Roy. Belg., *Bull. Classe Lettres et Sciences Mor. et Pol.*, 5ᵐᵉ série, t. xvii, n. 12, 7 Déc. 1931, pp. 463–93, 'L'épopée byzantine et ses rapp. avec l'ép. turque et l'ép. romane'), who shows, p. 482, that this is for Γουλαμίους (Arabic *ghulam*), of which the Μαγούλιοι of TRE 811, 1482; AND 1343, 2348, is a metathetic form.

48 ἀδνουμιάτας. See Sof. *Lex. Byz.* s.v. ἀδνούμιον (ad-nomen).

διαδραμὼν Χαρζιανήν, Καππαδοκίαν φθάνει,
καὶ εἰς οἶκον τοῦ στρατηγοῦ ἀθρόως ἐπιπίπτει.

Τὰ δὲ πραχθέντα ἐν αὐτῷ τίς εἰπεῖν ἐξισχύσει;
πάντας γὰρ ἐθανάτωσε τοὺς ἐκεῖ εὑρεθέντας,
πλοῦτον ἀφείλετο πολύν, ἐσκύλευσε τὸν οἶκον,   60
καὶ κόρην ᾐχμαλώτευσε πάνυ ὡραιοτάτην,
θυγατέρα τοῦ στρατηγοῦ, τυγχάνουσαν παρθένον.
Ὑπῆρχε δὲ ὁ στρατηγὸς ἐν ἐξορίᾳ τότε,
καὶ οἱ τῆς κόρης ἀδελφοὶ ἔτυχον εἰς τὰς ἄκρας·
ἡ μήτηρ δέ, τὰς τῶν ἐθνῶν ἀποφυγοῦσα χεῖρας,   65
ἅπαντα γράφει παρευθὺς τοῖς υἱοῖς τὰ συμβάντα,
τὴν τῶν ἐθνῶν τὴν ἔλευσιν, τὴν ἁρπαγὴν τῆς κόρης,
τῆς φιλτάτης τὸν χωρισμόν, τῶν συμφορῶν τὸ πλῆθος.
Προσέθηκε δὲ τῇ γραφῇ καὶ τάδε μετὰ θρήνων·
" Ὦ τέκνα ποθεινότατα, οἰκτείρατε μητέρα   70
ψυχὴν ἀθλίαν ἔχουσαν καὶ μέλλουσαν τεθνᾶναι·
ἀγάπης μνημονεύσατε ἀδελφῆς τῆς ἰδίας,
ἐλευθερῶσαι σπεύσατε ἀδελφὴν καὶ μητέρα,
τὴν μὲν δουλείας τῆς πικρᾶς, κἀμὲ δὲ τοῦ θανάτου.
Δώσομεν πᾶσαν ὕπαρξιν ἕνεκεν τῆς φιλτάτης·   75
ζωὴν μὴ προτιμήσητε διὰ τὴν ἀδελφήν σας,   2 vᵒ.
ἀδελφὴν ἐλεήσατε, τέκνα μου, τὴν ἰδίαν·
ἀπέλθετε μετὰ σπουδῆς εἰς ἀνάρρυσιν ταύτης·
εἰ δ' οὖν, θανοῦσαν ὄψεσθε μητέρα ὑπὲρ τέκνου·
καὶ τὴν κατάραν τὴν ἐμὴν λήψεσθε καὶ πατρῴαν,   80
εἰ τοῦτο οὐ ποιήσητε καθὼς ὑμῖν ὑπέσχον."

Οἱ δὲ ταῦτα ἀκούσαντες, στενάξαντες ἐκ βάθους,
καὶ δακρύων κατάβροχοι οἱ πέντε γεγονότες,
ἀλλήλους προεπέμποντο τοῦ ἀπελθεῖν σπουδαίως,
" Ἂς ἀπέλθωμεν," λέγοντες, "σφαγῶμεν ὑπὲρ ταύτης."   85
Λῦθις ἵππων ἐπέβησαν καὶ ᾤχοντο τοῦ δρόμου,
συνεπομένους ἔχοντες ὀλίγους στρατιώτας·
καὶ μηδὲν ἀμελήσαντες, ὕπνου μὴ κορεσθέντες,
διὰ βραχέων ἡμερῶν ἔφθασαν τὰ φουσσᾶτα,
εἰς τὴν κλεισοῦραν τὴν δεινὴν ἣν Δύσκολον καλοῦσι·   90
καὶ μακρόθεν πεζεύσαντες ἔνθα τὰς βίγλας εὗρον,

85 ἆς, partout ainsi.   89 φουσσάτα, partout ainsi.

_____

65 τῶν ἐθνῶν. The gentiles or pagans,   74 τῆς πικρᾶς omitted in translation.
as in N.T. So below 362 ἐθνικός.   89 τὰ φουσσᾶτα here bears its original

6

Ran through Harzianê, came to Kappadokia,
And on the general's dwelling fell in force.
What things were done therein who now can tell?
For all he put to death whom there he found,
And took away much wealth, and sacked the house,   60
And captive took a very lovely girl,
The general's daughter, and she was a virgin.
The general himself was then in exile;
The girl's brothers happened to be on the borders.
Her mother, having escaped the pagans' hands,
Forthwith wrote all had happened to her sons,
The pagans' coming, the Rape of the Girl,
The parting from her dearest, crowds of woes;
And this she added writing with lament:
    'O children dear, have pity on your mother,   70
Her soul in wretchedness and soon to die.
Be mindful of the love you bear your sister.
Hasten to free your sister, and your mother,
Her from captivity, and me from death.
We would give all existence for her sake.
Prefer not life to your sister's account;
Have mercy, children mine, on your own sister;
Go out in haste to her deliverance;
Else you shall see me dead, mother for child;
And shall receive your father's curse, and mine,   80
If this you do not as I have proposed.'
And having heard these words they deeply sighed,
The five of them, and all bedrenched with tears,
Urging each other to go forth in haste,
'Let us go', saying, 'and be slain for her.'
Therewith they mounted and went on the way,
With a few soldiers following behind.
Nothing neglecting, taking no fill of sleep,
In a few days they came to the encampment,
At the dread pass which they call Difficult.   90
Far off dismounting where they found the sentries,

meaning (*fossatum*), not the common
Byzantine derived sense 'army'.
Again, see below, 210.

91 βίγλας. βίγλα, the watch, outpost,
used of either the place or the man.

δι' ὑπομνήσεως αὐτῶν δεήσεως ἐγγράφου,
ἤχθησαν πρὸς τὸν ἀμηρᾶν τῇ ἐκείνου προστάξει.
Ὑπῆρχε δὲ καθήμενος ἐφ' ὑψηλοῦ τοῦ θρόνου,
χρυσοκολλήτου, φοβεροῦ, ἀπέξωθεν τῆς τένδας·   95
κύκλῳ αὐτοῦ παρίσταντο πλήθη ἀνδρῶν ἐνόπλων.
Καὶ πλησίον γενόμενοι, ἀκούει τούτων λόγους,
καὶ προσκυνήσαντες αὐτὸν μέχρι τρίτου ἐδάφους,
μετὰ δακρύων ἔλεγον τῷ ἀμηρᾷ τοιάδε·
" Ἀμηρᾶ, δοῦλε τοῦ Θεοῦ καὶ πρῶτε τῆς Συρίας,   100
νὰ φθάσῃς εἰς τὴν Πάνορμον, ἴδῃς τὸ μασγιδίον,
νὰ προσκυνήσῃς, ἀμηρᾶ, τὸν κρεμάμενον λίθον,   3 r°.
καὶ ἀξιωθῇς ἀσπάσασθαι τὸ μνῆμα τοῦ Προφήτου,
νὰ ἀκούσῃς τῆς προσευχῆς τῆς καθιερωμένης!
Κόρην τερπνὴν ἀφήρπαξας, ἀδελφὴν ἡμετέραν·   105
πώλησον ταύτην πρὸς ἡμᾶς, δοῦλε Θεοῦ ὑψίστου,
καὶ ἀντ' αὐτῆς σοι δώσομεν πλοῦτον ὅσον κελεύεις·
θρηνεῖ γὰρ δι' αὐτὴν ὁ πατὴρ ὡς μὴ ἔχων ἑτέραν,
θανεῖν ἡ μήτηρ βούλεται ταύτην μὴ καθορῶσα·
ἡμεῖς δὲ πόθον ἄπειρον πρὸς αὐτὴν κεκτημένοι,   110
πάντες ἐπωμοσάμεθα ὅρκοις φρικωδεστάτοις
ἂν τὴν οὐχ ὑποστρέψωμεν καὶ οἱ πάντες νὰ σφαγῶμεν."
Ἀκούων ταῦτα ὁ ἀμηρᾶς καὶ τὴν τόλμην θαυμάσας,
πρὸς τὸ μαθεῖν δῆτα στερεῶς εἰ τύγχανον ἀνδρεῖοι
(ἀκριβῶς γὰρ ἠπίστατο τὴν τῶν Ῥωμαίων γλῶτταν),   115
ἠρέμα ἀπεκρίνατο, λέγων αὐτοῖς τοιάδε·
" Εἰ ποθεῖτε τὴν ἀδελφὴν ποιῆσαι ἐλευθέραν,
εἷς χωρισθήτω ἀφ' ὑμῶν ὃν ἔχετε γενναῖον,
καὶ ἂς καβαλλικεύσωμεν ἐγώ τε καὶ ἐκεῖνος,
καὶ ἂς μονομαχήσωμεν ἐγώ τε καὶ ἐκεῖνος.   120
Καί, εἰ μὲν τρέψω τον ἐγώ, δούλους ὑμᾶς νὰ ἔχω·
εἰ δὲ κακεῖνος τρέψει με, χωρὶς λόγου παντοίου
νὰ λήψεσθε τὴν ἀδελφήν, μηδὲν ζημιωθέντες,

102 προσκυνήσεις.   112 οὐχ', partout ainsi.   114 Peut-être serait-il
préférable d'écrire τυγχάνουν.

101 Panormos, Palermo, was captured   of the poem—the songs, the tradi-
by the Arabs in 831 and by the Nor-   tions, the chronicles, the ballads, the
mans in 1072. The period of the   historians, the literary monks—all
origins as well as of the completion   fall within the two hundred years

By their transmission of written request
They were brought to the Emir by his command.
There he was seated on a lofty throne,
Plated with gold, awful, outside the tent;
Around him stood a crowd of men full-armed.
When they came near he listened to their words.
Having made reverence up to the third step,
With tears they began to speak thus to the Emir:
'Emir, servant of God, and prince of Syria,   100
May you come to Palermo, see the Mosque,
May you worship, Emir, the Hanging Stone,
Be found worthy to adore the Prophet's Tomb;
So may you hear the consecrated prayer.
You carried off a comely girl, our sister.
Servant of Highest God, sell her to us,
For her we will give you all the wealth you want.
Her father mourns her, as he had none other;
Her mother wants to die not seeing her.
Ourselves possessed of boundless love for her   110
Have sworn, and all of us, with frightful oaths,
Even to be killed if we bring her not back.'
    This hearing the Emir admired their daring,
And for to learn firmly if they were brave
(For he exactly knew the Roman tongue),
Gently replied saying these words to them:
'If you desire to set your sister free,
Let one of you, whom you think brave, be chosen,
And let us mount together he and I,
And let us fight together he and I.   120
And if I beat him, you shall be my slaves;
If he beat me, without all argument
You shall receive your sister, nothing losing,

850–1050. For the Suspended Tomb of Aristotle, not the Suspended Stone, at Palermo see Hasluck, *Christianity and Islam*, p. 17, n. 2; and for a Hanging Stone at Damascus, p. 395, n. 6. This is the only reference in the poem to any place in Europe (with the possible exceptions of Bathyrryaki, below 3743; and of Achaia in the much later version of Andros, AND 2419). For other cases of miraculous suspension see Dawkins, *Makhairas*, ii. 45.

καὶ ἕτερα αἰχμάλωτα παρ᾽ ἐμοῦ εὑρεθέντα·
ἄλλως γὰρ οὐ πεισθήσομαι τὴν ἀδελφὴν παράξαι,   125
εἰ καὶ τὸν πλοῦτον δώσετε πάσης τῆς Ῥωμανίας.   3 vᵒ.
Ἀπέλθετε, σκοπήσατε ὅπερ ὑμῖν συμφέρει.''
Εὐθὺς ἐξῆλθον ἅπαντες χαίροντες τῇ ἐλπίδι·
ἀλλ᾽, ἵνα μὴ φιλονεικοῦν ποῖος νὰ πολεμήσῃ,
λαχνοὺς θεῖναι προέκριναν καὶ ἔλυσαν τὴν ἔριν·   130
ἔλαχε δὲ τὸν ὕστερον τὸν μικρὸν Κωνσταντῖνον,
ὃς δίδυμος ἐτύγχανε μετὰ τῆς αὐταδέλφης.
Ὁ πρῶτος νουθετῶν αὐτὸν ἤλειφε πρὸς ἀγῶνας,
" Μὴ ὅλως," λέγων, "ἀδελφέ, φωναὶ καταπτοήσουν,
μικρόν τι δειλιάσωσι, πληγαί σε ἐκφοβήσουν·   135
κἂν γυμνὸν ἴδῃς τὸ σπαθίν, φυγεῖν οὕτω μὴ δώσῃς,
κἂν ἄλλο τι δεινότερον εἰς τροπὴν μὴ ἐκφύγῃς·
νεότητος μὴ φεῖσαι σὺ παρὰ μητρὸς κατάραν,
ἧς εὐχαῖς στηριζόμενος τὸν ἐχθρὸν καταβάλεις·
οὐ γὰρ παρόψεται Θεὸς δούλους ἡμᾶς γενέσθαι·   140
ἄπιθι, τέκνον, εὔθυμον, μὴ δειλιάσῃς ὅλως."
Καί, στάντες πρὸς ἀνατολάς, Θεὸν ἐπεκαλοῦντο·
" Μὴ συγχωρήσῃς, δέσποτα, δούλους ἡμᾶς γενέσθαι."
Καί, ἀσπασάμενοι αὐτόν, προέπεμψαν εἰπόντες·
" Ἡ τῶν γονέων μας εὐχὴ γένηται βοηθός σου! "   145
Ὁ δὲ ἐφ᾽ ἵππου ἐπιβὰς μαύρου, γενναιοτάτου,
σπαθὶν διαζωσάμενος, λαμβάνει τὸ κοντάριν,
ἐβάσταξε καὶ τὸ ῥαβδὶν εἰς τὸ ῥαβδοβαστάκιν·
τὸ δὲ σημεῖον τοῦ σταυροῦ φραξάμενος παντόθεν,
τὸν ἵππον ἐπελάλησεν, εἰς τὸν κάμπον ἐξῆλθε·   4 rᵒ.   150
ἔπαιξε πρῶτον τὸ σπαθίν, εἶθ᾽ οὕτως τὸ κοντάριν·
καί τινες τῶν Σαρακηνῶν ὠνείδιζον τὸν νέον·
" Ἴδε ποῖον ἐξέβαλον πρὸς τὸ μονομαχῆσαι
τὸν τρόπαια ποιήσαντα μεγάλα εἰς Συρίαν! "
Εἷς δέ τις τῶν Σαρακηνῶν ἀκρίτης διλεβίτης   155
γαληνὰ πρὸς τὸν ἀμηρᾶν τοιόνδε λόγον ἔφη·

126 δώσητε et un ε au-dessus de l'η.   127 σκοπίσατε.   135 σι.   139
καταβάλης.   148 Il faut sans doute lire ῥαβδοβαστάγιν.   149 φραγξάμενος.
156 ἀμυρὰν, partout orthographié avec υ. Je n'adopte l'η que parce que cette
orthographe est généralement reçue. A l'accusatif, ce mot porte partout l'accent
grave.

124 αἰχμάλωτα. For this use of the   below 1320 and 3173.
neuter plural see note on οἰκεῖα

And other captures that are found with me.
Else will I not consent to yield your sister
Even if you give all Romania's wealth.
Go and consider where your interest lies.'
Forthwith they all went out glad with the hope;
And that they should contend not who should fight,
Decided to cast lots, and ended strife.   130
The lot fell on the latest born, young Constantine,
Him that was the twin brother of his sister.
The first, anointing for the fight, advised him,
Saying, 'No wise, brother, let the shouts affright you
Nor ever shrink, nor let the blows appal you;
If you see the sword naked, give not way,
Or anything more terrible, never fly;
Heed not your youth, only your mother's curse,
Whose prayers supporting you, you shall prevail.
God shall not suffer us ever to be slaves.   140
Go child, be of good heart, fear not at all.'
And standing towards the east they called on God:
'O Lord, never allow us to be slaves.'
Having embraced they sent him forth, saying,
'So may our parent's prayer become your helper.'
He mounting on a black, a noble horse,
Having girt on his sword, took up the lance;
He carried his mace in the mace-holder,
Fenced himself all sides with the sign of the cross,
Impelled his horse and rode into the plain,   150
Played first the sword and then likewise the lance.
Some of the Saracens reviled the youth:
'Look what a champion is put out to fight
Him who great triumphs made in Syria.'
But one of them a Dilemite borderer
Spoke softly to the Emir a word like this:

---

130 λαχνοὺς θεῖναι. Read λαχμούς, for
which see Sof. *Lex.* s.v.
135 μικρόν τι δειλιάσωσι. Awkward and
probably corrupt.
150 τὸν ἵππον ἐπελάλησεν. ἐπιλαλῶ,
sometimes used abs., was a technical
term of riding, to 'address' your

horse, not necessarily with words.
From the abs. use it appears cor-
ruptly in some of the later literature
as ἱππιλαλῶ. But see below 226.
155 Read Διλεμίτης (see above 45); and
note that an Arab is here called
ἀκρίτης.

" Ὁρᾷς τὸ καταπτέρνισμα ἐπιδέξιον ὅπως,
σπαθίου τὴν ὑποδοχήν, γύρισμα κονταρίου·
ταῦτα πάντα ἐμφαίνουσι πεῖραν τε καὶ ἀνδρείαν·
ὅρα λοιπὸν μὴ ἀμελῶς τὸ παιδίον προσκρούσῃς. "   160
Ἐξέβη καὶ ὁ ἀμηρᾶς εἰς φάραν καβαλλάρης·
θρασύτατος ὑπάρχει γὰρ καὶ φοβερὸς τῇ θέᾳ,
τὰ ἄρματα ἀπέστιλβον ἡλιακὰς ἀκτῖνας·
κοντάριν ἐμαλάκιζε βένετον, χρυσωμένον·
καὶ πάντες συνεξήλθασιν εἰς θέαν τοῦ πολέμου.   165
Ὁ φάρας ἔπαιξε τερπνῶς πάντας ὑπερεκπλήττων·
τοὺς γὰρ πόδας τοὺς τέσσαρας εἰς ἓν ἐπισυνάγων,
καθάπερ ὡς ἐν μηχανῇ, ἐκάθητο ἐκεῖσε·
ἄλλοτε δὲ ἐφαίνετο λεπτοπυκνοβαδίζων,
ὡς δοκεῖν μὴ περιπατεῖν, ἀλλὰ χαμαὶ πετᾶσθαι.   170
Ὁ δ᾽ ἀμηρᾶς τερπόμενος καθώσπερ ἐπεγέλα,
παρευθὺς ἐπελάλησεν, εἰς τὸν κάμπον ἐξῆλθε,
κραυγάζων ὥσπερ ἀετὸς καὶ συρίζων ὡς δράκων,   4 vº.
ὡς λέων ὠρυόμενος καταπιεῖν τὸν νέον.
Ὁ δὲ τοῦτον δεξάμενος εὐθέως καὶ συντόμως,   175
καὶ κονταρέας δώσαντες, ἐκλάσθησαν τῶν δύο,
ἑτέρου μὴ ἰσχύσαντος τὸν ἕτερον κρημνῖσαι·
καὶ τὰ σπαθία σύραντες, ἔσωθεν χεῖρας δόντες,
ἀλλήλους ἐσυνέκοπτον ἐπὶ πολλὰς τὰς ὥρας·
τὰ ὄρη ἀντιδόνησαν, οἱ βουνοὶ βροντὰς εἶχον·   180
τὸ αἷμα δὲ κατέρρεε τὴν γῆν ἐκείνην ὅλην·
οἱ ἵπποι ἠγανάκτησαν, πάντας ἔκπληξις εἶχεν·
ὁλόπληγοι γεγόνασι, μηδεὶς τροπὴν ποιῶν τε·
Ὡς δὲ καὶ τὸ παράδοξον Σαρακηνοὶ κατεῖδον,
καὶ τὸ πολὺ θαυμάσαντες τὸ πρόθυμον τοῦ νέου,   185
ἔκστασιν δὲ τὴν ἄπειρον καὶ τὴν γενναίαν τόλμην,
ἅπαντες πρὸς τὸν ἀμηρᾶν ὁμοφώνως ἐλάλουν·
" Ἀγάπην ἐπιζήτησον, τὸν δὲ πόλεμον ἄφες,
ὁ Ῥωμαῖος δεινός ἐστι, μή σε κακοδικήσῃ."
Καὶ πρὸς φυγὴν ὁ ἀμηρᾶς εὐθέως ἐξετράπη,   190

162 Il faut peut-être lire ὑπῆρχε.   169 ἄλλως τε. δὲ manque. J'emprunte
cette correction au manuscrit d'Andros, vers 350.   171 ἐπηγγείλω. Correction suggérée par le ms. d'Andros, vers 351.   176 κονταραίας.   177 κρη-
μνίσαι.   181 γὴν.   189 δεινὸς ἐστί.   190 ἀμυρᾶς, partout ainsi.

161 φάραν. See index.   164 ἐμαλάκιζε βένετον. See below 1230.
163 See note, below 2777.   166 ὁ φάρας. See index.

'You see him spurring, and how cleverly,
His sword's parry, the turning of his lance.
All this exhibits skill as well as courage;
See then you meet the child not carelessly.'   160
Forth came the Emir riding upon a horse,
Most bold he was and terrible to view,
His arms were glittering with sunny rays;
The lance he wielded was of blue and gold.
And all came out at once to watch the battle.
The charger amazed all with pretty sporting,
For gathering his four hoofs to one spot,
As if caught in a trap, he there would stay;
Or again showed so quick and delicate a trot
That he seemed not to tread but skim the ground.   170
The Emir delighting seemed to smile on him,
Straightway impelled him, rode into the plain,
An eagle shrieking, and a hissing serpent,
A lion roaring to devour the youth.
The other soon and swiftly there received him.
They gave play with their spears, and both were broken,
Strength neither having to unseat the other;
Then having drawn their swords within arm's length
Together smote each other many hours.
The mountains echoed, thunders held the hills,   180
The blood ran down there over all the ground,
The indignant horses raged, all were amazed;
All wounded were they both, yet neither winning.
And when the Saracens beheld the wonder,
Admiring the great ardour of the youth,
His boundless instancy and noble daring,
All with one voice they called to the Emir:
'Ask for a truce now, and have done with fighting,
Strong is the Roman and may do you hurt.'
Straightway the Emir turned right away in flight;   190

168 ὡς ἐν μηχανῇ. Cf. *Ach. Tat.* VII.
xv. 2 ὡς ἀπὸ μηχανῆς βληθείς.
178 ἔσωθεν χεῖρας δόντες. Cf. below
3148.
183 ὀλόπληγοι. A curious formation
like modern ὀλόμαυρος, ὀλόγυμνος,

κ.τ.λ.
186 ἔκστασιν probably a mistake for
ἔνστασιν.
188 ἀγάπην. Cf. below 2738.
189 κακοδικήσῃ. Cf. below 2515, 1521,
1715.

13

καὶ ὁ πολλὰ καυχώμενος ἡττήθη κατὰ κράτος·
καὶ γὰρ καύχησις ἅπασα οὐκ ἀγαθὴ τυγχάνει.
Πόρρωθεν ῥίπτει τὸ σπαθίν, χεῖρας εἰς ὕψος ἄρας,
τοὺς δακτύλους ἐσταύρωσεν, ὡς ἦν αὐτοῖς τὸ ἔθος,
καὶ ταύτην πρὸς τὸν ἄγουρον τὴν φωνὴν ἐπαφῆκεν·   195
" Παῦσαι, καλὲ νεώτερε· σὸν γάρ ἐστι τὸ νῖκος·
δεῦρο λάβε τὴν ἀδελφὴν καὶ τὴν αἰχμαλωσίαν."
Καὶ λύσαντες τὸ θέατρον, ἀπῆλθον εἰς τὴν τένδαν·
καὶ ἦν ἰδεῖν τοὺς ἀδελφοὺς χαρμονῆς ἐμπλησθέντας.
Χεῖρας εἰς ὕψος ἄραντες Θεὸν δοξολογοῦσι   200
" Ἡ δόξα", πάντες λέγοντες, " σοὶ μόνῳ Θεῷ πρέπει·
ὁ γὰρ ἐλπίζων ἐπὶ σὲ οὐ μὴ καταισχυνθείη."   5 rᵒ.
Τὸν ἀδελφὸν ἠσπάζοντο μετὰ περιχαρίας·
οἱ μὲν φιλοῦσι χεῖρας του, ἄλλοι τὴν κεφαλήν του·
τὸν δ' ἀμηρᾶν ἀμφότεροι θερμῶς παρακαλοῦσι·   205
" Δός, ἀμηρᾶ, τὴν ἀδελφήν, καθὼς ἡμῖν ὑπέσχου,
καρδίαν παραμύθησον τὴν λύπῃ βαρυνθεῖσαν."
Ὁ ἀμηρᾶς δὲ πρὸς αὐτοὺς οὐκ ἀληθεύων ἔφη·
" Σφραγίδα λάβετε ἐμήν, γυρεύσατε τὰς τένδας·
πανταχοῦ ἐρευνήσατε, ἴδετε τὰ φουσσάτα·   210
τὴν ἀδελφὴν γνωρίσαντες, λαβόντες πορευθῆτε."
Οἱ δὲ μετὰ πολλῆς χαρᾶς τὴν σφραγίδα λαβόντες,
τὸν δόλον ἀγνοήσαντες, ἐπιμελῶς ἠρεύνουν.
Καὶ πανταχοῦ γυρεύσαντες, μηδὲν δὲ εὑρηκότες,
λυπούμενοι ὑπέστρεφον πρὸς ἀμηρᾶν εὐθέως,   215
καὶ καθ' ὁδὸν Σαρακηνῷ ἀγροίκῳ συναντῶσιν·
ἐκεῖνος ἔφη πρὸς αὐτοὺς διὰ τοῦ δρουγουμάνου·
" Τίνα ζητεῖτε, ἄγουροι, τίνος χάριν θρηνεῖτε; "
Οἱ δὲ ἀνταπεκρίθησαν λέγοντες μετὰ θρήνων·
" Κόρην ἠχμαλωτεύσατε ἀδελφὴν ἡμετέραν,   220
καὶ ταύτην μὴ εὑρίσκοντες οὐ ζῆν θέλομεν ἔτι."
Στενάξας δ' ὁ Σαρακηνὸς τοιόνδε λόγον ἔφη·
" Διέλθετε εἰς τὸ ὑπαύχενον· εὑρήσετε ῥυάκιν,

191 κατακράτος.   196 γὰρ ἐστὶ.   207 παραμύθισον.

_____

198 λύσαντες τὸ θέατρον. This seems to
be exactly, as translated, 'breaking
the ring' with no consciousness of

any dramatic performance.
205 ἀμφότεροι seems to imply, with
little Constantine, three brothers in

14

Who boasted much was beaten from the field—
(For and all boasting never was a virtue).
He threw his sword away, put up his hands,
He crossed his fingers as their custom was,
And to the boy he cried aloud these words:
'Cease, my good youth, the victory is yours.
Come take your sister and the captive band.'
Breaking the ring they went off to the tent.
Then was to see the brothers filled with joy.
They raised their hands on high, glorified God,　　　　200
All saying, 'Glory be to thee God alone;
Who puts his hope in thee shall not be shamed.'
Then with rejoicing they embraced their brother;
Some kiss his hands and others kissed his head.
Then warmly both of them implored the Emir:
'Give us, Emir, our sister, as you promised,
Comfort the heart has been weighed down with grief.'
To them the Emir, speaking no truth, replied:
'Take you my signet, search about the tents;
Seek everywhere you will, inspect the camp;　　　　210
Your sister found, take her and go your way.'
They with great joy having received the seal,
Not knowing the deceit, searched diligently;
After seeking everywhere and finding nothing,
In grief were returning straight to the Emir,
And on the way they met a Saracen peasant;
He said to them, by their interpreter,
'Whom do you seek, boys, for whom are you mourning?'
They answered him again, saying with tears,
'You have a captive girl who is our sister;　　　　220
Not finding her we want to live no more.'
Sighing the Saracen spoke such words as these:
'Go through to the undercliff; you will find a ditch.

---

all. But there are five above 83, five
below 1996, and five at AND 402,
and five TRE 67. For this loose use
of ἀμφότεροι cf. 581, 1193, 2638.
210 φουσσᾶτα. Cf. above 89.
223 ὑπαύχενον. Difficult but not necessarily corrupt (like the μπάμορφον

of AND 424). αὐχήν may mean a
'neck' of land, a ridge, or the 'gorge'
of a river, in which sense Herodotus
uses it of the Danube. It is simpler
therefore to take it as meaning 'the
part below the narrows or ridge',
and to translate 'lower gorge' or

χθὲς ἐν αὐτῷ ἐσφάξαμεν εὐγενικὰς ὡραίας,
διότι οὐκ ἐπείθοντο εἰς ἃ ταῖς ἐλαλοῦμεν."   225
Ἐλάλησαν τοὺς ἵππους των, ἀπῆλθον εἰς τὸ ῥυάκιν·
πολλὰς σφαμμένας εὕρηκαν εἰς τὸ αἷμα βαπτομένας·   5 vᵒ.
ὦν μὲν αἱ χεῖρες ἔλειπον, κρανία τε καὶ πόδες·
ὦν δὲ τὰ μέλη ἅπαντα, καὶ τὰ ἔγκατα ἔξω,
γνωρισθῆναι ὑπό τινος μὴ δυνάμενα ὅλως.   230
Καὶ ταῦτα θεασάμενοι, ἔκπληξις τούτους εἶχεν,
καὶ χοῦν λαβόντες ἀπὸ γῆς ταῖς κεφαλαῖς προσραίνουν,
ὀδυρμούς τε ἐκίνησαν καὶ θρήνους ἐκ καρδίας·
"Ποίαν χεῖρα συγκόψομεν, ποίαν κλαύσομεν κάραν;
ποῖον μέλος γνωρίσαντες τῇ μητρὶ κομιοῦμεν;   235
Ὢ ἀδελφὴ παγκάλλιστε, πῶς ἀδίκως ἐσφάγης;
ὦ γλυκυτάτη μας ψυχή, πῶς σοι τοῦτο συνέβη;
πῶς δὲ παρ' ὥραν ἔδυνας καὶ ἔσβεσας τὸ φῶς μας,
πῶς κατεκόπης μεληδὸν ὑπὸ χειρὸς βαρβάρων;
πῶς οὐκ ἐνάρκησεν ἡ χεὶρ τοῦ ἀσπλάγχνου φονέως,   240
τοῦ μὴ κατελεήσαντος σοῦ τερπνὴν ἡλικίαν,
τοῦ μὴ κατοικτειρήσαντος φωνήν σου τὴν ὡραίαν;
Ὄντως εὐγενικὴ ψυχή, παρὰ τὴν ἀχρειοσύνην,
ἡρετίσω τὸν θάνατον καὶ σφαγὴν ὀλεθρίαν·
ἀλλ', ὦ ἀδελφὴ παγκάλλιστε, ὦ ψυχὴ καὶ καρδία,   245
πῶς σε διαχωρίσομεν ἐκ τῶν λοιπῶν σωμάτων;
ἔξομεν τοῦτο κἂν μικράν τινα παραμυθίαν;
Ὢ ὥρα πανδεινότατε καὶ δολία ἡμέρα,
μὴ ἴδοις ἥλιόν ποτε, μὴ φῶς σοι ἀνατείλοι·
σκότους ἐμπλήσοι σε Θεός, ὅταν τὴν ἀδελφήν μας   250
ἀνηλεῶς κατέκοπτον οἱ ἄνομοι ἀδίκως!
Ποῖον μητρὶ ἐλεεινῇ μήνυμα κομιοῦμεν;
Ἥλιε, τί ἐφθόνησας τὸ ὡραῖον μας ἀδέλφιν,   6 rᵒ.

231 C'est par ce vers que commence le ms. de Trébizonde.   233 ὀδυρδούς.
236 παγκάλιστε.   243 διὰ, au lieu de παρά, que je n'hésite pas à adopter en
m'appuyant sur les mss. de Trébizonde (vers 27) et d'Andros (vers 462). ἀχρειωσύ-
νην.   245 παγκάλιστε.   247 μικρὰν τινά.   249 ἥλιον ποτέ. ἀνατείλη.

'undercliff', than to make ingenious
suggestions such as ἀπαυχένιον (from
ἀπαυχενίζω) which might mean a
'slaughter-house', or ὑπόκενον (from
ὑποκενέω) which might mean a

'drain or sewer'.
226 ἐλάλησαν τοὺς ἵππους, for the usual
ἐπελάλησαν as above 150 et pass.,
suggests that the author thought that
ἱππιλάλησαν was the proper forma-

There yesterday we killed some lovely ladies,
Because they would not do the things we told them.'
They urged their horses, went off to the ditch;
And many slain they found, bathed in their blood,
Of whom some had no hands, no heads nor feet,
Some had no limbs at all, and their guts out,
Not to be known by anyone at all.   230
And this having beheld, dismay seized them,
They took and poured on their heads dust of the earth,
Wailings were stirred and mourning from their hearts:
'What hand join we to wail, what head to weep?
How recognize a limb to bring our mother?
All-fairest sister, why unjustly slain?
O sweetest soul of ours, how come to this?
How set before your time, put out our light!
How cut up limb from limb by barbarous hands!
Why stiffened not the ruthless killer's hand   240
Who had no mercy on your lovely form,
Who had no pity for your voice of beauty?
O noble soul indeed, rather than baseness
You chose to die and dreadfully be slain.
But, fairest sister, O our heart and soul,
How shall we part you from the other bodies?
Shall we have even this small consolation?
All-dreadful hour and miserable day,
See not the sun ever, nor light arise,
But God fill you with darkness, when our sister   250
These wicked sinners cruelly cut down.
What message shall we bring our piteous mother?
O sun, why did you envy our fair sister

tion; see above 150.
231 The Trebizond version begins with
the line corresponding to this.
234 συγκόψομεν, 'join in mourning for'.
The middle, not the active, would
be usual in this sense. Who would
believe that συγκόπτειν could ever
have such a meaning, beating the
breast (and pouring dust on the
head) being unknown in England?

241 ἡλικίαν. Might be translated
'youth', but that elsewhere in the
poem it is always given the meaning
of 'stature'.
251 κατέκοπτον of course means 'were
cutting up'; but the translator for
once refused the literal rendering.
253 τὸ ἀδέλφιν. Neuter form, the
ordinary feminine being used in 250
and 255.

17

ἀδίκως ἐθανάτωσας δι' οὗ ἀντέλαμπέ σου! "

Ἀλλ' ὅμως ὡς οὐκ ἴσχυσαν εὑρεῖν τὴν ἀδελφήν των,   255
τάφον ἕνα ποιήσαντες κατέθαψαν ἁπάσας,
καὶ θρηνοῦντες ὑπέστρεφον πρὸς ἀμηρᾶν εὐθέως,
θερμὰ κινοῦντες δάκρυα ἐκ μέσης τῆς καρδίας·
" Δός, ἀμηρᾶ, τὴν ἀδελφήν, εἰ δ' οὐ θανάτωσόν μας·
οὐδεὶς ἡμῶν ἄνευ αὐτῆς ὑποστρέφει ἐν οἴκῳ,   260
ἀλλὰ σφαγῶμεν ἅπαντες διὰ τὴν ἀδελφήν μας."
Ἀκούων ταῦτα ὁ ἀμηρᾶς, ὁρῶν δὲ καὶ τοὺς θρήνους,
ἤρξατο τούτους ἐρωτᾶν· " Τίνος ἐστὲ καὶ πόθεν;
γένους ποίου τυγχάνετε; ποῖον θέμα οἰκεῖτε; "
" Ἡμεῖς ἐκ τὸ ἀνατολικόν, ἐξ εὐγενῶν Ῥωμαίων,   265
ὁ πατήρ μας κατάγεται ἀπὸ τῶν Κινναμάδων·
ἡ δὲ μήτηρ μας Δούκισσα, γένους τῶν Κωνσταντίνου·
στρατηγοὶ μὲν οὖν δώδεκα ἐξάδελφοι καὶ θεῖοι.
Ἐξ ὧν ὅλοι τυγχάνομεν μετὰ τῆς αὐταδέλφης.
Ὁ πατήρ μας ἐξόριστος διά τινα μωρίαν,   270
ἣν αὐτῷ προεξένησάν τινες τῶν συκοφάντων·
οὐδεὶς ἀφ' ἡμῶν ἔτυχεν εἰς τὴν ἐπέλευσίν σου,
καὶ γὰρ ἡμεῖς ὑπήρχομεν στρατηγοὶ εἰς τὰς ἄκρας·
εἰ γὰρ ἐκεῖ ἐτύχομεν, οὐκ ἂν τοῦτο συνέβη,
οὐκ ἂν εἰς οἶκον μᾶς ποτε εἴχετε πορευθῆναι·   275
ἀφ' οὗ δὲ οὐκ ἐτύχομεν, καλῶς νὰ τὸ καυχᾶσαι.
Ἀλλ', ὦ ἀμηράδων μέγιστε καὶ πρῶτε τῆς Συρίας,
νὰ προσκυνήσῃς τὸν Βαγδᾶ· εἰπὲ καὶ σὺ τίς εἶ γε·   6 vº.
καὶ εἰ στραφοῦν οἱ συγγενεῖς ἀπὸ τοῦ ταξιδίου,
φέρουν καὶ τὸν πατέρα μας ἀπὸ τὴν ἐξορίαν,   280
νά σε καταζητήσωμεν ὅπου δ' ἂν καὶ τυγχάνῃς·
οὐ γὰρ ἂν ἀνεκδίκητον ἐάσομεν τὴν τόλμην."
" Ἐγώ, καλοὶ νεώτεροι," ὁ ἀμηρᾶς ἀντέφη,
" Χρυσοβέργου υἱός εἰμι, μητρὸς δὲ τῆς Πανθίας·
Ἄμβρων ὑπῆρχέ μου παππούς, θεῖος μου ὁ Καρόης·   285
τέθνηκε γάρ μου ὁ πατὴρ ἔτι νηπίου ὄντος·
παρὰ μητρὸς ἐδόθην δὲ εἰς συγγενεῖς Ἀράβους,
οἵτινές με ἀνέθρεψαν εἰς τὸ εὖ μετὰ πόθου·

259 δὸς ἡμῖν, ἀμυρᾶ. Le second mot est de trop et rend le vers hypermètre.
272 ἔλευσιν.   275 μᾶς ποτέ.   278 προσκυνήσεις.   279 ταξειδίου.
281 ναί σε καταζητήσομεν. τυγχάνεις.   284 υἱὸς εἰμί.

265 ἀνατολικόν. The Anatolic theme   lay immediately to the west of the

And kill unjustly for outshining you?'
For all that, when they could not find their sister,
Making one grave they buried all of them,
And wailing returned straight to the Emir,
With warm tears stirring from their inmost heart.
'Give us, Emir, our sister, or else kill us.
Not one of us without her will turn home,   260
But all be murdered for our sister's sake.'
This hearing, the Emir, seeing their grief,
Began to ask, 'Whose sons are you and whence?
Come from what family? Dwell in what theme?'
'We from the Eastern theme, of noble Romans;
Our father is descended from the Kinnamades;
Our mother a Doukas, of Constantine's family;
Twelve generals our cousins and our uncles.
Of such descend we all with our own sister.
Our father banished for some foolishness   270
Which certain slanderers contrived for him,
And none of us was there at your attack,
For that we were commanding on the borders;
For if we had been there, this had not been,
Into our home you had not ever come.
But since we were not, you may boast it well.
O greatest of Emirs and chief of Syria,
To Bagdad may you bow, say who you are;
And if our kinsmen come from their campaign,
And bring our father back from banishment,   280
Know we will seek you out wherever you be,
And never leave your daring unavenged.'
'I,' the Emir replied, 'my good young men,
Am son of Chrysoverges, and of Panthia;
My grandfather was Ambrôn, my uncle Karoês;
My father died while I was still a baby;
My mother gave me to my Arab kinsmen,
Who brought me up in faith of Mohamet.

Cappadocian. See above 56.
288 εἰς τὸ εὖ μετὰ πόθου. This is certainly corrupt, and so is AND 519
μὲ ἀμετρήτους πόθους. TRE 81 εἰς
ἀμετμέ τοῦ πόθου, emended by
Sathas and Legrand to εἰς Μωαμὲτ
τοῦ πόθου, is better. I read εἰς
Μωαμὲτ τὴν πίστιν.

όρῶντες δέ με εὐτυχῆ εἰς πάντας τοὺς πολέμους,
ἐξουσιαστὴν ἐποίησαν εἰς ὅλην τὴν Συρίαν, 290
καὶ ἐκλεκτούς μοι ἔδωκαν τρισχιλίους κονταράτους·
πᾶσαν Συρίαν ὑπέταξα καὶ ἐπίασα τὸ Κοῦφερ,
καὶ μικρόν τι καυχήσομαι πρὸς ὑμᾶς ἀληθεύων,
τὴν Ἡράκλειαν ὕστερον ἐξήλειψα ταχέως·
τὸ Ἀμόριν δὲ καταλαβὼν ἄχρι τοῦ Ἰκονίου, 295
πλήθη λῃστῶν ὑπέταξα καὶ πάντα τὰ θηρία.
Ἐμοὶ οὐκ ἀντεστάθησαν στρατηγοί, οὐ φουσσᾶτα·
γυνὴ δέ με ἐνίκησε πάνυ ὡραιοτάτη,
ταύτης τὰ κάλλη φλέγουν με, τὰ δάκρυα μαραίνουν·
οἱ στεναγμοὶ φλογίζουν με, τί ποιῆσαι οὐκ ἔχω· 300
δι' αὐτὴν ὑμᾶς ἐπείραζον ἵνα τὸ βέβαιον μάθω,
οὐδέποτε γὰρ παύεται ὑπὲρ ὑμῶν θρηνοῦσα·
πάντως ἐξαγορεύω σας, τὴν ἀλήθειαν λέγω· 7 rº.
εἰ οὐκ ἀπαξιώνετε τοῦ ἔχειν με γαμβρόν σας,
διὰ τὰ κάλλη τὰ τερπνὰ τῆς ὑμῶν αὐταδέλφης 305
νὰ γένωμαι χριστιανός, στραφεὶς εἰς Ῥωμανίαν·
καὶ μάθετε τὸ βέβαιον, μὰ τὸν μέγαν Προφήτην,
οὔτε φίλημά μ' ἔδωκεν, οὔτε τινὰ λαλίαν·
δεῦτε οὖν εἰς τὴν τένδαν μου· ἴδετε ἣν ζητεῖτε."
Ἐκεῖνοι ταῦτα ὡς ἤκουσαν, ἀπὸ περιχαρείας 310
τὴν τένδαν ἀνεσήκωσαν καὶ ἔσωθεν εἰσῆλθον·
εὗρον κλίνην χρυσόστρωτον, χαμαὶ δὲ τὸ κορίτζιν·
ὡς ἔκειτο, Χριστέ, ἐκεῖ, ἔλαμπεν ὡς ἀκτῖνες·
οἱ ὀφθαλμοὶ κατάβροχοι ἦσαν ἐκ τῶν δακρύων.
Ἣν ἰδόντες οἱ ἀδελφοὶ ἀνέστησαν σπουδαίως, 315
καὶ ταύτην μετ' ἐκπλήξεως ἕκαστος κατεφίλει·
ἀπροσδοκήτου γὰρ χαρᾶς ἐλθούσης παρ' ἐλπίδα,

292 κοῦφε.   304 ἤ.

---

292 The MS. reads κοῦφε which
Legrand has emended to κοῦφερ
from TRE ii. 86 and AND 524. But
see Grégoire, op. cit., p. 492, and
Byzantion, xii, p. 699, who shows that
this refers to Kufah, the old capital
of southern Mesopotamia, a sacred
city which usurpers of the ninth
century always began by visiting.
(There was also a famous school of

grammarians there: see Nicholson,
Lit. Hist. Arab., p. 189; and *Camb.
Med. Hist.* iv, p. 291.)
295 ἄχρι τοῦ Ἰκονίου. Iconium is not
'as far as' Amorium. I think it
probable that these words are corrupt and conceal the name of
Akroinon in Phrygia which was the
scene of much fighting in the Arab
wars of the early eighth century, and

Seeing me fortunate in all my wars
They made me ruler over all Syria,   290
Gave me three thousand lancers chosen men.

All Syria I subdued and captured Kufah,
Little I boast in telling you the truth,
Soon afterwards I wiped out Hêrakleia;
Seizing Amorion, far as Ikonion,
I laid low hordes of thieves and all wild beasts.

No generals resisted me, nor armies;
A woman though has conquered me most lovely,
Whose beauties burn me and whose tears consume;
Her sighs enflame; I know not what to do.   300
For her sake but to know for sure I tried you;
She never ceases ever weeps for you.

Now wholly I confess and speak the truth:
If you deign have me as your sister's husband,
For the sweet beauty of your own dear sister
I will become a Christian in Romania.

And, listen to the truth, by the great Prophet,
She never kissed me, never spoke to me.
Come then into my tent: see whom you seek.'

    They when they heard these words were overjoyed   310
And lifted up the tent and went within.

They found a gold-laid bed, the girl reclining;
Christ, there she lay, and seemed to shine with light;
Her eyes were overwatered with her tears.

Whom seeing, her brothers gravely raised her up,
And each began to kiss her, with surprise,
For unexpected joy coming unhoped

where the Turkish hero Sayyid Battal was killed in 740. (See *Camb. Med. Hist.* iv. pp. 120–1, and Grégoire, Διγ. Ἀκρ., pp. 35–38.) But for Ikonion see below 2122.

306 νὰ γένωμαι. Constructions with νά are used throughout the poem with future sense as here. The ancient future is falling into disuse, but the modern θά, or its original form θέλω νά, is not yet common. But see, e.g., 348 below ἔχειν θέλομεν, and 357 ὄψομαι.

315 σπουδαίως, 'gravely', 'busily', 'carefully', 'losing no time'—a little of all these meanings.

317 The gnome 'unexpected joy causes tears' is expressed more fully, more clumsily, and more sinkingly than in TRE ii. 111, 112. It is not helped by the redactor's ending lines 317 and 318 παρ' ἐλπίδα and ἀνελπίστως. There is no doubt at all that so far from avoiding such repetitions, throughout the poem he deliberately aims at the repetition of the same

χαίρονται πάντες οἱ αὐτῆς τυχόντες ἀνελπίστως·
ὁμοῦ θλῖψιν ὑπέφερον τὰ δάκρυα καὶ πόνους
καὶ χαρὰν τὴν πανθαύμαστον τὴν τότε γεναμένην.   320
Ὡς δὲ ταύτην ἠσπάζοντο μετὰ περιχαρείας,
καὶ δάκρυα προσέβαλλον ποιοῦντες μετὰ θρήνων·
καὶ " Ζῆς " ἔλεγον " ἀδελφή, ζῆς, ψυχὴ καὶ καρδία,
ἡμεῖς θανοῦσαν σε εἴχομεν καὶ σπαθοκοπημένην·
ἀλλ᾽ οὖν τὰ κάλλη ζῶσαν σε ἐτήρησαν, φιλτάτη,   325
τὰ κάλλη γὰρ καὶ τοὺς ληστὰς ἡμέρους ἐκποιοῦσι,
καὶ πολεμίους φείδεσθαι νεότητος καὶ κάλλους."
Εἶθ᾽ οὕτως, βεβαιώσαντες τὸν ἀμηρᾶν μεθ᾽ ὅρκου
γαμβρὸν ἵνα τὸν λάβωσιν, ἂν ἔλθῃ εἰς Ῥωμανίαν,   7 vᵒ.
τὰ βούκινα ἐδώκασιν, ὑπέστρεφον εὐθέως,   330
καὶ πάντες ἐξεπλήσσοντο λέγοντες πρὸς ἀλλήλους·
" Ὤ θαῦμα ὅπερ βλέπομεν, δύναμις τῶν Ῥωμαίων,
αἰχμάλωτα ἀναλύουσι, φουσσᾶτα καταλύουν,
πίστιν ἀρνεῖσθαι πείθουσι, θάνατον μὴ φοβεῖσθαι."
Καὶ ἀκουστὸν ἐγένετο εἰς τὸν σύμπαντα κόσμον   335
ὅτι κόρη πανεύγενος, μετὰ τερπνά τῆς κάλλη,
φουσσᾶτα ἐκατέλυσε περίφημα Συρίας.

319 θλίψιν.   336 Il faut sans doute lire μὲ τὰ.

22

All must rejoice who without hope attain it;
At once they suffered grief, and tears, and pain,
And that all-wondrous joy that then began.   320
So when they were embracing her with gladness,
Tears would come on them too, and they would groan,
Would say, 'You live, live, sister, heart and soul;
We thought that you were dead, ripped by the sword,
But your beauties have kept you, dear, alive,
For beauties make even the robbers mild,
And make the enemies spare youth and beauty.'
  So with an oath they promised the Emir
To be their sister's husband in Romania,
Sounded the trumpets and returned at once   330
And still astonished, saying to each other,
'O wonder that we see, and passions' power,
They free the captive, they destroy armies,
Make man deny his faith and not fear death.'
And it was noised about the entire world
How that a noble girl with her sweet beauties
Had broken up the famed armies of Syria.

---

or similar words. It is a principle of
composition which tries to satisfy a
demand which was subsequently met
by the introduction of rhyme.
332 MS. and Legrand read δύναμις
τῶν ῾Ρωμαίων. But TRE 126 (and
also AND 564) read δύναμιν τῶν
ἐρώτων which makes sense and has

been translated.
333 αἰχμάλωτα ἀναλύουσι, φουσσᾶτα
καταλύουν might be translated 'break
down prisons, break up armies'.
φουσσάτα καταλύουν is echoed in 337.
See remarks above on verbal repetitions.

ΠΕΡΙ ΤΗΣ ΓΕΝΝΗΣΕΩΣ ΤΟΥ ΑΚΡΙΤΟΥ

ΛΟΓΟΣ ΔΕΥΤΕΡΟΣ

Ἐπειδὴ ὅρκους προύβάλλοντο γαμβρόν να τον ἐπάρουν,
ἐπῆρε τοὺς ἀγούρους του ὁ ἀμηρᾶς εὐθέως,
εἰς Ῥωμανίαν ὑπέστρεφε διὰ τὴν ποθητήν του.
Ὅταν δὲ κατελάμβανε μέρη τῆς Ῥωμανίας,
ἠλευθέρωνεν ἅπαντας οὓς εἶχεν αἰχμαλώτους,   5
ἑκάστῳ δοὺς ἐφόδια εἰς τὴν ὁδὸν ἀρκοῦντα.
Οἱ δὲ τῆς κόρης ἀδελφοὶ τῇ μητρὶ πάντα γράφουν·
τῆς ἀδελφῆς τὴν εὕρεσιν, τοῦ ἀμηρᾶ τὸν πόθον,
τὸ πῶς πίστιν ἠρνήσατο, συγγενεῖς καὶ πατρίδα·
καὶ " Ὢ μῆτερ παμπόθητε, μή τινα θλῖψιν ἔχῃς·   10
γαμβρὸν γὰρ ἔχειν θέλομεν πάγκαλον καὶ ὡραῖον·
τὴν χρείαν δὲ ἑτοίμασον ἅπασαν τὴν τοῦ γάμου."
Ἡ δὲ ταῦτα ἀκούσασα, τῷ Θεῷ ηὐχαρίστει,
" Δόξα, Χριστέ μου," λέγουσα, " τῇ σῇ φιλανθρωπίᾳ·
δόξα τῇ δυναστείᾳ σου, ἐλπὶς τῶν ἀνελπίστων,   15
ὅσα γὰρ θέλεις δύνασαι, οὐδὲν ἀδυνατεῖ σοι·   8 r°.
αὐτὸν γὰρ τὸν πολέμιον ἥμερον κατειργάσω,
καὶ θυγατέρα τὴν ἐμὴν ἐρρύσω ἐκ θανάτου.
Ἀλλ᾽, ὦ θύγατερ ποθεινή, φῶς τῶν ἐμῶν ὀμμάτων,
πότε σε ζῶσαν ὄψομαι, φωνῆς τῆς σῆς ἀκούσω;   20
ἰδοὺ καὶ γάμον γὰρ τὸν σὸν ηὐτρέπισα καὶ χρείαν,
ἆρα νυμφίος ἔσται σοι παρόμοιος τοῦ κάλλους;
ἆρα τὴν γνώμην θέλει σχεῖν τῶν εὐγενῶν Ῥωμαίων;
φοβοῦμαι, τέκνον μου καλόν, μὴ ἄστοργος ὑπάρχῃ,
μὴ θυμώδης ὡς ἐθνικός, καὶ ζῆν με οὐ συμφέρῃ."   25
Ταῦτα μὲν ἡ στρατήγισσα χαίρουσα ἐμελῴδει.
Ὁ δ᾽ ἀμηρᾶς καὶ μετ᾽ αὐτοῦ οἱ ἀδελφοὶ τῆς κόρης

10 θλίψιν ἔξεις (sic) et en marge ἔχης.   11 γὰρ manque. πάγκαλλον.   16 ἀδυνατοῖ.   21 ηὐπρέπισα.   25 συμφέρει.

339 ἀγούρους, his 'boys'; see above 47.
360 γνώμην, 'character' or 'nature'; for other refs. see index.
363 Apparently a song has been lost,

and in the corresponding passage TRE 157 Sathas marks a lacuna, as he does elsewhere where a song is indicated. The words χαίρουσα ἐμε-

OF THE BIRTH OF THE BORDERER

SECOND BOOK

SINCE they had vowed that he should wed their sister
The Emir straightway taking his company
Returned for his beloved to Romania.   340
And when he came into the Roman country
Began to free all those whom he held captive,
Giving each one provision for the way.
The girl's brothers wrote all things to their mother,
The finding of their sister, the Emir's love,
How he denied his faith, his kin and country,
And, 'O beloved mother, have no grief,
For we shall have a bridegroom fine and fair;
Make ready all things needful for the wedding.'
She having heard these things gave thanks to God,   350
Saying, 'My Christ, praise to thy loving-kindness,
Hope of the hopeless, praise be to thy power,
All thy will doing, nothing impossible,
For and this enemy thou hast made tame,
And hast delivered my daughter from death.
But, O my daughter dear, light of my eyes,
When shall I see thee living, hear thy voice?
For lo thy wedding and thy needs prepared,
But shall a groom be found to match thy beauty?
His be the nature of the noble Romans?   360
I fear, my good child, that he may be loveless,
Fierce as a pagan, and I not care to live.'
Thus in her joy the General's wife did sing.
    Meanwhile the Emir and with him the girl's brothers

λῴδει can hardly refer to the doubts and fears she has just uttered. But possibly the redactor departed from his archetype and rewrote a speech which in the original was either a more joyful utterance or perhaps a lyrical lamentation like the well-known μοιρολόγι for a lost daughter (Polites, Ἐκλογαί, No. 221):
'Sun going round the world, sun shining clear,
Last night I lost a girl, a daughter dear.'

χαίροντες ἄμφω τῆς ὁδοῦ ἤρχοντο μετὰ μόχθου·
ἡνίκα δ᾽ ἐπλησίασαν εἰς τὸν ἴδιον οἶκον,
λαὸς πολὺς καὶ συγγενεῖς εἰς ἀπαντὴν ἐξῆλθον,   30
εἶθ᾽ οὕτως ἡ στρατήγισσα μετὰ δόξης μεγάλης.
Τὴν δὲ χαρὰν τὴν ἄπειρον τὴν τότε γιναμένην
τίς φράσαι ὅλως δυνηθῇ, ἢ ὅλως παρεικάσαι;
Τὰ τέκνα γὰρ ἠσπάζοντο μητέρα μετὰ πόθου,
καὶ ἡ μήτηρ εὐφραίνετο ἀληθῶς ἐπὶ τέκνοις·   35
ἰδοῦσα δὲ καὶ τὸν γαμβρὸν περιχαρῆ τῷ ὄντι,
χάριν Θεῷ ἀνέπεμψεν ἐξ ὅλης τῆς καρδίας·
" Κύριε", λέγουσα, " Χριστέ, πᾶς ὁ εἰς σὲ ἐλπίζων
οὐκ ἀπέτυχε πώποτε τῶν ἐπιθυμουμένων."
Εἰς δὲ τὸν οἶκον φθάσαντες ἐποίησαν τοὺς γάμους,   40
καὶ τῷ θείῳ βαπτίσματι τὸν γαμβρὸν τελειοῦσι·   8 vᵒ.
ἡ δὲ χαρὰ ἐπηύξανε ἡ πάνδημος ἐκείνη·
ἔχαιρε γὰρ ὁ ἀμηρᾶς τυχὼν τῆς ἐρωμένης·
οὐ γάρ ἐστιν ἐρωτικῆς ἀγάπης χαρὰ κρείττων·
ὅσον φλέγεται ὁ ἐρῶν ἐπὶ ἀποτυχίᾳ   45
τοσοῦτον χαίρει ὁ ἐρῶν τυχὼν τῆς ἐρωμένης.
Μετὰ δὲ τὴν συνάφειαν συνέλαβεν ἡ κόρη,
καὶ ἔτεκε τὸν Διγενῆ Βασίλειον Ἀκρίτην·
ἔτι δὲ μᾶλλον ηὔξανε τοῦ ἀμηρᾶ ὁ πόθος.
Ἡ δὲ μήτηρ τοῦ ἀμηρᾶ γραφὴν ἀπὸ Συρίας   50
θρήνου μεστὴν ἐξέπεμψεν, ὀνειδισμοῦ καὶ ψόγου·
" Τὰ ὀμμάτια μου ἐτύφλωσας καὶ ἔσβεσας τὸ φῶς μου,
ὦ τέκνον ποθεινότατον, πῶς μητρὸς ἐπελάθου;
πῶς ἀπηρνήσω συγγενεῖς, καὶ πίστιν καὶ πατρίδα,
καὶ ἐγενήθης ὄνειδος εἰς πᾶσαν τὴν Συρίαν;   55
Βδελυκτοὶ δὲ γεγόναμεν ἀπὸ παντὸς ἀνθρώπου,
ὡς ἀρνηταὶ τῆς πίστεως, ὡς παραβάται νόμου,
ὡς μὴ τηρήσαντες καλῶς τοὺς λόγους τοῦ Προφήτου.
Τί συνέβη σοι, τέκνον μου, πῶς αὐτῶν ἐπελάθου;
πῶς γὰρ οὐκ ἐμνημόνευσας τὰς πράξεις τοῦ πατρός σου,   60

28 A ἄμφω il serait peut-être préférable de substituer ἄμα que donne le ms. de
Trébizonde (vers 159) et celui d'Andros (vers 597).   36 Le ms. de Trébizonde
(vers 169) et celui d'Andros (vers 607) donnent περικαλλῆ, mais la leçon περιχαρῆ
peut s'expliquer.   44 οὐδὲ γὰρ ἐστιν.   56 βδελλυκτοί.

365 ἄμφω. See above 205.   Psalms from which this is a quotation
372 TRE 167 refers explicitly to the   (LXX, Ps. cxii. 9; A.V. Ps. cxiii. 9).

Gladly together took the toilsome road
And when they were come near to their own house,
Much company and kin came out to meet them,
And then the General's wife with great array.
The limitless rejoicing then arose
Who now can wholly tell, wholly imagine?   370
The children lovingly embraced the mother,
She was verily a joyful mother of children.
And when she saw the bridegroom glad indeed
She sent up thanks to God with all her heart,
Saying, 'Lord Christ, whoever hopes in thee
Has never failed of all that he desired.'
  And coming to the house they made the wedding,
Fulfilled the groom with holy baptism.
And so increased that universal joy;
For the Emir rejoiced to have his love,   380
And greater joy is none than loving passion;
For as the lover burns in unsuccess,
So much the lover joys to have his love.
After their union the girl conceived,
And brought forth Digenes Basil Akrites;
So much the more the Emir's passion grew.
  The Emir's mother a letter from Syria
Sent him full of sorrow, blame, and reviling:
'You have put out my light, blinded my eyes;
Dear child, your mother how have you forgotten,   390
Denied your kindred and your faith and country,
And have become a reproach in all Syria?
To every man we are become abominable,
Deniers of the faith, the law's transgressors
Not having well observed the Prophet's words.
What came to you, child, how could you forget them?
How not remember what your father did,

---

373 περιχαρῆ. Legrand suggests that it
would be better to read περικαλλῆ
with TRE 169, AND 607. But it
would be simpler to read περιχαρῆς
(i.e. not the bridegroom but his
future mother-in-law was 'over-
joyed').

376 In TRE the second book ends with
the line corresponding to this, and
the passage recording the baptism
and marriage and the birth of
Digenes (as in AND ii. 611–27) has
disappeared altogether.

27

ὅσους Ῥωμαίους ἔσφαξε, πόσους ἔφερε δούλους;
οὐκ ἐγέμισε φυλακὰς στρατηγῶν καὶ τοπάρχων;
οὐκ ἐκούρσευσε θέματα πολλὰ τῆς Ῥωμανίας,
καὶ αἰχμαλώτους ἔφερεν εὐγενικὰς ὡραίας;
μὴ ἐπλανήθη ὥσπερ σὺ γενέσθαι παραβάτης;   65
Ὅταν γὰρ τὸν ἐκύκλωσαν φουσσᾶτα τῶν Ῥωμαίων,
οἱ στρατηγοί τον ὤμνυον ὅρκους φρικωδεστάτους   9 rᵒ.
πατρίκιος νὰ τιμηθῇ παρὰ τοῦ βασιλέως,
νὰ γένῃ πρωτοστράτορας, ἂν ῥίψῃ τὸ σπαθίν του.
Ἀλλ' ἐκεῖνος, προστάγματα φυλάττων τοῦ Προφήτου,   70
δόξης μὲν κατεφρόνησε, πλοῦτον δὲ οὐ προσέσχε·
καὶ μελῃδόν τον ἔκοψαν, καὶ ἀπῆραν τὸν σπαθίν του.
Σὺ δέ, ἀνάγκην μὴ εἰδώς, πάντα ὁμοῦ παρεῖδες,
τὴν πίστιν μέν, τοὺς συγγενεῖς, κἀμὲ τὴν σὴν μητέρα.
Ὁ ἀδελφός μου, ὁ θεῖός σου, ὁ Μουρσῆς ὁ Καρόης   75
εἰς Σμύρνην ἐταξίδευσεν εἰς τὸ παραθαλάσσιν,
τὴν Ἄγκυραν ἐκούρσευσε, τὴν Ἄβυδον τὴν πόλιν,
τὴν Ἀφρικήν, τὴν Τέρενταν, καὶ τὴν Ἑξακωμίαν,
καὶ ταῦτα τροπωσάμενος ἐστράφη εἰς Συρίαν·
σὺ δὲ ὁ δυστυχέστατος ἐποίησας ταξίδιν.   80
Ὅταν ἤθελες δοξασθῆν παρ' ὅλην τὴν Συρίαν,
τὰ πάντα προσαπώλεσας δι' ἀγάπην χανζυρίσσης
καὶ κατάρατος γέγονας εἰς πάντα μασγιδίον.
Εἰ μὴ παρέλθῃς γὰρ ταχὺ καὶ ἔλθῃς εἰς Συρίαν,
οἱ ἀμηρᾶδες βούλονται ἐμὲ νὰ ποταμήσουν,   85
τὰ τέκνα σου νὰ σφάξωσιν ὡς πατρὸς ἀποστάτου,
τὰ τερπνά σου κοράσια νὰ παραδώσουν ἄλλοις,
ἃ καὶ στενάζουν διὰ σέ, ὑπομονὴν οὐκ ἔχουν.
Ὦ τέκνον μου γλυκύτατον, οἰκτείρησον μητέρα·
μὴ καταγάγῃς γῆρας μου εἰς ᾅδου μετὰ λύπης,   90
καὶ μὴ θελήσῃς τέκνα σου τοῦ σφαγῆναι ἀδίκως·
μὴ δὲ παρίδῃς δάκρυα τερπνῶν σου κορασίων,   9 vᵒ.

---

69 πρωτοστάτωρας.   72 Je préfèrerais τὸ σπαθίν.   76 μύρνην ἐταξεί-
δευσεν.   78 Il faut peut-être lire Τεφρικήν. ἐξακομίαν.   80 ταξείδιν.   81
δοξασθεῖν.   82 πρσαπώλεσας (sic).   92 Peut-être μηδὲ serait-il préférable.

---

405 πατρίκιος. See below 2128; and
Theoph., p. 310. And compare the
promises of Pharas, one of the
officers of Belisarius, to the be-
leaguered Vandal, Gelimer, at the
end of the African War (A.D. 533):
'That generous prince [Justinian]
will grant you a rich inheritance of
lands, a place in the Senate, and the
dignity of patrician.' Gibbon, ch.

How many Romans slew, how many enslaved?
Did he not fill the prisons with generals and captains?
Did he not ravage many Roman themes,   400
And bring in captive many noble beauties?
Was he not led, like you, towards transgression?
For when the Roman armies ringed him round
The generals swore to him with frightful oaths
The emperor should make him a patrician,
Master of horse, if he threw down his sword.
But he keeping the Prophet his commandments,
Despised all honour, gave no heed to wealth;
They cut him limb from limb, and took his sword.
You, knowing no compulsion, gave up all,   410
Your faith, your kinsmen, even me your mother.
My brother and your uncle, Moursês Karoës,
Led his army to Smyrna by the sea,
Ravaged Ankyra, the city of Abydos,
And Tefrike, and Tarenta, and the Six Towns,
And from these victories turned to Syria.
You made an expedition, most unblessed,
And when you might have had all Syria's praise,
Have all forgone for a swine-eater's love
And are become accursed in every mosque.   420
If soon you come not forth and come to Syria
The emirs will have it in their minds to drown me,
To kill your children whose father was a renegade,
And give to other men your pretty damsels;
Which they lament for you and not endure.
O sweetest child of mine, pity your mother.
Bring not my old age to the grave in sorrow,
Nor let your children be unjustly slain,
Nor yet ignore your pretty damsels' tears,

xli, following Procopius, *Bell. Vand.* ii. 6.
412 See Genealogical table. AND iii. 656 refers to another uncle, Mousour of Tarsus, and so does TRE iii. 201.
415 Leg. Τεφρικήν . . . Τάρανταν. For Taranda see Honigmann, pp. 55, 56. No Six-towns appears to be known; for Πεντακωμία see Honigm. 16;

and Procop. *Aedific.* ii. 9.
419 προσαπώλεσας, i.e. 'in addition to not winning praise you have also lost'. χανζυρίσσης Arab. *hanzir.* ESC 269 χατζιροφαγοῦσα cf. Lyb. Rod. 2312.
421 For παρέλθῃς perhaps we should read προσέλθῃς, 'surrender'; cf. προσελθόντες below 3170; or 'show yourself'—cf. ἐπερχομένην 3647.

καὶ ἐκδαφίσῃ σε Θεὸς ὁ μέγας ἐκ τοῦ κόσμου.

Ἰδοὺ ἔστειλά σοι, ὡς ὁρᾷς, ἐπίλεκτα φαρία·
τὴν βάδεαν καβαλλίκευε, παράσυρε τὴν μαύρην,   95
ἡ δ' ἀγάλ' ἃς ἀκολουθῇ, καὶ οὐδεὶς οὐ μή σε φθάσῃ·
λάβε καὶ τὴν Ῥωμάϊσσαν, εἰ δι' αὐτὴν λυπῆσαι·
εἰ δὲ καὶ παρακούσῃς μου, ἔσῃ κατηραμένος."
Λαβόντες δὲ τὰ γράμματα ἐκλεκτοὶ Ἀραβῖται
διὰ πολλῆς ταχύτητος ἦλθον εἰς Ῥωμανίαν·   100
ἦν δέ τις οἶκος μήκοθεν τόπος ἡ Λακκοπέτρα,
ἐκεῖσε ἡμπλικεύσασι τοῦ μὴ φανερωθῆναι·
οἱ καὶ τούτῳ ἐδήλωσαν διὰ γραμματηφόρου·
" Τὸ φέγγος λάμπει ὁλονυκτί, ὁδεύσωμεν, εἰ βούλει."
Ὡς δὲ εἶδεν ὁ ἀμηρᾶς τὴν γραφὴν τῆς μητρός του,   105
ἐσπλαγχνίσθη κατὰ πολὺ ὡς υἱὸς τὴν μητέρα,
τὰ τέκνα κατηλέησε καὶ τὰς αὐτῶν μητέρας·
ζῆλος ἀνήφθη εἰς αὐτὸν εἰ περιλάβουν ἄλλους
(οὐ γὰρ ποτὲ λανθάνεται ἀρχὴ ἑτέρου πόθου,
τοῦτον δὲ κατημαύρωσεν ἡ ἀγάπη τῆς κόρης·   110
πόνος γὰρ ὁ σφοδρότατος ἀμαυροῖ τὸν ἐλάσσω),
καὶ ἵστατο διαπορῶν, θέλων τι διαπρᾶξαι.
Εἰς τὸ κουβούκλιν δ' εἰσελθὼν λέγει τὴν ποθητήν του·
" Λόγον τινὰ ἀπόκρυφον βούλομαί σοι θαρρῆσαι,
ἀλλὰ φοβοῦμαι, πάντερπνε, μὴ οὔκ ἔνι εἰς ἀρεστόν σου·   115
ἰδοὺ καιρὸς ἐφέστηκε τὸ βέβαιον νὰ μάθω,
ἐὰν ἀγάπην εἰς ἐμὲ ἔχῃς καθαρωτάτην."
Ἡ δὲ ταῦτα ἀκούσασα ἐδήχθη τὴν καρδίαν,   10 rᵒ.
καὶ στενάξασα βύθιον τοιόνδε λόγον λέγει·
" Ὦ ἄνερ μου γλυκύτατε, αὐθέντα καὶ προστάτα,   120
ποτὲ λόγον οὔκ ἤκουσα μὴ οὔκ ἔνι εἰς ἀρεστόν μου·
ποία δέ γε περίστασις χωρίσει με σοῦ πόθου;
πάντως κἂν δέῃ με θανεῖν, οὐκ ἀπαρνήσομαί σε·
οἶδε γὰρ ἡ περίστασις φιλίαν δοκιμάζειν."
" Οὐ πρὸς θάνατον, φίλτατε," ὁ ἀμηρᾶς ἀντέφη,   125
" τὸ δοκεῖς καὶ βουλεύεσαι μὴ γένοιτο, ψυχή μου·

93 ἐκδαφίσει.   95 βάδαιαν.   96 Sans doute δαγάλ'. ἀκολουθεῖ.   99
ἀραβίται.   106 καταπολύ.   112 δικπράξαι.   118 ἐδίχθη.   121 σου, au
lieu de μου.

432 On the led horse (para-veredus or   433 Read δαγάλ', as in TRE 222 and
palfrey) see Kyriakides, Διγενής, pp.   below 3178.
92 ff. and Soph. Lex. s.v. συρτόν.   438 Read οἴκου, from TRE 230

And have great God uproot you from the world.   430
I send you, as you see, some chosen mounts;
Ride you the bay and lead the black beside,
And let the chestnut follow, none shall catch you;
Take the Roman girl too, if you are sorry for her.
But if you hark not you shall be accurst.'
   Taking her letter picked Arabians
With much speed came into Romania.
   There was a lonely place called Hollow Stone,
Where they encamped, that they should not be seen,
And him informed by one that bore the letter: 440
'The moon shines nightlong, go we, if you will.'
The Emir when he saw his mother's writing
Felt all a son's compassion for his mother;
Was sorry for his children and their mothers;
Jealousy blazed lest they should others clasp—
(First love is not forgotten in another,
Only this maiden's love had obscured it,
For and a stronger pain obscures the less)—
And he stood wondering, wanting to act.
   Entering her room he said to his beloved: 450
'There is a secret I would dare to tell,
But I fear, dearest, lest it please you not.
Now is the time come I must learn for sure
If that your love for me is unadulterate.'
She when she heard these words her heart was stung,
And deeply sighing spoke such words as these:
'My sweetest husband, master and defender,
When have I heard you speak and not please me?
What circumstance shall part me from your love?
Even if I must die I will not deny you.   460
For circumstance can test affection.'
   'Not of death, dearest,' the Emir replied;
'Come not what you ponder and think, my soul;

441 For φέγγος of moonlight see
below 1451.
445 εἰ περιλάβουν ἄλλους—'lest they
should embrace others'. For περι-
λαμβάνω in this sense see Xanthoudides, *Erotokritos*, glossary. But TRE

and AND evidently not understanding the word read πῶς μέλλουσι
παραλαβεῖν ἄλλοι τὰ τέκνα τούτου.
458 Read with TRE iii. 256, AND iii.
706 πότε σου λόγον ἤκουσα οὐκ εἶναι
ἀρεστόν μου.

31

ἀλλὰ μητρὸς ἀπέλαβον γραφὴν ἀπὸ Συρίας,
καὶ κινδυνεύει δι' ἐμέ, βούλομαι δὲ ὑπάγειν·
ἐὰν καὶ σύ, ψυχίτζα μου, ἔρχεσαι μετ' ἐμέναν,
οὐ θέλω χωρισθῆναι σοι οὐδὲ πρὸς ὥραν μίαν·   130
καὶ πάλιν ὑποστρέψομεν διὰ πολλοῦ τοῦ τάχους."
" Μετὰ χαρᾶς, ὦ κύρκα μου," ἡ κόρη ἀπεκρίθη,
" τούτου χάριν μὴ θλίβεσαι· ὅπου κελεύεις ἔλθω."
Θεὸς δέ τι θαυματουργῶν παράδοξον ἐνταῦθα,
καὶ τὸ κρύφιον βούλευμα κατ' ὄναρ εἰς φῶς ἄγει·   135
ὁ γὰρ ὕστερος ἀδελφὸς τῆς κόρης ὄναρ εἶδεν·
καὶ ἐκ τοῦ ὕπνου ἀναστάς, τοὺς ἀδελφοὺς καλέσας,
τὸ ὄναρ διηγήσατο τῆς νυκτὸς ὅπερ εἶδεν.
" Ἤμην καθήμενος", φησίν, " ἐπάνω ἐν τῷ οἴκῳ,
καὶ ἱέρακας ἔβλεπον ἐπὶ τὴν Λακκοπέτραν,   140
καὶ φάλκωνα πολεμικὸν διώκων περιστέραν·
ὡς δὲ ταύτην ἐδίωκε καὶ τελείωσιν εἶχεν,
ἀμφότεροι εἰσῆλθοσαν ἔνδον τοῦ κουβουκλίου,
ἔνθα διάγει ὁ γαμβρὸς μετὰ τῆς αὐταδέλφης.
Συντόμως ἐξεπήδησα, ἔδραμον νά την πιάσω·   10 vo. 145
συνεταράχθη μου ἡ ψυχή, ἔξυπνος ἐγενόμην."
Τότε ὁ πρῶτος ἀδελφὸς τὸ ὅραμα συγκρίνει·
" Ἱέρακες, ὡς λέγουσιν, ἄνδρες ἅρπαγες εἶναι,
φάλκωνα δὲ ὃν ἔβλεπες, φοβοῦμαι τὸν γαμβρόν μας
περιστερὰν τὴν ἀδελφὴν μήπως την ἀδικήσῃ·   150
ἀλλ' ἂς ἀπέλθωμεν ἐκεῖ ἔνθα τὸ ὄναρ εἶδες,
ἔνθα καὶ τοὺς ἱέρακας ἔβλεπες πετωμένους."
Καβαλλικεύουν παρευθύς, ἀπῆγον εἰς τὴν πέτραν·
τοὺς Ἀραβίτας ηὕρηκαν μετὰ καὶ τῶν φαρίων·
ἰδόντες δ' ἐξεπλάγησαν, τὸ ὅραμα θαυμάζουν,   155
" Καλῶς ἤλθετε," λέγοντες, " ἄγουροι τοῦ γαμβροῦ μας·
πῶς ὧδε ἡμπλικεύσατε, τὸν οἶκον μας ἀφέντες; "
Οἱ δέ γε μὴ δυνάμενοι ἀντειπεῖν ὡμολόγουν

150 ἀδικήσει.   153 παρ' εὐθύς.   157 ὧδε.

469 *κύρκα μου*. Below *passim*, also TRE
1981 and AND 2943 *et passim*. See
also Polites, Ἐκλογαί, p. 281, No. 4,
Κύρκατης; and Passow, 438, and
Παχτίκου, 260 Δημ. Ἑλλ. Ἄισμ.,
p. 22 *Κύρκος*. A woman's pet-name

for her lover, usually (e.g. in editorial
glossaries of AND and TRE) said to
be the same as modern *κούρκος*, a
turkey, said by Meyer to be Slavonic.
Though unconvinced I have little
better to suggest. Prof. R. M.

I have letters from my mother in Syria,
Through me endangered, and I want to go.
If you too, my dear soul, will come with me,
Not for an hour will I be parted from you;
And very soon we will return again.'
'With great delight, my pet,' the girl replied,
'Fret not for that, I come wherever you bid.'   470
But God strange wonders to perform herein
The secret counsel brings in dream to light;
For the girl's youngest brother saw a dream,
And rising out of sleep, calling his brothers,
Told them the dream which he had seen by night.
'I was sitting', he said, 'up in the house,
And watching hawks over the Hollow Stone,
A warring falcon too that chased a dove;
And following it as he brought the chase to end,
Both of the birds entered into the chamber,   480
Wherein the bridegroom lives with our own sister;
I leaped up quickly and I ran to catch her;
My soul was all in trouble, I awoke.'
The eldest brother then judges the vision:
'Hawks, as they say, you saw be robber men,
The falcon that you saw, I fear our groom
May do some injury to the dove our sister.
But let us go to where you saw the dream,
And where you were watching the hawks in flight.'
Mounting at once they rode off to the Stone,   490
And found there the Arabians with their beasts;
Mazed at the sight they wondered at the vision,
Saying, 'Welcome, companions of our groom,
Why are you here encamped, far from our house?'
And they, unable to deny, confessed

Dawkins suggests a connexion with
Turkish *köroğlu*, 'son of the blind
man', a folk-tale hero. It may be
possible, I believe, to trace a connexion with the ancient word κίρκος,
'a kind of hawk or falcon' (*Iliad*
xxii. 139; *Od*. xiii. 87), for which
see L. & S.; but more evidence is
required. Kalonaros (on AND 2943)
suggests that it is a hypocoristic form
of κύρ or κύρης.
478 See *Iliad* xxi. 493 φύγεν ὥς τε πέλεια
. . . and Edgar Wallace, *Jack o'
Judgement*, p. 90 (ch. 14): '. . . she
dreamt he was flying after her, she
a pigeon and he a hawk.'

τὸ βέβαιον ἐκφαίνοντες, οὐδὲν δὲ ἀπεκρύβη.
Φόβος γὰρ ἀπροσδόκητος ἀληθείας ἐκφέρει,　　　　　　160
ὁ δέ γε προσδοκώμενος γεννᾷ ἀπολογίας.
Οἳ παρευθὺς λαβόμενοι εἰς τὸν γαμβρὸν ἀπῆλθον,
κατονειδίζοντες αὐτὸν ὡς κακόβουλον ὄντα,
μᾶλλον δὲ καὶ ὁ ὕστερος θρασύτατος ὑπάρχων·
" τὸ ἐνεθυμήθης," ἔλεγε, "μὴ τὸ ἀποδοκιμάσῃς,　　　　165
καὶ γίνωσκε, Σαρακηνέ, οὐ μὴ ἴδῃς τὴν Συρίαν·
ἀλλ᾽ ἐπειδὴ παράνομος καὶ ἐχθρὸς ἀπεφάνθης,
τὴν ἀδελφήν μας ἔασον, τὸ τέκνον σου ἀρνήσου,
καί, λαβὼν ἅπερ ἔφερες, πορεύου ὅθεν ἦλθες."
Ἀκούων ταῦτα ὁ ἀμηρᾶς καὶ τοὺς ἐλέγχους βλέπων,　　170
μὴ δυνάμενος ἀντειπεῖν παντελῶς ἐσιώπα,　　　　　　11 rᵒ.
αἰσχύνης, φόβου, θλίψεως ἀνάμεστος ὑπάρχων·
ᾐσχύνετο γὰρ φωραθείς, ὡς ξένος ἐφοβεῖτο,
ἐλυπεῖτο μὴ χωρισμὸν ὑποστῇ τῆς φιλτάτης.
Μὴ ἔχων τι ποιήσειεν, εἰς τὴν κόρην εἰσῆλθε·　　　　175
ταύτην γὰρ μόνην ἤλπιζεν εὑρεῖν παρηγορίαν,
μὴ γινώσκων ὅ, τι θεὸς ἐδήλωσε κατ᾽ ὄναρ·
" καὶ τί τοῦτο ἐποίησας; " ἐπεφώνει δακρύων·
" αὕτη ἔνι ἡ ἀγάπη σου καὶ οὕτως μοι ὑπέσχου;
οὐχί μου πᾶσαν τὴν βουλὴν εἰς σὲ προσανεθέμην;　　　180
οὐχὶ συνέθου τοῦ ἐλθεῖν μετὰ περιχαρίας;
μὴ γάρ σε κατηνάγκασα ἢ παρεβίασά σε;
μᾶλλον σύ με ἠνάγκασας μετ᾽ ἐμοῦ πορευθῆναι,
καὶ καθ᾽ ὁδοῦ συγχαίρεσθαι καὶ πάλιν ὑποστρέψαι·
σὺ δὲ φόβον μὴ ἔχουσα θεοῦ πρὸ ὀφθαλμῶν σου,　　　185
τοὺς ἀδελφοὺς ἠνάγκασας ἵνα με θανατώσουν·
οὐ μνημονεύεις ἐξ ἀρχῆς τί μετὰ σοῦ ἐποίουν;
αἰχμάλωτόν σε ἥρπαξα, ἐτίμουν ὡς κυρίαν·
δούλην σε ἔχειν ἤθελον, μᾶλλον εἶχές με δοῦλον·
τοὺς γονεῖς καὶ τὴν πίστιν μου διὰ σὲ ἠρνησάμην,　　190
καὶ διὰ τὴν ἀγάπην σου ἦλθον εἰς Ῥωμανίαν·
σὺ δὲ θάνατον ἀντ᾽ αὐτῶν ἐμνημόνευσας, κόρη,
βλέπε, καλή, μὴ παραβῇς τοὺς ἐν τῷ μέσῳ ὅρκους·
μὴ ἀρνηθῇς τὸν ἔρωτα ὃν εἴχομεν ἐκ πόθου·

162 παρ᾽ εὐθύς.　　　　184 Il faut sans doute écrire καθ᾽ ὁδόν.

499 TRE 321 has the better reading οὓς παρευθύς.

34

And what was sure declared, nothing was hidden.
(For unexpected fear brings truths to light,
Which if expected often breeds excuses.)
They straightway taking them went to the groom,
Reviling him as one of ill intent;   500
Therewith the youngest being overbold,
'This was your plan,' he said, 'do not reject it.
Know, Saracen, you shall not see Syria.
Yet having shown yourself a lawless foe,
Forgo our sister, and deny your child,
And taking what you brought go whence you came.'
    This hearing, the Emir, seeing his accusers,
Unable to reply, was wholly silent,
Being replete with shame and fear and grief,
Shamed by detection, and as a stranger frightened,   510
Pained at the thought of parting from his dear,
Not knowing what to do, went to the girl;
In her alone hoped to find consolation,
Not knowing what God had in a dream revealed.
'Why did you do this?' he exclaimed in tears,
'Is this your love? Thus did you promise me?
Did I not all my will repose on you?
Did you not gladly agree to come with me?
Did I constrain or do you violence?
Rather you forced me you should go with me   520
And on the way rejoice and back again;
But with no fear of God before your eyes
You urged your brothers they should murder me.
Do you not recall what first I did with you?
I took you captive, yet I honoured you.
I wanted you my slave, but I am yours;
My parents and my faith denied for you,
And for your love I came to Romania.
You for all this, girl, have called up my death.
See you transgress not, dear, the vows between us;   530
Do not deny the love we had of passion;

502 Note classical use of ἐνθυμοῦμαι.   μνημονεύεις of 524.
529 The unusual use of ἐμνημόνευσας   531 The adverbial ἐκ πόθου (for which
  repeats as is the author's habit the   see below 677, 931, 2908, 3463) seems

35

εἰ γὰρ καταναγκάσουν με θλίβοντες οἱ ἀδελφοί σου,   195
πάντως νὰ σύρω τὸ σπαθὶν καὶ σφάξω ἐμαυτόν μου,
καὶ κρίνειν ἔχει ὁ θεὸς μέσον τῶν ἀμφοτέρων·   11 vᵒ.
σὲ δὲ τὰ εὐγενικόπουλα πάντα νά σε ὀνειδίζουν,
ὅτι ἀνδρὸς μυστήριον οὐκ ἴσχυσας φυλάξαι,
ὡς Δαλιδὰ δὲ τὸν Σαμψὼν παρέδωκας σφαγῆναι."   200
Πάντα θρηνῶν ὁ ἀμηρᾶς ἔλεγε πρὸς τὴν κόρην,
ταύτην γὰρ ὑπελάμβανε τὴν βουλὴν φανερῶσαι·
ὁ ἔρως γὰρ ἀτιμασθεὶς φέρει κακολογίας.
Καὶ ἡ κόρη, ὡς ἤκουσεν, ἐννεὸς ἐγεγόνει,
μήτε λόγον προπέμψασθαι μηδόλως δυναμένη·   205
ἔμεινε δὲ στυγνάζουσα ἐπὶ πολλὰς τὰς ὥρας·
πᾶς γὰρ ὁ πταίων ἕτοιμος φέρειν ἀπολογίας,
ὁ δὲ μὴ πταίων σιωπᾷ, μὴ ἔχων τί λαλῆσαι.
Μόλις ποτὲ δὲ ἑαυτὴν ὡς εἰς πέρας λαβοῦσα·
" τί μάτην ὀνειδίζεις με; " ἐπεφώνει δακρύοις,   210
" τί, ἄνερ μου, κατηγορεῖς τὴν σὲ πολλὰ ποθοῦσαν;
οὐκ ἔστι μοι, μὴ γένοιτο, τὴν βουλὴν φανερῶσαι·
εἰ γὰρ τοῦτο ἐποίησα, ζῶσαν ἡ γῆ με πίοι,
νὰ γένωμαι παράδειγμα πᾶσι τοῖς ἐν τῷ κόσμῳ,
ὡς τοῦ ἀνδρὸς μυστήρια κατάδηλα ποιοῦσα."   215
Καὶ βλέπουσα τὸν ἀμηρᾶν αὐξήσαντα τὸν θρῆνον,
παρὰ μικρὸν δὲ γέγονε παράφρων ἐκ τὴν θλῖψιν,
(τὸ γὰρ πολὺ τῆς θλίψεως γεννᾷ παραφροσύνην,
ἐντεῦθεν καὶ παράνομον πολλοὶ κατατολμῶσι),
ἐφοβήθη μὴ ἑαυτὸν ἀναιρέσῃ τῷ ξίφει·   220
ἐξῆλθε πρὸς τοὺς ἀδελφοὺς τὰς τρίχας ἀνασπῶσα·
" ὦ γλυκύτατοι ἀδελφοί, τί μάτην ἐνοχλεῖτε
τὸν μηδὲν ἀδικήσαντα; ἰδοὺ γὰρ ἀποθνήσκει·   12 rᵒ.
ἰδοὺ ἀναιρέσει ἑαυτὸν ἀπὸ παραπληξίας·
μή, πρὸς θεόν, ἀδέλφια μου, μὴ ἀδικηθῇ ὁ ξένος,   225
ὃς δι' ἐμὲ ἠρνήσατο συγγενεῖς καὶ τὴν πίστιν,

197 ὁ θεὸς ἔχει.   198 εὐγενικόπουλλα. ὠνειδίζουν.   213 πίῃ.   217
θλίψιν.   220 ἀναιρέσει.   225 ἀδέλφιά.

to be used like the Homeric κηρόθι (always followed by μᾶλλον) to fill up the line.
535 εὐγενικόπουλα. Not 'the noble children', but contemptuous—'your crowd of noble relations—not that I think much of them'. The modern usage is the same. Cf. Μακρυγιάννης,

For if your brothers hurtfully constrain me,
Surely I will draw my sword and kill myself,
And God shall have to judge between us both;
And all the little nobles shall revile you,
Because you could not keep your husband's secret,
But like Delilah gave him to be slain.'
   So spoke the Emir all weeping to the girl,
For he supposed she had revealed his plan—
(And love being dishonoured brings on chiding).   540
The girl when that she heard these words was dumb,
In no wise could she utter any word,
But many hours remained in silent gloom—
(For who is guilty has excuses ready,
Who guiltless silent, with no word to say).
She scarcely at length coming to herself
'Why vainly scold me,' she exclaimed with tears,
'Why, husband, charge the one who loves you so?
Not mine, nor ever be, to tell your plan,
For if I did, earth swallow me alive,   550
That I be made a warning to the world
As one who has made known her husband's secrets.'
And seeing the Emir's increasing grief,
Who nearly was become insane with sorrow—
(For the excess of sorrow madness breeds,
And many therefrom venture what is lawless)—
He with his sword she feared might kill himself,
She went out to her brothers tearing her hair.
'Sweetest brothers, why are you vainly vexing
One who has done no wrong? Here he is dying,   560
Here he will kill himself in frenzy-stroke.
Brothers, in God's name, let not a guest be wronged
Who for my sake denied his kin and faith.

Ἀπομνημονεύματα, vol. i, p. 182: ἦταν κι κάτι ἀρχοντόπουλα; and Κ. Πολίτης, Λεμονοδάσος, p. 18: αὐτὸ τὸ κοριτσόπουλο.
537 τὸν Σαμψών omitted in translation.
541 ἐννεός, 'dumb', a rare classical word; see L. & S. TRE 377 has ἄφωνος.
543 στυγνάζουσα: classical.

546 This line is certainly corrupt, the sense being that she did not come to herself before the evening (see TRE 381, AND 832); εἰς πέρας can hardly be translated and perhaps conceals ὡς ἑσπέραν.
562 ξένος, 'guest', implying of course 'the stranger within our gates'.

οὐ γὰρ ἐνάντιόν ποτε καθ᾽ ὑμῶν ἐβουλήθη·
ἀρτίως δέ, φοβούμενος κατάραν τῆς μητρός του,
εἰς Συρίαν ἀπέρχεται, σὺν αὐτῇ ἐπανήκει·
ἐξεῖπε γάρ μου τὴν βουλήν, ἔδειξε καὶ τὸ γράμμα.   230
Καὶ πῶς ὑμεῖς, φειδόμενοι κατάρας τῆς μητρός μας,
μόνοι κατετολμήσατε ἐλθεῖν εἰς χιλιάδας
καὶ πόλεμον συνάψασθαι δι᾽ ἐμοῦ εἰς κλεισοῦραν,
μὴ φοβηθέντες θάνατον, ἀλλὰ μητρὸς κατάραν;
Δέδοικε ταῦτα καὶ αὐτός, βούλεται πορευθῆναι."   235
Καὶ ταῦτα πρὸς τοὺς ἀδελφοὺς ἡ κόρη πάντα λέγει,
θερμὰ κινοῦσα δάκρυα, τίλλουσα καὶ τὴν κόμην.
Οἱ δὲ μὴ φέροντες ὁρᾶν τὴν ἀδελφὴν θρηνοῦσαν,
ὁμοφώνως ἀνέκραζον, ταύτην καταφιλοῦντες·
" σὲ γὰρ οἱ πάντες ἔχομεν ψυχὴν καὶ θυμηδίαν·   240
ἐπεὶ δὲ βούλει καὶ αὐτὴ τὸν γαμβρόν μας ἐκπέμψαι,
θεὸν παράσχοι μάρτυρα τάχιον ὑποστρέψαι,
ἡμεῖς δὲ νὰ εὐχώμεθα καλῶς εὐοδωθῆναι."
Καὶ ἀμφότεροι παρευθὺς εἰς τὸν γαμβρὸν εἰσῆλθον,
συγχώρησιν αἰτούμενοι τῶν πρώην λαληθέντων·   245
" καὶ μὴ μνησθῇς ἡμῶν, γαμβρέ, ἀγνωσίας ῥημάτων
οὐ γὰρ ἡμῶν τὸ αἴτιον, πάντως γὰρ σὸν τὸ κρῖμα,
τοῦ μὴ γνωρίσαντος ἡμῖν ἅπερ ἐβούλου πράξειν."
Ὁ δὲ καὶ συνεχώρησε πάντας καταφιλήσας·
σταθεὶς δὲ πρὸς ἀνατολάς, χεῖρας εἰς ὕψος ἄρας·   13 vᵒ.   250
" Χριστέ μου, " ἐξεφώνησεν, "υἱὲ θεοῦ καὶ λόγε,
ὁ ὁδηγήσας με πρὸς φῶς τῆς σῆς θεογνωσίας,
τοῦ σκότους λυτρωσάμενος καὶ τῆς ματαίας πλάνης,
ὁ γινώσκων τὰ κρύφια καὶ λογισμοὺς καρδίας,
εἰ ἐπιλάθωμαί ποτε γαμετῆς τῆς φιλτάτης,   255
ἢ τοῦ τερπνοῦ ἀνθήματος τέκνου τοῦ παμποθήτου,
καὶ οὐχ ὑποστρέψω τάχιον ἐκ τὴν ἐμὴν μητέρα,
θηρίοις γένωμαι βορὰ καὶ πετεινοῖς ἐν ὄρει,
μὴ καταλογιζόμενος χριστιανοῖς ἐν μέρει! "
Καὶ ἀπὸ τότε ἤρξατο τῆς ὁδοῦ εὐτρεπίζειν,   260

227 ἐνάντιον ποτὲ.   235 A ταῦτα il faut peut-être substituer ταύτην, qui se lit
dans le ms. de Trébizonde (vers 406) et dans celui d'Andros (vers 858).   255
ἐπιλάθωμαι ποτὲ.

---

581 ἀμφότεροι. See above 205 for an-   be explained here as 'both the
other apparently loose use. It might   brothers on the one hand and the

For never did he plan aught against you;
But presently fearing his mother's curse
Is going to Syria, to return with her.
He told me his intention, showed the letter.
And how did you, heeding our mother's curse,
Venture alone to go against his thousands
And for my sake join battle in the pass,   570
Not fearing death, but only mother's curse?
The same he also fears, and plans to go.'
The girl in this wise tells her brothers all
Shedding warm tears while and plucking her hair.
They not bearing to see their sister weep
All with one voice cried out and kissing her:
'We all think you our soul, our heart's delight,
And since you too want to send forth the groom
God be his witness quickly to return,
And let us pray he have a happy journey.'   580
      And straightway both went in unto the groom,
Asking forgiveness of their former speech:
      'Remember not our thoughtless words against us,
For ours was not the fault, the guilt was yours
Not making known to us what you would do.'
And he forgave them and embraced them all;
Then standing towards the east, his hands on high,
'O Christ,' he said, 'O Son and Word of God,
Who to the light of God's knowledge hast led me,
From darkness hast redeemed and error vain,   590
Knowing the heart's secrets and reasonings,
If ever I forget my dearest wife
Or that sweet flower our most cherished child,
And do not return quickly from my mother,
May I be food for mountain beasts and birds
Nor ever more be numbered among Christians.'
      Then he began preparing for the road,

sister on the other'. Note, however, also that although as noted on 205 above one version of the story certainly includes five brothers, a two-brother version is suggested by the fact that only two, a πρῶτος and a ὕστερος, are ever mentioned as individuals.

καὶ συσκευάσας ἅπαντα ἡμερῶν δεκαπέντε,
γνωστὴ πᾶσιν ἐγένετο ἡ ἐξέλευσις τούτου,
καὶ πᾶν πλῆθος συνήρχετο συγγενῶν τε καὶ φίλων.
Καὶ ἦν ἰδεῖν τὸν ἔρωτα ὅνπερ εἶχον οἱ δύο·
κρατήσας γὰρ ὁ ἀμηρᾶς ἐκ τῆς χειρὸς τὴν κόρην,   265
εἰσῆλθε μόνος μετ᾽ αὐτῆς ἔνδον εἰς τὸ κουβοῦκλιν,
καὶ δάκρυα ἐκίνησαν ὡς ὄμβρος ἐκ καρδίας·
οἱ στεναγμοὶ ἀνέπεμπον ἦχον παρηλλαγμένον·
" δός μοι λόγον, αὐθέντρια, δός μοι σὸν δακτυλίδιν,
ἃς τὸ φορῶ, καλόγνωμε, ἕως οὗ ὑποστρέψω."   270
Ἡ δὲ κόρη στενάζουσα τὸν ἀμηρᾶν ἐλάλει·
" βλέπε, χρυσὲ αὐθέντα μου, μὴ παραβῇς τους ὅρκους
καὶ θεὸς ἀποδώσει σοι, εἰ περιλάβῃς ἄλλην·
θεὸς γὰρ δίκαιος κριτὴς ἀξίως ἀποδίδων."
" Εἰ τοῦτο πράξω, φίλτατε, " ὁ ἀμηρᾶς ἀντέφη,   275
" ἢ ἀθετήσω ἔρωτα ὃν ἔχομεν ἐκ πόθου,
ἢ θλίψω τὴν καρδίαν σου, ὦ πανευγενεστάτη,   13 rᵒ.
χανοῦσα γῆ με λήψεται, ᾅδης με καταπίοι,
καὶ μὴ ἐχάρην εἰς ἐσέ, τὴν μοσχομυρισμένην! "
Περιλαβόντες δὲ τερπνά, ἀπλήστως κατεφίλουν,   280
ὡς καὶ τὴν ὥραν εἰς πολὺ παρακατεκταθῆναι·
καὶ γέγοναν κατάβροχοι ἐκ τῶν πολλῶν δακρύων,
μόλις δὲ ἠδυνήθησαν ἀλλήλοις ἀποστῆναι,
τὸ πλῆθος μὴ αἰδούμενοι τῶν ἐκεῖ ἀθροισθέντων·
ἡ γὰρ ἀγάπη ἡ φυσικὴ φέρει ἀναισχυντίαν,   285
καὶ τοῦτο πάντες οἴδασιν οἱ τὸ φιλεῖν μαθόντες.
Εἶτα καὶ τέκνον τὸ αὐτοῦ λαβὼν εἰς τὰς ἀγκάλας,
θρηνῶν ταῦτα ἐφθέγγετο εἰς ἐπήκοον πάντων·
" ἆρα ποιήσει με θεὸς ἄξιον τοῦ ἰδεῖν σε,
ὦ παιδίον γλυκύτατον, καβαλλάρην ἐμπρός μου;   290
ἆρα, υἱέ μου διγενές, διδάξω σε κοντάριν,
ὡς ἂν καυχήσωνται ἐν σοὶ πάντες οἱ συγγενεῖς σου."
Καὶ ἐδάκρυσαν ἅπαντες τὸν ἀμηρᾶν ὁρῶντες·
εἶθ᾽ οὕτως ἵππον εὔθειον καὶ κομιδῇ γενναῖον

268 στεναγμόν.   276 et 277 On pourrait peut-être écrire εἰ au lieu de ἤ.
278 καταπίῃ et οι au-dessus de η.   280 στερπνά.   281 παρακατακταθῆναι.
290 καβαλλάριν.

605 ἦχον παρηλλαγμένον. This may   usual or wonderful sound; see below
mean only an extravagantly un-   2638 where it is used of dress.

And all made ready within fifteen days,
So that his going out was known to all
And a whole crowd assembled, friends and kinsmen.　　600
Then was to see the love they had, those two;
The Emir holding the girl by the hand
Went in with her alone into the chamber;
The tears were moved out of their hearts like rain,
Their sighs sent up an alternating sound.
'Give me your word, lady, give me your ring,
Let me wear it, kind fair, till I return.'
And the girl sighing spoke to the Emir:
'My golden master, see you keep your vows,
Or God will pay you, if you clasp another;　　610
For God is a just judge who pays in full.'
'If I do that, dear,' the Emir replied,
'Or disregard our love from passion sprung,
Or if I grieve your heart, noblest and best,
Let the earth gape and Hades swallow me,
Nor I have had in you sweet-scented joy.'
　　Then fondly embracing endlessly they kissed,
So that the time of it was long drawn out,
And they became drenched with the many tears,
And hardly could they from each other part,　　620
The multitude not heeding there assembled.
(Love that is natural brings shamelessness,
And all must know this who have learned to love.)
Then, having taken his child into his arms,
Weeping he spoke these words that all could hear:
'Will ever God make me worthy to see you,
My sweetest child, in front of me on horseback?
Shall I, my twyborn son, teach you the spear,
That all your kin may have their boast in you?'
And all shed tears beholding the Emir.　　630
　　Then, each on a swift horse and thoroughbred

---

607 καλόγνωμε, i.e. 'kind-natured'. Cf.
　above 360, γνώμη.
613 ἐκ πόθου. Above 531.
628 υἱέ μου διγενές. The use of the ad-
　jective here seems to show that it was
always applied to the hero with a
full consciousness of its meaning and
never became a mere proper name
as it is in the ballads.
631 εὔθειον. See below 1245, 1222.

ἐπιβάντες οἱ ἄγουροι ἐξήλθασι τοῦ οἴκου,   295
καὶ ὕστερον ὁ ἀμηρᾶς εἰς φάραν καβαλλάρης.
Ἦτον τὸ πλῆθος δὲ πολὺ συγγενῶν τε καὶ φίλων.
καὶ συνεξέβαλον αὐτὸν μέχρι τριῶν μιλλίων·
καὶ πάντας ἀσπασάμενος ἐποίει ὑποστρέψαι,
αὐτὸς τῆς ὁδοῦ ἥπτετο ἅμα σὺν τοῖς ἀγούροις.   300

298 μιλίων.

Note

There seems to be an error in Legrand's reference to the pagination of the
Grottaferrata MS. at line 250 of this book (above p. 38) where his 13v°
should evidently be 12v°. This is followed correctly by 13r° at line 277 (p. 40);
and 13v° is presumably a blank, the Third Book beginning on 14r° (p. 44).

Mounting, his young men rode out of the court,
And after the Emir riding his mare.
Great was the crowd of kinsmen and of friends;
And they together took him three miles out,   635
Where he embracing made them all turn back,
Himself with his companions took the road.

635 μέχρι τριῶν μιλλίων. Cf. below 2272 and 1879. What was the significance of the three-mile limit? It was still apparently observed in Persia in recent times in connexion with the *Istiqbal* or ceremonial meeting of distinguished visitors. See Morier's *Journey to Persia*, p. 97: 'An *Istiqbal* of fifty horsemen of our Mihmandar's tribe met us about three miles from our encampment. . . . Then came two of the principal merchants of Shiraz. . . . They however incurred the Envoy's displeasure by not dismounting from their horses, a form always observed in Persia by those of lower rank when they meet a superior.' (Quoted in Atkinson, *Shah Nameh*, p. 522.) Cf. also the fourth-century *Peregrinatio ad Loca Sancta* of the nun Sylvia, (quoted in Muller and Taylor, p. 127) where the Persians at Edessa advance 'ita ut usque tertium miliarium de civitate essent.'

Η ΑΠΟ ΣΥΡΙΑΣ ΥΠΟΣΤΡΕΨΙΣ ΜΕΤΑ ΚΑΙ ΤΗΣ ΜΗΤΡΟΣ ΑΥΤΟΥ

ΛΟΓΟΣ ΤΡΙΤΟΣ

Οὗτως δοῦλος πᾶς ὁ ἐρῶν τοῦ ἔρωτος ὑπάρχει·   14 rᵒ.
ἔστι γὰρ οὗτος δικαστὴς βασανίζων καρδίας
τῶν μὴ τηρούντων ἀκριβῶς τὰς ὁδοὺς τῆς ἀγάπης·
εὐστόχως πέμπει τὰς βολὰς καὶ τοξεύει καρδίας,
καὶ ἵσταται μετὰ πυρὸς τὸν λογισμὸν φλογίζων·   5
πᾶς δὲ ὃς τοῦτον κέκτηται οὐ δύναται ἐκφεῦξαι,
κᾶν τῶν ἐνδόξων τίς ἐστι, κᾶν τῶν πλουσιωτάτων,
ἐπαιρόμενος γὰρ αὐτοῦ ταχέως τοῦτον φθάνει.
Οὗτω τυχὼν ὁ ἀμηρᾶς ὁ θαυμαστὸς ἐκεῖνος
δόξης μὲν κατεφρόνησε καὶ ἀρχῆς τῆς μεγίστης,   10
ἐπελάθετο συγγενῶν, γονέων καὶ πατρίδος·
πίστιν δὲ ἀπηρνήσατο διὰ κόρης ἀγάπην
τερπνῆς τῷ ὄντι ἀληθῶς καὶ πανευγενεστάτης·
καὶ ὅ ποτε πολέμιος δοῦλος ἔρωτος ὤφθη,
εἰς Ῥωμανίαν ᾤκησε διὰ τὴν ποθητήν του.   15
Γραφὴν ἀπολαβὼν αὐτὸς μητρὸς ἀπὸ Συρίας
ἐτύπωσε τοῦ ἀπελθεῖν δεδιὼς τὴν κατάραν·
πάντως γὰρ δίκαιόν ἐστι γονεῖς μὴ παροργίζειν.
Καὶ γενομένης συμβουλῆς καὶ ὅρκου ἐν τῷ μέσῳ
πάντων προέπεμψαν αὐτὸν μετὰ περιχαρείας,   20
καὶ τραγῳδεῖν ἀπήρξατο παραμυθῶν τὴν κόρην·
" ἄγουροι, δυναμώνεσθε· φαρία, μὴ κατοκνεῖτε,
τὰς ἡμέρας σπουδάζετε, τὰς νύκτας ἀγρυπνεῖτε,
βροχάς, χιόνας, παγετοὺς ἀντ' οὐδενὸς ἡγεῖσθε,
μὴ βραδύνω τὸ σύνολον κατὰ τὴν ὡρισμένην,   25
καὶ ὀνειδιστῶ εἰς ὑποστροφὴν καὶ ζῆν με οὐ συμφέρη."

---

6 ἐφεῦξαι.   7 ἐστί.   14 ὅ ποτὲ.   17 δεδοιως.   20 πάντες ^(ων) (sic).

22 δυναμώννεσθε. κατοκνεῖτε ^(η) (sic).   24 μιμεῖσθε.   25 Peut-être τὸ ὡρισμένον comme dans le ms. d'Andros (vers 913). Mais on peut aussi sous-entendre ὥραν.   26 συμφέρει.

---

645 ἐπαιρόμενος. That this means 'flying over him' and not 'seizing

44

RETURN FROM SYRIA AND HIS MOTHER CAME TOO

THIRD BOOK

THUS every lover is the slave of Love,
For he is as a judge tormenting hearts
Of who keep not rightly the roads of love;   640
Straightly he aims his bolts and shoots at hearts,
And stands with fire to enflame consideration.
Whoever has him can no more escape,
One of the famous even or very rich,
For he uprising quickly catches him.
Thus happening that wonderful Emir,
Despising fame and great authority,
Forgot his kin, his parents, and his country,
Even denied his faith for a girl's love,
One indeed truly fair and very noble.   650
The one-time foe was seen the slave of love;
For his beloved he dwelled in Romany;
From Syria had a letter from his mother,
Resolved to go away fearing her curse—
(For it is righteous not to anger parents).
A council being made and vows between them
All sent him forth with gladness on his way.
 Then he began a song the girl consoling:
 'Young men, be strong, and horses idle not,
Hasten by day, and do not sleep at night,   660
Think nothing of the rains and snows and frosts,
Lest I be late for the appointed hour,
Return to scolding, and care not to live.'

---

him' (mod. παίρνω) is shown by AND i. 185 καὶ ἂν φύγῃ φθάνει τὸν ταχὺ μὲ τὰ πτερὰ ὁπό' 'χει. Note that the first eight lines of this third book are the foundation of the elaborate picture of the God of Love in Andros Book I; also that the first 37 lines of this third book are a repetition rather than a recapitulation of the end of the last book.

653–7 This part of the recapitulation can be traced in TRE 451–6.

662 τὸ σύνολον omitted in translation.

Εἶτα " χαίρεσθε," προσειπών, " ὦ συγγενεῖς καὶ φίλοι,"
καὶ πάντας ἀσπασάμενος εὔχεσθαι παρεκάλει. 14 vº.
Ὅ δὴ καὶ πεποιήκασι παρευθὺς ὁμοφώνως·
" ὁ θεὸς ὁ φιλάνθρωπος ἵνα σε εὐοδώσῃ, 30
καὶ καταξιωθείημεν διὰ τάχους ἰδεῖν σε."
Κἀκεῖθεν μὲν ὑπέστρεφον πάντες ἐπὶ τὸν οἶκον,
στυγνοὶ ὄντες καὶ σκυθρωποὶ ὡς δεινὸν πεπονθότες.
Τοιοῦτος γὰρ ὁ χωρισμὸς πάντων τῶν ἀγαπώντων·
διότι καίει τὰς ψυχάς, δαμάζει τὰς καρδίας, 35
ταράσσει καὶ τοὺς λογισμοὺς παντελῆς χωρισία.
Ἥπτετο δὲ ὁ ἀμηρᾶς μετὰ σπουδῆς τοῦ δρόμου,
καθ᾽ ἑκάστην ἐξέπεμπε γραφὰς τῇ ποθητῇ του·
" μὴ λυπηθῇς, παρακαλῶ, τοῦτο δ᾽ εὔχεσθαι μᾶλλον."
Ἀγούρους δὲ τοὺς ἑαυτοῦ ἱκέτευεν ἐκ πόθου· 40
" ἄρχοντες," λέγων, " ἄγουροι, φίλοι καὶ ἀδελφοί μου,
ἀγρυπνήσατε δι᾽ ἐμὲ καὶ κόπον ὑποστῆτε,
συνταγὰς γὰρ ποιήσατε καὶ πολλὰς ὑποσχέσεις,
ἃς ὑπέσχεσθε λέγοντες δι᾽ ἐμοῦ ἀποθνήσκειν,
τοῦτο δὲ οὐ πρὸς θάνατον, ἐρωτικὸς ὁ μόχθος· 45
φλέγεται γάρ μου ἡ ψυχή, καίεται ἡ καρδία,
κατανοῶν τὸ ἄπειρον διάστημα τοῦ δρόμου·
πότε κάμπους τοὺς φοβεροὺς διέλθωμεν, ἀγοῦροι,
καὶ τοὺς βουνοὺς τοὺς φοβεροὺς καὶ τὰς δεινὰς κλεισούρας,
καὶ τὴν Ῥαχὰβ θεάσομαι, ἴδω μου τὴν μητέρα; 50
καὶ πότε πάλιν ἅπαντα ταῦτα διαπεράσω, 15 rº.
ἐν τοῖς μέρεσιν ἔλθωμεν τῆς καλῆς Ῥωμανίας,
καὶ τὴν ἐμὴν θεάσομαι πέρδικαν τὴν ὡραίαν,
καὶ ἄνθος τὸ πανεύγενον, τὸν πάγκαλον υἱόν μου;
τίς μοι παράσχοι πτέρυγας καὶ πετάσαι, φιλτάτη, 55
καὶ εἰς ἀγκάλας δὲ τὰς σὰς πρὸς ὥραν καταπαῦσαι;
Πόσα στενάζει καὶ αὐτὴ δι᾽ ἐμὲ ἀγρυπνοῦσα,
καὶ σκοπεύουσα τὰς ὁδοὺς καθ᾽ ἑκάστην ἡμέραν;
Πεφύκασι γὰρ μέριμναι πολλαὶ τοῖς ποθουμένοις
καὶ φροντίδες διηνεκῶς, κίνδυνοί τε καὶ φόβοι. 60
Ἀλλ᾽, ὦ καλοὶ νεώτεροι, εὐγενικοί μου ἀγοῦροι,
ὕπνον ἀποτινάξατε καὶ πᾶσαν ῥᾳθυμίαν,

29 ὁμοφρόνως, et un ω au-dessus du ρ. 38 καθεκάστην. 40 ἱκετεύῶν (sic).

686 Note that he says nothing about
crossing the Euphrates, which would
have been the biggest obstacle on a
ride from Cappadocia to Edessa.

Then, 'Farewell,' said again, 'kinsmen and friends',
And having all embraced asked them to pray;
The which they did straightway with one accord:
  'God the compassionate give you good journey,
And may we be vouchsafed to see you soon.'
  Therefrom they all returned towards the house
Doleful and downcast as from suffering sore—   670
(For such the parting of all those who love,
For that the souls are burned, and hearts subdued,
Reasons troubled by complete severance).
  The Emir set out in haste upon the way
And every day sent letters to his love:
'Grieve not, I beg you, rather pray for me.'
His own companions lovingly implored,
'Princes,' saying, 'companions, friends, and brothers,
Watch now for my sake and endure the toil,
For disciplines you took and many promises   680
You promised saying you would die for me;
Now this is not for death, but love's the labour.
My soul is flaming, and my heart is burned,
Minding the boundless distance of the way.
When shall we cross the dreadful plains, companions,
The dreadful mountains and the terrible passes,
And when behold Rahab, and see my mother?
When shall I traverse all these back again,
Come to the places of fair Romania,
And I behold my beautiful my pet,   690
And that all-noble flower my best of sons?
Who will provide me wings and flight, my dearest,
And give me in your arms an hour's repose?
How often will she too sigh, awake for me,
And every day watching the roads for me?
(For many cares arise for the beloved,
Anxieties endlessly, fears and dangers.)
But, O good youths, noble companions,
Now shake off sleep and every indolence

687 τὴν Ραχάβ. Edessa.   469) the translator has had to depart
690 πέρδικαν τὴν ὡραίαν, 'my beautiful   from the literal.
  partridge'. As with κύρκα (above

47

ὡσὰν ταχέως φθάσωμεν εἰς τὸ 'Ραχὰβ τὸ κάστρον,
εἶθ' οὕτως θέντες ἔλθωμεν πάλιν εἰς 'Ρωμανίαν·
οὗ πολλάκις ἐρρύσθητε δι' ἐμὲ ἐκ κινδύνων· 65
καί, παρεάσας τὰ πολλά, ἐν ὑμῖν ὑπομνήσω,
ὃ καὶ πρὸς ὥραν γέγονεν εἰς τὰ Μελλοκοπία,
ὁπότε μας ἐκύκλωσαν οἱ στρατηγοὶ ἀθρόως
καὶ ὥσπερ τεῖχος γύρωθεν ἔστησαν τὰ φουσσᾶτα,
ὑμεῖς δὲ εἰς ἀπόγνωσιν κατήχθητε θανάτου, 70
ἀποκλεισθέντες ἔνδοθεν πάντες ὥσπερ ἐν τάφῳ,
μὴ ἐλπίζοντες τὶς ὑμῶν ἐξελθεῖν τῶν ἐκεῖσε·
ἐγὼ δὲ ἐπελάλησα, μέσον αὐτῶν εἰσῆλθον,
ὅσους εἰς ᾅδην ἔπεμψα οὐδ' ὑμεῖς ἀγνοεῖτε,
μόνος δὲ τρέψας ἅπαντας καὶ φυγάδας ποιήσας, 75
ἀβλαβεῖς διεσώθημεν μὲ τὴν αἰχμαλωσίαν.
Ἄρτι δ' οὐκ ἔστι πόλεμος, ἐρωτικὸς ὁ μόχθος, 15 vᵒ.
καὶ ἐν τούτῳ παρακαλῶ συνεργοί μου γενέσθαι."
    Ταῦτα καὶ ἄλλα πλείονα τοῖς σὺν αὐτῷ ἐλάλει
ὁ ἀμηρᾶς ἐν τῇ ὁδῷ μετὰ πόνου καρδίας· 80
οὕτως γὰρ φλέγει τοὺς αὐτῷ ὑπηκόους ὁ ἔρως,
ὡς πάντων μὲν καταφρονεῖν, αὐτὸν δὲ προσαγγέλλειν.
    Καὶ ἀκούσαντες ἔλεγον οἱ ἄγουροι εὐθέως·
" ὅπου θέλεις, αὐθέντα μου, ἂς γίνουν τ' ἄππλικτά σου,
οὐ γὰρ εὑρίσκεις ἐφ' ἡμῖν ἀφορμὴν ῥᾳθυμίας." 85
Καὶ ἦν ἰδεῖν θαῦμα φρικτόν, ἀλλ' οὐκ ἄπιστον πᾶσι
(ἔρως γὰρ ἦν ὁ ὑπουργῶν καὶ συνεργῶν εἰς πάντα),
τρεῖς γὰρ μονὰς διήρχοντο καθ' ἑκάστην ἡμέραν.
    Ὅτε δὲ κατελάμβανεν εἰς ἀοίκους κλεισούρας,
διήρχετο γὰρ γύρωθεν φυλάττων τοὺς ἀγούρους. 90
Ἐν μιᾷ οὖν ὁδεύοντες εἰς πάνδεινον κλεισοῦραν,
λέοντα εὗρον φοβερὸν κρατοῦντα ἐλαφῖναν·
ὡς δὲ τοῦτον ἐσκέψαντο οἱ ἄγουροι, εὐθέως
θροηθέντες ἀνέδραμον πάντες ἐπὶ τὸ ὄρος·
καὶ λυπηθεὶς ὁ ἀμηρᾶς πρὸς τὸν λέοντα ἔφη· 95
" πῶς τοῦτο κατετόλμησας, δεινότατον θηρίον,
καὶ παρεμπόδισας ὁδὸν ἐρωτικῆς φιλίας;
ἀλλ' ἐγὼ τὴν ἀνταμοιβὴν ἀξίαν σοι παράσχω."
Μὲ τὸ ῥαβδίν τον ἔδωκε πλήρης εἰς τὴν μεσίαν,
καὶ εὐθὺς ἔμεινε στυγνὸς εἰς γῆν ἐξηπλωμένος. 100

84 ἄπληκτά.   92 ἐλαφίναν.   97 παρεμπόδησας.

That we may quickly come to castle Rahab,   700
So having done return to Romania.
Often through me have you been saved from dangers,
Most of which passing I will recall you one,
Which lately happened at Mellokopia,
When that the generals closely circled us,
And like a wall stood armies round about,
And you were driven down to death's despair,
Shut up within them all as in a tomb,
Not hoping one of you to come out thence.
But I urged on, went in the midst of them,   710
How many sent to Hades well you know,
Alone I beat and turned them all to flight,
And with our captures we were saved unhurt.
But now it is not war, love is the labour,
In which I pray be my accomplices.'
These things and much else spoke to those with him
The Emir along the road with aching heart.
(For so love those enflames who are his subjects
That they all else despising him acknowledge.)
And hearing him his young men said at once: 720
'Where you please, master, your encampments be,
You shall not find in us delay's occasion.'
Dread wonder was it, one not all will doubt
(For love in all was working for and with them),
Three stages they went over every day.
    And when he came to the unpeopled passes
He would go round guarding his company;
Once as they travelled through an awful pass
They found a fierce lion holding a doe;
When they beheld him straightway his companions   730
All in a fright ran up into the hill;
And grieving the Emir said to the lion,
'How did you venture so, most dreadful beast,
And stand across the road of passionate love?
I'll give you recompense as you deserve.'
He struck him with his staff full in the middle
And straight he was stretched baleful on the ground.

710 ἐπελάλησα here used without ἵππον.   728 Read ἐν μίᾳ. See below 3568, 2190.

Καὶ εὐθέως προσέταξε τοὺς ἰδίους ἀγούρους·
" Τοὺς ὀδόντας ἐκσπάσατε πάντας τοὺς τοῦ θηρίου,
ὡσαύτως καὶ τοὺς ὄνυχας τῆς δεξιᾶς χειρός του,
ἵνα, ὁπότε σὺν Θεῷ στραφῶ εἰς Ῥωμανίαν,   16 rᵒ.
φορέσωμεν αὐτούς, φημί, τὸν πάγκαλον υἱόν μου,   105
τὸν Διγενῆ Καππάδοκα 'Ακρίτην τὸν γενναῖον."
Καὶ αὖθις πάλιν ἥπτετο τῆς ὁδοῦ μετὰ πόθου,
ἀλλήλοις προτρεπόμενος τοῦ προθύμως βαδίζειν.
Οὐδεὶς ἐν τούτῳ ῥᾴθυμος, οὐδεὶς ὕπνου μετέσχεν·
ἔρως γὰρ ἦν μέσον αὐτῶν τίς νικήσει τὸν ἄλλον.   110
"Οτε δὲ ἐπλησίασαν εἰς τὸ Ῥαχὰβ τὸ κάστρον,
προσέταξεν ὁ ἀμηρᾶς ἔξω στῆσαι τὰς τένδας,
καὶ δύο τῶν ἀγούρων του εἰσελθεῖν εἰς τὸ κάστρον,
ὡσὰν εἴπωσι τῇ μητρὶ τὴν ἐπέλευσιν τούτου.
Καὶ πορευθέντες τάχιον πεποιήκασι τοῦτο.   115
Ἡ δὲ μήτηρ ὡς ἤκουσε τοιαύτην ἀγγελίαν,
μικρόν περ καὶ ὠρχήσατο ἀπὸ περιχαρείας·
ὁμοίως καὶ οἱ συγγενεῖς ἐν γνώσει γεγονότες,
συνεξήλθασιν ἅπαντες εἰς ἀπάντησιν τούτου·
καὶ πλησίον γενόμενοι ἔνθα ἦσαν αἱ τένδαι   120
προϋπήντα ὁ ἀμηρᾶς πεζὸς μετὰ τζαγγίων·
ὃν ἐπιγνόντες καὶ αὐτοὶ ἐπέζευον εὐθέως
ἐμπεπλησμένοι ἡδονῆς, δακρύων γεμισμένοι
(φέρει γὰρ δάκρυα χαρά, ἀθρόως ὅταν ἔλθῃ),
καὶ κατησπάζοντο αὐτὸν μοιράζοντες τὸν πόθον,   125
ἐντεῦθεν μὲν οἱ συγγενεῖς, ἐκεῖθεν δὲ ἡ μήτηρ,
καὶ τὰ αὐτοῦ κοράσια ἀληθῶς μετὰ τέκνων
περιεπλέκοντο αὐτόν, ἀπλήστως κατεφίλουν,
καὶ χωρισθῆναι ἀπ' αὐτοῦ οὐκ ἤθελον οὐδ' ὅλως.
Εἰς δὲ τὴν τένδαν φθάσαντες ἐκάθισαν εὐθέως,   16 vᵒ.   130
καὶ λέγειν οὕτως ἤρξατο τοῦ ἀμηρᾶ ἡ μήτηρ·

---

102 τὰς, au lieu du second τοὺς.   105 πάγκαλλον.

---

742 φορέσωμεν with double accusative, 'give him them to wear'.
744 μετὰ πόθου for the more usual ἐκ πόθου, but I think there is a slight distinction of sense.
745 ἀλλήλοις προτρεπόμενος. See also

177, 179, and below 783 for loss of classical meaning.
757 γενόμενοι, the customary nominative absolute.
758 πεζὸς μετὰ τζαγγίων. See Ducange and Sophokles s.vv. τζάγγα, τζάγγιον

Straightway he commanded his own companions,
'Knock out the teeth all of them of the beast,
Likewise the talons of his right forepaw,   740
That when, with God, I return to Romania,
We'll give them to wear, I say, to my good son,
Twyborn brave Kappadokian Borderer.'
Then eagerly again he took the road,
Each urging other to march cheerfully;
Here none was idle and none paused to sleep,
Love was with them for one to beat another.
        And when they were come near to Fort Rahab
The Emir bade them pitch the tents without,
Two of his boys to go into the fort   750
That they might tell his mother of his coming;
And quickly going forward this they did.
His mother when she heard such a message
Did even almost dance from so much joy,
Likewise his kinsmen too, being informed,
Went out together all of them to meet him.
And, coming near to where the tents were pitched,
The Emir came first to meet them, on foot, booted,
Whom recognizing they at once dismounted
Fulfilled of pleasure and brimming with tears—   760
For joy brings tears when it comes in a flood—
And they embraced him, sharing their affection,
On the one hand his kinsmen, there his mother,
His damsels too verily with their children,
Hung all about him, kissed him endlessly,
And would not anywise be parted from him.
Then when they reached the tent they straight sat down,
And thus began to speak the Emir's mother:

for the special red boots of the Byzantine emperors. These three words
πεζὸς μετὰ τζαγγίων occur in the
poems of Ptochoprodromos (see
Maurofrydes, Ἐκλογὴ Μνημείων
(Athens, 1866), p. 39, line 67; cf.
Legrand, Bibl. Gr. Vulg., vol. i
(Paris, 1880), p. 78, line 69), where,
however, the boots are certainly not
honorific.

750–60 In the corresponding passage
(TRE 505, AND 1018) there is a
quotation from Iliad ii. 489.
761 Cf. above 317 ff.
764 ἀληθῶς μετὰ τέκνων. This seems to
be an implied and rather inappropriate reference to the quotation
from the Psalms, above 372; otherwise the insertion of ἀληθῶς is pointless.

" Ὦ τέκνον μου γλυκύτατον, φῶς τῶν ἐμῶν ὀμμάτων,
καὶ παραμύθιον ψυχῆς τῆς ἐμῆς ἐν τῷ γήρει,
καὶ τερπνὸν ἀγαλλίαμα, ἡ ἐμὴ θυμηδία,
εἰπέ μοι τί ἐβράδυνας, τέκνον, εἰς Ῥωμανίαν; 135
ἐγὼ γὰρ μὴ ὁρῶσα σε οὐκ ἤθελον φῶς βλέπειν,
οὔθ᾽ ἥλιον τὸν λάμποντα, οὔτε ζῆν ἐν τῷ κόσμῳ.
Μὴ θαύματα παράδοξα γίνονται εἰς Ῥωμανίαν
οἷα τελοῦνται, τέκνον μου, εἰς τὸ μνῆμα τοῦ Προφήτου,
εἰς ὃ κατῆλθες μετ᾽ ἐμοῦ εἰς εὐχὴν ἀγομένης; 140
Εἶδες θαῦμα παράδοξον πῶς, τῆς νυκτὸς παρούσης
καὶ φωτὸς μὴ ὑπάρχοντος, φέγγος ἦλθεν ἐξ ὕψους
καὶ ἀπορρήτως ἔπλησε φωτὸς τὸν ὅλον οἶκον;
Εἶδες ἄρκτους καὶ λέοντας, λύκους μετὰ προβάτων,
καὶ ζώων γένη πάμπολλα ὁμοῦ συμβοσκομένων, 145
μὴ βλάπτοντα τὸ ἕτερον τὸ ἕτερον οὐδ᾽ ὅλως,
ἀλλὰ πάντα προσμένοντα μέχρις εὐχῆς καὶ τέλους,
εἶθ᾽ οὕτως γόνυ κλίναντα εὐθὺς ὑποχωροῦσι;
Μὴ τούτων θαυμαστότερον εἶδες εἰς Ῥωμανίαν;
οὐ παρ᾽ ἡμῖν τὸ Νέευμα ὑπάρχει τὸ μανδίλιν 150
ὃς βασιλεὺς ἐγένετο μετὰ τῶν Ἀσσυρίων,
καί, διὰ πλῆθος ἀρετῶν, θαυμάτων ἠξιώθη;
Πῶς τούτων πάντων, τέκνον μου, γέγονας παραβάτης,
ἀρχῆς δὲ κατεφρόνησας καὶ τῆς μεγίστης δόξης;
Οἱ πάντες σε ἐφρόντιζον τῆς Αἰγύπτου κρατῆσαι, 155
σὺ δὲ τύχης τῆς ἑαυτοῦ ἐμποδιστὴς ἐγένου,
διὰ μίαν Ῥωμάϊσσαν τὰ πάντα ἀπολέσας." 17 rᵒ.
Ἔτι δὲ λέγειν θέλουσα καὶ ἕτερα τοιαῦτα,
ἐκκόψας ὁ νεώτερος τῇ μητρὶ οὕτως λέγει·
" τούτων πάντων, ὦ μῆτερ μου, καθέστηκα ἐν γνώσει· 160
μήπω φωτός τε μετασχών, ὡς ἀληθῶς ἐτίμων
τὰ σκότους ὄντως ἄξια καὶ πάσης ἀπωλείας·
ἡνίκα δὲ ηὐδόκησε Θεὸς ὁ ἐν ὑψίστοις,

138 θαυμαστά.   139 Lire comme s'il y avait 's au lieu de εἰς.   145
πάμπολα.   150 Il faut sans doute lire Νεεμάν.   151 ὡς.

769 φῶς τῶν ἐμῶν ὀμμάτων. Note that
φῶς means not only the state of being
seen, *visibility*, but also the state
of seeing, *vision*; i.e. 'light' but also
'sight'. Cf. δρόμος, 'running' or 'road';

μέθη, 'being drunk' or 'drunk-making-
ness'; βῆμα, 'a pace' or 'a platform';
καλός, 'good' or 'beautiful; σπου-
δαῖος, 'studious' or 'deserving study'.

'O sweetest child of mine, light of my eyes,
And consolation of my soul in age,   770
Pleasant delight and gladness of my heart,
Say why you tarried, child, in Romania;
Not seeing you, I would not see light at all,
Nor sun shining, nor in the world to live.
Do strange wonders happen in Romania
Such as are done, child, at the Prophet's tomb,
Where you went with me going to my prayers?
Saw you a wonder strange how in the night,
Without a light, came radiance from on high,
Filled the whole house with light unspeakable?   780
Did you see bears and lions, wolves with sheep,
And many kinds of beasts together feeding,
Not hurting one another, not at all,
But all there waiting till the final prayer,
Then how bending the knee they straight retired?
Did you see greater wonder in Romania?
Is there not with us Naaman's kerchief,
Who was a king among the Assyrians,
Thought worthy of wonders for his host of virtues?
How did you come, child, to transgress all this,   790
And power did despise and greatest fame?
They all believed that you would conquer Egypt,
But you turned obstacle of your own fortune,
And gave up everything for a Roman girl.'
Her wishing still to speak more on this wise
The young man stopped and thus said to his mother:
'All this, O mother, I have knowledge of.
Before I shared the light, I truly honoured
Things really worthy of darkness and all destruction.
But when God in the highest did think good   800

---

780 cf. Board, *Newsgirl in Egypt*, (1938),
p. 230. 'The most holy hajjis have seen
the light over the tomb of Mohammed
at Mecca that ascends to Paradise.'
783 μὴ βλάπτοντα τὸ ἕτερον τὸ ἕτερον.
Another example of the loss of
ἄλληλα, for the decay of which cf.

above 177, 179, and 745; and for
correct use see below 936.
787 τὸ Νέευμα ὑπάρχει τὸ μανδίλιν. Leg.
τοῦ Νεεμάν. See LXX, 4 Kings v.
This passage is discussed in the
introduction.
791 ἀρχῆς, translated 'power'.

ὁ δι' ἐμὲ ἑκούσιον πτωχείαν ὑπομείνας,
καὶ τὴν ἐμὴν ἀσθένειαν βουληθεὶς τοῦ φορέσαι,   165
ἀφαρπάσαι τοῦ φάρυγγος τοῦ νοητοῦ θηρίου,
καὶ τοῦ λουτροῦ ἠξίωσε τῆς παλιγγενεσίας,
ταῦτα πάντα κατήργησα λήρους ὄντα καὶ μύθους
καὶ πρόξενα ὑπάρχοντα πυρὸς τοῦ αἰωνίου·
οἱ γὰρ σεβόμενοι αὐτὰ πάντοτε τιμωροῦνται,   170
ὁ δὲ πιστεύων εἰς Θεὸν πατέρα τῶν ἁπάντων,
ποιητὴν οὐρανοῦ καὶ γῆς καὶ ἀοράτων πάντων,
καὶ εἰς Χριστὸν τὸν κύριον, υἱὸν Θεοῦ καὶ λόγον,
τὸν γεννηθέντα ἐκ πατρὸς πρὸ πάντων τῶν αἰώνων,
φῶς ἐκ φωτὸς ὑπάρχοντα, Θεὸν ἀληθῆ, μέγαν,   175
τὸν κατελθόντα ἐπὶ γῆς δι' ἡμᾶς τοὺς ἀνθρώπους,
καὶ γεννηθέντα ἐκ μητρὸς Μαρίας τῆς παρθένου,
τὸν ὑπομείναντα σταυρὸν δι' ἡμῶν σωτηρίαν,
καὶ ταφέντα ἐν μνήματι ὃ καὶ αὐτὴ θαυμάζεις,
καὶ ἀναστάντα ἐκ νεκρῶν ἐν τῇ τρίτῃ ἡμέρᾳ,   180
καθὼς ἡμᾶς διδάσκουσιν αἱ γραφαὶ αἱ ἅγιαι,
τὸν ἀεὶ καθεζόμενον τοῦ Πατρὸς δεξιόθεν,
οὗ βασιλείας τῆς αὐτοῦ οὐκ ἔσται ποτὲ τέλος·
καὶ εἰς Πνεῦμα τὸ ἅγιον ζωοποιοῦν τὰ πάντα,   17 vº.
ὃ προσκυνῶ σὺν τῷ Πατρὶ καὶ τῷ Υἱῷ καὶ Λόγῳ·   185
ἐν βάπτισμα ὁμολογῶν εἰς ἄφεσιν πταισμάτων,
καὶ προσδοκῶ ἀνάστασιν πάντων τῶν τεθνεώτων,
ἑκάστου ἀνταπόδοσιν καὶ τῶν πλημμελημένων,
τῶν δὲ δικαίων ἄφεσιν, καθώσπερ ἐπηγγέλθη,
ζωὴν τὴν ἀτελεύτητον τοῦ μέλλοντος αἰῶνος.   190
Πᾶς ὁ πιστεύων ἐν αὐτῇ τῇ ἁγίᾳ Τριάδι,
καὶ βαπτισθεὶς εἰς ὄνομα τοῦ Πατρὸς τοῦ ἀνάρχου,
καὶ τοῦ Υἱοῦ τοῦ ἐξ αὐτοῦ ἀχρόνως γεννηθέντος,
καὶ τοῦ ἁγίου Πνεύματος τοῦ ζωοῦντος τὰ πάντα,
οὐκ ἀπόλλυται πώποτε, ἀλλὰ ζῇ εἰς αἰῶνας.   195
Ὁ δὲ μὴ ταῦτα ἐγνωκώς, ὦ γλυκυτάτη μῆτερ,
εἰς τὴν γέενναν τοῦ πυρὸς ἐσαεὶ τιμωρεῖται·
κλαυθμὸς πολὺς ἐκεῖ ἐστι καὶ βρυγμὸς τῶν ὀδόντων."

181 ἅγίαι (sic).   184 ζωοποιοῦντα πάντα.   198 ἐστί.

803 τοῦ νοητοῦ θηρίου. Cf. Meliten.
1966 χοροὶ τῶν νοητῶν ἀγγέλων. In
both places R. M. Dawkins tells me

he would read νοερός for νοητός as
being a more ordinary ecclesiastical
word in the sense of 'spiritual'. But

DIGENES AKRITES

(Who willingly for me endured poverty
And had desired to put on my own weakness)
To snatch me from the throat of the cunning Beast
And thought me worth the water of rebirth,
I put all these away as tales and fables,
And as occasions of the eternal fire.
For who revere these things are always punished,
But who believes on God the father of all,
Maker of heaven and earth and of all things invisible,
And in Christ the Lord, the Son and Word of God,   810
Begotten of His Father before all ages,
Being light of light, and very God, and great,
Who for mankind came down on earth for us,
And from the virgin mother Mary born,
Suffered the cross for our salvation,
Was buried in a tomb, which you too honour,
And risen up from the dead on the third day,
Even as the holy scriptures do instruct us,
Sits ever on the right hand of the Father,
And of His kingdom there shall be no end;   820
And in the holy Spirit, making all things live,
Which with the Father and the Son and Word I worship,
Confessing one baptism for the remission of sins;
I await the resurrection of all the dead,
And everyone's requiting of his trespasses,
The forgiveness of the righteous as was promised,
And the unending life of the world to come.
Everyone believing on this holy Trinity,
Baptized in the name of the Father eternal,
And of the Son by Him timelessly begotten,   830
And of the holy Spirit quickening all things,
Shall never perish but for ever live.
Who has not known these things, my sweetest mother,
In the gehenna of fire is punished for ever;
There is much weeping there and gnashing of teeth.'

cf. Dapontes, *Κῆπος Χαρίτων* (1880),
p. 20, where *νοητός* seems to be used
in the sense of 'the cunning one'—
the opposite of *ἀνόητος*.
816 *ὃ καὶ αὐτὴ θαυμάζεις*. Another trace
of GRO's familiarity with Moslem
practice. For Moslem respect for the
Holy Sepulchre see Hasluck, *Christianity and Islam*, p. 7, n. 1.

55

Ταῦτα εἰπὼν ὁ ἀμηρᾶς καὶ ὁδὸν ὑπανοίξας
τῆς ἀμωμήτου πίστεως τῇ μητρὶ οὕτως λέγει·   200
" Ἐγώ, μῆτερ, ἀπέρχομαι πάλιν εἰς Ῥωμανίαν,
τὴν πίστιν ἐπιβεβαιῶν τῆς ἁγίας Τριάδος,
οὐ γὰρ ἀντάξιός ἐστι μιᾶς ψυχῆς ὁ κόσμος·
εἰ γὰρ πάντα κερδήσωμεν, ψυχὴν ζημιωθῶμεν,
πάντως οὐδὲν τὸ ὄφελος ἐν ἐκείνῃ τῇ ὥρᾳ,   205
ὅταν Θεὸς ἐξ οὐρανοῦ ἔλθῃ κρῖναι τὸν κόσμον,
καὶ παραστήσῃ ἅπαντας ἀποδώσοντας λόγον·
ὅταν φωνῆς ἀκούσωμεν πορευθῆναι λεγούσης
εἰς τὸ πῦρ τὸ ἐξώτερον τὸ κεκατηραμένον,
εἰς αἰῶνα ἐσόμενοι μετὰ τοῦ διαβόλου,   18 rº. 210
ὡς προσταγμάτων τῶν αὐτοῦ ἀπειθεῖς γεγονότες·
οἱ δέ γε ἐν Χριστῷ πιστεύοντες, ὡς θέμις,
καὶ ἐντολὰς τηρήσαντες αὐτοῦ τὰς σεβασμίας,
ὡς ἥλιος ἐκλάμψουσιν ἐν ἐκείνῃ τῇ ὥρᾳ
καὶ τῆς φωνῆς ἀκούσωσι τοῦ ἀγαθοῦ δεσπότου·   215
' Δεῦτε κληρονομήσατε, Πατρὸς εὐλογημένοι,
ἣν ὑμῖν προητοίμασα οὐρανῶν βασιλείαν.'
Καὶ οὗτοι μὲν πορεύσονται εἰς ζωὴν αἰωνίαν·
κριτὴς γὰρ δίκαιός ἐστιν ἀξίως ἀποδίδων.
Καὶ εἴπερ βούλει, μῆτερ μου, ζωῆς ἀξιωθῆναι,   220
λυτρωθῆναι τε τοῦ πυρὸς καὶ σκότους αἰωνίου,
πλάνης ματαίας ἔκφυγε καὶ πεπλασμένων μύθων,
καὶ τὸν Θεὸν ἐπίγνωθι τὸν ἐν τρισὶ προσώποις,
ἀσυγχύτως ἐνούμενον ἐν μιᾷ ὑποστάσει·
πείσθητι δὲ τῷ σῷ υἱῷ καὶ ἐλθὲ μετ' ἐμέναν,   225
πατὴρ δέ σου γενήσομαι ἐν Πνεύματι ἁγίῳ,
καὶ βαπτισθεῖσαν δέξομαι ἐν τῇ ἀναγεννήσει."
Τοιαῦτα μὲν ὁ ἀμηρᾶς τῆς δὲ μητρός, ὁποία
οὐ παρῃτήσατο παιδὸς συμβουλὴν τὴν καλλίστην,
ἀλλ', ὥσπερ γῆ τις ἀγαθὴ δεξαμένη τὸν σπόρον,   230
εὐθὺς προσήγαγε καρπόν, φθεγξαμένη τοιαῦτα·
" Πιστεύω, τέκνον, διὰ σοῦ Θεῷ τῷ ἐν Τριάδι,
καὶ μετὰ σοῦ πορεύσομαι καλῶς εἰς Ῥωμανίαν,

203 ἀντάξιος ἐστὶ.   209 ἐξότερον.   212 Le premier hémistiche de ce vers
est incomplet de deux syllabes.   215 La correction ἀκούσουσι est inutile.
219 δίκαιος ἐστὶν.   224 μία.   228 ὁποία.   230 τὶς.

849 Perhaps read οἱ δὲ εἰς Χριστὸν τὸν Κύριον.

Thus having spoken the Emir, and opened the way
Of the faith blameless, thus said to his mother:
'I, mother, am going back to Romania,
My faith confirming in the Trinity,
For the world is not worth a single soul;　　　　840
For if all things we gain and lose the soul
None verily the profit in that hour
When God shall come from heaven to judge the world
And set all men to give account before Him;
When we shall hear a voice bidding us go
Into the outer and accursed fire,
There to abide for ever with the devil,
As having His commandments disobeyed.
But those who in Christ the Lord believe, as is right,
And have observed his worshipful commands,　　　850
Shall shine out even as the sun in that hour,
And they shall hear the voice of their good master,
"Come and inherit, by the Father blest,
Heavens' kingdom which I have prepared for you."
And these shall go into eternal life;
The judge is just and rightly He repays.
Mother, if you wish to be thought worthy of life,
From fire redeemed and the eternal dark,
Fly from vain error and invented tales,
And recognize the God in three persons,　　　860
United in one substance unconfounded.
Listen to your own son and come with me,
I will be your father in the holy Spirit,
And when baptized your sponsor in rebirth.'
　　Such the Emir and such his mother, who
Did not refuse her son's excellent counsel,
But like good earth, having received the seed,
Straightway she brought forth fruit, speaking these words:
'Child, I believe through you on God in Trinity,
With you I will journey well to Romania,　　　870

864 δέξομαι. δέχομαι here for ἀναδέχο-
μαι which is of course a technical
term.
865 τοιαῦτα μὲν ὁ ἀμηρᾶς τῆς δὲ μητρός.
This is presumably to be translated

'Such (words spoke) the Emir, and
such (were the words) of his mother'.
The position of δέ shows that the
genitive cannot here be a modern-
ism (genitive for dative).

βαπτισθεῖσα εἰς ἄφεσιν τῶν πολλῶν μου σφαλμάτων,
χάριν ὁμολογοῦσα τε διὰ σοῦ φωτισθῆναι."   18 vᵒ.   235
Ὡσαύτως καὶ οἱ συγγενεῖς οἱ ἐκεῖσε τυχόντες
καὶ οἱ λοιποὶ οἱ μετ᾿ αὐτῆς ἐλθόντες πολὺ πλῆθος
μίαν φωνὴν ἀνέκραξαν Χριστὸν ὁμολογοῦντες·
" Μεθ᾿ ὑμῶν γὰρ ἐρχόμεθα πάντες εἰς Ῥωμανίαν,
καὶ βαπτισθέντες τύχοιμεν ζωῆς τῆς αἰωνίου! "   240
Καὶ θαυμάσας ὁ ἀμηρᾶς τὴν τούτων προθυμίαν·
" Δόξα σοι ", ἔφη, " τῷ Θεῷ τῷ μόνῳ φιλανθρώπῳ,
τῷ μὴ θέλοντι θάνατον ἁμαρτωλοῦ μηδ᾿ ὅλως,
ἀλλ᾿ ἀναμένων τὴν εἰς σὲ ἐπιστροφὴν οἰκτίρμων,
ὡσὰν ποιήσῃς κοινωνοὺς πάντας σῆς βασιλείας."   245
Εἶτα πλοῦτον τὸν ἄπειρον μεθ᾿ ἑαυτῶν λαβόντες,
ὁμοῦ πάντες ἐξῆλθασι πρὸς τὰ τῆς Ῥωμανίας.
Ὅτε δὲ καὶ κατέλαβον Καππαδοκίας μέρη,
βουλεύεται ὁ ἀμηρᾶς τοὺς ἑαυτοῦ ἀγούρους·
" Ἔννοιά τις εἰσῆλθέ μοι, ὦ καλοὶ στρατιῶται,   250
τοῦ προλαβεῖν με ἑαυτὸν καὶ συγχαρίκια δοῦναι·
εἰ γὰρ προλάβῃ ἕτερος, πάντως κατηγοροῦμαι
ὡς ὀκνηρὸς καὶ ῥᾴθυμος παρὰ τῆς ποθητῆς μου."
Οἱ δὲ ἀνταπεκρίθησαν καλὸν τοῦτο ποιῆσαι,
ἄξιον γὰρ ἐρωτικὴν ἐκπληρῶσαι ἀγάπην.   255
Ἐκεῖνος δὲ τὸ βούλευμα καλῶς ἐπινοήσας,
ἤμειψε τὴν στολὴν εὐθύς, περιβαλὼν ρωμαίαν,
θαυμαστὸν ἐπιλούρικον, χρυσὸν ῥεραντισμένον,
ὀξέον, λευκοτρίβλαττον, γρύψους ὡραϊσμένους,
φακεώλιν χρυσόγραμμον, πολυτίμητον, ἄσπρον·   19 rᵒ.   260
μοῦλαν ἐκαβαλλίκευσε βάδεαν, ἀστεράτην·
καὶ τρεῖς λαβὼν μεθ᾿ ἑαυτοῦ τῶν ἰδίων ἀγούρων,
καί, τὸ τοῦ λόγου, πετασθεὶς ἔφθασεν εἰς τὸν οἶκον,
καὶ ἔβαλεν εὐθὺς φωνὴν χαρᾶς ἐμπεπλησμένην·
" Περιστερά μου πάντερπνε, δέξαι τὸ σὸν γεράκιν,   265
καὶ παραμύθησον αὐτὸ ἀπὸ τῆς ξενιτείας! "
Καὶ διὰ ταύτην τὴν φωνὴν αἱ βάγιαι παρακύπτουν,

---

243 μὴ δ᾿.   244 οἰκτίρμον.   245 ὡσᾶν ποιησεις et un η au-dessus de ει.
258 Équivaut sans doute à χρυσῷ ῥεραντισμένον.

888 τοῦ προλαβεῖν με ἑαυτὸν καὶ συγχαρίκια δοῦναι. See below 948, 1866.
896 λευκοτρίβλαττον. Βλαττίον, originally purple, came to be used of any precious textile or silk tissue. See Ducange pro quovis panno sericeo, and

Baptized for remission of my many faults,
And grateful to have had the light through you."
   Likewise the kinsmen also who were there
And others who had come with her a crowd
All with one voice cried out confessing Christ:
   'With you we are all coming to Romania,
And when baptized may we win life eternal!'
And the Emir wondering at their zeal
Said: 'Praise to Thee the only, merciful God,
Who desirest not at all the death of a sinner,   880
But pitying waitest his return to Thee,
To make all men partakers in Thy kingdom.'
   Thereon taking with them their boundless wealth
Together all set out towards Romania.
And when they came to Kappadokian land
The Emir took counsel with his company:
   'The thought has come to me, my good soldiers,
To go ahead myself for joy's reward;
For if another goes I shall be charged
As being slow and idle by my beloved.'   890
They answered it was good he so should do,
For it was right love should be satisfied.
He having well considered the proposal,
He straightway changed, put on a Roman dress,
A tabard wonderful, sprinkled with gold,
Violet, white, and thick purple, griffin-broidered,
A turban gold-inscribed, precious and white;
He mounted a bay mule with one white star,
Took with him three of his own company,
And, as the saying, flew, and reached the house,   900
And straightway raised a shout fulfilled with joy,
"All-sweet my dove, welcome your homing hawk,
And comfort him after his wandering.'
And at the cry the nurserymaids looked out,

see e.g. βλαττίον ἐξάμιτον κόκκινον, quoted from a church inventory by A. Frolov, 'La Podea', in *Byzantion*, xiii, 1938, p. 492 (but without date). The word is of Latin origin. See Lewis & Short, s.v. *blatta*, a clot of blood, hence purple colour; or possibly from *blatta*, 'a moth', hence 'the silkworm'. See Maigne D'Arnis, s.v.
896 γρύψους. N.B. γρύψος for class. γρύψ.
902 'homing' inserted by translator.

καί, ὡς τοῦτον ἐσκέψαντο, τὴν κυρὰν οὕτω λέγουν·
" Χαίροις, χαίροις, αὐθέντρια· ὁ αὐθέντης μας ἦλθεν."
Ἐκείνη δὲ ὡς ἄπιστον ἐλογίζετο τοῦτο   270
(ὁ γὰρ τυχὼν αἰφνίδιον τοῦ ἐπιθυμουμένου
ὄναρ δοκεῖ φαντάζεσθαι ἀπὸ περιχαρείας),
καὶ πρὸς τὰς βάγιας ἔλεγε· " Φαντάσματα ὁρᾶτε; "
Ἔτι δὲ λέγειν θέλουσα καὶ πλείονα τοιαῦτα,
ὡς εἶδε τὸν νεώτερον ἐξαίφνης ἀνελθόντα,   275
λίαν ὠλιγοψύχησεν εἰς ἔκπληξιν ἐλθοῦσα,
καὶ χεῖρας περιπλέξασα τὰς αὐτῆς τῷ τραχήλῳ
ἀπεκρεμάσθη ἄφωνος, δάκρυα μὴ κινοῦσα.
Ὡσαύτως καὶ ὁ ἀμηρᾶς γέγονεν ὥσπερ ἔνθους,
καὶ τὴν κόρην περιλαβὼν καὶ βαλὼν εἰς τὸ στῆθος,   280
συμπεπλεγμένοι ἔμειναν ἐπὶ πολλὰς τὰς ὥρας.
Καί, εἰ μὴ ἡ στρατήγισσα ἔβρεχε τούτους ὕδωρ,
εἰς γῆν ἂν ἔπεσον εὐθὺς ἀπ' ὀλιγοθυμίας.
Ἀγάπη γὰρ ὑπέρμετρος γεννᾷ πολλὰ τοιαῦτα
καὶ χαρὰ ὑπερβάλλουσα εἰς θάνατον ἀπάγει,   285
ὡς καὶ αὐτοὶ παρὰ μικρὸν ἔμελλον ὑποστῆναι.   19 vº.
Μόλις δὲ ἠδυνήθησαν αὐτοὺς ἀποχωρῖσαι·
ἐφίλει γὰρ ὁ ἀμηρᾶς τοὺς ὀφθαλμοὺς τῆς κόρης,
περιεπλέκετο αὐτήν, μεθ' ἡδονῆς ἠρώτα·
" Πῶς ἔχεις, φῶς μου τὸ γλυκύ, πάντερπνόν μου δαμάλιν;   290
πῶς ἔχεις, φίλτατε ψυχή, ἐμὴ παραμυθία,
περιστερά μου πάντερπνε, πανώραιόν μου δένδρον,
μετὰ τοῦ σοῦ ἀνθήματος, τέκνου τοῦ παμποθήτου; "
Ἡ κόρη δ' ἀνανεοῦσα τὸν ἔρωτα ἐκ πόθου,
τοιαῦτα πρὸς τὸν ἀμηρᾶν ἐφθέγγετο γλυκέως·   295
" Καλῶς ἦλθες, ἐλπὶς ἐμή, ἀναψυχὴ τοῦ βίου,
μεγίστη μου ἀντίληψις, ψυχῆς μου θυμηδία,
τὰ γὰρ ἡμέτερα καλῶς τῇ τοῦ Θεοῦ δυνάμει,
τοῦ ἡμᾶς ἀξιώσαντος θεάσασθαι ἀλλήλους·

287 ἀποχωρίσαι.   290 δαμάλην.   291 La correction φιλτάτη est inutile.
294 Pour rendre ce vers correct, on pourrait écrire: ἡ κόρη δὲ τὸν ἔρωτα ἀνανεοῦσ'
ἐκ πόθου.

907 ἄπιστον for ἀπίστευτον.
913 λίαν ὠλιγοψύχησεν. This amorous
swoon is a commonplace of the
novels. Cf. Chariton, viii. i. 110; Ach.
Tat. iii. xvii. 7; Kallimachos and Chrysor-

roe, 1812; Heliodorus ii. vi.
924 Legrand's ἀποχωρῖσαι is unnecessary; for ἀποχωρίσαι see Lysias 16. 16.
927 πάντερπνόν μου δαμάλιν, translated

When they beheld him, thus said to their mistress:
'Rejoice, madam, rejoice, our master 's come.'
But she thought this was unbelievable—
For who gets suddenly the thing desired
Believes he sees a dream from his much joy—
And to the maids was saying, 'You see visions?'   910
And, still wanting to say more on this wise,
When suddenly she saw him coming up
She sorely fainted in a wonderstroke,
And having wound her arms about his neck
She hung there speechless, nor let fall her tears.
Likewise the Emir became as one possessed,
Clasping the girl, holding her on his breast,
So they remained entwined for many hours;
And had not the General's wife thrown water on them
They had straight fallen fainting to the ground.   920
(Love beyond measure often breeds such things,
And overpassing joy leads on to death,
Even as they too were nigh to suffer it.)
And hardly were they able to sever them;
For the Emir was kissing the girl's eyes,
Embracing her, and asking with delight:
'How are you, sweet my light, my pretty lamb,
How are you, dearest soul, my consolation,
Most pretty dove, and my most lovely tree
With your own flower, my beloved son?'   930
The girl, her love passionately renewing,
To the Emir spoke sweetly on this wise:
'Well come, my hope, refreshment of my life,
My chief supporter, and my soul's delight,
All is well with us by the power of God,
Who has thought us worthy to behold each other.

'lamb' instead of 'heifer'. The translator has also shied at 'partridge' and
'turkey' in similar contexts. This term
of endearment is not found in any of
the other versions; but cf. the Byzantine street-song of A.D. 600 (*Krumbacher*,
p. 792) εὑρῆκε τὴν δαμάλιδα ἁπαλὴν
καὶ τρυφεράν; and *Anth. Pal.* v. 292.

10 γλυκερὴν δάμαλιν; also below 1846.
931 ἐκ πόθου again—'eagerly' or 'passionately'—or 'to heart's content'?
933 καλῶς ἦλθες. The quite modern
formula of welcome.
936 ἡμᾶς . . . ἀλλήλους. Correctly used;
see above 783.

61

εἰπὲ καὶ σύ, αὐθέντα μου, τὰ περὶ σοῦ πῶς ἔχουν." 300
" Πάντα καλῶς," ἀντέφησε, " χάριτι τοῦ Χριστοῦ μου,
τοῦ καρδίας φωτίσαντος μητρὸς καὶ συγγενῶν μου
καὶ ὁδηγήσαντος αὐτοὺς πρὸς φῶς θεογνωσίας,
οὓς μετ᾽ ὀλίγον ὄψεσθε ἐρχομένους ἐνταῦθα."
Εἶτα καὶ τέκνον τὸ αὐτοῦ λαβὼν εἰς τὰς ἀγκάλας, 305
τοιαῦτα ἀπεφθέγγετο ἐκ βάθους τῆς καρδίας·
" Πότε, γεράκιν μου καλόν, τὰς πτέρυγας ἁπλώσεις,
καὶ κυνηγήσεις πέρδικα, λῃστάδας ὑποτάξεις; "
Καὶ ταῦτα μὲν ὁ ἀμηρᾶς τὸ παιδίον ἐλάλει.
Ἔλευσιν δὲ τὴν ἑαυτοῦ πάντες ἀναμαθόντες, 310
εἰς τοὺς οἴκους ἀπέτρεχον εἰπεῖν τὰ συγχαρίκια·
καὶ γέγονε πολλὴ χαρά, ἀμήχανον τὸ λέγειν· 20 rº.
καὶ χοροὺς συστησάμενοι χορείας ἐποιοῦντο.
Ἐν τῇ χαρᾷ πάλιν χαρὰ ἐπέρχεται ἑτέρα,
ἦλθε γάρ τις τὴν τῆς μητρὸς ἄφιξιν ἐπαγγέλλων· 315
καὶ ἦν ἰδεῖν πάντας ὁμοῦ, ἄνδρας τε καὶ γυναῖκας,
ἐξελθόντας εἰς ἀπαντὴν μετὰ τῆς στρατηγίσσης,
ὥστε μὴ σώζειν εὐχερῶς τούτους ἀπαριθμῆσαι.
Ὄντως θαῦμα παράδοξον ἔργον ὀρθῆς ἀγάπης·
τίς τοῦτο μὴ καταπλαγῇ; τίς μὴ θαυμάσῃ μᾶλλον, 320
καὶ καταμάθῃ ἀκριβῶς ἔρωτος τὰς δυνάμεις,
πῶς ἀλλοφύλους ἥνωσεν, εἰς μίαν φέρων πίστιν;
Καὶ πλησίον γενόμενοι ἐπέζευον εὐθέως
καταμανθάνοντες αὐτούς, ἀκριβῶς ἐρωτῶντες·
ἡ νύμφη μὲν τὴν πενθερὰν καὶ τοὺς λοιποὺς ἰδίους, 325
ἡ δὲ τοὺς συγγενεῖς αὐτῆς χαίρουσα κατεφίλει·
αἱ φάραι χρεμετίζουσαι ἔχαιρον σὺν ἀλλήλαις,
καὶ χαρὰ πᾶσι γέγονε μείζω τῆς προλαβούσης.
Εἰς δὲ τὸν οἶκον φθάσαντες, γάμους εὐθὺς ποιοῦσι·
καὶ τὴν μητέρα τὴν αὐτοῦ ὁ ἀμηρᾶς βαπτίσας, 330
αὐτὸς ταύτην ἐδέξατο ἐν τῇ ἀναγεννήσει,
ὡσαύτως καὶ τοὺς συγγενεῖς τοὺς σὺν αὐτῷ ἐλθόντας·

---

315 τὴν manque dans le manuscrit.   327 σχηματίζουσαι.

944, 945 These admirable lines are not in AND or TRE.
945 λῃστάδας: early use of modern plural; but below 995 τοὺς λῃστάς.
948 συγχαρίκια. See above 888, below 1866.

950 χοροὺς . . . χορείας: another verbal echo.
959 ἀλλοφύλους ἥνωσεν, i.e. brought the foreigners into communion, not 'joined different races in one'.

But say, my master, how goes it with you?'
'All well,' he answered, 'by the grace of Christ,
Who lighted the hearts of my mother and my kin
And guided them to light of God's knowledge;   940
Whom in a little you shall see come here.'
And then taking his child into his arms
Uttered such words from the deep of his heart:
'When, my fine hawk, will you unfold your wings,
And hunt the partridge, and subdue the robbers?'
Thus the Emir was speaking to the child.
And all the people having learned his coming
Ran to the house to say congratulations;
Much joy was there, impossible to tell;
And forming choirs they began to dance.   950
Into this joy came yet another joy,
Someone came telling the arrival of his mother.
Then men and women, all were to be seen
Going out to meet her, with the General's wife,
So it was hardly possible to count them.
(Strange wonder truly, work of upright love;
Who would not be amazed? Who would not wonder,
And here learn off the exact powers of Love,
How he joined foreign races in one faith?)
When they were come near straightway they dismounted,
Closely questioning, learning all about them;   961
The bride her husband's mother and other kindred,
And she her kinsmen gladly was embracing.
The horses whinnied gladly to each other,
More joy had all than that had gone before.
They reached the house and straight they made marriage;
And the Emir baptizing his own mother
Did sponsor her on her regeneration,
Likewise his kinsmen who had come with her,

961 This line, which appears to be an absent-minded echo of 958, illustrates the redactor's trick of irrelevant verbal repetition.

966 γάμους εὐθὺς ποιοῦσι. This seems to be another reflection (from 377, the previous arrival at the castle),

as no wedding was now required. Γάμος can hardly be used in the general sense of 'feast'. Line 971 is also almost exactly repeated from 379.

969 τοὺς σὺν αὐτῷ ἐλθόντας. Leg. σὺν αὐτῇ.

καὶ πατὴρ πάντων γέγονεν ἐν Πνεύματι ἁγίῳ.
Ἡ χαρὰ δὲ ἐπηύξανεν ἡ πάνδημος ἐκείνη·
ἔχαιρε γὰρ ἐπὶ μητρὶ υἱὸς τῇ πιστευσάσῃ,   335
ἡ δὲ μήτηρ εὐφραίνετο ἐπὶ υἱῷ φιλτάτῳ.
Μέρος δέ τι ὁ ἀμηρᾶς τοῦ οἴκου ἀφορίσας,
συγγενεῦσιν ἀπένειμεν ἐνδιαίτημα ἔχειν.   20 vᵒ.
Τὸ δὲ παιδίον ηὔξανεν ὁ Διγενὴς Ἀκρίτης,
χάρισμα ἔχων ἐκ Θεοῦ παράδοξον ἀνδρείας,   340
ὥστε πάντας ἐκπλήττεσθαι τοὺς αὐτὸν καθορῶντας,
καὶ θαυμάζειν τὴν σύνεσιν καὶ τὴν γενναίαν τόλμην.
Φήμη δὲ ἦν περὶ αὐτοῦ εἰς ἅπαντα τὸν κόσμον.

And was their father in the holy Spirit. 970
And so increased that universal joy;
The son rejoiced his mother had believed,
The mother too was glad in her dear son.
The Emir divided off part of the house,
And gave it to his kin for habitation.
    So the child grew, the Twyborn Borderer,
Having from God strange favour of manliness,
So that all looking on him were amazed,
Admired his wisdom and his noble daring;
And fame about him was in all the world. 980

ΛΟΓΟΣ ΤΕΤΑΡΤΟΣ

Άνδραγαθίαι ἄρχονται ἐντεῦθεν τοῦ Ἀκρίτου,
καὶ πῶς τὴν κόρην ἥρπαξε τὴν πάγκαλον ἐκείνην
καὶ περὶ γάμου τοῦ αὐτοῦ λόγος τέταρτος ἔστιν.

*   *   *

Καὶ εὐθὺς περὶ ἔρωτος ὑμᾶς ἀναμιμνήσκω·
ῥίζα γὰρ οὗτος καὶ ἀρχὴ καθέστηκεν ἀγάπης,   5
ἐξ ἧς φιλία τίκτεται, εἶτα γεννᾶται πόθος,
ὃς αὐξηθεὶς κατὰ μικρὸν φέρει καρπὸν τοιοῦτον,
μερίμνας μὲν διηνεκεῖς, ἐννοίας καὶ φροντίδας,
εὐθὺς κινδύνους παμπληθεῖς καὶ χωρισμὸν γονέων.
Νεότης γὰρ ἀκμάζουσα καρδίας ἀνασπάει,   10
εἶτα πάντα κατατολμᾷ τῶν ἀνεπιχειρήτων·
θαλάττης μὲν ἐφίκεσθαι, πῦρ μηδ᾽ ὅλως πτοεῖσθαι·
δράκοντας δὲ καὶ λέοντας καὶ τὰ λοιπὰ θηρία
οὐδοτιοῦν λογίζεται στερεωθεὶς ὁ πόθος
καὶ τοὺς λῃστὰς τοὺς τολμηροὺς ἀντ᾽ οὐδενὸς ἡγεῖται,   15
νύκτας ἡμέρας προσδοκᾷ καὶ τὰς κλεισούρας κάμπους,
ἀγρυπνίαν ἀνάπαυσιν, καὶ τὰ μακρὰν πλησίον·
πολλοὶ καὶ πίστιν τὴν αὐτῶν ἀρνοῦνται διὰ πόθον.
Καὶ τοῦτο μηδεὶς ἄπιστον ἐξ ὑμῶν λογισθήτω,   21 rᵒ.
μάρτυρα γὰρ ἐπαινετὸν εἰς μέσον παραστήσω   20
ἀμηρᾶν τὸν πανεύγενον καὶ πρῶτον τῆς Συρίας,
ὃς εἶχε κάλλη πάντερπνα καὶ τόλμην θηριώδη,
καὶ μέγεθος πανθαύμαστον, ἰσχὺν γενναιοτάτην,
καὶ μᾶλλον δεύτερος Σαμψὼν αὐτὸς ἐπενοήθη·
ἐκεῖνος γὰρ ἠρίστευσε χερσὶ λέοντα σχίσας,   25
οὗτος δὲ πλῆθος ἄπειρον ἀπέκτεινε λεόντων.
    Παύσασθε γράφειν Ὅμηρον καὶ μύθους Ἀχιλλέως
ὡσαύτως καὶ τοῦ Ἕκτορος, ἅπερ εἰσὶ ψευδέα.
Ἀλέξανδρος ὁ Μακεδὼν δυνατὸς ἐν φρονήσει,
Θεόν τε ἔχων συνεργὸν γέγονε κοσμοκράτωρ.   30

2 πάγκαλλον.   4 ἀναμιμνήκω.   12 μὴ δ᾽.   16 προσδοκᾶν.   27 ἀχιλέως.

984–6 ἔρως . . . ἀγάπη . . . φιλία . . .
πόθος. The distinction between these
different forms of 'love' is not always
     observed, and the translator can
     only hope that the series Desire . . .
     Love . . . Affection . . . Passion is a

FOURTH BOOK

HEREFROM begin the Borderer his feats,
And how he carried off that lovely Girl,
And about his wedding the Fourth Book is.

* * *

Straightway about Desire I readvise you,
For He is root and origin of Love,
From which is born Affection; then comes Passion,
Which growing by degrees brings forth such fruit,
As constant cares, anxieties, and troubles,
Dangers at once crowding, parting from parents.
For youth when at the bloom uproots the hearts,   990
And then dares all things that are unattempted,
To reach the sea and not fear fire at all;
Dragons and lions and all other beasts
Passion confirmed considers not at all,
Reckons as nothing the undaunted robbers,
Believes that nights are days, the mountains flat,
That waking is repose and far things near;
And many do deny their faith for passion.
Let none of you think this incredible;
I'll set a worthy witness in your midst   1000
The most highborn Emir and chief of Syria,
Who had sweetest beauties, daring like a beast's,
A wondrous stature, and most noble strength,
Indeed was made to be a second Sampson;
He shone who tore a lion with his hands;
The other would slay a countless host of lions.
    Cease writing of Homer, fables of Achilles,
And likewise those of Hektor, which are false.
Macedonian Alexander, strong in wisdom,
With God to help was master of the world;   1010

satisfactory rendering. For further
generalizations about these four sorts
see below 1420 ff. and 1604 ff.
989 χωρισμὸν γονέων, i.e. parting from
parents, not parting of one parent
from another.
992 θαλάττης . . . ἐφίκεσθαι. This
evidently refers to the raids of the
hero and his father and uncles in
Asia Minor. See above 413.

Αὐτὸς δὲ φρόνημα στερρὸν ἔχων Θεὸν ἐπέγνω,
ἐκέκτητο καὶ μετ' αὐτοῦ ἀνδρείαν τε καὶ τόλμην.
Φιλοπαπποῦ τοῦ γέροντος, Κινν́αμου καὶ Ἰωαννάκη
οὐδ' ὅλως ἔστιν ἄξιον τὰ αὐτῶν καταλέγειν,
οὗτοι γὰρ ἐκαυχήσαντο μηδὲν πεποιηκότες·   35
τούτου δὲ πάντα ἀληθῆ καὶ μεμαρτυρημένα.
Ἄμβρων ὑπῆρχεν ὁ παππούς, θεῖος του ὁ Καρόης·
διαλεκτοὺς τὸν ἔδωκαν τρισχιλίους κονταράτους,
πᾶσαν Συρίαν ὑπέταξεν, ἐπίασε τὸ Κοῦφερ·
εἶθ' οὕτως ἐν τοῖς μέρεσιν ἦλθε τῆς Ῥωμανίας,   40
κάστρα πολλὰ ἐκούρσευσε, χώραν τοῦ Ἡρακλέος,
Χαρζιανὴν ἐπραίδευσε καὶ τὴν Καππαδοκίαν·
κόρην τερπνὴν ἀφήρπαξεν εὐγενῆ τῶν Δουκάδων,
διὰ κάλλος τὸ θαυμαστὸν καὶ τερπνὴν ἡλικίαν,   21 vº.
τὰ πάντα ἀρνησάμενος, πίστιν ὁμοῦ καὶ δόξαν,   45
καὶ γέγονε χριστιανὸς ὀρθόδοξος διὰ ταύτην·
καὶ ὅ ποτε πολέμιος δοῦλος ὤφθη Ῥωμαίων.
Ἐξ ὧν παιδίον τίκτεται περικαλλὲς τῷ ὄντι,
καὶ ἐξ αὐτῆς γεννήσεως Βασίλειος ἐκλήθη·
λέγεται δὲ καὶ Διγενὴς ὡς ἀπὸ τῶν γονέων,   50
ἐθνικὸς μὲν ἀπὸ πατρός, ἐκ δὲ μητρὸς Ῥωμαῖος·
φοβερὸς δὲ γενόμενος, ὡς ὁ λόγος δηλώσει,
Ἀκρίτης ὀνομάζεται τὰς ἄκρας ὑποτάξας.
Τούτου πάππος Ἀντάκινος ἀπὸ τῶν Κινναμάδων,
ὃς τέθνηκεν ἐξόριστος προστάξει βασιλέως   55
Βασιλείου τοῦ εὐτυχοῦς, ἀκρίτου τοῦ μεγάλου·
πολὺς ὢν κλῆρος ἐν αὐτῷ καὶ ἀνείκαστος δόξα
μέγας μὲν ἐφημίζετο στρατηγὸς παρὰ πάντων·
μάμμη δὲ ἡ στρατήγισσα εὐγενὴς τῶν Δουκάδων·
θείους εἶχε τοὺς θαυμαστοὺς ἀδελφοὺς τῆς μητρός του,   60
οἳ καὶ ἐμονομάχησαν διὰ τὴν ἀδελφήν των
τὸν ἀμηρᾶν τὸν θαυμαστὸν τὸν ἑαυτοῦ πατέρα.
Οὗτος ἐβλάστησε φυλῆς ἐξ εὐγενῶν Ῥωμαίων,
καὶ γέγονε περίβλεπτος εἰς τὰς ἀνδραγαθίας.

41 χώρας.   47 ὁ ποτὲ.   51 ῥωμαίας.   54 Je n'ose remplacer Ἀντάνικος
par Ἀνδρόνικος que donnent le ms. de Trébizonde (vers 834) et celui d'Andros
(vers 1367).

1018 Metre requires τρισχιλίους.   1019 Κοῦφερ. See above 292.

But he firm-minded recognized his God,
Therewith possessed daring and manliness.
Old Philopappos, Kinnamos, Ioannakes,
Nothing of theirs is worth telling at all,
Who vainly boasted, for they did nothing.
But all his deeds are true and well attested.
Ambrôn his grandfather, Karoës his uncle,
They granted him three thousand chosen spearmen,
All Syria he subdued, laid hold of Koufah;
Then came he to the parts of Romania,   1020
Plundered many forts, the land of Hêrakles,
Harzianê he ravaged, and Kappadokia;
Carried off the Doukas's fair noble daughter,
For her fair stature and her wondrous beauty,
Denying everything, his faith and fame,
Became a Christian Orthodox for her.
Their former foe was seen the Romans' slave.
To them a child is born, indeed most fair,
Who from his very birth was named Basil,
Called also Twyborn as from his parents,   1030
A pagan father and a Roman mother;
Grown formidable, as the tale shall show,
The borders quelled, is surnamed Borderer.
Antakinos was his grandfather, of the Kinnamades,
Who died exiled by order of the emperor
Basil the blessed, the mighty borderer.
Great was his portion, and unmatched his fame,
By all reputed a great general;
His grandmother the general's wife, a noble Doukas;
His uncles were his mother's wondrous brothers,   1040
Who fought, in single combat for their sister,
The wonderful Emir who was his father.
So sprang he from a line of noble Romans,
And was illustrious for his braveries.

1024 θαυμαστόν. The metre requires
θαυμάσιον.
1029 ἐξ αὐτῆς γεννήσεως. TRE 830
(wrongly numbered 850), having
misunderstood ἐξ αὐτῆς, says that he
was christened Basil when six years

old—ἐξαετής.
1031 ἐθνικός. 'Pagan' or 'gentile'?
1034 Ἀντάκινος. TRE 834, AND 1367,
have Ἀνδρόνικος.
1036 Βασιλείου. TRE 836, AND 1369,
have Ῥωμανοῦ.

Ἤδη λοιπὸν ἀρξώμεθα τὰ αὐτοῦ καταλέγειν.   65
Οὗτος τοίνυν ὁ θαυμαστὸς Βασίλειος Ἀκρίτης
παιδόθεν εἰς καθηγητὴν παρὰ πατρὸς ἐδόθη·
καὶ τρεῖς ὅλους ἐνιαυτοὺς μαθήμασι σχολάσας,
τῇ τοῦ νοὸς ὀξύτητι πλῆθος ἔσχε γραμμάτων·   22 rº.
ἐντεῦθεν ἱππηλάσια καὶ κυνηγεῖν ποθήσας,   70
μετὰ πατρὸς ἐσχόλαζε καθ' ἑκάστην ἐν τούτοις.
Μιᾷ τοίνυν τῶν ἡμερῶν, τὸν πατέρα του λέγει·
" Πόθος, αὐθέντα καὶ πατήρ, ἐσέβη εἰς τὴν ψυχήν μου
τοῦ δοκιμάσαι ἐμαυτὸν εἰς θηρίων πολέμους·
καὶ, εἴπερ ὅλως ἀγαπᾷς Βασίλειον υἱόν σου,   75
εἰς τόπον ἃς ἐξέλθωμεν ἔνθα εἰσὶ θηρία,
καὶ πάντως βλέψεις λογισμὸν ἀεί με ἐνοχλοῦντα."
Λόγους τοιούτους ὁ πατὴρ ἀκούων τοῦ φιλτάτου,
ἠγάλλετο τῷ πνεύματι, ἔχαιρε τῇ καρδίᾳ·
μετὰ πολλῆς τῆς ἡδονῆς τοῦτον ἐκατεφίλει·   80
" Ὦ τέκνον ποθεινότατον, ὦ ψυχὴ καὶ καρδία,
θαυμαστοὶ μὲν οἱ λόγοι σου, γλυκεῖα καὶ ἡ γνώμη,
πλὴν οὐ παρέστηκε καιρὸς τῆς θηριομαχίας·
θηρίων γὰρ ὁ πόλεμος δεινότατος ὑπάρχει,
καὶ σὺ παῖς δωδεκάχρονος ἢ βίσεξτος ὑπάρχεις,   85
ἀνάξιος παντάπασι πολεμεῖν τὰ θηρία·
μή, γλυκύτατον τέκνον μου, τοῦτο εἰς νοῦν ἐμβάλῃς·
μηδὲ ῥόδα σου τὰ καλὰ πρὸ καιροῦ ἐκτρυγήσῃς·
ὅταν δέ, θέλοντος Θεοῦ, ἀνὴρ τέλειος φθάσῃς,
τότε λοιπὸν λόγου ἐκτὸς πολεμεῖν τὰ θηρία."   90
Καὶ ὡς ταῦτα ἀκήκοε τὸ εὐγενὲς παιδίον,
ἐλυπήθη κατὰ πολύ, ἐτρώθη τὴν καρδίαν·
καὶ δακρύσας τοῖς ὀφθαλμοῖς λέγει πρὸς τὸν πατέρα·
" Εἰ μετὰ τὴν τελείωσιν ἀνδραγαθήσω, πάτερ,
τί μοι ἐκ τούτου ὄφελος; τοῦτο πάντες ποιοῦσιν·   22 vº.   95
ἄρτι ποθῶ δεξάσασθαι καὶ τὸ γένος λαμπρῦναι,
πληροφορῶ δὲ καὶ ἐσὲ τὸν ἐμὸν εὐεργέτην

71 καθεκάστην.   85 βήσεκστος.   86 ἀνάξιον.   88 μὴ δὲ.

1045 καταλέγειν. Cf. the modern use
of καταλόγια, e.g. as a heading, in
the Polites collection of folk-songs,
for the narrative ballads.

1049 γραμμάτων, i.e. book-learning.
1062 γνώμη. Perhaps 'your nature'; see
above 360.
1065 δωδεκάχρονος ἢ βίσεξτος. There

So let us now begin his tale to tell.
This Basil then the wondrous Borderer
His father gave from childhood to a teacher,
And three whole years devoting to his lessons
With his keen mind much learning he acquired.
Then when he wanted horsemanship and hunting,   1050
To these each day devoted with his father.
And so one day he says to his father:
'Desire is in my soul, master and father,
To try myself in fighting with wild beasts,
And, if you love at all your son Basil,
Let us go out to a place where there are beasts,
And you shall see the purpose that still irks me.'
Such words the father hearing from his dear,
Was glad in spirit and in heart rejoiced;
With great delight he covered him with kisses: 1060
'O soul and heart, O my most darling child,
Wonderful are your words, and sweet your will,
But the time is not come for beast-fighting;
The war with beasts is very terrible,
You are a twelve-year-old, a child twice six,
Wholly unfit to battle with the beasts;
This put not in your mind, my sweetest child,
Nor harvest your fair rose before its time;
When, God willing, you are a full-grown man,
Then without saying shall you fight with beasts.'   1070
And when the noble child had heard these words
He was sore grieved and wounded was his heart,
Tears filled his eyes, he said to his father:
'If when grown up I do my deeds, father,
What good is that to me? So all men do.
I want fame now, to illustrate my line,
And I make known to you, my benefactor,

seems no point in calling the child
a 'twelve-year-old or double-six'—
unless possibly the redactor had been
following a version which had the
reading ἑξαετής (above 1029) which
survives in TRE 830; in which case
a point might have been made of

being christened at six—initiated at
twelve. Βίσεξτος properly means
'intercalary'—the extra day in leap
year, so called because it was a
duplication of the sixth day before
the Kalends of March.
1076 δεξάσασθαι. Leg. δοξάσασθαι.

ὅτι δοῦλον θέλεις ἔχειν με ἀνδρειότατον, μέγαν,
καὶ συνεργὸν καὶ βοηθὸν εἰς πάντας τοὺς πολέμους."
Καὶ κατένευσεν ὁ πατὴρ τῇ προθυμίᾳ τοῦ νέου·   100
φύσεως γὰρ τὸ εὐγενὲς ἐκ παιδόθεν προφαίνει.
Τῇ δὲ ἐπαύριον λαβὼν τὸν γυναικάδελφόν του
τὸν γεννηθέντα ὕστερον, τὸν χρυσὸν Κωνσταντῖνον,
καὶ τὸν υἱὸν μεθ᾽ ἑαυτοῦ Ἀκρίτην τὸν γενναῖον,
καὶ ἀπὸ τῶν ἀγούρων του τινὰς καβαλλαρίους,   105
εἰς τὴν ἕλην παρευθὺς ἐξῆλθον εἰς τὰ ἄλση·
καὶ μακρόθεν ἐσκέψαντο ἄρκτους φοβερωτάτους·
ἄρσεν καὶ θῆλυ ὑπήρχασιν ἀρκοπούλια δύο·
βάλλει φωνὴν ὁ θεῖος του· " Βασίλειε, ἄρτι ἃς ἴδω·
πλὴν τὸ ῥαβδίν σου ἔπαρον, ξίφος μηδὲν βαστάσῃς·   110
ἄρκτους οὐκ ἔνι ἐπαινετὸν πολεμεῖν μετὰ ξίφους."
Καὶ ἦν θαῦμα φρικτὸν ἰδεῖν καὶ ξένον τοῖς ὁρῶσι·
καὶ γὰρ φωνῆς ὡς ἤκουσε τοῦ θείου τὸ παιδίον,
παραυτίκα ἐπέζευσε καὶ λύει τὸ ζωνάριν,
ἐκδύεται τὸ ὑπολούρικον, ἦτον πολὺς ὁ καύσων,   115
καὶ τὰς ποδέας ὀχυρῶς πήξας εἰς τὸ ζωνάριν,
καμηλαυκίτζιν χαμηλὸν βαλὼν εἰς τὸ κεφάλιν,
ὡς ἀστραπὴ ἐξεπήδησεν ἀπὸ περιστηθίου,
μηδὲν ἐπιφερόμενος εἰ μὴ λιτὸν ῥαβδίτζιν,
εἶχε δὲ δύναμιν πολλήν, ἀκολουθὸν τὸ τάχος·   23 rᵒ.   120
καὶ πλησίον γενόμενοι ἔνθα ἦσαν οἱ ἄρκτοι,
προϋπαντᾷ τὸ θηλυκὸν φθονοῦν διὰ τὰ παιδία,
καὶ σφόδρα μυκησάμενον πρὸς ἐκεῖνον ἐξῆλθεν.
Ἐκεῖνος ὢν ἀπείραστος εἰς θηριομαχίαν,
οὐκ ἐγυρίσθη ὄπισθεν νὰ τοῦ δώσῃ ῥαβδέαν,   125
ἀλλ᾽ ἐπεσέβη σύντομα, ἐκ τὴν μέσην τὸ πιάνει,

106 Il manque une syllabe dans le premier hémistiche, peut-être τὸ avant
παρευθύς.   108 ἀρκοπούλλια.   117 καμιλαυκίτζιν χαμιλόν.   120 Il faut
vraisemblablement écrire ἀκόλουθον ou ἀκολουθοῦν.   125 ὄπισθε. δώσει ῥαβδαίαν.

1082 γυναικάδελφον. In previous references he has always been called
γαμβρός.
1083 See above 131.
1086 τὴν ἕλην. Ἕλη (fem.) for ἕλος
(neut.) seems to be rare. (See also
below 1109.) 'Swamp' or 'marsh',

the ordinary translation, is rather
too wet; it means something more
like 'water-meadows' or 'withy-beds'.
Legrand points out that a syllable
is missing at the beginning of the
line, and I think the true reading
was ἀπὸ τὴν ἕλην—'from the water-

A brave great servant you shall have in me
To help and fight with you in all your battles.'
The father to the youngster's zeal assented 1080
(A well-born nature shows from childhood forth).
  And on the morrow taking his wife's brother,
The latest born, the golden Constantine,
His son with him, the noble Borderer,
And a few riders of his company,
They went straight through the marsh into the woods,
And from afar spied most ferocious bears;
There were a male and female and two cubs.
His uncle cried: 'Now, Basil, let me see;
But only take your club, carry no sword; 1090
It is no credit to fight bears with swords.'
A wonder dread it was and strange to see:
For when the boy had heard his uncle's voice,
Straightway he dismounted, loosened his belt,
Took off his tabard, for the heat was great,
Fastened his kilts up firmly in his belt,
And putting a low cap upon his head,
Like lightning he jumped out of his breastplate,
And carried nothing but a simple staff;
Great strength he had, and speed attending it; 1100
And when they were come near where the bears were,
The female met him jealous for her cubs,
And loudly roaring she came out towards him.
He, as he was untried in beast-fighting,
Did not turn back so as to swing his cudgel,
But jumped in quick and caught it by the middle,

meadows they rode up into the wooded foothills'.

1088 καμηλαυκίτζιν. See also 3177. The cubs are not mentioned in TRE 904, but reappear in ESC 757 (κουλούκια). Read ὑπῆρχασι καὶ.

1095 ὑπολούρικον translated 'tabard' as if it was the same as ἐπιλούρικον; but it may be 'tunic' worn under the cuirass, as the name implies.

1097 καμηλαυκίτζιν. See also 3177. Seems to have been a small cap probably of fur. See Ducange, Meursius, and Sophokles s.v. καμη-λαύκιον, and Maigne d'Arnis s.v. camelaucum. See also Gibbon, vi, p. 536, quoting Const. Porph. de Adm. (13. 29, 34) on barbarian requests which must never be granted for 'imperial robes and crowns of the kind called Kamelaukia'. See also Papadopoulos in Epet. Byz. Spoud. 1928, p. 293. See also O.E.D. 'cala-manco, glossy Flemish woollen stuff; Dutch: kalamink'. From this word also came the name of the modern priest's hat usually written καλυμμαύχι.

καὶ σφίξας τοὺς βραχίονας εὐθὺς ἀπέπνιξέ τον·
καὶ τὰ ἐντὸς ἐξήρχετο ἐκ τοῦ στόματος τούτου·
ἔφυγε δὲ τὸ ἀρσενικὸν εἰς τὴν ἔλην ἀπέσω·
Ὁ θεῖος του τὸν ἐφώνησε· " Βλέπε, τέκνον, μὴ φύγῃ." 130
Κἀκεῖνος ἀπὸ τῆς σπουδῆς ἀφῆκε τὸ ραβδίν του,
καὶ πετάσας ὡς ἀετὸς ἔφθασε τὸ θηρίον·
ἡ ἄρκτος ἐστράφη πρὸς αὐτὸν στόμα χανοῦσα μέγα,
καὶ ὥρμησε τὴν κεφαλὴν τοῦ παιδὸς ἐκλαφῦξαι.
Τὸ δὲ παιδίον σύντομα τὸ μάγουλόν του πιάνει 135
καὶ τινάξας ἀπέκτεινε χαμαὶ βαλὼν τὸ θηρίον,
στρέψας τὸν τράχηλον αὐτοῦ ἐξεσφονδύλισέ το,
καὶ παρευθὺς ἀπέψυξεν εἰς τὰς χεῖρας τοῦ νέου.
    Ἐκ δὲ τῶν ἄρκτων τοὺς βρυγμοὺς καὶ τῶν ποδῶν τοὺς κτύπους,
ἔλαφος ἐξεπήδησε μέσον τῆς παγαναίας· 140
ὁ ἀμηρᾶς ἐλάλησε· " Δέχου, τέκνον, ἐμπρός σου."
Καὶ τοῦ πατρὸς ὡς ἤκουσεν, ὥσπερ πάρδος ἐξέβη,
καὶ εἰς ὀλίγα πηδήματα φθάνει τὴν ἐλαφῖναν,
καὶ τῶν ποδῶν δραξάμενος αὐτῆς τῶν ὀπισθίων,
ἀποτινάξας ἔσχισε ταύτην εἰς δύο μέρη. 145
Τίς μὴ θαυμάσῃ μέγεθος Θεοῦ τῶν χαρισμάτων, 23 vᵒ.
καὶ τὴν αὐτοῦ ἀσύγκριτον δύναμιν μεγαλύνῃ;
ὄντως ἔργον παράδοξον τὰς ἐννοίας ἐκπλῆττον
πῶς τὴν ἔλαφον ἔφθασε παιδίον χωρὶς ἵππου,
πῶς τοὺς ἄρκτους ἐφόνευσε μηδὲν ἐν χερσὶν ἔχον, 150
ὄντως Θεοῦ τὸ δώρημα καὶ δεξιᾶς ὑψίστου.
Ὢ πόδες ὡραιότατοι, ἐφάμιλλοι πτερύγων,
οἱ δορκάδος νικήσαντες τὸ τάχος παραδόξως,
καὶ συντρίψαντες δύναμιν τῶν φοβερῶν θηρίων!
    Ἅπερ ὁρῶντες οἱ ἐκεῖ τότε παρατυχόντες, 155
τὸ θαῦμα ἐκπληττόμενοι ἔλεγον πρὸς ἀλλήλους·
" Θεοτόκε, τὸ θέαμα ὃ βλέπομεν εἰς τὸν νέον!
οὐκ ἔστιν τοῦτος ἄνθρωπος ὥσπερ οἱ ἐκ τοῦ κόσμου·
ὁ Θεὸς τοῦτον ἀπέστειλε διὰ τοὺς ἀνδρειωμένους,

---

127 σφίγξας.   133 ἄκτος.   134 ἐκλαφύξαι.   135 συντόμως.   137 ἀπε-
σφονδήλισέ, et ἐξε au-dessus de ἀπε   143 ἐλαφίναν.   147 μεγαλύνει.
152 ἐφάμιλοι.

1113 The male bear is suddenly called   culine throughout (TRE 905 ὁ ἄρκος).
ἡ ἄρκτος, although above (and below   1116 Read χαμαὶ βαλὼν ἀπέκτεινε τινάξας
1130) the word is masculine. The   τὸ θηρίον.
feminine is classical. In TRE it is mas-   1117 ἐξεσφονδύλισέ το, i.e. dislocated

And tightening his arms choked it at once;
Its inward parts were coming from its mouth.
The male ran off into the marshy flats.
His uncle called 'See it doesn't get away, child.'   1110
He in his hurry let his cudgel go,
Flew like an eagle and caught up the beast.
The bear turned on him gaping wide its mouth
And rushed the boy's head for to swallow down.
But the boy quickly seized it by the chap,
And shook the beast, killed, threw it on the ground,
Twisted its neck about and broke its spine,
Which straightway in the youngster's hands expired.
    From the bears' roars and beating of their feet
A deer jumped from the middle of the covert.   1120
The Emir spoke up, 'Mark, child, in front of you.'
He heard his father, went off like a pard,
In a few strides he overtook the deer,
And by the hind legs seizing hold of it,
With a quick shake he tore it in two parts.
    Who should not wonder at God's mighty favours,
Magnify his incomparable strength?
Strange deed in truth astonishing the thought,
How a boy without horse caught up the hind,
How nothing in his hands he killed the bears,   1130
The gift of God and of the Highest's right hand.
O feet most beautiful and rivalling wings
That strangely beat the speed of the gazelle,
And overcame the strength of dreadful beasts!
Which when they saw who happened to be there,
Struck by the wonder began to tell each other:
'Mother of God, the sight we see in the youth!
This is no man as those are in the world;
God must have sent him forth to show the brave,

its spine. Legrand in TRE 908 wrongly translates ἀποσφονδυλίζω 'asséner un coup de poing', and fails to notice a lacuna after TRE 904 corresponding to AND 1415-41.
1120 μέσον τῆς παγαναίας. See note of Legrand in TRE gloss., with quota-tion from Valaorites, and add refs. to Passow 501. 16, and Soph. s.v. παγανός. The ordinary modern mean-ing of παγανιά is a 'drive' or 'battue' of game, rather than a 'covert'.
1139 διὰ τοὺς ἀνδρειωμένους. In modern Greek culture οἱ ἀνδρειωμένοι, 'the

νά τον βλέπουν πῶς χαίρεται, πῶς πολεμεῖ, πῶς τρέχει." 160
'Ως δὲ ταῦτα ἐλέγασιν ὁ πατὴρ καὶ οἱ θεῖοι,
λέων ἐξέβη μέγιστος ἀπὸ τοῦ καλαμιῶνος
καὶ εὐθὺς περιεστράφησαν ἰδεῖν τὸν ἀγουρίτζην,
εἰς ἕλην τον ἐσκέψαντο σύρνοντα τὰ θηρία.
Μὲ τὴν δεξιὰν ἔσυρνε γὰρ οὖς ἐφόνευσεν ἄρκτους, 165
καὶ μετὰ τὴν ἀριστερὰν σύρει τὴν ἐλαφῖναν.
Ὁ θεῖος του τὸν ἐλάλησεν· "'Ελθέ, τέκνον, ἐνθάδε·
καὶ τὰ νεκρὰ κατάλειψον, ἔχομεν ἄλλα ζῶντα,
ἐν οἷς καὶ δοκιμάζονται τῶν εὐγενῶν οἱ παῖδες."
Ὁ παῖς ἀνταπεκρίνατο λέγων αὐτῷ τοιάδε· 170
" Εἰ θέλημα Θεοῦ ἐστι τοῦ εὐδοκοῦντος πάντα,
εἰ ἔχω τοῦ πατρὸς εὐχὴν καὶ τῆς καλῆς μητρός μου, 24 rº.
νεκρὸν θεάσῃ καὶ αὐτὸν ὥσπερ τοὺς δύο ἄρκτους."
Καὶ ὥρμησε ξίφους χωρὶς εἰς τὸν λέοντα ὑπάγειν.
Καὶ λέγει τον ὁ θεῖος του· " "Επαρον τὸ σπαθίν σου· 175
οὗτος οὐκ ἔστιν ἔλαφος ἵνα τον σχίσῃς μέσον."
Εὐθὺς δὲ ὁ νεώτερος τοιόνδε λόγον ἔφη·
" Ὁ Θεὸς οὐκ ἀδυνατεῖ, θεῖε μου καὶ αὐθέντα,
παραδοῦναι εἰς χεῖρας μου καθάπερ καὶ ἐκεῖνον."
Καί, τὸ σπαθὶν δραξάμενος, κινᾷ πρὸς τὸ θηρίον· 180
ὅταν δὲ ἐπλησίασεν, ἀποπηδᾷ ὁ λέων,
καὶ χαρζανίσας τὴν οὐρὰν ἔδερε τὰς πλευράς του,
καὶ μέγα βρυχησάμενος εἰς τὸν νέον ἐξῆλθε.
Τὸ δὲ παιδίον τὸ σπαθὶν εἰς ὕψος ἀνατείνας
κρούει τον κατὰ κεφαλῆς πλήρης εἰς τὴν μεσίαν, 185
καὶ διεσχίσθη ἡ κεφαλὴ ἄχρι τῶν ὤμων κάτω.
Καὶ πρὸς τὸν θεῖον του ὁ Διγενὴς τοιόνδε λόγον ἔφη·
" Ὁρᾷς, χρυσὲ αὐθέντα μου, Θεοῦ τὰ μεγαλεῖα·
οὐ κεῖται ἄφωνος, νεκρὸς ὥσπερ οἱ δύο ἄρκτοι; "
Καὶ κατεφίλησαν αὐτὸν ὁ πατὴρ καὶ ὁ θεῖος· 190
χεῖρας τε καὶ βραχίονας, ὀμμάτια καὶ στῆθος·

163 ἀγουρίτζιν.   165 με, toujours ainsi.   166 ἐλαφίναν.   169 οἷς.
171 ἐστὶ. Ce vers est répété en tête du feuillet 24 rº.   178 ἀδυνατοῖ.   182
ἔδαιρε.   183 μεγάλα (correction empruntée aux mss. de Trébizonde (vers 958)
et d'Andros (vers 1495).

brave', constitute an ideal class of national heroes. This is an early example of the usage found in the Hymn of Solomos and there certainly inspired by one of the ballads commemorating the Parga episode

To see how he rejoices, fights, and runs.'   1140
As thus they spoke his father and his uncles,
A lion huge came from the withy-bed,
And quickly they turned round to see the boy,
Beheld him in the marsh dragging the beasts.
In his right hand dragging the bears he had killed,
With his left hand he was dragging the hind.
His uncle called to him, 'Come hither, child,
And leave the dead, we have others alive,
And some that well-born lads are tested by.'
The boy answered him saying on this wise: 1150
'If it is God's will who approves all things,
If I have father's and my dear mother's prayer,
Dead you shall see him too like the two bears.'
And with no sword he ran to meet the lion.
His uncle said to him: 'Take up your sword,
This is no deer for you to tear in two.'
The youth at once spoke such a word as this:
'My uncle and my master, God is well able
To give him, like the other, into my hands.'
Snatching his sword he moved towards the beast,   1160
And when he had come near out sprang the lion,
And brandishing his tail he lashed his sides,
Bellowing loudly at the youth he came.
The boy then stretching up his sword on high
Struck him upon the head full in the middle
And split his head apart down to the shoulders.
Then to his uncle thus said Digenes:
'My golden master, you see God's greatness:
Lies he not voiceless, dead as the two bears?'
    Father and uncle covered him with kisses,   1170
His hands and his arms, his eyes and his breast,

(1819). See Polites, 'Εκλογαί, 9.
Β'. 15, καὶ τἀντρειωμένα κόκκαλα
ξεθάψτε τοῦ γονιοῦ σας.
1145 μὲ τὴν δεξιάν. Note the ordinary
modern μέ and in the same sentence
the transitional use of μετά with
accusative from which it originated.
1157 ὁ νεώτερος. Used regularly in
positive and substantival sense as

equivalent of νέος, see e.g. 698.
1162 χαρζανίσας. See Ducange s.v.
χαρζάνιον: 'est igitur idem quod
ἵμας'. See also Soph. The lion was
cracking his tail like a whip. This
explains χαρζανιστί below vi. 550
(3011), and see ESC 509 and
Sophokles s.v. μαγκλάβιον.

καὶ ἀμφότεροι χαίροντες εἶπον αὐτῷ τοιάδε·
" Πᾶς ὁ βλέπων τὴν ἔμνοστον ἡλικίαν καὶ κάλλος
τὸ σόν, ὦ περιπόθητε, ὄντως οὐ μὴ ἀμφιβάλῃ,
ἀλλὰ βεβαίως δέξεται τὰς σὰς ἀνδραγαθίας." 195
   Εἶχε γὰρ ὁ νεώτερος εὔνοστον ἡλικίαν,
κόμην ξανθήν, ἐπίσγουρον, ὀμμάτια μεγάλα, 24 vᵒ.
πρόσωπον ἄσπρον, ῥοδινόν, κατάμαυρον ὀφρύδιν,
καὶ στῆθος ὥσπερ κρύσταλλον, ὀργυιὰν εἶχε τὸ πλάτος.
Τοῦτον ὁρῶν ἡγάλλετο ὁ πατὴρ αὐτοῦ λίαν, 200
καὶ χαίρων ἔλεγεν αὐτῷ μεθ᾽ ἡδονῆς μεγάλης·
ὅτι " τὸ καῦμα ἔστι πολύ, ἔνι καὶ μεσημέριν,
καὶ τὰ θηρία κρύβονται ἀπάρτι εἰς τὴν ἕλην·
καὶ δεῦρο ἂς ἀπέλθωμεν εἰς τὸ ψυχρὸν τὸ ὕδωρ,
καὶ νῖψον σου τὸ πρόσωπον ἐκ τῶν πολλῶν ἱδρώτων· 205
ἀλλάξεις δὲ καὶ τὰ φορεῖς, εἰσὶ γὰρ μεμιασμένα
ἐκ τῶν θηρίων τοὺς ἀφροὺς καὶ λέοντος τὸ αἷμα·
καὶ τρισμακάριστος ἐγὼ ἔχων τοιοῦτον παῖδα,
πλύνω δὲ καὶ τοὺς πόδας σου μὲ τὰς ἰδίας χεῖρας·
ἀπάρτι πᾶσαν μέριμναν ῥίψω ἐκ τὴν ψυχήν μου, 210
νὰ εἰμὶ καὶ ἀφρόντιστος ἔνθα σε ἀποστείλω,
εἴς τε τὰ κούρση τὰ πολλὰ καὶ πολεμίων βίγλας."
   Καὶ παρευθὺς ἀμφότεροι εἰς τὴν πηγὴν ἀπῆλθον,
ἣν δὲ τὸ ὕδωρ θαυμαστόν, ψυχρὸν ὡς τὸ χιόνιν·
καὶ καθεσθέντες γύρωθεν, οἱ μὲν ἔνιπτον χεῖρας, 215
οἱ δὲ τὸ πρόσωπον αὐτοῦ, ὁμοίως καὶ τοὺς πόδας.
Ἔρρεεν ἔξω τῆς πηγῆς καὶ ἔπινον ἀπλήστως,
ὡς ἂν ἐκ τούτου γένωνται κἀκεῖνοι ἀνδρειωμένοι.
Ἄλλαξε δὲ καὶ τὸ παιδὶν τὴν ἑαυτοῦ ἐσθῆτα,
βάλλει στενὰ μοχλόβια διὰ τὸ καταψυχῆσαι, 220

194 ἀμφιβάλει.   205 νίψον.   207 ἀφρούς.   218 ἐκ τόν (sic).

1173 ἔμνοστον, 1176 εὔνοστον. See
Lampros, *Romans grecs*, gloss. s.v.
See below 1361.
1177 ἐπίσγουρον. TRE 972 has ὑπό-
σγουρον, which is more probable.
1179 See additional note on p. 141.
1191 νὰ εἰμί. Note modern νά (for ἵνα)
with ancient εἰμί.
1193 ἀμφότεροι. See above 581.
1198 A curious piece of magic—drink-
ing the hero's bath-water to share his

strength—which does not appear in
any other version. I have heard that
a similar incident was to be found in
a Russian ballad, but have not been
able to trace it. For a modern par-
allel from Africa see J. Roscoe, *The
Bakitara* (Cambridge, 1923), p. 94.
1200 στενὰ μοχλόβια. Legrand in
his *index verborum* suggests reading
μαχλάβια (as below 3176), but does
not say what this would mean. It is

And both rejoicing spoke him on this wise:
'Whoever sees that comely form and beauty
Of yours, darling, truly shall never doubt,
But surely shall accept your braveries.'
    Indeed the young man had a comely stature,
And fair hair, curling a little, and large eyes,
A white and rosy face, a brow all black,
His breast like crystal was a fathom broad.
Looking on him his father was most glad,   1180
Spoke joyfully to him with great delight,
How that 'The heat is great, it is midday,
Now the beasts hide themselves within the marsh;
Come let us go aside to the cool water,
And you wash the much sweating from your face;
And you shall change your clothes, for they are soiled
With the beasts' foaming and the lion's blood.
Thrice blessed am I that I have such a son,
And I will wash your feet with my own hands.
Now will I cast all care from off my soul,   1190
That I be heedless where I send you out,
To many raids and posted enemies.'
    Forthwith they both went off towards the spring;
There was the water wondrous, cold as snow.
Sitting round, some began to wash his hands,
Others his face, likewise also his feet.
The spring ran over, thirstily they drank,
So that they too might become brave therefrom.
And afterwards the boy changed his clothing;
Thin singlets he put on to cool himself,   1200

better to compare AND 3715, and read here πτενὰ μαχλάμια. (Grégoire in his paper referred to in note on 47 above, dealing with the change of m to b, makes the same correction.) The ed. of AND in his gloss suggests a connexion of μαχλάμι with χλαμύς. But the real connexion is with Turkish mahramas, a veil, which appears in English in 'macramé' and in Greek may be found in Passow 474. 56; and turns up in Cacavelas, Siege of Vienna (ed. F. H. Marshall), in the form χραμάδα; and in Chios (Pyrghi) as χράμια—said to be 'coarse homewoven sheets of sheep's wool'. See Argenti and Rose, Folklore of Chios (1949), p. 892. Another word which seems to be involved in the confusion is μαγνάδι, a veil (?), AND 2987; Callim. and Chrys. 1878; SPE, p. 308, magnitom; ESC 1462 μαγδαΐτην; see Lampros, Romans grecs, gloss. s.v.; Meursius, s.v.;

τὸ μὲν ἐπάνω κόκκινον μὲ τὰς χρυσὰς τὰς ρίζας, 25 rᵒ.
αἱ δὲ ρίζαι του χυμευταὶ μετὰ μαργαριτάρων,
τὸν τράχηλόν του γεμιστὸν ἄβαρ ὁμοῦ καὶ μόσχον,
τρανὰ μαργαριτάρια εἶχεν ἀντὶ κομβίων,
τὰ δὲ θηλύκια στρεπτὰ ἐκ καθαροῦ χρυσίου, 225
τουβία ἐφόρει ἐξάκουστα, γρύψους ὡραϊσμένους,
τὰ πτερνιστήρια πλεκτὰ μετὰ λίθων τιμίων,
ἐπὶ τῶν ἔργων τῶν χρυσῶν εἶχε λυχνίτας λίθους.
Πάμπολλα δὲ ἐσπούδαζε τὸ εὐγενὲς παιδίον
εἰς τὴν μητέρα ἀπελθεῖν μὴ δι᾽ αὐτὸν λυπῆται, 230
καὶ ἠνάγκαζεν ἅπαντας εἰς τὸ καβαλλικεῦσαι.
Ἵππον ἐμετεσέλλισεν ἄσπρον ὡς περιστέριν,
πλεκτὸς ἦτον ὁ σγόρδος του μετὰ λίθων τιμίων,
καὶ κωδωνίτζια χρυσὰ μέσον τῶν λιθαρίων·
πάμπολλα κωδωνίτζια, καὶ ἦχος ἐτελεῖτο 235
ἐνήδονος καὶ θαυμαστός, πάντας ὑπερεκπλήττων·
πράσινον, ρόδινον βλαττὶν εἶχεν εἰς τὸ καποῦλιν,
καὶ τὴν σέλλαν ἐσκέπαζε νὰ μὴ κονιορτοῦται·
τὸ σελλοχάλινον πλεκτὸν μετὰ χρυσῶν σβερνίδων,
τὰ ὅλα ἔργα χυμευτὰ μετὰ μαργαριτάρων. 240
Ἦτον ὁ ἵππος τολμηρὸς καὶ θρασὺς εἰς τὸ παίζειν,
τὸ δὲ παιδίον εὔθιον εἰς τὸ καβαλλικεύειν·
πᾶς ὁ βλέπων ἐθαύμαζε τὸν ἄγουρον ἐκεῖνον,
πῶς μὲν ὁ ἵππος ἔπαιζε κατὰ γνώμην τοῦ νέου,
πῶς δὲ αὐτὸς ἐκάθητο ὥσπερ μῆλον εἰς δένδρον. 245
Καὶ ὥρμησαν τοῦ ἀπελθεῖν εἰς τὸν ἴδιον οἶκον·
οἱ μὲν ἄγουροι ἔμπροσθεν κατὰ τάξιν ὑπάγουν, 25 vᵒ.
ἀπ᾽ αὐτοῦ δὲ ὁ θεῖος του καὶ ὁ πατὴρ ὀπίσω,
καὶ μέσον ὁ νεώτερος, ὡς ἥλιος ἀστράπτων,

223 τὸ, au lieu de τὸν. 226 γρύψους. 233 ὁ σγόρδος του πλεκτὸς ἦτον
234 et 235 κοδονίτζια. 237 On est tenté d'écrire πρασινορρόδινον, mais cela
n'est pas absolument nécessaire.

Xanthoudides, *Erotok.*, gloss. s.v. μα-
γνιά. (Erotokr. B. 507) and Ducange,
s.v. μαγγάδι.
1201 ρίζας. See Ducange: ρίζαι videntur
dici limbi vestis seu orae inferiores.
1202 χυμευταί. No translation suits all
the passages in which this word
occurs. See below 1220.

1203 ἄβαρ. Either origanum or habroto-
num. But TRE 998 has ἄμπαρ which
is ambergris.
1213 σγόρδος also below 3014 (vi. 553)
σγοῦρδος, and in *Lyb. Rhod.* and
Achill., not in any of the dictionaries:
neither 'mane' nor 'tail' but 'forelock'.
1217 πράσινον, ρόδινον. Leg. πρασινορρό-

80

The upper one was red with golden hems,
And all the hems of it were fused with pearls,
The neck was filled with southernwood and musk,
And distinct pearls it had instead of buttons,
The buttonholes were twisted with pure gold;
He wore fine leggings with griffins embellished,
His spurs were plaited round with precious stones,
And on the gold work there were carbuncles.
But passing eager was the well-born child
To go to his mother lest she grieve for him,   1210
Began constraining everyone to horse;
Changed saddle to a horse white as a dove,
His forelock was plaited with precious stones,
And little golden bells among the stones;
So many little bells a noise was made
Delightful, wondrous, and amazing all.
A green and rosy silk was on his croup
Covered the saddle to keep the dust away;
Saddle and bridle plaited with gold tags
And all the handicraft studded with pearls.   1220
The horse was spirited and bold in play
And so the boy was quick in riding it.
Whoever saw him wondered at the youth,
How that the horse played at the youngster's will,
And he sat like an apple on a tree.
So hurried they to go off home again;
His young companions go in line ahead,
Then his uncle and his father after him,
The youth between them, flashing like the sun,

δινον, as in TRE 1012, and as suggested by Legrand.
1219 σβερνίδων. Meaning unknown.
AND 2258 has χρυσῶν σμυρίδων,
which ought to mean (see Soph. s.v.)
'golden emery-stones'. Possibly connected with mod. σβάρνα a harrow,
and hence 'studs' or 'pegs'.
1220 χυμευτής means either an alche-
mist or a jeweller-goldsmith; hence
χυμευτός means decorated with
precious stones or with gold; or in
a suitable context it might mean

enamelled, as the cloisonné enamels
of this period must have been the
work of a χυμευτής.
1222 The boy is called παιδίον, ἄγουρος,
νέος, and νεώτερος here and in the
next few lines; his companions or
palikars as usual ἄγουροι.
εὔθιον. Leg. εὔθειον. See above 638
1245.
1225 Cf. the ballad of *Hugh Spenser*
(version B, stanza 27, Child, p. 381):
He turn'd him in his saddle
Like an apple on a tree.

κοντάριν ἐμαλάκιζε μετὰ τὴν δεξιάν του   250
πρασινοαραβίτικον μετὰ χρυσοῦ διβέλλου.
'Ωραῖος ἦν εἰς ὅρασιν, τερπνὸς εἰς συντυχίαν,
μόσχος εἰς τὸ ἀνάβλεμμα ὅλος μεμυρισμένος.

*   *   *

Καὶ ὅτε ἔφθασαν ὁμοῦ καὶ εἰς τὸν οἶκον ἦλθον,   TRE 1028
κ' ἔφαγόν τε καὶ ἔπιον κ' ἔχαιρον καθ' ἑκάστην.
'Ο δὲ πατήρ του ἀμηρᾶς, ἐξ ἐκείνων τῶν χρόνων   1030
τῶν κύκλωθεν τοῦ οὐρανοῦ τρεχόντων δι' ἡλίου,
διῆγε μελετώμενος τὰς ὁδοὺς τοῦ Κυρίου,
καὶ καθ' ἑκάστην ἔχαιρε μετὰ καὶ τῆς συζύγου,
καὶ μετὰ τῶν υἱῶν αὐτοῦ καὶ μετὰ φίλων πάντων,
ἕως εἰς πύλας ἔφθασεν τοῦ γήραος ἐκεῖνος,   1035
ἐγκαταλείψας τῷ υἱῷ πάσας ἀνδραγαθίας.
  "Οτε δὲ ὁ εὐγενικὸς Διγενὴς ὁ ὡραῖος
αὐτὸς εἰς μέτρον ἔφθασεν τῆς αὐτοῦ ἡλικίας,
καὶ εἰς τοὺς ἄνδρας εὔθειος ἀνὴρ προσεγεγόνει,
τότ' ἐν μιᾷ τῶν ἡμερῶν πηδᾷ, καβαλλικεύει,   1040
ἀπῆρε τὸ κοντάριον καὶ τὴν ῥάβδον ἣν εἶχεν,
καὶ συναθροίσας τε λαὸν ἔλαβεν ἴδιόν του,
καὶ ὡς ἐκεῖ διήρχοντο τὴν στράταν μετὰ μόχθου,
δι' ἀπελάτων ἤκουσεν ἄγαν ἀνδρειωμένων,
ὅτι κρατοῦσι τὰ στενά, ποιοῦν ἀνδραγαθίας,   1045
καὶ ζῆλος ἦλθεν εἰς αὐτὸν τοῦ εἰδέναι ἐκείνους.
Καὶ μόνος ἀπερχόμενος νεροκάλαμον εὗρε
κ' εἶχε λέοντα φοβερὸν ἔνδον ἀποδαρμένον
'Ιωαννικίου ἐκ τῶν χειρῶν τοῦ θαυμαστοῦ ἐκείνου·
καί, ὡς εἶδε τὸν λέοντα ὁ Διγενὴς Ἀκρίτης,   1050
ἐκ βάθους ἀναστέναξε ψυχῆς, καὶ εἶπεν οὕτως·
  " Πότε ἰδῆτε, ὀφθαλμοί, τοὺς ἀνδρείους ἐκείνους; "   (F. 30)

1036 ἀνδραγαθείας.   1038 ἔφθανσε.   1044 ἀνδρειομένων.   1052 ἰδεῖτε.

1230 ἐμαλάκιζε. See gloss. Xanth.,
  Erotokr.; gloss. Lib. Rod.
1231 διβέλλου. See Ducange and
  Meursius s.v.
1233 There is a lacuna after this line
  in GRO, which passes straight from
  the Hunting to the Courtship. The
  omission is here supplied from TRE
  1028–1108. (See also AND 1566–

1673, part of which can be used to
fill a lacuna after TRE 1078.) This
part of TRE is very perfunctory. It
seems possible that the archetype
of all three versions had a lacuna
between the Hunting and the Courtship, and that the interposed passages of TRE and AND are copyists'
attempts to fill the gap. The original

In his right hand was brandishing a spear   1230
Arabian, green, with a pennon of gold.
Lovely he was to see, in converse sweet,
Musk in his gaze, of fragrance all compact.

*   *   *

And when they came together to the house
They ate and drank and day by day rejoiced.
His father the Emir from those times forth
That with the sun went circling round the sky
Lived meditating the ways of the Lord,
And every day in gladness with his wife,
Together with his son and all his friends,   1240
Until he reached the gateways of old age,
Having left all feats of bravery to his son.
And when the well-born Digenes the fair
Himself came to the measure of his prime
And among men was counted a right man;
Then on a day he sprang to horse and rode,
Took up the spear and took the club he had,
Gathered his company and took them with him.
And as they went with toil along the way
He heard tell about reivers passing brave   1250
That hold the narrows and do braveries,
And envy came on him to know the men.
So going off alone he found a reed-bed;
In it there was a dreadful lion, flayed
By the hands of the wondrous Iôannikios.
Digenes the Borderer, when he saw the lion,
Sighed from the bottom of his soul, and said:
'O eyes of mine, when shall you see those braves?'

cause of the lacuna was probably the similarity of the lines about the Way Home with which the Hunting ends and the Courtship begins (cf. TRE 1108 with TRE 1020). The unfilled lacuna in GRO is perhaps another mark of its earliness.

1240 μετὰ τῶν υἱῶν. Leg. from AND 1572 μετὰ τοῦ υἱοῦ.

1245 εὔθειος. See above 631, 1222; also TRE 2077; AND 1577. For the medieval formation from εὐθύς see Hatzidakis, Μεσ. καὶ Νέα Ἑλληνικά ii. 12 (but that does not explain the accent). The ed. of AND in his glossary alone notices that some explanation is required, but does not give any.

1253 νεροκάλαμον, i.e. a 'reed-and-water'.

Τὸν ὑδροφόρον εὗρηκε τῶν ἀπελάτων τότε,
καὶ ἀνηρώτησεν αὐτὸν διὰ τοὺς ἀπελάτας·
ὁ ὑδροφόρος παρευθὺς τὸν Διγενὴν ἐλάλει·   1055
" Τί τοὺς θέλεις, νεώτερε καλέ, τοὺς ἀπελάτας; "
Ἐκεῖνος ἀπεκρίθηκε πάλιν τὸν ὑδροφόρον·
" Ζητῶ κ' ἐγὼ νὰ γένωμαι ὡς εἷς τῶν ἀπελάτων."
Καὶ τότ' ἐκεῖνος ἔλαβε τὸν Διγενῆ, καὶ ἦλθον
'ς τὸ λησταρχεῖον ἔνδοθεν τὸ φοβερὸν καὶ ξένον.   1060
Καὶ εὗρε τὸν Φιλόπαππον ὅτ' ἔκειτο εἰς κλίνην,
πολλῶν θηρίων δέρματα εἶχεν ἀπάνω κάτω·
καὶ κύψας ὁ νεώτερος Βασίλειος Ἀκρίτης
προσεκυνήσατο αὐτὸν καὶ ἐχαιρέτησέ τον.
Καὶ ὁ γέρων Φιλόπαππος οὕτως τὸν ἀπεκρίθη·   1065
" Καλῶς ἦλθες, νεώτερε, ἂν οὐκ ἔσῃ προδότης."
Καὶ τότε ὁ Βασίλειος οὕτως ἀνταπεκρίθη·
" Προδότης ἐγὼ δέν εἶμαι, ἀλλὰ ζητῶ γενέσθαι
ἄρτι ἐν τῇδε τῇ μονῇ μεθ' ὑμῶν ἀπελάτης."
Ὁ γέρων δὲ ὡς ἤκουσεν, οὕτως ἀπηλογήθη·   1070
" Ἂν καυχᾶσαι, νεώτερε, ἔσεσθαι ἀπελάτης,
τὴν ῥάβδον ταύτην ἔπαρον καὶ κάτελθε εἰς βίγλαν·
καὶ ἂν νηστεῦσαι δύνασαι ἡμέρας δεκαπέντε,
μηδ' ὕπνον εἰς τὰ βλέφαρα λάβῃς τῶν ὀφθαλμῶν σου,
καὶ μετὰ ταῦτα ἀπελθὼν τοὺς λέοντας ἂν κτείνῃς,   1075
καὶ πάντων τὰ δερμάτια ἂν φέρῃς ὧδε πάντα,
καὶ πάλιν ἐὰν δύνασαι εἰς βίγλαν καταβῆναι,
ὅταν περνοῦν οἱ ἄρχοντες μετὰ πολλοῦ τοῦ πλήθους . . .

*   *   *

ἔχοντας νύμφην καὶ γαμβρὸν νὰ ἔμπῃς εἰς τὸ μέσον,   AND 1617
νὰ πάρῃς τὴν νεόνυμφον ἐδῶ νὰ τὴν ἐφέρῃς,   1619
τότε πληροφορήθητι νὰ γίνῃς ἀπελάτης."   1620
Ὁ Διγενής, ὡς ἤκουσεν, οὕτως τὸν ἀπεκρίθη

1057 ἀπεκρίθικε.   1065 φιλόπαππούς.   1076 φέρεις.   1078 Après
πλήθους, le ms. ajoute λοίπη (λείπει). Il y a en effet ici une lacune considérable.
1617-43 Λείπουν ἐν χειρ. Τρ.   1619 Ὁ στίχος περιττεύει.

1268 ἀπάνω κάτω. This might just mean   'all over the place'. As a modern
'under and over' him, i.e. that he   colloquialism ἀπάνω κάτω means
was lying on skins and covered by   'more or less, approximately', while
skins. But it more probably means   ἄνω κάτω means 'upside down, in

Then he met with the reivers' water-carrier,
And he did question him about the reivers.　　　　　1260
The water-carrier said to Digenes:
'What would you with the reivers, good young man?'
He answered the water-bearer again:
'I too want to be as one of the reivers.'
Then he took Digenes and so they came
Into the robbers' den dreadful and strange.
He found Philopappos lying on a couch,
And skins of many beasts were all about.
And bowing down the young Basil Akrites
Made reverence to him and greeted him.　　　　　1270
Old Philopappos then thus answered him:
'Welcome, young man, if you'll not be a traitor.'
And then Basil made answer thus again:
'I am no traitor, but I want to be
Presently in this camp with you a reiver.'
The old man when he heard thus answer made:
'If you boast, young man, you will be a reiver,
Then take this cudgel and go down on guard.
And if you can go fasting fifteen days,
And sleep not close the eyelids of your eyes,　　　　1280
And after that go off and kill the lions,
If you bring here the skins of all of them,
And if you can go down on guard again,
When princes with great company go by,

*　　　*　　　*

With bride and groom, if you can go among them,
And take the new-made bride, and bring her here,
Then, to be sure, you may become a reiver.'
Digenes, when he heard, thus answered him:

disorder'.

1272 Note οὐκ ἔσῃ followed by 1274 δέν εἶμαι.

1275 ἐν τῆδε τῇ μονῇ. Wrongly translated by Legrand 'dans cette solitude'. Of course μονῇ here means a stopping-place or camp, as above 725.

1278 εἰς βίγλαν. Either 'on guard' or 'to the look-out'.

1284 There is a lacuna after this line (TRE 1078) which has to be filled by the corresponding passage in ANDROS (1617–43). But AND 1618, 1619 are alternative lines, one of which, 1618 for choice, has to be dropped.

" Ταῦτα, ὦ γέρον, μὴ λαλῇς, μικρὸν γὰρ τὸ ἐποίουν,
μόνον τοιούτως λέγω σοι, Φιλόπαππε, ἀνδρεῖε,
λαγὼν εἰς τὸν ἀνήφορον τρίτον νὰ τὸν πιάσω,
τὴν χαμοπετοῦσαν πέρδικα ν᾽ ἁπλώσω νὰ τὴν λάβω." 1625
Καὶ τότες ὁ Φιλόπαππος τοῖς ἀπελάταις εἶπεν   Σ. 129
ἔφεραν ἀργυρὸν σελλὶν καὶ κάθισεν ὁ Ἀκρίτης,
τράπεζαν ἔθεντο αὐτῷ ἔμπροσθεν θαυμασίαν,
ἔφαγον δὲ καὶ ἔπιον ἅπαντες χαριέντως,
καὶ μετὰ ταῦτα ἔλεγον ἕκαστος ἐξ ἐκείνων   1630
ὅτι δύνανται πολεμεῖν πολλοὺς ἐκ τῶν ἀνδρείων.
Ἀκούσας δ᾽ ὁ Φιλόπαππος εἶπε πρὸς τὸν Ἀκρίτην·
" Σὺ δέ, καλὲ νεώτερε, πόσους δύνασαι κρούειν; "
Ὁ δὲ Βασίλειος εὐθὺς οὕτως ἀπηλογήθη·
" Ἐλάτε, ἀγοῦροι, νὰ πάρωμεν ὑπόκοντα ραβδία,   1635
καὶ πορευθῶμεν ἄπωθεν 'ς τὴν ὁμαλίαν πάντες,
καὶ κάθε εἷς νὰ δώσωμεν ραβδέας ὑπ᾽ ἀλλήλων,
καὶ εἴ τις νικήσει τὸν ἕτερον ἂς πάρῃ τὸ ραβδί του."
Τότε ἐκεῖνοι ἔλαβον ὑπόκοντα ραβδία,   Σ. 130
ὁ Κίνναμος ὁ θαυμαστὸς μετὰ Ἰωαννικίου,   1640
καὶ σὺν αὐτοῖς ὁ Διγενὴς μετὰ καὶ ἄλλων πλείστων,
καὶ ὅλοι ἐπορεύθησαν κάτω 'ς τὴν ὁμαλίαν,
καὶ ἔδιδον εἰς ἕκαστος τὸν ἕτερον ραβδέας.

*   *   *

Καὶ τότε ὁ Βασίλειος ὁ Διγενὴς ἐκεῖνος   TRE 1079
ἐπῆρε τὸ ραβδίον του καὶ εἰς τὸ μέσον ἦλθεν,   1080
τοὺς μὲν ραβδέας ἔκρουε, τοὺς δ᾽ ἄλλους σφονδυλέας,
καὶ πάντων ὑπελύθησαν αἱ χεῖρες τῶν ἀνδρείων·
καὶ ἐπάρας ὁ Διγενὴς ἐκείνων τὰ ραβδία,
ἔφθασε πρὸς τὸν γέροντα λέγων αὐτῷ τοιαῦτα·
" Δέξαι ραβδιά, Φιλόπαππε, πάντων τῶν ἀπελάτων (F. 31) 1085
καὶ ἂν οὐδὲν ἀρέσῃ σοι καὶ σοὶ τὸ θέλω ποίσειν! "
Ταῦτα οὖν ὁ θαυμάσιος Ἀκρίτης ἐκτελέσας,
ὑπέστρεψε πρὸς τὴν ὁδὸν ἔνθα ἦν ὁ λαός του,

1079 διγενεῖς.   1081 ραβδαίας. σφονδηλαίας.   1085 ραβδαίαν φιλόπαππου.
1086 ἀρέσει.

─────────────

1291 τρίτον seems to be pointless. Read   1302 ὑπόκοντα ραβδία. I am not sure
τρέχοντα. See additional note p. 141.   what 'quarterstaffs' are, but they

'Talk not of that, old man, I did it as a child;
Only I tell you, brave Philopappos, thus: 1290
A hare running uphill and I will catch it,
Or stretch and snatch a partridge flying low.'
   Thereupon Philopappos told the reivers,
They brought a silver chair, Akrites sat,
They spread a wondrous table there before him,
And all with courtesy they ate and drank,
Thereafter each of them began to say
That they could fight with many of the brave.
And hearing Philopappos asked Akrites:
'And you, good youth, how many can you knock?'   1300
And straightway Basil answered on this wise:
'Come along, boys, let us take quarterstaffs
And let us all go off into the plain,
And each of us give stick-play with the rest,
Whoever beats a man shall take his staff.'
Thereupon they did take their quarterstaffs
The wondrous Kinnamos with Iôannikios,
And with them Digenes and many others,
And all of them went down onto the level
And there began to give each other stick-play.   1310

                    *   *   *

And thereupon that Basil Digenes   1310a
Took up his staff and came into the midst
Some with his staff smote others with his fists
And soon of all those braves the hands were loosed.
Digenes taking up the staffs of them
Came to the old man saying to him thus:
'Take the staffs, Philopappos, of all your reivers;
If it displease, I'll do the same to you.'
   This then performed, the wondrous Borderer
Returned to the road where his people were,

seem to fit in here: except that a
quarterstaff according to *O.E.D.* was
6–8 feet long. These ῥαβδία must
have been more like singlesticks.
1312 ῥαβδέας . . . σφονδυλέας, blows
with stick or fist.
1313 ὑπελύθησαν αἱ χεῖρες. Seems to be a
reminiscence of the Homeric ὑπέλυντο
δὲ γυῖα.

καὶ μετὰ ταῦτα ἦλθοσαν πάντες εἰς τὰ οἰκεῖα.
Ἔχαιρε δὲ ὁ Διγενὴς ἐν πάσαις ταῖς ἡμέραις 1090
ὁ θαυμαστὸς Βασίλειος, ἡ δόξα τῶν ἀνδρείων,
καὶ πάντες ἔφριττον αὐτὸν ἐκ τῶν αὐτοῦ πολέμων.

* * *

Λοιπὸν πάλιν, ὦ φίλτατε, προσλέξω σοι καὶ ταῦτα, TRE V 1100
ὅτ' ἐν ἐκείνῳ τῷ καιρῷ ὁ Δούκας ὁ ὡραῖος,
ὁ στρατηγὸς ὁ θαυμαστὸς μέρους τῆς Ῥωμανίας,
εἶχε κόρην πανεύμορφον κλημένην Εὐδοκίαν,
ἧς πάντοτε τὸ ὄνομα ἤκουεν ὁ Ἀκρίτης,
εἶχε γὰρ κάλλος ἄπειρον, παράδοξον τὸ γένος. 1105
Καὶ ἐν μιᾷ τῶν ἡμερῶν πηδᾷ, καβαλλικεύει,
ὑπῆρε τοὺς ἀγούρους του, ὑπάγει εἰς κυνῆγιν.
Ἀφοῦ δὲ ἐκυνήγησαν, ἤρχοντο εἰς τὸν οἶκον.

* * *

Οἶκος ὑπῆρχε καθ' ὁδὸν στρατηγοῦ τοῦ μεγάλου, GRO IV 254
καὶ πλησιάσαντος αὐτοῦ ἀναφώνημα εἶπε· 255
" Ἄγουρος ὅταν ἀγαπᾷ κόρην ὡραιοτάτην,
ὅταν ἐκεῖ ἀπέρχεται καὶ βλέπει της τὰ κάλλη,
δαμάζεται ἡ καρδίτζα του, οὐ θέλει ζῆν εἰς κόσμον."
Τῆς ἡδονῆς ὡς ἤκουσαν τῷ οἴκῳ οἱ παρόντες,
ἐξέστησαν ὥσπερ ποτὲ ὁ Ὀδυσσεὺς ἐκεῖνος, 260
ὅτε τὸ μέλος ἤκουε Σειρήνων ἐν τῷ πλοίῳ.
Ἀλλ' οὐδ' ἡ κόρη ἔμεινεν ἀνήκοος τοῦ νέου
πάγκαλος ἡ διάφημος ἡ ἀκουστὴ ἐκείνη,
ἧς τὸ κάλλος ἀμήχανον, παράδοξον τὸ γένος,
οὐσίαν τε καὶ κτήματα καὶ ἑτέραν πλουσίαν 265
ἀδύνατον ἀπαριθμεῖν ἢ ἀπεικάζειν ὅλως.
Μόνον γὰρ οἶκον τὸν αὐτῆς οὐδεὶς ἐγκωμιάσει·
ἅπας γὰρ χρυσομάρμαρος, ὅλος μεμουσιωμένος·

1090 πάσαι.   1108 ἐκινήγισαν.   263 πάγκαλος.

1320 εἰς τὰ οἰκεῖα. For this use of the neuter plural see Lampros, *Romans grecs*, gloss. s.v. γονικός, and below (3173).
1323 After this line, the last of TRE Book IV, we omit TRE 1093-9 (which are not part of the narrative but only the introductory argument to Book V) and carry on with the begin-

ning of Book V, TRE 1100 to 1108.
1329 παράδοξον τὸ γένος. This use of παράδοξος 'famous' in place of the meaning of 'unexpected' (παρὰ δόξαν) arose by confusion with περίδοξος.
1331 Leg. ἐπῆρε.
1332 After TRE 1108 we return to GRO iv. 254.
1335-7 Seems to be the incorporation

And after that they all came to their homes.   1320
So Digenes rejoiced in all his days,
The wondrous Basil, glory of the brave,
And all trembled before him after his fights.

*   *   *

So then this also will I tell you, dearest,
How that at that same time the handsome Doukas,
Wondrous general of part of Romania,
Had a most lovely girl called Evdokia,
Whose name the Borderer was always hearing,
Boundless her beauty, glorious her descent.
   So on a day he leapt to horse and rode,   1330
And took his boys and went off to the chase.
And when the chase was done, they made for home.

*   *   *

The great general's house was on the road;
When they came near to it he gave a call:
'When a boy loves a very lovely girl,
And there he passes by and sees her beauties,
His heart is tamed, he would not live on earth.'
Those in the house when the sweet sound they heard
They were amazed as once was that Odysseus
When in his ship he heard the Sirens' song.   1340
Nor of the youth unhearing stayed the Girl,
All-beautiful, renowned, herself far-heard,
Her beauty priceless, glorious her descent,
Whose substance, and possessions, all her wealth
Impossible to count or quite imagine.
Only her dwelling none can celebrate;
All gold and marble was it, all mosaicked;

of a folk-song (see e.g. καρδίτζα)
which TRE 1112 ff. comically translates into more dignified Greek. TRE
also inserts a negative in 1113.
1338 ἡδονῆς. For this use of ἡδονή—'a
pleasant sound'—see ESC 1151,
2119; Lyb. Rod. (Scalig.) 1046; and
below 1515, 3471, 2501. There was
possibly some confusion with ἀηδόνι.
1340 TRE 1117 has μέλη σειρήνια, but
omits any reference to Odysseus.

1341 ἡ Κόρη. From this point onwards she is always referred to as
Korè, the Gilr par excellence. Her name
Evdokia (above TRE 1103) does not
occur in GRO. I am prepared to
defend 'the Girl' as on the whole the
best translation of KOPH with its
innumerable connotations ancient
and modern.
1346 μόνον, i.e. 'even her dwelling
alone'.

τὸ μοναχὸν κουβούκλιον ἔνθα ἦτον ἡ κόρη
ἀπέξωθεν ὁλόχρυσον, ὅλον μεμουσιωμένον, 270
ὃ καὶ ἐπωνομάζετο τῆς κόρης τὸ κουβοῦκλιν.
Αὕτη τοίνυν ἡ πάμπλουτος καὶ πανωραία κόρη,
ὡς εἶδε τὸν νεώτερον, καθὼς ἐκδιηγούμαι, 26 rº.
ἐφλέχθη ἡ καρδίτζα της, οὐ θέλει ζῆν εἰς κόσμον·
πόνος ἀνήφθη εἰς αὐτήν, ὡς τὸ δίκαιον ἔχει, 275
οὗ γὰρ κάλλος ὀξύτατον καὶ τὸ βέλος τιτρώσκει·
καὶ δι᾽ αὐτῶν τῶν ὀφθαλμῶν εἰς ψυχὴν ἐπανήκει·
ἤθελε μὲν τοὺς ὀφθαλμοὺς ἐκ τοῦ νέου ἀπᾶραι,
ἀλλὰ πάλιν οὐκ ἤθελε τοῦ κάλλους χωρισθῆναι,
ἀλλὰ εἷλκεν αὐτοὺς ἐκεῖ προδήλως ἡττηθέντας· 280
καὶ πρὸς τὴν βάγιαν ἔλεγε γαληνὰ εἰς τὸ ὠτίον·
" Παράκυψαι, βαγίτζα μου, ἴδε ἔμνοστον νέον,
ἴδε κάλλος πανθαύμαστον καὶ ξένην ἡλικίαν·
ἂν ἤθελεν ὁ κύρης μου γαμβρὸν νὰ τὸν ἐπῆρε,
νὰ εἶχε, πίστευσον, γαμβρὸν οἷον ἄλλος οὐκ ἔχει." 285
Ἀπέμεινε δὲ βλέπουσα ἐκ τῆς ὀπῆς τὸν παῖδα·
ὁ δὲ νέος ἠρώτησεν ἀληθῶς μὴ γινώσκων·
" ὁ οἶκος οὗτος τίνος ἐστὶν ὁ φοβερὸς καὶ μέγας;
μὴ οὗτος ἔνι τοῦ στρατηγοῦ τοῦ ἀκουστοῦ ὃν λέγουν;
καὶ ἡ κόρη ἡ πανεύφημος ἐνταῦθα καταμένει; " 290
" Ναί, τέκνον μου γλυκύτατον, " ὁ πατὴρ ἀπεκρίθη,
" δι᾽ ἧς πολλοὶ ἀπώλοντο τῶν εὐγενῶν Ῥωμαίων."
" Καὶ πῶς, πάτερ, ἀπώλοντο; " αὖθις ὁ παῖς ἠρώτα.
" Ἠβουλήθησαν, τέκνον μου, τὴν κόρην ἀφαρπάσαι
διὰ τὰ κάλλη τὰ τερπνὰ ἅπερ ἔχει, ὡς λέγουν· 295
καὶ τούτους γνοὺς ὁ στρατηγός, τῆς κόρης ὁ γεννήτωρ,
ἐγκρύμματα ἐποίησε καὶ ἐκράτησε πάντας,

278 ἐπάραι.   280 ἀλλ᾽.   284 κύρις.   288 ἔνι, au lieu de ἐστίν.
On pourrait aussi construire ce vers de la sorte: τίνος ἔνι ὁ φοβερὸς οἶκος οὗτος
καὶ μέγας. Mais nous préférons la correction ἐστίν, forme qui n'est pas rare dans
cette épopée.   293 ἀπώλλοντο.   297 ἐγκρίμματα.

1353 οὐ θέλει ζῆν εἰς κόσμον. Repeated
from above 1337.
1355 οὐ γὰρ κάλλος. Leg. τὸ γὰρ κάλλος
TRE 1128, cf. AND 1691.
1356 See the well-known folk-song
Passow 528, and Polites, Ἐκλογαί 93.
In a poem attributed to Const.
Manasses, who wrote in the first half

of the twelfth century, and was much
influenced by the popular language,
occur these lines: τὸ κάλλος γὰρ
ὀξύτερον τιτρώσκει καὶ βελέμνου καὶ
δι᾽ ὀμμάτων εἰς ψυχὴν ἐπιρριζοῦν
εἰσρέει. (Poème moral de Const.
Manassès, ed. Emm. Miller in Ann.
de l'Ass. d'Ét. gr., 1875, line 488). It

The separate chamber where the maiden was,
All gold without and was all mosaicked,
The which also was called the Maiden's Chamber.   1350
    And so this wealthy and all-lovely Girl,
When that she saw the youth, as I am telling,
Her heart was fired, she would not live on earth;
Pain kindled in her, as is natural;
Beauty is very sharp, its arrow wounds,
And through the very eyes reaches the soul.
She wanted from the youth to lift her eyes,
Yet wanting not from beauty to be parted,
Plainly defeated drew them there again;
And said to her Nurse quietly in her ear: 1360
'Look out, dear Nurse, and see a sweet young man,
Look at his wondrous beauty and strange stature.
If but my lord took him for son-in-law
He would have, believe me, one like no one else.'
So she stayed watching the boy from the opening.
And the youth asked and not knowing in truth:
'Whose is the house this awful house and great?
Is this the General's whose renown they tell?
And here abides the Girl so widely famed?'
'Yes, my sweet child,' his father answered him,   1370
'For whom have perished many noble Romans.'
'How perished, father?' asked the boy again.
'They planned, my child, to carry off the Girl,
For the sweet beauties, as they say, are hers.
Knowing of them the General, her sire,
Made ambuscades for them, and took them all;

is remarkable that this folk-song should have found its way into all three versions of Digenes (AND 1692, TRE 1128) as well as into the poem of Const. Manasses. It may have come originally from Heliodorus, *Aethiop.* iii. 7 τῶν ἐρώτων γένεσις . . . διὰ τῶν ὀφθαλμῶν τὰ πάθη ταῖς ψυχαῖς εἰστοξεύονται. And also from Ach. Tat. i. 4.

1361 ἔμνοστον νέον. See above 1173. ἔμνοστος was the medieval form of εὔνοστος and disappeared after trans-

ferring its meaning to the modern νόστιμος. See below 3284 πανεύμνοστος.

1365 Ἀπέμεινε, i.e. she stayed as long as she wanted to. For the force of ἀπό see below 3239 ἀποπλύσασα; and see A. Mirambel, 'The Determinate Aspect in Mod. Greek', in *The Link*, No. 1, June 1938.

1366 In TRE 1140, which from this point again diverges considerably, Digenes only pretends not to know whose house it is.

τοὺς μὲν ἀπεκεφάλισεν, τοὺς δὲ τυφλοὺς ἐποίησεν·
ἔχει γὰρ δύναμιν πολλὴν καὶ δόξαν εἰς τὴν χώραν."   26 vᵒ.

Στενάξας δὲ ὁ Διγενὴς ἔφη πρὸς τὸν πατέρα·   300
" Εὔχου, πάτερ, μὴ δόξῃ με ἵνα την ἀφαρπάσω,
ὅτι ἐμὲ ἐγκρύμματα ποτὲ οὐ θορυβοῦσι·
τοῦτο δὲ μόνον εὔχομαι, εἴπερ ἀποδεκτόν σοι,
νὰ μηνύσῃς τὸν στρατηγὸν διὰ συμπενθερίαν·
καὶ εἰ μὲν ἴσως ἀρεσθῇ γαμβρὸν νά με ἐπάρῃ,   305
ἵνα τὸν ἔχω πενθερὸν τῇ ἰδίᾳ του γνώμῃ·
εἰ δὲ μή, γνώσῃ, πάτερ μου, μετὰ ταῦτα τὸ τέλος."
" Πολλάκις τον ἐμήνυσα, γλυκύτατε υἱέ μου,
ἀλλ' οὐδὲ ὅλως πείθεται εἰς τοῦτο κατανεῦσαι."
'Ως δὲ τοιαῦτα ὁ πατὴρ ἔλεγε πρὸς τὸν παῖδα,   310
ἐσκέφθη ὁ νεώτερος ἐκ τῆς ὀπῆς τὴν κόρην·
καὶ ταύτην θεασάμενος ἐμπρὸς οὐ βηματίζει,
ἀλλ' εἶχεν ἔκπληξις αὐτὸν καὶ τρόμος τὴν καρδίαν·
τὸν βοῦλχαν ἐπελάλησε, πλησιάζει τῇ κόρῃ,
καὶ πρὸς αὐτὴν ἠρέμα τε λόγον εἶπε τοιόνδε·   315
" Γνώρισόν μοι, κοράσιον, ἔχεις με εἰς νοῦν σου,
καὶ εἰ ποθεῖς κατὰ πολὺ τοῦ λαβεῖν σε γυναῖκα·
εἰ δ' ἀλλαχοῦ τὸν νοῦν ἔχεις, πολλὰ οὐ παρακαλῶ σε."
Τὴν βάγιαν δὲ παρακαλεῖ τὴν ἑαυτῆς ἡ κόρη·
" Κατάβα, βάγια μου καλή, εἰπὲ τὸν ἀγουρίτζην·   320
τὸν Θεόν σε πληροφορῶ εἰς τὴν ψυχήν μου ἐσέβης·
ἀλλ' οὐκ οἶδα, νεώτερε, ποίου γένους τυγχάνεις·
εἰ μὲν εἶ σὺ Βασίλειος ὁ Διγενὴς Ἀκρίτης,
ὑπάρχεις μὲν τῶν εὐγενῶν καὶ τῶν πλουσιωτάτων
καὶ συγγενὴς ἡμέτερος ὡς ἀπὸ τῶν Δουκάδων·   27 rᵒ.   325
ἀλλ' ὁ πατήρ μου ὁ στρατηγὸς διὰ σὲ βίγλας ἔχει,
ἤκουσε γὰρ κατὰ πολὺ τὰς σὰς ἀνδραγαθίας·
καὶ φυλάττου, νεώτερε, δι' ἐμοῦ κινδυνεύσῃς

---

298 Il faut prononcer ἐποίησεν comme si ce mot était accentué ἐποιῆσεν.
316 Au lieu de εἰ, le ms. donne εἰς.   318 On peut écrire εἰ δ' ἔχεις τὸν νοῦν
ἀλλαχοῦ, ou considérer ἔχεις comme enclitique, ce qu'il est quelquefois en
pareil cas.   320 ἀγουρίτζιν.   321 ἐσέβεις.

1383 συμπενθερίαν. The relation between the parents of the bridegroom
and the parents of the bride; the
connexion of two families by marriage—a word which appears in
many forms in modern Greek and is
still in common use. See Ducange.
See below 1939.

Some of them he beheaded, some made blind;
He has much power and glory in the land.'
Then Digenes sighing said to his father:
'Pray, father, I think not to take her off,   1380
For ambuscades do never frighten me;
Only I pray you, if acceptable,
Advise the General for intermarriage,
If he might please take me for son-in-law,
And be my father-in-law of his own will;
If not, father, he shall know the end hereafter.'
'Often have I told him, my sweetest son,
Never is he persuaded to agree.'
Even as the father spoke thus to his son,
The youth through the embrasure saw the Girl,   1390
And gazing on her, forward made no step,
Amazement took him, trembling took his heart;
He urged his charger, drew near to the Girl,
And to her quietly spoke words like these:
'Acquaint me, maid, if you have me in mind,
If you much wish I should take you for wife;
If elsewhere be your mind, I'll not entreat you.'
And the Girl thereon did entreat her nurse,
'Go down, good nurse, and say you to the boy,
"Be sure, God's name, you are come into my soul;   1400
But I know not your family, young man.
If you are Basil, Twyborn, Borderer,
You are of well-born and most wealthy people,
Our kinsman too, sprung from the Doukases.
But father the General sets watch for you,
For he has heard much of your braveries.
Take care, young man, nor risk yourself for me,

1385 γνώμη here means 'will'.
1393 τὸν βούλχαν. Strange word for a horse (below 1455, 3013); probably a dialectic variation of βρόχα common in TRE. See Ducange, s.v. βουρίχος. Legrand (TRE gloss., p. 287) also refers to French *bourrique* and Latin *burichus* (Ducange, *Med. Inf. Latin.*).
1395 Read εἰ ἔχεις με from TRE 1169.
1400 τὸν θεὸν σὲ πληροφορῶ hardly

makes sense. TRE 1175 reads θεὸς πληροφορήσει σε. Cf. AND 1736.
1406 κατὰ πολύ, 'much' or 'often'. In the following lines, and generally, I have kept as far as possible one conventional meaning for each word: ἀγάπη, 'love'; πόθος, 'desire'; ψυχή, 'soul'; καρδία, καρδίτζα, 'heart'; ἔρως, 'passion'; φιλία, 'love, affection', &c.

καὶ στερηθῇς νεότητος τῆς πανωραιοτάτης·
οὐδ᾽ ὅλως γάρ σου φείσεται ὁ ἄσπλαγχνος πατήρ μου." 330
Καὶ αὖθις ὁ νεώτερος πρὸς τὴν κόρην ἀντέφη·
" Παράκυψον, ὀμμάτια μου, ἃς ἴδω σου τὸ κάλλος,
ἃς ἔμβῃ εἰς τὴν καρδίτζαν μου ἡ ἀπειρός σου ἀγάπη·
εἰμὶ γὰρ νέος, ὡς ὁρᾷς· οὐκ οἶδα τί ἔνι ὁ πόθος·
οὔτε γινώσκω κἂν ποσῶς τὰς ὁδοὺς τῆς ἀγάπης, 335
καὶ εἰ μὲν εἰσέλθῃ ὁ πόθος σου εἰς τὴν ψυχήν μου ἀπέσω,
ὁ πατήρ σου ὁ στρατηγὸς καὶ τὸ συγγενικόν του
καὶ ἅπαντες οἱ μετ᾽ αὐτοῦ, ἐὰν γένωνται βέλη
καὶ ξίφη ἀπαστράπτοντα, οὐ δύνανταί με βλάψαι."
Καὶ ἦν ἰδεῖν οὐδέποτε τέλος ἐκείνων λόγοις· 340
ἔρως τότε παρώξυνεν ἄσεμνον διαπρᾶξαι,
δουλοῖ γὰρ τὰ φρονήματα ἔρως ὡς ὢν δεσπότης,
ὑποτάσσει τὸν λογισμὸν ὡς ἡνίοχος ἵππον·
καὶ διὰ τοῦτο ὁ ποθῶν εὐταξίαν οὐκ ἔχει,
οὐ συγγενεῖς αἰσχύνεται, οὐ γείτονας πτοεῖται, 345
ἀλλ᾽ ἔστιν ὅλως ἀναιδὴς δοῦλος ὢν τῆς φιλίας,
ὥσπερ καὶ ἡ πανεύγενος κόρη πέπονθε τότε,
καὶ παρέκυψε μερικῶς ἐκ τὴν χρυσῆν θυρίδα·
τὰ κάλλη τοῦ προσώπου της κωλύουν τοὺς ὀφθαλμούς του
καὶ οὐ δύναται καλῶς ἰδεῖν τὴν ἡλιογεννημένην· 350
ὡς γὰρ ἀκτὶς ἀνέτειλεν ἐν μέσῳ τοῦ προσώπου,
ἦν γὰρ ἡ κόρη ἀληθῶς ὥσπερ ἱστορισμένη· 27 vº.
ὄμμα γοργὸν ἐνήδονον, κόμην ξανθὴν καὶ σγοῦρον,
ὀφρὺν εἶχε κατάμαυρον, ἄκρατον δὲ τὸ μέλαν,
ὡς χιόνα τὸ πρόσωπον, μέσον δὲ βεβαμμένον, 355
οἷα πορφύρα ἐκλεκτὴ ἦν βασιλεῖς τιμῶσι.
Οὕτως ἰδὼν ὁ θαυμαστὸς ἐκεῖνος νεανίας,
εὐθὺς ἐτρώθη τὴν ψυχήν, ἐπλήγη τὴν καρδίαν,
καὶ πόνον εἶχεν ἄπειρον, ἀδημονῶν εἱστήκει.
Κόρη δὲ ἡ πανεύγενος, οὕτως αὐτὸν ἰδοῦσα, 360
οὐ παρεῖδε κατὰ πολὺ τῷ ἄλγει ἐπιμένειν,
ἀλλὰ ταχέως ἔστειλε πρὸς αὐτὸν τὴν ἀγάπην
πολλῆς χαρᾶς ἀνάπλεων, ἡδονῆς μεμιγμένην,

332 ὀμμάτιά.   343 ἡνίοχος.

1411 ὀμμάτια μου—'my eyes'—here   1416 τὸ συγγενικόν του. See above 1320,
translated 'light'—the commonest of   below 1532.
modern Greek endearments.   1427 ἐκ with accusative, below 1621.

94

And be cut off from your all-lovely youth.
My ruthless father surely will not spare you. " '
Again the young man answered to the Girl: 1410
'Look out, my light, and let me see your beauty,
And let your boundless love enter my heart;
For I am young, you see; know not desire,
Nor recognize at all the ways of love;
But if desire for you come into my soul,
The General your father, and his kinsmen,
And all his company, if they turn to arrows
And lightning-flashing swords, can never hurt me.'
    So never was there end of talk for them.
Passion was urging to some wanton deed,   1420
For Passion, as being master, enslaves the mind,
As charioteer the horse, subdues the reason;
Wherefore the lover has no discipline,
No shame of kindred, no respect for neighbours,
But is all shameless being slave of love.
Even so then suffered the all-noble Girl,
And partly leaned out of the golden window.
The beauties of her face prevent his eyes
Nor can he clearly see the sunborn maid;
Some radiance was dawning in her face;   1430
In truth the girl was like a picture painted;
A bright and charming eye, hair blond and curly,
A brow she had all black, unmixed the sable,
A face like snow, and tinctured in the middle,
As with the chosen purple kings do prize.
So gazing there the wonderful young man
His soul was straightway wounded, hurt his heart,
Boundless his pain, and there distressed he stood.
And the all-noble Girl thus seeing him,
Left him not long in anguish to remain,   1440
But quickly sent to him, so that his love
With joy was much fulfilled, mingled with pleasure,

1429 ἡλιογεννημένη. The beauty that
dazzles like sunlight is a novelist's
commonplace. See e.g. Chariton IV.
i. 9.

1432. Much confusion arose later be-

tween σγοῦρος (accented on either
syllable) 'curly', connected with
γυρός, and σκοῦρος 'dark', connected
with *obscurus*.

1442 ἀνάπλεων. Might be a feminine

τὸ δακτυλίδιν ἔδωκεν εἰποῦσα πρὸς ἐκεῖνον·
" "Απιθι χαίρων, ἄγουρε, κἀμοῦ μὴ ἐπιλάθῃς."   365
Ὁ δὲ δεξάμενος αὐτὸ εἰς τὸν ἴδιον κόλπον,
εὐθὺς ἀνταπεκρίνατο· " Αὔριόν με ἐκδέχου."
Καὶ χαρᾶς ὅλως ἐμπλησθεὶς ὤδευε μετὰ πάντων·
εἰς δὲ τὸν οἶκον φθάσαντες, εὐθὺς φροντίδας εἶχε,
καὶ τὸν Θεὸν ἱκέτευεν ἐξ ὅλης τῆς καρδίας·   370
" Δέσποτα ", λέγων, " ὁ Θεός, ἐπάκουσον εὐχῆς μου,
καὶ δῦνόν μου τὸν ἥλιον, ἀνάτειλον τὸ φέγγος,
ὡσάν μοι γένῃ συνεργὸς ἐν τῇ δουλείᾳ ταύτῃ·
ἐπειδὴ γὰρ μονώτατος βούλομαι πορευθῆναι."
Καὶ κατ᾽ ἰδίαν ἔλεγε τὸν πρωτοστράτορά του·   375
" Ἀπόστρωσαι τὸν βοῦλχαν μου, στρῶσον μου δὲ τὸν μαῦρον,
δύο κίγκλας τον κίγκλωσον καὶ δύο ἐμπροσθελίνας,   28 rᵒ.
καὶ κρέμασε εἰς τὴν σέλλαν μου τὸ ὡραῖον μου σπαθορράβδιν,
καὶ θὲς βαρὺ τὸ μάσσημα ἵνα γοργὸν γυρίζῃ."
Καὶ εἰς τὸν δεῖπνον προσκληθεὶς οὐ μετέσχε βρωμάτων,   380
οὐ πόσεως τὸ σύνολον θέλοντα τοῦ γευθῆναι,
τὴν κόρην στρέφων κατὰ νοῦν, τὸ κάλλος εἰκονίζων·
καὶ ποτὲ μὲν οὐκ ἔχρῃζε ταύτην ἀπογινώσκων·
ἄλλοτε δ᾽ ἐφαντάζετο ἔχων χρηστὰς ἐλπίδας,
καὶ τοῖς πᾶσιν ἐφαίνετο ἐν ὀνείρῳ θεᾶσθαι.   385
Ὃν καὶ ἡ μήτηρ ἡ αὐτοῦ ἵστατο ἀποροῦσα·
" Τί συνέβη σοι, τέκνον μου, καὶ λυπεῖς τὴν ψυχήν μου;
μὴ θηρίον προσέκρουσε καὶ ἐτάραξε φόβος;
μὴ δαίμων σε ἐβάσκανε, βλέπων σου τὴν ἀνδρείαν;
ἀνάγγειλόν μοι τάχιον, μὴ θλίβῃς τὴν ψυχήν μου·   390
ὁ γὰρ κρύπτων τὸ νόσημα ὑπ᾽ αὐτοῦ δαπανᾶται."
" Οὔτε θηρίον προσέκρουσεν, " ὁ νέος ἀπεκρίθη,
" ἀλλ᾽ οὔτε πάλιν θόρυβος ἐτάραξε ψυχήν μου,
εἴπερ δέ τις μ᾽ ἐβάσκανε, μή με τὴν καταρᾶσαι,

373 ὡς ἄν.   375 πρωτοστάτορά.   378 σπαθοράβδην.   384 ἄλλωστε.
394 ὑπὲρ δὲ τὴν.   καταράσαι.

accusative of the classical Attic form
ἀνάπλεως 'full up', agreeing with
ἀγάπην. But it may also be an indeclinable (feminine nominative agreeing with κόρη) participle of ἀναπλέω
in the sense of ἀναπληρόω—and this
is easier to construe. But AND 1778,
where she sends her maid, βάϊαν,

makes it possible that there is some
corruption.
1451 φέγγος, used as here specifically
of moonlight, and the origin of the
modern φεγγάρι, can be traced from
classical times. See L. & S. ref. to
Plato, *Rep.* 508 c; see also L. W.
Lyde on Pindar (Manch. Univ.

Gave him her ring, and unto him saying:
'Go your way gladly, boy, and forget me not.'
He taking it into his own bosom,
Answered at once, 'Tomorrow wait for me.'
All filled with joy he went with all his men;
But home arrived, straight had anxieties
And was imploring God from all his heart:
Saying 'O God and Master, hear my prayer,   1450
Sink me the sun and make the moon to rise,
To be my complice in this business,
For I shall have to go one and alone.'
And privately he spoke to his chief groom:
'Unsaddle this horse, saddle me the black,
With double girths and double martingales,
Hang at the saddle my fine sword and club,
Put on a heavy bit to turn him quickly.'
When he was called to dinner he took no food,
No drink at all was he willing to taste,   1460
Turning the girl in mind, imaging her beauty;
Sometimes despairing wanted her no more,
And sometimes fancied that his hopes were good,
And seemed to all men gazing in a dream,
Whom his own mother stayed then, questioning:
'What's happened to you, child, and you grieve my soul?
Has beast resisted and some fear disturbed you?
Or god bewitched seeing your bravery?
Inform me quickly, do not hurt my soul—
(Who hides his illness is by it consumed).'   1470
'Neither has beast withstood,' the youth replied,
'Nor any trouble yet disturbed my soul;
And if one has bewitched, curse me not her,

Press, 1935) arguing that φάος is a glaring, φέγγος a subdued light. Also below 1484 and above 441.

1453 μονώτατος, used by Ar. and Theocr.

1455 τὸν βούλχαν. Above 1393.

1457 σπαθορράβδιν. It is natural to take this as a *dvandva* compound 'sword and club'; but below iv. 645 (1724) shows that it is one weapon, probably

the same as the σπαθοβάκλιον quoted by Soph. from Porph. *Cer.* 72. 18.

1458 μάσσημα, 'bit'—i.e. 'something to bite on'.

1460 θέλοντα. Indeclinable participle in the accusative form, a step towards the modern form θέλοντας.

1469 At this point TRE 1218 and AND 1810 explicitly introduce a quotation from *Iliad* i. 363.

τὴν μηδὲν ἀδικήσασαν· ἐγὼ γὰρ ὑγιαίνω." 395
Εἴτα κἀκεῖθεν ἀναστὰς ἀνέβη εἰς τὸ κουβοῦκλιν,
καὶ λαβὼν ὑποδήματα λαμβάνει καὶ κιθάραν,
ψιλαῖς δὲ πρῶτον ταῖς χερσὶ τὰς χορδὰς ἐκτινάξας
(κάλλιστα δ' ἐπεπαίδευτο ἐν μουσικοῖς ὀργάνοις),
καὶ ταύτην ἁρμοσάμενος ἔκρουε ψιθυρίζων· 400
" Ὅστις φιλήσειεν ἐγγύς, τοῦ ὕπνου οὐχ ὑστερεῖται,
ὁ δὲ φιλῶν ἀπόμακρα μὴ ἀμελῇ τὰς νύκτας·
ἐγὼ μακρόθεν ἀγαπῶ καὶ γοργὸν ἃς ὑπάγω, 28 vº.
ἵνα μὴ θλίβω τὴν ψυχὴν τὴν δι' ἐμὲ ἀγρυπνοῦσαν."
Ὅταν ἔδυνε ὁ ἥλιος, κατέλαβε τὸ φέγγος, 405
μόνος ἐκαβαλλίκευσε κρατῶν καὶ τὴν κιθάραν·
ἧτον δάος ὁ μαῦρος του, τὸ φέγγος ὡς ἡμέρα,
σύναυγα δὲ κατέλαβε τῆς κόρης τὸ κουβοῦκλιν.
Ἐκείνη δὲ ὡς ἐδέχετο ὁλονυκτὶ ἀγρυπνοῦσα,
τὴν αὐγὴν ἐρραθύμησε καὶ εἰς ὕπνον ἐτράπη· 410
ὡς δὲ ταύτην οὐκ ἔβλεπε τὸ εὐγενὲς παιδίον,
ἠνιᾶτο κατὰ πολύ, ἐταράττετο σφόδρα,
λογισμοὶ ἔκοπτον αὐτοῦ πονηροὶ τὴν καρδίαν,
θλῖψιν εἶχεν ἀφόρητον καὶ ὀδύνην μεγίστην·
ἔλεγε γὰρ ἐν ἑαυτῷ· " Ἄρα μετεμελήθη; 415
ἄρα πτοεῖται τοὺς γονεῖς μήπως αὐτὴν νοήσουν;
τί πρὸς ταῦτα βουλεύσομαι; πῶς τὸ βέβαιον μάθω;
ἐξαπορεῖ γάρ μου ὁ νοῦς, οὐκ ἔχω τι διαπρᾶξαι·
εἰ γὰρ λαλήσω, κράζοντος ἕτεροί μου ἀκούσουν,
δώσουν, ὑπονοήσουν με οἱ φυλάττοντες ὧδε, 420

402 ἀμελεῖ. 405 ἔδυνεν. Je supprime καὶ après ἥλιος, cette conjonction rendant le vers hypermètre. 410 ἐραθύμησε. 414 θλίψιν. 418 ἀπορεῖ. 420 ὧδε.

1477 ψιλαῖς . . . ταῖς χερσί. This might mean with his bare hands, i.e. without a plectrum, which was ordinarily used (see below 1509), but more probably means here without singing, as ψιλός was regularly used of music unaccompanied by the voice (see classical references in L. & S.). In Ach. Tat. 1. v. 4 it clearly means 'without a plectrum'. Cf. also ἐψιλοτραονέι in an akritic song from Karpathos (Polites, Eklogai, No. 69)

which seems to mean 'sing without accompaniment', and ψιλοῖς λόγοις, Plato, Symp. 215 c.

1480 This seems to be the literary version of a folk-song, which may have been a rather meaningless jingle; the version in AND 1844 is quite meaningless. Hesseling (Laografia, iii, p. 547) quotes a similar song from Passow (dist. 700, p. 550).

1484 κατέλαβε, the moon 'took over' or overtook; the word is characteristi-

Who never did me wrong, for I am well.'
Then rising thence he went up to his room,
He fetched his boots, and then he took his lute,
First with his hands alone the strings vibrated
(Well was he trained in instruments of music)
And having tuned he struck it murmuring:
'Who loves near by shall not be short of sleep,   1480
Who loves afar let him not waste his nights:
Far is my love and quickly let me go,
That I hurt not the soul that wakes for me.'
The sun was setting and the moon came up
When he rode out alone holding his lute.
The black was swift, the moon was like the day,
With the dawn he came up to the Girl's pavilion.
   As she had waked and waited all the night
She at the dawn relaxed and turned to sleep.
And when he saw her not the noble youth   1490
Was much distressed and sorely was he troubled,
And evil thoughts began to strike his heart,
With woe unbearable and greatest pain.
For in himself he said, 'Has she repented?
Is she afraid her parents notice her?
What then shall I devise? How learn the truth?
My mind bemused, I know not what to do:
For if I speak, others will hear me calling,
Rush out and find me, who are here on guard,

cally repeated 1487, of his arrival at her κουβούκλι, evidently a separate building. Legrand's omission of καὶ is quite unnecessary.

1486 δάος. This mysterious word, used Lyb. Rod. often and substantivally (like μαῦρος here) for a horse, remains dark. In Chron. Mor. 3378 ἄλογον τοῦ δάου seems to mean a mountain horse (Turk. dagh), but the reading is doubtful. Kyriakides (Dig. Akr., p. 82), who characteristically prefers the reading of ESC 844 (in which it is the black horse which shines like the moon), discusses the word at length, but throws no more light on it than a black horse. An Arabic root is probable; and it may be connected with δαγάλης see below 3178, TRE 222, 697, and 2549 (translated by Legrand 'chestnut') and AND 673, &c.

1499 δώσουν in this sense is an extension of the meaning 'strike' for which see refs. in Soph. It is also possible to take με with δώσουν as well as with ὑπονοήσουν, in which case it would mean 'hit' not in the sense of 'strike' but in the sense of 'not miss'; cf. Lyb. Rod. (Scal.) 1206, 2432; and could be translated 'find me'.

καὶ πρὸ τῆς πράξεως γνωσθῶ μὴ τυχὼν τῆς φιλτάτης,
ὡς ἂν μὴ ἔχων εὐχερῶς ἰδεῖν τὴν ποθουμένην·
καὶ τί μοι ἔστιν ὄφελος ζῆν ἐν τῷδε τῷ βίῳ; "
Ταῦτα λέγων ἐν ἑαυτῷ ἐκπληττόμενος σφόδρα,
δέον εἶναι προέκρινε τοῦ κροῦσαι τὴν κιθάραν,   425
ὅπως λάβῃ ἀπόπειραν περὶ ὧν ἠδημόνει·
" Φείσασθαι", λέγων, " ἐμαυτῷ δοκιμάζων τὴν κόρην
κιθάραν ταύτην συνεργὸν παραστήσω ἐν μέσῳ,
καὶ τοῦ Θεοῦ τὸ θέλημα πάντως ἔχει γενέσθαι."   29 rº.
Καὶ ταύτην ἁρμοσάμενος τῷ πλήκτρῳ τε πατάσσων,   430
μέλος γὰρ πάνυ ἥδιστον ἐτέλει ψιθυρίζων·
" Πῶς ἐπελάθου, πάντερπνε, νέας ἡμῶν ἀγάπης,
καὶ ἡδέως καθύπνωσας ἀμερίμνως, εὐκόλως;
ἀνάστα, ῥόδον πάντερπνον, μῆλον μεμυρισμένον·
ὁ αὐγερινὸς ἀνέτειλεν, δεῦρο ἃς περιπατῶμεν."   435
Ὡς δὲ κιθάρας ἤκουσε τῆς ἡδονῆς ἡ κόρη,
τῆς κλίνης ἐξεπήδησε, σφίγγει της τὸ ζωνάριν,
καὶ χαμηλὰ προκύψασα λέγει τὸν ἀγουρίτζην·
" Ἐγώ, κύρκα, σε ὠνείδισα, δι' οὗ πολλὰ βραδύνας,
ὡς ὀκνηρὸν καὶ ῥάθυμον πάντα νά σε ὀνειδίζω,   440
τὴν δὲ κιθάραν ἦν κρούεις, δοκεῖς τὸ ποῦ εἶσαι οὐκ οἶδας,
καλέ, ἂν σε νοήσῃ ὁ κύρης μου νά σε κακοδικήσῃ,
καὶ νὰ ἀποθάνῃς δι' ἐμέ, ὦ τῆς παρανομίας,
ὁ Θεὸς γὰρ ἐπίσταται ὁ τῶν κρυφίων γνώστης,
ὅτι ἐρριζώθη ὁ πόθος σου εἰς τὴν ἐμὴν καρδίαν,   445
καὶ συμφορὰν λογίζωμαι τὴν σὴν ἀποτυχίαν·
σώζου λοιπόν, ψυχὴ ἐμή, πρὶν τὸ φῶς καταλάβῃ,
καὶ μνήσκου μου διὰ παντὸς τῆς σὲ πολλὰ ποθούσης·
καὶ γάρ, καλὲ νεώτερε, οὐ θέλω ἐλθεῖν μετά σου·
οἶδα ὅτι ὁ πόθος φλέγει σε, καὶ ἡ ἀγάπη ἡ ξένη,   450
ὁ λογισμὸς εἰσπείθει σε δι' ἐμοῦ ἀποθνήσκειν·
ἀλλ' ἂν παροδηγήσῃς με καὶ ἔλθω μετὰ σένα,   29 vº.
καὶ γνώσουν το τὰ ἀδέλφια μου καὶ τὸ συγγενικόν μου,

434 ἀλλ' ἀνάστα.   438 ἀγουρίτζιν.   441 ἦσε.   442 κύρις. κακοδικήσει.
445 ἐριζώθη.   449 σοῦ.   453 ἀδέλφιά.

1515 ἡδονῆς. See above 1338.
1516 σφίγγει της τὸ ζωνάριν. Cf. AND
1872 τὴν ζώνην. But ESC 853 has
ἐπῆρε τὸ λουρίν τῆς—which Kyriakides (Dig. Akr., p. 84) translates

'put on her jacket' (sc. λουρίκιον) and
laboriously defends. Having assumed that ESC because more vernacular gives a better text, he tries
to show that λουρί is here not a strap

And known before the act, losing my dear,   1500
I so should hardly even see my love;
What were the use of life in this world then?'
So saying to himself and sore affrayed,
He judged it right that he should strike his lute
To make a trial of the things he feared.
Saying, 'To test the girl, sparing myself,
This lute a partner I will set between us;
And what God wills shall surely come to pass.'
So having tuned he struck it with the quill,
And made a pleasing music murmuring: 1510
'How have you, dear, forgotten our young love,
Fallen sweet asleep, carelessly, easily?
Rise up, my lovely rose, my scented apple,
The morning star is risen, let us go.'
When the Girl heard the sweet sound of the lute
She jumped out of the bed, tightened her belt
And low down leaning out says to the boy:
   'I scolded you, my pet, you were so late,
Shall always scold if you are slack and slow,
And lute-playing, as if you don't know where you are,   1520
Dear, if my father hear and do you harm,
And you die for me, O the crime of it,
For God who knoweth secrets understands
That love of you is rooted in my heart,
And where you fail I reckon my disaster.
Be gone, my soul, before the light arrests you,
And always think of me who loves you much;
For and, dear youth, I will not come with you:
I know desire enflames you, and alien love,
And reason urges you to die for me;   1530
But if you misguide me, and I come with you,
And if my brothers know it and my kin,

---

but a λουρίκι, and that λουρίκι is here
not a cuirass but a jacket. Of course
λουρί, 'strap', is just what the island
bard of ESC, trying to recite the
story from memory, would say instead of ζώναρι.
1518 κύρκα. See above 469, below 2566.

1521 καλέ has a remonstrative force as
in modern colloquial Greek—'my
good man'.
   κακοδικήσῃ. Above 189, below
1715, and 2515; always with sense of
physical injury. Cf. also 1733, ἀδικήσῃς.

καὶ καταφθάσῃ σε ὁ πατὴρ ὁ ἐμὸς μετὰ πλήθους,
πῶς ἔχεις ἐξιβάλειν με καὶ σῶσαι τὴν ψυχήν σου; "   455
Καὶ λυπηθεὶς ὁ θαυμαστὸς πρὸς τὴν κόρην ἀντέφη·
" Ἐπαινῶ σου τὴν ἔκστασιν, ὦ πανευγενεστάτη,
τὸ γὰρ ἐνάντιον σκοπῶν τῶν μελλόντων συμβαίνειν,
προκρίνεις γὰρ τὰ βέλτιστα σαφῶς λογιζομένη·
σὺ δὲ μηδὲν γινώσκουσα τὰ κατ' ἐμὲ οὐδ' ὅλως,   460
εἰ γὰρ ἐν γνώσει γέγονας ἐμῶν ἀνδραγαθίων,
οὐκ ἂν ἔλεγες ἀδελφοὺς καὶ τὸ συγγενικόν σου
φθάσουν καὶ ἐγκρημνίσουν με καὶ σὺ δι' ἐμὲ λυπῆσαι·
ἀλλ' ἔστω σοι τοῦτο γνωστὸν καὶ βέβαιον, ψυχή μου,
ὅτι φοσσᾶτα προσδοκῶ μόνος καταπονέσαι,   465
νικῆσαι τε παραταγὰς καὶ κράτη ὑποτάξαι·
τὸν δὲ πατέρα τε τὸν σὸν καὶ τοὺς αὐτοῦ ἀγούρους
ὡσαύτως καὶ τοὺς ἀδελφοὺς μετὰ τῶν συγγενῶν σου
πάντως βρέφη λογίζομαι καὶ μηδὲν ὅλως ὄντα·
τοῦτο μόνον ζητῶ μαθεῖν παρὰ τῶν σῶν χειλέων   470
εἰ προθυμεῖς κατὰ πολὺ ἐμοὶ ἀκολουθῆσαι,
ὡς ἂν ὁδοὺς ἐξέλθωμεν τοὺς στενωποὺς πρὶν φέξῃ·
ῥύμαι γὰρ καὶ στενώματα ἀποκτείνουν ἀνδρείους·
εἰς δὲ τοὺς κάμπους ἄνανδροι τολμηροὶ ἐκποιοῦνται·
εἰ δ' ἴσως ἐμετέγνωσας, ἑτέρου ᾑρετίσω,   475
καὶ διὰ τοῦτο ἀφορμὰς προβάλλεσαι τοιαύτας,
μὰ τοὺς ἁγίους μάρτυρας τοῦ Χριστοῦ Θεοδώρους,
οὐκ ἂν ἄλλος, ζῶντος ἐμοῦ, εἰσακουσθῇ ἀνήρ σου."
Αὖθις ἡ ἡλιόκαλος πρὸς τὸν ἄγουρον ἔφη·   30 rᵒ.
" Σὺ μὲν οὖν, ὦ παμπόθητε, ἀπείραστος ὡς πρῶτον   480
πάσης ἀγάπης πέφυκας καὶ φιλίας, ὡς ἔφης·
νυνὶ δὲ πάσχεις δι' ἐμὲ καὶ ἴσως ἀληθεύεις,
ἐκ τῶν ὁμοίων καὶ αὐτὴ τοῦτο τεκμαιρομένη·
εἰ γὰρ καὶ λίαν ἀπρεπὲς τὰ κατ' ἐμὲ εἰπεῖν σοι,
ὅμως ἐρῶ σοι ἅπαντα τῷ πόθῳ δουλωθεῖσα·   485
πολλοὶ ἐμὲ τῶν εὐγενῶν ἄρχοντες μεγιστᾶνες

---

455 ἐξηβάλειν.   464 ἔστι (correction empruntée au ms. d'Andros, vers
1902).   469 λογίζονται.   472 φέξει.   473 ἀποκτένουν, et αι au-dessus
de έ.   476 δια (sans accent).   479 ἡλιόκαλλος.

1534 ἐξιβάλειν. For this form see   1537 σκοπῶν. Note masculine parti-
Πόλεμος τῆς Τρωιάδος, ed. Mauro-   ciple; but in the next line but one
frydês, Eklogé, p. 207, l. 697 τὰ   γινώσκουσα.
σωθικὰ ἐξήβαλαν.

My father with a crowd should overtake you,
How could you get me out and save your life?'
  And grieved the hero to the Girl replied:
'Your trouble, noblest lady, I commend,
For looking at the front of things to come
Reasoning clearly you forejudge most well;
Yet nothing knowing about me at all,
For if you were acquainted with my deeds,   1540
You would not say your brothers and your kin
Will catch and cast me down, and you be sorry.
But be this known and sure to you, my soul,
Alone I look to overcome armies
Subdue their powers, and conquer their arrays;
As for your father and his company
Likewise your brothers and with them your kinsmen,
I reckon them just babies being nothing.
Only this I want to learn from your own lips,
If you are most eager to follow me,   1550
That we may leave the by-ways before dawn,
(Brave men are killed by lanes and alley-ways,
And in the open cowards are made brave);
But if you have repented, chosen another,
Therefore put forward this sort of excuses,
Then by the Saints Theodore, Christ's witnesses,
None other, while I live, shall be called your husband.'
  Again spoke to him the sun-lovely Girl:
'You then, dearest of all, untried, as first,
Are of all love and affection, as you said,   1560
And now suffer for me, and perhaps speak true;
Myself likewise this also testify,
Though to tell you about myself be wrong,
Yet by desire enslaved I will tell you all:
Me many noble princes, many captains

1542 ἐγκρημνίσουν. Soph. refers to Genes. 106. 18.
1545 παραταγάς, classical παρατάξεις (which comes below 1567).
1556 Cf. AND 1921 μὰ τὸν ἅγιον Θεόδωρον τὸν μέγαν ἀπελάτην. AND follows fairly closely, but GRO alone refers to the possibility of a rival.
1558 ἡλιόκαλος seems to be *hap. leg.* In the speech which follows the translation reproduces some of the confusion in syntax which may be intended by the poet to express the Maiden's hesitation.

καὶ βασιλέων συγγενεῖς ἐζήτησαν καὶ τέκνα
βασιλικὴν παράταξιν ἔχοντες καὶ ἐσθῆτα,
καὶ ποθοῦντες θεάσασθαι τὸν ἐμὸν χαρακτῆρα,
πυκνότερον διήρχοντο τοῦ οἴκου μου πλησίον,   490
ἀλλ᾿ οὐδενὶ τὸ σύνολον ἠρκέσθη ὁ πατήρ μου·
οὐ τὴν σκιὰν δὲ τὴν ἐμὴν τὶς ἰδεῖν ἠξιώθη,
φωνῆς οὐδείς μου ἤκουσεν ἢ συντυχίας ὅλως,
οὐ γέλωτος μειδίασμα, οὐ βαδίσματος ψόφον·
τῆς θυρίδος οὐδέποτε τὴν κεφαλήν μου ἦγον,   495
ἀλλοτρίοις ἀθέατον ἐμαυτὴν διετήρουν·
ἐκτὸς γάρ μου τῶν συγγενῶν καὶ τῶν γνωστῶν ἰδίων,
οὐδείς μου εἶδε πώποτε προσώπου χαρακτῆρα,
τάξιν τηροῦσα ἀκριβῆ τὴν πρέπουσαν παρθένοις·
τούτων δὲ γέγονα ἐκτὸς καὶ τοὺς ὅρους παρῆλθον   500
καὶ ἐγενόμην ἀναιδὴς διὰ τὴν σὴν ἀγάπην·
καὶ ἡ μηδέποτε ἀνδρὶ ἀλλοτρίῳ ὀφθεῖσα
λόγους νῦν μεταδίδωμι ὅλως μὴ αἰδουμένη,
καὶ τὸ ὄντως ἐλεύθερον φρόνημα παρθενίας
δοῦλον ὁρῶ γινόμενον καὶ ἀναιδὲς ἀθρόως.   30 vᵒ. 505
Ἀφ᾿ ἧς γὰρ ὥρας πρόσωπον τὸ σὸν εἶδον, ὦ νέε,
ὡς πῦρ κατέφλεξεν εὐθὺς τὴν σώφρονα ψυχήν μου,
μετήλλαξε τὸν λογισμὸν ὁμοίως καὶ τὴν γνώμην,
τὸ φρόνημα ἐδούλωσεν, ἀναίσχυντόν με ποιήσας
εἰς σὲ καὶ μόνον, ποθητέ, καὶ πρὸς τὴν σὴν ἀγάπην·   510
πείθομαι νῦν καὶ βούλομαι μετὰ σοῦ πορευθῆναι,
δι᾿ οὗ ἀρνοῦμαι συγγενεῖς, γονέας ὑστεροῦμαι,
ἀλλοτριοῦμαι ἀδελφῶν καὶ τοῦ ἀπείρου πλούτου,
καὶ μετὰ σοῦ πορεύομαι ὅπου δ᾿ ἂν καὶ κελεύῃς,
Θεὸν ἔχουσα μάρτυρα τὸν πᾶσι βοηθοῦντα   515
ἐκδικητὴν παγκάλλιστον, μή με παροδηγήσῃς·
σὲ μὲν ἡ ἀγάπη φλέγει σε, ἡ ἀγάπη παροξύνει,
καὶ πείθει σε ὁ λογισμὸς δι᾿ ἐμὲ τοῦ θανεῖν σε,
ὅπερ ἀπεύχομαι ἰδεῖν ἢ τοῖς ὠσὶν ἀκοῦσαι."
Ὡς δὲ ταῦτα ἐφθέγγετο ἡ πανώραιος κόρη,   520
ἐδάκρυσε τοῖς ὀφθαλμοῖς, ἐστέναξε μεγάλως,
καὶ ἑαυτὴν ἐμέμφετο τῆς πολλῆς ἀναιδείας·

517 καὶ σὲ μέν.   521 ἀδελφοῖς, au lieu de ὀφθαλμοῖς. On traduirait ce premier hémistiche par *ses yeux se mouillèrent de larmes*.

1568 χαρακτῆρα. See below 1577 προσώπου χαρακτῆρα, of which it is the

Have sought, and kinsmen and the sons of kings,
Having their kingly retinue and vesture,
Desiring to behold my countenance,
They would go thickly by before my house;
With none at all my father was contented,   1570
Not one was thought worthy to see my shadow,
None heard my voice at all or my converse,
My laughing or the sound of my footfall.
At the casement I never showed my head,
Unseen by other eyes I kept myself
(For save my kinsmen and my own familiars
No one has ever seen my countenance),
Keeping the strictness which becomes a maid;
But I am out and, overstept these bounds,
Am become shameless on your love's account,   1580
And who was never seen by a strange man
Now share my talk without all shame at all,
While the free purpose of virginity
I see become a slave and shameless quite.
For from the hour, O youth, I saw your face,
As it were fire burnt up my temperate soul,
Altered my reason and likewise my nature,
Enslaved my purpose, making me immodest,
To you alone, my dear, and to your love.
Now I obey, and wish to go with you,   1590
For whom I deny kin, am reft of parents,
Estranged from brothers and from boundless wealth,
And go with you wherever you may bid,
Holding God witness, helper of us all,
And best avenger, you lead me not astray.
You too love burns you, and love pricks you on,
And reason tells you you would die for me,
The which I pray never to see or hear.'
    While she was speaking thus the all-lovely Girl
Filled up her eyes with tears and deeply sighed,   1600
And blamed herself for her great shamelessness;

equivalent; see below v. 159 (2331).   1586 εὐθύς omitted in translation.
1571 This line is identical with AND   1587 γνώμην. See above 360, 607, 1062.
1933.

καί, θέλουσα κατὰ πολὺ μεταβαλεῖν τὴν γνώμην,
ὁ ταύτης ἔνδον ἄπειρος οὐ συνεχώρει πόθος.

Δύναμις γὰρ τοῦ ἔρωτος, πόθος καὶ ἡ φιλία,   525
ἅπερ τὴν τάξιν ἀκριβῶς τηροῦντα τὴν ἰδίαν,
σώφρονα νοῦν κατέχων τις, ὁ πόθος πολεμεῖ τον·
καὶ διὰ τοῦτο ὁ ποθῶν εὐταξίαν οὐκ ἔχει,
οὐ συγγενεῖς αἰσχύνεται, οὐ γείτονας πτοεῖται,
ἀλλ᾿ ἔστιν ὅλος ἀναιδὴς καὶ δοῦλος τῆς φιλίας·   530
ὡς καὶ οὕτως πεπόνθασιν οἱ παγκάλλιστοι νέοι.   31 r°.

Εἶτα ὁ θαυμαστὸς ἰδὼν δακρύσασαν τὴν κόρην
μετὰ δακρύων καὶ αὐτὸς ἀντέλεγε τοιαῦτα·
" Ἐγώ, κόρη παγκάλλιστε, τὰ περὶ σοῦ γινώσκω·
τὸν πλοῦτον γὰρ τὸν ἄπειρον ὃν κέκτηται ὁ πατήρ σου, 535
δι᾿ οὗ πολλοὶ τῶν εὐγενῶν ἐπόθουν τοῦ λαβεῖν σε
ἐν γνώσει πάντων γέγονα ἀκριβῶς ἐρευνήσας,
ἐγὼ γάρ, φιλτάτη ψυχή, οὐκ ἐφίεμαι πλούτου,
οὐ κτήματα ἐπιθυμῶ, οὐκ ὀρέγομαι δόξης,
πάντα χόρτον λογίζομαι ἐντρυφῶν τοῦ σοῦ κάλλους, 540
ἀφ᾿ ἧς ὥρας, μαυρόμματε, ὠψόμεθα ἀλλήλους,
οὐκ ἀπέστης ἐκ τὴν ἐμὴν ψυχὴν ὠρίτζαν μίαν·
ἐρριζώθης γὰρ ἔσωθεν καὶ συνεπλέχθης ταύτῃ,
καὶ σὲ πάντα φαντάζομαι καὶ βλέπω σε μὴ οὖσαν·
οὐ γὰρ ἡράσθην πώποτε οἱουδήποτε κάλλους,   545
οὐ τὰς ὁδοὺς ἐγνώρισα κἂν ποσῶς τῆς ἀγάπης·
δεῦρο, τὸ φῶς μου τὸ γλυκύ, ἔπου τῷ ἐραστῇ σου·
ἤνπερ ἔχεις ἀπέσωθεν ἐμφάνισον ἀγάπην·
ἀκριβὴς γὰρ ἀπόδειξις συνίσταται ἐξ ἔργων,
καὶ συμβιώσομεν Θεοῦ νεύσει χαίροντες ἄμφω·   550
ἐπὶ τοῦτο γεννήτορες καὶ οἱ σοὶ εὐφρανθῶσιν,
γαμβροῦ οἵου τετύχηκαν ἐν γνώσει γεγονότες·
καὶ οὐδεὶς ὀνειδίσει σε, μᾶλλον δὲ μακαρίσει."
Ταῦτα καὶ ἕτερα πολλὰ φθεγξάμενος ὁ νέος,

---

528 δια (sans accent).   529 συνεγγεῖς, correction empruntée au ms.
d'Andros (vers 1950). Le copiste avait sans doute pensé à σύνεγγυς.   531
παγκάλιστοι.   532 ἰδὼν manque dans le manuscrit.   534 παγκάλιστε.
542 Après ψυχήν, je supprime κἂν, qui rendrait le vers hypermètre. On pourrait
aussi écrire κἂν ὥραν μίαν.   543 ἐριζώθης.   550 συμβιώσωμεν νεύσε θεοῦ.

1604–6. The sentence is rather muddled   line by line. The general meaning is
and seems to have been composed   that love, constant in its own nature,

And yet, though wishing much to change her mind,
Boundless desire within would not allow her.
(The power of love, desire and affection,
Things which exactly keep their proper station—
One has a temperate mind, desire attacks him,
Wherefore the lover has no discipline,
No shame of kindred, no respect for neighbours,
But is all shameless, and a slave of love;
Even so suffered they, the young so fair).   1610
The hero then seeing the Girl weeping,
Himself in tears made answer to her thus:
'O lovely maid, I know your circumstance,
The boundless riches which your father owns,
For which many nobles wanted to take you,
All this I know by exact inquisition;
For I, my dearest soul, aim not at riches,
Want no possessions, reach not after fame,
Count it all grass, being rich in your beauty;
For from the hour, black-eyes, we saw each other,   1620
You went not from my soul one little hour,
Rooted within, you were entwined in it;
My fancy sees you when you are not there;
For never yet have I loved any beauty,
Nor have I known at all the ways of love.
Come then, my sweet light, follow your lover;
Show forth the affection which you have within,
For a strict demonstration is in deeds,
By God's assent we will live in joy together.
Your parents too will be made glad on this,   1630
When they have heard what a son-in-law they have gotten;
And none shall blame but rather call you blessed.'
This and much else the young man having uttered,

produces inconstancy and disorder
in the person it attacks. The redactor
has made this, the disorderliness of
love, the theme of the whole episode.
See above 984 ff. and 1421 ff. Lines
1607–9 are an exact repetition of
1423–5.
1620, 1621 μαυρόμματε . . . ὠρίτζαν.

Two words straight from the vocabulary of folk-song, not found in the
corresponding passage of AND
(1962).
1621 ἐκ τὴν ἐμὴν ψυχήν. For ἐκ with
accusative cf. below 1664 and above
1427.

" Εν σοί μου πᾶσα ἡ ἀρχή", ἔφησε, " καὶ τὸ τέλος   555
σὺν Θεῷ ἐναρχόμενον μέχρι τῆς τελευτῆς μου·
καὶ εἰ πώποτε βουληθῶ λυπῆσαι σε, ψυχή μου,   31 vᵒ.
καὶ οὐ φυλάξω ἀθόλωτον τὴν πρὸς ἐμέ σου ἀγάπην
πόθον τε καθαρώτατον ἄχρι τῆς τελευτῆς μου,
νὰ μὴ ἀποθάνω χριστιανός, νὰ μὴ κατευοδοῦμαι,   560
νὰ μὴ κερδίσω τὰς εὐχὰς τῶν ἐμῶν γεννητόρων·
καὶ αὐτὴ δέ, πανεύγενε, τὰ ὅμοια φυλάξοις! "
Ταῦτα ἡ κόρη τοῖς ὠσὶν ἐνηχηθεῖσα εἶπεν·
" Εἰ καὶ λίαν παράνομον τοῦ ἐμαυτὴν προδοῦναι
(ἡ τάξις γὰρ ἡ ἀληθὴς εὐγένεια καλεῖται,   565
ἤνπερ κἀγὼ ἠθέτησα, οὐκ οἶδα τι παθοῦσα),
πόθος γὰρ ὅμως ἀκραιφνής, ἀγάπη σου ἡ βεβαία
προτιμοτέραν ἔπεισε σῇ καλλίστῃ ἀγάπη."
Εἴθ' οὕτως ὅρκον μ' ἔρωτος ἡ κόρη φθεγξαμένη·
" Καταλιμπάνουσα γονεῖς, ἀδελφοὺς καὶ οἰκίαν,   570
ἀπὸ τὸν Θεόν, ὦ ἄγουρε, σοὶ ἐμαυτὴν πιστεύω,
αὐτόν μοι δίδου μάρτυρα ὅλως μή με λυπῆσαι,
ἀλλὰ γυναῖκαν ἔννομον ἄχρι τέλους ποιῆσαι·
καὶ γὰρ πολλοὶ τῶν ἐραστῶν ἠθετήκασι λόγους,
ταῖς ποθουμέναις πρῴην γὰρ ἐρωτικῶς δειχθέντες."   575
Καὶ ὡς τὸ ἤκουσεν ὁ παῖς ἐξεπλάγη θαυμάζων
τῆς παρθένου τὴν σύνεσιν· ἐπώμοσε δὲ ὅμως·
" Μὰ τὸν Πατέρα καὶ Υἱὸν καὶ τὸ ἅγιον Πνεῦμα,
οὐ λυπήσω σε πώποτε, ὦ πανευγενεστάτη,
ἀλλὰ κυρίαν τῶν ἐμῶν καὶ δέσποιναν ποιήσω,   580
γαμετήν τε καὶ σύνοικον μέχρι τέλους ζωῆς μου,
εἰ καθαρὸν τὸν πρὸς ἐμὲ διατηρήσεις πόθον,
καθώσπερ καὶ προέφην σοι, ὦ ποθεινὴ ψυχή μου."   32 rᵒ.
Καὶ ἐμπεδώσαντες καλῶς ἀλλήλους ἐκ τῶν ὅρκων,
ἡ παρθένος προκύψασα ἐκ τὴν χρυσῆν θυρίδα,   585
ὁ παῖς την ὑπεδέξατο ὀρθωθεὶς ἐν τῷ ἵππῳ·
ἡ πέρδικα ἐξεπέτασεν, ὁ ἱέραξ τὴν ἐδέχθη·

562 φυλάξῃς.

_____

1644-7 These lines are almost un-   καλλίστην ἀγάπην (perhaps the right
translatable and may be corrupt,   reading). (See above 1604 ff. for the
especially the last three words, which   redactor's previous efforts in the
I have translated as if they were σὴν   same style.) And I have taken ἀγάπη

'In you all my beginning, and my end,' he said,
'With God begun, unto my taking off;
And should I ever will, my soul, to grieve you,
And not keep untroubled your love for me
And most pure passion till my dying day,
Let me not die a Christian, never prosper,
Never obtain the prayers of my parents;   1640
May you keep, noble maid, the like resolve.'
This sounding in her ears the Girl replied:
'Though sore transgression be to give myself
(For order true is called nobility,
Which I have set at nought, I know not how),
Yet sudden passion, and my sure affection,
Made me your fair affection to prefer.'
Then uttering thus the Girl her vow of love,
'Leaving my house, my brothers, and my parents,
From God, dear youth, I trust myself to you,   1650
Him take to witness not to grieve me at all,
But make me till the end your lawful wife.
(For many lovers set their words at nought
Who first to those desired showed loving selves.)'
When the boy heard surprised he wondered at
Her virgin wisdom. Yet he swore again:
'By the Father and Son and by the Holy Ghost,
I will not ever grieve you, noble maid,
But make you lady and mistress of all mine,
My spouse and helpmate until my life's end,   1660
If pure you keep your desire towards me,
Even as I said before, my darling soul.'
    Having well bound each other by their vows,
The maiden leaned out of the golden casement,
The boy upstanding on his horse received her,
The partridge flew out and the falcon caught her.

σου ἡ βεβαία (1646) as 'my love for
you'; but am not sure about it.
1648 ὅρκον μ' ἔρωτος. Leg. ὅρκον
ἔρωτος. One might guess that this
wandering μ had originally been
written in the margin as a correction
of σου (1646), which should probably
be μου.
1666 The same simile of the hawk
stooping to catch the partridge is
used AND 2073, but to describe the
ferocity of Digenes when he attacks
his pursuers.

καὶ κατεφίλησαν τερπνῶς, ὡς ἔπρεπεν, ἀλλήλους,
ἀνεκλαλήτως χαίροντες καὶ δακρύοντες ἄμφω,
πεφύκασι γὰρ ἀκαρῆ ἐν χαρμονῇ μεγίστη,   590
καὶ δάκρυα μεθ᾿ ἡδονῆς θερμότατα ἐκίνουν·
ὁ δέ γε παῖς ὑπὸ χαρᾶς κινηθεὶς καὶ ἀνδρείας,
σταθεὶς τοῦ οἴκου ἄντικρυς ἐξεφώνησε λέγων·
" Εὖξαι μου, κύρη πενθερέ, μετὰ τῆς θυγατρός σου·
εὐχαρίστει δὲ τῷ Θεῷ ἔχων γαμβρὸν τοιοῦτον."   595
Τῆς δὲ φωνῆς ὡς ἤκουσαν τοῦ στρατηγοῦ αἱ βίγλαι,
διελάλησαν ἅπασιν εἰς τὸ καβαλλικεῦσαι.
Καὶ ὁ στρατηγὸς παρευθὺς ἐξάπινα ἀκούσας
ἄλλος ἐξ ἄλλου γέγονεν οὐκ ἔχων ὅ, τι δρᾶσαι·
καὶ ἐκ βάθους ἀνέκραξεν· " Ἀπώλεσα τὸ φῶς μου,   600
θυγάτηρ ἡ μονογενὴς ἐξ ὀφθαλμῶν μου ἤρθη."
Στρατήγισσα δ᾿ ὡς ἤκουσεν ἠλάλαζε βοῶσα·
" Οἴχεται ἡ μονογενής, ἡρπάγη ἡ θυγάτηρ."
Οἱ ἀδελφοὶ ἑτέρωθεν θρηνοῦντες ἀνεβόων·
" Τίς τοῦτο κατετόλμησε τὸ ἀνόμημα πρᾶξαι;   605
τίς ἀφ᾿ ἡμῶν τὴν ἀδελφὴν ἀπέσπασεν ἀθρόως; "
Ἔκλαιον αἱ οἰκέτιδες, οἰμωγὰς ἀνεβόων,
ὀδυρμὸς ἀκατάσχετος διὰ παντὸς ἐχώρει·
στρατός τε πολὺς ἔνοπλος εἰς δίωξιν τοῦ νέου
καὶ ὀπίσω ὁ στρατηγὸς μετὰ τῶν δύο τέκνων·   32ᵛ°. 610
ἀλλ᾿ οὐδὲ ἡ στρατήγισσα κατελείφθη ἐν οἴκῳ,
τῆς θυγατρὸς τὸν χωρισμὸν μὴ φέρουσα οὐδ᾿ ὅλως·
πλῆθος γὰρ οἰκετίδων τε μεθ᾿ ἑαυτῆς λαβοῦσα,
πεζῇ ὡς εἶχεν εἵπετο, λυσίκομος, θρηνοῦσα·
" Φιλτάτη ψυχή," κράζουσα, " ποῦ πορεύῃ οὐκ οἶδα."   615
Οὐδεὶς δὲ ἐναπέμεινε γηραιὸς οὔτε νέος
ὃς οὐκ ἐκαβαλλίκευσεν εἰς δίωξιν τοῦ νέου,
πάντα ὑπεραλγήσαντες τὴν ἁρπαγὴν τῆς κόρης,
ὡς μὴ ἰσχύειν ἀκριβῶς ἀριθμῆσαι τὸ πλῆθος.
Καὶ τοῦ φωτὸς αὐγάζοντος ἀπάρτι τῆς ἡμέρας,   620
ἐκεῖ τοὺς ἐκατέλαβον εἰς τοὺς ἀδήλους κάμπους·

590 ἀκαρὴ.   594 κύρι.   598 εὐθύς.   599 δράσαι.

1678 ἄλλος ἐξ ἄλλου. For the usual
ἔξαλλος; cf. below 1916.
1679 ἐκ βάθους, sc. τῆς καρδίας. AND

2005–7 and ESC 922 give more racy
words to the General, who calls to
his men φθάσατε ᾿ς τὸν παγκόπελον,

Sweetly they kissed each other as was right,
Unspeakably rejoicing and both weeping,
For they were in an instant in great bliss
And fervently were shedding tears of pleasure.   1670
Thereon the boy with joy and bravery moved
Stood opposite the house and shouted saying,
   'Bless me, lord father-in-law, with your daughter,
And then thank God for such a son-in-law.'
   The General's sentries when they heard the cry,
Proclaimed to everyone the call to horse.
Straightway the General hearing suddenly,
Beside himself, not knowing what to do,
Cried from his heart out, 'I have lost my light,
My only daughter lifted from my eyes.'   1680
The General's wife when she heard cried wailing,
'She is clean gone our only daughter ravished.'
Her brothers elsewhere mourning cried aloud,
'Who can have dared to do this lawless thing?
Who snatched our sister clean away from us?'
The housemaids were weeping with loud laments
And everywhere went mourning unrestrained.
A large force armed went in the youth's pursuit,
The General behind with his two sons.
Nor was the General's wife left in the house,   1690
Not bearing to be parted from her daughter,
For taking with her many of the housemaids,
On foot she followed, hair unbound, weeping,
Crying, 'Dear soul, I know not where you go.'
Not one remained there neither old nor young,
Who did not ride in pursuit of the youth,
All overgrieved at the Girl's ravishment,
So none could strictly count the company.
   And when dawned presently the light of day
They overtook them in the darkling plains;   1700

ἐπῆρε μου τὴν κόρην—'Catch the all-bastard, he has taken my daughter' —where Kyriakides surprisingly says that Pankopelos must be the name of a place (*Dig. Akr.*, p. 27, n. 3). See Introduction,.

1689 In AND 2075 there are three brothers, as in TRE 1267: but see PAS 359.

1693 ὡς εἶχεν, 'just as she was', omitted in translation.

οὖσπερ ἰδοῦσα μήκοθεν ἡ πανώραιος κόρη
(καὶ γὰρ ἔβλεπεν ὄπισθεν σκοπεύουσα ὀξέως,
ἐν ταῖς ἀγκάλαις οὖσα τε τοῦ πανηγαπημένου),
πρὸς αὐτὸν ταῦτα ἔλεγε, σφικτὰ τοῦτον κρατοῦσα·   625
" Ἀγωνίζου, ψυχίτζα μου, μή μας ἀποχωρίσουν,
καὶ ἴσχυε κατὰ πολὺ τὸν μαῦρον ἀποπλήττων·
ἰδοὺ γὰρ μέλλουσιν ἡμᾶς οἱ διώκοντες φθάνειν."
Ὡς ταῦτα δὲ ὁ θαυμαστὸς ἤκουσε νεανίας,
θάρσους εὐθέως ἐμπλησθεὶς καὶ τῆς ὁδοῦ ἐκκλίνας,   630
δένδρον εὑρίσκει διφυὲς, κλάδους φέρον τε δύο,
καὶ τὴν κόρην ἀποβαλὼν μέσον τῶν δύο κλάδων·
" Αὐτοῦ κάθου, παγκάλλιστε, καὶ σὸν φίλτατον βλέπε."
Καὶ πρὸς πόλεμον ἑαυτὸν καθοπλίζει εὐθέως·
καὶ τότε τὸ ἡλιογέννημα τὸν ἄγουρον ἐλάλει·   635
" Τοὺς ἀδελφούς μου πρόσεχε μὴ τοὺς κακοδικήσῃς."   33 rᵒ.
Ξένον πρᾶγμα ἐδείκνυτο τοῖς ἐκεῖσε παροῦσι
πῶς μόνος κατετόλμησε συμβαλεῖν χιλιάσιν·
καὶ ἐν βραχεῖ ἀπέκτεινε στρατιώτας ἀπείρους
καθωπλισμένους, ἱππικούς, πολέμου γυμνασμένους,   640
οἷς συμβουλεύειν ἤρξατο στραφῆναι εἰς τὰ ὀπίσω,
καὶ μὴ πεῖραν τῆς ἑαυτοῦ μεταλαβεῖν ἀνδρείας.
Ἐκεῖνοι δὲ τὴν τοῦ ἑνὸς αἰσχυνόμενοι ἧτταν,
τὸ θανεῖν ἡρετίσαντο ἢ θανεῖν ὑπ' ἐκείνου.
Κἀκεῖνος ἐπελάλησε, σύρνει τὸ σπαθορράβδιν,   645
καὶ πρὶν ἐλθεῖν τὸν στρατηγὸν οὐδὲ εἷς ὑπελείφθη.
Καὶ τοῦ πολέμου πέρας τε ὁ παῖς ἀποπληρώσας,
ὡς νικητὴς ὑπέστρεφε πρὸς τὴν παρθένον χαίρων,
καὶ ἐκ τοῦ ἵππου καταβὰς καὶ μυρία φιλήσας·
" Ἔχεις με, κόρη πάντερπνε, ἀπόδειξιν τῶν ἔργων."   650
Ἡ δὲ κόρη τὸν ἄγουρον ὡραΐζουσα πλέον,
ἡδέως ὑπεδέχετο φιλημάτων τοὺς ψόφους,
ἠρέμα πρὸς τὸν ἄγουρον οὑτωσὶ φθεγξαμένη·

629 θαύμαστος.   633 παγκάλιστε.   645 σπαθοράβδιν.

1705 ψυχίτζα μου (and below 1887).
1710 In TRE (which has just recom-
     menced after a long lacuna) 1255,
     and AND 2063, he sits her on a rock.
1714 ἡλιογέννημα. Again below 1886.
1715 κακοδικήσῃς. Again below 2515.
1723 τὸ θανεῖν ἡρετίσαντο ἢ θανεῖν ὑπ'

ἐκείνου. The second θανεῖν may be
corrupt, but it is difficult to suggest
an emendation and no help is given
by the other versions which are less
elaborate at this point. The general
sense is clear: ashamed of being
beaten by one man they preferred to

Whom seeing from afar the all-lovely Girl
(For she was looking back and sharply gazing
In the arms as she was of her beloved),
Holding him tightly spoke these words to him:
'Struggle, my darling, that they part us not,
Be very strong and whip the black horse up,
For look those who pursue are going to catch us.'
Whenas he heard these words the wondrous youth,
Straight filled with courage, turning from the way,
Found there a forking tree with two branches,   1710
And putting down the Girl between the branches—
'Sit there, my loveliest, and watch your dear';
He said and quickly armed himself for battle.
And then the sun-child spoke unto the boy,
'My brothers mind you do not injure them.'
To those there present was shown a strange thing,
How that he dared alone to encounter thousands;
In a short time he killed countless soldiers,
Accoutred, mounted, exercised in war,
Whom he began advising to turn back,   1720
And not to share a trial of his valour.
But they ashamed by one to be defeated,
Preferred to die than to be spared by him.
     Then he drove forward, drew his mace and sword,
Before the General came not one was left;
And having paid his fill and more of battle
Returned a victor to the maid rejoicing,
Dismounted, and a thousand kisses giving,
'You have in me, sweet girl, proof of my deeds.'
The Girl herself, the more admiring him,   1730
Accepting with delight his noisy kisses,
Quietly spoke on this wise to the boy:

face him and meet their death; they
would rather die than be killed—
an unsuccessful euphuism.

1724 σπαθορράβδιν. See above 1457.

1730 ὡραΐζουσα πλέον seems to mean
'calling or finding him more beautiful'. For modification of the verbal
meaning in the substantive cf.
ὡραΐσεις (fem. plur.) in the sense of

ὡραιότητες in Meliten. 102 and 108.
But ὡραΐζω may possibly here have
the sense of ὡραΐζεσθαι, 'to give one-
self airs' or 'to bloom with youthful
beauty' (see L. & S. and quotation
from Cratinus by Phrynichus fr.
370). Cf. also above 41, ἀνδρείαν
θαυμάζων—'making his bravery to
be a wonder'.

" Μὴ ἀδικήσῃς, ὦ ψυχή, τοὺς ἐμοὺς αὐταδέλφους·
ἐκείνους γὰρ οὖσπερ ὁρᾷς πρὸς ἡμᾶς ἐρχομένους 655
ἐκ τῶν ἵππων τεκμαίρομαι ἀδελφοὺς ἐμοὺς εἶναι·
καὶ ὁ τρίτος ὁ μετ' αὐτῶν ὁ πατήρ μου τυγχάνει·
τούτους μοι σώους χάρισον, ἀβλαβεῖς συντηρήσας."
" Γενήσεται ὅπερ αἰτεῖς ", ὁ παῖς τῇ κόρῃ ἔφη,
" εἰ μή τι ἕτερον συμβῇ ἐκ τῶν ἀπροσδοκήτων· 660
ὁ γὰρ ἐχθρῶν φειδόμενος ἐν ὥρᾳ τοῦ πολέμου
ὑπ' ἐκείνων ἀσυμπαθῶς κατεβλήθη πολλάκις." 33 vᵒ.
Ταῦτα εἰπὼν εἰσπήδησεν ἐν τῷ ἰδίῳ ἵππῳ
καὶ τοῖς περὶ τὸν στρατηγὸν σπουδαίως ὑποπίπτει.
Οἱ δὲ τῆς κόρης ἀδελφοὶ ζήλου πολλοῦ πλησθέντες 665
ἀνελεῖν τοῦτον ἔλεγον τοῖς ἰδίοις ἀγούροις,
τὸν φόνον προσδοκώμενοι ὑφ' ἑτέρων γενέσθαι·
ὁ δὲ παῖς τὸ παράγγελμα φυλάττων τῆς φιλτάτης
εὐτέχνως τούτους ὑπελθὼν σοφῶς ἀνεῖλε πάντας·
οἱ δ' ἀδελφοὶ ὁρμήσαντες μανικῶς ὑπ' ἐκεῖνον, 670
οὕτως αὐτοὺς ἐκύκλευσεν ἐκ τῶν ἵππων εἰσρίψας
ὡς ἂν μὴ βλάψαι ἀκριβῶς ἢ ὅλως τραυματίσαι·
καὶ στραφεὶς πρὸς τὸν στρατηγὸν μακρόθεν καὶ πεζεύσας,
σφικτὰ δήσας τὰς χεῖράς του, χαμηλὰ προσκυνήσας,
ἤρξατο λέγειν πρὸς αὐτὸν θαρσαλέᾳ τῇ ὄψει· 675
" Συγχώρησόν μοι, αὐθέντα μου, μηδέν με καταμέμφου·
ὁ στρατός σου ἦτον χωρικὸς τοῦ κρούειν καὶ λαμβάνειν,
καὶ διὰ τοῦτο οἱ πλείονες εἰς τὸν ᾅδην ἀπῆλθον·
οὐ γὰρ εἰμὶ τῶν ἀγενῶν οὐδὲ τῶν ἀνανδρίων,
καὶ εἰ ποτὲ προστάξῃς με ποιῆσαί σοι δουλείαν, 680
τότε λοιπὸν βεβαιωθῇς οἷον γαμβρὸν ἐπῆρες·
εἰ δὲ καὶ πεῖραν λάβῃς μου ἀκριβῆ ἐκ τῶν ἔργων,
τῆς εὐτυχίας ἑαυτὸν μακαρίσεις πολλάκις."
Αὐτίκα δὲ ὁ στρατηγός, χεῖρας εἰς ὕψος ἄρας
καὶ ὄμμα πρὸς ἀνατολάς, τῷ Θεῷ ηὐχαρίστει· 685
" Δόξα σοι," λέγων, "ὁ Θεὸς ὁ συμφερόντως πάντα
οἰκονομῶν τὰ καθ' ἡμᾶς σοφίᾳ τῇ ἀρρήτῳ·
ὡς γὰρ αὐτὸς ἠθέλησα γαμβροῦ κατηξιώθην 34 rᵒ.
ὡραίου τε καὶ εὐγενοῦς, σώφρονος καὶ ἀνδρείου,

---

663 εἰπὼν manque dans le ms.   674 σφικτὰς. χαμιλλά.   675 θαρσαλαία.
677 Après καὶ, je supprime μὴ.   678 δια (sans accent).   679 Faut-il
écrire ἀνανδρείων?

'Harm not, my soul, those own brothers of mine;
For those whom you see coming now towards us,
By the horses I judge they are my brothers,
The third man who is with them is my father;
Grant me them safe, and keep them without hurt.'
'What you ask shall be', the boy said to the Girl,
'If nought else happen unexpectedly;
(Whoever spares his foes in time of war   1740
Is often ruthlessly struck down by them).'
So having said he jumped on to his horse
Fell fast on those about the General.
The brothers of the Girl filled with much zeal,
Were telling their own men to finish him,
Counting his death should be by other hands;
But the boy, keeping his dear one's injunction,
With skill attacking wisely finished all.
The brothers then rushing madly on him,
He circled so and threw them from their horses   1750
As strictly not to harm or wound at all.
Then to the General turned far off dismounting,
Tightly clasping his hands and bowing low
Began to say to him with cheerful mien:
'Forgive me, master, blame me not at all:
Your troops were boorish at the give and take,
And therefore most of them have gone to Hades;
For I lack not nobility or valour,
And if you ever bid me do you service
You shall know all about your son-in-law;   1760
And if you try me strictly by my deeds
Often shall bless yourself for your good fortune.'
Straightway the General lifting high his hands
And his face to the east gave thanks to God:
Saying, 'Glory to thee O God who all things well
Rulest for us in unspeakable wisdom:
Just as I wished I am vouchsafed a son-in-law,
Noble and fair and temperate and brave,

οἵου οὐδεὶς ἐπέτυχε πώποτε εἰς τὸν κόσμον." 690
Ταῦτα ἐξ ὅλης τῆς ψυχῆς Θεῷ εὐχαριστήσας,
πρὸς τὸν παῖδα ἐφθέγξατο ἐπιεικῶς τοιάδε·
" Χάρις μέν, ὦ χρυσόγαμβρε, τῷ Θεῷ ἐπὶ πᾶσι,
τῷ τὰ συμφέροντα ἡμῖν καλῶς οἰκονομοῦντι·
ἔπαρον δέ, παγκάλλιστε, ἣν ἔλαβες ἐκ πόθου· 695
εἰ μὴ γὰρ πόθον ἄπειρον πρὸς αὐτὴν πάντως εἶχες
οὐκ ἂν μόνος ἐτόλμησας ἐμβῆναι εἰς χιλιάδας·
δεῦρο οὖν ἃς ἀπέλθωμεν εἰς τὸν ἐμὸν τὸν οἶκον,
καὶ μὴ λογίζου παρ' ἡμῶν λυπηρὸν ὑποστῆναι,
ἀλλ' ἵνα καὶ τὰ σύμφωνα ποιήσωμεν τοῦ γάμου 700
συμβόλαια ἐν γράμμασι, τοῦ πατρός σου παρόντος,
τάχιστα γὰρ ὡς μηνυθεὶς πρὸς ἡμᾶς ἐπανήξεις
καὶ τὴν προῖκα τῆς θυγατρὸς τῆς ἐμῆς ἀπολήψεις·
ποιήσω καὶ τοὺς γάμους σου ἀκουστοὺς εἰς τὸν κόσμον,
νὰ λάβῃς καὶ τὴν προῖκα σου ἀπ' αὐτῆς τῆς ἡμέρας 705
κεντηνάρια εἴκοσι νομίσματα παλαῖα,
ἃ πρὸ καιροῦ ἐχώρισα καὶ ἐθέμην ἰδίως
τῆς φιλτάτης εἰς ὄνομα, καὶ ἀργυραῖα σκεύη,
βιστιάριον χρῆζον τε πεντακοσίας λίτρας,
κτήματα πολλὰ ἀκίνητα τριανταὲξ εἰσόδων, 710
βάγιας ἑβδομήκοντα σὺν τῷ μητρῴῳ οἴκῳ,
περιφανεῖ τυγχάνοντι καὶ πολυτίμῳ ὄντως·
ὡσαύτως καὶ ἐξαίσια κόσμια τῆς μητρός της,
στέφανον τὸν παγκόσμιον, ἀξιέπαινον ἔργον 34 vᵒ.
συντεθειμένον ἐκ χρυσοῦ, λίθων τιμιωτάτων· 715
καὶ μετὰ τούτων πάντων εὑρισκόμενα ζῶα,
πρωτεῖα τετρακόσια, στράτορας ὀγδοήντα,
μαγείρους δεκατέσσαρας καὶ μάγκιπας ὡσαύτως,
καὶ ἕτερα ψυχάρια ἑκατὸν καὶ πενήντα·

695 παγκάλιστε.   706 παλαῖα, au lieu de παλαιά, est une accentuation par-
ticulière au grec médiéval.   710 εἰσόδων τριανταὲξ.   716 Le premier
hémistiche est incomplet d'une syllabe.   717 στράτωρας.   719 πενῆντα.

1772 χρυσόγαμβρε. Cf. μαυρόμματε, above 1620, for the successful use of vernacular appellatives.
1785 κεντηνάρια. Legrand (TRE 1307) translates 'quintaux', and Constantinides' dictionary gives 'quintal', and O.E.D. gives 'quintal' as meaning a

hundredweight (Arab. qintār). See Legrand's note (TRE, p. 281): 'Le quintal ou centenarium vaut cent livres ou litrae byzantines.' Gibbon on the finances of Justinian (chapter xl) makes a centenary of gold the equivalent of four thousand pounds.

Such as none ever found yet in the world.'
Thus giving thanks with all his soul to God   1770
These words he uttered kindly to the boy:
'Thanks above all, my golden groom, to God,
Who governs well what things are good for us.
Take her, fair youth, whom you desired to have;
If you had not boundless desire for her
You would not dare alone encounter thousands.
Come then let us go hence into my house;
And think not to meet at our hands any hurt,
But that we make agreements for the marriage,
Contracts in writing, in your father's presence,   1780
And soon advised you shall return to us,
And you shall bear away my daughter's dowry.
I will make the wedding famous in the world,
And from this day you shall receive your dowry,
Twenty centenaries of ancient coins,
Which long ago I sorted and put by
In her my dearest's name, and silver vessels,
A wardrobe valuing five hundred pounds,
Many estates of income, thirty-six,
Seventy handmaids, with her mother's house,   1790
Which is illustrious and truly precious,
Likewise her mother's marvellous ornaments,
Her world-famed crown, an admirable work
Of gold compounded and most precious stones;
And with all these the cattle that are there,
Four hundred prizewinners, and eighty grooms,
And fourteen cooks, the same number of bakers,
And other serfs, one hundred and fifty.

1788 βιστιάριον, i.e. *vestiarium*. *Vestiarium* can mean, to quote Maigne
d'Arnis, 'locus ubi non modo vestes
asservantur sed etiam cimelia, atque
adeo thesaurus et pecuniae'. So here
it may be explanatory of the σκεύη,
'a treasure chest of silver plate worth
five hundred pounds'.
1792 κόσμια 'ornaments'.
1795 This line (TRE 1310) should

apparently come after 1789. Leg. τὰ
εὑρισκόμενα.
1796 πρωτεῖα (a favourite word of
Psellos) is difficult here; but see
below 2245, where it is unmistakably
used of horses.
1798 ψυχάρια. *Mancipia*, Ducange
quoting Const. Porph. *de Adm. Imp.* 32
(55). ἀντέδωκαν ... ψυχάρια δύο φαλ-
κώνια δύο. (Also *ib.* 9. 52.)

δώσω σοι καὶ προτίμησιν τῶν λοιπῶν μου παιδίων   720
πλοῦτον πολὺν καὶ ἄπειρον, κτήματα οὐκ ὀλίγα,
σὺν τούτοις ἄλλα πλείονα παράσχω τῶν ῥηθέντων,
πρὸ τοῦ γενέσθαι, τέκνον μου, τὴν ἱερολογίαν,
ποιήσω καὶ τοὺς γάμους σου ἀκουστοὺς εἰς τὸν κόσμον,
τοῦ μὴ κράζειν σε πώποτε κλεψίγαμον οἱ νέοι,   725
καὶ ὅτι κόρην ἥρπασας πραγμάτων ἀμοιροῦσαν,
ὅπερ αἰσχύνη πέφυκε πᾶσι τοῖς εὖ φρονοῦσιν·
καὶ ταῦτα πῶς οὐκ ἐκφυγεῖν ῥαδίως ἐξισχύσεις,
εἰ μὴ τανῦν σὺ μεθ' ἡμῶν ὑποστραφῇς ἐν οἴκῳ,
ὅπως καὶ ἡ στρατήγισσα παρηγορίαν λάβῃ   730
(οὐδαμῶς γὰρ ἐπίσταται ποῖος ἄρα τυγχάνεις),
καὶ χαίρουσα τῶν ἀγαθῶν μεγαλύνη δοτῆρα·
πείσθητι οὖν, καλὲ γαμβρέ, καὶ ἐλθὲ μετ' ἐμένα."
Ταῦτα εἰπὼν ὁ στρατηγὸς κολακεύων τὸν νέον,
παρευθὺς ὁ νεώτερος τῷ στρατηγῷ ἀντέφη·   735
" Πεισθῆναι σου τῆς συμβουλῆς ἀρίστης ὑπαρχούσης,
αὐθέντα μου καὶ πενθερέ, δίκαιόν με τυγχάνει,
καὶ δέδοικα μὴ κίνδυνος ἐκ τούτου μοι ἐπέλθῃ,
καὶ μετ' αἰσχύνης θάνατον οἰκτρότατον ὀφλήσω,
ὡς ἐχθρὸς καὶ ἐπίβουλος καὶ ἐχθρὸς γεγονώς σου·   35 rᵒ.   740
πείθει με γὰρ τὸ συνειδὸς τηρεῖν τὰ ἐναντία,
καὶ τὴν ὄψιν ἐρυθριῶ ἰδεῖν τῆς στρατηγίσσης·
ἐγώ, κύριε μου πενθερέ, ἐπιθυμίαν εἶχον
τὴν θυγατέρα σου λαβεῖν διὰ τὸ ταύτης κάλλος,
οὐχὶ δὲ πλούτου εἵνεκα ἢ διὰ τῶν κτημάτων·   745
ταῦτα πάντα χαρίζομαι τοῖς γυναικαδελφοῖς μου·
ἀρκοῦν ἐμοὶ τὰ κάλλη της ἀντὶ πολλῶν προικίων,
πλοῦτον παρέχει ὁ Θεὸς καὶ πενίαν ὡσαύτως,
καὶ ταπεινοῖ καὶ ἀνυψοῖ, κατάγει καὶ ἀνάγει·
ὑπὲρ δὲ τοῦ ὑποστραφῆν, οὐ μή σε παρακούσω·   750
ἀλλ' ἂς ἀπέλθω πρότερον εἰς τὴν ἐμὴν μητέρα,
ἵν' ἴδῃ ὁ ἐμὸς πατὴρ νύμφην ἣν θέλει ἔχειν
καὶ νὰ δοξάσῃ τὸν Θεὸν καὶ ταχὺ ὑποστρέφω·
ἀλλὰ μὴ τοῦτο λυπηθῇς, ὑπερεύχου δὲ μᾶλλον,
τέκνα σου γὰρ τυγχάνομεν καὶ δοῦλοι τῆς ψυχῆς σου."   755
Καὶ θαυμάσας ὁ στρατηγὸς τὴν σύνεσιν τοῦ νέου·

729 τανῦν. σὺ manque dans le ms. ὑποραφῇς.   732 μεγαλύνει.   743
κύριέ μου.   750 ὑποστραφεῖν.   753 νὰ manque dans le ms.

I will give you honour above my other children,
Much wealth and boundless, not a few estates,   1800
With these provide more else than has been said,
Before, my child, the sacred rite is done;
And make your wedding famous in the world,
The boys shall never cry you stole the match,
And snatched a girl that had no share of goods,
Which is disgrace to all are minded well;
And this you will not easily escape,
Unless you turn home presently with us,
So that my lady may have consolation
(For no wise does she know who you may be),   1810
And gladly praise the dispenser of blessings;
So, good groom, be persuaded, come with me.'
    So said the General, flattering the boy,
Straightway the youth answered the General:
'To obey your counsel which is excellent,
Master and father-in-law, is right for me,
But that I fear lest danger come therefrom,
And I with shame pay due of piteous death,
As having been your foe, your traitorous foe.
Conscience persuades me keep the opposing course,   1820
And I should blush to see your lady's face.
I, my lord father-in-law, had the wish
To take your daughter for her beauty's sake,
Not for her riches or for her possessions;
All these I give them to my wife's brothers.
To me her beauty stands for many dowries.
God bestows wealth and likewise poverty,
He humbles and exalts, brings down, lifts up.
As for returning I will not hearken to you;
Let me first go hence to my own mother,   1830
That my father may see his daughter-in-law to be,
And may praise God, and I will soon return.
Do not regret this, rather pray for us;
We are your children, servants of your soul.'
    The General admired his understanding,

" Ὁ Θεός," ἔφη, " τέκνον μου, ἵνα σε εὐλογήσῃ
καὶ ἀξιώσῃ χαίρεσθαι τὰ ἔτη τῆς ζωῆς σου! "
Καὶ ἀσπασάμενος αὐτὸν ἐπέβηκε τοῦ ἵππου·
καὶ εἰς τὴν κόρην μὲν αὐτός, στρατηγὸς δὲ ἐν οἴκῳ,   760
συνοδοιπόρους τοὺς υἱοὺς ἐκ τοῦ πώματος ἔχων,
σφόδρα ὑπερθαυμάζοντες τὴν τοῦ παιδὸς ἀνδρείαν.
Ὁ δέ γε ὄντως θαυμαστὸς ἐκεῖνος νεανίας
ἐν τῷ τόπῳ καταλαβὼν ἔνθα ἦτον ἡ κόρη·
" Δεῦρο, γλυκύτατόν μου φῶς," ἐξεφώνησε λέγων,   765
" δεῦρο, ἄνθος γλυκύτατον, ρόδον μεμυρισμένον,
δεῦρο, δάμαλις ἡ ἐμὴ ἣν ἔζευξεν ὁ ἔρως,   36 rᵒ.
τὴν ὁδὸν διανύσωμεν, οὐδεὶς γὰρ ὁ κωλύων,
δρόμον οὐδείς, πανεύμορφε, ἐστὶν ὁ ἐμποδίζων,
μόνον πατρὸς καὶ ἀδελφῶν τῶν σῶν περισωθέντων·   770
οὐ γὰρ τὸ πρόσταγμα τὸ σὸν ἠθέλησ' ἀθετῆσαι."
Καὶ ἐκ τοῦ δένδρου παρευθὺς κατελθοῦσα ἡ κόρη,
χαρᾶς καὶ ἡδονῆς πολλῆς ὑποπλησθεῖσα λίαν,
περιπατοῦσα γαληνὰ τὸν ἄγουρον ὑπήντα
καί, πλησίον γενόμενοι, μετὰ πόθου ἠρώτα·   775
" Πάντως οὐδὲν ἐνάντιον συνέβη σοι, ψυχή μου,
ἀνάγγειλόν μοι τάχιον περὶ τῶν ἀδελφῶν μου."
" Μὴ θλίβεσαι, ψυχίτζα μου," ὁ ἄγουρος ἀντέφη,
" ἐκτὸς γὰρ τῶν ἐπαινετῶν ἀγούρων τοῦ πατρός σου,
οὐδεὶς ὑπέστη μερικῶς οὔτε καθόλου βλάβην."   780
Καὶ κύψας εἵλκυσεν αὐτὴν ἐπάνω ἐν τῷ ἵππῳ,
καὶ ὑποδέχεται αὐτὴν ἐν τῷ ἰδίῳ ἵππῳ·
φιλήματός τε καθαροῦ ἡδέως κορεσθέντες
καὶ χαίροντες διώδευον μεθ' ἡδονῆς μεγάλης.
Καὶ ὡς ἐσκέψαντο αὐτὸν αἱ βίγλαι τοῦ πατρός του   785
ἐν ταῖς ἀγκάλαις φέροντα τὴν ροδόμορφον κόρην,
μετὰ σπουδῆς ἀπέτρεχον εἰπεῖν τὰ συγχαρίκια.
Ὡς δὲ ἤκουσεν ὁ πατὴρ τὴν τούτου ἔλευσιν ὅλως,

---

767 Le verso du f. 35 resté blanc a été rempli ultérieurement par des prières et
des invocations écrites d'une main assez peu expérimentée.   778 θλίβεσε.
787 ἀπέτρεχεν.

1839 The construction is muddled with   less; we must of course read πτώμα-
   the characteristic changes of subject.   τος, 'after their fall'.
1840 ἐκ τοῦ πώματος. This is meaning-

'May God,' he said, 'my child, give you his blessing,
Grant you enjoy all the years of your life.'
And having embraced him he mounted his horse;
He to the Girl; the General went home,
With him faring, after their fall, his sons,   1840
Very much wondering at the boy's valour.
    Meanwhile wondrous indeed the youth himself,
When he had reached the place where the Girl was,
Called to her saying, 'Come, sweetest my light,
Come, sweetest flower, perfume-breathing rose,
My little heifer, come, whom love has yoked,
Let us begin the way, for none prevents,
None is there, loveliest, who bars the road,
Only your father is left and your brothers,
Because I would not disregard your bidding.'   1850
Then from the tree straightway the Girl descending,
Filled with exceeding joy and great delight,
Quietly walking went to meet the boy,
And coming near she asked him lovingly,
'At all events no ill befell you, my soul,
Inform me quickly now about my brothers.'
'Grieve not, my darling soul,' the boy replied,
'Except your father's honourable boys,
No one was hurt partially or at all.'
Stooping he drew up her on to the horse,   1860
Accommodating her on his own horse.
Of pure kissing they gladly took their fill
And joyfully they fared with great delight.
And when his father's watchmen sighted him
Bearing the roselike Girl within his arms
In haste they ran to tell deserving news.
And when his father fully heard his coming

1857, 1858 ἄγουρος . . . ἀγούρων. The
  awkwardness of this repetition and
  of the 'horse' repetition in 1860, 1861
  has been intentionally reproduced.
1863 ἡδονὴ here in classical sense, as
  below 1934.
1865 ῥοδόμορφον. Must be 'rose-lovely'
  (ῥοδο-εὔμορφος) rather than 'rose-

shaped'.
1866 συγχαρίκια. Here means not the
  reward given for good news but the
  news which deserves rewarding. See
  above 888, 948. And *Sacrifice of
  Abraham*, 1095. See Ducange s.vv.
  συγχαριάρια, συγχαρίκια.

πλήρης γενόμενος χαράς εὐθὺς καβαλλικεύει,
οἱ πέντε γυναικάδελφοι, τρισχίλιοι ἀγοῦροι, 790
δώδεκα σελλοχάλινα ἔστρωσαν γυναικεῖα,
δύο ὑπῆρχον χυμευτὰ μετὰ μαργαριτάρων
καὶ τὰ λοιπὰ ὁλόχρυσα μάλιστα μετὰ ζώων·
πέπλα δὲ εἶχον ἅπασαι αἱ σέλλαι παγκαλλίστως· 36 vᵒ.
βλαττία ἦσαν σκεπαστοὶ οἱ ἵπποι πάντες μάλα 795
ὑπ᾽ αὐτῶν καλυπτόμενοι καὶ τοῦ πολλοῦ χρυσίου·
ὄπισθεν τούτων σάλπιγγες καὶ βούκινα βαρέα,
τύμπανά τε καὶ ὄργανα ἐκρούοντο εἰς ἄκρον,
καὶ ἦν ἦχος ἐξάκουστος ἐν ἐκείνῃ τῇ ὥρᾳ·
ὡς ἄχρι τρία μίλλια τοῦ οἴκου προσελθόντες, 800
οὕσπερ ἰδοῦσα μήκοθεν ἡ πανώραιος κόρη
σύντρομος ὅλη γέγονε τοὺς ὄντας ἀγνοοῦσα,
καὶ πρὸς τὸν παῖδα ἔφησε λίαν συντετριμμένη·
" Ἐὰν ξένοι τυγχάνωσιν, ἡμᾶς ἀποχωρίσουν."
" Μὴ φοβοῦ, φῶς μου τὸ γλυκύ," ὁ νέος ἀπεκρίθη, 805
" ὁ πενθερός σου ἔνι αὐτός, διὰ σὲ ἐκοπώθη."
Πάλιν τὸ ἡλιογέννημα τὸν ἄγουρον ἀντέφη·
" Ἐντρέπομαι, ψυχίτζα μου, δι᾽ οὗ μόνη τυγχάνω·
εἰ τοῦ πατρός μου ἤκουσας καὶ μετ᾽ ἐμοῦ ἐστράφης,
ἄρτι νὰ εἶχον τὰς βάγιας μου καὶ τὴν ἐξόμπλισίν μου, 810
νὰ ἐγίνωσκε καὶ ὁ σὸς πατὴρ τίνος παιδὶν ἀπῆρες·
ἀλλ᾽ ὅμως ὡς τὸ ἐδίκησας, ἀπολογίας ἔχε."
" Μὴ λυπεῖσαι, πανεύγενε, διὰ τὴν μοναξίαν,
σὲ γὰρ πάντες γινώσκουσι κἂν καὶ μόνη τυγχάνεις,
καὶ τούτου μέμψις ἕνεκα ὑπάρχει οὐδεμία." 815
Ὅτε δὲ ἐπλησίασαν, χαιρετίζουν ἀλλήλους·
ἐπέζευσεν ὁ νεώτερος μετὰ τῆς ποθητῆς του,
ἐπέζευσε καὶ ὁ ἀμηρᾶς, ἠσπάσατο τοὺς δύο·
" Ὁ Θεός," ἔφη, " τέκνον μου, ἵνα σας εὐλογήσῃ,
αὐξήσῃ καὶ τὰ ἔτη σου ἐν εἰρήνῃ καὶ πλούτῳ, 37 rᵒ. 820

792 χιμευτά. 800 μίλια. 806 αὐτὸς ὁ πενθερός σου ἔνι. 810 βάγιάς
μου. 813 λυπῆσα. 815 οὐδὲ μία.

1870 σελλοχάλινα. One of the common
dvandva compounds.
1871 See above 1220.
1872 μάλιστα μετὰ ζώων. The ζῶα must
be taken in the sense of ζωίδια and
like the ζώων συγκοπαί below 1988.

See Ducange, s.v. ζώδιον. See also
L. & S. showing that even in Hdt.
and Plato ζῷον can mean any painting or design, not necessarily of an
animal.

Being filled with joy at once he mounted horse,
His wife's five brothers, with three thousand men,
Twelve women's saddles and bridles they prepared,   1870
Two of them were all jewelly with pearls,
The others all of gold, with figured beasts,
And all the saddles beautifully draped;
The horses all were hung with purple silk
By which they were enwrapped and with much gold;
Behind these trumpets were and heavy horns,
And drums and organs they were loudly playing,
And at that time there was a noise far heard.
As far as three miles from the house advancing,
Whom seeing from afar the lovely Girl,   1880
Not knowing who they are was all atremble,
And to the boy she said in sore affliction,
'If they are strangers they will sever us.'
'Fear not, my sweet light,' the youth made answer,
'That is your father-in-law, for you his pains.'
Again the sun-child answered to the boy,
'Darling, I am shamed, because I am alone;
If you had turned back with me, heeding my father,
That I should have my maids and my array,
Your father too should know whose child you have taken, 1890
But you decided, yours be the excuses.'
'Most noble do not grieve to be alone,
For they all know you, even if you are alone,
There is no blame at all on that account.'
    When they came near they greeted each other;
The young man then dismounted with his loved one,
The Emir dismounted and embraced them both.
'May God,' he said, 'my child, give you His blessing,
Therewith increase your years in peace and wealth,

1879 The three-mile limit. See above 635 and below 2272.
1885 ἐκοπώθη. 'He has taken all this trouble.' The classical κοπόω is here used in the sense of the modern κοπιάζω, for which see Soph. s.v. κοπιάω, who refers to Theoph. 728. 18, where it is used in exactly the sense of the present passage—'to take the trouble, or have the great kindness, to come'. For similar use of κουράζομαι see *Sacrifice of Abraham* 766, where the correct reading is κουρασθῇ.
1889 ἐξόμπλισιν. Leg. ἐξόπλισιν with TRE 1349, AND 2212.
1891 GRO noticeably gives the Girl a character and allows her to be critical.

καὶ βασιλείας τῆς αὐτοῦ ἐπιδείξῃ μετόχους! "

Εἰς δὲ σέλλαν τὴν χυμευτὴν καθίσαντες τὴν κόρην,
καὶ πολύτιμον στέφανον αὐτῇ περιβαλόντες,
καὶ ἕκαστος τῶν συγγενῶν τῶν ἐκεῖ εὑρεθέντων
δῶρα αὐτῇ προσήνεγκαν ὑπέρτιμα τῷ ὄντι·   825
καὶ, τὸν παῖδα κοσμήσαντες ὡς ἔπρεπε τῷ νέῳ,
τὰ βούκινα ἐδώκασιν, ὑπέστρεφον εὐθέως,
ἠλάλαζον αἱ σάλπιγγες, τὰ τύμπανα ἐφώνουν,
ἐκρούοντο τὰ ὄργανα, ἐμελῴδουν τὰ πάντα·
κιθάραι ἦχον ἔπεμπον καὶ πᾶν μουσικὸν εἶδος,   830
ᾀδόμενα ὑπέστρεφον ἐν τῷ οἴκῳ συντόμως.
Χαρὰν τὴν ὑπερβάλλουσαν τὴν γιναμένην τότε
τίς ἑρμηνεῦσαι δυνηθῇ ἢ εἰπεῖν ἐξισχύσει;
Ἐδόκουν γὰρ ὡς καὶ ἡ γῆ ἐν ᾗ περιεπάτουν
καὶ αὐτὴ συνετέρπετο περιπατούντων πάντων·   835
καὶ πᾶς ὅστις ἐτύγχανεν εἰς τὴν χαρὰν ἐκείνην
ἄλλος ἐξ ἄλλου γέγονεν ἀπὸ τῆς θυμηδίας·
τὰ βουνία ἐσκίρτιζον, ἐχόρευον αἱ πέτραι,
ἀνέβλυζον οἱ ποταμοί, ἠγάλλοντο τὰ δένδρα,
ὁ ἀὴρ ἐφαιδρύνετο ἐν τῇ χαρᾷ ἐκείνῃ.   840
Ὡς δὲ τοῦ οἴκου ἔμελλον ἀπάρτι πλησιάσαι,
πλῆθος ἄπειρον γυναικῶν αὐτοῖς συναπαντῶσιν·
ἦν γὰρ καὶ ἡ στρατήγισσα πρὸς ἀπαντὴν τῶν νέων,
καὶ σὺν αὐτῇ ἡ πάντερπνος μήτηρ ἡ τοῦ Ἀκρίτου,
οἰκέτιδές τε εὐπρεπεῖς λαμπρῶς ἠγλαϊσμέναι,   845
αἱ μὲν ἄνθη κατέχουσαι ῥόδα τε καὶ μυρσίνας,   37 vᵒ.
τὸν ἀέρα μυρίζουσαι ὀσμαὶ θυμιαμάτων·
ἕτεραι χειροκύμβαλα ἔκρουον μελῳδοῦσαι
μέλος λίαν ἡδύτατον, ἐπαινοῦσαι τὸν παῖδα
καὶ τὴν παρθένον μετ᾽ αὐτοῦ καὶ γονεῖς ἀμφοτέρων·   850
ἔδαφος ἐπανέστρωτο μυρσίνας τε καὶ δάφνας,
ῥόδα, ναρκίσσους καὶ πολλὰ εὐωδέστατα ἄνθη.
Ἡ πενθερὰ τὴν ἑαυτῆς κατησπάζετο νύμφην,
ἔργα αὐτῆς ἐξαίρετα φιλοτίμως παρέχει,

---

821 ἐπιδείξει.   827 βύκινα.   829 ἐκρόουντο.

1901 χυμευτήν. I think 'jewelled' is as   1916 ἄλλος ἐξ ἄλλου. Above 1678.
fair a translation as we can get,   1922 στρατήγισσα. I.e. the Emir's
meaning that it had been decorated   mother-in-law, grandmother of Di-
by a goldsmith or jeweller.   genes. See below 1995.

And show you to be sharers in His kingdom.'   1900
   Sitting the Girl upon the jewelled saddle
They set a precious crown upon her head,
And each one of the kinsmen who were there
Offered her presents truly of great price;
The boy adorning, as beseemed the youth,
They blew the horns, began straight to return,
The trumpets blaring and the drums were sounding,
The organs playing, everything was singing,
Sounding the lutes and every kind of music,
With song they returned quickly to the house.   1910
   The overtopping joy that there was then
Who shall interpret or have power to tell?
It seemed as even the earth on which they walked
Delighted with them as they walked on it;
Everyone who happened in that gladness
Was quite beside himself with his rejoicing,
The hills were skipping and the rocks were dancing,
The rivers gushing up, the trees made merry,
And with that joy the air was made to shine.
   When they were now about to approach the house   1920
A boundless crowd of women came to meet them;
There was the General's wife to meet the young ones,
With her the charming mother of the Borderer;
And comely housemaids brilliantly adorned,
Some bearing flowers, roses, myrtle boughs,
With balmy odours perfuming the air;
Others were beating cymbals as they sang
A song exceeding sweet, praising the boy,
The virgin with him, and the parents of both;
The ground was strewed with myrtles and with bay,   1930
Narcissus, rose, and many fragrant flowers.
Her mother-in-law fondly embraced the bride,
Presented honouring her finest work;

1924 This charming feature of the reception is not found in any other version: and the 'system of housemaids' and flowers is repeated below 1957 ff.

1933 ἔργα αὐτῆς ἐξαίρετα. I.e. needlework or weaving or embroidery. Women's work, as in Hom. *Od.* 20. 72, *Il.* 9. 390, or Theocr. 15. 37 τοῖς δ' ἔργοις καὶ τὰν ψυχὰν ποτέθηκα.

καὶ ἦν ἄπληστος ἡδονὴ καὶ μεγίστη τερπνότης. 855

Εἰς δὲ τὸν οἶκον φθάσαντες, ὁ ἀμηρᾶς εὐθέως
γυναικαδελφοὺς τοὺς ἑαυτοῦ καὶ στρατὸν οὐκ ὀλίγον
συναριθμήσας ἔστειλε τρισχιλίους ἀγούρους
νὰ εἴπωσι τὸν στρατηγὸν ἵν᾽ ἔλθη εἰς τοὺς γάμους·
" Κέλευσον, ὦ συμπενθερέ, τοῦ ἐλθεῖν εἰς τοὺς γάμους, 860
οὓς ὁ Θεὸς ἡτοίμασεν, ἡμῶν μὴ βουλομένων."
Ὡς δὲ καὶ τούτων ἤκουσεν μὴ ἀμελήσας ὅλως,
ἅπαντα ἅπερ εἰς τιμὴν τῶν φιλτάτων [προσῆκον]
μεθ᾽ ἑαυτοῦ παραλαβὼν ἀνείκαστόν τε πλῆθος
τῇ ἑξῆς ἐπορεύετο μετὰ τῆς στρατηγίσσης· 865
οὐδὲν γὰρ εἶχον τι λέγειν ἢ ποσῶς ἀμφιβάλλειν,
οἵου γαμβροῦ τετύχηκαν γεγονότες ἐν γνώσει·
σὺν προθυμίᾳ τὸ λοιπὸν καὶ χαρμονῇ μεγίστη
τὴν ὁδὸν μᾶλλον ἤνυον ᾄδοντες τὰ τοῦ γάμου
καὶ οἱ τῆς κόρης ἀδελφοὶ μετὰ τῶν συμπαρόντων· 870
ἄφιξιν δὲ τὴν ἑαυτῶν ὁ τοῦ παιδὸς ἀκούσας
πατὴρ πρὸς ὑπαντὴν καλὴν μετὰ λαοῦ ἐξῆλθε·
βουλόμενος δ᾽ ὁ θαυμαστὸς κατελθεῖν ἐκ τοῦ ἵππου, 38 rᵒ.
ὁ στρατηγὸς ἐκώλυσεν ἑαυτὸν ἐξορκίσας·
ἀλλήλους τε ὡς ἔπρεπεν ἀσπασάμενοι μάλα 875
ἐπὶ τὸν οἶκον ἔσπευδον καὶ ὀλίγον προβάντων
πεζοπόροι ἀπήντησαν ἀναρίθμητον πλῆθος,
καὶ μετ᾽ ἐκείνους ἕτεροι σύστημα οἰκετίδων·
τοῦ οἴκου δὲ τὰ σύνορα καταλαβόντες ἤδη
μετὰ κόσμου τοῦ πρέποντος πλήθους θυμιαμάτων 880
ῥοδόσταμμα καὶ τῶν λοιπῶν παντοίων μυρισμάτων.
Ταῦτα ἡ μήτηρ τοῦ παιδὸς ἤγαγεν ἡ ὡραία·
τὰ δὲ ἐντεῦθεν ποῖος νοῦς φράσαι ὅλως ἰσχύσει;
τὴν θαυμαστὴν ὑποδοχὴν τοῦ ἀμηρᾶ ἐκείνην,
τὴν καλὴν συναναστροφὴν τῆς ἑαυτοῦ συζύγου, 885
εὐωχίαν τὴν εὔτακτον καὶ ἁρμόδιον τάξιν,
ἐδεσμάτων τὴν ἄπειρον πολυποίκιλον θέαν

875 ἀσπασάμενος.   881 ῥοδοστάμματα.   887 ἐδαισμάτων.

1939 κέλευσον, ὦ συμπενθερέ. A confusion of direct and indirect narration; cf. below 2328.
1942 προσῆκον is presumably supplied

by Legrand.
1948 ᾄδοντες τὰ τοῦ γάμου. Perhaps
the traditional Greek νυφιάτικα
τραγούδια.

So there was endless pleasure and great delight.
When they came to the house the Emir straightway
His own wife's brothers with no small company
Mustered and sent three thousand men-at-arms
To tell the General to come to the wedding:
'Bid my fellow father-in-law come to the wedding,
Which God has settled with no will of ours.'   1940
He when he heard them not neglecting aught,
All things in proper honour of his dears
Taking with him, in number not imagined,
On the next day set forth with his lady.
For they had naught to say, or room to doubt,
Having learned what a bridegroom they had found;
Eagerly then and with greatest gladness
The way they speeded with the marriage songs,
And the Girl's brothers with those there attending.
Of their arrival then hearing the boy's   1950
Father went out to welcome with his folk;
And when the famous one would have dismounted,
The General prevented him adjuring.
Having embraced each other as was meet,
They hastened toward the house, and on a little
Met them on foot a countless company,
Others with them, an assembly of housemaids,
And as they reached the precincts of the house
In meet array an incense-bearing crowd
With rosewater and all other perfumes.   1960
These the boy's mother led, the beautiful.
What then ensued what mind has power to tell?
That wonderful reception by the Emir,
The lovely conversation of his spouse,
The ordered banqueting and due array
Of meats, the endless-varied spectacle,

1952 ὁ θαυμαστός, used absolutely, usually means, as noted elsewhere, 'the Hero', i.e. Digenes. Here it is used of the Emir, ὁ τοῦ παιδὸς πατήρ of the preceding lines, who had also been a Hero in his own right, as Grégoire has reminded us.

1957 μετ' ἐκείνους ἕτεροι σύστημα οἰκετίδων. An example of the habitual confusion of genders, as the three lines following are of the confusion of cases.

τὴν ἐκ πάντων παράθεσιν ζώων ἀναριθμήτων;
τῶν μίμων τὰς μεταβολάς, αὐλητῶν μελῳδίας,
χορευτρίων λιγύσματα, ποδῶν τὰς μεταβάσεις, 890
τῶν χορῶν τὸ ἐνήδονον καὶ ξένην μελῳδίαν;
κάλλος γὰρ εἶχον ἅπαντα τέρψιν ἄλλο πρὸς ἄλλο.
Προικὸς δὲ τὰ συμβόλαια τῇ ἑξῆς πληρωθέντα,
τὰ ἐν αὐτοῖς ἀδύνατον κατ' ἔπος ἐξιέναι·
ἅπερ δὲ οὐ συνέθεντο ἀμφότεροι τοῖς τέκνοις 895
καλῶς τε καὶ τὰ κτήματα εὐαρίθμητα ὄντα
μὴ λέξαι ἐξ ὀνόματος ἀπρεπέστατον ἔστιν
τῶν τε ζώων τὸν ἀριθμὸν καὶ τῶν λοιπῶν πραγμάτων.
Δέδωκε μὲν ὁ στρατηγὸς ἵππους δώδεκα μαύρους,
τερπνὰ φαρία δώδεκα εὐμορφότατα λίαν, 38 vᵒ. 900
δώδεκα μούλας ἐκλεκτὰς μετὰ σελλοχαλίνων
ἀργυρῶν τε καὶ χυμευτῶν, ἔργων ἀξιεπαίνων·
οἰκέτας νέους δώδεκα, στράτορας χρυσοζώνους,
δώδεκα παρδοκυνηγοὺς λίαν δοκιμωτάτους,
χιονίδας ἱέρακας δώδεκα Ἀβασγίας, 905
φαλκωνάρια δώδεκα καὶ φάλκωνας ὡσαύτως·
εἰκόνας δύο χυμευτὰς ἁγίων Θεοδώρων,
καὶ τένδαν χρυσοκέντητον, ὡραίαν, παμμεγέθη,
ζώων ἔχουσαν συγκοπὰς πολυμόρφους ἰδέας,
τὰ σχοινία μεταξωτά, ἀργυροὶ δὲ οἱ πάλοι, 910
κοντάρια κυπρίζοντα ἀραβίτικα δύο,
καὶ τοῦ Χοσρόου τὸ σπαθὶν τὸ διαφημισμένον.
Καὶ ταῦτα μὲν ὁ στρατηγὸς χαρίσματα παρέσχε
γαμβρὸν αὐτοῦ τὸν Διγενῆ· ὁ δ' ἀμηρᾶς ὡσαύτως
θεώρετον πολύτιμον παρέδωκε τῇ κόρῃ· 915
ὁμοίως καὶ ἡ στρατήγισσα ἡ μάμμη τοῦ Ἀκρίτου·
οἱ πέντε γυναικάδελφοι καὶ συγγενεῖς οἱ ἄλλοι

890 Il y a bien dans le ms. χορευτρίων et non χορευτριῶν. 900 εὐμορφώ-
τατα. 907 χυτάς.

1967 παράθεσιν. The uses of this word
(see Soph.) show that it refers to the
presentation of animals for food.
1969 λιγύσματα. Leg. λυγίσματα.
1974 ff. The translation reproduces the
confusion of the Greek. Possibly the
negative in 1974 ought to be dropped.
1984 χιονίδας ἱέρακας. 'Snowy', perhaps
by a misunderstanding of ἄχρωμος,

used ESC 1512 and elsewhere as a
stock epithet of the hawk and apparently meaning 'colourless', but
now well explained by Lambert
(*Lyb. Rod.* gloss.) as meaning 'un-
blushing', i.e. 'fearless'. See also
Goossens in *Byzantion* xxii (1952)
p. 260.
1985 φαλκωνάρια should probably be

Setting before them of all countless beasts,
The changes of the mimes, flute-players' tunes,
The bending dancing-girls, the shifting feet,
The delight of the dances, and strange music?   1970
Each had more charm and beauty than the other.
The bonds next day completed for the dowry
The contents word for word cannot be told;
Not but what both contracted for their children,
And the possessions which can well be counted,
These not to tell by name is most unseemly,
The number of the beasts and other things.

  The General presented twelve black horses,
Twelve handsome palfreys very beautiful,
Twelve chosen mules with saddle and bridles,   1980
Silver, enjewelled, admirable works;
With twelve young housemen, golden-belted grooms,
Twelve hunting leopards, strictly trained and tried,
Twelve snowy hawks brought from Abasgia,
Twelve falconers, also as many falcons.
Two jewelled pictures of Saints Theodore,
A gold-embroidered tent, immense and fair,
With manifold shapes of inlaid animals,
And silken ropes for it and silver poles;
Therewith were two Arabian spring-wood spears,   1990
And the renowned sword of Chosroës.
These were the gifts the General presented
His son-in-law Digenes. Likewise the Emir
Gave a most precious bride-gift to the Girl;
So did the General's wife, Akrites's grandmother.
His wife's five brothers and the other kinsmen,

φαλκωναρίους, as translated.
1988 ζώων . . . συγκοπὰς πολυμόρφους
ἰδέας. For συγκοπή in sense of tessel-
lated work see Ducange, and Soph.
who refers to Theoph. Cont. 143. 23.
1990 κυπρίζοντα. This can hardly mean
'made of copper'; or 'green' (oxidized
copper); or 'made of cypress'; but
κυπρίζω is used in LXX (Cant. ii. 13
and 15; vii. 13) of young vines blooming, and I have preferred to follow

this clue (LXX ἄμπελοι κυπρίζουσιν;
AV. 'The vines with the tender
grape'). For 'spring-wood' see O.E.D.
1991 TRE 1405, AND 2269.
1994 θεώρετρον. The gift on seeing the
bride; see Ducange s.v. θεώρητρον,
and cf. ὀπτήρια and ἀνακαλυπτήρια;
cf. also Homeric ἔδνα and Germ. Mor-
gengabe.
1996 i.e. the Emir's five brothers-in-
law.

μαργαριτάριν ἄπειρον, χρυσίον καὶ λιθάριν,
καὶ βλαττία πολύτιμα ἄπειρα καὶ ὀξέα·
ἡ δέ γε τούτου πενθερὰ παρέδωκεν ὡσαύτως   920
πράσινον λευκοτρίβλαττον καὶ ζώνας πολυτίμους,
τέσσαρα χρυσογράμματα φακεώλια ἄσπρα,
καββάδδην τε χρυσοφυῆ ὄπισθεν γρύψους ἔχον·
ὁ πρῶτος γυναικαδελφὸς δέδωκε δέκα νέους
ἀσκευάστους καὶ εὐειδεῖς καὶ τῇ κόμῃ ὡραίους,   925
ἠμφιεσμένους περσικὴν στολὴν ἀπὸ βλαττίου   39 rᵒ.
καὶ χρυσομάνικα καλὰ εἰς τοὺς αὐτῶν τραχήλους·
θάτερος γυναικαδελφὸς σκουτάριν καὶ κοντάριν·
ἄλλοι δὲ τούτου συγγενεῖς ἔδωκαν ἄλλα πλεῖστα,
ὧν οὐκ ἐξὸν ἀπαριθμεῖν τὸ εἶδος τῶν πραγμάτων.   930
Καὶ τρεῖς μῆνας ἐποίησε τελούμενος ὁ γάμος,
ἡ δὲ χαρὰ οὐκ ἔληγεν ἡ πάνδημος ἐκείνη·
Μετὰ δὲ τὸ συντελεσθῆν τὸν τριμηναῖον γάμον,
παραλαβὼν ὁ στρατηγὸς πάντας τοὺς συμπενθέρους
καὶ τὸν γαμβρὸν τὸν ἴδιον, ἦλθεν εἰς τὴν οἰκίαν,   935
καὶ γάμος ἄλλος γέγονεν φαιδρότερος τοῦ πρώτου.
Ἠγάλλετο ὁ στρατηγὸς τοῦ παιδὸς ὡς ἑώρα
τὴν εὔτακτον κατάστασιν, τὴν νουνεχῆ ἀνδρείαν,
τῶν ἠθῶν τὴν πραότητα καὶ λοιπὴν εὐκοσμίαν·
ἡ στρατήγισσα ἔχαιρε καθορῶσα τὸ κάλλος   940
καὶ τὴν αὐτοῦ πανευπρεπῆ καὶ ξένην ἡλικίαν·
οἱ τούτου γυναικαδελφοὶ ἐπισκέπτοντες σφόδρα
οἱ ταῖς αὐτῶν καυχώμενοι ἀεὶ ἀνδραγαθίαις,
καὶ δόξα τῷ μόνῳ ἀγαθῷ ἐπιτελοῦντι ἔργον.
Ἐν γὰρ ταῖς διοικήσεσι τῶν μεγίστων πραγμάτων   945
ὁ Θεὸς συνεισέρχεται, καὶ μηδεὶς ἀπιστείτω·
εὐλόγως τοίνυν πρὸς Θεὸν ἀναπέμψωμεν χάριν,
αὐτὸς γὰρ πάντων ὁ δοτὴρ τῶν ἀγαθῶν ὑπάρχει.
Ἐκεῖσε τοίνυν ἱκανὰς ποιήσαντες ἡμέρας,

933 συντελεσθεῖν.   943 αὐτῶν.

1998 βλαττία . . . ὀξέα. See above 896 ff.
2001 φακεώλια. See above 897.
2002 καββάδδην. Lampros, *Romans
grecs*, gloss. s.v. καβάδι (OXF 2917)
—'caftan, mot persan signifiant un
habit de guerre' (so that Kabbadias

and Caftanzoglu are different forms
of the same name).
2004 ἀσκευάστους. For the meaning of
this word, which does not seem to
occur elsewhere in this sense, see
L. & S. s.vv. σκεῦος and σκευή. It is

A boundless store of pearls, and gold, and stones,
And boundless precious cloths of purple silk;
His own mother-in-law likewise presented
Green and white threefold silk, and precious girdles,   2000
And four white turbans with gold monograms,
A gold-webbed cloak, with griffins at the back.
His wife's eldest brother gave him ten boys,
Sexless and handsome with lovely long hair,
Clothed in a Persian dress of silken cloth
With fine and golden sleeves about their necks;
Her younger brother gave a shield and spear;
And others of his kin many other things,
Of which the sorts cannot be numbered here.

Three months lasted the marriage celebration   2010
And never ceased that universal joy.
After the three months' wedding was accomplished,
The General taking all his marriage-kin,
With the bridegroom himself, going to his home,
Had a new wedding grander than the first.
The General was glad when he saw the boy's
Ordered condition, and sagacious valour,
His gentle temper and other good behaviour.
The General's wife rejoiced seeing his beauty,
And his most good-looking and strange stature.   2020
His wife's own brothers much frequenting him,
They always boasting their own braveries,
Gave praise to the one Good that crowned the deed.
For in the governments of great affairs
God enters in, let no one disbelieve.
With reason then send we our thanks to God,
For that He is the giver of all good things.
There then having continued several days

remarkable that these twelve beautiful eunuchs are not mentioned in any of the other versions except the prose PAS, p. 361. So that an unexpected connexion is established between PAS and GRO.

2020 ξένην ἡλικίαν. For this use of ξένος 'marvellous', cf. 3359.

2021–3 A line in which the brothers-in-law expressed their admiration o Digenes seems to have been lost. Otherwise 2023 is a more than usually startling *non sequitur*, even if the lack of a main verb is not in itself remarkable, the redactor being very forgetful.

2028 ποιήσαντες. Cf. above 2010 ἐποίησε. ἐκεῖσε for ἐκεῖ.

ὁ ἀμηρᾶς ὑπέστρεψεν ἐν τῷ ἰδίῳ οἴκῳ,   950
καὶ μετ᾽ αὐτοῦ ὁ Διγενὴς καὶ ἡ τούτου φιλτάτη
μεγίστης προσελεύσεως γεναμένης καὶ αὖθις.
Εἶθ᾽ οὕτως λίαν δόκιμος ἀποφανθεὶς ὁ νέος   39 vº.
γέγονε δὲ περίφημος ἐν ταῖς ἀνδραγαθίαις,
ὥστε σχεδὸν εἰς ἅπαντα βεβαιωθεὶς τὸν κόσμον·   955
καὶ μόνος ἡρετίσατο διάγειν εἰς τὰς ἄκρας,
τὴν κόρην φέρων σὺν αὐτῷ καὶ ἰδίους οἰκέτας·
πόθον γὰρ εἶχεν ἄπειρον τοῦ μόνος συνδιάγειν
καὶ τοῦ μόνος περιπατεῖν δίχα τινὸς ἑτέρου.
Ἔνθα γὰρ ἐπορεύετο τένδαν εἶχεν ἰδίαν,   960
εἰς ἣν ἡ κόρη καὶ αὐτὸς συνεδίαγον μόνοι·
καὶ τένδαν ἄλλην εἴχασιν αἱ βάγιαι αἱ δύο,
ἑτέραν δὲ οἱ θαυμαστοὶ ἀγοῦροι τοῦ Ἀκρίτου,
ἐκ διαστήματος πολλοῦ ἀπέχοντες ἀλλήλοις.

Πολλοὶ δὲ τῶν ἀπελατῶν τοῦτο ἀναμαθόντες,   965
συμβούλιον ἐποίησαν τὴν κόρην ἀφαρπάσαι·
καὶ πάντας συναπέκτεινε καθυποτάσσων τούτους,
ὅπως τε κατεπτόησε πᾶσαν τὴν Βαβυλῶνα,
Ταρσὸν ὁμοῦ καὶ τὸν Βαγδᾶ, τοὺς Μαυροχιονίτας,
καὶ ἄλλα μέρη ἱκανὰ τῶν δεινῶν Αἰθιόπων.   970

Ταῦτα τὰ κατορθώματα ὁ βασιλεὺς ἀκούσας
ὁ τηνικαῦτα τὴν ἀρχὴν τοῖς Ῥωμαίοις διέπων,
Βασίλειος ὁ εὐτυχὴς καὶ μέγας τροπαιοῦχος,
ὁ καὶ συνθάψας μεθ᾽ ἑαυτοῦ τὴν βασίλειον δόξαν
(ἔτυχε γὰρ κατὰ Περσῶν ποιῶν τὴν ἐκστρατείαν   975
ἐν ἐκείνοις τοῖς μέρεσιν ἐν οἷς ὁ παῖς διῆγεν),
καὶ μαθὼν τὰ περὶ αὐτοῦ ἐξεπλήττετο σφόδρα.
Ποθήσας οὖν κατὰ πολὺ θεάσασθαι τὸν νέον,

957 αὐτῷ.   971 Après ταῦτα, je supprime τοίνυν, qui rend le vers hypermètre.   975 Au lieu de κατὰ, le ms. porte μετὰ. εὐστρατείαν.

2035 These curious details are found in
all the primary versions. See AND
2312 ff., TRE 1448 ff. Only TRE
(1460) and AND (2324) give the
strange story of how Digenes blinded
with an angry blow one of his cooks
who offended him—a story probably
derived from an incident in the
Alexander legend (Alexander's rage

with his cook for finding and losing
the Water of Life). See Pallis, Φυλ-
λάδα τοῦ Μεγ᾽ Ἀλεξάντρου (Athens,
1935), p. 54.
2044, 2045 These lines, the substance
of which is repeated with equal
brevity in AND 2335, 2336, and
TRE 1469, 1470, have been over-
worked by Polites and others who

The Emir returned again to his own house
And with him Digenes and his beloved   2030
And yet again there was a great concourse.
Thus the youth being proved most estimable
Was become famous in his braveries,
So almost was affirmed in all the world;
And on the borders chose to live alone,
Taking the Girl with him and his own servants;
Boundless desire he had to live alone
And walk alone without anyone else.
For where he journeyed he had his own tent,
In which the Girl and he would live alone.   2040
The two maidservants had another tent,
The Borderer's fine men-at-arms another,
Each standing a great distance from the other.
    Now many of the reivers learning this
Made a conspiracy to steal the Girl;
And all of them he overcame and slew
Even as he overwhelmed all Babylon,
Tarsus with Bagdad, and the Blacksnowmen,
And many other places of the dread Aethiops.
    These great achievements when he heard, the King   2050
Who at that time held sway over the Romans,
Basil the blessed, the great trophy-bearer,
Who buried with himself the kingly glory,
Taking his arms by chance against the Persians
In those same places where the boy was living,
And learning about him was much amazed.
So much desiring to behold the youth,

are determined to find in the Epic
some trace of the Akritic Ballad
Cycle, in which Digenes is quite a
minor character without a wife of
his own. It is in fact a commonplace
of European balladry, the Lochinvar
theme of the Stolen Bride.
2047 ὅπως τε suggests that a line has
been lost (like TRE 1471).
2048 Μαυροχιονῖται, probably the same
as the Μαυρονῖται of 3742, possibly
from the Μαῦρον Ὄρος between

Antioch and the sea.
2050 Βασιλεύς I have translated 'King'
and Βασιλεία 'majesty' throughout—
even in 2106, where 'kingdom'
might be more suitable.
2052, 2053 Βασίλειος . . . τὴν βασίλειον
δόξαν. A mild pun, not reproduced
in the translation, which also satisfies
the redactor's itch for verbal repetition. Basil II, Boulgaroktonos, 960–
1025, was probably the emperor here
referred to.

γραφὴν πρὸς αὐτὸν ἔστειλε περιέχουσαν τάδε· 40 rᵒ.

" Τὰ περὶ σοῦ, ὦ τέκνον μου, ἡ ἐμὴ βασιλεία 980
μαθοῦσα κατορθώματα εὐφράνθημεν ἐν τούτοις,
τῷ συνεργοῦντί σοι Θεῷ ἀναπέμποντες χάριν·
ἐν ἐφέσει δὲ γεγόναμεν αὐτοψεὶ τοῦ ἰδεῖν σε,
καὶ παρασχεῖν σοι ἀμοιβὰς τῶν σῶν ἔργων ἀξίας·
ἐλθὲ τοίνυν ὡς πρὸς ἡμᾶς χαίρων ἀνενδοιάστως, 985
μὴ ὑποπτεύων λυπηρὸν παρ' ἡμῶν ὑποστῆναι."
Ὁ δὲ ταύτην δεξάμενος ἀντιγραφὴν ἐκπέμπει·
" Ἐγὼ μὲν δοῦλος ἔσχατος τοῦ σοῦ κράτους τυγχάνω,
εἰ καὶ πάντων τῶν ἀγαθῶν ἀμέτοχος ὑπάρχω·
ποῖον δέ, δέσποτα, ἐμὸν κατόρθωμα θαυμάζεις 990
τοῦ ταπεινοῦ καὶ εὐτελοῦς καὶ παντελῶς ἀτόλμου;
ἀλλ' ὅμως πάντα δυνατὰ τῷ πρὸς Θεὸν θαρροῦντι·
καὶ ἐπειδήπερ βούλεσαι ἰδεῖν τὸν σὸν οἰκέτην,
μετ' ὀλίγων παραγενοῦ πρὸς ποταμὸν Εὐφράτην,
κἀκεῖ με ὄψει, δέσποτα ἅγιε, ὅταν βούλει. 995
Καὶ μὴ νομίσῃς ἀπειθῶ πρὸς σὲ παραγενέσθαι·
ἀλλ' ὅτι κέκτησαι τινὰς ἀπείρους στρατιώτας,
καὶ εἰ μὲν ἴσως εἴπωσι τινὲς ὅπερ οὐ δέον,
ποιήσω σε εἰς τὸ βέβαιον ἄμοιρον τῶν τοιούτων,
τοῖς γὰρ νέοις, ὦ δέσποτα, συμβαίνουσι τοιαῦτα." 1000
Καὶ τὴν γραφὴν ὁ βασιλεὺς διεξιὼν κατ' ἔπος,
ἐθαύμαζε τὴν τοῦ παιδὸς ταπείνωσιν τοῦ λόγου,
καὶ ἔχαιρε κατανοῶν τὸ ὕψος τῆς ἀνδρείας.

Σφόδρα δὲ ὀρεγόμενος ἰδεῖν τὸν νεανίαν
παραλαβὼν μεθ' ἑαυτοῦ ἑκατὸν στρατιώτας 40 vᵒ. 1005
καὶ δορυφόρους ἱκανούς, ἦλθεν εἰς τὸν Εὐφράτην,
πᾶσιν ἐπαγγειλάμενος τοῦ φθέγξασθαι μηδ' ὅλως
λόγον τινὰ ἐπίμωμον ἔμπροσθεν τοῦ Ἀκρίτου.
Οἱ δέ γε τούτου ἕνεκα φυλάττειν συνταχθέντες,
παρὰ μικρὸν ἀπήγγειλαν τὴν ἄφιξιν συντόμως 1010
βασιλέως πρὸς Διγενῆ τὸν θαυμαστὸν Ἀκρίτην.
Καὶ πρὸς αὐτὸν ὁ Διγενὴς μονώτατος ἐξῆλθεν,
ὃς μέχρι γῆς τὴν ἑαυτοῦ κεφαλὴν ὑποκλίνας·
" Χαίροις," ἔφη, " ὁ ἐκ Θεοῦ λαβὼν τὴν βασιλείαν,
καὶ δι' ἀσέβειαν ἐθνῶν ἅπασι κυριεύσας, 1015

1002 De λόγου il n'y a plus de visible que la première lettre. 1007 μὴ δ'.

Sent him a letter with these words therein:
'Concerning you, my child, my majesty
Learning your deeds, we have been glad therein, 2060
Sending up thanks to God who works with you;
Our purpose is with our own eyes to see you
And give you recompense worthy your deeds.
Come then towards us gladly undoubtingly
Suspecting nothing grievous at our hands.'
Receiving this he sent back a reply:
'I am the lowest servant of your power,
Even though I have no share of benefits;
What deed of mine, master, do you admire,
Of me quite humble, worthless, and undaring? 2070
Yet all things can he do who with God ventures;
Inasmuch as you wish to see your servant,
In a few days be by Euphrates river;
There, holy master, you shall see me when you will.
Think not that I refuse to come before you;
But that you have some inexperienced soldiers,
And if some chanced to say what they ought not,
I should for certain make you miss such men;
For with the young, master, such things occur.'

 The King perused the writing word by word, 2080
Admired the modest diction of the boy,
And gladly understood his lofty valour.

 Desiring eagerly to see the youth,
Taking with him a hundred soldiers
And a few spearmen he came to the Euphrates,
Enjoining all not anywise to utter
A word of blame before the Borderer.
So those posted to watch on that account
Shortly announced the coming imminent
To Digenes the wondrous Borderer of the King. 2090
Digenes went out towards him all alone,
And bowing down his head unto the ground,
Said, 'Hail, who take your majesty from God,
Lord of all nations, through their wickedness,

2059 The poet is no doubt trying to epistolary style of the Byzantine
reproduce or represent the stilted court.

πόθεν μοι τοῦτο γέγονεν ὁ γῆς πάσης δεσπόζων
παραγενέσθαι πρὸς ἐμὲ τὸν ἐξουθενημένον; "
Τοῦτον ἰδὼν ὁ βασιλεὺς καὶ ἐκπλαγεὶς τὴν θέαν,
παντὸς ἐπιλαθόμενος ὄγκου τῆς βασιλείας,
μικρὸν τοῦ θρόνου προσελθὼν κατησπάζετο χαίρων,   1020
κατεφίλει περιχαρῶς ἡλικίαν θαυμάζων,
καὶ τὴν πολλὴν κατάθεσιν τοῦ εὐμεγέθους κάλλους·
" Ἔχεις," λέγων, " ὦ τέκνον μου, ἀπόδειξιν τῶν ἔργων·
τοῦ γὰρ κάλλους ἡ σύνθεσις ἀνδρείαν εἰκονίζει·
εἴθε τοιούτους τέσσαρας εἶχεν ἡ Ῥωμανία!   1025
Λέγε λοιπόν, ὦ τέκνον μου, πεπαρρησιασμένως,
καὶ ὅπερ βούλει λάμβανε τῆς ἐμῆς βασιλείας."
" Τὰ πάντα ἔχε, δέσποτα," ὁ παῖς ἀνταπεκρίθη,
" ἐμοὶ γὰρ ἔστιν ἱκανὴ μόνον ἡ σὴ ἀγάπη·
οὐ δίκαιον δὲ τοῦ λαβεῖν ἀλλὰ διδόναι μᾶλλον,   1030
ἔχεις καὶ γὰρ ἐν τῷ στρατῷ ἐξόδους ἀνεικάστους·
ἀξιῶ καὶ ἀντιβολῶ τῆς σῆς δόξης τὸ κράτος   41 rº.
ἀγαπᾶν τὸ ὑπήκοον, ἐλεεῖν πενομένους,
τοὺς ἀδικοῦντας ῥύεσθαι καὶ καταπονουμένους,
τοῖς παρὰ γνώμην παίουσι συγχώρησιν παρέχειν,   1035
μὴ προσέχειν διαβολαῖς, ἄδικον μὴ λαμβάνειν,
αἱρετικοὺς ἀποσοβεῖν, ὀρθοδόξους κρατύνειν.
Ταῦτα γάρ, δέσποτα, εἰσὶν ὅπλα δικαιοσύνης,
μεθ᾽ ὧν δυνήσῃ τῶν ἐχθρῶν πάντων περιγενέσθαι·
οὐ γὰρ ἔστι δυνάμεως κρατεῖν καὶ βασιλεύειν,   1040
Θεοῦ μόνον τὸ δώρημα καὶ δεξιᾶς ὑψίστου·
ἐγὼ δὲ ὁ πανευτελὴς τῷ σῷ κράτει δωροῦμαι
ὃ ἐδίδου κατὰ καιρὸν τέλος τῷ Ἰκονίῳ
ἄλλο τοσοῦτον σε λαβεῖν παρ᾽ ἐκείνων ἀκόντων,
καὶ ποιήσω σε, δέσποτα, ἀμέριμνον ἐκ τούτου,   1045
ἄχρις ἂν ἡ ἐμὴ ψυχὴ ἐκ τοῦ σκήνους ἐξέλθῃ."
Καὶ ἐχάρη ὁ βασιλεὺς ἐπὶ τούτοις τοῖς λόγοις,

1033 πενωμένους.   1034 Il faut considérer ἀδικοῦντας comme ayant ici le
sens passif, ou lire ce vers comme dans le ms. de Trébizonde (vers 1527) et celui
d'Andros (vers 2393) : ἐξ ἀδικούντων ῥύεσθαι τοὺς καταπονεμένους.   1036 δια-
βουλαῖς et o au-dessus de ου.   1037 ἀποσοβῶν. κρατύνων.

2113 τοὺς ἀδικοῦντας ῥύεσθαι καὶ κατα-   Otherwise, with TRE 1527, AND
πονουμένους. ἀδικοῦντας must be   2393, read ἐξ ἀδικούντων ῥύεσθαι τοὺς
taken to mean here 'suffering injus-   καταπονεμένους.
tice'. Stranger things have happened.

Why has this happened to me that all the earth's master
Comes before me who am of no account?'
Him seeing the King, astonished at the sight,
Forgetting all the weight of majesty,
Came from his throne a little, embraced him gladly,
Joyfully kissed him, admiring his stature,   2100
And the great store of his full-grown beauty,
Saying, 'You have, my child, proof of your works,
For beauty so compounded shows forth valour.
Would there were four such men in Romania!
Speak therefore, O my child, fully and freely,
And of my majesty take what you will.'
'Master, keep everything,' the boy replied,
'Your love alone is quite enough for me.
It is not right to be taking but rather giving;
You have unmatched expenses in your army.   2110
I claim and I entreat your glory's power,
To love obedience, pity the poor,
Deliver from injustice the oppressed,
Accord forgiveness to unwilling faults,
Not to heed slanders, accept no injustice,
Scatter the heretics, confirm the orthodox.
These, master, are the arms of righteousness,
With which you can overcome all your enemies.
For rule and kingship belong not to might,
Only God grants it and the Highest's right hand.   2120
I worthless as I am grant to your power
The tribute once it paid Iconium
As much again from their unwilling hands;
From this care, master, I will set you free,
Until my soul goes from its tabernacle.'
    Upon these words of his the King rejoiced,

2114 παίουσι. Leg. πταίουσι. Cf. TRE
1528, AND 2394 πταίσματα.
2122 The reference to the tribute of
Iconium is not found in TRE or
AND. It can hardly be correlated
with the Emperor Basil. Can it echo
the defeat of Romanos Diogenes in
1071? The reference must not any-

how be taken too seriously, if, as
suggested in the introduction, the
poet is giving a romantic and
foreshortened view of the past two
centuries from a peaceful period in
the middle of the eleventh century
(Constantine IX Monomachos, 1042–
54).

καὶ φησίν· "῏Ω θαυμάσιε, κάλλιστε νεανία,
ἡ βασιλεία ἡ ἐμὴ πατρίκιόν σε ἔχει,
δωρουμένη σοι ἅπαντα κτήματα τοῦ σοῦ πάππου, 1050
καὶ ἐξουσίαν νέμω σοι τοῦ διοικεῖν τὰς ἄκρας·
ταῦτα δὲ εἰς χρυσόβουλλον σῶα ἐπικυρώσω,
καὶ ἐσθῆτας βασιλικὰς παρέχω πολυτίμους."
Ταῦτα εἰπὼν ὁ βασιλεύς, εὐθὺς ὁ νέος προστάξας
ἕνα τῶν ἵππων τῶν αὐτοῦ ἀγροικῶν, ἀδαμάστων, 1055
κομίσαι ἔμπροσθεν αὐτῶν σιδήροις δεδεμένον·
ὃν λῦσαι ἔφη τοῖς παισὶν καὶ "Ἀφετέ τον τρέχειν."
Καὶ τὰς ποδέας ὀχυρῶς πήξας εἰς τὸ ζωνάριν, 41 vᵒ.
ἤρξατο τρέχειν ὄπισθεν τοῦ καταλαβεῖν τοῦτον·
καὶ εἰς ὀλίγον διάστημα τῆς χαίτης τε κρατήσας, 1060
ὄπισθέν τον ἐγύρισε τὸν ἀγροικὸν καὶ μέγαν,
λακτίζων, στροινιάζων τε, φυγεῖν ὅλως εἰκάζων·
καὶ ἔμπροσθεν τοῦ βασιλέως ἐλθόντος τοῦ γεννάδα
κάτω τον ἐκατέρραξεν εἰς γῆν ἐφηπλωμένον.
Καὶ πάντες ἐξεπλάγησαν τῇ παραδόξῳ θέᾳ. 1065
Ὑποχωρεῖν βουλόμενος, λέων τις ἐκ τοῦ ἄλσους
ἐξελθὼν διεπτόησε τοὺς μετ' αὐτοῦ παρόντας
(πολλοὶ γὰρ λέοντες εἰσὶν ἐν ἐκείνῳ τῷ τόπῳ),
καὶ πρὸς φυγὴν δὲ καὶ αὐτὸς ὁ βασιλεὺς ἐτράπη.
Ὁ δὲ παῖς πρὸς τὸν λέοντα ὑποδραμὼν εὐθέως, 1070
ποδὸς αὐτοῦ δραξάμενος ἑνὸς τῶν ὀπισθίων,
ἀποτινάξας ἰσχυρῶς καὶ τῇ γῇ καταρράξας,

1055 ἀγροικῶν est bien périspomène dans le ms. 1057 ἄφετε τόν. 1061
ὄπισθεν. ἀγροικὸν est bien oxyton dans le ms. 1062 τε manque. 1063 Il
faut prononcer βασιλέως comme si ce mot était accentué βασιλεὼς, εω étant
diphtongue. 1066 Après ὑποχωρεῖν, je supprime δὲ, qui fausse le vers.

2128 πατρίκιόν σε ἔχει. 'Dignitas in-
venta a Constantino M. ut scribit
Zosimus lib. 2 . . . deferebatur viris
qui de Republica bene meruerant'
(Ducange). See above 405.
2129 The banished grandfather: see
above 63, 270.
2134 ἀγροικῶν. Ducange refers to
Joannes Cinnamos for ἀγρίμι used
of a wild horse.
2137 'girding up his loins'. Cf. above
1096.

2141 στροινιάζων. Ducange quotes from
a MS. στρινιάζειν of a fish; L. & S.
give στρηνύζω of elephants trumpet-
ing and στρηνής of a harsh sound, as
well as στρηνιάω and στρῆνος, 'wantonness'; so the unbroken horse here
is either 'kicking and plunging' or
'kicking and screaming' (notice
both participles nominative agreeing
with accusative in the line before).
See also in N.T. (Tim. i. 5, 11)
καταστρηνιάω of the young widows

And said, 'O wondrous, excellent young man,
My majesty appoints you a patrician,
Granting you all your grandfather's estates;
I assign you authority to rule the borders;   2130
These things I will fast confirm in a Golden Bull,
And precious royal vestments I bestow.'
   So spoke the King; straightway the youth commanding
One of his horses fresh from grass, unbroken,
To be brought before them hobbled in irons;
Bade his boys loose him, saying 'Let him run';
And tucking fast his kilts into his girdle,
Began to run behind to catch him up,
And in a little distance seizing the mane
He turned round backwards the great beast and wild,   2140
Kicking and plunging, all thinking to escape;
And when the brave boy came before the King,
He dashed it down spread out upon the ground.
All were astounded at the marvellous sight.
As he was going, a lion from the grove
Came out and startled those were there with him
(For there are many lions in that place)—
Even the King himself was turned to fly.
The Boy at once running up to the lion
And snatching hold of one of its hind legs,   2150
Mightily shook and dashed it on the ground,

who 'wax wanton against' Christ
(Souter gives 'exercise youthful
vigour against'), and in Revelation
xviii. 3, 7, 9, στρῆνος and στρηνιάω in
senses of 'wantonness', 'live wanton-
ly' (A.V. 'live deliciously'). Morosi,
Dialetti Greci della Terra d'Otranto
(1870), gives '*strignazo, strionno* . . .
sbizzarrisco (dei cavalli, dei tori
ecc.); στροιβινιάζω e στροιβόνω p.
στροιβάω, στροιβιλέω GR. ANT.' The
variation from στροινιάω to στρηνιάω,
developing before the onset of
itacism, is of course, in onomato-
poeic words of this sort, no more
than the difference between 'whine'
and 'whinny'. Vlasto, Συνώνυμα καὶ
Συγγενικά, gives στρινιάζω s.v. φω-

νάζω.
   To the N.T. references above
should be added from LXX 4 Reg.
xix. 28, στρῆνος (A.V. 2 Kings xix.
28 'Thy *tumult* is come up into my
ears'). Suidas quotes this and adds
'στρηνιῶ–ἀτακτῶ'. Phrynichus (*Eclog.*
357) says στρηνιῶ is wrongly used
by writers of the New Comedy for
τρυφῶ; and Rutherford in his edition, p. 475, gives two references
from Middle Comedy, and adds, 'in
neither of these passages is it a
synonym of τρυφῶ, but expresses the
fighting-cock feeling of a man who
has just risen from a hearty meal'.
2142 γεννάδα. Classical; see L. & S.

νεκρὸν αὐτὸν ἀπέδειξε πάντων ὁμοῦ βλεπόντων.

Τοῦτον κρατῶν ἐν τῇ χειρί, καθάπερ τις τὸν πτῶκα,
πρὸς βασιλέα ἤνεγκε· "Δέξαι ", λέγων, " κυνῆγιν   1075
τοῦ σοῦ οἰκέτου, δέσποτα, διὰ σοῦ θηρευθέντα."
Καὶ πάντες ἐξεπλάγησαν ἔντρομοι γεγονότες,
τὴν ὑπεράνθρωπον αὐτοῦ ἰσχὺν κατανοοῦντες.
Καὶ τὰς χεῖρας ὁ βασιλεὺς πρὸς οὐρανὸν ἐκτείνας·
" Δόξα σοι," ἔφη, " δέσποτα, ποιητὰ τῶν ἁπάντων,   1080
ὅτι με κατηξίωσας τοιοῦτον ἄνδρα βλέψαι
ἐν τῇ παρούσῃ γενεᾷ ἰσχυρὸν παρὰ πάντας."
Καὶ τὴν δορὰν τοῦ λέοντος ἐπαρθῆναι κελεύσας
καὶ πλείστας πρὸς τὸν θαυμαστὸν ἐποίει ὑποσχέσεις·   42 r⁰.
ἀλλήλους ἀσπαζόμενοι, ὑπεχώρουν εὐθέως   1085
πρὸς τὸν στρατὸν ὁ βασιλεύς, ὁ δὲ παῖς πρὸς τὴν κόρην.
Ἔκτοτε κῦρος ἔλαβε παρ' ἁπάντων ὁ λόγος,
καὶ τὸν παῖδα ὠνόμαζον Βασίλειον Ἀκρίτην,
τοῦ χρυσοβούλλου εἵνεκα τοῦ ἄρχειν εἰς τὰς ἄκρας.
Ἡμεῖς δὲ καταπαύσωμεν τὸν λόγον μέχρις ὧδε,   1090
τῶν ἐφεξῆς ἐχόμενοι συντάξεως ἑτέρας·
κόρος γὰρ λόγου, ὡς φησὶν ὁ ἐμὸς θεολόγος,
ταῖς ἀκοαῖς πολέμιος διὰ παντὸς ὑπάρχει.

1084 πλείστα. ἐποιή (sic).   1085 εὐθεως.   1087 παραπάντων.   1089
χρυσοβούλου.   1090 ὧδε   1093 διαπαντός.

140

And turned it dead before the gaze of all.
This in his hand as one would hold a hare
He brought to the King, saying, 'Accept the quarry,
Master, hunted down for you by your servant.'
All were astounded then being afraid
Understanding his superhuman strength.
And the King, stretching out his hands to heaven,
Said 'Glory to thee, Master, maker of all things,
Who hast thought me worthy to see such a man   2160
Mighty above all in this generation';
And bidding them take up the lion's hide
Made many a promise to the wondrous boy.
Having embraced each other straight they went
The King to his army, and the boy to the Girl.
Thenceforth the saying was confirmed abroad;
They called the boy Basil the Borderer,
From the Gold Bull that he should rule the borders.
    And we will cease our discourse at this point
Keeping what follows for another book;   2170
Surfeit of discourse, as my Preacher says,
Is always enemy of listening.

2152 ἀπέδειξε. This usage is classical.
Cf. Ar. *Ran.* 1011. Cf. below 2177
δείκνυται and 2246 ἔδειξα.
2153 πτῶκα. The cowering animal;
classical in poets; see L. & S.
2161 This passage is slightly but not

decisively reminiscent of the exhibition of bull-throwing by Theagenes
in Heliodorus, *Aethiop.* x. 30.
2171 ὁ ἐμὸς θεολόγος. Does this suggest
that the redactor is a novice under
instruction?

ADDITIONAL NOTES

1179 στῆθος ὥσπερ κρύσταλλον. See also TRE 974. Cf. Psellos, *History*, cxxvi, of
Constantine IX, (1042–1055) κρυστάλλῳ δὲ τὸ λοιπὸν σῶμα καθαρωτάτῳ καὶ
διαυγεῖ. See also a dirge from Arahova (Polites, ᾿Εκλογαί, no. 195)... ἄγουρε
δροσερὲ κρουσταλλοβραχιονᾶτε.

1185. Legrand's change of accent, νῦψον for νίψον, seems to be unnecessary.

1291 Ducange s.v. κουράζειν quotes from a MS. γνώθη ὁ λαγὸς ὅτι οἱ ἄνθρωποι καὶ
οἱ κύνες πολλὰ γοργὸν κουράζονται ὅταν τὰ ὄρη τρέχουν.

1486. δάος. In support of the possible connection with Turkish *dagh*, I owe to
Impellizzeri a reference to Triantafyllides, *Die Lehnwörter der mittelgriechischen
Vulgärlitteratur*, Strasburg, 1909, p. 133, which I have not been able to verify.

1983. παρδοκυνηγούς· Must mean 'hunting leopards', and not 'leopard-huntsmen'
or 'leopard-grooms' as understood by Kalonaros (for which see Ducange s.v.
παρδόβαλλοι).

ΛΟΓΟΣ ΠΕΜΠΤΟΣ

Νεότης πᾶσα ἀληθῶς ματαιότης ὑπάρχει,
ὁπηνίκα πρὸς ἡδονὰς ἐκτείνει τὰς ἀτάκτους·
ὁ δέ γε ταύτης ἀσφαλῶς τὰς ἡνίας ἰθύνων
ἀχείρωτος τοῖς πάθεσιν ἐσαεὶ διαμένει,
καὶ κληρονόμος δείκνυται ζωῆς τῆς αἰωνίου,   5
ἀντὶ προσκαίρου ἡδονῆς τῆς αἰσχρᾶς καὶ βεβήλου.
Ὃς γὰρ τρυφᾷ, ἀδύνατον τυχεῖν τῆς αἰωνίου·
ὡς γὰρ οὐκ ἔστιν ἐμπρησμὸν μετὰ ἐλαίου σβέσαι,
οὐδὲ τρυφῶν τις δυνατὸν φυγεῖν τὴν ἁμαρτίαν,
δι' ἧς τὸ πῦρ ἐκτρέφεται πᾶσι τοῖς ἀκολάστοις.   10
Καὶ γὰρ οὗτος ὁ θαυμαστὸς καὶ γενναῖος Ἀκρίτης,
ὁ τοῖς χαρίσμασι Θεοῦ πᾶσι πεπλουτισμένος,
πρὸς ὀλίγον τὴν ἑαυτοῦ νεότητα χαυνώσας
ἀμελῶς περιπέπτωκεν ἐγκλήματι μοιχείας·
ὕστερον δὲ μετάμελος γεγονὼς ὑπὲρ τούτου   42 vº. 15
τοῖς ἐντυγχάνουσιν αὐτῷ ἀνήγγειλε τὸ σφάλμα,
οὐ καυχήσεως ἕνεκεν, ἀλλὰ μεταμελείας.
Καὶ γὰρ μιᾷ τῶν ἡμερῶν ἐντυχὼν Καππαδόκι,
τὴν ἑαυτοῦ βουλόμενος ἁμαρτίαν φαυλῆσαι,
πρὸς αὐτὸν διηγήσατο τάδε μετρίως λέγων·   20
" Ὁπηνίκα ἐθελοντὶ τοῦ πατρὸς ἐχωρίσθην
καὶ ἐν ταῖς ἄκραις κατοικεῖν μόνος ἡρετισάμην,
ταξιδεῦσαι ἠθέλησα εἰς τὴν ἔνδον Συρίαν,
ἔτος πεντεκαιδέκατον ἄγων τῆς ἡλικίας·
ἀνύδρους τε καταλαβὼν κάμπους τῆς Ἀραβίας,   25
τὴν ὁδόν, ὥσπερ εἴωθα, μόνος μου διοδεύων,
φάραν ἐπικαθήμενος, βαστάζων καὶ κοντάριν,
ἔνδιψος ὅλος γέγονα (πολὺς γὰρ ἦν ὁ καύσων),
καὶ πανταχοῦ ἐσκόπευα ποῦ τὸ ὕδωρ ὑπάρχει·

16 αὐτῷ.   23 ταξειδεῦσαι.   24 πέντε καὶ δέκατον. τὴν ἡλικίαν.   28
ἔδιψος.

2176 ἀχείρωτος, 'unconquered'.
2177 δείκνυται. Like ἀπέδειξεν, above
2152; below 2246. Cf. *Barlaam and
Joasaph* xiv. 122.
2182 δι' ἧς. Perhaps a better translation would be rather '(sin) for the
sake, or on account of which, fire is
fed for the unchaste'.
2185 χαυνώσας in classical sense. πρὸς
ὀλίγον perhaps for παρ' ὀλίγον.

FIFTH BOOK

ALL youthfulness is vanity indeed
When reaching out after unruly pleasures,
But he who firmly manages its reins
Ever remains unconquered by the passions
And is made heir of the eternal life,
Instead of brief pleasure base and unclean.
Who waxes wanton cannot win the eternal;
As fire can never be with oil extinguished,   2180
Neither can the wanton ever escape sin,
By which the fire is fed for all the unchaste.

   So this wondrous and noble Borderer,
Who was enriched by all the gifts of God,
Within a little making vain his youth
Fell heedlessly into adultery's sin.
And afterwards being penitent for this
To those who met him he would tell his fault
Not for the sake of boasting but of penitence.

   So on a day meeting a Kappadokian   2190
Wishing to show the baseness of his sin
He told this tale to him in humble words:
'When I was parted from my father willingly
And on the borders chose to live alone,
I wanted to journey into inner Syria
Then being in my fifteenth year of age.
Reaching the waterless plains of Araby,
Faring my way, as I was wont, alone,
Sitting my horse and carrying a spear,
I was all thirsty, for the heat was great,   2200
And looking everywhere water could be.

2190 The Cappadocian listener appears
only in this version. The other versions mention only the dear friends
with whom he sat. TRE 1574, AND
2462.
2191 φαυλῆσαι. For this unusual sense,
'to say or think or make to appear
base', cf. χαυνώσας above 2185, and

ὡραΐζουσα above 1730.
2192 μετρίως, humbly.
2195 ταξιδεῦσαι seems to be used here
in the modern sense of making a
journey or excursion, not in the
Byzantine sense of making a military
expedition or raid.

δένδρον ὁρῶ ἀπόμηκα πρὸς τὴν δασέαν βάλτον, 30
καὶ τὴν φάραν ἐπιλαλῶ, νομίσας ὕδωρ ἔχειν·
καὶ οὐδαμῶς ἀπέτυχον· φοῖνιξ δὲ ἦν τὸ δένδρον,
καὶ ἐκ τῆς ῥίζης θαυμαστὴ ἀνεπέμπετο βρύσις.
Ταύτῃ δ' ὡς ἐπλησίαζον ὀλολυγμοὺς ἀκούω,
καὶ κλαυσώδεις ὀλοφυρμοὺς μετὰ πλείστων δακρύων· 35
ἡ δὲ θρηνοῦσα κόρη ἦν πάνυ ὡραιοτάτη·
κἀγὼ νομίσας φάντασμα τὸ ὁρώμενον εἶναι,
ἔκδειλος ὅλος γέγονα, τριχῶν μου ὀξυνθέντων,
καὶ τὸ φρουροῦν με δὴ ἀεὶ διεχάραττον ὅπλον·
ἦν γὰρ ὁ τόπος ἔρημος, ἄβατος καὶ ἀλσώδης. 40
Ἐκείνη δὲ ὡς εἶδε με, ἀνέθορεν εὐθέως,
καὶ αὐτὴν περιστείλασα ἐν τῷ πρέποντι κόσμῳ, 43 rᵒ.
τάς τε βροχὰς τῶν ὀφθαλμῶν ἄρασα τῇ ὀθόνῃ,
πρός με λέγειν ἀπήρξατο περιχαρῶς τοιάδε·
" Πόθεν, καλὲ νεώτερε, καὶ ποῦ μόνος ὁδεύεις; 45
μὴ διὰ πόθον καὶ αὐτὸς ἐπλανήθης ἐνταῦθα;
ἀλλ' ἐπειδή, ὡς ἔοικεν, ἐκ Θεοῦ ὡδηγήθης
τῆς ἐρημίας ὅπως με τὴν ἀθλίαν ἑλκύσῃς,
πρὸς μικρὸν ἀναπαύθητι, κύριέ μου, ἐνταῦθα,
ἵν' ὅπως ἀκριβέστερον τὰ κατ' ἐμοῦ ἀκούσῃς, 50
καί τινα τῶν ὀδυνῶν παρηγορίαν λάβω,
λόγοις γὰρ συνεπαίρεται ἐκ τῆς ψυχῆς ἡ λύπη."
Ταῦτα κἀγὼ ὡς ἤκουσα, εἰς χαρὰν μετεβλήθην,
ἀληθὲς τὸ φαινόμενον ἀκριβῶς ἐννοήσας·
μετὰ πολλῆς τῆς ἡδονῆς ἐπέζευον εὐθέως, 55
ἥψατο γάρ μου τῆς ψυχῆς τὸ ἀπόρρητον κάλλος,
ὥστε δευτέραν τῆς ἐμῆς ταύτην εἶναι νομίσαι.
Καὶ τὸν μὲν φάραν ἔδησα εἰς τοῦ δένδρου τὸν κλῶνα,
τὸ δὲ κοντάριν ἔστησα μέσον αὐτοῦ τῆς ῥίζης,
καί, ὕδατος μεταλαβών, πρὸς αὐτὴν τάδε ἔφην· 60

51 Après τινα on pourrait peut-être suppléer γε, afin de rétablir la mesure.
57 νομίσας.

2209 (and TRE 1642, AND 2528).
This is the first of many couplets in
the next two books which seem to be
echoed from the Allegorical Poem of
Meliteniotes (ed. M. Miller, Notices
et Extr. des Manuscrits de la Bibl.
Imp., t. xix, seconde partie, 1858),

Meliten. 140, 141. See Appendix A.
2211 διεχάραττον. Probably an extension
of the meaning of χαράττω 'to
sharpen', for which see Hesiod Op.
573; but possibly an extension of
the ordinary medieval and modern
use of χαράττειν of the day 'breaking'.

I saw a tree far off, near a thick swamp,
Pressed my horse, thinking there was water there,
And was not wrong; a date-palm was the tree
And from its root a wondrous spring gushed up.
When I came near to it I heard moaning
Lamentations with weeping and much tears.
The mourner was a girl most beautiful;
But I believing that I saw a spirit,
Was all affrighted and, hair standing up,   2210
Began to draw the steel which always guards me;
The place was desert, pathless, overgrown.
She when she saw me up she jumped at once,
Wrapping herself about in decent order,
Wiped with her linen the showers from her eyes,
And gladly thus began to speak to me:
"Whence fare you alone, and whither, good young man?
Surely you too are not strayed here for love?
But since, it seems, by God you have been guided
To save me in my misery from the desert,   2220
Rest yourself here, my lord, a little while,
That rightly as may be you may hear about me,
And I take consolation for my woes
(For grief is lifted from the soul by words)."
I too when I heard this was changed to joy,
Rightly understanding the apparition real;
So straightway with much pleasure I dismounted;
Her beauty unspeakable had touched my soul,
So that I thought her a second to my own.
My horse I tied up to the branching tree,   2230
And set my spear to stand between its roots,
Then took some water and spoke to her thus:

2229 δευτέραν τῆς ἐμῆς. Some classical
scholars may feel bound by the genitive to translate this 'Second to [i.e.
only surpassed in beauty by] my own
beloved'. Even if we can supply the
'only', this is a feeble description of
the ἀπόρρητον κάλλος, and I believe
that this line was intended by the
writer to mean 'so that I thought she

was another like my own'. The
numeral here, as in 'A second
Adam', connotes not inferiority but a
perfect match. Cf. δεύτερον ἄχος,
Iliad xxiii. 46; and Drayton's 'If
Time . . . Can shew a Second to so
pure a Love'.
2230 τὸν φάραν: masc. as above 166,
&c., but fem. 2203, &c. See index.

" Λέγε μοι, κόρη, πρότερον πῶς ἐνταῦθα διάγεις;
καὶ τίνος χάριν ᾤκησας ἐν τῇ ἐρήμῳ ταύτη,
εἶθ᾽ οὕτως γνώσῃ καὶ αὐτὴ ποῖος κἀγὼ ὑπάρχω."
Εἶτα καθίσαντες ὁμοῦ ἐν θώκῳ χαμαιζήλῳ,
τάδε λέγειν ἀπήρξατο, στενάξασα ἐκ βάθους·   65
" Ἐμὴ πατρίς, νεώτερε, τὸ Μεφερκὲ τυγχάνει·   43 vᵒ.
τὸν Ἀπλορράβδην ἤκουσας, τὸν ἀμηρᾶν τῶν πάντων,
οὗτος πατὴρ ἐμός ἐστί, μήτηρ ἡ Μελανθία.
Ῥωμαιογενῆν ἠγάπησα ἐπὶ κακῷ ἰδίῳ,
ὄντινα εἶχε δέσμιον τρεῖς χρόνους ὁ πατήρ μου·   70
καὶ γὰρ ἐνδόξου στρατηγοῦ υἱὸς ἔλεγεν εἶναι·
τῶν δεσμῶν ἠλευθέρωσα, φυλακῆς ἐρρυσάμην,
φαρία τον ἐχάρισα, πρωτεῖα τοῦ πατρός μου,
ἄρχοντα τοῦτον ἔδειξα περιφανῆ Συρίας,
μετὰ βουλῆς καὶ τῆς μητρός, τοῦ πατρός μου ἀπόντος,   75
ἐν τοῖς πολέμοις γὰρ ἀεὶ εἴωθεν ἀσχολεῖσθαι.
Ἐφαίνετο δὲ εἰς ἐμὲ πολλὴν ἔχων ἀγάπην,
καὶ θνήσκειν εἰ συμβέβηκε πρὸς ὥραν μὴ ἰδεῖν με·
ὑπῆρχε δὲ ἐπίπλαστος, ὡς ἔδειξε τὸ τέλος.
Καὶ γὰρ μιᾷ τῶν ἡμερῶν, δρασμὸν ὑπονοήσας,   80
βουλόμενος τοῦ ἐξελθεῖν ἐπὶ τὴν Ῥωμανίαν,
καὶ τὴν βουλὴν ἐξεῖπέ μοι, καὶ ὅνπερ εἶχε φόβον
διὰ πατέρα τὸν ἐμὸν μήποτε ἐπανήξῃ·
καὶ ἐμὲ κατηνάγκαζε σὺν αὐτῷ πορευθῆναι,
ὅρκοις ἐπαγγειλάμενος λίαν φρικωδεστάτοις   85
μὴ ἀρνηθῆναί με ποτέ, ἀλλὰ σύμβιον ἔχειν.
Οἷσπερ κἀγὼ πιστεύσασα, συμφυγεῖν κατεθέμην·
ἄδειαν εἶτα ἐφευρεῖν ἄμφω διεσκοποῦμεν
τὸν πλοῦτον ὅπως ἄρωμεν τῶν ἐμῶν γεννητόρων.
Καὶ δή, κατά τινα πικρὰν καὶ δαιμονίαν τύχην,   90
νόσος ἐπῆλθε τῇ μητρὶ θανάτῳ γειτνιῶσα·

67 ἀπλοράβδιν. που πάντως, la correction est empruntée aux mss. de Trébizonde
(vers 1664) et d'Andros (vers 2552).

2236 θώκῳ χαμαιζήλῳ. θῶκος (Ion. for
θᾶκος) is Homeric.
2238 Μεφερκέ. Mayyafariqin or Mar-
tyropolis, one of the Arab frontier
towns like Melitene which were the
scenes of much fighting in the tenth
century. Haplorrabdes probably con-

ceals the name of Abu Taghlib of
M. who was an ally of Bardas
Skleros in 976 (Honigmann, p. 150).
2239 τὸν ἀμηρᾶν τῶν πάντων is obscure,
but occurs in all three versions;
probably sc. Μεφερκίτων.

"First tell me, girl, how are you living here?
For what cause made your dwelling in this desert?
So then shall you learn also who I am."
We sat together on a groundling seat,
And deeply sighing she began to speak:
"My own country, young man, is Meferkeh.
You have heard of Haplorrabdes, the Emir of all,
He is my father, my mother Melanthia.   2240
I loved a Roman to my own despite,
One whom my father held captive three years;
He said he was a famous general's son;
I loosed his chains, delivered him from prison,
Gave him horses, my father's champions,
Made him an eminent chief in Syria,
With my mother's consent, my father absent,
Who always used to be engaged in wars.
Then he appeared to have much love for me,
Would die if he chanced not see me for a while;   2250
But he was false as the event did show.
For on a day, having planned to run away,
And wishing to depart to Romania,
His will he told me, and the fear he had
Because of my father in case he should return.
He tried to force me to set out with him,
Promising and with the most dreadful vows,
Never to deny me but make me his spouse,
Which I trusting agreed to fly with him.
We both began to look for an occasion   2260
That we might take the riches of my parents.
Then by some bitter and fateful mischance
Disease came on my mother, nearing death;

2241 'Ρωμαιογενής. TRE 1666, AND
2554 'Ρωμογενής.
2240 Μελανθία. Notice another Greek-
named wife of an Arabian emir,
recalling Σπαθία, mother of the emir
Mousour (TRE 488 ff.), called Πανθία
(above 284, and PAS 323).
2245 πρωτεῖα. See above 1796.
2246 ἔδειξα. See above 2177.
2252 δρασμόν. See below 2978.

2256 κατηνάγκαζε. Exactly as below
3268, not 'compelled', but 'tried to
compel', 'was violently persuading'.
2260, 2266 ἄδειαν, 'opportunity'—between the ancient meaning of
'security' and modern meaning of
'permission'.
2263 μητρὶ . . . γειτνιῶσα. A fine
example of participial disagreement.
But TRE 1694 γειτνιώσῃ.

καὶ οἱ μὲν ἄλλοι ἅπαντες πρὸς θρήνους οἱ ἐν οἴκοις
ἔτρεχον ἀνοιμώζοντες ἔνθα θάνατος ἤγεν·
ἐγὼ δέ, ἡ παντάλαινα, ἀδείας ἐντυχοῦσα,
πλοῦτον πολὺν διάρασα τῷ πλάνῳ συνεξῆλθον,   95
ὑπουργησάσης τῆς νυκτὸς εὐχερῶς πρὸς τὸ ἔργον,   44 rᵒ.
ἀσέληνος γὰρ ἔτυχε καὶ ἀφώτιστος πάντη.
Ἐφ᾽ ἵπποις δὲ ἀμφότεροι τοῖς προητοιμασμένοις
ἐποχηθέντες, τῆς ὁδοῦ ἠρχόμεθα σπουδαίως,
καὶ φόβον μέγαν εἴχομεν ἄχρι τοῦ τριμιλλίου·   100
ὡς δὲ παρήλθομεν αὐτὸ ὑπ᾽ οὐδενὸς γνωσθέντες
τὰ λοιπὰ διηνύομεν ἀδεῶς μετὰ μόχθου,
τροφῆς μεταλαμβάνοντες ὅτε καιρὸς ἐκάλει,
ὕπνου τε κορεννύμενοι καὶ τροφῆς μετασχόντες·
ἐρώτων δὲ μυστήρια ἐρυθριῶ τοῦ λέγειν   105
ἀγάπην τὲ τὴν πρὸς ἐμὲ παρ᾽ αὐτοῦ δεικνυμένην·
ψυχὴν γάρ με ὠνόμαζε, φῶς ὀφθαλμῶν ἐκάλει,
καὶ μετ᾽ ὀλίγον γαμετὴν ἔλεγε καὶ φιλτάτην,
ἀκορέστως καταφιλῶν, κρατῶν με ταῖς ἀγκάλαις.
Οὕτως ἐν πάσῃ τῇ ὁδῷ συγχαίροντες ἀλλήλοις,   110
ἐν ταύτῃ κατελάβομεν τῇ ὁρωμένῃ βρύσει·
καὶ τρεῖς ἀναπαυσάμενοι ἡμέρας τε καὶ νύκτας,
ἐρωτικὰς μεταβολὰς τελοῦντες ἀκορέστως,
γνώμην αὐτοῦ τὴν ἔνδοθεν δολίως κεκρυμμένην
ἀνακαλύπτειν ἄρχεται ὁ· δεινὸς παραβάτης.   115
Καὶ γὰρ ὁμοῦ καθεύδοντες ἐν τῇ νυκτὶ τῇ τρίτῃ,
λάθρα τῆς κοίτης ἀναστὰς ἐπέστρωσε τοὺς ἵππους,
τόν τε χρυσὸν ἀφείλετο καὶ τὰ κρείττονα σκεύη.
Ὡς δὲ τοῦτο ἐπέγνωκα τοῦ ὕπνου ἀναστᾶσα,
ἐμαυτὴν ὡς πρὸς τὴν ὁδὸν ηὐτρέπιζον εὐθέως,   120
εἰς νεανίσκου τὴν στολὴν μεταβαλοῦσα εἶδος·
τοιούτῳ γὰρ τῷ σχήματι τῆς πατρίδος ἐξῆλθον.   44 vᵒ.
Ἐφ᾽ ἵππου τοίνυν ἐπιβὰς τοῦ ἰδίου ἐκεῖνος
εἷλκε χερσὶ τὸν ἕτερον καὶ ᾤχετο τοῦ δρόμου.
Τοῦτο γοῦν τὸ παράλογον ἀνέλπιστον ὡς εἶδον,   125
πεζῇ ὡς εἶχον ἔτρεχον κατόπισθε βοῶσα·

100 τριμιλίου.

2268 εὐχερῶς. TRE 1698 εὐκαίρως. But   2280 γαμετὴν for class. γαμέτιν.
see below 2365.   2286 γνώμην, 'purpose'.
2272 ἄχρι τοῦ τριμιλλίου. Cf. above 635.   2288 καὶ γὰρ ὁμοῦ καθεύδοντες ἐν τῇ

All others mourning who were in the house
As death was driving them ran off lamenting;
And miserable I, occasion found,
Much riches seized, went off with the deceiver;
Night being the deed's timely minister,
Happened to be moonless and all unlit.
On horses both that were prepared before   2270
We mounted, and began the way in haste,
And had much fear until the three-mile mark;
But when we passed it recognized by none
Fared without fear thereafter, wearily,
Taking some food when the occasion called.
We had our fill of sleep and took our food;
The secrets of our loves I blush to tell,
And the affection toward me shown by him;
His soul he would name me, call me his eyes' light,
And soon he said I was his wife, his dearest,   2280
Unfilled with kissing held me in his arms.

    Thus all the way rejoicing in each other
We arrived at this fountain which you see;
For three days here reposing and three nights,
Love's changes celebrating without fill,
His inner purpose craftily concealed
The dire transgressor now began to show.
For while we slept together the third night,
He rose up secretly, saddled the horses,
And took the gold and better furniture.   2290
This when I noticed rising up from sleep,
I quickly made me ready for the road,
In a boy's dress transforming my appearance,
For I had left my country in that guise.
But then he having mounted his own horse,
Took lead of the other and started on the way.
When I saw this so strange and unexpected,
On foot as I was I ran after him screaming,

νυκτὶ τῇ τρίτῃ. This line, identical in
TRE 1714, becomes in AND 2603
ἀντάμα ἐκοιμούμεσθεν ἐν τῇ νυκτὶ
τῇ τρίτῃ—which Legrand (GRO,

introd., p. xv) calls 'macaronisme
choquant et fastidieux'.
2293 Other versions (TRE 1719, AND
2608) have misunderstood this detail.

" Ἀπέρχεσαι, ὦ φίλτατε, ἐμὲ λιπὼν ποῦ μόνην;
ἐπελάθου τῶν ἀγαθῶν ὧν σοι ἐνεδειξάμην;
οὐ μνημονεύεις ἐξ ἀρχῆς τοὺς ἐξαιρέτους ὅρκους; "
'ὼς δὲ οὐχ ὑπεστρέφετο, ἔτι μᾶλλον ἐφώνουν·   130
" Ἐλέησον, οἰκτείρησον, σῶσον με τὴν ἀθλίαν,
μὴ ἐνταῦθα ἐάσῃς με ὑπὸ θηρῶν βρωθῆναι."
Καὶ ἄλλα πλείονα αὐτῷ ἔλεγον θρηνῳδοῦσα·
ὁ δὲ γέγονεν ἀφανὴς μὴ φθεγξάμενος ὅλως·
ἐμοῦ δὲ ἤδη τῶν ποδῶν ἀπάρτι ἀποκαμόντων   135
τοῖς τῶν πετρῶν προσκρούσμασι πάντοθεν αἱμαχθέντων,
ἐκεῖσε που κατέπεσον νεκρὰ ἐφηπλωμένη·
καὶ μεθ᾽ ἡμέρας ἑαυτὴν μόλις ἀναλαβοῦσα,
ἐν τῇ πηγῇ ὑπέστρεψα ἀνάγκῃ βαδιοῦσα,
καὶ εἰμὶ πάντων ἔρημος, μὴ ἔχουσα ἐλπίδας·   140
οὐ γὰρ τολμῶ εἰς τοὺς γονεῖς τοὺς ἐμοὺς ὑποστρέψαι,
αἰσχύνομαι τοὺς γείτονας, τὰς συνομήλικάς μου.
Ποῦ εὑρεῖν τὸν πλανήσαντα παντελῶς οὐ γινώσκω,
καὶ δέομαί σου μάχαιραν τοῦ δοῦναί μοι εἰς χεῖρας,
καὶ κατασφάξω ἐμαυτὴν ὡς πράξασαν ἀφρόνως·   145
οὐ γὰρ συμφέρει μοι τοῦ ζῆν πάντων ἀποτυχοῦσα.
Ὦ τῶν ἐμῶν ἀτυχιῶν, ὦ συμφορῶν μεγίστων,
ἠλλοτριώθην συγγενῶν, γονέων ἐχωρίσθην
πρὸς τὸ κερδῆσαι φίλτατον, καὶ αὐτοῦ ὑστερήθην."
'Ως δὲ ταῦτα ἐφθέγγετο ἡ κόρη θρηνῳδοῦσα,   45 rᵒ.   150
τοὺς βοστρύχους συντέμνουσα, τύπτουσα καὶ τὴν ὄψιν,
ἐγὼ ταύτην, ὡς δυνατόν, ἀνέστειλα τοῦ θρήνου,
τὰς χεῖράς τε τῶν πλοκαμῶν ἀνέσπασα ἐν μέτρῳ
ἔχειν παραμυθούμενος ἐλπίδας χρηστοτέρας.
Καὶ ἐπερώτησα μαθεῖν πόσαι εἰσὶν ἡμέραι   155
ἀφ᾽ ἧς ὁ πλάνος μόνην σε κατέλιπεν ἐνταῦθα.
Ἡ δὲ αὖθις στενάξασα· " Δέκα ἡμέρας ", ἔφη,
" μέχρι τοῦ νῦν ἐπλήρωσα ἐν ταύτῃ τῇ ἐρήμῳ,
μὴ ἰδοῦσα ἐκτός σου ἕτερον ἀνθρώπου χαρακτῆρα

137 ποῦ.   153 Je ne suis pas sûr d'avoir lu exactement le dernier mot de ce
vers.   159 Au lieu de ἕτερον, le ms. porte ἄλλον. Cette correction m'est
suggérée par le ms. de Trébizonde (vers 1758).

2310 μεθ᾽ ἡμέρας, 'after a day', or more   below 2912; but in 3306 it certainly
  probably as here translated. See   means 'after a day'.

'Going, dearest? Where are you leaving me alone?
Have you forgotten the kindnesses I showed you?   2300
Remember not our first especial vows?'
And when he turned not back still more I cried:
'Have mercy, pity me, save me in my misery,
Nor leave me here to be by beasts devoured.'
Much else I said to him in lamentation;
But he was gone from sight without a word.
Now I, my feet presently tired out,
By bruising of the stones all smeared with blood,
Fell down somewhere there stretched out as one dead;
And with the day hardly recovering,   2310
I came back treading painfully to the spring.
I am bereft of all, without all hopes;
For to my parents I dare not return,
I am ashamed of neighbours, and companions.
Where to find my traitor I know not at all.
I beg you give a knife into my hands,
And I will kill myself for folly done.
It boots me not to live now all is lost.
O my misfortunes and most great disasters!
From kin I was estranged, from parents parted   2320
To win a lover, and have been robbed of him."
And while the mourning girl was speaking thus,
Tearing her locks, with beating of her face,
I stayed her, as I could, from her lament,
Drew back her hands in measure from her hair,
Comforting her to have some better hopes,
And asked to know, "How many are the days
Since the deceiver left you here alone?"
And she, sighing again, "Ten days", she said,
"Have I spent up to now in this desert,   2330
Not seeing other face of man but you,

2311 ἀνάγκῃ. Cf. Soph. *Phil.* 205
φθογγά του στίβον κατ' ἀνάγκαν
ἕρποντος.
2325 ἐν μέτρῳ seems to mean no more
than ὡς δυνατόν in the preceding line.
2327 πόσαι—ἐνταῦθα; Legrand omits
inverted commas here, making this

an indirect question. This could be
accepted as a mixture of direct and
indirect, as above 1939. But it is
simpler to add the inverted commas.
2331 Legrand's reading of ἕτερον for
ἄλλον is quite unnecessary. χαρακτῆρα.
See above 1568, 1577.

καί τινος ἄλλου γηραιοῦ, κατὰ τὴν χθὲς ἡμέραν·   160
ὃς ἔλεγε καὶ τὸν υἱὸν αὐτοῦ παρὰ Ἀράβων
ἀφαιρεθῆναι πρὸ μικροῦ καὶ αἰχμάλωτον εἶναι,
καὶ σπεύδειν εἰς ἀνάρρυσιν αὐτοῦ εἰς Ἀραβίαν.
Οὗτος μοι διηγήσατο, τὰ κατ' ἐμὲ ἀκούσας,
ὅτι, πρὸ πέντε ἡμερῶν, εἰς τὸ Βλαττολιβάδιν,   165
παιδὶν ξανθόν, ἀρτιγενές, μακρὸν τῇ ἡλικίᾳ,
εἰς φάραν ἐποχούμενον καὶ συρτὸν ἄλλον φέρον,
ὁ Μουσοὺρ ἐστασίασε καὶ σπαθέαν τον ἐδῶκε·
καί, εἰ μὴ ὁ νεώτερος ὁ Ἀκρίτης εὑρέθη,
ἐφόνευε τὸν ἄγουρον ἐν τῇ ὥρᾳ ἐκείνῃ·   170
λέγω δὲ τοῦτον ἐκ παντὸς τὸν παραβάτην εἶναι,
ταῦτα γὰρ τὰ γνωρίσματα ἐκεῖνον βεβαιοῦσι.
Οἴμοι, οἴμοι, παντάλαινα καὶ παναθλία τύχη,
ἡ ἀδοκήτως ἀγαθοῦ τοιούτου στερηθεῖσα,
ἡ τὸ γλυκὺ πρὸ τοῦ πιεῖν ἀπολέσασα κάλλος,   175
καὶ ὡς δένδρον νεόφυτον πρὸ καιροῦ ξηρανθεῖσα! "   45 vᵒ.
Ταῦτα ἡ κόρη λέγουσα, δακρύουσα ἀσχέτως,
καὶ Ἀραβοι ἐξῇεσαν ἄφνω ἀπὸ τῆς ἕλης
ὑπέρτεροι τῶν ἑκατόν, πάντες δὲ κονταρᾶτοι·
οὕτως δέ μοι ὑπέπεσαν ὡς γῦπες εἰς τὸ βρῶμα·   180
καὶ ὁ φάρας πολλὰ φθαρεὶς ἀπέσπασε τὸν κλῶνον,
ἐγὼ δὲ τοῦτον κατασχὼν ἐχόμενον τοῦ δρόμου,
μετὰ σπουδῆς ἐπέβαινον κατέχων τὸ κοντάριν,
καὶ πρὸς αὐτοὺς ἐπιδραμὼν πολλοὺς τούτων ἀνεῖλον·
τινὲς δέ με γνωρίσαντες ἔλεγον πρὸς ἀλλήλους·   185
" Αὕτη ἡ τόλμη ἀληθῶς καὶ ἡ πολλὴ ἀνδρεία
τὸν Ἀκρίτην ἐμφαίνουσιν· ἀπωλόμεθα πάντες."
Οἱ δὲ τοῦτο ἀκούσαντες ἔφυγον εἰς τὴν ἕλην,

161 αὐτοῦ, après lequel je supprime ποτὲ.   170 ἐφόνευέ τον ἐκ παντὸς (ces
deux derniers mots sont répétés dans le vers suivant). La correction est empruntée au ms. de Trébizonde (vers 1768) et à celui d'Andros (vers 2664).
176 νεώτατον, et au-dessus νεόφυτον.   179 κονταράτοι.   184 τούτους.
Correction empruntée au ms. d'Andros (vers 2688).   187 ἀπολλόμεθα.

2338 ἀρτιγενές, 'freshly-born' in the
sense of 'young' is hardly possible
here. Read ἀρτιγένειον or better still
ἀρχιγένειον, or better still ξανθοαρχι-
γένειον, for which see Malalas (Bonn)
104 ξανθοαρχιγένειος, and 105 ἀρχι-

γένειος.
2339 On συρτά, led horses, see Kyriakides, Διγενής, pp. 92 ff., and Soph.
Lex. s.v.
2340 The sudden mention of Mousour,
as if everybody knew who he was, is

And someone else, an old man, yesterday,
Who said that his own son also by Arabs
Taken not long ago was now a captive,
To deliver him he was hurrying to Arabia;
This man told me, when he had heard about me,
That five days earlier, at Blattolivadi,
A fair youth, downy-cheeked and tall of stature,
Riding a mare and leading another horse,
Mousour attacked, and struck him with his sword,   2340
And, had not the young Borderer been there,
He would that very hour have killed the boy.
I say that this was surely my transgressor,
The same tokens make certain it was he.
Alas most hapless and most wretched fate,
Of such good suddenly to be bereft,
Sweetness of beauty to have lost untasted,
Untimely parched like a new-planted tree!"
    The girl thus speaking and her tears unchecked,
Arabs dashed suddenly out of the marsh,   2350
More than a hundred and all armed with spears;
They fell on me like vultures on the prey.
My horse, much startled, broke away the branch;
I caught him up when he was on the road,
In haste I mounted and caught up my spear,
And charging at them killed many of them.
Some said to each other recognizing me,
"This daring truly and much gallantry
Show forth the Borderer; we are all lost."
And those who heard this fled into the marsh,   2360

a fault in an otherwise well managed
narrative. This shows that the redactor of GRO was rearranging a version in which, as now in TRE and
AND, Digenes's fight with Mousour,
the border bandit and highwayman,
had been described at the beginning
of the book (TRE 1617, AND 2504).
The redactor of GRO rightly cut
out this preliminary to begin at once
with the palm-tree and the weeping
lady, but forgot to add some ex-

planation of Mousour here, although
he brings it in later, 2388.
2340 ἐστασίασε. Perhaps read ἐνστασίασε,
from TRE 1766, ἐνστασιάσας; cf. uses
of ἐνστατικός (L. & S.), and below
of ἔνστατος (2695) and ἐνστατικῶς.
(3208).
2349 A typical nominative absolute.
2353 πολλὰ φθαρείς. For this use of
φθείρω, cf. Eur. Andr. 708 εἰ μὴ
φθερῇ ... τῆσδ' ἀπὸ στέγης.

τὰ κοντάρια ῥίψαντες ἔνιοι καὶ ἀσπίδας,
μήτε μίαν προσμείναντες κἂν στιγμὴν τὸ παράπαν.　　190
Ὡς δὲ καὶ μόνον ἑαυτὸν εἶδον περιλειφθέντα,
πρὸς τὴν πηγὴν ὑπέστρεφον ἔνθα ἦτον ἡ κόρη·
ἐκείνη δὲ εἰς εὐχερὲς δένδρον ἐπανελθοῦσα,
ἑώρα τὰ γενόμενα καὶ γεγονότα πάντα·
ἰδοῦσα δέ με πρὸς αὐτὴν ἀπερχόμενον μόνον,　　195
ἐκ τοῦ δένδρου κατήρχετο καὶ σπουδαίως ὑπήντα,
παρεκάλει τὲ λέγουσα μετὰ δακρύων τάδε·
" Κύριέ μου καὶ τῆς ἐμῆς πρόξενε σωτηρίας,
εἰ ὁ Ἀκρίτης ἀληθῶς σὺ ὑπάρχεις ἐκεῖνος
ὁ τὸν ἐμὸν ῥυσάμενος φίλτατον ἐκ θανάτου,　　200
οὗ τὸ ὄνομα ἔφριξαν καὶ νῦν οἱ Ἀραβῖται,
ἀπάγγειλόν μοι, δέομαι, μὴ ἀποκρύψῃς ὅλως　　46 rº.
καὶ τὴν σπαθέαν τοῦ Μουσοὺρ εἰ μετεῖχε θανάτου."
　　Ἐμὲ δὲ εἶχεν ἔκπληξις καὶ θαυμάζειν ἐποίει
τῆς κόρης βλέπων τὴν πολλὴν ἀγάπην πρὸς τὸν παῖδα　　205
τὸν ταύτη προξενήσαντα συμφορὰς ἀνεικάστους,
τῶν γεννητόρων χωρισμόν, ἀφαίρεσιν τοῦ πλούτου,
καὶ φρικώδη κατάλειψιν ἐν ἐρήμῳ ἀβάτῳ,
μὴ προσδοκῶσα ἄλλο τι ἢ τὸ θανεῖν ἀδίκως·
καὶ τότε πρῶτον ἔπαθον ἀγάπην γυναικείαν　　210
θερμοτέραν κατὰ πολὺ ὑπάρχειν τῶν ἀρρένων·
φθείρει δὲ μᾶλλον ἄθεσμος καὶ παράνομος μῖξις.
　　Ἐγὼ δὲ ἔφην πρὸς αὐτήν· " Παῦσαι, κόρη, τοῦ κλαίειν
καὶ τοῦ θρηνεῖν ὑπὲρ αὐτοῦ τοῦ δι' ἐμοῦ σωθέντος·
ἐγὼ εἰμὶ ὁ τὸν Μουσοὺρ δικαίως θανατώσας　　215
τὸν ὁδοστάτην καὶ λῃστήν, τὸν τὰς ὁδοὺς κρατοῦντα,
ὡς μηδένα κατατολμᾶν διελθεῖν τοῖς ἐκεῖσε·
ἐγὼ εἰμὶ ὁ ἐξ αὐτοῦ ἑλκύσας καὶ θανάτου
ὃν οὐκ οἶδα πῶς ἀγαπᾷς καὶ ἐπὶ μνήμην φέρεις
φίλτατον τὸν ἀβέβαιον ὀνομάζουσα παῖδα·　　220
ἀλλὰ δεῦρο καὶ πρὸς αὐτὸν ἐγώ σε ἀπαγάγω,

　　203 σπαθαίαν.　　212 μίξις.　　218 ὁ manque.

2365 εὐχερές makes it possible that
above 2268 εὐχερῶς may after all be
the right reading.
2375 Her question seems pointless as
she has just said that her lover had
been saved from death. The other

versions (TRE 1784, AND 2729)
make it clear that the substance of
her question was 'tell me some more
about my lover whom Mousour
nearly killed'.
2378, 2381 The redactor for once gets

Throwing their spears away and some their shields,
Not tarrying a single moment even.
And when I saw myself left there alone,
I turned back where the girl was to the well.
She had climbed into a convenient tree
Watched what was doing and all that had been done;
Seeing me coming back to her alone,
She came down from the tree, hurried to meet me,
Began to entreat, saying thus with tears,
"My lord, and procurer of my salvation,   2370
If and in truth you are that Borderer,
Who did deliver my beloved from death,
Whose name awed the Arabians even now,
Tell me, I beg you, nor conceal at all,
If Mousour's sword-stroke too had death in it."
Amazement held me then and made me wonder
Seeing the girl's much love for the young man,
Who had procured her unimagined woes,
Parting from parents, taking wealth away,
Awful desertion in the pathless wild   2380
To wait for nothing but death undeserved;
And first I learned then that the love of women
Is warmer a great deal than that of men,
But wrong and lawless union more corrupts it.
And then I said to her, "Cease, girl, from weeping
And mourning over him was saved by me.
I am the man who justly slew Mousour,
Robber and highwayman, who held the roads,
That no one dared at all to pass thereby;
I am the man who saved from him and death   2390
The one you love, how I know not, and remember,
Calling the unsteady boy your best beloved.
Yet thither and to him I will conduct you,

his participle προξενήσαντα in agreement, but soon retreats to the safety
of the nominative absolute προσδοκῶσα.
2382 ἔπαθον. Leg. ἔμαθον. This passage,
the sense of which is that women are
more passionate but less faithful, is
not found in other versions. For the
redactor's curious trick of verbal
repetition note πρόξενε 2370, προξενήσαντα 2378, φθαρείς 2353, φθείρει
2384; παρασκευάσω 2394, παρεσκεύασε
2425, παρασκευάζει 2471.
2390 ἐλκύσας for the more usual ῥύσας.

παρασκευάσω τε αὐτὸν τοῦ γαμετήν σε ἔχειν,
εἰ καὶ τὸ σέβας ἀρνηθῇς τῶν αἰσχρῶν Αἰθιόπων."
Ἡ δὲ τοῦτο ἀκούσασα, χαρᾶς ἐμφορηθεῖσα·
" Κύριέ μου," ἀντέφησε, " μέγιστε ἀντιλῆπτορ,   225
καὶ τοῦ θείου βαπτίσματος γέγονα ἐν μεθέξει
πρὶν συναφθῆναι τῷ ἀνδρί, παρ' αὐτοῦ κελευσθεῖσα·
οὐδὲν γὰρ εἶχον δυνατόν, τῷ πόθῳ δουλωθεῖσα,   46 vᵒ.
τὰ παρ' αὐτοῦ λεγόμενα μὴ ἀγαγεῖν εἰς ἔργον,
δι' ὃν γονεῖς καὶ ἀγχιστὰς εἰς οὐδὲν ἐλογίσθην."   230
Ταῦτα, φίλε, ὡς ἤκουσα ἐκ στόματος τῆς κόρης
καθάπερ φλὸξ εἰς τὴν ἐμὴν καρδίαν ἐπεισῆλθεν,
καὶ προσέφερεν ἔρωτα καὶ παράνομον μῖξιν·
καὶ πρῶτα μὲν ἀνέστελλον τὴν ἀκάθεκτον γνώμην,
καὶ ἤθελον, εἰ δυνατόν, φυγεῖν τὴν ἁμαρτίαν·   235
ἀλλὰ πάντως ἀδύνατον πῦρ παραμεῖναι χόρτῳ.
Ὡς γὰρ ταύτην ἀνήγαγον ἐν τῷ ἰδίῳ ἵππῳ,
καὶ τῆς ὁδοῦ ἡπτόμεθα ὡς πρὸς τὴν Χαλκουργίαν
(τόπος γὰρ οὗτος πέφυκε πλησίον τῆς Συρίας),
οὐκ εἶχον ὅτι γένωμαι, πῦρ ὅλος ἐγενόμην,   240
τοῦ ἔρωτος ὁλοσχερῶς ἐν ἐμοὶ αὐξηθέντος·
καταβαλόντες τὸ λοιπὸν χρείαν τάχα ποιῆσαι
ἐν τῷ κάλλει τοὺς ὀφθαλμούς, ἐν τῇ ἀφῇ τὰς χεῖρας,
τὸ στόμα τοῖς φιλήμασι καὶ ἀκοὴν τοῖς λόγοις,
ἠρξάμην ἅπαντα ποιεῖν πράξεως παρανόμου·   245
καὶ γεγόνασιν ἅπαντα ὅσα ἤθελον ἔργα,
καὶ ἐμιάνθη ἡ ὁδὸς ἀπὸ τῆς ἀνομίας,
συνεργείᾳ σατανικῇ καὶ ψυχῆς ἀμελείᾳ,
εἰ καὶ πολλὰ ἀνθίστατο ἡ κόρη πρὸς τὸ ἔργον,
εἰς Θεὸν καθορκίζουσα καὶ εἰς ψυχὰς γονέων.   250
Ἀλλὰ ὁ ἀντικείμενος, τοῦ σκότους ὁ προστάτης,
ὁ ἐχθρὸς καὶ πολέμιος τοῦ ἡμετέρου γένους,
καὶ αὐτοῦ παρεσκεύασε Θεοῦ ἐπιλαθέσθαι
καὶ τῆς ἀνταποδόσεως τῆς φοβερᾶς ἡμέρας,   47 rᵒ.

223 ἀρνήσῃ.   233 μίξιν.   244 τῷ στόματι φιλήματα. Correction
empruntée au ms. de Trébizonde (vers 1815).

2395 Αἰθιόπων. Cf. above 32, 2049; and
introduction on the southern Arabs
of Bagdad and Egypt being (literally)
denigrated. This, like so many other

things, was first pointed out by
Grégoire.
2396 ἐμφορηθεῖσα. Not 'carried away
by' but 'gorged with' as is shown by

And make him ready to take you to wife,
If the base Aethiops' faith you will deny."
   This when she heard, being fulfilled of joy,
"My lord," she answered, "and most great protector,
Of divine baptism I had partaken
Before being joined to this man, at his bidding;
For nothing could I, by desire enslaved,   2400
Not bring to pass of what was said by him,
For whom parents and kin I counted nothing."
This when I heard, my friend, from the girl's mouth
As it were a flame came up into my heart,
Offered me love and lawless union.
First I put off my unrestrained purpose,
And wanted, if I could, to escape sin;
But fire cannot ever stay with grass.
And when I took her up on my own horse
And we set out to go to Coppermines   2410
(That was a place near by in Syria)
I knew not what I was, I was all fire,
Passion increasing utterly within me;
So when we rested as for natural need—
My eyes with beauty and my hands with feeling,
My mouth with kisses and with words my hearing—
I started to do all of lawless action,
And every deed I wanted all was done.
By lawlessness our journey was defiled
By Satan's help and my soul's negligence,   2420
Although the woman much opposed the doing
Calling on God and on her parents' souls.
The Adversary, champion of the dark,
The foe and enemy of all our race,
Made me ready to forget God Himself
And the requiting of the dreadful day

---

quotations in L. & S.
2397 ἀντιλῆπτορ. LXX.
2406 γνώμην, 'purpose'.
2410 Χαλκουργίαν, Coppermines. TRE
1810, AND 2757 Χαλκογοῦρνα (so
PAS 372; but 373 Χοχλακοῦρα,
which also appears in TRE 1827

(corrected by editors).
2414 καταβαλόντες τὸ λοιπόν. This line
and this excuse for stopping is in no
other version. For καταβάλλω in this
intrans. sense, like καταλύω, cf.
κατάβολος, a port of call. This line
would fit better after 2416.

ἐν ᾗ πάντα τὰ κρύφια πταίσματα φανεροῦνται 255
τῶν ἀγγέλων ἐνώπιον καὶ τῶν ἀνθρώπων πάντων.
Εἶτα παραγενόμενος ἐπὶ τὴν Χαλκουργίαν,
ἐκεῖσε τὸν πλανήσαντα ταύτην εὕρομεν παῖδα.
Ἦν δὲ ἄρα τοῦ στρατηγοῦ υἱὸς τοῦ Ἀντιόχου,
τοῦ πρὸ χρόνων ἐν τῷ ζυγῷ ὑπὸ Περσῶν σφαγέντος. 260
Ὡς γὰρ αὐτὸν ἀπὸ χειρῶν τοῦ Μουσοὺρ ἐρρυσάμην,
ἔμπροσθέν μου οὐκ εἴασα τοῦ πορευθῆναι τοῦτον,
γνωστὸν δὲ πᾶσιν ἔφηνα καὶ παράνομον μάλα·
καὶ τοῦτον παραδέδωκα πρὸς τοὺς ἐκεῖ μου φίλους,
ὡς ἂν διάγῃ μετ' αὐτῶν ἄχρις οὗ ὑποστρέψω· 265
" Εἰ δ' οὖν καὶ ταύτην ἐκβαλεῖν τὴν κόρην βουληθείης,
μὰ τὸν σωτῆρά μου Χριστόν, πλεῖον ζωὴν οὐχ ἕξεις."
Φήσας αὐτῷ μὴ ἀδικεῖν τὴν κόρην μήτε βλάπτειν,
τοῦτον ἐκεῖ καταλιπὼν πλεῖστά τε νουθετήσας,
καὶ δεύτερον ἐντειλάμενος μὴ ταύτην ἀθετῆσαι, 270
ἀλλ' ἔχειν, ὡς ὑπέσχετο, γαμετὴν διὰ νόμου,
διηγησάμην ἅπασι πῶς τε εὗρον τὴν κόρην
καὶ πῶς ταύτην ἀφήρπασα ἀπὸ τῶν Ἀραβίτων·
τὰ δὲ μὴ δέον ἐξειπεῖν παρέτρεχον τῷ λόγῳ,
ἵνα μὴ σκάνδαλον ὁ παῖς εἰς διάνοιαν λάβῃ. 275
Εἶτα τὸν πλοῦτον ἅπαντα παραδοὺς ἀμφοτέροις,
ὃν ἡ κόρη ἀφείλετο ἐξ οἰκείων γονέων,
καὶ ἵππους δύο τοὺς αὐτῶν ἀπέπεμπον ἐκεῖσε,
αὖθις ἐπαγγειλάμενος τῷ νέῳ δημοσίως
τοῦ μηδέποτε ἄδικον ἔτι τῇ κόρῃ πρᾶξαι. 47 vᵒ. 280
Καὶ μετ' ὀλίγον καὶ αὐτὸς ἦλθον εἰς τὴν καλήν μου,
τοῦ ἀπριλίου τρέχοντος πρὸς μεσότητα ἤδη,
τὸ συνειδὸς κατήγορον φέρων τῆς ἁμαρτίας
καὶ ταλανίζων ἐμαυτὸν ἐν τῇ ἀθέσμῳ πράξει·
ὁπηνίκα τὸν ἥλιον, τὴν ἐμὴν ψυχὴν εἶδον, 285
ὡς αἰσχυνόμενος αὐτὴν μεγάλως ἀδικήσας,
μετ' ὀλίγον γὰρ ἔδοξα μετοίκησιν ποιῆσαι

259 ἄρα υἱὸς στρατηγοῦ τοῦ ἀντιόχου. Correction empruntée au ms. de Trébizonde (vers 1829) et à celui d'Andros (vers 2778). 261 ἐρυσάμην. 265 Je
crois devoir adopter la leçon αὐτῶν du ms. de Trébizonde (vers 1834) au lieu de
αὐτῆς. A mon avis, ce mot pourrait aussi se rapporter à κόρης sous-entendu.
267 τον (sans accent). 282 ἀπριλλίου.

2437 Legrand reads μετ' αὐτῶν (from TRE 1834) instead of MS. μετ' αὐτῆς.

Wherein all secret faults shall be revealed
Before the face of angels and of men.
Thereafter when I came to Coppermines,
There did we find the boy who had seduced her   2430
(Son was he of the General Antiochos
Slain years ago under the yoke by Persians)—
For when I rescued him from Mousour's hands
I let him not go forth before my face,
But made him known to all, a lawbreaker,
And gave him over to my friends were there
To stay with them until I should return—
"If you should think of casting out this girl,
By Christ my Saviour you shall live no more—"
Telling him not to wrong the girl nor harm   2440
And having left him there and much admonished,
Now again bade him not to disregard her
But make her, as he promised, wife by law;
I told them all how I had found the girl,
And rescued her from the Arabians;
My tale passed over what was wrong to tell
That the boy's mind should not receive offence.
Then to both handing over all the wealth
The girl had taken off from her own parents,
And their two horses, I sent them away,   2450
Having again enjoined the youth in public
Never to do the girl wrong any more.
    Soon I myself came back to my good wife,
April already running to mid-month,
With the accusing conscience of my sin,
Calling me wretched for my forbidden act.
Whenever I saw the sun, I saw my soul,
Being ashamed as having greatly wronged her,
And soon resolved to make a change of dwelling—

Μετ' αὐτῆς accords better with
the two lines which follow; μετ'
αὐτῶν better with the line which
precedes. The fact is that the redactor was evidently in a momentary
muddle between the two interviews
with the son of Antiochus; the first
after his rescue from Mousour, the
second on returning to find him in
safe keeping and to give him his
deserted and rescued bride.

(διὰ τὸ γνῶναι καὶ αὐτὴ τὴν παράνομον μῖξιν),
ἢν δὴ καὶ πεποιήκαμεν ἀπάραντες ἐκεῖθεν.

288 μίξιν.

(Because she knew of the unlawful union)— 2460
The which we did removing from that place.'

2460 This line looks like an interpolation and if retained must be put in brackets so that ἦν, 2461, may refer to μετοίκησιν, 2459.

ΛΟΓΟΣ ΕΚΤΟΣ

Ὁ ἕκτος λόγος ὁ παρὼν πλείστων ἀνδραγαθίων
διεξιὼν τὰ θαύματα τοῦ Διγενοῦς Ἀκρίτου,
ὡς αὐτὸς διηγήσατο πρὸς τοὺς ἰδίους φίλους.

*   *   *

Εἰ βασιλέα τῶν μηνῶν θεῖναι τις ἐβουλήθη,
μάϊος ἐβασίλευσεν εἰς ἅπαντας τοὺς μῆνας,   5
κόσμος οὗτος τερπνότατος γῆς ἁπάσης τυγχάνει,
ὀφθαλμὸς πάντων τῶν φυτῶν καὶ τῶν ἀνθῶν λαμπρότης,
τῶν λειμώνων ἐρύθημα καὶ κάλλος ἀπαστράπτον,
ἔρωτας πνέει θαυμαστῶς, ἀφροδίτην ἐπάγει·
γῆν τοῦ μιμεῖσθαι οὐρανὸν αὐτὴν παρασκευάζει,   10
ἀγλαΐζων τοῖς ἄνθεσι ῥόδοις τὲ καὶ ναρκίσσοις.
Ἐν τούτῳ δὴ τῷ θαυμαστῷ μηνὶ τῷ γλυκυτάτῳ,
ἠθέλησα μεταβαλεῖν μόνος μὲ τῆς καλῆς μου,
τοῦ στρατηγοῦ τῆς θυγατρὸς τοῦ Δουκὸς τῆς ὡραίας.
Καὶ δὴ πρός τινα θαυμαστὸν λειμῶνα ἀπελθόντες,   15
ἐκεῖ τὴν τένδαν ἔστησα καὶ τὴν ἰδίαν κλίνην,
κύκλωθεν ταύτης τεθεικὼς πάντων φυτῶν τὰ εἴδη.   48 rᵒ.
Κάλαμοι ἐπεφύοντο εἰς ὕψος ἐπηρμένοι,
ὕδωρ ψυχρὸν ἀνέβλυζεν ἐν μέσῳ τοῦ λειμῶνος
καὶ πανταχοῦ διέτρεχεν τῆς γῆς ἐκείνης πάσης·   20
ὀρνέων γένη ἱκανὰ ἐνέμετο τῷ ἄλσει,
ταῶνες χειροήθεις τε ψιττακοὶ καὶ οἱ κύκνοι,
οἱ ψιττακοὶ κρεμώμενοι ἐπὶ τοῖς κλώνοις ᾖδον,
οἱ κύκνοι ἐν τοῖς ὕδασι τὴν νομὴν ἐποιοῦντο·
οἱ ταῶνες τὰς πτέρυγας κυκλοῦντες εἰς τὰ ἄνθη,   25
ἀντέλαμπον τῇ τῶν ἀνθῶν ἐν ταῖς πτέρυξι χρόᾳ·

1 Le premier ὁ manque.   3 Au lieu de ὡς, il n'est pas nécessaire de lire
ἇς, comme dans le ms. de Trébizonde (vers 1858).   6 τερπνότητος.   8
ἀπαστράπτων.   13 με.   16 ἔστησαν. Correction fournie par le ms. de
Trébizonde (vers 1878) et celui d'Andros (vers 2834).   23 κλώνοι. Correction
fournie par le ms. de Trébizonde (vers 1896) et celui d'Andros (vers 2825).

2465 For this set piece on the King of
Months, which appears also in other
versions (TRE 1861 ff., AND 2816–
23, 2871, 2872), see Ach Tat. II. i. 2,
and Meliten. 32 ff. See also 'On a
May mornynge' at the beginning of

Piers the Plowman, and Skeat, ad loc.,
who says that 'On a May morning'
is nearly equivalent to 'Once upon
a time'—so common is it in the
Early English poets.
2467 κόσμος, 'ornament'—rare in this

SIXTH BOOK

THE sixth and present book of many gests
Recording the wonders of Digenes the Borderer,
Even as himself told them to his own friends.

*　　*　　*

'If any would suppose a king of months
Of all the months the month of May is king;
He is all earth's most pleasant ornament,
Eye of all plants and brilliance of the flowers,
The blush and beauty of the meadows flashing,
Breathes wondrous passions, brings in love-making;　　2470
He sets the earth to imitate the sky
Decking with blooms of rose and daffodil.
　　And in this wonderful this sweetest month
I pleased to move, alone with my good wife
The lovely daughter of the General Doukas.
So to a wondrous meadow when we came
There I set up my tent and my own bed,
Having put round it every sort of plants.
Rushes were growing there rising on high,
In the mid-meadow gushing up cool water　　2480
Was running everywhere through all that land.
Several kinds of birds lived in the grove,
Tame peacocks there and parrots and the swans,
The parrots hanging on the branches sang,
The swans found their own pasture in the waters,
Circling their wings the peacocks in the flowers
Flashed back the hue of flowers in their wings;

---

sense so late, but classical; also below 3757.

2469 ἀπαστράπτων agreeing with μάϊος; but Legrand unnecessarily reads ἀπαστράπτον.

2471 αὐτὴν παρασκευάζει. Leg. αὐτός from TRE 1867.

2474 μὲ τῆς καλῆς μου. See above 2453, &c. I think καλή is always used with the connotation of 'wife', as in the modern language.

2486, 2487 πτέρυγας, πτέρυξι; 2488

πτερά; but there is no distinction of meaning.

2487 ἀντέλαμπον. At first sight this line would seem to mean 'outshone the flowers with their wings'. But ἀντιλάμπω cannot mean 'outshine'; and the line must mean rather 'answered the colour of the flowers with the brightness of their wings'. Cf. below 3349, where the line is repeated with slight variations. Line 2479 is also repeated below 3329.

αἱ δὲ λοιπαὶ ἐλεύθερα τὰ πτερὰ κεκτημέναι
ἔπαιζον ἐποχούμεναι εἰς τῶν δένδρων τοὺς κλώνους.

Καὶ τὸ κάλλος τῆς εὐγενοῦς κόρης ὑπεραστράπτον
κρεῖττον ταῶνος ἔλαμπε καὶ τῶν φυτῶν ἁπάντων·   30
ναρκίσσου γὰρ τὸ πρόσωπον τὴν χροίαν ἐμιμεῖτο,
αἱ παρειαὶ ὡς εὔθαλλον ἐξανέτελλον ῥόδον·
ἄνθος ῥόδον ἀρτιφυὲς ὑπέφηνε τὰ χείλη,
ὁπηνίκα ταῖς κάλυξιν ἄρχεται ἀνατέλλειν·
βόστρυχοι ἐποχούμενοι τῶν ὀφρυδίων λίαν   35
χρυσοτερπεῖς ἀνέπεμπον ἀκτινοβόλους μάλα,
καὶ διὰ πάντων ἄρρητος ὑπῆρχεν εὐφροσύνη.

Περὶ τῆς κλίνης πέμματα ἐκάπνιζον παντοῖα·
μόσχοι, νίται καὶ ἄμβαρα, καμφοραὶ καὶ κασσίαι·
καὶ ἦν πλείστη ἡ ἡδονὴ καὶ ὀσμὴ εὐφροσύνης·   40
τοσαύτην ὁ παράδεισος τὴν τερπνότητα εἶχεν.

Ἐν ὥρᾳ τῇ μεσημβρινῇ πρὸς ὕπνον ἀνετράπην,
ῥοδόσταμμα τῆς εὐγενοῦς ῥαντιζούσης με κόρης,
ἀδονίδων καὶ τῶν λοιπῶν ὀρνίθων μελῳδούντων.   48 vᵒ.

Ἡ δὲ κόρη διψήσασα πρὸς τὴν πηγὴν ἀπῆλθε·   45
καί, ὡς ἐκεῖσε ἔβρεχε τοὺς πόδας τερπομένη,
δράκων, μορφώσας ἑαυτὸν εἰς εὐειδὲς παιδίον,
πρὸς αὐτὴν παρεγένετο, βουλόμενος πλανῆσαι·
ἡ δέ, τὸν ὄντα οὐδαμῶς ἀγνοήσασα, ἔφη·
" Ἄφες, δράκον, ὃ βούλεσαι· ἐγὼ οὐκ ἀπατοῦμαι,   50
ὁ φιλῶν με ἠγρύπνησε καὶ ἀρτίως καθεύδει
(ἔλεγε γὰρ ἐν ἑαυτῇ· δράκων οὗτος ὑπάρχει,
πώποτε οὐ τεθέαμαι ὧδε τοιαύτην ὄψιν)·
εἰ ἐγερθῇ καὶ εὕρῃ σε, νά σε κακοδικήσῃ."

29 ὑπεραστράπτων.   32 ἐξανέτελλε   35–36 Entre ces deux vers, il y
en a probablement un ou plusieurs d'oubliés.   38 πέγματα.   40 ἡ
manque.   44 ἀδωνίδων.   53 πώποτε. ὧδε.

2492 TRE 1906 has ἡλίου for ναρκίσσου,
and so has AND 2865.
2495 and TRE 1910 ff. There seems
to be a reflection here from Meliten.
2842 ff., but nothing decisive.
2499 πέμματα ought to mean 'cakes',
'sweetmeats', but in view of the next
line it seems to mean 'perfumes'.
2500 μόσχοι, νίται, καὶ ἄμπαρα. For

ἄμπαρα, ambergris not amber, see
above 1203. TRE 1918 has the same
list with ξυλαλόαι (bitter aloes) sub-
stituted for νίται. Legrand puts νίται
in his Index de mots remarquables without any explanation. The solution is
in Ducange, appendix ad gloss., s.v.
Νέτ—which he defines as galla musca-
ta (which ought to mean a nutmeg);

The others in freedom their wings possessing
Played riding on the branches of the trees.
The noble Girl her beauty overgleaming   2490
Brighter than peacock shone and all the plants.
Her face had copied the narcissus hue,
And like a rose in bloom her cheeks were dawning,
Her lips showed forth a rose-flower just opening
What time begins the dawning of its cup.
Curls that were riding just above her brows
Scattered about fair-flashing gleams of gold,
And joy unspeakable was over all.
All sorts of confections smoked round the bed,
Musk, allspice, ambergris, camphor, and cassia,   2500
Great was the pleasure and smell of gladness:
So much delightfulness the garden had.
   About the midday hour I turned to sleep
While the noble Girl sprinkled me with rosewater
And nightingales with other birds made music.
The Girl being thirsty went down to the spring,
And as she wetted her feet playing there
A serpent, self-changed to a handsome youth,
Came up towards her wanting to seduce her.
She said, not ignorant of what he was,   2510
"Serpent, give up your plan: I am not deceived.
Who loves me has been watching; now he sleeps"
(For to herself she said, He is a serpent;
I never saw before such visage here)—
"If he wakes up and finds you, he shall hurt you."

quoting Psellos, and then a Spanish medical dictionary: 'Ned, composition aromatica o neda. Ned primum, sahumerio muy aromatico.' Prof. V. Minorsky tells me the word 'is a bastard of *nardos*, Pers. *nard*, Arab. *nārdīn* or *nēzdīn*, all derived from Sanskr. *narada | nalada*'.
2501 ἡδονή here, especially as combined with ὀσμή, may mean 'sound'; see above 1338.

2505 ἀδονίδων. TRE 1923 and AND 2883 ἀηδόνων. Ἀδόνιν was a recognized modern formation perhaps especially Cretan; see Ducange s.v.
2508 δράκων. Like the δράκων of *Iliad* xi. 39 and xii. 202 no ordinary snake, and well on the way to becoming the δράκος, or ogre, of modern Greek folk tales.
2514 ὄψιν, either 'face' or 'appearance'.
2515 νά σε κακοδικήσῃ. For κακοδικῶ

Ὁ δὲ πηδήσας ἀναιδῶς βιάζειν ἐπεχείρει· 55
καὶ φωνὴν ἔπεμπεν εὐθὺς καλοῦσα με ἡ κόρη·
" Ἐξύπνησον, αὐθέντα μου, καὶ λάβε τὴν φιλτάτην."
Τῆς δὲ φωνῆς εἰς τὴν ἐμὴν καρδίαν ἠχησάσης,
τάχιον ἀνεκάθισα καὶ τὸν ὀχλοῦντα εἶδον·
ἄντικρυς γάρ μου ἡ πηγὴ ἦν ἐξεπιτηδείως, 60
καὶ ἐξελκύσας τὸ σπαθὶν εἰς τὴν πηγὴν εὑρέθην,
οἱ γὰρ πόδες μου ἔτρεχον ὡς πτέρυγες ὀξέως·
καὶ τοῦτον τε καταλαβών, φάντασμά μοι ἐδείκνυ
φρικῶδες τε καὶ φοβερὸν ἐν ἀνθρώποις καὶ μέγα,
τρεῖς εὐμεγέθεις κεφαλὰς πυρφλογιζούσας ὅλως· 65
ἐξ ἑκατέρων ἔπεμπεν ἐξαστράπτουσαν φλόγα·
ἐκ τόπου δὲ κινούμενος βροντῆς ἦχον ἐτέλει,
ὥστε δοκεῖν σαλεύεσθαι γῆν τε καὶ πάντα δένδρα.
Σῶμα παχύνων, κεφαλὰς εἰς ἓν ἐπισυνάγων,
ὄπισθεν λεπτυνόμενος καὶ οὐρὰν ἀποξύνων, 49 rᵒ. 70
ποτὲ μὲν συστελλόμενος, ἐξαπλούμενος δ᾽ αὖθις,
καὶ ἐπάνω μου ἅπασαν τὴν ὁρμὴν ἐποιεῖτο.
Ἐγὼ δέ, τὰ ὁρώμενα ἀντ᾽ οὐδενὸς νομίσας,
εἰς ὕψος ὅλῳ τῷ θυμῷ τὸ σπαθὶν ἀνατείνας,
εἰς κεφαλὰς κατήγαγον θηρὸς τοῦ δεινοτάτου, 75
καὶ ἀπάσας αἱρῶ ὁμοῦ· ὃς καὶ πρὸς γῆν ἡπλώθη,
ἄνω καὶ κάτω τὴν οὐρὰν κινῶν τὰ τελευταῖα.
Καὶ ἀπομάξας τὸ σπαθὶν καὶ βαλὼν εἰς τὴν θήκην,
πόρρωθεν ὄντας τοὺς ἐμοὺς προσεκαλούμην παῖδας,
καὶ ἀρθῆναι προσέταττον τὸν δράκοντα εὐθέως. 80
Ὡς δὲ τοῦτο ἐγένετο ταχέως ὑπὲρ λόγον,
οἱ παῖδες μὲν ἀπέτρεχον εἰς τὰς ἰδίας τένδας,
ἐπὶ τὴν κλίνην δὲ κἀγὼ ὑπνωσόμενος αὖθις,
ἡδὺς γὰρ ὃν ἐκάθευδον εἷλκε με πάλιν ὕπνος·
οὔπω γὰρ τούτου κορεσθεὶς ἀφύπνωσα τὸ πρῶτον. 85
Ἡ δὲ κόρη πρὸς γέλωτα ἄμετρον κινηθεῖσα,
φαντάσματα τοῦ δράκοντος φέρουσα ἐπὶ μνήμης
καὶ τὸν σύντομον θάνατον ἐκείνου τοῦ μεγέθους,
πρὸς τὸ μὴ ἐξυπνῆσαι με ἐξῆλθε πρός τι δένδρον,

---

65 κεφαλὰς εὐμεγέθεις.   84 ὧν. Correction fournie par le ms. de Trébizonde
(vers 1963) et celui d'Andros (vers 2924).

---

see above 1521. νά here expresses something between a wish, and a future.

He sprang and shamelessly tried violence:
The Girl at once cried out calling for me:
"Wake up, my master, and take back your darling."
And when her voice had sounded in my heart,
I sat up quickly and I saw the troubler   2520
(For by design the spring was opposite)—
I drew my sword, and I was at the spring,
For and my feet ran dazzlingly like wings;
And when I reached him he showed me an appearance
Horrible, dreadful among men, and great,
Three well-grown heads he had all fiery-flaming,
From each of them a flashing flame sent out;
Moving from his place he made a noise of thunder,
So the earth seemed to shake and all the trees.
His body thick, joining the heads in one,   2530
Behind was slender, tapering to a tail,
Now gathered himself up, and then stretched out,
And right against me all his onset made.
But I counting as nothing what was seen
On high with all my spirit raised my sword,
Down brought it on the dreadful beast his heads,
Took all together; on the ground stretched out
He lashed his tail up and down for the last time.
I wiped my sword and put it in its sheath,
Called up my servants who were some way off   2540
And bade them straightway take the serpent up.
When this was done quickly beyond the telling
My boys ran off again to their own tents,
And I too to my bed to sleep again;
Sweet sleep I had been slumbering drew me back,
For I had woken still unsatisfied.
The Girl now moved to measureless laughter,
Remembering the snake's appearances
And of that magnitude the quick-cut death,
So as not to wake me went away to a tree,   2550

2518 TRE 1935 more vividly χαόνεις
τὴν καλήν σου.
2523 ὀξέως—of motion, quite classical.
2527 ἑκατέρων. It is possible that only
the two outside heads breathed fire;

but it is more likely that ἑκάτερος is
used loosely here, like ἀμφότεροι
above 205, 1193, instead of ἕκαστος.
2533 ἐπάνω μου, modern colloquial
sense.

167

παρηγορίαν τε λαβεῖν μικρὰν ἀπὸ τοῦ φόβου.   90
Καὶ ἰδοὺ λέων φοβερὸς ἐξῆλθεν ἐκ τοῦ ἄλσους,
ὃς πρὸς τὴν κόρην καὶ αὐτὸς τὴν ὁρμὴν ἐποιεῖτο·
ἡ δὲ φωνὴν ἐξέπεμψε βοηθόν με καλοῦσα·
καὶ ἐπακούσας τάχιστα ἐπανέστην τῆς κλίνης·
καὶ ὡς εἶδον τὸν λέοντα συντόμως εἰσπηδήσας,   95
φέρων ῥάβδον ἐν τῇ χειρὶ τοῦτον εὐθὺς ἐκπίπτω,
πατάξας δὲ εἰς κεφαλήν, ἔθανε παραχρῆμα·   49 vᵒ.
ὡς δὲ καὶ οὗτος μήκοθεν ἐρρίφη τὲ ὁ δράκων,
ἡ κόρη [μου] εἰς ἐμαυτὴν καθώρκισεν εἰποῦσα·
"Ἄκουσόν μου, αὐθέντα μου, νά με ἐπιχαρείης,   100
ἔπαρον τὴν κιθάραν σου, κροῦσον αὐτὴν ὀλίγον
μεταβαλών μου τὴν ψυχὴν ἐκ τοῦ θηρὸς τοῦ φόβου."
Καὶ ὡς οὐκ ἦν μοι δυνατὸν παρακοῦσαι τῆς κόρης,
ταύτην ἀνέκρουον εὐθύς, ἡ δὲ ἐνετραγῴδει·
"Εὐχαριστῶ τῷ ἔρωτι γλυκὺν δόντι μοι κύρκαν,   105
καὶ χαίρω βασιλεύουσα, μηδένα φοβουμένη,
κρίνον ὑπάρχει εὐθαλές, μῆλον μεμυρισμένον,
καὶ ὡς ῥόδον πανεύοσμον θέλγει μου τὴν καρδίαν."
Ὡς δὲ τὸ ῥόδον ἔλεγεν ἡ κόρη μελῳδοῦσα,
ἐνόμιζον ὅτι κρατεῖ ῥόδον ἐπὶ τὰ χείλη,   110
ἐοίκασι γὰρ ἀληθῶς ἄρτι ἀνθοῦντι ῥόδῳ.
Τῆς δὲ κιθάρας ἡ ᾠδὴ καὶ ἡ φωνὴ τῆς κόρης
ἦχον τερπνὸν ἀνέπεμπον, ὀρέων ἀντηχούντων,
ὡς καὶ τοὺς ὄντας μήκοθεν αἰσθάνεσθαι τοῦ μέλους.
Καὶ τοῦτο ἐπεγνώκαμεν ἐκ τούτου τοῦ σημείου·   115
κατὰ τύχην διήρχοντο, ἐν ἐκείνῃ τῇ ὥρᾳ,
στρατιῶται ἐν τῇ ὁδῷ τῇ καλουμένῃ Τρώσει,
ἐν ᾗ πολλοὺς συμβέβηκε πολλὰ τραυματισθῆναι,
καὶ δῆλον ἐκ τὸ ὄνομα ὃ εἴληφεν ὁ τόπος.
Ὑπῆρχον δέ, ὡς ὕστερον παρ' αὐτῶν τοῦτο ἔγνων,   120
Ἰωαννάκης θαυμαστὸς καὶ νέος ἀπελάτης,   50 rᵒ.
Φιλοπαπποῦς ὁ γέρων τε καὶ ὁ Κίνναμος τρίτος·

96 ῥᾶβδον.

2557 Leg. ἐμπίπτω.
2560 εἰς ἐμαυτήν. Leg. ἑαυτήν.
2563 μεταβαλών μου τὴν ψυχήν, i.e.
'making me think of something
else'. TRE 1984 μετεώρισον.

2566 κύρκαν. See above 469, 1518.
2570-5 Only in GRO.
2578 Τρώσει. The place called Trôsis,
'Wounding', has been identified by
Grégoire with the modern Trusch.

To have a little comfort after her fear.
And lo came from the grove a dreadful lion,
And he too made his onset on the girl.
She gave a cry calling on me her helper;
I heard, and swiftly rose up from the bed,
And when I saw the lion, quickly jumped
With staff in hand, and straightway fell on him,
And struck him on the head; he died forthwith.
When he too, with the snake, was thrown far off,
The Girl adjured me on her life, saying,   2560
"Listen, my master, grant me this favour,
Take up your lute, and play on it a little,
Refresh my soul from terror of the beast."
And as I could not disobey the Girl
Began at once to play, and she sang to it:
"To love my thanks who gave me my sweet darling,
I joy to be his queen, afraid of none,
Who is a lily in bloom, a scented apple,
Like a perfuming rose enchants my heart."
And as the Girl spoke of that rose in song   2570
I thought she held a rose between her lips,
For truly they were like a new-blown rose.
The music of the lute and the Girl's voice
Sent up a pleasant sound, the hills echoed,
Even they heard it who were far away.
And this we knew of by this testimony:
It chanced that at that hour were passing by
Some soldiers, by the way that is called Wounding
(Where many happened to have been much wounded,
The name declares it which the place had taken).   2580
These were, as afterwards I learned from them,
Ioannakes, a young and wondrous Reiver,
Old Philopappos, and Kinnamos the third.

(see introd.). It is not mentioned
here in the other versions (TRE
2002, AND 2966, but see TRE
2289) which from this point differ considerably. GRO's forty-five
στρατιῶται become three hundred
ἀπελάται. The tomb of Digenes was
also erected at Trôsis (see below
3776), and has been identified by
Grégoire with the existing ruin of a
Commagene monument.
2581–3 These lines should come below
after 2641.

καί, ὡς ᾤχοντο τῆς ὁδοῦ, ἤκουσαν τῶν ᾀσμάτων,
μίλλιον ἓν ἀπέχοντες ἀφ᾽ ἡμῶν, ὡς εἰκάζω,
καὶ ταύτης ἐκστρατήσαντες ἦλθον ἡμῶν πλησίον.   125
Καὶ ὡς μόνην ἐσκέψαντο τὴν περίβλεπτον κόρην,
ὡς ὑπὸ βέλους τὰς ψυχὰς ἐτρώθησαν τῷ κάλλει,
καὶ εἰς ἔρωτα ἄπειρον ἐκινήθησαν πάντες,
σώζοντες τὸν σαρακοστὸν ἀριθμὸν πρὸς τοῖς πέντε,
ἐμὲ δὲ μόνον βλέποντες λόγοις ἤλπιζον τρῶσαι·   130
" Ἄφες τὴν κόρην ", λέγοντες, " καὶ σῶσον ἑαυτόν σου·
εἰ δ᾽ οὔ, κερδίσῃς θάνατον, ἀπείθειαν ὡς ἔχων."
Ἀκμὴν γὰρ οὐκ ἠπίσταντο ποῖος ἄρα τυγχάνω.
Ἡ δὲ ἡλιογέννητος ἄφνω τούτους ἰδοῦσα
ἁρματωμένους ἅπαντας ἐφ᾽ ἵππους καθημένους,   135
λόγοις αὐτῶν πιστεύσασα ἐδειλίασε σφόδρα,
καὶ τῇ ὀθόνῃ τὰς αὐτῆς καλυψαμένη ὄψεις,
ἐπὶ τὴν τένδαν ἔδραμε, παντελῶς φοβηθεῖσα.
Ἐγὼ δὲ ἔφην πρὸς αὐτήν· " Τί οὐ λαλεῖς, φιλτάτη; "
" Ὅτι ", φησί, " πρὸ τῆς ψυχῆς τέθνηκεν ἡ φωνή μου·   140
ἰδοὺ γὰρ χωριζόμεθα καὶ ζῆν οὐ θέλω φέρειν."
" Παῦσαι," ἔφην, " ψυχὴ ἐμή, λογίζεσθαι τοιαῦτα·
οὓς ὁ Θεὸς συνέζευξεν, ἄνθρωποι οὐ χωρίσουν."
Εὐθὺς τὴν ῥάβδον εἴληφα καὶ τὸ χειροσκουτάριν,
ὡς ἀετὸς πρὸς πέρδικας ἀφ᾽ ὕψους ἐκπετάσας,   145
ὅσους ἡ ῥάβδος ἡ ἐμὴ ἔφθασε τοῦ προσψαῦσαι,
ζωῆς ἐν τούτοις λείψανον οὐδαμῶς ὑπελείφθη·
πολλοὶ δὲ θέλοντες φυγεῖν, κατελάμβανον τούτους,   50 vᵒ.
οὐ γὰρ ἐνίκησεν ἐμὲ ἵππος ποτὲ εἰς δρόμον.
Καὶ οὐ σεμνύνων ἐμαυτὸν ταῦτα διαγορεύω,   150
ἀλλ᾽ ἵνα καταμάθητε τὰς δωρεὰς τοῦ πλάστου.
Τινὲς δέ με ἐλάνθανον εἰς βάλτα κρυβηθέντες·
καί, πρὶν ὀλίγον ἅπαντας θανάτῳ παραδῶσαι,
ἕνα ζωγρήσας μοναχὸν παρ᾽ οὗ ἔμαθον τίνες
ὑπῆρχον οἱ ἀσύνετοι καὶ παράφρονες οὗτοι·   155

124 μίλιον.   129 τεσσαρακοστόν. πρὸ τῶν.   137 αὐτῆς.   144 ῥάβδον.
146 ῥάβδος.   153 παραδώσας.

2598 ὄψεις may mean her 'face' as if it were ὄψιν. It may indeed be a mistake for ὄψιν, which is the reading of TRE 2022. It may also mean 'her eyes'; cf. above 2514, where ὄψιν means either 'thing seen' or 'face'.

As they went on the road they heard our songs,
Distant one mile from us, as I suppose,
And riding off from it came near to us.
When they beheld the wonderful Girl alone,
Their souls wounded as by her beauty's arrow,
They were moved all of them to boundless love,
Forty of them in number and five more,   2590
Saw me alone and hoped to wound with words,
Saying, "Give up the girl and save yourself;
Or else you shall win death for disobedience."
For yet they did not know me who I am.
The sunborn maid suddenly seeing them
All of them armed there sitting on their horses,
Their words believing feared exceedingly,
And with her veil covering up her face
She ran quite terrified into the tent.
I said to her, "Why, dearest, speak you not?"   2600
"Because", she said, "my voice died ere my soul;
Look we are parted, I will not bear to live."
I answered, "Cease, my soul, to think such things;
Whom God has joined men shall not put asunder."
I took at once my club and handbuckler,
Flew out as eagle on partridges from a height,
As many as my club but only touched
No trace of life was left in them at all;
Many wanting to fly, I caught them up,
For no horse ever beat me at running.   2610
(This I declare not to exalt myself
But that you fully learn the Creator's gifts.)
A few escaped me hidden in the marshes;
And just before putting them all to death,
Took one alone alive, from him learned who
They were, these senseless ones, out of their wits;

For ὀθόνη AND 2987 has μαγνάδι
for which see Xanth. *Erotokr.*, gloss.
s.v. μαγνάδι.
2601 πρὸ τῆς ψυχῆς τέθνηκεν ἡ φωνή
μου. This line is taken word for word
from Ach. Tat. iii. xi. 2; and the
corresponding passages (TRE 2024,
AND 2990) are subsequent adaptations.
2604 Matt. xix. 6. GRO follows closely
the words of the Gospel, but TRE
2030 and AND 2995 paraphrase and
expand the reference.

καὶ ὑπερζέσας τῷ θυμῷ οὐδενὸς ἐφεισάμην,
εἶθ' οὕτως ῥίπτω τὸ σπαθὶν καὶ τὸ χειροσκουτάριν,
καὶ τὸ μανίκιν ἔσειον καὶ πρὸς τὴν κόρην ἦλθον.
Ἡ δὲ κόρη, ὡς εἶδε με μόνον περιλειφθέντα,
ἐξῆλθεν εἰς ἀπάντησιν χαρᾶς ἐμπεπλησμένη,   160
καὶ ῥοδόσταμμα ἔρριπτε μὲ τὰς ἰδίας χεῖρας,
φιλοῦσά μου τὴν δεξιὰν καὶ ʒῆν ἐπευχομένη·
Κἀγὼ ταύτης βουλόμενος τὸ δέος ὀνειδῖσαι,
λόγους μεθ' ὑποκρίσεως ἐρωτικοὺς ἐκίρνων·
" Μὴ γὰρ ἐγὼ πρὸ τοῦ παθεῖν ὥσπερ σὺ ἀποθνήσκω; "   165
Ἡ δὲ συνιεῖσα ἃ λαλῶ γλυκερῶς ἐμειδία·
" Τὸ πλῆθος εἶδον ", λέγουσα, " τῶν ἱππέων ἐξαίφνης
ἀρματωμένους ἅπαντας, σὲ δὲ πεζὸν καὶ μόνον·
ἐπὶ τούτῳ, αὐθέντα μου, ὁ φόβος μοι ἐπῆλθε."
Καὶ μυρία φιλήσαντες ἤλθομεν εἰς τὴν τένδαν,   170
καὶ τῇ ἑξῆς πρὸς ποταμὸν λουθῆναι ἀπηρχόμην,
ὅπως ἀλλάξω τὴν στολὴν τὴν αἵματι χρανθεῖσαν·
καὶ τῇ κόρῃ παρήγγειλα ἑτέραν ἀγαγεῖν μοι.
Καὶ δὴ παραγενόμενος τοῦ ὕδατος πλησίον,
ἐπί τι δένδρον καθεσθεὶς τὴν κόρην ἐκδεχόμην·   51 rº.   175
καὶ ἰδοὺ τρεῖς ἀνέφανον ὡραῖοι καβαλλάροι,
στολάς τε ἀνεφέροντο ἄμφω παρηλλαγμένας,
καὶ πρὸς ἐμὲ ἀνήρχοντο τὸν ποταμὸν κρατοῦντες·
εἶδον γάρ με καθήμενον εἰς τοῦ δένδρου τὴν ῥίζαν,
καὶ πλησίον γενόμενοι ἐχαιρέτισαν πάντες·   180
ἐγὼ δὲ οὐκ ἠγέρθην τους, ἀλλ' ἐκαθούμην μᾶλλον.
" Μὴ στρατιώτας, ἀδελφέ, οἵους ἐνταῦθα εἶδες; "
Κἀγὼ ἀντέφην πρὸς αὐτοὺς μὴ δειλιάσας ὅλως·
" Ναί, εἶδον," ἔφην, " ἀδελφοί, κατὰ τὴν χθὲς ἡμέραν,
ἤθελον γὰρ καὶ τὴν ἐμὴν γαμετὴν ἀφαρπάσαι,   185

161 με (sans accent)   163 ὀνειδίσαι.   168 ἀρματωμένους.   170
φιλήσαντας.   184 ἀλλ', et en marge ναί.

2619 τὸ μανίκιν ἔσειον (also TRE 2048,   version of the Ballad of Armoures
AND 3013, ESC 1185). This means   published by Hedwig Lüdeke in
primarily and literally the shaking   Byzantion, xiv (1939), p. 254.
down of a loose long sleeve which   2623 A lacuna follows the correspond-
has been rolled up for the fight; but   ing line in TRE (2052) which begins
also connotes a gesture of shaking the   again at the line corresponding to
fingers, implying 'good riddance'.   2648.
See Laografia iii. 701, and iv. 327.   2632 The river, presumably the
It is to be found also e.g. in a Cypriot   Euphrates, on whose banks the

And with rage overboiling I spared none,
Then threw aside my sword and handbuckler,
And shook my sleeve, and came back to the Girl.

And the Girl when she saw me left alone   2620
Came out to meet me, filled with joyfulness,
With her own hands threw on me rosewater,
Kissing my right hand as she wished me life.
And I, wishing to scold her for her fear,
Began to mix with feigning words of love:
"Do I, as you do, die before I am hurt?"
She knowing what I spoke of smiled sweetly:
Saying, "I saw suddenly the crowd of horsemen,
All of them armed and you on foot alone;
That, master, was why fear came over me."   2630
We kissed a thousand times, went in the tent.

Next day I was going down to the river, to wash,
That I might change my garment, stained with blood,
And told the Girl to bring me out another.
So then I came down to the waterside,
Sat on a tree and waited for the Girl.
When lo there showed up three fine cavaliers,
All were dressed up in exquisite array,
And up to me they came, holding the river;
They saw me sitting at the tree's root there,   2640
And coming near they all saluted me.
I rose not for them, rather sat the more.
"Have you seen such-like soldiers, brother, here?"
I answered to them with no fear at all:
"Yes," I said, "brothers, yesterday I saw them,
For and they wanted to carry off my wife;

interview with the Emperor had taken place (above 2073) suddenly reappears on the scene instead of the spring (2480 and 2506).

2638 ἄμφω after τρεῖς in the preceding line; cf. ἀμφότεροι (above 205, 581, 1193).

παρηλλαγμένας. The word seems to be used of exquisite or unusual finery, as ἐξηλλαγμένος of poetic diction removed from the ordinary in Aris-

totle, *Poet.* 1458 ᵃ 5 and 20. Cf. also the στολὴ ἔξαλλος worn by David when he danced before the ark, LXX, 2 Reg. vi. 14. See also above 605 ἦχον παρηλλαγμένον.

2639 κρατοῦντες, i.e. 'hugging the bank'.

2646 Another trace of the Stolen Bride theme of the Ballads, for which see above 2044.

καί, μὰ τὸν λόγον τοῦ Θεοῦ, οὐδὲ ἵππου ἐπέβην·
τί δὲ αὐτοῖς συμβέβηκε γνώσεσθε μετὰ ταῦτα."
Οἱ δὲ ταῦτα ἀκούσαντες ἐθεώρουν ἀλλήλους,
πρὸς αὐτοὺς ψιθυρίζοντες, χείλη κινοῦντες μόνα·
" Μὴ οὗτος ἔνι ὃν λέγουσι Βασίλειος Ἀκρίτης;   190
ἀλλὰ πάντως γνωσόμεθα δοκιμάσαντες τοῦτον."
Καὶ λέγει μοι ὁ πρόκριτος· " Πῶς ἔχομεν πιστεῦσαι
ὅτι μόνος καὶ ἄοπλος, πεζός, καθάπερ λέγεις,
μετ᾽ αὐτῶν κατετόλμησας μάχην ἐπισυνάψαι;
Ἅπαντας γὰρ δοκιμαστοὺς εἴχομεν ἐν ἀνδρείᾳ·   195
ἀλλ᾽, εἴπερ λέγεις ἀληθῆ, φάνηθι ἐκ τῶν ἔργων,
ἕνα ἔκλεξον ἀφ᾽ ἡμῶν τῶν τριῶν ὅνπερ βούλει,
καὶ μονομάχησον αὐτῷ καὶ γνωσόμεθα πάντες."
Καὶ μειδιάσας πρὸς αὐτοὺς ἐγὼ ἀνταπεκρίθην·
" Εἰ βούλεσθε, πεζεύσατε καὶ δεῦτε οἱ τρεῖς εἰς ἕνα,   200
εἰ δ᾽ ἴσως οὐκ αἰσχύνεσθε, δεῦτε καὶ καβαλλάροι,
καὶ ἐκ τῶν ἔργων μάθετε ποῖος ἄρα τυγχάνω   51 vº.
καί, εἰ δοκεῖς, ἀρξώμεθα τῆς μάχης ἀπεντεῦθεν."
Ῥαβδὶν λαμβάνω σύντομα, ὄρθιος ἐγενόμην,
καὶ τὸ χειροσκουτάριν μου, καὶ γὰρ ἐκράτουν ταῦτα,   205
καὶ πρὸς ὀλίγον προσελθὼν " Εἰ κελεύετε," ἔφην.
Καὶ ὁ πρῶτος ἐφώνησεν· " Οὐ ποιοῦμεν ὡς λέγεις,
ἡμεῖς ἔθος οὐκ ἔχομεν ἐλθεῖν οἱ τρεῖς εἰς ἕνα,
οἱ θαρροῦντες μετακινεῖν ὁ καθεὶς χιλιάδας·
ἐγὼ γὰρ ὁ Φιλοπαπποῦς εἰμὶ ὅνπερ ἀκούεις,   210
Ἰωαννάκης οὗτος δὲ καὶ Κίνναμος ὁ τρίτος,
καὶ αἰσχυνόμεθα οἱ τρεῖς πολεμῆσαι εἰς ἕνα·
ἀλλ᾽ ἐπίλεξον ἀφ᾽ ἡμῶν ἕνα οἷον κελεύεις."
Κἀγὼ " Ναί," ἔφην πρὸς αὐτούς, " δεῦρο λοιπὸν ὁ πρῶτος."
Καὶ εὐθὺς ὁ Φιλοπαπποῦς κατῆλθεν ἐκ τοῦ ἵππου,   215
σπαθὶν ἀράμενος αὐτοῦ ἅμα καὶ τὴν ἀσπίδα,

187 τίς. Correction empruntée au ms. d'Andros (vers 3050). 198 Peut-être
πάντως, comme au vers 191. 203 δοκεῖ est la leçon fournie par le ms. de
Trébizonde (vers 2128). 211 ἰωαννάκην. 214 κἀγὼ manque et est emprunté au ms. de Trébizonde (vers 2141) et à celui d'Andros (vers 3139). 216
αὐτοῦ.

2661 At this point in TRE (2069) and
AND (3066) Digenes gives the
strange reply that he is an only son
who walks by himself (a declaration

also found in this version, but only
after the fight, below 2750, where
it is repeated in TRE 2223 and
AND 3221), and then proceeds to

And, by God's word, I did not even mount;
What happened to them you shall know hereafter."
This when they heard they gazed at each other,
Whispering together, lips only moving,   2650
"Can this be whom they call Basil the Borderer?
But we shall know when we have tried him out."
The chief says to me, "How can we believe
That alone, unarmed, and, as you say, on foot
You ever dared to join combat with them?
For we had tried out all of them in valour.
But if you speak true, show it by your deeds:
Out of us three choose out one, whom you will,
Fight him singly, and all of us will know."
And with a smile to them I made reply: 2660
"Dismount, if you like, and come on three to one,
Or, if you are not ashamed, come on your horses,
And by my deed be taught just who I am;
And, if you like, let us start the fight at once."
I quickly took my club, I stood upright,
And my handbuckler, for I had them there,
Went a bit forward, and said "At your bidding."
The leader cried, "We do not as you say,
Our use is not to attack all three to one,
We trust to shift each one of us his thousands.   2670
For I am Philopappos, whom you hear,
This Ioannakes, Kinnamos the third;
We are ashamed we three to fight one man;
But take your choice of us one at your bidding."
"Yes," I replied, "Then let the first come on."
Straight Philopappos got down from his horse,
And took his sword up and his shield as well,

tell the cautionary story of Ankylas,
which is only found in TRE 2071–
2123, AND 3068–3120, OXF 2495 ff. I
have left it out because although not
inappropriate it is a later interpolation
and lacks to my ear the heroic note;
Digenes seems to have become a
professional.
2668 πρῶτος called πρόκριτος above 2653.
2670 μετακινεῖν. TRE 2135 has τοῦ νικᾶν.

2671 The appearance of Philopappos
here, as if for the first time, exhibits
the poem as a collection of episodes
rather than a connected narrative.
2677 ἀσπίδα might suggest that the
shield of Philopappos was of a different, heavier type than the σκουτάρι
or χειροσκουτάρι of Digenes; but the
shield of Philopappos is also called
σκουτάρι below 2686 and 2693.

τρανῶς εἰσῆλθε πρὸς ἐμὲ πτοῆσαι με ἐλπίζων·
εἶχε καὶ γὰρ ὡς ἀληθῶς ὁρμὴν ἀνδρειοτάτην,
καὶ σπαθέαν μου δώσαντος τρανὰ εἰς τὸ σκουτάριν,
ἐν τῇ χειρὶ τὸ κράτημα μόνον μοι ἀπελείφθη.   220
Οἱ δύο ἀντεφώνησαν ἄντικρυς καθορῶντες·
" Ἄλλην μίαν, Φιλοπαπποῦ γέρον μου, τὸν ἐπίθες."
Ὁ δὲ αὖθις βουλόμενος τὴν σπάθην ἀνατεῖναι,
τῇ ῥάβδῳ κατὰ κεφαλῆς τοῦτον ἐγὼ πατάσσω,
καί, εἰ μὴ ταύτην ἐφύλαττε καθόλου τὸ σκουτάριν,   225
σῶον οὐκ ἔμενεν ὀστοῦν ἐν αὐτῇ τὸ παράπαν.
Ὅμως ὁ γέρων τραλλισθείς, κατὰ πολὺ τρομάξας,
βοῦς ὥσπερ μυκησάμενος, ἐπὶ τὴν γῆν ἡπλώθη.
Καὶ τοῦτο θεασάμενοι οἱ ἕτεροι ὡς εἶχον   52 r°.
καβαλλάροι ἐπάνω μου ἤρχοντο παραχρῆμα,   230
μηδαμῶς αἰσχυνόμενοι, ὡς πρώην ἐκαυχῶντο.
Τούτων ὡς εἶδον τὴν ὁρμήν, ἁρπάζω τὸ σκουτάριν
ἀπὸ χειρῶν τοῦ γέροντος, καὶ πρὸς αὐτοὺς ἐκτρέχω.
Γεναμένης δὲ συμπλοκῆς καὶ ἐνστάτου πολέμου,
ὁ μὲν Κίνναμος ὄπισθεν ἔσπευδε τοῦ λαθεῖν με·   235
Ἰωαννάκης ἔκρουεν εὐθέως καὶ συντόμως,
καὶ τότ' εἶδον πολεμιστὰς ὡς ἀληθῶς δοκίμους,
ἀλλ' οὐδεὶς τούτων ἴσχυσεν ἐμοὶ περιγενέσθαι·
καὶ γάρ, ἡνίκα τὴν ἐμὴν ἀπετίνασσον ῥάβδον,
ὅλοι ὡς ἀπὸ λέοντος ἔφευγον ἐναντίον,   240
ὡσεὶ πρόβατα μήκοθεν ἐμὲ περισκοποῦντες,
καὶ αὖθις πάλιν ἤρχοντο ὡς κύνες ὑλακτοῦντες.
Ὡς δὲ οὕτως ἐγένετο ἐφ' ὥραν οὐκ ὀλίγην,
καὶ ἡ κόρη κατέλαβε, πλὴν ἵστατο μακρόθεν,
ἀντικρὺς ἐξεπίτηδες τοῦ παρ' ἐμοῦ ὁρᾶσθαι·   245
καὶ ὡς εἶδε κυκλοῦντας με τοὺς δύο ὡσεὶ κύνας,
λόγον μοι ἐνετόξευσεν ἐπίκουρον εἰποῦσα·
" Ἀνδρίζου, ὦ παμφίλτατε! " Καὶ εὐθὺς σὺν τῷ λόγῳ
ἰσχὺν ἀναλαβόμενος, πλήττω τὸν Ἰωαννάκην
ἐν τῇ χειρὶ τῇ δεξιᾷ ἄνωθεν τοῦ ἀγκῶνος·   250
τὰ ὀστᾶ συνετρίβησαν, ἡ χεὶρ ὅλη ἡπλώθη,

219 σπαθαῖαν.   239 ῥάβδον.   246 με manque et est emprunté au ms.
de Trébizonde (vers 2180).   249 πλήττει.

2678 τρανῶς: 2680 τρανά.   3154 have ζαλισθείς which may be
2688 τραλλισθείς. TRE 2156, AND   the correct reading.

Came sharply at me hoping to frighten me;
For and he had in truth a brave attack,
Gave me a swordcut sharply on the buckler,   2680
Left in my hand only the hold of it.
The two looking on opposite shouted over,
"Another, old Philopappos, let him have it."
But when he would have raised his sword again,
I struck him with my staff upon the head,
And if his shield had not guarded it at all
Not a bone whole would have been left in it.
The old man though being dazed, and much afraid,
Roared like a bull, fell flat upon the ground.
This when they saw, the others as they were   2690
Mounted charged down on me immediately,
Nothing ashamed, as they before had boasted.
Their onset when I saw, I snatched the shield
Out of the old man's hands, and ran to meet them.
There was a melly and a stubborn fight;
Kinnamos was keen to dodge me from behind,
Ioannakes was hitting fast and straight,
And then I saw them warriors truly tried,
But none of them had power to overbear me.
Whenever I would brandish my staff about   2700
All of them fled before me, as from a lion,
Watching about me from afar like sheep,
And then like barking dogs came on again.
As it was so for not a little time,
The Girl understood, though standing far away
Opposite, on purpose to be seen by me;
And when she saw both circling me like dogs,
She shot at me a helping word, saying,
"All-dearest, be a man"; straight with that word
My strength recovering I struck Ioannakes   2710
On the right arm above the elbow-joint.
The bones were shattered, the whole arm spread out,

2708 (and TRE 2181, AND 3181 . . .
ὑπήκοον μοῦ ἔρριξεν . . .). See Heliodorus, Aethiop. v. 32 Ἡ Χαρίκλεια
λόγον ἐπίκουρον τῷ Θεαγένει διετό-
ξευσεν, Ἀνδρίζου, φίλτατε . . ..

2712 ἡπλώθη, 'was spread out flat', i.e.
limp. English although familiar with
'doubling up', has no similar use of
'singling out'.

καὶ τὸ σπαθὶν ἐπὶ τὴν γῆν πέπτωκε παραχρῆμα·
ὀλίγον δέ μου παρελθὼν πέπτωκεν ἐκ τοῦ ἵππου,
καὶ εἰς πέτραν ἀκούμπησεν, ἐχόμενος τοῦ πόνου.

Βουληθεὶς δὲ ὁ Κίνναμος μόνος ἀνδραγαθῆσαι,   52 vᵒ.   255
ἄνω καὶ κάτω τὸν αὐτοῦ ἵππον ἐπιλαλήσας,
τεθαρρηκὼς ὁ δείλαιος τὸν λέοντα πτοῆσαι,
ὡς πρὸς ἐμὲ κατήρχετο σὺν τῷ ἰδίῳ ἵππῳ,
ῥαβδέαν τοῦτον ἔπληξα μέσον τῶν δύο ὤμων,
ἀφ᾿ ὧν αἷμα ποταμηδὸν ἔρρεε παραχρῆμα   260
ἔκ τε κροτάφων καὶ αὐτοῦ τοῦ στόματος τοῦ φάρα,
καὶ αὐτίκα συμποδισθεὶς πίπτει σὺν τῷ Κιννάμῳ·
τὸν δὲ φόβος ἐλάμβανε καὶ δειλία συνεῖχε,
νομίζων ὅτι κείμενον θέλω αὐτὸν πατάξαι.

Λέγω δ᾿ ἐγώ τε πρὸς αὐτόν· "Ὦ Κίνναμε, τί τρέμεις;   265
τὸν πεσόντα οὐδέποτε ἔθος ἔχω τοῦ κρούειν·
ἀλλ᾿, εἰ βούλει, ἀνάστηθι καὶ λάβε σου τὰ ὅπλα,
καὶ δώσομεν εἰς πρόσωπον, ὡς δοκεῖ τοῖς ἀνδρείοις·
τὸ δὲ πατάσσειν πτώματα τοῖς ἀδρανέσι πέλει."
Ἐκεῖνος δὲ τοῖς νεύμασιν ὑποταγὴν ἐδείκνυ·   270
οὐκ ἴσχυε γὰρ τοῦ λαλεῖν ἐχόμενος τοῦ τρόμου.
Ἐκεῖ τοῦτον ἀφέμενος ὄπισθεν ἐστρεφόμην,
καὶ ὁρῶ τὸν Φιλοπαπποῦν εἰς ἑαυτὸν ἐλθόντα,
κινοῦντα τὲ τὴν κεφαλὴν καὶ λέγοντα τοιαῦτα·
"Μὰ τὸν Θεὸν τὸν ποιήσαντα οὐρανὸν καὶ γῆν πᾶσαν,   275
τὸν σὲ κατακοσμήσαντα τοῖς χαρίσμασι πᾶσι,
κατάλειπε τὸν πόλεμον καὶ ποίησον ἀγάπην,
καὶ δοῦλοί σου ἐσόμεθα, εἴπερ αὐτὸς κελεύεις,
παρὰ σοῦ προστασσόμενοι καὶ ποιοῦντες ἀόκνως."

Ὡς ταῦτα φίλα ἤκουσα κατηλέησα τούτους   53 rᵒ.   280
(πραΰνουσι γὰρ τὸν θυμὸν ὑποπίπτοντες λόγοι),
καὶ μειδιάσας πρὸς αὐτὸν μετ᾿ εἰρωνείας ἔφην·
"Φιλοπαπποῦ, ἐξύπνησας καὶ ὁράματα λέγεις·
ἀλλ᾿, ἐπεὶ εἰς κατάνυξιν μετέστρεψας τὸ γῆρας,
ἀνάστα, λάβε τοὺς σὺν σοί, ἄπελθε ὅπου βούλει,   285
οἰκείους ἔχων ὀφθαλμοὺς μάρτυρας τοῦ πραχθέντος,

256 αὐτοῦ.   259 ῥαβδαῖαν.   275 μὰ manque dans le manuscrit.
282 εἰρωνίας.   283 βλέπεις, et en marge λέγεις.

_____

2720 μέσον τῶν δύο ὤμων, 'two shoulders'. This seems to be the expression giving

178

Immediately his sword fell to the ground;
A little past me he fell off his horse,
And leaned against a rock clutching the pain.
Kinnamos wanting to play the brave alone,
Now having urged his own horse up and down,
Trusting the wretch that he should scare the lion,
Came charging down upon me with his horse;
My staff struck it a blow between the withers,   2720
From which blood in a river flowed at once,
From its temples and from the nag's very mouth,
Straightway in a heap it fell with Kinnamos.
Then terror seized on him and fear constrained,
Thinking that I would hit him lying down.
I said to him, "Kinnamos, why are you trembling?
My use has never been to strike the fallen.
But, if you like, rise up and take your weapons,
And we will face to it, as brave men should.
It is for weaklings to hit carcasses."   2730
And he by signs was showing his subjection,
For in his fright he had no power to speak.
Leaving him there I turned backwards again
Saw Philopappos coming to himself,
Moving his head and speaking on this wise:
"By God who made the heaven and all the earth,
Who has embellished you with all His favours,
Abandon war and make an understanding,
And we will be your servants, as you bid,
By you enjoined and working without rest."   2740
Hearing such friendliness I pitied them
(Anger is softened by submissive words)—
And smiling at him said with irony,
"Awake, Philopappos, telling us your dreams?
Since you have turned your old age to contrition,
Rise, take those with you, and go where you will,
Your proper eyes shall witness what was done;

rise to ESC 1137 τὰς δισουμέας.
2730 πατάσσειν πτώματα is only a
repetition of (2727) τὸν πέσοντα
κρούειν and of (2725) κείμενον

πατάξαι; but I have translated πτώματα as if it connoted some additional contempt.
2736 Omit second τόν.

179

καὶ οὒς ζητεῖτε πίστευσον νὰ λείψουν ἐκ τὸ ἀδνούμιν.

Ἄρχειν δὲ οὐκ ἐφίεμαι, ἀλλὰ μόνος διάγειν,
ἐπειδὴ καὶ μονογενὴς πέφυκα τοῖς γονεῦσιν·
ὑμῖν δὲ ἄρχειν ἔξεστι καὶ συνεργεῖν ἀλλήλοις   290
ἐφ' οἷς ἔχετε δυνατὸν ποιεῖσθαι καὶ τὰ κούρση·
καί, εἰ πολλάκις θέλετε πάλιν με πολεμῆσαι,
ἄλλους ἀνθολογήσατε ἐκ νέου ἀπελάτας
τοὺς μὴ εἰδότας πεῖραν μου, μηδὲ γινώσκοντάς με·
εἶδον γὰρ ὅσοι πεῖραν μου ὑμῖν οὐ συνεργήσουν."   295
Καὶ ἐχάρη ὁ Φιλοπαππούς δεξάμενος τὴν λῦσιν,
καὶ ἐφώνει τοῖς μετ' αὐτοῦ λύτρωσιν ἐκμηνύων·
οὐδεὶς γὰρ τούτων ἤλπιζε ζωῆς ἀξιωθῆναι,
ἀλλ' εἶχον ἤδη τὰς ψυχὰς πρὸς πύλας τοῦ θανάτου.
Καί, ὡς ἤκουσαν τῆς φωνῆς, ἀνελάμβανον ταύτας,   300
καὶ τὸ στόμα διήνοιγον πλεῖστα εὐχαριστοῦντες,
" Ὄντως εἴδομεν", λέγοντες, "ἔργα νικῶντα φήμην,
καὶ τὴν σὴν ὑπεράνθρωπον μεγίστην εὐσπλαγχνίαν,
ἣν οὐδεὶς ὑπεδείξατο ἐν τῷ παρόντι βίῳ·
καὶ ἀντιδῴη σοι Θεὸς ἀντάξια τῆς γνώμης   54 rº.   305
μείζονα τὰ χαρίσματα καὶ ζῆν μετὰ συμβίου
εἰς ἀπεράντους χρόνους τε τερπόμενοι ἀλλήλοις."
Εἶτα τὴν πολυώραιαν λαβὼν ἐν ταῖς ἀγκάλαις,
πόρρωθεν ἐκαθέσθημεν ὑποκάτω εἰς δένδρον,
οὐρανοῦ μέσον ἥλιος ἀπάρτι διατρέχων.   310
Ἐκεῖνοι δὲ συνήχθησαν οἱ τρεῖς εἰς ἕνα τόπον,
καὶ θαυμάζοντες ἔλεγον οἱ δύο πρὸς ἀλλήλους
νεωτέρας οἱ ἄγοντες ἡλικίας καὶ φρένας·
" Ὄντως λίαν τὸ ὁραθὲν καὶ παράδοξον ξένον,
ἄνθρωπος ἄοπλος, πεζός, ῥάβδον κατέχων μόνην,   315
ἡμᾶς τοὺς ἐν τοῖς ἅρμασι καλῶς καθωπλισμένους,
τοὺς μυριάδας τρέψαντας καὶ πόλεις κατασχόντας,
καθολικῶς ἐνίκησεν ὥσπερ τινὰς ἀπείρους,
καὶ αἰσχύνης ἐνέπλησε καὶ δειλίας καὶ φόβου·

287 ἀδνούμην.   294 μὴ δὲ.   302 λέγοντες manque et est emprunté au
ms. d'Andros (vers 3237).   304 Le verso du feuillet 53 est blanc.   308
πολυωραίαν.   315 ῥάβδον.   316 ἅρμασι.   318 ὥσπέρ τινας.

2748 ἀδνούμιν. See above 48.
2750 μονογενής. Above 2661 n.; TRE
2223, AND 3221. See below p. 215.
2753 πολλάκις (also confirmed by TRE

2226) is strange here as 'often' is
hardly the sense expected; but taken
with πάλιν 'often again' is almost
equivalent to 'as often as'.

Those whom you seek, trust me, will miss the muster.
I do not want to rule, but to live alone,
Being alone-begotten to my parents.   2750
Be yours to rule and work with one another,
As you find possible, and make your raids;
And if again you often want to fight me,
Pick out afresh another bunch of reivers,
Those who have had no trial of me or knowledge;
For who have tried me will not work with you."

    Philopappos was glad to accept release,
And called to tell those with him their deliverance;
For none of them hoped to be granted life,
They had their souls already at death's gates;   2760
And when they heard him shout, they took them back,
And opened wide their mouths giving much thanks,
Saying, "Verily we have seen deeds passing praise,
Your great compassion passing that of men,
Such as none in this present life has shown;
May God reward you as befits your nature
With greater gifts, and with your spouse to live
To boundless years in mutual delight."

    Then in my arms taking her of many beauties
Far off we sat down underneath a tree,   2770
The sun now crossing the middle of the sky.

    Those other three were gathered in one place
And wondering to each other spoke the two
Who younger bodies had and younger minds:
"Truly most marvellous and strange the sight,
A man unarmed, on foot, with staff alone,
Us properly equipped with all our weapons,
Us who have routed thousands, captured cities,
Beat us all round, as if some untried few,
Filled us with fear and cowardice and shame;   2780

After the corresponding line in TRE (2226) there is a lacuna; TRE resumes at the line corresponding to GRO vi. 355 (below 2816).
2757 λῦσιν often used by Byzantine authors (e.g. Ptochoprod. ed. Koraes ii. 550) of an imperial rescript.

2774 ἡλικίας καὶ φρένας clearly shows the physical sense of ἡλικία.
2777 τοῖς ἅρμασι. Note that τὰ ἅρματα (= Latin arma; sing., if ever found, τὸ ἅρμα) is a Byzantine word, nothing to do with classical τὸ ἅρμα, 'a chariot'.

βέβαιον γόης πέφυκεν ἢ στοιχεῖον τοῦ τόπου, 320
ἐπεὶ αὐτὸς ἀντ᾽ οὐδενὸς ἡγεῖτο τὰς σπαθέας,
καὶ ἀνυπόστατον θυμὸν εἶχεν ἐπὶ τὴν ῥάβδον·
εἰ γὰρ ὑπῆρχεν ἄνθρωπος ὥσπερ οἱ ἐκ τοῦ κόσμου,
εἶχεν ἂν σῶμα καὶ ψυχήν, θάνατον ἐδεδοίκει,
καὶ οὐ μὴ ὥσπερ ἄσαρκος ξίφεσι κατετόλμα· 325
ἀλλὰ στοιχεῖον ἐκ παντὸς ἐτύγχανε τοῦ τόπου,
καὶ φαντασίᾳ μεθ᾽ ἡμῶν τὸν πόλεμον συνῆψε.
"Ἴδετε καὶ τὸ ἄπειρον κάλλος τῆς φαινομένης
τηλαυγέστερον πέμπον τι ἡλιακῶν ἀκτίνων,
καὶ ὥσπερ στήλη ἔμψυχος ἡμῖν νομιζομένη." 330
Ταῦτα καὶ τούτοις ὅμοια λέγοντες ἀσυνέτως,
ὁ γέρων ὁ Φιλοπαπποῦς γηραιὸν ἔφη λόγον· 54 vo.
" Ταῦτα πάντα, ὦ τέκνα μου, εἰσὶ παραμυθίαι,
περιγραφαὶ ἀτυχιῶν, ψυχῶν παρηγορίαι·
ἐγὼ δὲ εἶδον ἀληθῶς δοκιμώτατον ἄνδρα, 335
τοῖς τοῦ Χριστοῦ χαρίσμασι πᾶσι πεπλουτισμένον,
κάλλος, ἀνδρείαν, φρόνησιν καὶ πολλὴν εὐτολμίαν,
ἔχει καὶ δρόμον ἄπειρον τῶν ἀγαθῶν προσθήκην·
ἡμῖν δὲ τοῦτο γέγονε μόνον παρηγορία
ὅτι οὐκ εὑρέθησάν τινες εἰς θέαν τοῦ πολέμου· 340
ὄνομα δὲ ὃ εἴχομεν τὸ τῆς ἀνδρείας μέγα,
τοῦτο νῦν ἀπωλέσαμεν ὑφ᾽ ἑνὸς ἡττηθέντες·
ἀλλ᾽, εἴπερ θέλετε βουλήν, ὦ ἡμέτερα τέκνα,
μηδαμῶς ἀμελήσωμεν τὴν ὕβριν ἐκδικῆσαι,
ἀλλὰ παντοίους σπεύσωμεν ἐφευρεῖν τοὺς οἰκείους· 345
εἰ γὰρ καὶ ἐκαυχήσατο, ἀλλ᾽ οὐ πάντας ἀνεῖλε,
καί, εἰ θελήσει ὁ Θεὸς καὶ περισυσταθοῦμεν
ἵνα του ἐπιπέσωμεν ἐν νυκτὶ ἀδοκήτως,
καὶ εἰ κατάσχωμεν αὐτόν, ἀφαιρεθῇ ὁ πόνος,

322 ῥάβδον. 324 θανάτου. 329 τι.

2781 στοιχεῖον τοῦ τόπου. (Also AND 3273.) The Mod. Greek sense of στοιχεῖον, a spirit or 'elemental', is found in Theoph. Cont. 379. 14 (Soph.), perhaps deriving from St. Paul, Ep. Col. ii. 8. See Bury, *Eastern Roman Empire*, p. 443, n. 3, for this word in magical practices in the ninth century. ESC 1328 has a characteristic muddle showing dependence on sound, θηρίον τὸν τόπον του βλέπει ('a dragon guards his beat').

2791 στήλη ἔμψυχος. Also AND 3277; cf. below 2874 (= TRE 2296, AND 3385) εἰκὼν ἔμπνους. See Anna

Wizard is he surely or spirit of the place,
For that himself thought nothing of our sword-thrusts,
Bore in his staff wrath irresistible.
Had he been man as are they in the world,
He would have had body and soul, would have feared death,
Nor as if fleshless have out-dared our blades.
For sure he was the spirit of the place,
And in our fancy joined with us in battle.
You saw her boundless beauty who appeared,
More brightly flashing than the sunny rays,   2790
Seeming to us an image come to life."
This and such-like they speaking senselessly,
Old Philopappos said an old man's word:
"All these, my children, are only assuagements,
Descriptions of mishaps, souls' comfortings.
But I saw truly a most worthy man,
By all the favours of the Christ enriched,
Beauty and bravery, wisdom and much daring
He has, and boundless speed adds to these gifts.
But for us this alone is consolation: 2800
That none were found within view of the fight;
The name we had was great for bravery,
This we have lost by one man now defeated.
But if you want advice, O children mine,
Let us no wise omit to avenge the insult,
But haste to find our friends of every sort;
For though he boasted, he has not all destroyed,
And, if God will we rally round together,
To fall on him unexpectedly at night,
And if we take him, gone will be the hurt   2810

Comnena (*Alex.* 3. 3), who describes her mother Eirene as ἔμπνουν ἄγαλμα καλλονῆς καὶ στήλην ἔμβιον εὐρυθμίας. Cf. also Ach. Tat. v. xi. 5 γυναῖκα . . . πάνυ καλήν, ὥστε ἂν ἰδὼν αὐτὴν εἴποις ἄγαλμα. For στήλη in sense of 'statue' (not classical) see Theoph. (Bonn), p. 347; and 358 στήλη ἔφιππος 'Ιουστινιανοῦ.
2794 παραμυθίαι. The redactor seems

to be deliberately using this as the equivalent of the vernacular παραμύθια (pl.) 'fables', and the following line 'descriptions of misfortune, used to comfort the soul' is his attempt to explain the derivation of παραμύθι, a 'story', from the classical παραμυθία 'consolation'. The mod. παραμύθι is noted by Ducange but without refs.

ὃν εἰς ψυχὰς κατέσπειρε τὰς ἡμῶν ὁ γεννάδας,   350
καὶ ἡ κόρη εἰς ὄνομα σόν, Ἰωαννάκη, ἔσται·
ῥηθῆναι δὲ ἀμήχανον τὸ κάλλος της εἰκάϳω·
καὶ ἀληθῶς οὐδέποτε τοιοῦτον ἐν ἀνθρώποις
κάλλος τις ἐθεάσατο, ὥσπερ ὑπολαμβάνω.
Καὶ γὰρ πεντηκοστὸν ἐγὼ δεύτερον ἔτος ἄγω,   355
πλείστας πόλεις διέδραμον χώρας τε οὐκ ὀλίγας,
ἀλλ᾽ ἡττήθησαν ἅπασαι, οἷα χορὸς ἀστέρων,
ὁπηνίκα ὁ ἥλιος τὰς ἀκτῖνας ἐκτείνει.   55 rᵒ.
Ἀλλὰ θάρσει, παγκάλλιστε, σοῦ τοῦ λοιποῦ ὑπάρχει."

Ταῦτα ὁ γέρων εἰρηκὼς καλῶς ἔδοξε λέγειν·   360
καὶ ἀνῆλθον εἰς τὸν φανὸν τὴν σύναξιν ποιοῦντες,
τῇ δὲ νυκτὶ ἐπὶ πολὺ τὸν πυρσὸν δᾳδουχοῦντες,
καὶ τὸ παράπαν οὐδὲ εἷς παρῆν τῶν δοκουμένων·
οἱ δὲ περὶ Φιλοπαπποῦν λέγειν ἄρχονται τάδε·
" Τί, γέρον ἀνδρικώτατε, κόπους ἡμῖν παρέχεις;   365
οὐχὶ πιστεύων εἴληφας τῆς ἡμῶν εὐτολμίας,
ἐξ ὧν οἶδας ἀριστειῶν καὶ μεγίστων ἐπάθλων
τῶν τελεσθέντων παρ᾽ ἡμῶν ἐν κραταιοῖς πολέμοις;
οὐ πολλάκις ἐθαύμασας ἡμᾶς ὡς ἀηττήτους,
τὰς παραδόξους καθορῶν ἀεὶ ἀνδραγαθίας,   370
καὶ παρ᾽ αὐτοῦ ἡττήθημεν ὡς ἄπειροι πολέμου·
περὶ ἐκείνων ἀπιστεῖς μὴ παρ᾽ αὐτοῦ κτανθῆναι;
ἀλλ᾽, εἰ κελεύεις, πείσθητι τῇ βουλῇ τῶν σῶν τέκνων,
καταλείψωμεν τοὺς πολλοὺς καὶ ἀνονήτους μόχθους,
καὶ ἄπελθε πρὸς Μαξιμοῦν τὴν ἡμῶν συγγενίδα,   375
καὶ παρακάλεσον αὐτὴν ἡμῖν τοῦ συνεργῆσαι,
λαὸν γὰρ ἔχει ἐκλεκτὸν ὡς καὶ αὐτὸς γινώσκεις·
πλὴν τὰ συμβάντα πρὸς αὐτὴν μηδαμῶς ἀναγγείλῃς,
εἰ γὰρ ἐν γνώσει γένηται, οὐ πεισθῇ συνελθεῖν σοι·
ἀλλ᾽ ὡς ἐχέφρων, νουνεχής, ποίησον ἀποκρίσεις,   380
ὅπως ἑλκύσῃς εἰς βουλὴν τὴν ἡμετέραν ταύτην·

354 τὶς.   355 ἐγὼ manque et est emprunté au ms. de Trébizonde (vers
2227).   359 παγκάλιστε ὑπάρξει, et un χ au-dessus du ξ.   363 τῶν
φαινομένων, et en marge τῶν δοκουμένων.   366 τὰς. Correction empruntée
au ms. de Trébizonde (vers 2250).   377 αὐτὴ.

2811 γεννάδας. Above 2142 and below
3732. The emphasis here seems to
be on youth rather than on nobility.
2816 Here TRE resumes after lacuna.

2827 οὐχὶ πιστεύων εἴληφας τῆς ἡμῶν
εὐτολμίας. Cf. TRE 2250 οὐκ εἴληφας
τὸ πάμπιστον . . . . Leg. οὐχὶ πίστευ-
σιν . . . .

Which in our souls the braveling has implanted;
The Girl, Ioannakes, shall be in your name.
I think her beauty never can be spoken;
Truly of such a sort none among men
Ever beheld such beauty, I suppose.
For I am in my fifty-second year,
Have traversed many cities, countries not a few,
But all were vanquished, like a choir of stars,
Whenever that the sun extends his beams.
Cheer up, my fairest, she is yours henceforward."   2820
Thus when he spoke they thought the old man said well.
They went up to the beacon, for the gathering,
Long in the night with torches fed the fire,
But never one appeared of those expected.
Then those round Philopappos began to say,
"Why give us all this trouble, brave old man?
Have you not taken warrant of our boldness,
From championships you know and great achievements
That were performed by us in mighty wars?
Have you not often admired us as unbeaten,   2830
Our wondrous gallantries ever beholding,
And by him we were beaten as untried in war.
Those others doubt you they were killed by him?
But, if you please, hark to your childrens' counsel;
Leave we these great unprofitable toils,
And go to Maximo our kinswoman,
And beg of her that she should work with us;
She has a picked company as you know:
Only nowise inform her what has happened,
For if she knows she will not agree to help you.   2840
Be prudent and discreet to do your errand,
That you may draw her on to this our plan;

2833 This line must refer to the forty-five horsemen at Trosis whose disappearance Philopappos was investigating. See above 2590, 2643. The same line, TRE 2256, is translated by Legrand: 'Tu ne croiras rien de ce que nous disons, si nous ne sommes pas tués par lui'!

2836 Note that in GRO she is always called *Maximou*, but the Maximo of TRE and AND has been adopted for euphony in the translation.
2841 ἀποκρίσεις. Byzantine sense (always in plural) 'an embassy'. Cf. ἀποκρισιάριος. The warning not to tell Maximo the truth is only in GRO.

καὶ ἐὰν τοῦτο γένηται ἐξόμεθα τὸ νῖκος·
ἡμεῖς δὲ ἐνωθοῦμεν σοι, τὸν πυρσὸν ὅταν δείξῃς."
Καὶ ἤρεσεν ἡ συμβουλὴ τῷ γέροντι ἀσμένως·   55 vᵒ.
εὐθὺς ἐφ᾽ ἵππου ἐπιβὰς πρὸς Μαξιμοῦν ἀπῆλθε.   385
Αὕτη δὲ ἦν ἀπόγονος γυναικῶν Ἀμαζόνων,
ἃς βασιλεὺς Ἀλέξανδρος ἤγαγεν ἐκ Βραχμάνων·
εἶχε δὲ τὴν ἐνέργειαν μεγίστην ἐκ προγόνων,
βίου ἀεὶ τὸν πόλεμον καὶ τέρψιν ἡγουμένη.
Πρὸς ταύτην ὁ Φιλοπαπποῦς γεγονώς, ὡς ἐρρέθη,   390
προσηνῶς κατησπάζετο· "Πῶς ἔχεις", ἐπερώτα.
Τῆς δὲ εἰπούσης· "Ζῶ καλῶς, τῇ τοῦ Θεοῦ προνοίᾳ·
ἀλλὰ σύ, ὦ πανάριστε, πῶς μετὰ τέκνων ἔχεις;
χάριν δὲ τίνος πρὸς ἡμᾶς τούτων χωρὶς ἐπῆλθες;"
Αὖθις ὁ γέρων ἔφησε τάδε, οὐκ ἀληθεύων·   395
"Οἱ μὲν παῖδες, κυρία μου, Κίνναμος καὶ Ἰωαννάκης,
καλῶς ἔχοντες σὺν Θεῷ ἀπῆλθον εἰς τὰς βίγλας,
τοὺς ἀτάκτους ὁλοσχερῶς σπεύδοντες ἀφανίσαι·
τῶνδε κἀγὼ ἀπολυθεὶς ἀναπαύσεως χάριν,
ἢ μᾶλλον οἰκονομικῶς Θεοῦ τῇ εὐδοκίᾳ   400
εἰς τοῦ καλοῦ ἀνεύρεσιν καὶ ἀτιμήτου δώρου,
ὡς γὰρ οὐκ ἦν μοι πώποτε τέλεον ἠρεμῆσαι,
μετὰ τὴν ὑποχώρησιν τῶν ἐμῶν παμφιλτάτων,
μόνος τοῦ ἵππου ἐπιβὰς ἀνέτρεχον τὰς ὄχθας
καὶ τοὺς πόρους ἐσκόπευον ἰδεῖν τοὺς ἐναντίους·   405
ὡς δὲ ἦλθον ἐν τῇ ὁδῷ τῇ καλουμένῃ Τρώσει,
πρὸς μέρος τὸ εὐώνυμον ἐν τῷ δασεῖ λειμῶνι,
θηράματι ἐνέτυχον χρυσοῦ τιμιωτέρῳ,
κόρῃ, οἵαν οὐδέποτε οἱ ὀφθαλμοί μου εἶδον.
Ἐν τῷ κάλλει ἀμήχανον τὴν φαιδρότητα εἶχεν,   410
ἐξ ὀφθαλμῶν ἀπόρρητον ἀνέπεμπε τὴν χάριν,   56 rᵒ.
ἔρνος ὥσπερ εὐθέατον τὴν ἡλικίαν ἔχων,
καὶ θέλγει πάντων τὰς ψυχάς, εἰκὼν καθάπερ ἔμπνους·

---

387 ἦν, au lieu de ἇς. Correction fournie par le ms. de Trébizonde (vers 2270)
et celui d'Andros (vers 3358). βραγμάνων. Correction fournie par les mêmes mss.
(*ibid.*).   398 ἀφανίσαι.   409 οἵαν.

2848 ἐκ Βραχμάνων. I.e. from the   2859 Legrand's ἀφανῖσαι is unnecessary.
Indians.   2865 ὄχθας, which brings us to the
2850 βίου. Leg. βίον with TRE 2272.   river again; but TRE 2287 has

And if this be we shall obtain the victory:
And we will join you when you show the fire."
    This counsel pleased and made the old man glad:
Straight mounting horse he went to Maximo.
She was descended from Amazon women,
King Alexander brought from the Brahmanes.
Great was the strength she had from her forebears,
Finding in war her life and her delight.   2850
    Come to her, Philopappos, as was said,
Gently saluted: "How are you?" he asked.
She saying, "By God's providence, I live well;
You, best of men, how are you with your children?
For what sake came you to us without them?"
The old man spoke again, not saying truth,
"The children, lady, Kinnamos and Ioannakes,
Are well, with God's help, and gone off to the posts,
Keen to wipe out the freebooters entirely;
And I by them released for sake of rest,   2860
Or rather, by dispensation, with God's favour,
To finding of a good and priceless gift;
For since complete repose was never mine,
After my dearest ones had gone away,
Mounting my horse alone I went up the banks
And watched the fords to spy on those against us;
And when I came into the way called Trosis,
On the left side and in the thick meadow
I found a quarry more precious than gold,
A girl such as my eyes have never seen.   2870
She had a peerless brilliance in her beauty,
And from her eyes shed grace unspeakable;
With stature like a young plant good to see;
She charms the souls of all, a breathing picture.

ἄκρας, which is also used below, 2892.

2869 θήραμα: but below 2892 κυνῆγιν.

2871 ἀμήχανον. Cf. TRE 2293 ἀμήχανον τὸ κάλλος, which Legrand translates 'une beauté dépourvue d'artifices'!

2873 ἔρνος εὐθέατον. This, being too difficult for the redactor of TRE, becomes TRE 2295 ἔργον ἐνθέατον, which Legrand translates 'un chef-d'œuvre des mains de Dieu'!

ἡλικίαν. See above 2774. εὐθέατος, used by Genesius in sense 'easily seen' (cf. Aristotelian εὐσύνοπτος), here means 'good to look at'.

2874 εἰκὼν ἔμπνους. See above 2791.

ἔστι δέ, ὡς ἀνέμαθον, τοῦ Δουκὸς ἡ θυγάτηρ,
ἣν λόγῳ οἰκειούμεθα τοῦ Χρυσοϊωαννάκη·   415
ἕτερος δὲ προέλαβεν, ἀγνοῶ ποίῳ τρόπῳ,
καὶ μετ᾽ αὐτῆς ἐφαίνετο νυνὶ ἐν τῷ λειμῶνι.
Καί, εἴπερ ὅλως συγγενοῦς κήδεσαι τοῦ φιλτάτου,
ὑπὲρ αὐτοῦ κοπίασον, δέξαι καὶ ἀγρυπνίαν,
τὴν ἀγάπην βεβαίωσον, κυρία μου, ἐξ ἔργων·   420
ὁ γὰρ προθύμως κοινωνῶν θλίψεσι τῶν φιλτάτων,
ἐκεῖνος φίλος ἀληθὴς καὶ συγγενὴς ὑπάρχει."
Γέρων δὲ ὁ Φιλοπαπποῦς τοιαῦτά τε λαλήσας,
κατὰ πάντα πειθήνιον τὴν Μαξιμοῦν ποιεῖται·
καὶ γὰρ εὐεξαπάτητον φρόνημα γυναικεῖον.   425
Οὐδαμῶς γὰρ ἠρεύνησε τίς ὁ τὴν κόρην ἔχων,
ἀλλ᾽ αὐτίκα περιχαρῶς καλεῖ τὸν Μελιμίτζην,
ὃν εἶχε πρῶτον ἄγουρον ἐξάρχοντα τῶν ἄλλων,
καὶ μειδιῶσα πρὸς αὐτὸν περιχαρῶς ἐξεῖπεν·
" Ἔμαθες ὡς ὁ θαυμαστὸς Φιλοπαπποῦς ὁ γέρων   430
κυνῆγιν εὗρε κάλλιστον ἀρτίως εἰς τὰς ἄκρας,
καὶ ἀξιοῖ μεθ᾽ ἑαυτοῦ καὶ ἡμᾶς πορευθῆναι,
τῆς τε χαρᾶς μεταλαβεῖν καὶ τρυφῆς τῆς ἐντεῦθεν;
ἀλλὰ τάχιον ἄπελθε, εὑρὲ τοὺς ἀπελάτας,
καὶ ἀπὸ πάντων ἑκατὸν ἔκλεξαι τοὺς δοκίμους,   435
ἵππους τε ἔχοντας καλούς, ὀχυρώτατα ὅπλα,
ἵνα ᾧπερ ἐντύχωμεν, κατάσχωμεν ῥαδίως."   56 vᵒ.
Ὁ δὲ πρόσταγμα μὴ τολμῶν δεσποίνης ἀθετῆσαι,
ἐν τῇ βίγλᾳ γενόμενος, ἐν ταύτῃ τῇ ἑσπέρᾳ,
καὶ ἐπιδείξας τὸν πυρσόν, καὶ πλείστους συναθροίσας   440
πρὸς χιλίων ἐπέκεινα δοκίμους στρατιώτας,
ἐκ τούτων ἀπεχώρισεν ἑκατὸν τοὺς γενναίους·
καὶ τούτους συμπαραλαβὼν πρὸς τὴν κυρίαν ἦλθεν.
Ἡ δὲ τὰς χρείας ἅπασας εἰκότως ἐπιδοῦσα,
ἐνετείλατο τῇ ἑξῆς γενέσθαι ἐν τοῖς ὅπλοις·   445
μεθ᾽ ὧν ὥρμησε κατ᾽ ἐμοῦ ζήλῳ πολλῷ πλησθεῖσα,

---

416 ἀγνοῶν.   435 ἑκατὸν manque et est emprunté au ms. de Trébizonde
(vers 2320) et à celui d'Andros (vers 3409).   444 ἁπάσας. C'est la seule correction possible.

2875 (and above 2475) τοῦ Δουκός, not   (so also AND), which seems to be
as in TRE τοῦ Δούκα.   the better form.
2888 Μελιμίτζην. TRE 2311 Μελεμέντζην   2889 πρῶτον ἄγουρον (see above 47,

She is, as I found out, Doukas his daughter;
We talked of making her our darling John's,
Another got her first, I know not how,
And with her in the meadow has appeared.
So, if you care at all for your dear kinsman,
Bestir yourself, be ready to watch for him,   2880
My lady, and confirm your love by deeds—
For who shares willingly his dear ones' griefs
He is a kinsman and a friend indeed."
Thus having spoken old man Philopappos
Made Maximo in all respects submissive—
For woman's mind is easily deceived.
She nowise asked who it was had the girl,
But straightway cheerfully called Melimitzes,
First of her band and prefect of the rest,
And smiling at him cheerfully spoke out: 2890
"Wondrous old Philopappos, have you heard,
Has lately found fine quarry on the borders,
And asks us also to go out with him,
And share the joy and revel that is there.
Therefore go quickly forth and find the reivers,
And from them all pick out a worthy hundred,
Those with good horses and the strongest arms,
So that with ease we capture whom we find."
His mistress' order daring not neglect
He that same evening coming to the watch,   2900
And having shown the beacon, and gathered a host
Of well-tried fighting men, beyond a thousand,
A gallant hundred set apart from these;
Taking them with him came to his lady.
She having duly all their wants supplied
Bade them the next day to attend in arms;
With whom most zealously she set out against me,

339, &c.) ἐξάρχοντα τῶν ἄλλων. TRE
2312 ἔξαρχον ἀπελάτων. So below
2895, Maximo's followers are called
ἀπελάται.
2900 βίγλα. Ducange s.v. quotes a

gloss φρυκτωρία ἐστὶν ἡ παρ' ἡμῖν
λεγομένη βίγλα, ἢ φανός, ἢ λαμπάς,
which shows the double sense of
βίγλα like 'beacon' in English.

τοῦ στρατοῦ προηγούμενος Φιλοπαπποῦς ἐν πόθῳ.
Ἐν δὲ τῷ ἀναστήματι γενόμενοι τοῦ λόφου,
ὁ γηραιὸς τὸ σύνθημα τοῖς φίλοις προσμηνύει,
πυρσὸν ἐξῆπτε τῇ νυκτὶ τοῖς περὶ Ἰωαννάκην·   450
καὶ μεθ' ἡμέρας καὶ αὐτοὶ ἐν τῷ στρατῷ παρῆσαν,
ἀσμένως πρὸς τῆς Μαξιμοῦς λίαν ἀποδεχθέντες,
ἑτοίμους γὰρ ὡς ἀγχιστὰς τούτους καὶ ὡς συμμάχους
ἐδέξατο ἡ Μαξιμοὺ ὁλοσχερῶς τερφθεῖσα.
Πρὸς δὲ ὄχθας τοῦ ποταμοῦ πλησιάσαντες ἤδη,   455
ἄρχεται τοῦ δημηγορεῖν Φιλοπαπποῦς τοιάδε·
" Ὁ μὲν τόπος, κυρία μου καὶ ὑμεῖς στρατιῶται,
ὑπάρχει δυσκολώτατος ἐν ᾧ τὴν κόρην εὗρον·
καὶ μὴ πάντες ἀπέλθωμεν ὡς κρότον ἐμποιοῦντες,
διάγνωσιν παρέχοντες τῷ φυλάττοντι ταύτην,   460
καί, πρινὴ πλησιάσομεν, δύνωσιν ἐν τῷ ἄλσει,
καὶ οὐδ' ὅλως ἰσχύσωμεν τὸ θήραμα κρατῆσαι,
καὶ γένηται διακενῆς πάντων ἡμῶν ὁ κόπος·
ἀλλ', εἰ δοκεῖ, προλάβωμεν δύο ἢ καὶ τρεῖς μόνοι,
λάθρα ἐπισκοπεύοντες ποῦ ἡ κόρη ὑπάρχει·   57 rº.   465
καὶ οἱ μὲν δύο μείνωμεν ταύτην ἐπιτηροῦντες,
ὁ δέ γε τρίτος πρὸς ὑμᾶς ἐπανελθὼν δηλώσει,
καὶ σὺν αὐτῷ ἐλεύσεσθε μηδαμῶς πλανηθέντες."
Πρὸς δὲ ταῦτα ἡ Μαξιμοὺ τῷ γέροντι ἀντέφη·
" Ὦ γέρον τε καὶ νουνεχές, σοὶ τὴν ἀρχὴν πιστεύω·   470
πράττε λοιπὸν ὡς βούλεσαι, πάντων σοι πειθομένων."
Καὶ εὐθὺς ὁ Φιλοπαπποῦς, λαβὼν τὸν Μελιμίτζην
καὶ τὸν Κίνναμον σὺν αὐτῷ, τὸν ποταμὸν διῆλθε,
τοῖς ἄλλοις ἐντειλάμενος προσκαρτερεῖν ἐκεῖσε,
ἄχρις ἂν μήνυμα αὐτοῖς ἐκ τούτων ἐπανέλθῃ.   475
Ἐμοὶ δὲ τότε ἔτυχε διάγειν ἐν τῇ βίγλᾳ,
ἵππον κρατῶν τοῦ χαλινοῦ καθέζεσθαι ἐν πέτρᾳ,
καὶ τούτων τε διὰ παντὸς τὴν ἔλευσιν ἐτήρουν.

453 On pourrait adopter au lieu d'ἑτοίμους, ἐτίμα qui est la leçon des mss. de Trébizonde (vers 2335) et d'Andros (vers 3424).   462 ἰσχύσομεν.   475 αὐτῆς.   478 τε manque et est emprunté au ms. de Trébizonde (vers 2360).

2908 ἐν πόθῳ seems to mean like ἐκ πόθου (above 531) 'with a will'.
2910 σύνθημα. At first sight this seems to mean that he told his friends the 'password' and it is so translated by

Legrand (TRE 2331); but the real meaning must be that he told his new companions (Melimitzes and his men) the 'arrangement' he had made for communicating with Ioan-

Philopappos heading the company at his wish.
When they came to the rising of the hill,
The old man told his friends the sign arranged,   2910
Lit the night-fire for those with Ioannakes;
When the day came they too were with the troop,
And joyfully received by Maximo;
As ready next of kin and as allies
Maximo welcomed them with full delight.
When they were coming near the river banks
Philopappos began a discourse of this sort:
"The place, my lady and you men-at-arms,
In which I found the girl, is very difficult.
Let us not all go on, making a noise,   2920
Giving who guards her our discovery,
That, ere we come, they plunge into the grove,
So we should have no power to seize our quarry,
And vain should be the labour of us all.
Let two or three, if you please, go first alone,
Secretly spying out where the girl is,
Then two of us stay keeping watch on her,
While the third coming back to you shall tell,
And you shall come with him and not get lost."
On this Maximo answered the old man: 2930
"O old and wise, I trust you to command,
Do as you will then, all obeying you."
Philopappos straightway taking Melimitzes
And Kinnamos with him, they crossed the river,
Having ordered the others to wait there
Until a message should come back from them.
It happened then that I was at the watch,
Sat on a rock holding my horse's bridle;
For I was looking always for their coming.

nakes. σύνθημα is used in exactly the same sense, of an agreement to light a beacon, in Thuc. iv. 112. Cf. also meaning 'covenant' below, 3735.

2914 ἑτοίμους is almost certainly a mistake for ἐτίμα which can be supplied from TRE 2335. The next line 2915 would then be a copyist's attempt to supply the lost verb. But

as the couplet makes good sense as it stands I have preferred to translate it uncorrected.

2934 διῆλθε: i.e. 'they crossed to my side of the river': cf. below 2979, where Philopappos crosses back again.

2937 βίγλᾳ. Note that Digenes also had a 'beacon' or look-out post (translated 'watch') as part of his camp.

Ἰδών με ὁ Φιλοπαπποῦς λέγει τὸν Μελιμίτζην·
" Ὁρᾷς ἐκεῖνον" (τῇ χειρὶ ἐμὲ ὑποδεικνύων) 480
" τὸν ἐν πέτρᾳ καθήμενον ἐπὶ τὴν ἀκρωρείαν;
αὐτὸς ὑπάρχει, γίνωσκε, ὁ τὴν κόρην κατέχων·
μὴ τοίνυν ἐλευσώμεθα κατὰ πρόσωπον τούτου·
ἀλλὰ ἃς ἐρευνήσωμεν ὅπου τὴν κόρην ἔχει,
καὶ εἶθ' οὕτως γνωρίσωμεν τῷ λαῷ, ὡς ἐρρέθη· 485
εἰ γὰρ καὶ μόνος πέφυκεν, πλὴν καλὸς εἶναι πάντως·
οἶδα γὰρ οἷος καὶ αὐτὸς ὑπάρχει ἐν ἀνδρείᾳ,
καὶ παραινῶ μηδὲ ποσῶς μόνοι αὐτῷ φανῆναι."
Ὡσαύτως καὶ ὁ Κίνναμος ἐπαινῶν τὰ λεχθέντα,
ἀλλ' οὐδαμῶς συνέθετο τούτοις ὁ Μελιμίτζης 490
εἰρηκὼς ὡς " Οὐ δύναμαι νῦν ὑμᾶς ἐπιγνῶναι·
εἰς χιλίους οὐδέποτε συνεργοῦ ἐδεήθην,
καὶ εἰς τὸν ἕνα λέγετε τὸν λαὸν περιμένειν;
πάντως εἰ τοῦτο ἀκουσθῇ πρὸ τῆς ἐμῆς κυρίας
καταμεμφθῶ ὡς ἄνανδρος, τὸν ἕνα δειλιάσας, 495
καὶ ζῆν οὐκέτι βούλομαι, εἰ ἄτολμος ἀκούσω."
Οὕτως εἰπόντος κατ' ἐμοῦ ὅλῳ θυμῷ ἐκινήθη,
τὰς τοῦ γέροντος παρ' οὐδὲν θέμενος παραινέσεις·
ἔστι γὰρ καὶ τὸ βάρβαρον δύσπιστον ἔθνος ἅπαν.
Τούτου ὡς εἶδον τὴν ὁρμήν, τοὺς δὲ ἐφεπομένους 500
(καὶ αὐτοὶ γὰρ παρείποντο σκοπεύοντες τὸ μέλλον),
τοῦ ἵππου μου ἐπέβαινον καὶ αὐτοῖς προσυπήντων·
ὡς δὲ ἔμπροσθεν ἤρχετο πάντων ὁ Μελιμίτζης,
τὸ μὲν κοντάριν ἴθυνε δοῦναί μοι κονταρέαν·
τοῦτο δὲ τέχνῃ παρελθὼν ἐν τῷ με παρατρέχειν, 505
τῇ ῥάβδῳ τοῦτον ἔπληξα καὶ πρὸς γῆν κατηνέχθη·
ἱστάμην δὲ ἐγὼ τηρῶν εἰ ἐγερθῆναι ἔχει·
καὶ ὡς ἐν τούτῳ μου τὸν νοῦν εἰς ὥραν ἐσχολούμην,
λαθών με ὁ Φιλοπαπποῦς καὶ ἐλθὼν ἐκ πλαγίου,
κονταρέαν ἐν τῷ μηρῷ τιτρώσκει μου τὸν ἵππον· 510
ὑπῆρχον δὲ συνηρεφῆ καὶ θαμινὰ τὰ δένδρα,
τοῦ ἵππου δὲ πονέσαντος καὶ ταραχθέντος λίαν,
ἐπιστραφεὶς τὸν γέροντα φευγόμενον κατεῖδον,
καὶ ἐπεφώνησα αὐτῷ· "Τί με ἀποδιδράσκεις;

---

486 καλὸν. πάντας.   488 μὴ δὲ.   504 et 510 κονταραίαν.   511 συνηρρεφῆ.

2952 ὑμᾶς ἐπιγνῶναι. ἐπιγιγνώσκω is rare in this sense, 'acknowledge' or

Philopappos saw me, said to Melimitzes,   2940
"You see him," pointing at me with his hand,
"Him sitting on the rock up on the ridge?
That is the man, you know, has got the girl;
So let us not come face to face with him,
But let us find out where he has the girl,
And then acquaint the company, as was said.
For though he be alone, he is good all through.
I know what sort he is in manliness;
I say by no means show ourselves alone."
While Kinnamos approved what he had said,   2950
Melimitzes by no means agreed with them,
Saying, "I cannot now acknowledge this;
I never wanted help against a thousand;
You say for one we wait our company?
Surely if this be heard before my lady
I shall be called unmanly, frightened of one,
And want to live no more if called a coward."
So saying he moved on me with all his might,
Counting for nothing the old man's advice
(Barbarians are all an unbelieving race).   2960
When I beheld his charge, and those behind—
For they too followed, watching what was coming—
I mounted on my horse and went to meet them.
As Melimitzes came before them all
He aimed his spear to give me a spear-thrust;
With skill avoiding this, as he ran past me,
I struck him with my staff, to earth he fell,
And I stood there watching if he could rise.
And as I set my mind some time on this,
I saw not Philopappos from one side,   2970
He came and in the quarter spears me my horse;
The trees were over-roofed and thickly grown;
My horse being in pain and very frightened;
I turned and saw the old man running away,
And shouted at him, "Why do you run from me?

'approve' rather than 'recognize', but is found in N.T. See 1 Cor. xvi. 18.
2954 There is a lacuna in TRE from half-way through the line corresponding to this (2384); it begins again at the line corresponding to 3011 below.

ἔκδεξαί με δὲ εἰς πρόσωπον, ἐὰν ᾖς στρατιώτης,   515
καὶ μὴ ὥσπερ κυνάριον λυσσῶν λάθρα με δάκῃς."
Ὁ δὲ μᾶλλον σφοδρότερον τὸν δρασμὸν ἐποιεῖτο
καὶ διῆλθε τὸν ποταμὸν ἅμα σὺν τῷ Κιννάμῳ·
κἀγὼ ἄχρι τοῦ ὕδατος αὐτοῖς ἀκολουθήσας,
ὡς εἶδον πέρα τὸν λαόν, πάντας καθωπλισμένους,   520
οὐκ ἔκρινα τοῦ ἀπελθεῖν πρὸς αὐτοὺς χωρὶς ὅπλων,
μάλιστα δ᾿ ὅτι ὤκλαζεν ὁ ἵππος ἐν τῇ τρώσει·
καὶ αὐτίκα ὑπέστρεψα πρὸς τὴν κόρην εὐθέως,
εἶτα βαλὼν τὰ ἅρματα, ἀλλάξας καὶ τὸν ἵππον,
πρὸς τὴν ὡραίαν εἴρηκα· " Δεῦρο, φῶς μου, ἐν τάχει,   525
ἵν᾿ ὅπως σε ἐν τῇ κρυπτῇ τοῦ λόφου ἐπαγάγω·
κἀκεῖθεν βλέπε τοὺς ἐχθροὺς ἡμῶν ἀπολλυμένους,
καὶ μάθε τίνα σοι ὁ Θεὸς ἐκδικητὴν παρέσχε,
καὶ τὸ πανάγιον αὐτοῦ κράτος καὶ νῦν δοξάσεις."
Ἡ δὲ εὐθὺς ἐπέβηκεν ἐφ᾿ ἵππῳ τῷ ἰδίῳ,   530
καὶ γὰρ τὴν ἔφοδον αὐτῆς προηυτρέπισα μάλα·
ὡς δὲ καὶ κατελάβομεν ἐν τῷ ῥηθέντι τόπῳ,
τὴν μὲν ἐν τῇ περιωπῇ ἀφέμενος τοῦ ὄρους,
ἐν ᾧ ἄντρον αὐτοφυὲς ὡς οἴκημα ὑπῆρχεν,
ὑπὸ δένδρων κρυπτόμενον καὶ δυσεύρετον λίαν,   535
τοῦ ὁρᾶν μὲν τὰ πόρρωθεν πραττόμενα παρεῖχε,
καὶ μηδὲ τὸ κρυπτόμενον παρά τινος ὁρᾶσθαι·
ἐκεῖσε, ὡς δεδήλωται, τὴν κόρην κατακρύψας,
καὶ παραγγείλας μηδαμῶς δειλιᾶν τὰ συμβάντα,
μηδὲ μὴν ἐν ταῖς συμπλοκαῖς φωνῆσαι τὸ παράπαν,   540
ἵνα μὴ τούτοις γένηται ὁδηγὸς ἡ φωνή σου,
καὶ ἐπανέλθωσι πρὸς σέ, ἐμοῦ ἀσχολουμένου,
καὶ προφανὴς ὁ κίνδυνος ἐκ τούτου μοι ἐπέλθῃ.
Καὶ ὥρμησα πρὸς ποταμὸν τὸν λαὸν ἔνθα εἶδον,
καὶ τὰς ὄχθας ἀνέτρεχον ἵνα τὸν πόρον εὕρω·   545
καὶ θεωρῶ τὴν Μαξιμοῦν τῶν λοιπῶν χωρισθεῖσαν   58 vᵒ.

520 εἶδε. Correction empruntée au ms. d'Andros (vers 3504).   524 ἅρματα.
526 κρηπῇ. J'écris κρυπτῇ (cachette) sans hésiter, bien que l'accentuation normale
soit κρύπτῃ; car on ne peut songer à un synonyme vulgaire de κοηπίς.   540
μὴ δὲ.

2978 δρασμὸν ἐποιεῖτο. See above 2252.　　2987 κρύπτῃ, or κρυπτή, usually means
2985 βαλὼν τὰ ἅρματα. Leg. λαβὼν　　a 'crypt' or a vault, but here
with AND 3508.　　obviously means a hiding-place—or

Wait for me face to face, if you be a soldier,
And bite me not by stealth like a mad whelp."
He all the harder made his running off
And went with Kinnamos across the river;
I having followed them down to the water,   2980
When I saw beyond the company, all armed,
Deemed not to start against them without arms,
The more that from his wound my horse was lame,
And straight returned directly to the Girl.
Then taking arms and having changed my horse,
Spoke to my fair one, "Come, my light, quickly,
Let me take you to the hide-out on the hill:
Look thence and see our enemies destroyed,
Learn what avenger God has given you,
And you shall praise again His all-holy might."   2990
Straightway she mounted up on to my horse,
For her supplies I had prepared before.
And when we reached the place I spoke about,
I left her in the look-out of the hill,
Wherein there was a natural cave for dwelling,
Hidden by trees and very hard to find,
Allowing view of what was done far off,
Not what was hid by any to be viewed.
There, as was said, I hid away the Girl,
Bidding her have no fear of what took place,   3000
Nor in the fighting to cry out at all—
"For fear your voice should be a guide to them,
And they come back to you, myself engaged,
And thereby manifest danger come on me."
I sped to the river where I had seen the band,
And trotting along the banks to find the ford,
I beheld Maximo parted from the others,

in fact a 'grotto' on the hill-top.
2992 ἔφοδος used here for ἐφόδιον
(= *viaticum*). See above 343.
3002 The usual mixture of direct and
indirect narration—'I told *her* not
to cry out for fear they should hear
your voice' a mixture rather like drawing two eyes in a profile face.

3005 λαόν as usual, here translated
'band', for the 'company' of ἄγουροι.
3006 There had been no difficulty before in finding the ford; but cf.
below 3034.
3007 τῶν λοιπῶν: i.e. parted from her
λαός.

καὶ σὺν αὐτῇ τοὺς τέσσαρας μεγίστους ἀπελάτας,
Φιλοπαπποῦν τὸν γέροντα, Κίνναμον καὶ Ἰωαννάκην,
καὶ τὸν δόκιμον Λέανδρον τὸν μέγαν ἐν ἀνδρείᾳ·
χαρζανιστὶ κατήρχοντο τοῦ ποταμοῦ τὸ χεῖλος,   550
δύο ἔνθεν κακεῖθεν τε, ἡ Μαξιμοῦ δὲ μέσον,
ἐποχουμένη εἰς βουλχᾶν λευκὸν καθάπερ γάλα,
χαίτην ἔχων καὶ τὴν οὐράν, τὸν σγοῦρδον καὶ τὰ ὦτα,
ὄνυχάς τε τοὺς τέσσαρας κοκκίνους βεβαμμένους,
ἅπαν τὸ σελλοχάλινον χρυσῷ πεποικιλμένον·   555
τὸ λουρίκιν ἀπέστραπτε χρυσέας ρίζας ἔχον.
Στραφεῖσα πρὸς τὸν γέροντα ἐπιμελῶς ἠρώτα·
" Λέγε μοι, ὦ Φιλόπαππου, τίς ὁ τὴν κόρην ἔχων; "
Ὁ δὲ φησίν· " Οὗτός ἐστι," κἀμὲ τῇ χειρὶ δείξας.
Ἡ δέ· " Καὶ ποῦ οἱ σὺν αὐτῷ ", ἤρετο, " στρατιῶται;   560
" Οὗτος," φησί, " κυρία μου, τῶν συνεργῶν οὐ δεῖται,
ἀλλ' εἰς τὴν ἄπειρον αὐτοῦ ἐπιθαρρῶν ἀνδρείαν,
μόνος ὁδεύει πάντοτε, καύχημα τοῦτο ἔχων."
Ἡ δέ· " Ὢ τρισκατάρατε γέρον," ἀνταπεκρίθη,
" καὶ διὰ ἕνα κόπους μοι καὶ τῷ λαῷ παρεῖχες,   565
πρὸς ὃν μόνη περάσασα, σὺν Θεῷ καυχωμένη,
ἀρῶ αὐτοῦ τὴν κεφαλήν, ὑμῶν μὴ δεηθεῖσα; "
Ταῦτα εἰποῦσα ἐν θυμῷ, ὥρμησε τοῦ περάσαι.
Ἐγὼ δὲ λέγω πρὸς αὐτήν· " Μαξιμού, μὴ περάσῃς·
ἀνδράσι καὶ γὰρ πέφυκεν ἔρχεσθαι πρὸς γυναῖκας·   570
ἔλθω λοιπὸν ἐγὼ πρὸς σέ, ὡς τὸ δίκαιον ἔχει."
Καὶ αὐτίκα τὸν ἵππον μου κεντήσας ταῖς περόναις,
πρὸς τὸ ὕδωρ ἐξώρμησα, ἀποτυχὼν τοῦ πόρου·   59 rᵒ.
ἦν δὲ πολὺς ὁ ποταμὸς καὶ ἔπλευσεν ὁ ἵππος·
ὕδατος τούτου ἔκχυσις ἄποθεν δὲ ὑπῆρχεν   575
βραχυτάτην ἐμφαίνουσα λίμνην συχνήν τε πόαν·
ἐν ᾗπερ στᾶσα ἀσφαλῶς λίαν εὐτρεπισμένη
ἡ Μαξιμοῦ τὴν προσβολὴν τὴν ἐμὴν ἐπετήρει·
οἱ δὲ συνόντες ἄλλοι μὲν ἔτρεχον πρὸς τὸν πόρον,

557 Je supprime καὶ avant στραφεῖσα.   561 μου manque.   562 αὐτοῦ.
569 μαξιμοῦ.

3011 χαρζανιστί. See above 1162. An
attempt by Grégoire to interpret
this in connexion with the name of
the Harzianian theme cannot be

accepted; but it might possibly
mean 'on a zigzag path'. With this
line TRE (2385) begins again after
lacuna.

And with her the four chiefest of the Reivers,
Old Philopappos, Kinnamos, Ioannakes,
And the well-tried Leander, great in manliness,   3010
Descending on the lash the river's lip,
Two on each side, Maximo in the middle,
Riding upon a charger white as milk,
Having his mane and tail, forelock and ears
Dyed red, his four hoofs also dyed with red,
Saddle and bridle all picked out with gold,
Her breastplate flashing with its golden hems.
Turning to the old man she asked intently,
"Tell me, Philopappos, who is it has the girl?"
He said, "That is the man", pointing at me.   3020
And then she asked, "Where are the soldiers with him?"
"Lady," he said, "he has no need of helpers,
But trusting in his boundless manliness,
Fares ever alone, making a boast of it."
"You thrice accurst old man," she answered him,
"So me and my people you troubled for one man,
To whom I will cross alone, boasting with God's help
I will bring back his head, not needing you?"
So saying in her rage she rushed to cross.
But I called to her, "Cross not, Maximo: 3030
It is the lot of men to come to women,
So I will come to you, as it is right."
Forthwith pricking my horse on with my spurs,
I charged down to the water, missing the ford;
Full was the river and my horse was swimming.
On the other side this water's overflow
Had made a shallow pool and thick herbage,
Wherein securely standing well prepared
Maximo was watching for my attack.
Of those with her some ran towards the ford,   3040

3013 βουλχᾶν. See above 1393.
3014 σγοῦρδον. See above 1213 and
Lyb. Rod. where Lambert's glossary gives 'queue ou crinière'. The
present passage shows that it can
mean neither of these, and must mean
'forelock'. Probably connected with

σγοῦρος (for σγοῦρρος).
3016 σελλοχάλινον. The usual *dvandva*
compound.
3017 ρίζας. See above 1201.
3040, 3041 ἄλλοι μέν . . . ἔτεροι δέ . . . .
Cf. below 3148-50. οἱ μέν . . . ἄλλοι
δέ . . . ἔτεροι δέ . . . .

ἕτεροι δὲ ἐνήδρευον ἐγκρύμματα ποιοῦντες.   580
Ἐγὼ δέ, ὅταν ἔγνωκα εἰς γῆν πατεῖν τὸν ἵππον,
τρανὰ αὐτὸν ἠρέθιζον, καὶ τὸ σπαθὶν ἑλκύσας
ὁλοψύχως πρὸς Μαξιμοῦν εὐτέχνως ἀπηρχόμην.
Ἡ δέ, ὡς προηυτρέπιστο, προσαπαντᾶν δραμοῦσα,
κονταρέαν μοι δέδωκεν ξυστὴν εἰς τὸ λουρίκιν·   585
καὶ μηδαμῶς ἀδικηθεὶς ἔκοψα τὸ κοντάριν,
τινάξας δ᾿ αὖθις τὸ σπαθὶν ταύτης ἐνεφεισάμην·
τοῦ δὲ βοῦλχα ἀποτεμὼν τὴν κεφαλὴν εὐθέως,
καὶ τὸ μὲν πτῶμα χαλεπῶς ἐπὶ γῆν κατηνέχθη·
ἡ δὲ ἀναποδίσασα, τρόμῳ συνεχομένη,   590
προσπίπτουσα ἐφθέγγετο· " Ὦ νέε, μὴ ἀποθάνω·
πεπλάνημαι γὰρ ὡς γυνὴ Φιλοπαππού πεισθεῖσα."
Καὶ ταύτης μὲν εὐλαβηθείς, εἰσακούων τοῖς λόγοις
κάλλος τε τὸ θαυμάσιον ὃ εἶχεν ἐλεήσας,
ἐκεῖ ταύτην ἀφέμενος, πρὸς τοὺς λοιποὺς ἐξῆλθον·   595
ὅπως τὲ πάντας ἴσχυσα αἰσχύνομαι τοῦ λέγειν,
ἵνα μὴ ὡς καυχώμενον λογίσησθέ με, φίλοι·
ὁ γὰρ ἐκδιηγούμενος ἰδίας ἀριστείας
κενόδοξος λογίζεται ὑπὸ τῶν ἀκουόντων.
Ἐγὼ δὲ οὐ καυχώμενος ταῦτα ὑμῖν ἐκφαίνω,   59 vᵒ.   600
οὔ, μὰ τὸν διδόντα ἰσχὺν καὶ γνῶσιν τοῖς ἀνθρώποις,
αὐτὸς γὰρ μόνος πάροχος τῶν ἀγαθῶν ὑπάρχει·
διὰ τοῦτο ῥηθήσονται ὡς γεγόνασι πάντα,
συγγνώμην ὅπως παρ᾿ ὑμῶν ἔξω τῶν ἀκουόντων.
Αὖθις καὶ γὰρ ὠλίσθησα εἰς βόθυνον μοιχείας,   605
δι᾿ ἐλαφρότητα φρενῶν καὶ ψυχῆς ἀμελείαν,
ὑπὲρ τούτου κατὰ πολὺ ὁ λόγος μὲν δηλώσει·
ἔχει δὲ οὕτω καθεξῆς ὥσπερ ὑμῖν ἐξεῖπω.
Ἡ Μαξιμού, τὸν ἴδιον ἀπολέσασα ἵππον,
ἀπελείφθη ἐν τῇ ποᾷ, ὡς ἄνωθεν ἐρρέθη,   610
καὶ πρὸς τοὺς ἄλλους ἐκδραμὼν τὸν πόλεμον συνῆψα·
καί, πρὶν λάβωσι πεῖραν μου, εἰσήγοντο μὲν πρός με·
ὡς δὲ πάντας τοὺς μετ᾿ ἐμοῦ συμβεβληκότας εἶδον,
κατερραγμένους ἐπὶ γῆν, ἀφ᾿ ἵππον ἀπωσμένους,

585 *κονταραίαν.*   589 *καὶ* manque et est emprunté au ms. de Trébizonde
(vers 2420) et à celui d'Andros (vers 3587).   590 *τὴν δὲ ἀναποδίσασαν τρόμω*
συνεχομένην. Cf. le ms. de Trébizonde (vers 2602) et celui d'Andros (vers 3588).
593 *μὲν* manque.

And others making ambush lay in wait.
I when I knew my horse was treading ground
Stirred him up sharply, and drawing my sword
With all my soul and skill advanced on Maximo.
She, being well prepared, charged on to meet me,
Gave me a grazing spear-thrust on the breastplate;
And I in no wise hurt cut off the spear-head,
Brandished the sword again, sparing herself
Then swiftly sliced right off her charger's head,
And heavily his body fell to earth.   3050
She springing back and in a grip of fear
Crouched down, and said, "Let me not die, young man;
I erred woman-like, Philopappos told me.
And I respected her, hearing her words,
Pitied the wondrous beauty that was hers,
And left her there and turned against the rest.
How I had power on all I shame to say,
My friends, lest you should reckon me a boaster
(For he who tells the tale of his own feats
Is reckoned by his listeners a braggart).   3060
These things I show forth to you not as boasting,
No, by the Giver of power and knowledge to men,
For He alone is provider of good things;
Therefore as things happened shall all be told,
That I may have pardon from you who hear me.
Again I slipped into adultery's pit,
Through my lightheartedness and soul's negligence,
Thereof in measure my discourse shall show;
Even as I tell you thus was it in order.
Maximo then having lost her own horse   3070
Was left there in the grass, as told above,
And charging on the others I joined battle.
Before they had me tried, they would come at me,
But when they saw that all those who had met me
Lay broken on the ground, thrown off their horses,

3051 ἀναποδίσασα. See below 3225,
where it is suggested that the redactor thought ἀναποδίζω meant 'I rise
to my feet' or 'get up after a fall'.

3052 προσπίπτουσα may mean 'sup-
plicating'.
3061 See above 2189.

καὶ ἐξ αὐτῶν ἐγνώρισαν τῶν ἔργων ὅστις ἤμην, 615
φυγῇ μόνῃ ἐπίστευον ἰδεῖν τὴν σωτηρίαν·
καὶ ἐκ πάντων ὀλιγοστοὶ ἴσχυσαν ἀποδρᾶσαι.
Καί, τοῦ πολέμου παύσαντος, ὄπισθεν ἐστρεφόμην,
καὶ ἐξαίφνης τοὺς τέσσαρας καθορῶ ἀπελάτας
Φιλοπαπποῦν καὶ Λέανδρον, Κίνναμον καὶ Ἰωαννάκην, 620
τοῦ ἄλσους ἀνακύψαντας καὶ πρός με ἐρχομένους·
Λέανδρος δὲ καὶ Κίνναμος ἤρχοντο ἐκ προσώπου,
ὁ γέρων δὲ καὶ οἱ λοιποὶ ἤλαυνον ἐξοπίσω,
ἐλπίζοντές με ἀνελεῖν μέσον αὐτῶν βαλόντες,
ἀλλ᾽ ἠνέχθησαν μάταια καὶ κενὰ μελετῶντες· 625
ὡς γὰρ εἶδον τοὺς ἔμπροσθεν σφόδρα ἐπιλαλοῦντας, 60 r°.
πρὸς αὐτοὺς ὥρμησα εὐθύς, τῶν ἄλλων μὴ φροντίσας.
Ὁ Λέανδρος ἐπέδραμεν, οὐ γὰρ εἶχέ μου πεῖραν·
ὃν καὶ πατάξας, ἐπὶ γῆν πέπτωκε σὺν τῷ ἵππῳ.
Τοῦτον ἰδὼν ὁ Κίνναμος ἐτράπη τῆς εὐθείας· 630
οἱ δὲ λοιποὶ συνάψαντες τοὺς ὤμους καὶ τὰ ξίφη
ἐκ πλαγίου προέβαλον δοῦναί μοι κονταρέας·
πρὸς οὓς συντόμως τὴν ἐμὴν ἀνθυποστρέψας σπάθην,
τὰ κοντάρια ἔτεμον παρευθὺς ἀμφοτέρων,
καὶ πρὸς φυγὴν ἐτράπησαν τοὺς ἵππους ἐκκεντοῦντες, 635
μηδαμῶς αὐτῶν ὄπισθεν θεάσασθαι τολμῶντες.
Οὕτως ὡς εἶδον ἔχοντας, μετὰ γέλωτος εἶπον·
" Στράφητε, οὐκ αἰσχύνεσθε τὸν ἕνα δειλιῶντες; "
Οἱ δὲ μᾶλλον σφοδρότερον τὸν δρασμὸν ἐπετέλουν·
καὶ οὐκ ἐδίωξα αὐτούς, τῆς συμφορᾶς οἰκτείρας 640
(ἔλεος καὶ γὰρ πάντοτε πρὸς τοὺς φεύγοντας εἶχον,
νικᾶν καὶ μὴ ὑπερνικᾶν, φιλεῖν τοὺς ἐναντίους),
ἀπέστρεφόν τε ὄπισθεν κατὰ σχολὴν βαδίζων,
πλησίον δὲ τῆς Μαξιμοῦς ἐλθών, τοιάδε ἔφην·
" Ἡ καυχωμένη ἄμετρα καὶ ἰσχύϊ θαρροῦσα, 645
ἄπελθε, ἐπισύναξον τοὺς φυγεῖν σωζομένους,
καὶ ἀνδραγάθει σὺν αὐτοῖς δυνατῶς ἔνθα ἔχεις,
ἔθος ὡς οἶσθα καὶ αὐτὴ καλῶς πεῖραν λαβοῦσα,

617 ἀποδράσαι.   621 τούς.   623 ἐξόπίσω.   624 αὐτῶν.   632
κονταραίας.   636 αὐτῶν.

3084 οἱ λοιποί. Who were the λοιποί, after three have been mentioned out of four? Presumably their attendant squires. In TRE and AND they were

And by those works they knew me who I was,
In flight alone they thought to find salvation;
Few of them all were able to escape.
And when the battle ended I turned back,
And suddenly I beheld the four Reivers,   3080
Philopappos, Leander, Kinnamos, Ioannakes,
Emerging from the copse, coming towards me.
Leander and Kinnamos came facing me,
The old man and the rest rode from behind,
Hoping to kill by catching me between them;
But vain and empty suffered they their plan.
For when I saw those in front urging hard
I charged straight at them, not caring for the others.
Leander came on, for he had not tried me,
Whom when I struck, he fell to earth with his horse.   3090
Seeing him Kinnamos turned from the straight;
The others fastening their swords to shoulder
Charged from the side to get me with their spears.
But quickly swinging round my blade against them
Straightway I sliced the spearheads of them both,
And they were turned to flight pricking their horses,
Not even venturing to look behind them.
Seeing them in that plight, I said laughing,
"Turn round, afraid of one and not ashamed?"
But they the harder made their running off.   3100
I did not chase them, sorry for their downfall—
Pity for those who fled was always mine,
To conquer and not more, to love my enemies—
But I turned back again, pacing at ease,
And coming near to Maximo spoke thus:
"Unmeasured in boasting, trusting in your strength,
Go, gather those who lived to run away,
And do your feats with them, where you have power,
As you have use, and having made good trial,

five in this episode, Melementzes
being one of them. But GRO rightly
remembers that he has already been
disposed of, above 2967.
3095 ἀμφοτέρων. See above 1193, 581,
205.

3100 δρασμόν. Above 2978.
3103 νικᾶν καὶ μὴ ὑπερνικᾶν, φιλεῖν τοὺς
ἐναντίους also in TRE 2511, AND
3679. For ὑπερνικᾶν cf. Ep. Rom.
viii. 37, 'We are more than con-
querors'.

ἐξ ὧν ἔπαθες μάνθανε καὶ μὴ ἀλαζονεύου·
Θεὸς γὰρ ἀντιτάσσεται πᾶσιν ὑπερηφάνοις." 650
Ἐκείνη δὲ πρὸς ὑπαντὴν ἐλθοῦσα ἡμετέραν,
τὰς χεῖρας αὐτῆς δήσασα πρεπόντως τὰς ἰδίας
καὶ μέχρι γῆς τὴν κεφαλὴν κλίνασα εὐκοσμίως·
" Ἁπάντων γενναιότατε," ἔφησε, " νῦν ἐπέγνων
τὴν σὴν ἀνείκαστον ἰσχὺν καὶ τὴν φιλανθρωπίαν, 655
ἣν οὐδεὶς ἔσχε πώποτε τῶν πάλαι ἐν ἀνδρείᾳ·
ἀφ' οὗ γάρ με ἐκρήμνισας, εἶχες καὶ τοῦ φονεῦσαι,
ἀλλ' ἐφείσω, ὡς θαυμαστὸς καὶ μέγας ἐν ἀνδρείᾳ·
ὁ Κύριος φυλάξοι σε, γενναῖε στρατιῶτα,
αὐθέντα μου πανθαύμαστε, μετὰ τῆς ποθητῆς σου, 660
εἰς χρόνους πλείονας καλοὺς ἐν δόξῃ καὶ ὑγείᾳ·
ὅτι πολλοὺς τεθέαμαι γενναίους στρατιώτας,
πολεμιστὰς περιφανεῖς καὶ στερροὺς ἐν τῇ μάχῃ,
ἀλλ' οὔτε κραταιότερον ἐν ταῖς ἀνδραγαθίαις
οὐκ εἶδον ἄλλον πώποτε παρ' ὅλον μου τὸν βίον." 665
Εἶτα περιλαβοῦσά μου τοὺς πόδας, κατεφίλει
τὴν χεῖρα μου τὴν δεξιάν, ἠρέμα φθεγγομένη·
" Εὐλογημένος ὁ πατὴρ καὶ μήτηρ ἡ τεκοῦσα,
καὶ οἱ μαστοὶ οἱ θρέψαντες μητρὸς εὐλογημένης·
τοιοῦτον γὰρ οὐδέποτε ἄλλον ἄνδρα κατεῖδον· 670
πληρῶσαι οὖν παρακαλῶ σὲ τὸν ἐμὸν δεσπότην
καὶ ἑτέραν μου αἴτησιν, ἐκ ταύτης ὅπως γνώσῃς
ἀκριβέστερον τὴν ἐμὴν ἐν τῷ πολέμῳ πεῖραν·
κέλευσόν με τοῦ ἀπελθεῖν καὶ ἐπιβῆναι ἵππου,
καὶ τὸ πρωὶ ἐλεύσομαι ἐν τῷ παρόντι τόπῳ, 675
ὅπως μονομαχήσωμεν μηδενὸς συμπαρόντος,
καὶ νὰ νοήσῃς, πάγκαλε, καὶ τὴ· ἐμὴν ἀνδρείαν."
" Μετὰ χαρᾶς, ὦ Μαξιμοῦ," πρὸς αὐτὴν ἐγὼ ἔφην,
" ἄπελθε ἔνθα βούλεσαι, κἀμὲ ὧδε εὑρήσεις· 61 rᵒ.
μᾶλλον δὲ φέρε καὶ τοὺς σοὺς ἑτέρους ὀτελάτας, 680
καὶ δοκίμασον ἅπαντας καὶ τοὺς κρείττονας μάθε."
Καὶ τότε ἕνα συλλαβὼν τῶν πλανωμένων ἵππων
τῶν πεπτωκότων σὺν αὐτῇ ἐν ὥρᾳ τοῦ πολέμου,

---

655 εὐχήν.   665 πῶποτε.   672 γνώσω. Cf. le ms. de Trébizonde (vers
2532) et celui d'Andros (vers 3700).   673 τὴν σήν. Cf. le ms. de Trébizonde
(vers 2533) et celui d'Andros (vers 3701).   677 πάγκαλε.   678 αὐτόν.
679 ὧδε.   681 μαθέ.

Learn from what you have suffered, and do not brag;   3110
For God is ranged against all overweeners."
And she then coming forward to our meeting
Her own hands having joined becomingly,
And decorously bowed her head to earth,
"Noblest of all," she said, "now have I known
Your unimagined strength, and clemency
Which none had ever who of old were brave:
For since you threw me off, you could have killed
But spared me, great and wonderful as brave.
The Lord preserve you, most noble soldier,   3120
My master most wondrous, with your beloved,
Many good years in glory and in health.
For many noble soldiers have I seen,
Far-famous warriors and firm in fight,
But not a mightier in feats of strength
Saw I another ever in all my life."
Then she embraced my feet, and then she kissed
My right hand, gently uttering these words:
"Blessed your father, and your mother who bore you,
And the blessed mother's breasts which nourished you;   3130
For such another man I never saw.
I beg you then my master to fulfil
One more request, that by it you may know
More strictly my experience in war:
Bid me to go away and mount my horse,
And in the morning I will come to this place,
That we may singly fight, none present with us,
And you shall see, good friend, my bravery."
"With joy, O Maximo," I said to her,
"Go where you will, and you shall find me here;   3140
Or rather bring your other reivers too,
And try them all, and find the better men."
   Then catching one of the straying horses
Of those who fell with her at the time of the fight,

3115 ἐπέγνων. Cf. above 2952.
3142 τοὺς κρείττονας μάθε. The first
meaning of κρείττων, says L. & S., is
'stronger in battle'.

ἤγαγον τοῦτον πρὸς αὐτὴν ἐπιβῆναι προστάξας.

'Ὡς γὰρ εἶδε με ὁ λαὸς κρημνίσαντα τὴν κόρην, 685
κύκλῳ περιεχύθησαν ὡς ἀετοὶ σπουδαίως·
οἱ μὲν σπαθέας ἔκρουον ἔσω χειρὶ συντόμως,
ἄλλοι δὲ κονταρέας μοι ἐδίδων κατὰ κράτος,
ἕτεροι δὲ τοῖς βέλεσιν αὐτῶν ἐξένυττόν με·
καὶ τότε τίς ὁ βοηθῶν; τίς ὁ φρουρῶν καὶ σκέπων; 690
οὐκ ἄλλος πάντως ἢ Θεὸς δικαιοκρίτης μέγας·
αὐτὸς γὰρ ἐξαπέστειλε βοήθειαν ἐξ ὕψους
καὶ ἐμὲ διεφύλαξεν ἀβλαβῆ παρ' ἐλπίδα,
ὡς δὲ εἰς μέσον κέκλεισμαι τοσούτων πολεμίων
καὶ πάντοθεν πληττόμενος τὴν φυγὴν ἠσχυνόμην· 695
εἶχον γὰρ ἄρματα καλὰ καὶ κατωχυρωμένα,
καὶ σὺν Θεῷ πεφύλαγμαι ἄτρωτος ἐν τῇ μάχῃ·
εἰς πολὺ δὲ οὐ γέγονεν ἡ ἐκείνων θρασύτης,
ἀλλὰ ταχέως ἔσβεσται, τοῦ Θεοῦ βοηθοῦντος·
ἔχων τε καὶ τοὺς μάρτυρας ἁγίους Θεοδώρους, 700
Γεώργιον, Δημήτριον, τούτους ἔτρεψα πάντας.
Κοντάριν γὰρ οὐκ ἔλαβον ἐν αὐτοῖς, οὐδὲ τόξον,
τὴν ἐμὴν σπάθην ἔσυρα καὶ ἦλθον ἔσω χεῖρας·
καὶ ὅσους μὲν ἐλάγχανον, ἔκοπτον τούτους μάλα,
καὶ γὰρ αὐτοὺς ἐλάμβανον ψυχὴν μὴ κεκτημένους· 705
ἄλλοι δὲ φεύγειν θέλοντες, κατελάμβανον τούτους,
καὶ μὴ δυνάμενοι ποσῶς ἐμοὶ προσαντιστῆναι,
ἐπέζευον τοὺς ἵππους των, ἔρριπτον τὰ ἄρματά των,
καὶ προσελθόντες ἔφευγον, ἐχόμενοι τοῦ τρόμου·
καὶ οὕτω τε ἀπέμενον ἵπποι πολλοὶ ἐκ τούτων, 710
ἐξ ὧν, ὡς ἔφην, δέδωκα τῇ Μαξιμοῦ τῷ τότε,
καὶ διῆλθον τὸν ποταμόν, ἡ δὲ πρὸς τὰ οἰκεῖα,
χάριν μοι, ὡς ἐφαίνετο, πολλὴν ὁμολογοῦσα.

---

685 ὁ manque. κνημίσαντα. 687 σπαθαίας. 688 κονταραίας. 701
μᾶλλον, et en marge πάντας. 708 ἄρματα. 711 δώδεκα.

3146–72 This passage describing the
rout of Maximo's 'company' is
placed earlier in TRE and AND—
after the line corresponding to 3056
above. (See TRE 2425–62; AND
3592 ff.)
3148 ἔσω χειρί should probably be
written as one word. TRE 2428 has

σπαθέας ἐσώχειρας. Cf. above 178
ἔσωθεν χεῖρας δόντες; and below
3164 ἔσω χεῖρας. συντόμως is awkward here as it must mean 'at short
intervals'.
3156 τὴν φυγὴν ἠσχυνόμην. Was Digenes
ever 'ashamed to fly'? Sense can be
made by translating 'disdained':

I brought it to her telling her to mount.
For when her men had seen me throw the Maid
They had poured round about me keenly like eagles;
Some aimed their sword-cuts quickly at arm's length,
And some with all their might were giving spear-thrusts,
While others tried to pierce me with their javelins.   3150
Who was my helper then? My shield and guardian?
None other only God, great judge and righteous:
For He sent forth assistance from on high,
Kept me unharmed against all expectation;
When I was shut up among so many foes,
From all sides smitten I disdained to fly:
I had good weapons that were strongly made,
With God's will in the fight was kept unwounded;
And all their boldness did not come to much,
But quickly was put out, with God helping;   3160
And with the Saints, the martyred Theodores,
George, and Demetrius, I beat them all.
For spear I did not take to them, nor bow,
But drew my sword and came within arm's length.
As many as I caught, I cut them down,
And the earth took them with no soul in them.
Others who would have fled I overtook them,
And quite unable to stand up to me,
Got off their horses, threw away their arms,
Gave themselves up and ran off terrified.   3170
So from them many horses had remained.
Of which, as said, I gave one then to Maximo.
    I crossed the river then, and she went home,
Much thanks, it seemed, acknowledging to me.

but there is a possibility that it may be due to a misunderstanding of a reading like that of TRE 2445, the redactor thinking ἐπίστευον was first person singular.

3161 The same four saints are mentioned in the introd. to Book I, above 21, 23, 25; and the Theodores also above 1986 (their pictures); one of them again below 3413.

3164 ἔσω χεῖρας. See above 3148. In

TRE 2458, 2428, Legrand translates this 'à deux mains'.

3166 καὶ γὰρ αὐτοὺς ἐλάμβανον. Leg. καὶ γῆ . . . ἐλάμβανεν as in TRE 2460, AND 3627.

3169 ἐπέζευον τοὺς ἵππους. Not at all classical; cf. below 3655.

3170 προσελθόντες ἔφευγον. Very classical; cf. Thuc. 3. 59. 3.

3173 τὰ οἰκεῖα. See above 1320.

Καί, εἰς τὴν τένδαν μου ἐλθών, ἀπέβαλον τὰ ὅπλα,
καὶ ἐδυσάμην θαυμαστὸν λεπτότατον μαχλάβιν, 715
βαλών τε καὶ σγουρούτζικον κόκκινον καμηλαύκιν,
καὶ ἵππον μετεσέλλισα δαγάλην, ἀστερᾶτον,
ὃς εἶχε γνώμην κάλλιστον ἐν ταῖς ἀνδραγαθίαις·
σπαθίν, σκουτάριν εἰληφὼς καὶ βένετον κοντάριν,
τὸν ποταμὸν ἐπέρασα, ἑσπέρας ἤδη οὔσης· 720
ἐπὶ τούτῳ καὶ ὤκνησα ἀνελθεῖν ἐν τῇ κόρῃ,
ἀλλ᾽ ἔστειλα τὰς ἑαυτῆς δύο θαλαμηπόλους·
εἴχομεν καὶ γὰρ ἱκανοὺς τοὺς ἡμῖν ὑπουργοῦντας,
τὴν οἴκησίν των ἔχοντας ἀπόμακρα τῆς τένδας,
οὐχὶ δὲ ἅπαντες ὁμοῦ, ἀλλ᾽ ἄνδρες μὲν ἰδίως, 725
καὶ αἱ γυναῖκες ὡσαύτως εἶχον αὐτῶν τὰς τένδας.
Περάσας οὖν, ὡς εἴρηκα, τὸν ποταμὸν Εὐφράτην,
ἐν τῷ λειμῶνι τῷ τερπνῷ ἑαυτὸν ἀνακλίνας,
τόν τε ἵππον ἀνέπαυσα διαγαγὼν τὴν νύκτα.
Πρὸς ὄρθρον δὲ ἐξαναστὰς καὶ ἐπιβὰς τοῦ ἵππου, 730
εἰς τὸ πεδίον ἀνελθών, ἱστάμην ἀναμένων.
Τῆς δὲ ἡμέρας τῷ φωτὶ ἄρτι διαυγαζούσης, 62 r°.
καὶ τοῦ ἡλίου λάμποντος ἐπὶ τὰς ἀκρωρείας,
ἰδοὺ μόνη ἡ Μαξιμοὺ ἐφάνη ἐν τῷ κάμπῳ.
Εἰς φάραν ἐπεκάθητο μαύρην, γενναιοτάτην, 735
ἐφόρει ἐπιλώρικον ὁλόσηρον καστόριν
φακεωλίτζιν πράσινον, χρυσὸν ῥεραντισμένον,
σκουτάριν ἔχον ἀετοῦ πτέρυγας γεγραμμένας,
κοντάριν ἀραβίτικον, καὶ σπαθὶν ἐζωσμένη.
Ταύτης ἐγὼ πρὸς ἀπαντὴν ἐκίνησα εὐθέως, 740
καὶ πλησίον γενόμενοι ἠσπασάμεθα ἄμφω·

716 καμαλαύκην. 717 γαδάλην ἀστεράταν et o au-dessus de αν. 726 Au
lieu de ὡσαύτως, qui fausse le vers, il faut sans doute lire ἄποθεν, comme dans
le ms. de Trébizonde (vers 2558). 736 ὁλόβυρον.

3176 λεπτότατον μαχλάβιν. See above
1200. TRE 2547 has here πτενώτατον
μαχλάμιν (also AND 3715).
3177 σγουρούτζικον καμηλαύκιν. See
above 1097. Note that Ducange con-
fuses σγουρός and derivatives with
σκοῦρος.
3178 μετεσέλλισα δαγάλην ἀστερᾶτον.
'Chestnut' (alezan) is Legrand's

translation for δαγάλην (or rather for
δαγάλλον TRE 2549), but I do not
know his authority. See also above
433, and see Chron. Mor. Schmitt,
gloss. s.v. δάος—with which it may
be connected.
3179 γνώμην. See above 360, &c.
3180 βένετον κοντάριν. See above 164,
1231. Why is a spear blue? A painted

I came into my tent, put off my arms,
Drew on a very thin and wondrous singlet,
And put on a red cap of curly fur,
Changed saddle to a chestnut horse white-starred,
His nature excellent for deeds of arms.
I took a sword, a shield, and my blue spear,   3180
And crossed the river; it was evening now.
Therefore I shrank from going up to the Girl,
But I sent her her own two chambermaids.
For we had several who waited on us,
Who had their dwelling distant from our tent,
Not all together, but the men apart,
And the women likewise had their own tents.
Crossing Euphrates river, as I said,
In that delightful meadow I lay down,
Resting my horse to pass the night away.   3190
Rising towards dawn, and mounting my horse,
I rode up to the plain, and stood waiting.
And as the daylight was just breaking through,
And the sun shining on the mountain tops,
Maximo appeared in the field alone.
She sat upon a black a noble mare,
Wearing a tabard, all of yellow silk
And green her turban was, sprinkled with gold,
She bore a shield painted with eagle's wings,
An Arab spear, and girdled with a sword.   3200
To meet with her I moved forward at once,
And when we were come near we both embraced,

shaft? Or a blue steel blade? And why is blue 'Venetian'? See below p. 214.

3186 The explanation is repeated from 2041, where the two θαλαμηπόλοι are called βάγιαι.

3195 κάμπῳ. Translation omits ἰδού. This scene is one of the poetic successes of the whole work.

3197, 3198 ἐπιλώρικον ὁλόσηρον καστόριν φακεωλίτζιν πράσινον. L. & S. record that Suidas says καστόριον may mean 'a kind of colour', and a colour is wanted with ὁλόσηρον. But if we take the obvious meaning of 'beaver-skin' it must go with the turban. The connexion of the beaver with musk offers another possible interpretation, for which cf. the scented scarf worn by Digenes above 1203. Ducange, s.v. κάστωρ, says 'crocus—apud Interpolat. Dioscor.' Cf. also ESC 1494 τοῦ βίου ὀξικάτορα, for which I read τουβία ὀξυκάστορα, 'boots of dark blue beaverskin'. See also Frolov. in Byzantion, xiii (1938), p. 474; and Grégoire in Byzantion, xiv (1939), p. 222.

χαιρετίσαντες, ὡς εἰκός, ἀλλήλους παμφιλτάτως,
τῆς μάχης τε ἠρξάμεθα, λαλήσαντες τοὺς ἵππους,
ἄνω καὶ κάτω πρὸς μικρὰν διαδραμόντες ὥραν,
κονταρέας δεδώκαμεν, μηδενὸς κρημνισθέντος.   745
Χωρισθέντες οὖν παρευθὺς εἱλκύσαμεν τὰς σπάθας,
καὶ κρούοντες ἐνστατικῶς, ἐμπεσόντες ἀλλήλοις·
ἐφειδόμην γάρ, βέλτιστε, τοῦ ἀδικῆσαι ταύτην·
ἀνδρῶν γὰρ ἔστι μωμητὸν οὐ μόνον τοῦ φονεῦσαι,
ἀλλ' οὐδὲ ὅλως πόλεμον μετὰ γυναικὸς στῆσαι.   750
Αὕτη δὲ ἦν ὀνομαστὴ τῶν τότε ἐν ἀνδρείᾳ,
τούτου χάριν τὸν πόλεμον οὐδαμῶς ἐπῃσχύνθην·
χεῖρα αὐτῆς τὴν δεξιὰν πλήξας τε πρὸ δακτύλων,
ἡ μὲν σπάθη ἐπὶ τὴν γῆν πέπτωκεν ἣν κατεῖχεν,
τρόμος δὲ ταύτην εἴληφε καὶ δειλία μεγίστη.   755
Ἐγὼ δὲ ἐξεφώνησα· " Μαξιμού, μὴ φοβεῖσαι,
οἰκτείρω γάρ σε ὡς γυνὴν καὶ κάλλους πεπλησμένην·
ἵνα δὲ γνώσῃ τίς εἰμι ἀκριβῶς ἐκ τῶν ἔργων,
τὴν ἰσχὺν ἐπιδείξω σοι τὴν ἐμὴν ἐν τῷ ἵππῳ."   62 vᵒ.
Καὶ σπαθέαν καταβατὴν εἰς τοὺς νεφροὺς εὐθέως   760
τοῦ φαρίου κατήγαγον καὶ διῃρέθη μέσον,
πεσόντος τοῦ ἡμίσεος εἰς μέρος μετ' ἐκείνης,
τοῦ δὲ λοιποῦ ἑτέρωθεν εἰς γῆν κατενεχθέντος.
Ἡ δὲ ἀναποδίσασα, λίαν τεταραγμένη,
συγκεκομμένη τῇ φωνῇ " Ἐλέησον," ἐβόα,   765
" ἐλέησόν με, κύριε, τὴν κακῶς πλανηθεῖσαν·
μᾶλλον, εἰ οὐκ ἀπαξιοῖς, ποιήσωμεν φιλίαν,
ἔτι παρθένος γὰρ εἰμὶ ὑπ' οὐδενὸς φθαρεῖσα·
σὺ μόνος με ἐνίκησας, σύ με ἀποκερδίσεις·
ἕξεις δέ με καὶ συνεργὸν εἰς τοὺς ὑπεναντίους."   770
" Οὐκ ἀποθνήσκεις, Μαξιμού," πρὸς αὐτὴν ἄρτι ἔφην,
" τὸ δὲ ἔχειν σε γαμετὴν οὐ δυνατόν μοι ἔσται,
νόμιμον ἔχω γαμετὴν εὐγενῆ καὶ ὡραίαν,
ἧς ἀγάπην οὐδέποτε τολμήσω ἀθετῆσαι.

742 χαιρετίσαντος.   745 κονταραίας.   750 στῆσαι μετὰ γυναικὸς. On
pourrait aussi écrire, στῆσαι μετὰ γυναίκας (génitif vulgaire). Mais je préfère
ma correction qui nous donne un accent sur la cinquième syllabe, comme l'affec-
tionne l'auteur de ce poème.   756 μαξιμοῦ. φοβῆσαι.   758 τὶς εἰμὶ.   760
σπαθαίαν.   772 ἔστι (sic).

3204 λαλῶ for usual ἐπιλαλῶ, see above   150. Xanth. Erotokr. gloss. s.v. records

Greeting each other lovingly, as was fair.
Then we began the fight, urging our horses,
And cantered up and down some little time,
We gave our spear-thrusts, no one was unhorsed.
We parted then and forthwith drew our swords,
Fell on each other giving stubborn blows;
And I forbore, my friend, from hurting her—
In men it is blamed not only to kill   3210
But even to join battle at all with woman;
She was of those then famed for bravery,
Wherefore was I to fight nowise ashamed—
On her right hand I struck above the fingers;
The sword that she was holding fell to earth,
And quaking seized her and great fearfulness.
I cried out, "Maximo, be not afraid,
I pity you as a woman and filled with beauty;
But that you know me strictly by my deeds
I will show you forth my strength upon your horse."   3220
Straight a descending sword-cut on the croup
I swung, the horse was severed in the middle,
And half of it fell on one side with her,
The other side the rest was borne to earth.
She started back, grievously terrified,
And in a broken voice "Mercy," she screamed,
"Have mercy on me, lord, I have sorely erred;
Rather let us make friends, if you disdain not.
I am a virgin still by none seduced.
You alone have conquered, you shall win me all;   3230
And have me helpmate too against your foes."
"You die not, Maximo," I said to her,
"But it cannot be for me to make you wife.
I have a lawful wife noble and fair,
Whose love I will never bear to set aside.

that λαλῶ has a distinct use for driving animals.

3206 Note that κρημνίζειν is the technical term for 'unhorsing'.

3212 ἀνδρεία here as always means 'fighting skill', i.e. the practice of a man's profession.

3218 γυνήν, accusative.

3225 ἀναποδίσασα (see above 3051) seems to be used here in the sense of 'starting to her feet'.

3230 ἀποκερδίσεις. Force of ἀπό is 'completely'.

Λοιπὸν δεῦρο ὑπὸ σκιὰν ἀπέλθωμεν τοῦ δένδρου, 775
καὶ διδάξω σε ἅπαντα τὰ κατ' ἐμὲ ὡς ἔχουν."
Ἐλθόντες δὲ πρὸς ποταμοῦ τὰ γειτνιῶντα δένδρα,
ἡ Μαξιμού, τὴν ἑαυτῆς ἀποπλύσασα χεῖρα,
καὶ δόκιμον ἐν τῇ πληγῇ ἄλειμμα ἐπιθεῖσα,
ὅπερ φέρειν εἰώθαμεν ἀεὶ ἐν τοῖς πολέμοις, 780
ῥίπτει τὸ ἐπιλώρικον, πολὺς γὰρ ἦν ὁ καύσων·
καὶ ὁ χιτὼν τῆς Μαξιμοῦς ὑπῆρχεν ἀραχνώδης.
πάντα καθάπερ ἔσοπτρον ἐνέφαινε τὰ μέλη,
καὶ τοὺς μαστοὺς προκύπτοντας μικρὸν ἄρτι τῶν στέρνων.
Καὶ ἐτρώθη μου ἡ ψυχή, ὡραία γὰρ ὑπῆρχε· 785

* * *

Καὶ ἐκ τοῦ ἵππου κατελθών, ἐφθέγγετο βοῶσα· TRE 2632
" Χαίροις, δεσπότης ὁ ἐμός," ἐπάνω μου δραμοῦσα,
" δούλη σου ὄντως γέγονα τῇ τοῦ πολέμου τύχῃ."
Καὶ χεῖρά μου τὴν δεξιὰν ἡδέως κατεφίλει· 2635
ὡς δὲ ἀνήφθη ὁ πυρσὸς ὁ τῆς ἐπιθυμίας,
οὐκ εἶχον ὅστις γένομαι, καθόλου ἐφλεγόμην·
πάντα λοιπὸν ἐσπούδαζα φυγεῖν τὴν ἁμαρτίαν,
καί, ἐμαυτὸν κατηγορῶν, ταῦτα ἐλογιζόμην·
" Ὦ δαίμων, διατί ἐρᾷς πάντων τῶν ἀλλοτρίων, 2640
πηγὴν ἔχων ἀθόλωτον, ὅλην μεμερισμένην; "
Ταῦτα διαλεγόμενος καθ' ἑαυτόν, ὦ φίλοι,
ἡ Μαξιμὼ τὸν ἔρωτα ἐξῆπτεν ἔτι μᾶλλον,
τοξεύουσα ταῖς ἀκοαῖς λόγοις παγγλυκυτάτοις,
ἦτον γὰρ νέα καὶ καλή, ὡραία καὶ παρθένος, (F. 75) 2645
ἡττήθη οὖν ὁ λογισμὸς βεβήλῳ ἐπιθύμει·

783 ἐμφαίνοντο. Cf. le ms. de Trébizonde (vers 2631), qui donne ὑπέφαινε.
785 ὡραῖα. Après ce vers, il manque un feuillet, enlevé sans doute par un lecteur
qu'avaient scandalisé les détails qui s'y trouvaient concernant l'adultère d'Acritas.
Nous comblons cette regrettable lacune à l'aide du ms. de Trébizonde (vers
2632–2672).   2644 παγγλυκυτάτοις.

3239 ἀποπλύσασα. Force of ἀπό is 'finished' washing.
3240 ἄλειμμα. TRE 2624 and AND 3794 have βότανον.
3242 ἐπιλώρικον. Nothing is said about taking off the breastplate, which should have come between ἐπιλώρικον and χιτών (3243).

3244 ἐνέφαινε. ἐμφαίνω is twice used by Plato of reflections in a mirror.
3245 τῶν στέρνων governed by προκύπτοντας; cf. above 3082 τοῦ ἄλσους ἀνακύψαντας; and refs. in L. & S. to Alciphr. 3. 10; Babr. 116. 3; and χιτωνίου τιτθίον προκύψαν Ar. Ran. 412. For στέρνων μαστοί cf. Anth. Pal.

Come let us go under the tree's shadow,
And I will teach you all that me concerns."
We came to the trees bordering the river,
And Maximo, when she had washed her hand,
And put a proper ointment on the wound   3240
We ever used to carry in our fighting,
Threw off her tabard, for the heat was great.
Maximo's tunic was like gossamer,
Which as a mirror all her limbs displayed,
And her small paps just peeping from her breast.
My soul was wounded, she was beautiful.

*   *   *

When I dismounted she cried out aloud,
" Hail, master mine," and running up to me,
"I am your slave indeed by war's fortune."
Sweetly she covered my right hand with kisses.   3250
And when the fire of lust in me was kindled
I knew not who I was, I was all burning.
Then I tried all means to escape from sin,
And I would reason thus myself accusing:
"Demon, why love you all things that are foreign,
With your own well untroubled all set apart?"
While I thus talked, my friends, within myself,
Maximo lighted up my love the more
Shooting upon my hearing sweetest words,
And she was young and fair, lovely and virgin,   3260
Reason was conquered by profane desire;

v. 13. 3. Much of this passage seems
to come from Ach. Tat. i. i. 11
(describing a painting of Europa):
τὸ δὲ σῶμα διὰ τῆς ἐσθῆτος ὑπε-
φαίνετο . . . μαζοὶ τῶν στέρνων ἠρέμα
προκύπτοντες. . . . καὶ ἐγίνετο τοῦ
σώματος κάτοπτρον ὁ χιτών. And the
passage is again reflected in the
Allegory of Meliteniotes 358 . . . τὰ
μέλη, καὶ τοὺς μαζοὺς προκύπτοντας
δεικνύουσαι τοῖς στέρνοις.
3246 After this line a page has been
torn out of the GRO MS. The

lacuna is supplied from TRE 2632–72.
3255 ἀλλοτρίων. Note that ἀλλότριος has
a technical sense as 'the stranger',
i.e. 'the Enemy'.
3256 μεμερισμένην. A reminiscence of
LXX. Prov. v. 17–18 μηδεὶς ἀλλότριος
μετασχέτω σοι· ἡ πηγή σου τοῦ
ὕδατος ἔστω σοι ἰδία. AND 3812
reads μεμυρισμένην wrongly.
3261 ἐπιθύμει. Note ἐπιθυμίς for ἐπιθυμία
and cf. ὡραῖσις in Meliten., θαύμασις
in the Achilleid, and ἐπίθυσις from
inscriptions.

αἰσχύνης γὰρ καὶ μίξεως ἁπάσης πληρωθείσης,
εἶτα αὐτὴν καταλιπών, προπέμψας τε ἐκεῖθεν,
λόγον ἐξεῖπον πρὸς αὐτὴν παραμυθίας δῆθεν·
" Ὕπαγε, κόρη μου, καλῶς καὶ μὴ μοῦ ἐπιλάθου."   2650
Καὶ ἐν τῷ ἵππῳ ἐπιβὰς τὸν ποταμὸν διῆλθον·
ἡ δὲ πρὸς ὕδωρ λούσασα αὐτῆς τὴν παρθενίαν,
ἐμὴν τὴν ὑποχώρησιν ἠνάγκαζε βαρέως.

Εἶτα παραγενόμενος πρὸς τὴν ἐμὴν φιλτάτην,   2655
κατῆλθον ἐκ τοῦ ἵππου μου, ταύτην φιλῶ ἀπλήστως,
" Εἶδες, ψυχή μου," ἔλεγον, " ἐκδικητὴν ὃν ἔχεις.
καὶ οἷαν σοι ἀντίληψιν ὁ πλαστουργὸς παρέσχεν; "
Ἡ δὲ τινὰ ἐν τῇ ψυχῇ ζηλοτυπίαν σχοῦσα,
" Ἐν ἅπασιν εὐχαριστῶ," ἀντέφη, " κύριέ μου,   2660
δάκνει μὲ δὲ τῆς Μαξιμοῦς ἡ πάντολμος βραδύτης,
τὸ τί ἐργάζου μετ᾿ αὐτῆς ἐγὼ γὰρ οὐ γινώσκω·
ἔστι καὶ τοίνυν ὁ Θεὸς ὁ τὰ κρυπτὰ γινώσκων,
ὃς συγχωρήσει σοι, καλέ, ταύτην τὴν ἁμαρτίαν·
ἀλλ᾿ ὅρα μή, νεώτερε, πάλιν καὶ τοῦτο πράξῃς,   2665
καὶ ἀποδώσῃ σοι Θεὸς ὁ κρίνων δικαιοσύνην·
ἐγὼ δὲ τὰς ἐλπίδας μου εἰς Θεὸν ἀνεθέμην,
ὅστις διαφυλάξει σε καὶ σώσει τὴν ψυχήν σου,
καὶ χαίρειν ἀξιώσει με τὰ πάντερπνά σου κάλλη
εἰς χρόνους πλείστους καὶ καλούς, πανεύμνοστέ μου κύρκα."

Λόγοις δ᾿ ὅμως πειθανικοῖς αὐτὴν παρεκρούομην,   2671
ἀγγέλλων τε τὸν πόλεμον τῆς Μαξιμοῦς ἀρχῆθεν,

* * *

χεῖρα ὅπως ἐπλήγωσα τὴν δεξιὰν ἐκείνης   GRO VI 826

* * *

προσέθηκα καὶ αἵματος ῥύσιν πολλὴν γενέσθαι,   TRE 2674
ἐξ οὗ θανεῖν τῇ Μαξιμῷ παρὰ μικρὸν συνέβη,   2675

* * *

2664 συγχωρήσεισει.   2666 ἀποδούσει.   2670 πανεύμνωστε.   2671
πιθανικοῖς.   2672 ἀγγέλων.   826 Avec ce vers nous reprenons le texte du
ms. de Grotta-Ferrata.   2674 πολὴν.

3263 προπέμψας ἐκεῖθεν. Almost 'saying   lously 'fut vivement affligée de mon
good-bye there'; cf. προπεμπτήριος   départ'.
λόγος, &c.   3272 ἀντίληψιν. Cf. 1 Cor. xii. 28
3268 ὑποχώρησιν ἠνάγκαζε. See above   ἀντιλήψεις, 'helps'.
2256 and TRE 1006 'tried to con-   3275 πάντολμος βραδύτης 'daring . . .
strain my returning'. Legrand ridicu-   slowness'; intentionally humorous.

Our shame and union being all fulfilled;
Leaving her then and sending her away
I spoke a word that might console perhaps,
"Go, my girl, go in peace, do not forget me."
I mounted on my horse and crossed the river.
She having bathed her maidenhead in water
Tried sorely to constrain me to return.
    Then having come back to my own beloved,
I got down from my horse, greedily kissed her   3270
And said, " See you, my soul your own avenger,
And helper the Creator has provided?"
She having in her soul some jealousy
Answered, "For all things I give thanks, my lord;
What stings me is Maximo's daring delay;
What you were doing with her I know not;
But there is surely God knows what is hidden,
And will forgive this sin of yours, my friend;
But see, young man, you do this not again,
Or God shall pay you back, who judges righteousness;   3280
And I have laid up all my hopes in God,
Who will preserve you and will save your soul,
And grant me to enjoy your sweetest beauties
For many years and good, my charming pet."
Yet did I cheat her with persuasive words
Telling Maximo's battle from the start,

*   *   *

How that I wounded her in the right hand,

*   *   *

I added that there was much flow of blood
From which nearly chanced Maximo to die,

*   *   *

3284 πανεύμνοστέ μου κύρκα. See above
1361, 2566.
3285 πειθανικοῖς seems to be unre-
corded. παρεκρουόμην classical in
this sense.
3287 GRO here resumes (vi. 826); but
just after the restart another couplet
has dropped out; or at least the
sense is defective, and to remedy it
a couplet has been taken from TRE.

(The couplet taken is numbered in
Legrand's text 2674, 2675; but
should be 2673, 2674; Legrand's
2655 is really 2654.) The defective
sense in GRO has led to the insertion
of an unmetrical καί at the beginning
of GRO vi. 827 which must be cut
out when the missing couplet is
restored.

καὶ εἰ μὴ θᾶττον ἐπέζευον καὶ ἐπέβρεχον ὕδωρ GRO VI 827
ταύτην οἰκτείρας ὡς γυνὴν καὶ ἀσθενῆ τῇ φύσει·
"Τὴν μὲν χεῖρα ἀπέπλυνα τὴν πληγὴν καταδήσας,
διὰ τοῦτο ἐβράδυνα, φῶς μου μεμυρισμένον, 830
ἵν' ὅπως μὴ ὀνειδισθῶ ὡς γυναῖκα φονεύσας."
Ταῦτα εἰπών, ἀναψυχὴν ἐλάμβανεν ἡ κόρη,
ἀληθεύειν νομίσασα ἐμὲ ἐν τοῖς ῥηθεῖσιν.

Εἶτα καὶ κατὰ νοῦν βαλὼν τὰ ῥήματα τῆς κόρης,
καὶ ὅλως τῷ θυμῷ αὐτὸς εἰς ἄκρον ὑπερζέσας, 835
καβαλλικεύω παρευθύς, δῆθεν εἰς τὸ κυνῆγιν,
καὶ ταύτην δὲ καταλαβὼν ἀνηλεῶς ἀνεῖλον,
μοιχείαν, φόνον τότε γὰρ ἐκτελέσας ἀθλίως·
καὶ οὕτως ὑποστρέψας γε ἔνθα ἦτον ἡ κόρη,
καὶ ἐκεῖσε τὴν ἅπασαν ποιήσαντες ἡμέραν 840
ἀμφότεροι κατήλθομεν τῇ ἐξῆς ἐν τῇ τένδᾳ,
καὶ ἐπὶ τὴν ἀπόλαυσιν τῶν λειμώνων ἐκείνων·
καὶ μεθ' ἡμέρας σκέψεως καὶ βουλῆς παγκαλλίστης,
ἐν τῷ Εὐφράτῃ ἔκρινα τὴν οἴκησιν ποιῆσαι,
κατασκευάσαι τε λαμπρὸν καὶ ἐξαίσιον οἶκον. 845

3290 Read εἰ μὴ θᾶττον.

ADDITIONAL NOTES

2749 ἀλλὰ μονος διάγειν. In the Norse Eddas Sigurd gives a similar answer to the
dying dragon Fafnir—'I am called the Wild-thing Glorious, and alone I wend
on the earth' (William Morris, *Sigurd the Volsung*, Bk. II) ; and Lord Raglan has
reminded us (*The Hero*, 1936; pp. 194, 273, etc.) that loneliness is a characteristic
of all popular heroes.

3180 The origin of βένετος seems to be unknown. The earliest ref. given by L.
& S. is Juv. iii. 170 (*veneto duroque cucullo*) where the connotation is vague; so it
is in Mart. iii. 74, 4, where *venetum lutum* sounds like blue lias used as a depilatory.
Florio (1598), as we learn from O.E.D., gives '*Veneto*, a light or Venice blew, a
Turkie colour'—(i.e. turquoise). So also Cotgrave (1611). But Venice blue is
unknown to modern colour merchants either in Paris or London. We cannot say
that any blue owes a name to Venice as Prussian blue is called after its discovery
in Berlin in 1704. As for the colours of the Circus their origin is as obscure as the
beginnings of the Circus itself, and so is their political significance; 'the problem
how the Demes came to be connected with the colours of the Circus has still to
be solved', says Bury (Gibbon vol. iv, App. 12). Blue colours may have been
adopted by victorious teams sent to Rome by Venetian horse-breeders. It is
equally possible that Malalas (Bonn, p. 176) is right when he says that the
colour was so called because ἐκεῖθεν ἐξέρχεται τὰ κυανὰ τοῦτ' ἐστὶ τὰ βενέτζια
βάμματα τῶν ἱματίων, although he does not inspire much confidence after telling
us that πράσινος is derived from *praesens*.

Had I not jumped off quickly and wetted it,   3290
Pitying her as a woman weak by nature:
"I washed her hand well binding up the wound;
Therefore I tarried, O my scented light,
That I should not be blamed for killing a woman."
When I said this the Girl had some relief,
Thinking the truth had been in what I said.
Then having taken the Girl's words to mind,
Myself all boiling over in much rage,
Forthwith I mounted as if for the chase,
And having caught I slew her ruthlessly,   3300
Adulteress, performed the sorry murder;
And so having returned where the Girl was,
When we had spent the whole day in that place,
We both came down the next day to the tent,
For the enjoyment of those meadows there.
After a day of thought and excellent counsel,
On the Euphrates I resolved to dwell,
And build a dwelling bright and marvellous."

3296 At this point TRE Book VII comes to an end. The next six lines of Christian murder are found only in GRO.

3301 μοιχείαν, a form not elsewhere recorded—'adulteress'—but μοιχεία, adultery, 3066.

3302 i.e. on top of the hill.

3306 μεθ' ἡμέρας. The sense here is clearly 'after a day'; but above 2310, 2912, 'with the dawn'.
βουλῆς παγκαλλίστης. The line seems to mean 'After a day's consideration and taking the best possible advice'.

ΛΟΓΟΣ ΕΒΔΟΜΟΣ

Βασίλειος ὁ θαυμαστὸς καὶ Διγενὴς Ἀκρίτης,
τῶν Καππαδόκων ὁ τερπνὸς καὶ πανευθαλὴς ἔρνος,
ὁ τῆς ἀνδρείας στέφανος, ἡ κεφαλὴ τῆς τόλμης,
πάντων τῶν νέων ὁ τερπνὸς καὶ παγκάλλιστος κόσμος,
μετὰ τὸ πάσας ἀνδρικῶς τὰς ἄκρας ὑποτάξαι,   5
πλείστας τε πόλεις κατασχὼν καὶ χώρας ἀπειθούντων,   63 vᵒ.
οἰκῆσαι ἡρετίσατο πλησίον τοῦ Εὐφράτου.
Οὗτος δὲ πάντων ποταμὸς ὁ κάλλιστος ὑπῆρχεν,
τὴν κρήνην ἔχων ἐξ αὐτοῦ μεγάλου παραδείσου·
διὰ τοῦτο γλυκύτητα ἔχει εὐωδεστάτην,   10
ψυχρότητα χιόνος τε ἀρτίως λελυμένης·
ἐξ αὐτοῦ δὲ τοῦ ποταμοῦ ὕδωρ μετοχετεύσας,
ἄλλον τερπνὸν παράδεισον ἐφύτευσεν ἐκεῖθεν,
ἄλσος ξένον, εὐθέατον τοῖς ὀφθαλμοῖς τῷ ὄντι.
Περὶ τὸ ἄλσος τεῖχος ἦν αὔταρκες μὲν εἰς ὕψος,   15
πλευρὰς δὲ ἔχον τέσσαρας ὑπὸ ξυστῶν μαρμάρων·
ἔσωθεν δὲ ἡ τῶν φυτῶν πανήγυρις ἐκόμα,
φαιδρῶς οἱ κλάδοι ἔθαλλον προσπίπτοντες ἀλλήλοις,
τοσαύτη τις ἐτύγχανε τῶν δένδρων ἀμιλλία·
ἄμπελοι ἑκατέρωθεν ἐξήρτηντο ὡραῖοι,   20
κάλαμοι ἐπεφύοντο εἰς ὕψος ἐπηρμένοι,
οἱ καρποὶ ἐξεκρέμαντο, ἀνθῶν τἄλλα ἐπ' ἄλλων,
ὁ λειμὼν φαιδρῶς ἔθαλλε τῶν δένδρων ὑποκάτω
ποικίλην ἔχων τὴν χρόαν τοῖς ἄνθεσιν ἀστράπτων,
τὰ μὲν εὐώδη νάρκισσα, ῥόδα τε καὶ μυρσίναι·   25
τὰ ῥόδα γῆς ἐτύγχανον πορφυρόβαφος κόσμος,
γάλακτος ἔστιλβον χρόαν οἱ νάρκισσοι ἐν μέρει,
τὰ ἴα ἀπαστράπτοντα χρόαν εἶχον θαλάσσης

---

2 Il serait peut-être mieux d'écrire τὸ τερπνὸν καὶ πανευθαλὲς, mais on risque, en
modifiant la langue, de corriger le poète. ἔρνος.   3 ἡ τῆς ἀνδρείας τόλμης.
et en marge, κεφαλὴ τῆς.   5 Ce vers est répété en tête du feuillet 63 verso.
8 ποταμῶν, que donne le ms. de Trébizonde (vers 2698) et celui d'Andros (vers
3900), serait plus correct.   10 διατοῦτο.   16 ἔχων.   22 ἀνθ' ὧν τ' ἄλλα.

3310 ἔρνος. See above 2873; and
εὐθέατον, the epithet there joined to
it, comes again below 3322.

3323–49 The first source of the whole
of this passage is Ach. Tat. I. xiv and
xv, too long to quote here; and see

BASIL the wondrous Twyborn Borderer,
The Kappadokians' sweet and blooming branch,   3310
The crown of bravery, the head of daring,
Sweet finest ornament of all the young,
After subduing bravely all the borders,
Taking many cities and lands of the unruly,
He chose to make his dwelling by Euphrates.
This was the fairest river of them all,
Having his source from that Great Paradise,
Wherefore he has a very fragrant sweetness,
And a coldness of freshly melted snow.
From that same river having channelled water,   3320
He planted there another pleasant paradise,
A strange grove good indeed for eyes to look on.
Round the grove was a wall in height sufficient,
And having its four sides of polished marbles.
Within the long-haired plants held festival,
Branches bloomed gladly falling on each other,
Such was the emulation of the trees.
On either side were hanging lovely vines,
Reeds growing there were lifted up on high,
The fruits hung down, and flowers one on another,   3330
The meadow brightly bloomed beneath the trees,
Its hue was dappled, and it flashed with flowers,
Sweet-smelling daffodils, roses, and myrtles;
Roses were earth's purple-dyed ornament,
Daffodils gleamed in turn a milky hue,
The twinkling violets had a hue of the sea,

also Longus iv. 2. Some of it (e.g. the parrots) reappears in ESC 1655ff. 3325 ἡ τῶν φυτῶν πανήγυρις ἐκόμα. See also TRE 2711. This sophisticated line comes from Meliten. 2451 (and in 2450 θεάμα ξένον, cf. above 3322); and originally from Ach. Tat. I. xv. It has become a common place; see e.g. Ψυχάρης, Τὸ Ταξίδι μου, p. 100

(ch. xiii). 3329 This line is repeated from 2479. 3330 τ' ἄλλα ἐπ' ἄλλων. A dislocation of ἀλλεπάλληλος, accumulative or successive, for which see the dictionaries. Cf. ἄλλος ἐξ ἄλλου above 1916. 3333 νάρκισσα, but 3335 νάρκισσοι. 3336 ff. See Ach. Tat. I. xv. 5 and Meliten. 2481 ff.

ἐν γαλήνῃ ὑπὸ λεπτῆς σαλευομένης αὔρας·
ὕδωρ ἀφθόνως πάντοθεν ἔρρεε τῷ λειμῶνι.   30
Ὀρνίθων γένη ἱκανὰ ἐνέμοντο ἐκεῖσε,   64 rᵒ.
τὰ μὲν κολακευόμενα τροφὴν ἐν τοῖς ἀνθρώποις,
τὰ δὲ λοιπὰ ἐλεύθερον τὸ πτερὸν κεκτημένα
ἔπαιζον ἐποχούμενα πρὸς τῶν δένδρων τὰ ὕψη,
τὰ μὲν ᾄδοντα ᾄσμασι λιγυρῶς τὰ ὀρνίθια,   35
τὰ δὲ ἀγλαϊζόμενα τῇ στολῇ τῶν πτερύγων,
χειροήθεις ταῶνες μέν, ψιττακοὶ καὶ οἱ κύκνοι,
οἱ μὲν κύκνοι ἐν ὕδασι τὴν νομὴν ἐποιοῦντο,
ἐν τοῖς κλώνοις οἱ ψιττακοὶ ᾖδον περὶ τὰ δένδρα,
οἱ ταῶνες τὰς πτέρυγας κυκλοῦντες εἰς τὰ ἄνθη,   40
ἀντέλαμπεν ἡ τῶν ἀνθῶν ἐν ταῖς πτέρυξι θέα.
    Μέσον αὐτοῦ τοῦ θαυμαστοῦ καὶ τερπνοῦ παραδείσου,
οἶκον τερπνὸν ἀνήγειρεν ὁ γενναῖος Ἀκρίτης
εὐμεγέθη, τετράγωνον ἐκ λίθων πεπρισμένων,
ἄνωθεν δὲ μετὰ σεμνῶν κιόνων καὶ θυρίδων·   45
τοὺς ὀρόφους ἐκόσμησε πάντας μετὰ μουσίου
ἐκ μαρμάρων πολυτελῶν τῇ αἴγλῃ ἀστραπτόντων·
τὸ ἔδαφος ἐφαίδρυνεν, ἐψήφωσεν ἐν λίθοις,
Ἔσωθεν δὲ τριώροφα ποιήσας ὑπερῷα,
ἔχοντα ὕψος ἱκανόν, ὀρόφους παμποικίλους,   50
ἀνδριάντας σταυροειδεῖς, πεντακούβουκλα ξένα
μετὰ μαρμάρων φαεινῶν λίαν ἀστραπηβόλων.
Τοσοῦτον δὲ ἐκάλλυνε τὸ ἔργον ὁ τεχνίτης,
ὥστε νομίζειν ὑφαντὰ τὰ ὁρώμενα εἶναι
ἔκ τε τῶν λίθων τῆς φαιδρᾶς καὶ πολυμόρφου θέας·   55
τὸ ἔδαφος κατέστρωσεν ἐκ λίθων ὀνυχίτων
ἠκονημένων ἰσχυρῶς, ὡς δοκεῖν τοὺς ὁρῶντας
ὕδωρ ὑπάρχειν πεπηγὸς εἰς κρυστάλλινον φύσιν.   64 vᵒ.
Ἀμφοτέρωθεν ἵδρυσε τῶν μερῶν ἐκ πλαγίου

    37 μὲν ταῶνες.   48 ἔδαφος [sic Legr.].   56 ἔδαφος.

3339 Line repeated from 2482 above.
Lines 3329, 3342, 3345–9 are all
repeated with slight variations from
the opening passage of Book VI
(above 2479–89).
3359 ἀνδριάντας σταυροειδεῖς πεντακούβουκλα ξένα. Read ἀνδρώνας δὲ.
See Meliten., op. cit. 829, 830, 838

ἀνδρῶνα . . . σταυροειδῆ . . . πεντακούβουκλα. The redactor of GRO
must have copied this, misreading
ἀνδρῶνα. It can hardly be supposed
that any writer would have misunderstood a familiar word like
ἀνδριάντας. For πεντακούβουκλα see
Ducange, s.v. κουβούκλειον: 'Tri-

When it is calm stirred by a gentle breeze.
Plenty of water flowed everywhere in the meadow.
There many sorts of birds had their living;
Some flattered for their food on humankind,   3340
The rest of them having their feathers free
Played riding on the summits of the trees,
Some little birds there singing their shrill songs,
Some with the vesture of their wings resplendent;
There peacocks tame and parrots were and swans;
The swans upon the waters had their living,
On the boughs the parrots sang about the trees,
The peacocks in the flowers circling their wings,
The show of flowers shone in their wings again.

Amid this wondrous pleasant paradise   3350
The noble Borderer raised a pleasant dwelling,
Of goodly size, four-square of ashlared stone,
With stately columns over and casements;
The ceilings with mosaic he all adorned,
Of precious marbles flashing with their gleam;
The pavement he made bright inlaid with pebbles;
Within he made three-vaulted upper chambers,
Of goodly height, the vaults all variegated,
And chambers cruciform, and strange pavilions,
With shining marbles throwing gleams of light.   3360
The artist had so beautified the work
That woven seemed to be what there was seen
From the stones' gay and many-figured show.
The floor of it he paved with onyx stones,
So firmly polished those who saw might think
Water was there congealed in icy nature.
He laid out in the wings on either side

clinium quinque cubicula complectens. Ita dictum triclinium M. Palatii Constantinopolitani apud Const. Porph. in Basilio [Vita Basil. Maced. Imp.].' See also Anna Comn. *Alex.* (Reiff.) ii, p. 313 μέρος ἕτερον τοῦ πεντορόφου οἰκήματος.

3361–3 Copied almost word for word from Meliten. 839–41.

3365, 3366 (cf. TRE 2834, AND 4034).

Almost word for word from Meliten. 912, 913. Note that Meliten. 912, 913 are repeated in Meliten. 681 ff.; and that Meliten. 824–6 and 861 are reflected in TRE 2768 and 2774— but not in GRO.

3367, 3368 See Meliten. 844–6. GRO seems again to have avoided the words ἀνδρώνων, ἀνδρώνας.

χαμοτρικλίνους θαυμαστούς, εὐμήκεις, χρυσωρόφους,   60
ἐν οἷς πάντων τὰ τρόπαια τῶν πάλαι ἐν ἀνδρείᾳ
λαμψάντων ἀνιστόρησε χρυσόμουσα, ὡραῖα,
τὴν τοῦ Σαμψὼν ἀρχίσας τε πρὸς ἀλλοφύλους μάχην,
λέοντα ὅπως ἔσχισε τῇ χειρὶ παραδόξως,
πύλας ὅπως μετὰ κλειθρῶν πόλεως ἀλλοφύλων   65
ἐν τῷ λόφῳ ἠγάγετο, ὁπότε ἀπεκλείσθη·
ἀλλοφύλων τοὺς ἐμπαιγμοὺς καὶ τὰς ἐξολοθρεύσεις·
τελευταῖον τὴν τοῦ ναοῦ κατάλυσιν ἀθρόαν
τὴν γεναμένην παρ' αὐτοῦ ἐν ταῖς πάλαι ἡμέραις,
καὶ αὐτὸν ἀπολλύμενον μετὰ τῶν ἀλλοφύλων.   70
Μέσον παράγει τὸν Δαβὶδ χωρὶς ὅπλων παντοίων,
μόνην σφενδόνην τῇ χειρὶ κατέχων καὶ τὸν λίθον·
ἐκεῖθεν δὲ τὸν Γολιὰθ μέγαν τῇ ἡλικίᾳ,
καὶ τῇ ἰδέᾳ φοβερὸν πολύν τε ἐν ἰσχύϊ,
πεφραγμένον ἐν κεφαλῇ μέχρι ποδῶν σιδήρῳ   75
καὶ τῇ χειρὶ ἀκόντιον φέροντα ὡς ἀττίον
ὁλοσίδηρον τῇ χροᾷ τῇ τοῦ ζωγράφου τέχνῃ·
ἔγραψε τούτου καὶ αὐτὰ τὰ κινήματα πολέμου·
λίθῳ εὐστόχως τε βληθεὶς ὁ Γολιὰθ εὐθέως
ἐπὶ τὴν γῆν κατέπεσε τρωμένος παραυτίκα,   80
καὶ τὸν Δαβὶδ δραμόντα τε καὶ ἄραντα τὸ ξίφος
καὶ τεμόντα τὴν κεφαλὴν καὶ λαβόντα τὸ νῖκος.

Εἶτα τὸν φόβον τοῦ Σαούλ, φυγὴν τοῦ πραοτάτου,
τὰς μυρίας ἐπιβουλάς, Θεοῦ τὰς ἐκδικήσεις.

Ἀχιλλέως ἱστόρησε τοὺς μυθικοὺς πολέμους·   65 rᵒ.   85
τὸ κάλλος Ἀγαμέμνονος, φυγὴν τὴν ὀλεθρίαν·
Πηνελόπην τὴν σώφρονα, τοὺς κτανθέντας νυμφίους·
Ὀδυσσέως τὴν θαυμαστὴν πρὸς τὸν Κύκλωπα τόλμην·

60 χρυσορόφους.   74 εἰδέα, et en marge ἰδαία.   78 Avant πολέμου, je
supprime τοῦ, afin de rendre le vers correct.   85 ἀχιλέως.   88 ὀδυσσέος.

3371 ἀλλοφύλους. The Philistines are always so called in LXX.
3375 ἐξολοθρεύσεις does not make very good sense. Perhaps read ἐξοφθαλμίσεις.
3381 ἡλικία, 'stature' as usual.
3382 ἰδέα, rare in sense of 'appearance'.
3383-6 See Meliten. 1967, 1973-7, Meliten. 1977 κινήματα κινεῖσθαι. In

Meliten. the statue of Goliath seems to move. Here the mosaics represented the successive stages of the battle. The simile of the weaver's beam is from LXX, 2 Kings (= A.V. 2 Sam.) xxi. 19. ἀττίον for the usual form ἀντίον (e.g. Ar. Thesm. 822) is the common vernacular denasalization.

Reclining-rooms, long, wondrous, golden-roofed,
Where the triumphs of all, of old in valour
Who shone, he painted fair in gold mosaic;   3370
Began with Sampson's fight against the gentiles,
How with his hands he strangely rent the lion,
How of the gentiles' town the gates and bars
He bore on to the hill, when he was prisoned;
The gentiles mocking him, and their destructions;
Lastly the temple's complete overthrow
By him accomplished in those days of old,
And himself being destroyed with the gentiles.
David midmost he showed, without all arms,
Sling only bearing in his hand and stone;   3380
Beyond Goliath too in stature great,
Dreadful to look at, mighty in his strength,
From head to foot in iron fenced about,
Bearing a javelin like a weaver's beam
In hue all iron by the painter's art.
He painted too the very moves of war:
Struck rightly by the stone Goliath straight
Fell wounded to the ground immediately;
How David running, lifting up his sword,
Cutting his head off had the victory.   3390
And then the fear of Saul, the meek one's flight,
The thousand plots, and God His vengeances.
   The fabled wars he painted of Achilles;
Agamemnon the fair, the baleful flight,
Penelope the wise, the suitors slain,
Odysseus' wondrous daring of the Kyklops;

3393 ἱστόρησε, 3386 ἔγραψε, 3385
ζωγράφου τέχνη, and 3370 ἀνιστόρησε:
various words for painting.
3393–6 TRE followed by AND differs
considerably from GRO in this book
but also shows indebtedness to
Meliteniotes. The corruption of GRO
3394, 3395 in TRE 2817—καὶ τοῦ
᾽Αλδελαγᾶ φησιν τὴν ὀλεθρίαν πάνυ
᾽Ολόπης τε τὴν συμφοράν—(the version
which was the first to appear—and
with a French translation), a cor-

ruption followed by AND 4022 and
PAS 400, led Krumbacher to speak
of 'eine sonst unbekannte Leidens-
geschichte des Paares Aldelagas und
Olope' (Byz. Litt. (1897), p. 855);
and the phantom lovers Aldelaga
and Olope (or, as in AND, Aldegala
and Elope) have since wandered into
Entwistle's European Balladry (1939),
p. 304, Oman's Unfortunate Col.
Despard (1922), p. 95, and other
works.

Βελλεροφόντην κτείναντα Χίμαιραν τὴν πυρφόρον·
Ἀλεξάνδρου τὰ τρόπαια, τὴν τοῦ Δαρείου ἧτταν·   90
Κανδάκης τὰ βασίλεια καὶ τὴν αὐτῆς σοφίαν,
τὴν πρὸς Βραχμᾶνας ἄφιξιν, αὖθις πρὸς Ἀμαζόνας,
λοιπά τε κατορθώματα τοῦ σοφοῦ Ἀλεξάνδρου,
ἄλλα τε πλήθη θαυμαστά, πολυειδεῖς ἀνδρείας.
Τὰ τοῦ Μωσέως θαύματα, πληγὰς τῶν Αἰγυπτίων,   95
Ἰουδαίων τὴν ἔξοδον, γογγυσμοὺς ἀγνωμόνων,
Θεοῦ τὴν ἀγανάκτησιν, θεράποντος δεήσεις,
καὶ Ἰησοῦ τὰς τοῦ Ναυῆ ἐνδόξους ἀριστείας.
Ταῦτα καὶ ἄλλα πλείονα ἐν τοῖς δυσὶ τρικλίνοις
ὁ Διγενὴς ἱστόρησε χρυσόμουσα ποιήσας,   100
ἃ τοῖς ὁρῶσιν ἄπειρον τὴν ἡδονὴν παρεῖχον.
Ἐντὸς τοῦ οἴκου τῆς αὐλῆς ὑπῆρχε τὸ πεδίον
πολὺ ἔχον διάστημα εἴς τε μῆκος καὶ πλάτος·
τούτου ἐν μέσῳ ἵδρυσε ναόν, ἔνδοξον ἔργον,
ἁγίου ἐν ὀνόματι μάρτυρος Θεοδώρου·   105
καὶ ἐν αὐτῷ τὸν ἴδιον πανέντιμον πατέρα
θάπτει κομίσας τὸν νεκρὸν ἀπὸ Καππαδοκίας,
λίθοις τὸ μνῆμα φαεινοῖς ὡς ἔπρεπε κοσμήσας.
Τότε πεῖραν ὁ θαυμαστὸς πρῶτον θλίψεως ἔσχε·
μαθὼν γὰρ νόσον τῷ πατρὶ περιελθοῦσαν τότε,   65 vᵒ. 110
καὶ ὅτι πέφυκε δεινὴ θανάτῳ γειτνιῶσα,
ἔσπευδε τοῦ καταλαβεῖν τὴν Καππαδόκων χώραν·
πλησίον δὲ τοῦ γονικοῦ ὡς ἐγένετο οἴκου,
ὀδυρομένους ἅπαντας ὁρᾷ τοὺς συναντῶντας·
καί, μαθὼν ὅτι ὁ πατὴρ ἀπέλιπε τὸν βίον,   115
τὴν ἐσθῆτα διέρρηξε καὶ τοῦ ἵππου κατῆλθεν,
ἔνδοθεν δὲ γενόμενος, περιπλακεὶς τὸ σῶμα,
θρηνῳδῶν ἀπεφθέγγετο μετὰ δακρύων τάδε·
"Ἀνάστα, πάτερ, θέασαι τὸ φίλτατόν σου τέκνον·
θέασαι τὸν μονογενῆ, λαλιὰν μικρὰν φθέγξον·   120
νουθέτησαι καὶ βούλευσαι, μή με σιγῶν παρέλθῃς."
Εἶτα πάλιν αὐξήσας γε ἐπὶ πολὺ τὸν θρῆνον,
βοῶν ἐναπεφθέγγετο εἰς εὐήκοον πάντων·

89 χίμαιρραν.   92 βραγμᾶνας.   112 καππαδώκων.

3399 τὰ βασίλεια. Perhaps a mistake for   usage in τὰ οἰκεῖα κ.τ.λ. noted above.
βασιλείαν or βασίλισσαν but probably   See Meliten. 2204 Κανδάκης τε
an extension of the neuter plural   βασίλεια. Κανδάκη appears in ESC

Bellerophon slaying the fiery Chimaira;
Alexander's triumphs, rout of Darius,
And Kandake her queenship and her wisdom,
His coming to the Brahmans, then to the Amazons,   3400
And other feats of the wise Alexander,
And hosts more marvels, manifold braveries.
Moses his miracles, the plagues of Egypt,
Exodus of the Jews, ungrateful murmurs,
And God's vexation, and His servant's prayers,
Joshua son of Nun his glorious feats.
This and much else in those two dining-halls
With gold mosaic Digenes depicted
Which gave to those who saw a boundless pleasure.
Within the house was the floor of the court,   3410
Both in length and in breadth having great dimension.
Herein he built a glorious work, a temple
In the name of Theodore the saint and martyr.
In it his own all-honourable father
He buried, the body brought from Kappadokia,
Duly with shining stones the tomb adorning.
Then first the hero had knowledge of mourning;
Learning disease then come upon his father,
And grievous that it was, neighbouring death,
He hastened to reach the Kappadokes' country.   3420
And when he was come near his parents' home,
He saw lamenting all who came to meet him;
And learning that his father had gone from life,
He rent his raiment, got down from his horse,
And being come within embraced the body,
Began to voice with tears this threnody:
'Father, arise, behold your dearest child,
Behold your only son, utter some word;
Counsel, advise, nor pass me by in silence.'
Then again louder lifting up the dirge,   3430
He cried his utterance that all should hear:

1671 as βασίλισσα τοῦ πρὸς Παρα-
σογάρδου (i.e. Πασαργάδα, Persia).
3407 τρικλίνοις. See above 3368; one in
each wing.
3415 Note explicit statement of the
move from Cappadocia to Euphrates.
3423 In TRE 2884, AND 4090, the
father ἐθνήσκει, was dying, not dead,
which involves some modifications.

" Οὐκ ἀποκρίνῃ μοι τῷ σῷ ποθεινοτάτῳ τέκνῳ;
οὐκ ἀποφθέγγῃ μοι λαλῶν ὡς ἔθος εἶχες πάντα;   125
οἴμοι σιγᾷ τὸ μαντικὸν καὶ θεηγόρον στόμα·
οἴμοι ἐκλείσθη ἡ φωνὴ ἡ πᾶσιν ἡδυτάτη·
ποῦ δὲ τὸ φῶς τῶν ὀφθαλμῶν, ποῦ τῆς μορφῆς τὸ κάλλος;
τίς τὰς χεῖρας ἐδέσμευσε; τίς τὴν ἰσχὺν ἀφεῖλε;
τίς τῶν ποδῶν ἐκώλυσε τὸν ἀνείκαστον δρόμον;   130
τίς ἀγάπην τὴν ἄπειρον τὴν πρὸς ἐμέ σου, πάτερ,
χωρῖσαι κατετόλμησεν; ὢ τῆς παρανομίας,
ὢ τῆς ἀθρόας συμφορᾶς, ὢ τῆς πικρᾶς ὀδύνης!
πῶς μετὰ πόνου τὴν ψυχὴν παρέδωκας καὶ λύπης,
καλῶν με ἐξ ὀνόματος ἄχρι τέλους ζωῆς σου;   135
ὢ εὐτυχέστατος ἐγὼ παρὰ βραχεῖαν ὥραν
πάντως εἰ ἤκουσα φωνῆς, εὐχῆς τῆς τελευταίας,   66 rᵒ.
καὶ ταῖς ἀγκάλαις τὴν ψυχὴν ταῖς ἐμαῖς ἐπαφῆκες,
λοῦσαι τὸ σῶμα ταῖς χερσὶν εἶχον ἂν ταῖς ἰδίαις,
καὶ καλύψαι τοὺς ὀφθαλμοὺς τοὺς σούς, ὢ καλὲ πάτερ·   140
νυνὶ δὲ ἀθλιώτερος εἰμὶ παντὸς ἀνθρώπου,
καὶ τὰ σπλάγχνα τιτρώσκει μου ἡ ἄμετρος ὀδύνη·
εἴθε μοι μᾶλλον τοῦ θανεῖν ἢ κατιδεῖν τοιαῦτα·
τί ἀγαθόν, ὢ θάνατε, ἐφθόνησας τοιοῦτον,
λαβεῖν ἐμὲ ἀντὶ πατρὸς καὶ τοῦτον φθάσαι ζῶντα,   145
καὶ ἀπεφάνθης ἄδικος παρὰ βραχεῖαν ὥραν; "
Ὡς ταῦτα καὶ τὰ ὅμοια ὁ Διγενὴς ἐθρήνει,
πεποίηκεν, ὡς λέγεται, καὶ τοὺς λίθους θρηνῆσαι,
καὶ σὺν αὐτῷ ἡ θαυμαστὴ μήτηρ ἡ τοῦ Ἀκρίτου·
καὶ οὕτω συνετέλεσαν κηδεύσαντες ἐντίμως   150
τοῦ πατρός τε τὴν τελευτὴν οὐκ ὀλίγας ἡμέρας.
Εἶτα λαβὼν ὁ θαυμαστὸς τὸ σῶμα τοῦ πατρός του,
καὶ τὴν μητέρα μετ' αὐτοῦ ἦλθεν εἰς τὰ οἰκεῖα,
καὶ οὕτω θάπτει δεύτερον ἐντίμως τὸν πατέρα
εἰς τὸν ναὸν ὅνπερ αὐτὸς ἀνήγειρεν ἐκ πόθου·   155
καὶ διῆγε μετὰ τοῦ υἱοῦ ἡ μήτηρ τοῦ Ἀκρίτου.
Τὰ δὲ μετέπειτα αὐτοῖς πολυέραστα ἔργα

132 χωρίσαι.   136 ἀτυχέστατος.

─────────────

3444 παρὰ βραχεῖαν ὥραν ought to mean
'except for a short time'—a meaning
which accords with the TRE version
(TRE 2901) 'I was not able to find

you alive except for a few minutes'.
This may suggest that the story that
the father was still alive (as in TRE)
was altered by the redactor of GRO.

'Will you not answer me, your most-loved child?
Utter me words as you were always wont?
Still the prophetic God-discoursing mouth,
Alas, closed up the voice to all most sweet.
Where are the eyes their light, the form's beauty?
Who bound your hands? Who took your strength away?
Who stayed the unmatched running of your feet?
And who your boundless love, father, for me
Has dared to put asunder? O transgression,   3440
O complete overthrow, and bitter ache!
With pain how gave you up your soul and sorrow,
Calling on me by name till your life's end?
Most happy I, but for a little time
If I had heard your voice at all, your last prayer,
If in my arms you had released your soul;
With my own hands I should have washed your body,
My good father, and covered up your eyes.
More wretched am I now than any man,
And measureless the ache pierces my bowels.   3450
Would I had rather died than seen such things.
O death, why did you grudge me such a boon,
To be taken instead, having found him alive,
Why prove your spite by such a little time?'
This and the like as Digenes was mourning,
Even the stones, they say, he had made mourn,
And with the Borderer his wondrous mother.
Thus honourably they paid the last offices
And funeral of his father for some days.
The hero then taking his father's body,   3460
His mother with him, came to his own house,
So buried his father honourably again
In the temple he had built to his desire.
And with her son abode the Borderer's mother.
  What were thereafter their most lovely doings,

3453 λαβεῖν ἐμὲ ἀντὶ πατρὸς καὶ τοῦτον
φθάσαι ζῶντα. A highly compressed
description of the boon death has
refused to grant: 'To take me instead
of my father, and me to have found
him still alive.'

3460 ὁ θαυμαστός. See above 3417.
3461 τὰ οἰκεῖα. See above 1320.
3463 ἐκ πόθου may mean only 'lovingly,
  with a will'; or referring to the temple
  'to his desire'. Cf. 2908 ἐν πόθῳ.
3465 πολυέραστα; cf. 3473 πολυώραια.

μικρὸν ἐναποφήναντες ὑμῖν λέξομεν τάδε.
Οὕτω διῆγον χαίροντες καθ' ἑκάστην ἡμέραν·
πολλάκις δὲ ἐλάμβανε κιθάραν πρὸ τοῦ τέλους   160
τοῦ ἀρίστου ὁ θαυμαστός, καὶ ἐπῇδεν ἡ κόρη
μέλος, ὁποῖον Σειρηνῶν ἢ ποῖον ἀηδόνων
ὑπερέβαινεν ἡδονήν, τὰς ἀκοὰς ἐκπλῆττον·
τὸν ἦχον δὲ πρὸς ὀρχησμὸν ἐκτρέπων τῆς κιθάρας,   66 vᵒ.
εὐθὺς ἡ πολυώραια ἀνίστατο τῆς κλίνης,   165
βλαττὶν ἐξήπλωνεν ἐν γῇ, ἐπέβαινεν ἐν τούτῳ.
Φράσαι δὲ ὅλως ἀπορῶ κινήματα τῆς κόρης,
τὰς τῶν χειρῶν μεταστροφάς, ποδῶν τὰς μεταβάσεις·
ῥάως ἐφέροντο συχνῶς ἑπόμεναι τῷ ἤχῳ,
λυγίσματα ἀκόλουθα κρούσμασι τῆς κιθάρας.   170
'Ὡς γὰρ μέλιτος γλύκασμα τοῖς ἀγνοοῦσι πέλει
ἐφικτόν, οὕτω τὴν χαρὰν οὐκ ἔστιν ἀπαγγεῖλαι
καὶ τέρψιν τὴν ἐξαίσιον ἰδιωμάτων ταύτης.
Εἶθ' οὕτως ἀνιστάμενοι τῆς τραπέζης προσῆκον
τῶν ἡδέων ἐτρέφοντο, εἶτα πρὸς τὸν λειμῶνα   175
τὸν δηλωθέντα ἄνωθεν ὡραίου παραδείσου
σφόδρα ἀγαλλιώμενοι, Θεῷ εὐχαριστοῦντες
οἱ νέοι οἱ περίβλεπτοι καὶ εὐγενεῖς τῷ ὄντι.
Ἐν μόνον τούτων τὰς ψυχὰς ἐλύπει καθ' ἑκάστην,
ἀτεκνίας ἡ ἄσβεστος καὶ δεινοτάτη φλόγα·   180
ἧς μόνοι πεῖραν ἔλαβον οἱ τέκνων ἀποροῦντες,
μεγίστην τε τὴν συμφορὰν προξενεῖ τοῖς ἐν βίῳ·
ὑπὲρ τούτου ἐδέοντο τοῦ Θεοῦ καθ' ἑκάστην.
Καὶ τῆς πρώτης τῶν ἀρετῶν ἐσεμνύνοντο σφόδρα,
τῆς εὐποιίας λέγω δὴ καὶ τῆς ἐλεημοσύνης·   185
ὅμως θελήματι Θεοῦ ἥμαρτον τῆς ἐλπίδος,
ἀλλὰ λίαν ὡς σώφρονες τῷ Θεῷ ηὐχαρίστουν,
τοῖς οἰκείοις δὲ σφάλμασιν ἔγραφον τὴν αἰτίαν.
Ἐν τούτῳ νόσος τῇ μητρὶ ἐλθοῦσα τοῦ Ἀκρίτου,

162 σύριγγον. J'avais d'abord pensé à écrire σύριγγων ou συριγγῶν.   165
πολυωραία.   166 ἐξήπλων (sic).   169 ἐφέρωντο. ἑπόμεναι.   178 Je
supplée le premier οἱ.   179 ὄν. καθεκάστην.   183 καθεκάστην.   189
τούτω.

3466 μικρὸν ἐναποφήναντες suggests that   3470 Σειρήνων. Leg. from AND 4204.
the redactor may have omitted some   3471 ἡδονήν. See above 1338.
domestic details as given in TRE   3474 βλάττίν. Any silken fabric. See
2970 ff., AND 4180 ff.   above 896.

In part revealing we will tell you this.
Thus they abode rejoicing every day.
Often would take his lute before the end
Of dinner the hero, and the Girl would sing
A song, such as of nightingales or Sirens   3470
Surpassed the sweetness, and amazed the hearing;
And as the lute changed to a dancing mood
Straight the most lovely rising from the couch
Would spread the floor with silk, and tread on it.
I cannot tell the movements of the Girl,
Turns of her hands and changes of her feet,
Made lightly, quickly following the music,
Bendings accorded to the beating lute.
Not honey's sweetness is for those not knowing
Conceivable; so the joy cannot be told   3480
The wondrous delight of all her attitudes.
Thus rising from the table they with due
Delights were fed; and then towards the meadow
Described above, in that fair paradise
Rejoiced exceedingly, and thanking God,
Verily young and noble and renowned.
One thing alone grieved their souls every day
The unquenched and dreadful flame of childlessness,
Which only those in want of children know,
To those in life greatest misfortune brings;   3490
For this they used to pray God every day;
Themselves they prided on the first of virtues,
On doing good, I mean, and almsgiving,
But by the will of God failed of their hope,
Yet in their prudence gave much thanks to God,
And to their own faults they ascribed the cause.
 Meanwhile sickness came to the Borderer's mother,

3476 μεταστροφάς . . . μεταβάσεις. Cf.
above 1969.
3479 ὡς γὰρ μέλιτος γλύκασμα. Leg. οὐ
γάρ, as a negative has to be supplied
to make sense. γλύκασμα is a LXX
word.
3481 ἰδιωμάτων. See TRE 791 ἰδίωμα
τερπνόν, and Xanthoudides, Erotok.

gloss. s.v. διῶμα. The present use is
that from which the popular use
would easily develop.
3482, 3483 τῶν ἡδέων ἐτρέφοντο. It is
not clear if these delights are meta-
phorical. The following passage is
also obscure and lacks a main verb.

227

διὰ τεσσάρων ἡμερῶν τὴν φωνὴν ἐπαφῆκε·   190
ἰσχυρῶς αὐτὴν ἔκλαυσε καὶ ἐπένθησε λίαν·   67 rᵒ.
ὁ Διγενὴς ἐν μνήματι σὺν τῷ πατρὶ κηδεύει.

Ζήσασα μετὰ τελευτὴν τοῦ ἀνδρὸς ἔτη πέντε,
καὶ πᾶσιν ἐντρυφήσασα ἀγαθοῖς ἐν τῷ κόσμῳ,
ἡ ὄντως ἀξιέπαινος ἐν γυναιξὶ φανεῖσα,   195
ἡ ἐν τῷ κάλλει τρέψασα ποτὲ τοὺς πολεμίους
πολλοὺς ἐλευθερώσασα δεινῆς αἰχμαλωσίας,
καὶ εἰρήνην βραβεύσασα πόλεσί τε καὶ κώμαις
καὶ γὰρ ἐκ ταύτης ἡ ἀρχὴ γέγονε τῶν κρειττόνων
συνεργίᾳ τῇ θεϊκῇ τὴν ἔχθραν καθελοῦσα   200
καὶ χαρὰν ἀντεισάξασα πανταχοῦ καὶ εἰρήνην,
ῥίζαν καὶ κλάδον εὐγενῆ τεκοῦσα καὶ ὡραῖον·
ὃς πάντων τῶν Ἀγαρηνῶν φρυάγματα καθεῖλε,
καὶ πόλεις προενόμευσε καὶ τῷ κράτει συνῆψε.

Πρὸ γὰρ τούτου τοῦ θαυμαστοῦ καὶ γενναίου Ἀκρίτου,   205
ἀδεῶς ἐξερχόμενα γένη τῶν Αἰθιόπων
ἀφειδῶς ἐξηφάνιζον τὰς πόλεις τῶν Ῥωμαίων,
καὶ οἱ τῶν δούλων ἔκγονοι παῖδας τῶν ἐλευθέρων
τοὺς τιμίους καὶ εὐγενεῖς ἐπὶ δουλείαν ἦγον.

Ἡνίκα δὲ ὁ δι᾽ ἡμᾶς γεννηθεὶς ἐκ παρθένου   210
ὡς ἀγαθὸς ηὐδόκησε πάντας ἐλευθερῶσαι
τὴν θαυμαστὴν καὶ ἔνδοξον ποιεῖ οἰκονομίαν
φίλον γενέσθαι τὸν ἐχθρὸν καὶ ἐξ αὐτοῦ τεχθῆναι
τὸν τῆς ἀνδρείας στέφανον, τὸν Διγενῆ Ἀκρίτην,
καὶ ἐγένετο ἀληθῶς ἐξ ἐχθρῶν σωτηρία,   215
τοσούτων γὰρ τῶν ἀγαθῶν παρ᾽ αὐτοῦ ἐκαρποῦτο
καὶ εἰς τέλος ἐπλήσθησαν οἱ αἰχμάλωτοι πάντες
ὡς δούλους κτῆσαι τοὺς αὐτῶν δεινοτάτους δεσπότας.

Ἆρα πόσης ἀπήλαυσαν οἱ συγγενεῖς ἐκείνων   67 vᵒ.
χαρμονῆς ὄντως τοὺς αὐτῶν δεξάμενοι γνωρίμους·   220
πόλεμος δὲ τὸ σύνολον ἢ ἀκοὴ πολέμου
οὐδαμῶς ἐγνωρίζετο ἐν ταῖς αὐτοῦ ἡμέραις,

190 διατεσσάρων.   194 Après ἀγαθοῖς, je supprime τοῖς, qui fausse le vers.
202 εἰρήνην, et en marge ὡραῖον.   203 φρυάγματα ἀγαρηνῶν.   218 αὐτῶν.
220 τους (sans accent) αὐτῶν.

3498 φωνήν. Perhaps leg. ψυχήν as   3507 The celebration of his mother as
above 3442.   source of the great peace which Di-
3506 εἰρήνην βραβεύσασα. Cf. below   genes imposed is peculiar to GRO,
3764.   which omits the details of his wealth

And within four days she gave up her speech;
Deeply he wept her and he greatly grieved,
And with his father Digenes entombed her.   3500
After her husband's end five years she lived,
Having in all the world's good things delighted,
Shown praiseworthy indeed among women,
Who had once routed foemen by her beauty,
Many delivered from dreadful captivity,
And had awarded peace to towns and villages.
For from her was the start of better things
Who with divine assistance put down hatred,
And brought instead joy everywhere and peace,
Bearing a root and branch noble and fair;   3510
Who put down all the Hagarenes' insolence
And plundered cities and joined them to his realm.
Before this wondrous noble Borderer
The tribes of Aethiopes fearlessly sallying
Would ruthlessly destroy the Romans' cities;
And, sprung from slaves, the children of the free,
The honourable and noble, would enslave.
But when He who for us was born of a Virgin
In His goodness was pleased to free us all,
He made the wondrous glorious dispensation   3520
Foe should turn friend and from him should be born
The crown of bravery, Digenes the Borderer,
And there was truly from the foe salvation,
So great a crop of goods by him was reaped,
And in the end the captives all were filled,
That slaves did own their own most dreadful masters.
Of them the kinsmen did enjoy what great
Gladness indeed receiving their familiars!
Then war in general or report of war
Was never known in those his days at all;   3530

and daily life (except the music and
dancing after dinner) and omits the
separate *moirologi* for the mother, all
of which are in TRE. Only AND 68
gives the mother's name as Eirene.
3511, 3514 It is clear that the Agarenes
and the Aethiops both refer to
Arabian border tribes.
3512 τῷ κράτει συνῆψε. This might
mean 'annexed them to the empire';
but in this panegyric the hero is
evidently regarded as an independent ruler. See below 3526 and 3535.

ἀλλ᾽ ἦν εἰρήνη πανταχοῦ, ἠρεμία μεγάλη,
καὶ πάντες ἄνθρωποι συχνῶς τῷ Θεῷ ηὐχαρίστουν,
καὶ ἅπαντες τὸν Διγενὴν ἐκάλουν εὐεργέτην,   225
ἀντιλήπτορα μέγιστον καὶ σὺν Θεῷ προστάτην·
καὶ πολλοὶ ἐπευφραίνοντο τῇ τούτου βασιλείᾳ
δοξάζοντες ἀσύγχυτον Τριάδα παναγίαν,
ᾗ πρέπει ἡ προσκύνησις εἰς ἅπαντας αἰῶνας.

228 *ἀσύγχητον.*

But peace was everywhere, great quietness,
And all men constantly gave thanks to God,
And all called Digenes their benefactor,
Most great protector, and with God their champion;
And many in his kingship did rejoice,   3535
Praising the all-holy Trinity unconfounded,
Which to all ages is to be adored.

ΤΗΣ ΑΥΤΟΥ ΤΕΛΕΥΤΗΣ

ΛΟΓΟΣ ΟΓΔΟΟΣ

Ἐπειδὴ πάντα τὰ τερπνὰ τοῦ πλάνου κόσμου τούτου
ᾅδης μαραίνει καὶ δεινὸς παραλαμβάνει Χάρων,
καὶ ὡς ὄναρ παρέρχεται καὶ σκιὰ παρατρέχει,
καπνὸς ὥσπερ λυόμενος πᾶς πλοῦτος τοῦδε βίου,
κατέλαβε καὶ θάνατος τοῦ θαυμαστοῦ Ἀκρίτου,   5
γεναμένης τῆς ἀφορμῆς ἀπὸ τοῦ βαλανείου.
   Ποτὲ γὰρ φίλοι πρὸς αὐτὸν ἐλθόντες ἐκ τὸ Ἔμελ,
ὀρθόδοξοι ἀπὸ πατρὸς συγγενεῖς αὐτοῦ ὄντες,
(οἱ γὰρ πλείονες συγγενεῖς ταῖς χρησταῖς νουθεσίαις
τοῦ πατρὸς ἐστηρίχθησαν πρὸς ὀρθόδοξον πίστιν),   10
εἶχον δὲ θέλημα πολύ, ἐπιθυμίαν πάντες
τοῦτον ὁμοῦ θεάσασθαι καὶ τὴν αὐτοῦ ἀνδρείαν·
τινὲς δὲ ὄντες ἀπ᾽ αὐτῶν τῆς πατρῴας θρησκείας
χριστιανοὶ γεγόνασιν Ἀκρίτου νουθεσίᾳ.   68 rº.
   Ἐκείνων, ὡς δεδήλωται, πρὸς τοῦτον ἀφιγμένων,   15
ἀσμένως τούτους δέχεται ἡ φιλάγαθος γνώμη·
τούτων ὡς ὄντων εὐγενῶν κρειττόνων τε καὶ ἄλλων,
δέδωκεν εἰς καταγωγὴν τερπνὸν ξενοδοχεῖον,
ὃ τῶν ἄλλων ἐτύγχανεν ἐγγύτερον τοῦ οἴκου·
καὶ μετ᾽ αὐτῶν ἐφ᾽ ἱκανὰς ἡμέρας διατρίψας,   20
πολλά τε καὶ ἐξαίσια ἀριστεύματα δράσας,
εἰς θήραν ἐξερχόμενος σὺν αὐτοῖς καθ᾽ ἑκάστην,
θάμβος μὲν εἶχεν ἅπαντας καὶ ἔκπληξις μεγίστη,
κατανοοῦντες τὴν ἰσχὺν καὶ τὸν ἄπειρον δρόμον·
οὐδέπω γὰρ τὸ εὑρεθὲν εἶχε τοῦ ἀποδρᾶσαι,   25
ἀλλ᾽ εἰς χεῖρας τὰς ἑαυτοῦ εἴ τι δ᾽ ἂν καὶ ὑπῆρχε,
κἂν λέων, κἂν τε ἔλαφος, κἂν ἄλλο τι θηρίον·
οὐκ εἶχε κύνας μετ᾽ αὐτοῦ ἢ πάρδους πολυδρόμους,
οὐχ ἵππου ἐπεκάθητο, οὐ ξίφεσιν ἐχρᾶτο,

---

22 καθεκάστην.   25 ἀποδράσαι.   27 ἄλλό.

3538 This line in almost the same   ESC 1695, PAS 406; but OXF 2975
words runs through all early ver-   has τὸν ψευστικὸν τὸν κόσμο.
sions: see TRE 3130, AND 4368,   3542 κατέλαβε, 'happened'. Cf. above

OF HIS END
EIGHTH BOOK

Since all the sweets of this deceiving world
Hell withers up and dreadful Charon takes,
Like a dream passes, like a shadow flies,   3540
Like smoke dissolving all wealth of this life;
Came also the wondrous Borderer his death,
The occasion arriving from the bath.
For friends once coming to him from Amida,
Orthodox kinsmen on his father's side
(Most of his kin by the good admonitions
Of his father where confirmed in the orthodox faith),
They had much will all of them and desire
Him to behold together and his bravery;
And some being of his paternal creed   3550
Turned Christian by the Borderer's admonition.
They having come to him, as has been said,
Gladly his kindly nature did receive them.
To them as nobles and to other chiefs
He gave for their lodging a pleasant guest-house,
Was nearer than the others to his house.
With them he spent his time for several days,
Performing many feats and marvellous,
Going out hunting with them every day;
Wonder and great amazement held them all,   3560
His strength observing and his boundless speed;
For what they found could never run away,
But fell into his hands whatever it was,
Lion, or deer, or any other beast;
He had no hounds with him, or running pards,
Nor sat upon a horse, nor used a sword,

1484 κατέλαβε τὸ φέγγος.
3543 This rationalistic view, ἀπὸ τοῦ
βαλανείου, seems to be derived by
GRO from Alexander's chill after
bathing in the river Kydnos.
3544 Ἔμελ. Leg. Ἔμετ, i.e. Amida

(Diarbekir). The Emir of Amida
was received by Constantine VII in
946. Also below 3744.
3565 πάρδους πολυδρόμους. See above
1983 παρδοκυνηγούς.

ἀλλ' ἦσαν ἅπαντα αὐτῷ χεῖρες μόνον καὶ πόδες.   30
Εἶτα προστάξας ἐν μιᾷ λουτρὸν εὐτρεπισθῆναι
κάλλιστον, ὃ πεποίηκε μέσον τοῦ παραδείσου,
τοῦ σὺν τοῖς φίλοις λούσασθαι, τὴν ἀφορμὴν ἐκεῖθεν
ἔσχεν ὁ πολυέραστος καὶ χρηστότατος οὗτος
νοσήματι περιπεσὼν λίαν χαλεπωτάτῳ,   35
ὃ παῖδες ὀπισθότονον τῶν ἰατρῶν καλοῦσιν.
Γνοὺς δὲ τοῦ πόνου τὸ σφοδρόν, καταλιπὼν τοὺς φίλους,
ἐπὶ τὸν οἶκον ἔρχεται, καὶ πεσὼν ἐπὶ κλίνης
τὴν ὀδύνην καθ' ἑαυτὸν καὶ τὸν πόνον συνεῖχε,
ἵνα μὴ θλίψῃ τὴν ψυχὴν τῆς πανεντίμου κόρης·   68 vº. 40
ὡς δὲ μᾶλλον δεινότερος καὶ σφοδρότερος ἔτι
ὁ πόνος ἔθλιβεν αὐτόν, καὶ γνοῦσα τοῦτο ἡ κόρη,
ἀπὸ βάθους στενάξασα· " Ὦ κύριέ μου," ἔφη,
"οὐκ ἐρεῖς μοι τί τὸ συμβὰν καὶ πιέζον σε ἄλγος;
οὐ λέγεις, ὦ παμφίλτατε, τίς ἡ ἀδημονία;   45
πλείονα γάρ μοι προξενεῖς σιωπῶν τὴν ὀδύνην,
καὶ τὴν ψυχὴν ἀναίρεις μοι, τὴν νόσον ἀποκρύπτων."
Ὁ δὲ μᾶλλον τῷ στεναγμῷ ταύτην ἀλγήσας πλέον,
οὐ γὰρ ἐβούλετο ποτὲ κατιδεῖν τεθλιμμένην·
" Οὐδὲν ἄλλο, ἐμὴ ψυχή, πιέζει καὶ συντρίβει,   50
εἰ μὴ πόνος ἀφόρητος τὰ ὀστᾶ μου ἀπέσω·
ὀσφὺν γὰρ πᾶσαν καὶ νεφρούς, ῥάχιν, ὀστᾶ καὶ πάντας
τοὺς ἁρμούς μου διέλυσε, καὶ οὐ φέρω τοὺς πόνους.
Τῶν ἰατρῶν καλείτω τις τῶν τοῦ στρατοῦ ἐν τάχει."
Οὗ καὶ ἐλθόντος τῇ ἑξῆς καὶ σφυγμοῦ ἁψαμένου,   55
ἐκ τῆς πυρᾶς τὴν δύναμιν ἐπέγνω παρελθοῦσαν·
ἡ γὰρ νόσος κατὰ πολὺ νενίκηκε τὴν φύσιν.
Στενάξας οὖν ὁ ἰατρὸς καθ' ἑαυτὸν καὶ κλαύσας,
ἐπέγνω ὁ θαυμάσιος φθάσαι τὸ τέλος ἤδη,
καὶ μηδὲν εἰρηκὼς αὐτῷ τοῦ ἐξελθεῖν προστάττει,   60
τὴν δὲ κόρην εἰς τὸ ἐντὸς ὑπάρχουσαν ταμεῖον
εὐθὺς ἐκάλει πρὸς αὐτόν, ἡ δὲ παρῆν δραμοῦσα·

45 πανφίλτατε.   47 νοσον (sans accent).   54 τὶς.   55 σφιγμοῦ.
57 κατα πολυ (sans accents).

3568 ἐν μιᾷ, 'one day'; cf. μιᾷ τῶν   M.N.E. i, p. 119.
ἡμερῶν above 2190 and 728. It may   3573 ὀπισθότονος, 'back-bending', te-
be connected with the vernacular   tanic spinal recurvation mentioned
ζιμιό, for which see Xanthoudides,   by Plato, Tim. 84 E. The Greek word
Erotokr. gloss. s.v., and Hatzidakes,   is still in medical use; it is, however,

Only his hands and feet were all to him.
So bidding once the bath to be prepared
Most fine, which he had made amid the garden,
There with his friends to bathe, the cause therefrom   3570
Had this beloved and most excellent man
To fall into a very grave disease
Which doctors' boys call opisthotonos.
Knowing the pain acute, leaving his friends
He came into the house, fell on a bed,
Kept to himself the aching and the pain
To hurt not in her soul the all-precious Girl.
And as more dreadful still and more acute
The pain oppressed him, knowing this the Girl
Sighed from the depth and 'O my lord,' she said,   3580
'Will you not tell me what happened, what hurt afflicts?
Say you not, dearest, what your trouble is?
You cause me more by keeping your pain secret,
And tear my soul out hiding your disease.'
He with his groaning still more hurting her,
For never did he want to see her grieved,
'Naught else, my soul, afflicts and crushes me
But pain unbearable within my bones.
For all my loins and kidneys, back, bones, all
My joints it melts, I cannot bear the pain.   3590
One of the army doctors be called quickly.'
He having come next day and felt his pulse
Knew by the fever that his strength was passing;
For the disease by much had conquered nature.
The doctor sighing to himself and weeping,
The hero knew his end already come,
And nothing saying bade him go away,
And the Girl, who was in the inner closet,
Straightway he called to him, and she came running.

not a disease but a sign of meningitis, tetanus, or strychnine poisoning.

3574 τὸ σφοδρόν. Technical in this sense, see L. & S. See Aelius Aristides and Celsus, de Med. iii, quoted in *Greece and Rome*, xxi. 61 (Jan. 1952);

and for Alexander the Great's cramp after bathing in the river at Tarsus in 333 B.C., see Arrian, *Anab*. ii. 4; and Pseudo-Callisth., Pallis, p. 104.

3593 πυρᾶς. For πυρετός not elsewhere recorded.

καὶ πνεῦμα συλλεξάμενος καὶ στενάξας ἐκ βάθους·
" Ὢ τῆς πικρᾶς ", ἐφθέγξατο, " φιλτάτης χωρισίας,
ὢ τῆς χαρᾶς καὶ τῶν τερπνῶν πάντων τοῦ κόσμου τούτου. 65
ἀλλὰ κάθισον ἄντικρυς, χορτάσω σε τοῦ βλέπειν,   69 rᵒ.
ἄλλο γὰρ οὐ θεάσεις με τὸν σὲ πολλὰ ποθοῦντα·
καὶ ἐρῶ σοι τὰ ἀπ' ἀρχῆς ἡμῖν συμβεβηκότα.
Μνήσκεσαι, ὢ ψυχὴ ἐμὴ καὶ φῶς τῶν ὀφθαλμῶν μου,
ὅπως μόνος τὴν ἁρπαγὴν ἐτόλμησα ποιῆσαι,   70
τοὺς σοὺς γονεῖς μὴ πτοηθείς, μὴ δεδοικὼς τὰ πλήθη;
τὸ τοῦ στρατοῦ ἀνείκαστον ἐπεχείρουν χωρῖσαι
ἡμᾶς, ὢ περιπόθητε, ἐν τῷ ἀδήλῳ κάμπῳ,
οὓς μὴ πεισθέντας τοῦ στραφῆν παρέδωκα θανάτῳ·
καὶ ἀδελφοὺς ὅπως τοὺς σούς, σὸν πρόσταγμα φυλάξας,   75
ἐκ τῶν ἵππων κατέβαλον μηδ' ὅλως τραυματίσας;
μέμνησαι ὅπως μόνην σε λαβεῖν ἡρετισάμην,
τῷ σῷ πατρὶ καταλιπὼν ἄχρι ζωῆς τὴν προῖκα;
πάντως διὰ τὴν ἄπειρον ἀγάπην σοῦ, φιλτάτη,
ταῦτα πάντα πεποίηκα ἵνα σε ἐκκερδίσω.   80
Μνημονεύεις, ψυχὴ ἐμή, εἰς τὸ Βλαττολιβάδιν,
ὅταν ὁ δράκων μόνην σε ἐν τῇ πηγῇ ὡς εὗρε,
καὶ ἀναιδῶς πλανῆσαί σε ὁ δεινὸς ἐπεχείρει;
σὺ δὲ φωνὴν ἐξέπεμψας καλοῦσα βοηθόν με,
ἧς ἐπακούσας τάχιον ἐν τῇ πηγῇ εὑρέθην,   85
καὶ τὰ αὐτοῦ φαντάσματα ἀντ' οὐδενὸς νομίσας,
τὰς κεφαλὰς ἀπέτεμον αὐτοῦ τὰς πυρφλεγούσας;
Ταῦτα δὲ κατετόλμησα διὰ τὴν σὴν ἀγάπην,
αἱρούμην γὰρ ἀποθανεῖν ἢ σὺ στενάξαι ὅλως.
Μέμνησαι καὶ τοῦ λέοντος εἰς τὸ αὐτὸ λιβάδιν,   90
ὅπως, ἐμοῦ καθεύδοντος, φῶς μου μεμυρισμένον,
ὥρμησε τοῦ σπαράξαι σε, σὺ δὲ φωνὴν ἀφῆκας,
ἧς ἐπακούσας πρὸς αὐτὸν κατεπήδησα θᾶττον,   69 vᵒ.
καὶ θανατώσας ἀβλαβῆ ἐκ τῶν ὀνύχων τούτου
σὲ ἐρρυσάμην, πάντερπνε, ἐμπεπλησμένην φόβου;   95

72 χωρίσαι.   74 στραφεῖν.   76 μηδ'.   81 ἐμή manque.

3600 πνεῦμα συλλεξάμενος. Cf. Eur.
Phoen. 850 συλλέξαι σθένος καὶ πνεῦμ'
ἄθροισον.
3601 With this dying speech GRO

returns to approximate agreement
with AND (4422) and TRE (3164).
3603 χορτάσω σε τοῦ βλέπειν, 'I will
give you your fill of seeing [me]'.

Then having gathered breath and deeply sighed,　　　3600
'O bitter', he said, 'parting from my dearest,
O for the joy and all this world's delights.
Sit opposite, and let me fill your sight;
You will not see me more who love you much;
I will tell you from the beginning what befell us.
Do you remember, my soul, ligh of my eyes,
How that alone I dared to make your capture,
Feared not your parents, shrunk not from their hosts?
The boundless army that did try to sever
Us, O beloved, in the darkling plain,　　　3610
Whom not consenting to turn back I slew?
And how your brothers, keeping your injunction,
I did unhorse not wounding them at all?
Remember how I chose to take you alone,
Leaving your father the dowry for life?
All for my boundless love of you, my dearest,
All these things did I to win you utterly.
Do you remember, my soul, at Blattolibadi,
When the snake found you at the well alone,
And shamelessly the brute tried to seduce you?　　　3620
And how you gave a cry calling my help,
Which hearing swiftly to the well I came,
And nothing recking of his apparitions
I cut away his fiery-flaming heads?
These are the things I ventured for your love,
Choosing my death before your single sigh.
Remember too the lion in the same meadow,
How while I was asleep, my scented light,
He sprang to tear you up, you gave a cry,
Which hearing I jumped quickly out at him,　　　3630
And killed him, and unhurt from out his claws
Delivered you, my sweet, brimmed up with fear?

TRE 3168 has χόρτασον μὲ βλέπειν
(cf. AND 4422).
3610 See above 1700.
3611 See above 1720.
3617 At this point TRE (3182 = AND
4436) comes to an end.
3623 φαντάσματα. I.e. his changes of

form. See above 2524.
3626 αἱρούμην γὰρ ἀποθανεῖν ἢ σὺ
στενάξαι ὅλως. 'I preferred to die
rather than that you should sigh at
all.' I have not been strictly literal
here because it is too good a line to
spoil.

κιθάρας δὲ τῷ κρούσματι θέλων μεταβαλεῖν σε,
οἱ ἀπελάται, τῷ σαυτῆς ἤχῳ ὁδηγηθέντες,
πρὸς ἡμᾶς ἦλθον ἀναιδῶς οἱ τοῦ Ἰωαννακίου,
οἳ καὶ τόλμῃ ἐχρήσαντο ἡμᾶς ἀποχωρῖσαι·
πάντως οἶδας, ψυχὴ ἐμή, τὰ εἰς αὐτοὺς πραχθέντα,   100
ἄνευ γὰρ ὕπνου ἅπαντας θανάτῳ παρεδόμην·
ταῦτα δὲ ἕνεκα τῆς σῆς ἀγάπης ἐποιούμην,
ἧς οὐ τὸν κόσμον, οὐ τὸ ζῆν εἶχον προτιμητέον.
Μνήσκεσαι καὶ τῶν θαυμαστῶν ἀπελατῶν, ψυχή μου,
Φιλοπαπποῦ τοῦ γέροντος, Κιννάμου καὶ Ἰωαννάκη,   105
τῶν ἐν ἀνδρείᾳ λαλητῶν, πάντη περιβοήτων,
ἄοπλον ἐν τῷ ποταμῷ ὅπως ἐνέτυχόν με,
φαρίοις ἐποχούμενοι, οἱ τρεῖς καθωπλισμένοι;
Οἶδας ὅσα ἐσπούδασαν ἐμὲ τοῦ ἀποκτεῖναι,
ἡνίκα σε ἐσκέψαντο πρός με ἐπερχομένην;   110
σὺ δὲ φωνήν μοι ἔπεμψας βοηθοῦσα τῷ λόγῳ·
" Ἀνδρίζου, ὦ παμφίλτατε, ἵνα μὴ χωρισθῶμεν."
Παρ' ἧς πλέον δυναμωθεὶς τούτους ἐτροπωσάμην,
καὶ κατὰ κράτος ἥττησα τῇ ῥάβδῳ τραυματίσας,
οἷς καὶ τὸ ζῆν ἐχάρισα δυσωπηθεὶς τοῖς λόγοις;   115
καὶ ταῦτα δι' ὑπερβολὴν ἐποιούμην ἀγάπης
τῆς σῆς, πανυπερπόθητε, ὅπως νά σε κερδήσω.
Τὴν Μαξιμοῦν ἐπέζευσα, τοὺς μετ' αὐτῆς ἀνεῖλον,
εἶτα πεισθεὶς τοῖς λόγοις σου, πάλιν ὀπίσω τρέχων
ἔσφαξα καὶ αὐτὴν λάθρα σοῦ μὴ εἰδυίας;   70 rᵒ.   120
Καὶ ἄλλα πολλῷ πλείονα διὰ τὴν σὴν ἀγάπην,
ἐμὴ ψυχή, πεποίηκα ἵνα σε ἐκκερδήσω,
καὶ τοῦ σκοποῦ ἀπέτυχον, ἥμαρτον τῆς ἐλπίδος·
καὶ γὰρ πληροφορήθητι βέβαιον ἀποθνῄσκω,
ὁ Χάρων δέ με ἐκ παντὸς τὸν ἀήττητον τρέπει,   125
ᾅδης χωρίζει τῆς πολλῆς ἀγάπης σου, φιλτάτη,
καὶ ὁ τάφος καλύπτει με πολὺν ἔχοντα πόνον,
καὶ ὀδύνην ἀφόρητον διὰ τὴν σὴν χηρείαν·

---

99 ἀποχωρίσαι.   114 κράττος, avec le premier τ exponctué.   120 Le
premier hémistiche est incomplet de deux syllabes.   124 τέλειον, et en marge
γράφε βέβαιον.

3633 μεταβαλεῖν σε. See above 2563.   3641 and 3606 μνήσκεσαι, 3614, 3627
To 'change,' i.e. 'refresh' you. Cf.   μέμνησαι, 3618 μνημονεύεις. There is
French altérer.   a scarcity of words in English.

238

And when I would have changed your thoughts with lute-playing
The reivers then, guided by your own song,
Came on us shamelessly, those of Ioannakes,
And tried with daring to dissever us.
You know, my soul, all that was done to them;
Without sleeping I gave them all to death.
These are the things I did for your love's sake,
To which not world nor life did I prefer.   3640
Do you recall, my soul, the wondrous Reivers,
Old Philopappos, Kinnamos, Ioannakes,
Talked of for courage everywhere extolled,
And how unarmed they found me at the river,
All three riding their chargers, fully armed?
You know how eagerly they tried to kill me
When they beheld you coming out before me;
And you sent me a cry, speaking your help:
"Be a man, dearest, that we be not parted,"
By which more fortified I routed them,   3650
Beat them by force maiming them with my staff,
Whom by their prayers abashed I granted life?
And these things for excess I did of love
For you, most longed for, so that I might win you.
I unhorsed Maximo, destroyed those with her,
Then, by your words convinced, ran back again
And slew her secretly, without your knowledge.
And many other things too, for your love,
My soul, I did, to win you utterly;
And yet I missed my aim, I lost my hope.   3660
For be assured certainly I am dying.
Me, the invincible, Charon quite routs,
Hades parts, dear, from my much love of you,
And the tomb covers me with all my pain
And grief unbearable for your widowing.

3647 ἐπερχομένην. See above 2706,
which shows that the meaning here
is 'showing yourself'.
3649 ἀνδρίζου. Above 2709.
3652 δυσωπηθείς. The proper meaning
of δυσωπέω is 'put out of countenance'
especially by prayer; in later

authors it means only 'beseech'; cf.
TRE 2603, 2953; AND 4535, 4575.
3654, 3666. πανυπερπόθητε. I think this
must be a mistake for παμπεριπόθητε.
3655 τὴν Μαξιμοῦν ἐπέζευσα. For another startling use of πεζεύω see
above 3169 ἐπέζευον τοὺς ἵππους.

ἀλλ᾽, ὦ πανυπερπόθητε, ποίαν σου κλαύσω λύπην;
πῶς σε παραμυθήσομαι; ποῦ σε ἀφῶ τὴν ξένην; 130
ποία μήτηρ συγκλαύσει σοι; τίς πατὴρ ἐλεήσει;
ἢ νουθετήσει ἀδελφός, τινὰ μὴ εὐποροῦσα;
ἀλλὰ φύλαξον τοὺς ἐμούς, ὦ παμφιλτάτη, λόγους
καὶ τελευταίαν βούλησιν ἐμοῦ μὴ ἀθετήσῃς,
ἵνα βιώσῃ τοῦ λοιποῦ τινὰ μὴ φοβουμένη. 135
Οἶδ᾽ ὡς οὐχ ἕξεις δυνατὸν χηρείαν ὑπομεῖναι.
ἀλλ᾽ ἄνδρα, μετὰ θάνατον ἐμόν, ἕτερον λάβῃς,
ἡ γὰρ νεότης ἐκ παντὸς βιάσει σε εἰς τοῦτο.
Καὶ βλέπεσαι μὴ πλανηθῇς εἰς πλοῦτον ἢ εἰς δόξαν,
ἀλλ᾽ εἰς ἀνδρεῖον ἄγουρον τολμηρὸν καὶ γενναῖον, 140
καὶ βασιλεύσεις ἐπὶ γῆς ὡς πρότερον, ψυχή μου."
Ταῦτα σὺν δάκρυσιν εἰπὼν ἀπέπαυσε τὸν λόγον·
ἡ δὲ κόρη στενάξασα πικρῶς ἀπὸ καρδίας,
καὶ δάκρυσι τὰς παρειὰς βρέξασα θερμοτέροις·
" Ὢ κύριέ μου," ἔφησεν, " εἰς τὸν Θεὸν ἐλπίζω, 145
καὶ εἰς τὴν ἄχραντον ἁγνὴν δέσποιναν θεοτόκον,
οὐδεὶς ἄλλος γνωρίσει με, εἰ μὴ σύ, μέχρι τέλους, 70 vᵒ.
καὶ τῆς δεινῆς λυτρώσει σε ἐν τάχει ἀρρωστίας."
Οὕτως εἰποῦσα ἔρχεται εἰς τὸ ἐντὸς ταμεῖον,
χεῖρας τὲ πρὸς ἀνατολὰς ἐκτείνασα καὶ ὄμμα, 150
δάκρυσί τε τὸ ἔδαφος καταβρέξασα ἅπαν,
πρὸς τὸν Θεὸν τὸν ὕψιστον ἐπηύξατο τοιάδε·
" Δέσποτα, δέσποτα Θεέ, ὁ κτίσας τοὺς αἰῶνας,
ὁ στερεώσας οὐρανὸν καὶ γῆν θεμελιώσας,
καὶ πάντα τὰ ὁρώμενα τῷ λόγῳ σου κοσμήσας, 155
ὁ ἐκ τῆς γῆς τὸν ἄνθρωπον σῇ χειρὶ πλαστουργήσας,
ὁ ἐκ μὴ ὄντων ἅπαντα παραγαγὼν εἰς εἶναι,
εἰσάκουσον δεήσεως ἐμοῦ τῆς ἀναξίας,
ἴδε μου τὴν ταπείνωσιν, ἴδε μου καὶ τὴν θλῖψιν·
καὶ ὡς ποτε παράλυτον ἐξήγειρας, οἰκτίρμον, 160
καὶ τὸ θυγάτριόν ποτε τὸ τοῦ ἑκατοντάρχου,
καὶ νεκρὸν τετραήμερον Λάζαρον ἐκ τοῦ τάφου,

---

136 εἰδὼς, et en marge οἶδ᾽ ὡς.   144 θερμοτέρως.   151 ἔδαφος.
159 θλίψιν.   160 ὡς ποτὲ.   161 θυγάτριον ποτὲ.

3669 τινὰ μὴ εὐποροῦσα. A startling
nominative; but participles are often

driven into the nominative by the
tendency to modern indeclinability.

240

O much-desired, how shall I weep your sorrow?
How shall I comfort, where leave you the stranger?
What mother shall weep with you, what father pity you,
Or brother shall advise, of nought provided?
But, dearest, O observe these words of mine,   367
And this my last wish do not set aside,
That you may live henceforth afraid of none.
Widowhood I know you will not be able to bear;
But after my death take another husband;
Youth will compel you certainly to this.
See that you stray not after wealth or fame,
But to a brave boy, courageous and noble,
And as before you shall reign on earth, my soul.'
This having said with tears, he ceased his speech.
The Girl bitterly sighing from her heart,   3680
With warmer tears having wetted her cheeks,
'O my lord,' she said, 'My hope is in God,
In the pure stainless Lady, God's Mother;
None else shall know me to the end but you,
From your dread sickness He shall soon redeem you.'
So saying she went into the inner closet,
Stretching her hands and eyes towards the east,
And having wetted all the floor with tears,
She prayed to God the most high on this wise:
'Lord, who hast built the ages, O Lord God,   3690
Made firm the heaven and founded the earth,
And all things visible ordered by Thy word,
Man by Thy hand created out of the earth,
And out of nothing brought all things to being,
Hearken to my prayer, unworthy that I am,
Look on my lowliness, look on my affliction,
As Thou didst raise the palsied once in mercy,
And the centurion's little daughter once,
And Lazarus, dead four days, out of the tomb,

See also 3672, τινὰ μὴ φοβουμένη.
3673 Cf. AND 4538 χηρείας καύσωνα, repeated PAS 408.
3675 AND 4544.
3683 Δέσποινα according to Sofokles is not applied to the Deipara before the tenth century. But see Moschos (ed. Hesseling, 1931), p. 65.
3687 ὄμμα. For ὄμματα, or perhaps for ὄψιν.

οὕτω καὶ νῦν ἀνάστησον νέον ἀπελπισμένον·
οἰκτείρησον ὡς ἀγαθὸς τὴν ἐμὴν εὐσπλαγχνίαν,
σπλαγχνίσθητι νεότητος, Χριστέ, τοῦ σοῦ οἰκέτου,   165
εἰ καὶ πολλὰ ἡμάρτομεν ἐνώπιόν σου, Λόγε,
καὶ παντελῶς ἀνάξιοι ἐσμὲν τοῦ σοῦ ἐλέους,
ἀλλ᾿ ὡς οἰκτίρμων δέησιν ἐκ ψυχῆς κατωδύνου
πρόσδεξαι καὶ ἀνάστησον νέον ἀπελπισμένον·
δάκρυα μὴ παρίδῃς μου, ἡ χαρὰ τῶν ἀγγέλων·   170
ἐλέησον, φιλάνθρωπε, τὴν ἐμὴν ξενιτείαν·
τὴν μοναξίαν οἴκτειρον, καὶ ἀνάστησον τοῦτον·
εἰ δ᾿ οὔ, κέλευσον, ὁ Θεὸς ὁ δυνάμενος πάντα,
πρὸ τούτου τελευτῆσαι με καὶ τὴν ψυχὴν ἀφεῖναι,
μὴ ἴδω τοῦτον ἄφωνον νεκρὸν ἐξηπλωμένον,   71 r°.   175
μὴ ἴδω χεῖρας τὰς καλὰς ἀνδραγαθεῖν μαθούσας
δεδεμένας σταυροειδῶς, μενούσας ἀκινήτους,
κεκαλυμμένους ὀφθαλμούς, πόδας συνεσταλμένους·
μή με τοσαύτην κατιδεῖν παραχωρήσῃς θλῖψιν,
ὦ ποιητά μου καὶ Θεέ, ὡς δυνάμενος πάντα."   180
Ταῦτα ἡ κόρη σὺν πολλῇ συντριβῇ τῆς καρδίας
δεηθεῖσα, ὑπέστρεψε τοῦ ἰδεῖν τὸν Ἀκρίτην,
καὶ ὁρᾷ τοῦτον ἄφωνον οἴμοι ψυχορραγοῦντα·
καὶ τὸν πόνον μὴ φέρουσα ὀδύνης τῆς ἀπείρου,
ἀπὸ ἀμέτρου καὶ πολλῆς πεσοῦσα ἀθυμίας   185
ἐπὶ τοῦ νέου συμπαθῶς ἐξέπνευσεν ἡ κόρη.
Οὐδέπω γὰρ ἡ θαυμαστὴ θλίψεως πεῖραν ἔσχε,
διὰ τοῦτο ὑπενεγκεῖν ταύτην οὐκ ἠδυνήθη.
Εἶτα ἰδὼν ὁ θαυμαστός, τῇ χειρὶ ψηλαφήσας,
καὶ γὰρ ἀκμὴν αὐτὸς ζῶν ἦν Θεοῦ τῇ εὐσπλαγχνίᾳ,   190
καὶ ταύτην θεασάμενος θανοῦσαν παραδόξως,
" Δόξα σοι," ἔφη, " ὁ Θεὸς οἰκονομῶν τὰ πάντα,
τοῦ μὴ φέρειν ἀφόρητον πόνον ἐν τῇ ψυχῇ μου,
διὰ τὸ μόνην εἶναι τὲ καὶ ξένην ἐν τοῖς ὧδε."
Καὶ τὰς χεῖρας σταυροειδῶς τελέσας ὁ γεννάδας   195
τὴν ψυχὴν μὲν παρέδωκεν ἀγγέλοις τοῦ κυρίου,
καὶ ἄμφω ἐτελεύτησαν οἱ περίβλεπτοι νέοι
ἐν μιᾷ ὥρᾳ τὰς ψυχάς, ἐκ συνθήματος ὥσπερ.

179 θλῖψιν.   190 Je supplée αὐτός.   194 ὧδε.

3700 ἀπελπισμένον. Mod. sense AND 4584.

Even so now raise a young man despaired of;   3700
In Thy goodness pity my own compassion,
Christ, have compassion on Thy servant's youth,
Though we have sinned before Thy face, O Word,
And we are quite unworthy of Thy pity,
Being merciful, the prayer of a soul in pain
Receive, and raise up a young man despaired of.
Overlook not my tears, the joy of angels;
In loving-kindness pity me in exile,
Have mercy on my loneliness, raise him up.
If not, O God who can do all, command   3710
Me die before him and give up my soul,
Let me not see him voiceless, stretched out dead,
See his fair hands that learned to be so brave
Clasped crosswise, and remaining motionless,
His eyes covered over, and his feet wrapped up:
Allow me not to see such great affliction,
O God my maker, who canst do all things.'
Thus the Girl with much contrition of heart
Having prayed, turned to see the Borderer,
Beheld him speechless, yielding up his soul;   3720
And not bearing the pain of boundless grief
From measureless and great despondence falling
On him in sympathy the Girl expired.
Never had she had knowledge of affliction,
And therefore was not able to endure it.
The hero seeing, and feeling with his hand,
For he was living still by God's compassion,
Having beheld her dying suddenly,
Said, 'Glory to Thee, O God, who orderest all,
That my soul bears not pain unbearable,   3730
That she should be alone here and a stranger.'
His hands setting crosswise the noble youth
Gave up his soul to the angels of the Lord;
Illustrious and young both brought to an end
Their souls at once, as if by covenant.

3714 δεδεμένας. Above 1753 δήσας τὰς   tion.
     χεῖρας.   3732 ὁ γεννάδας. Above 2811, below
3724 ἡ θαυμαστή omitted in transla-   3797.

Τούτων τὸν θάνατον ὁ παῖς οἰνοχόος ὡς εἶδε
τῷ δομεστίκῳ παρευθὺς δηλοῖ τῷ τραπεζίτῃ   200
μετὰ κλαυθμοῦ καὶ ὀδυρμοῦ· οἱ δὲ πάλιν τοῖς ἔξω.
Τῆς φήμης δὲ καὶ πόρρωθεν ἤδη διαδραμούσης,   71 vᵒ.
ἄρχοντες τῆς ἀνατολῆς παρεγένοντο πλεῖστοι,
Χαρζιανοί, Καππάδοκες, Κουκουλιθαριῶται,
Κονδανδῖται οἱ δόκιμοι, Θαρσῖται, Μαυρονῖται,   205
Βαγδαῖται οἱ ἐκλεκτοὶ σὺν Βαθυρρυακίταις,
Βαβυλώνιοι εὐγενεῖς καὶ πολλοὶ ἐκ τοῦ Ἔμελ,
ἔσπευσαν ὅπως εἰς ταφὴν φθάσωσι τοῦ Ἀκρίτου·
καὶ τὸ πλῆθος ἀνείκαστον ἦτον συνηθροισμένον,
ὡς καὶ πάντα τὰ ἔξωθεν τοῦ οἴκου πεπληρῶσθαι.   210
Τίς δὲ τοὺς θρήνους ἐξειπεῖν τοὺς τότε ἐξισχύσει;
τὰ δάκρυα, τοὺς ὀδυρμούς, τῶν συμφορῶν τὸ πλῆθος;
ἅπαντες γὰρ παράφρονες τῇ λύπῃ γεγονότες,
τὰς μὲν τρίχας ἀνέσπαον, ἔτιλλον γενειάδας,
ἐφώνουν· " Σείσθητι, ἡ γῆ· θρήνησον, πᾶς ὁ κόσμος·   215
ὦ ἥλιε, ζοφώθητι, κρύψον σου τὰς ἀκτῖνας·
σελήνη, μελανώθητι, μηκέτι δαδουχήσῃς·
αἱ τῶν ἀστέρων ἅπασαι σβέσθητε φρυκτωρίαι,
τὸ γὰρ ἄστρον τὸ φαεινὸν τὸ λάμψαν ἐν τῷ κόσμῳ,
ὁ Διγενὴς Βασίλειος, πάντων νέων ὁ κόσμος,   220
καὶ ἡ τούτου ὁμόζυγος, τῶν γυναικῶν ἡ δόξα,
ἐν μιᾷ ὥρᾳ ἔδυναν ἄφνω ἀπὸ τοῦ κόσμου.
Δεῦτε πάντες οἱ ἐρασταὶ καὶ φίλοι τῆς ἀνδρείας,
τὸν γενναῖον καὶ τολμηρὸν πενθήσατε Ἀκρίτην·
θρηνήσατε τὸν ἰσχυρὸν καὶ φοβερὸν τοῖς πᾶσι,   225
τὸν πάντα ὑπενάντιον ἀφανίσαντα ἄνδρα,
καὶ γαλήνην βραβεύσαντα καὶ βαθεῖαν εἰρήνην.

199 οἰνοχοὸς.   200 παρ᾽ εὐθὺς.   202 φήμη.   205 κονδανδίται. θαρσίται.
μαυρονίται.   206 βαθυριακίταις.

3736 ὁ παῖς οἰνοχόος seems to refer to
the παιδίον σμικρότατον who alone
waited at table according to TRE
2977, 2978, in the passage of
domestic detail which is omitted in
GRO.

3741 Κουκουλιθαριῶται. Most of the
other names here are those of well-
known themes, so it is safe to emend

this to Βουκελλαριῶται; and in the
next line Κονδανδῖται should certainly be Ποδανδῖται, i.e. those from
the Pass of Podandos in the Taurus—
Grégoire's emendation for Kopid-
nados—where a regimental officer
named Diogenes was killed in battle
in 788 and attained posthumous
glory as Digenes, according to Gré-

The boy winebearer, when he saw their death,
Forthwith he told the server of the table,
With grief and wailing, they to those without.
As presently the news was spread abroad
Came very many rulers of the East,   3740
Charzianians, Káppadokians, Boukellariots,
Worthy Podandites, Tarsites, Mauronites,
Elect Bagdadis, with some from Bathyrryaki,
Nobles from Babylon, many from Amida,
Hastened to attend the Borderer's burial.
Countless the multitude that was assembled,
So everywhere outside the house was full.

Who shall have strength to tell those lamentations?
The tears, the wails, the multitude of sorrows?
For all, become beside themselves with grief,   3750
Were tearing out their hair, plucking their beards,
Crying, 'Shake, earth, and all the world lament;
O sun, be darkened and conceal your rays;
Be blackened, moon, no longer show your fires;
And all the beacons of the stars, be quenched,
For the bright star that in the world did shine
Basil Digenes, of the world's youth the ornament,
And his own spouse, the glory of women,
Sank suddenly together from the world.
Come all lovers and friends of bravery   3760
Mourn the noble the daring Borderer;
Lament the mighty, the dreadful to all,
The man who made to vanish every adversary,
Awarding peace and deep tranquillity.

goire. See Theoph., Bonn p. 718; and Grégoire, Διγενὴς Ἀκρ. (N.Y. 1942), p. 37. Μαυρονῖται may be those from the district of the Μαῦρον Ὄρος, and may or may not be intended for the same people as the 'Blacksnowmen' of 2048. The only known place called Βαθυρρυνάκι seems to be that mentioned by Anna Comnena in *Alex.* ii. 6. 30, the scene of the battle outside the walls.
3744 Ἔμελ. Leg. Ἔμετ, as above

3544; i.e. Amida.
3754 δᾳδουχήσῃς. See above 2823.
3755 φρυκτωρίαι. See above 2901, n.
3757 πάντων νέων ὁ κόσμος (see above 2467); but the line before and the next line but one have the same word in a different sense.
3759 ἐν μιᾷ ὥρᾳ. I have translated this 'together' and above 3735 'at once'.
3764 γαλήνην βραβεύσαντα. Cf. above 3506.

Γυναῖκες, δεῦτε κλαύσατε καλλονὴν ὑμετέραν,
αἱ ἐν κάλλει καυχώμεναι, νεότητι θαρροῦσαι,   72 rᵒ.
τὴν ὡραίαν θρηνήσατε καὶ πανσώφρονα κόρην.   230
Οἴμοι, τί τὸ ὁρώμενον; ἄφνω δύο φωστῆρες
οἱ πάντα κόσμον λάμψαντες ἔδυναν πρὸ τῆς ὥρας! "
Ταῦτα καὶ τούτοις ὅμοια ἔλεγον θρηνῳδοῦντες
οἱ παρόντες πρὸς τὴν ταφὴν τῶν εὐγενῶν σωμάτων.

Τῶν ὕμνων δὲ πρὸς τὴν ταφὴν καλῶς ἐκτελεσθέντων,   235
καὶ ἅπαντα τοῖς πένησι δοθέντα τὰ ἐν οἴκῳ,
τὰ λείψανα ἐν μνήματι κηδεύσαντες πρεπόντως,
τούτων τὸν τάφον ἔστησαν ἐπάνω εἰς κλεισοῦραν
παρέκει Τρώσεως τινὸς τόπου τοῦ καλουμένου.
Ἐπ' ἀψίδος ἱστάμενος ὁ τάφος τοῦ Ἀκρίτου,   240
συντεθειμένος θαυμαστῶς ἐκ μαρμάρου πορφύρας,
ἵν' οἱ βλέποντες ἔξωθεν τοὺς νέους μακαρίζουν,
τῆς ἀκρωρείας πόρρωθεν δυνάμενος ὀφθῆναι·
τὰ γὰρ εἰς ὕψος ὄντα τὲ μήκοθεν θεωροῦνται·
Εἶτ' ἀναβάντες ἅπαντες οἱ τότε συνελθόντες,   245
οἱ μεγιστᾶνες, ἄρχοντες καὶ πάντες οἱ τῷ τότε
τὸν τάφον στεφανώσαντες καὶ κυκλώσαντες τοῦτον,
τοιαῦτα λέγειν ἄρχονται δακρύοντες ἀσχέτως·
" Ἴδετε ποῦ κατάκειται ἡ τόλμη τῆς ἀνδρείας,
ἴδετε ποῦ κατάκειται ὁ Διγενὴς Ἀκρίτης·   250
τῶν γονέων ὁ στέφανος, νέων πάντων ἡ δόξα,
ἴδετε ποῦ κατάκειται τὸ ἄνθος τῶν Ῥωμαίων,
βασιλέων τὸ καύχημα, εὐγενῶν ἡ λαμπρότης,
ὁ τοῖς λέουσι φοβερὸς καὶ πᾶσι τοῖς θηρίοις·
οἴμοι, οἴμοι τί γέγονεν ἡ τοσαύτη ἀνδρεία;   255
Θεέ, καὶ ποῦ ἡ δύναμις καὶ ποῦ ἡ εὐτολμία,   72 vᵒ.
ποῦ φόβος ὁ ἀνείκαστος τοῦ ὀνόματος μόνου;
Εἰ γὰρ Ἀκρίτου ὄνομα τοῦ Διγενοῦς ἠκούσθη,
φρίκη πάντας ἐλάμβανεν καὶ δειλία μεγίστη,
τοσαύτην χάριν ἐκ Θεοῦ εἴληφεν ὁ γεννάδας   260
ὡς μόνῳ τῷ ὀνόματι τρέπειν τοὺς ἐναντίους·
εἰ γὰρ ποτὲ ὁ θαυμαστὸς ἐξῆλθε τοῦ θηρεῦσαι,

3773 δοθέντα: nom. abs., after gen. abs.
   in preceding line.
3774 μνῆμα ought rightly to mean the

'monument', the erection of which
is described in the next line, where
it is called τάφος.

Come, women, come and weep for your own beauty,
Who boast in beauty and who trust in youth,
Mourn for the lovely and all-virtuous Girl.
Woe, what is it we see? Two lamps suddenly,
That lit the whole world, set before their time.'
This and the like they spoke in threnody   3770
Who came to burial of the noble bodies.
The burial hymns having been duly closed,
And all things in the house given to the poor,
They interred the corpses meetly in a grave,
And set their monument up on a pass
Beyond a certain place that is called Trôsis.
The Borderer's tomb, standing upon an arch,
Is wondrously composed of purple marble,
That those who see without bless the young pair,
The ridge being visible from far away   3780
(For things on a height are seen from a distance).
Then going up all who were then assembled,
The princes, rulers, all who at that time
Had garlanded the tomb and circled round it,
Such words began to speak with tears unchecked:
'Look where low lies the edge of bravery,
Look where low lies the Twyborn Borderer,
His parents' crown, the glory of all youth,
Look where low lies the flower of the Romans,
The boast of kings, the nobles' brilliancy,   3790
The dread of lions and of all wild beasts.
Woe, woe, what is become of all the bravery?
O God, where is the might, and where the courage,
Where the matchless dread of his name alone?
If Digenes the Borderer's name was heard
Horror seized all and greatest cowardice;
Such favour had the youth received from God
His name alone would rout his adversaries.
For if the hero ever went out hunting

3776 Τρώσεως. See above 2578.

3777 'Επ' ἀψίδος. These words seem to
show knowledge, or misunderstanding, of the Bridge built by Digenes
in ESC 1660.

3780 δυνάμενος. Indeclinable participle—'it being possible'.

θηρία πάντα ἔτρεχον εἰς τὴν ἕλην ἀπέσω·
ἀρτίως δὲ ὑπὸ μικροῦ κατακρατεῖται τάφου,
ἄπρακτος, ἀνενέργητος ὁρώμενος τοῖς πᾶσιν·   265
ἆρα τίς κατετόλμησε τὸν ἰσχυρὸν δεσμεῦσαι;
ἆρα τίς τὸν ἀήττητον ἴσχυσεν ὑποτάξαι;
Θάνατος ὁ πικρότατος καὶ παραίτιος πᾶσι,
Χάρων ὁ τρισκατάρατος καὶ πάντας συναναίρων,
καὶ Ἅιδης ὁ ἀκόρεστος, οἱ τρεῖς ἀνθρωποκτόνοι,   270
οἱ τρεῖς ἀνελεήμονες, οἱ πᾶσαν ἡλικίαν
καὶ πᾶν κάλλος μαραίνοντες, φθείροντες πᾶσαν δόξαν·
οὐ γὰρ τῶν νέων φείδονται, οὐ γηραιοὺς αἰδοῦνται,
οὐ φοβοῦνται τοὺς ἰσχυρούς, οὐ τιμῶσι πλουσίους,
τὰ κάλλη οὐ σπλαγχνίζονται, ἀλλὰ κόνιν ποιοῦσιν,   275
πηλὸν καὶ τέφραν ἅπαντα ἐργάζονται δυσώδη.
Οὗτοι καὶ νῦν τὸν θαυμαστὸν Ἀκρίτην συλλαβόντες,
ὁ τάφος μὲν κατακρατεῖ, γῆ δὲ τοῦτον μαραίνει,
καὶ σάρκας οἴμοι τὰς καλὰς σκώληκες δαπανῶσι,
ᾅδης μαραίνει τὰς καλὰς καὶ χιονώδεις σάρκας.   280
Καὶ διὰ ποίαν ἀφορμὴν ταῦτα ἡμῖν ἐπῆλθε;
τῇ παραβάσει τοῦ Ἀδὰμ καὶ Θεοῦ ἀποφάσει.
Ἀλλ', ὦ δέσποτα καὶ Θεέ, τοιοῦτον στρατιώτην   73 vᵒ.
οὕτω νέον, οὕτω καλὸν καὶ ἡδύτατον πᾶσι,
τί παρεχώρησας θανεῖν καὶ μὴ ζῆν παντὶ χρόνῳ;   285
ἀλλ' οὐκ ἔστιν ὃς ζήσεται, φησὶν ὁ Θεοπάτωρ,
καὶ οὐκ ὄψεται θάνατον· πρόσκαιρος γὰρ ὁ βίος,
πρόσκαιρα τὰ ὁρώμενα, ματαία πᾶσα δόξα.
Χριστέ, καὶ τίς ἀπέθανε τοιοῦτος ἐν τῷ κόσμῳ;
τὸ ἄνθος τῆς νεότητος, ἡ δόξα τῶν ἀνδρείων.   290
Χριστέ, καὶ ἃς ἀνέζησεν, ἃς ἔφερε τὸν νοῦν του,
ἃς τὸν ἐθεασάμεθα κρατοῦντα τὸ ῥαβδίν του,
ἃς ἀπεθάνομεν εὐθὺς καὶ μηδεὶς ὑπελείφθη!
Ὤμοι, φεῦ, φεῦ τῶν ἀγαθῶν πάντων τοῦ πλάνου κόσμου·
φεῦ τῆς τρυφῆς, φεῦ τῆς χαρᾶς, φεῦ νεότητος πάσης,   295
οὐαὶ τοῖς ἁμαρτάνουσι καὶ μὴ μετανοοῦσι,
τοῖς θαρροῦσι νεότητι, ἰσχύϊ καυχωμένοις!"
Ταῦτα καὶ τούτοις ὅμοια θρηνήσαντες ἐκ βάθους,

    281 ἀφορμήν.   292 τὸν ῥαβδίν.   294 ὄμοι.

3807 Death, Charon, and Hades regarded as a trinity.

All beasts would run to cover in the swamp.   3800
Now he is held down by a little tomb,
Vain, ineffectual for all to see.
Who is it greatly dared to bind the strong?
Who had strength to subdue the undefeated?
Bitterest Death, accessory of all,
Charon, thrice-cursed and common taker-off,
Hades insatiate, these three man-killers,
The three unpitying, and every age,
All beauty withering, wasting all glory.
The young they spare not, nor respect the old,   3810
Nor fear the strong, nor honour the wealthy;
Beauties they pity not, but turn to dust,
And all things work to mud and stinking ash.
They have now seized the wondrous Borderer,
The grave holds him down, and the earth withers him,
And worms, alas, expend his lovely flesh,
His lovely snowy flesh Hell withers up.
Through what occasion came these things on us?
By Adam's transgression and by God's decree.
But, O Master and God, such a soldier,   3820
So young, so lovely, and to all most sweet,
Why did You let him die, not all time live?
None is there who shall live, saith God the Father,
And not see death; for life is transitory,
Things visible transitory, all glory vain.
Christ, and who in the world has died like this,
The flower of youth, the glory of the brave?
Christ, let him have lived again, and brought his mind,
Let us have seen him holding of his staff,
And then be dead at once and not one left.   3830
Woe, alas, for all the goods of the erring world,
Woe for softness, woe for joy, woe for all youth,
Woe betide those who sin and repent not,
And those who trust in youth, who boast in strength.'
This and on this wise having deeply mourned

3808 ἡλικίαν. Here every 'age', in the   just mean 'stature' as elsewhere in
modern sense—perhaps. But it might   the poem.

οἴκαδε ἀνεχώρησαν οἱ ἐκεῖ ἀθροισθέντες
πρὸς τὴν ταφὴν τῶν εὐγενῶν καὶ εὐαγῶν σωμάτων.　　300
Ἀλλ', ὦ Χριστὲ παμβασιλεῦ καὶ ποιητὰ τῶν ὅλων,
Βασίλειον τὸν εὐγενῆ, πολυέραστον κλάδον,
ὁμόζυγον τὴν εὐθαλῆ καὶ ὡραίαν σὺν τούτῳ,
καὶ πάντας τερπομένους τε καὶ ζῶντας ὀρθοδόξως,
ὅταν καθίσῃς ἐπὶ γῆς κρῖναι ψυχὰς ἀνθρώπων,　　305
τότε, Χριστέ μου, τήρησον καὶ φύλαξον ἀτρώτους,
τοῖς δεξιοῖς συντάττων τὲ μέρεσι τῶν προβάτων·
ἡμᾶς δὲ τοὺς τὸ ζῆν παρὰ σοῦ ἐσχηκότας
κράτυνον, σκέπασον φρουρῶν ἀπὸ τῶν ἐναντίων,
ἵν' ὑμνῶμεν τὸ ἄχραντον καὶ μέγα ὄνομά σου　　310
Πατρὸς ἅμα καὶ τοῦ Υἱοῦ καὶ Πνεύματος ἁγίου,
Τριάδος ἀσυγχύτου τὲ ὁμοφυοῦς καὶ θείας,
εἰς ἀπεράντους καὶ μακροὺς αἰῶνας τῶν αἰώνων.

304 ὀρθοδόξ~ως~ (sic). Mais, malgré la correction, je crois devoir conserver
ὀρθοδόξως.　　　308 Le premier hémistiche est incomplet de deux syllabes.
312 ἀσυγχήτου. ὁμοφυοῦ.

They home departed who were gathered there
For burial of those pure and noble bodies.
  But, O Christ, king of all, maker of all things,
Basil the noble, much-beloved branch,
His beautiful his blooming spouse with him,   3840
And all who delight and live in orthodoxy,
When Thou shalt sit on earth to judge men's souls,
Then, my Christ, keep and guard them unwounded,
Ranging them on the right hand with the sheep;
And us, who have received our life from Thee,
Strengthen, shield, ward us from our adversaries,
That we may hymn Thy great and stainless name,
Together the Father's, the Son's, and the Holy Spirit's,
Trinity's unconfounded, of one nature, divine,
For ages of ages long and infinite.   3850

*   *   *   *   *   *   *

3839 πολυέραστον κλάδον. Cf. ἔρνος 2873, 3310.

APPENDIX A

GENEALOGY OF DIGENES

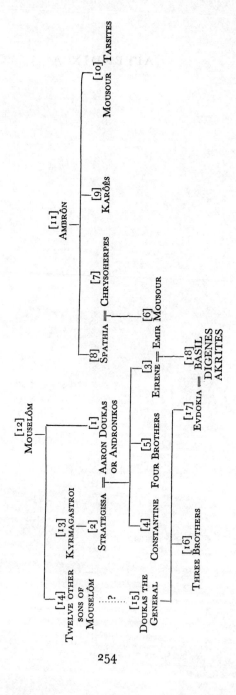

Key to the Genealogical Table

1. AARON DOUKAS, described as descended *apo tôn Kinnamadôn* TRE 54, AND 490, ESC 140; called *Antakinos apo tôn Kinnamadôn* GRO iv. 54; *Andronikos apo tôn Kinnamadôn Doukas* AND 20; Andronikos ('in Syrian Aaron') king OXF 7; *apo tôn Kinnamadôn* GRO i. 266; exiled by Romanos TRE 855, 1545; *Andronikos apo tôn Kinnamadôn*, banished by Romanos, AND 1367; banished by Basil, GRO iv. 56; PAS 323.

2. His wife, the STRATEGISSA, TRE 57, 839; called Anna AND 30, OXF 19; *ek genous tôn Doukadôn* TRE 839, AND 1372; *Doukissa genous tou Kostantinou* GRO i. 267; She is descended from [13] *Kyrmagastroi*, q.v.

3. Her daughter called EIRENE AND 68, OXF 67; of Doukas family TRE 817.

4. Her son CONSTANTINE TRE 303, 898; said to be his sister's twin GRO i. 132, SPE 307; the eldest TRE 303; goes hunting with his nephew TRE 898.

5. Four other sons TRE 311.

6. The EMIR MOUSOUR TRE 790-820, 3070; AND 302, 1339, 4304; GRO iv. 21, 37, PAS 342; after baptism called *Iôannes* AND 4307, PAS 495.

7. CHRYSOCHERPES, father of the emir Mousour, TRE 80, 187 ff.; called Chrysoberges GRO i. 284; surrounded by the Romans and cut to pieces rather than surrender GRO ii. 60 ff; TRE 187; called Chrysoterpes PAS 323, 327. (Chrysocheir the Paulician defeated and killed 873?)

8. SPATHIA, mother of the emir Mousour; of *Rouhá* (Edessa, Rahab), TRE 488 ff., 3067; AND 516, 4303; called Panthia GRO i. 284; PAS 323.

9. KARÔÊS, TRE 82, 807; AND 520, 4314; GRO i. 285, ii. 75; (where Mousrés seems to be corrupt, perhaps for Mousour); if so, Mousour of Tarsus is the same person as Karôês; PAS 324; Panthia explicitly calls him her brother GRO ii. 75. (Carbeas the Paulician?)

10. MOUSOUR OF TARSUS, TRE 201; AND 655 ff., 4313; PAS 327. Karôês and Mousour are the 'Arabian uncles' of TRE 80, 808. But they are apparently regarded as one and the same person in GRO ii. 75.

11. AMBRÓN, TRE 87, 807, 3064; AND 520, 4301; GRO 285; PAS 324. (Omar of Melitene defeated and killed 863?)

12. MOUSELÔM, TRE 56, AND 491, father of Aaron Doukas, ESC 146. (Alexis Mouseles?)

13. KYRMAGASTROI, rich family of the General's wife Anna, TRE 57, AND 490, ESC 138; called Magastranoi, AND 493; Magastreoi AND 29; Kyr Magistroi PAS 323. Probably corrupt. The explanations of Grégoire, Adontz, and Kyriakides are all unsatisfactory.

14. Twelve other sons of Mouselôm? The twelve uncles of Eirene who provided her with six cousins. TRE 59, AND 494, PAS 323. From these was perhaps descended the General [15] Doukas who was Evdokia's father—for Evdokia tells Digenes that she is related to him through the Doukases TRE 1179.

15. DOUKAS THE STRATÊGOS, TRE 1105; called Doukas Stratarhos OXF 1590.

16. His three sons TRE 1275, AND 2075, OXF 1962. But Evdokia has two brothers GRO iv. 610, PAS 359; and five brothers ESC 969.

17. EVDOKIA, TRE 1103, AND 2045; her name is not mentioned in GRO, which usually only calls her Kore.

18. BASIL DIGENES AKRITES.

APPENDIX B

CONSPECTUS OF VERSIONS
AND EPISODES

Description	GRO ed. E. Legrand, Paris, 1892	TRE ed. C. Sathas & E. Legrand, Paris, 1875	AND ed. A. Meliarakes, Athens, 1881	ESC ed. D. C. Hesseling, Laografia, 3, Athens, 1912	OXF ed. S. P. Lampros, Paris, 1880	PAS PROSE Laografia, 9, Athens, 1928	SPE RUSSIAN Byzantion, 10, Brussels, 1935; Kalonaros ii Athens, 1941	BALLADS
Lovely child ERRENE born to AARON ANDRONIKOS DOUKAS and ANNA in Cappadocia. At seven shut up in Palace; at twelve EIRENE has vision of God of Love.	i. 1–197		i. 1–279		i. 1–116	i. pp. 305–317		
Her father in exile, she goes for picnic. Emir MOUSOUR carries her off. Her brothers pursue. KONSTANTINE defeats Emir.			ii. 280–435		ii. 117–	ii. 317–	pp. 303–	
They cannot find sister. Emir produces her and asks for her hand. Return to Castle Doukas. Emir, converted, marries Eirene. Birth of BASIL DIGENES	198–337 ii. 1–49	ii. 1–172	436–622	1–220	–556	–326	–311	
Emir's mother writes to him. After quarrel with brothers he leaves bride, rides to Edessa, converts mother and family, and returns with them to Castle Doukas.	50–300 iii. 1–343	iii. 173–759	iii. 623–1285	221–609	iii. 557–1218	iii. 327–340	311–312	
Heroism and exploits of Emir. Education and first Hunting of BASIL DIGENES.	iv. 1–253	iv. 760–1036	iv. 1286–1574	702–738 610–620	iv. 1219–1400	iv. 341–347	313–316	
DIGENES visits PHILOPAPPOS, aged chief of Reivers, and asks to join his band.		1037–1092	1575–1657	739–791	1401–1544	347–349	Filipap and his daughter Maximiana 319	
DIGENES serenades EVDOKIA daughter of General DOUKAS and carries her off, pursued by brothers.	254–855	v. 1093–1385	v. 1658–2249	621–701	v. 1545–	v. 350–	321–328	pursuit by brothers Arch. Pont. i, no. 6, 69–75
Wedding of BASIL and EVDOKIA. List of wedding presents	856–952	1386–1436	2250–2300	792–	–2106	–362	329–330	
BASIL DIGENES on the Borders with EVDOKIA. Domestic arrangements. The Blinded Cook.	953–970	1437–1475	2301–2341	–1085 1086–1096	2107–2152	362–363		

	971–1093 Emp. Basil (Digenes catches horse, kills lion)	1470–1551 Emp. Romanos	2342–2443 Emp. Romanos		2153–2182 Emp. Romanos third person	363–365 Emp. Romanos	331–334 defeat of Emperor Basil	
Boasting of Digenes. Rescue, story, and seduction of deserted Bride at Oasis, daughter of Emir Haplorrabdes	v. 1–289	vi. 1552–1855	vi 2444–2810		vi. 2183–2384 third person	vi. 365–373 first person		
THE MONTH OF MAY							317	
The Serpent and the Lion at the Well. The Song in the Desert. A hundred Reivers driven off.	vi. 1–173	vii. 1856–2053 (300 Reivers)	vii. 2811–3017	1097–1197	vii. 2385–2466	vii. 374–378	319	
Three Horsemen hear the story of Ankylas who insulted Digenes and paid for it.		2054–2123	3018–3120		2467–2562	378–381		
Three chief Reivers, Philopappos, Kinnamos, and Ioannikios, defeated by Digenes and spared.	vi. 174–310	2124–2226	3121–3247	1198–1315	2563–2658	381–382		
They plan to steal Evdokia for Ioannikios: Maximo the Amazon, asked to help, calls up Melementzes and her best men.	311–475	2227–2357	3248–3447	1316–1420	2659–2726	383–387		Bride of Ioannikios Kyriakides, p. 140
Digenes drives away the Three Chiefs, hides Evdokia on hill-top, unhorses Maximo, scatters her men, defeats the Five Chiefs. Maximo asks him to fight again.	476–713	2358–2541	3448–3709	1421–1551	2727–2914	387–394		
Next morning he fights and loves Maximo and returns to Evdokia. *End of the Boasting*	714–845 Kills Maximo 835–839	2542–2682	3710–3879	1552–1605	2915–2964	394–397 end of first person	Filipap and Maximiana 319–332	
GARDEN AND PALACE BY EUPHRATES. Death of his Father in Cappadocia. His mother lives with them. Domestic arrangements.	vii. 1–229	viii. 2683– ix. –3038	viii. 3880–4214	1606–1659, 1095 builds bridge and tomb	viii. 2965–3008	vii. 397–403 ix. 403–405		
Death of his Mother Eirene			ix. 4215–4357	1660–1694				
Glory of Digenes as restorer of Peace and holder of office from Emperor Nikeforos		3039–3120			3009–3042	405		
Digenes falls ill. Talks to Evdokia about their life together. She dies and he dies.	viii. 1–198	x. 3121–3182	x. 4358–4618	1695–1867		x. 406–410		Death of Digenes— *Laografia*, i (1910), pp. 169–275
Their funeral and Mourning. Moral: the Vanity of this World.	199–313 tomb at Trôsis		4619–4778		3043–3062 3063–3094	410–412		

REFERENCE LIST OF LEADING TEXTS, COMMENTARIES, BOOKS, AND ARTICLES

I. TEXTS

1. C. SATHAS and E. LEGRAND. *Les Exploits de Digénis Akritas*: épopée byzantine du dixième siècle publiée pour la première fois d'après le manuscrit unique de Trébizonde. [With French translation.] Paris, 1875. (TREBIZOND.)

1A. S. IOANNIDES. *Epos Mesaiônikon ek tou Heirografou Trapezountos O Basileios Digenês Akritês O Kappadokês Ýpomnematisthen Ekdidotai ypo SABBA IÔANNIDOU*. Constantinople, 1887.

2. E. LEGRAND. *Les Exploits de Basile Digénis Acritas*: épopée byzantine publiée d'après le manuscrit de Grotta-Ferrata. Paris, 1892. [Reprinted 1902.] (GROTTAFERRATA.)

3. A. MÊLIARAKÊS. *Basileios Digenes Akritas: epopoiia byzantinê tês 10ês ekatontaetêridos kata to en Andrôi aneurethen heirografon*. Athens, 1881. [Reprinted 1920.] (ANDROS.)

4. S. P. LAMPROS. *Romans grecs en vers*. Paris, 1880. (pp. 111–238, and introd., pp. lxxxviii–cvii.) (OXFORD.)

5. D. C. HESSELING. *Le Roman de Digénis Akritas* d'après le manuscrit de Madrid. In *Laografia*, vol. iii, pp. 536–604. Athens, 1912. (ESCORIAL.)

6. D. PASCHALES. *Oi deka logoi tou Digenous Akritou: pezê diaskeuê* (*Meletiou Blastou*). In *Laografia*, vol. ix, 1928, pp. 305–440. (PASCHALES PROSE.)

7. P. PASCAL. *Le 'Digenis' slave, ou la 'Geste de Devgenij'*. [French translation.] In *Byzantion*, vol. x, fasc. 1, pp. 301–39. Brussels, 1935. (SPERANSKY SLAVONIC.) Greek translation of Russian text in *Kalonaros*, vol. ii, pp. 257–92. For a third MS. (c. 1760) of the Russian version newly discovered see V. D. KUZMINA. *Novy Spisok 'Devgeneva deyaniya'* in *Trudy otdela drevnerusskoi literatury*, ix. Moscow and Leningrad, 1953.

II. SECONDARY TEXTS

a. Akritic Songs

8. M. BÜDINGER. *Ein Mittelgriechisches Volksepos*. Leipzig, 1866.

9. W. WAGNER. *Mediaeval Greek Texts*. London (Philological Society), 1870. (pp. x, xiii n. 34, xxii–xxiv.)

10. S. ZAMPELIOS. *Pothen ê koinê lexis Tragoudô?* Athens, 1859. (pp. 38–43.)

11. E. LEGRAND. *Chansons populaires grecques*. Paris, 1874. (pp. 182–97.)

12. E. LEGRAND. *Chansons populaires grecques* (spécimen d'un recueil en préparation). Paris, 1876. (pp. 2, 10–19.)

13. P. TRIANTAFYLLIDES. *Oi Fygades: meta makrôn prolegomenôn peri Pontou.* Athens, 1870. (pp. 21–51; 169–75.)

14. *Archeion Pontou,* vol. i. Athens, 1928. (pp. 47–96.)

15. A. PASSOW. *Popularia Carmina Graeciae Recentioris.* Leipzig, 1860. [Akritic are: Nos. 439, 440, 448, 449, 474, 482, 486, 491, 508, 509, 510, (514, 515), 516, (517–19), 526, 527.]

16. S. P. KYRIAKIDES. *O Digenês Akritas.* Athens, n.d. [Six typical akritic songs printed in an appendix (pp. 119–50). Same as No. 27.]

17. N. G. POLITES. *O Thanatos tou Digenê. Laografia,* vol. i. Athens, 1910. (pp. 169–275.) [A collection of 72 songs dealing with the death of Digenes.]

18. N. G. POLITES. *Eklogai apo ta tragoudia tou Ellenikou laou.* Athens, 1925. [pp. 85–115; Nos. 69–78.]

19. R. M. DAWKINS. 'Some Modern Greek Songs from Cappadocia.' *American Journal of Archaeology,* vol. xxxviii (1934). [No. 1.]

Other Akritic songs and versions are to be found in nearly all collections of folk-songs and in various volumes of *Laografia, Archeion Pontou,* &c.

b. Related Texts

20. M. MILLER. *Poème Allégorique de Méliténiote.* (Notices et extraits de manuscrits de la Bibliothèque impériale, tome xix, seconde partie.) Paris, 1858.

21. H. ETHÉ. *Die Fahrten des Sajjid Batthâl.* [2 vols.] Leipzig, 1871.

22. J. ATKINSON. *The Shah Nameh of Firdausi,* translated and abridged. London, 1832.

23. J. GRIMM und A. SCHMELLER. *Lateinische Gedichte des X. und XI. JH.* Göttingen, 1838.

24. P. LE BAS. Eumathii Philosophi *de Hysmines et Hysminiae Amoribus.* (Erotici Scriptores.) Paris, 1856.

25. J. A. LAMBERT. *Lybistros kai Rodamne.* Amsterdam, 1935.

III. COMMENTARIES

26. N. G. POLITES. *Peri tou Ethnikou Epous tôn Neôterôn Ellênôn.* Athens, 1906. Reprinted in *Laografika Symmeikta,* i. Athens, 1920.

27. S. P. KYRIAKIDES. *O Digenês Akritas.* Athens, n.d. (1926).

28. A. RAMBAUD. *Une épopée byzantine au Xe siècle. Revue des Deux Mondes.* 15 Août 1875.

29. C. GIDEL. *Nouvelles Études sur la littérature grecque moderne.* Paris, 1878.

30. J. B. BURY. *Romances of Chivalry on Greek Soil.* Oxford, 1911.

31. H. PERNOT. *Études de littérature grecque moderne.* Paris, 1916.

32. J. PSICHARI. 'A propos de Digénis Akritas', and 'La Ballade de Lénore

en Grèce', in *Quelques Travaux de Linguistique, de Philologie et de Littérature helléniques*, tome i. Paris, 1930.

33. H. GRÉGOIRE. *O Digenês Akritas*. New York, 1942.

To these must be added very numerous articles by H. Grégoire, R. Goossens, N. Adontz, A. Hatzês, M. Canard, E. Honigmann, S. P. Kyriakides, and others in the volumes of *Byzantion*, the *Byzantinische Zeitschrift*, the *Byzantinisch-neugriechische Jahrbücher*, *Laografia*, and the *Epetêris Byzantinôn Spoudôn*. The beginning of this modern series of Akritic studies was Grégoire's article on 'Ancyre et les Arabes sous Michel l'Ivrogne', in *Byzantion*, vol. iv, pp. 437 ff. (1929). The offprint of his contribution to *Byzantion*, vol. ix (1934), gives on pp. 2 and 3 of the wrapper a list of twenty-four articles constituting the Gregorian campaign up to that date, of which two were the sole work of Goossens. A good summary of the earlier results claimed is given by Grégoire and Goossens in 'Les Recherches récentes sur l'épopée byzantine' in *L'Antiquité Classique*, Louvain, vols. i (1932) and ii (1933).

34. S. IMPELLIZZERI. *Il Digenis Akritas: L'Epopea di Bisanzio*. Florence, 1940.

35. P. P. KALONAROS. *Basileios Digenês Akritas*. 2 vols. Athens, 1941, 1942.

IV. WORKS OF REFERENCE

36. K. KRUMBACHER. *Geschichte der Byzantinischen Litteratur*. Munich, 1897.

37. J. B. BURY. *Cambridge Mediaeval History*, vol. iv. *The Eastern Roman Empire*. Cambridge, 1923.

38. —— *A History of the Eastern Roman Empire* (802–867). London, 1912.

39. C. DIEHL. *History of the Byzantine Empire*. Princeton, 1925.

40. N. H. BAYNES. *The Byzantine Empire*. London, 1925.

41. R. BYRON. *The Byzantine Achievement*. London, 1929.

42. S. RUNCIMAN. *Byzantine Civilisation*. London, 1933.

43. —— *Romanus Lecapenus*. Cambridge, 1929.

44. A. A. VASILIEV. *Histoire de l'Empire Byzantin*. Paris, 1932.

45. —— *Byzance et les Arabes*. Brussels, 1935.

46. E. HONIGMANN. *Die Ostgrenze des Byzantinischen Reiches* (363–1071). Brussels, 1935.

47. S. RUNCIMAN. *The Medieval Manichee*. Cambridge, 1947.

48. G. N. HATZIDAKIS. *Mesaiônika kai Nea Hellênika*. Athens, 1905, 1907.

49. S. XANTHOUDIDES. *Erôtokritos*. Candia, 1915.

50. F. J. CHILD. *English and Scottish Popular Ballads*. London, 1904.

51. J. MEURSIUS. *Glossarium Graeco-Barbarum*. Leyden, 1614.

52. DUCANGE. *Glossarium ad Scriptores Mediae et Infimae Graecitatis*. Leyden, 1688.

53. E. A. SOPHOCLES. *Greek Lexicon of the Roman and Byzantine Periods*. Harvard, 1914.

54. W. H. MAIGNE D'ARNIS. *Lexicon Manuale Mediae et Infimae Latinitatis*. Paris, 1866.

55. N. H. BAYNES and H. St. L. B. MOSS, edd. *Byzantium: an Introduction to East Roman Civilization*. 2nd imp. Oxford, 1949.

56. D. OBOLENSKY. *The Bogomils.* Cambridge. 1948.
57. C. M. BOWRA. *Heroic Poetry.* London. 1952.
58. Byzantské epos *Basilios Digenis Akritas.* Přeložil, úvodem a poznámkami opatřil K. Müller. V. Praze, nákladem České akademie věd a umění, 1938. [Czech translation of Book I from Oxford MS.: Books II–X from Trebizond MS.: and Book X from Oxford MS.; with introduction and notes.]*

*For notice of this work and other bibliographical information I am indebted to the kindness of Mr. John Simmons of the Taylor Institution at Oxford.

APPENDIX D

THE following are the chief passages from the *Kleitofon and Leukippe* of Achilles Tatius, the *Aithiopika* of Heliodorus, and the *Allegory* of Meliteniotes which show significant resemblance to passages in one or more versions of *Digenes*.

I. ACHILLES TATIUS

1. Ach. Tat. I. i. 11 = Dig. GRO vi. 782–4; Dig. TRE 2627–31; Mel. 357–9.
2. Ach. Tat. I. v. 4 = Dig. GRO iv. 397–400; Dig. TRE 1241–4.
3. Ach. Tat. I. xv. 1, 4, 5, 7 = Dig. GRO vii. 13–41 (vi. 18–41); Dig. TRE 2703–24 (1880–1910); Mel. 2450–97.
4. Ach. Tat. I. xv. 6 = Dig. TRE 2720.
5. Ach. Tat. III. xi. 2 = Dig. GRO 139, 140; Dig. TRE 2023–5.
6. Ach. Tat. II. i. 2 = Dig. GRO vi. 4–11; Dig. TRE 1861–8; Mel. 32–39.
7. Ach. Tat. II. i. 2, I. xix. 1 = Dig. GRO 32–34, Dig. TRE 1912,1913; = Mel. 2841–6.
8. Ach. Tat. III. ix. 2 = Dig. GRO 32 (?).

II. HELIODORUS

1. Heliod. II. vi = Dig. GRO iii. 280; TRE 715.
2. Heliod. III. vii = Dig. GRO iv. 275; TRE 1128; AND 1691. Cf. also Passow no. 528; and Const. Manass., *Poème Moral* (ed. Miller, *Ann. Ass. Études GR.* 1875).
3. Heliod. v. xxxii = Dig. GRO vi. 247; TRE 2181; AND 3181; ESC 1285.
4. Heliod. VI. xii: cf. Dig. GRO 230 ff. (but no verbal identities).
5. Heliod. VII. x = Dig. GRO i. 30 ff.
6. Heliod. VIII. xvi = Dig. GRO i. 46 ff.
7. Heliod. x. xxviii–xxx: cf. Dig. GRO iv. 1054.
8. Heliod. x. xxxviii: cf. Dig. GRO 168; and Ach. Tat. VII. xv.

III. MELITENIOTES

The text of this Allegorical Poem (for which see Krumbacher, p. 782, and Grégoire and Goossens in *Antiq. Class.* II. ii (1933), p. 470, n. 5) is not so easily accessible as the romances of Heliodorus and Achilles Tatius, but the relevant passages are too numerous to be reprinted in full.

1. Mel. 32–38 = GRO vi. 5–10; TRE 1862–7; AND 2818–23.
2. Mel. 140–1 = GRO v. 37–38; TRE 1642, 1643; AND 2528, 2529.
3. Mel. 358, 359 = GRO vi. 782–4; TRE 2627–30; AND 3797–800.

4. Mel. 681–3, 913, 914 = GRO vii. 57, 58; TRE 2834–5, AND 4039–40.

5. Mel. 824–7 = TRE 2766–9; AND 3969–72.

6. Mel. 828–30, 836, 838, 839 = GRO vii. 45, 49–53; TRE 2765, 2770, 2771; AND 3968, 3973, 3974.

7. Mel. 840, 841, 844–6 = GRO vii. 54, 55, 59, 60.

8. Mel. 857–63 = TRE 2772–7, 2787–9; AND 3975–80, 3990–2.

9. Mel. 935–7, 946, 947, 954, 955 = TRE 2782, 2783; AND 3985–7.

10. Mel. 1950, 1952, 1967, 1968, 1975, 1976, 1977 = GRO vii. 73–78; TRE 2803–7; AND 4007–10 (cf. also LXX II Reg. xxi. 19; I Reg. xvii. 7).

11. Mel. 2450, 2451–3, 2455, 2457, 2458, 2466, 2473, 2474, 2478 = GRO vii. 14–17; TRE 2704, 2711; AND 3906, 3913.

12. Mel. 2481, 2482, 2484, 2485, 2490, 2491, 2494–7 = GRO vii. 28, 29.

13. Mel. 2841–3 = GRO vi. 33–34; TRE 1912, 1913; AND 2871, 2872.

INDEX OF GREEK WORDS

INDEX TO INTRODUCTION

271

INDEX

ISBN 0–19–	Author	Title
8143567	ALFÖLDI A.	The Conversion of Constantine and Pagan Rome
6286409	ANDERSON George K.	The Literature of the Anglo-Saxons
8219601	ARNOLD Benjamin	German Knighthood
8228813	BARTLETT & MacKAY	Medieval Frontier Societies
8111010	BETHURUM Dorothy	Homilies of Wulfstan
8142765	BOLLING G. M.	External Evidence for Interpolation in Homer
814332X	BOLTON J.D.P.	Aristeas of Proconnesus
9240132	BOYLAN Patrick	Thoth, the Hermes of Egypt
8114222	BROOKS Kenneth R.	Andreas and the Fates of the Apostles
8203543	BULL Marcus	Knightly Piety & Lay Response to the First Crusade
8216785	BUTLER Alfred J.	Arab Conquest of Egypt
8148046	CAMERON Alan	Circus Factions
8148054	CAMERON Alan	Porphyrius the Charioteer
8148348	CAMPBELL J.B.	The Emperor and the Roman Army 31 BC to 235 AD
826643X	CHADWICK Henry	Priscillian of Avila
826447X	CHADWICK Henry	Boethius
8219393	COWDREY H.E.J.	The Age of Abbot Desiderius
8148992	DAVIES M.	Sophocles: Trachiniae
825301X	DOWNER L.	Leges Henrici Primi
814346X	DRONKE Peter	Medieval Latin and the Rise of European Love-Lyric
8142749	DUNBABIN T.J.	The Western Greeks
8154372	FAULKNER R.O.	The Ancient Egyptian Pyramid Texts
8221541	FLANAGAN Marie Therese	Irish Society, Anglo-Norman Settlers, Angevin Kingship
8143109	FRAENKEL Edward	Horace
8201540	GOLDBERG P.J.P.	Women, Work and Life Cycle in a Medieval Economy
8140215	GOTTSCHALK H.B.	Heraclides of Pontus
8266162	HANSON R.P.C.	Saint Patrick
8224354	HARRISS G.L.	King, Parliament and Public Finance in Medieval England to 1369
8581114	HEATH Sir Thomas	Aristarchus of Samos
2115480	HENRY Blanche	British Botanical and Horticultural Literature before 1800
8140444	HOLLIS A.S.	Callimachus: Hecale
8212968	HOLLISTER C. Warren	Anglo-Saxon Military Institutions
8219523	HOUSLEY Norman	The Italian Crusades
8223129	HURNARD Naomi	The King's Pardon for Homicide – before AD 1307
8140401	HUTCHINSON G.O.	Hellenistic Poetry
9240140	JOACHIM H.H.	Aristotle: On Coming-to-be and Passing-away
9240094	JONES A.H.M	Cities of the Eastern Roman Provinces
8142560	JONES A.H.M.	The Greek City
8218354	JONES Michael	Ducal Brittany 1364–1399
8271484	KNOX & PELCZYNSKI	Hegel's Political Writings
8225253	LE PATOUREL John	The Norman Empire
8212720	LENNARD Reginald	Rural England 1086–1135
8212321	LEVISON W.	England and the Continent in the 8th century
8148224	LIEBESCHUETZ J.H.W.G.	Continuity and Change in Roman Religion
8141378	LOBEL Edgar & PAGE Sir Denys	Poetarum Lesbiorum Fragmenta
9240159	LOEW E.A.	The Beneventan Script
8241445	LUKASIEWICZ, Jan	Aristotle's Syllogistic
8152442	MAAS P. & TRYPANIS C.A .	Sancti Romani Melodi Cantica
8142684	MARSDEN E.W.	Greek and Roman Artillery—Historical
8142692	MARSDEN E.W.	Greek and Roman Artillery—Technical
8148178	MATTHEWS John	Western Aristocracies and Imperial Court AD 364–425
9240205	MAVROGORDATO John	Digenes Akrites
8223447	McFARLANE K.B.	Lancastrian Kings and Lollard Knights
8226578	McFARLANE K.B.	The Nobility of Later Medieval England
9240205	MAVROGADO John	Digenes Akrites
8148100	MEIGGS Russell	Roman Ostia
8148402	MEIGGS Russell	Trees and Timber in the Ancient Mediterranean World
8142641	MILLER J. Innes	The Spice Trade of the Roman Empire
8147813	MOORHEAD John	Theoderic in Italy
8264259	MOORMAN John	A History of the Franciscan Order
9240213	MYRES J.L.	Herodotus The Father of History
8219512	OBOLENSKY Dimitri	Six Byzantine Portraits
8116020	OWEN A.L.	The Famous Druids
8131445	PALMER, L.R.	The Interpretation of Mycenaean Greek Texts
8143427	PFEIFFER R.	History of Classical Scholarship (vol 1)
8143648	PFEIFFER Rudolf	History of Classical Scholarship 1300–1850

8111649	PHEIFER J.D.	Old English Glosses in the Epinal-Erfurt Glossary
8142277	PICKARD–CAMBRIDGE A.W.	Dithyramb Tragedy and Comedy
8269765	PLATER & WHITE	Grammar of the Vulgate
8213891	PLUMMER Charles	Lives of Irish Saints (2 vols)
820695X	POWICKE Michael	Military Obligation in Medieval England
8269684	POWICKE Sir Maurice	Stephen Langton
821460X	POWICKE Sir Maurice	The Christian Life in the Middle Ages
8225369	PRAWER Joshua	Crusader Institutions
8225571	PRAWER Joshua	The History of The Jews in the Latin Kingdom of Jerusalem
8143249	RABY F.J.E.	A History of Christian Latin Poetry
8143257	RABY F.J.E.	A History of Secular Latin Poetry in the Middle Ages (2 vols)
8214316	RASHDALL & POWICKE	The Universities of Europe in the Middle Ages (3 vols)
8154488	REYMOND E.A.E & BARNS J.W.B.	Four Martyrdoms from the Pierpont Morgan Coptic Codices
8148380	RICKMAN Geoffrey	The Corn Supply of Ancient Rome
8141076	ROSS Sir David	Aristotle: Metaphysics (2 vols)
8141092	ROSS Sir David	Aristotle: Physics
8142307	ROSTOVTZEFF M.	Social and Economic History of the Hellenistic World, 3 vols.
8142315	ROSTOVTZEFF M.	Social and Economic History of the Roman Empire, 2 vols.
8264178	RUNCIMAN Sir Steven	The Eastern Schism
814833X	SALMON J.B.	Wealthy Corinth
8171587	SALZMAN L.F.	Building in England Down to 1540
8218362	SAYERS Jane E.	Papal Judges Delegate in the Province of Canterbury 1198–1254
8221657	SCHEIN Sylvia	Fideles Crucis
8148135	SHERWIN WHITE A.N.	The Roman Citizenship
9240167	SINGER Charles	Galen: On Anatomical Procedures
8113927	SISAM, Kenneth	Studies in the History of Old English Literature
8642040	SOUTER Alexander	A Glossary of Later Latin to 600 AD
8270011	SOUTER Alexander	Earliest Latin Commentaries on the Epistles of St Paul
8222254	SOUTHERN R.W.	Eadmer: Life of St. Anselm
8251408	SQUIBB G.	The High Court of Chivalry
8212011	STEVENSON & WHITELOCK	Asser's Life of King Alfred
8212011	SWEET Henry	A Second Anglo-Saxon Reader—Archaic and Dialectical
8148259	SYME Sir Ronald	History in Ovid
8143273	SYME Sir Ronald	Tacitus (2 vols)
8200951	THOMPSON Sally	Women Religious
8201745	WALKER Simon	The Lancastrian Affinity 1361–1399
8161115	WELLESZ Egon	A History of Byzantine Music and Hymnography
8140185	WEST M.L.	Greek Metre
8141696	WEST M.L.	Hesiod: Theogony
8148542	WEST M.L.	The Orphic Poems
8140053	WEST M.L.	Hesiod: Works & Days
8152663	WEST M.L.	Iambi et Elegi Graeci
9240221	WHEELWRIGHT Philip	Heraclitus
822799X	WHITBY M. & M.	The History of Theophylact Simocatta
8206186	WILLIAMSON, E.W.	Letters of Osbert of Clare
8208103	WILSON F.P.	Plague in Shakespeare's London
8114877	WOOLF Rosemary	The English Religious Lyric in the Middle Ages
8119224	WRIGHT Joseph	Grammar of the Gothic Language